Hong Kong Companies and Partnerships Laws

International Law & Taxation Publishers

London

Hong Kong Companies and Partnerships Laws

ISBN 1-893713-21-0

Copyright © 2001 International Law & Taxation Publishers

International Law & Taxation Publishers
London

http://www.internationallawandtaxationpublishers.com

Contents

COMPANIES ORDINANCE

(as amended, 1997)

CONTENTS

Authentication of Documents

PART II - SHARE CAPITAL AND DEBENTURES

Prospectus

Allotment

Commissions and Discounts

Financial assistance by a company for acquisition of its own shares
Provisions applying to all companies

Listed Companies

Unlisted Companies

Construction of References to offering Shares or Debentures to the Public

Issue of Shares at Premium, Redeemable Preference Shares, and Shares at Discount

Redeemable shares; Purchase by a company of its own shares

Redemption and purchase generally

Redemption or purchase of own shares out of capital (private companies only)

Supplementary

Miscellaneous Provisions as to Share Capital

Reduction of Share Capital

Variation of Shareholders' Rights

Transfer of Shares and Debentures, Evidence of Title

Accounts and Audit

Accounts of certain private companies

Inspection

Inspection of Companies' Books and Papers

Directors and other Officers

Avoidance of Provisions in Articles or Contracts relieving Officers from Liability

Arrangements and Reconstructions

Minorities

PART IVA - DISQUALIFICATION OF DIRECTORS

PART V - WINDING UP

(i) Preliminary

Modes of Winding Up

Contributories

(ii) Winding Up By The Court

Jurisdiction

Committees of Inspection

General Powers of Court in case of Winding Up by Court

(iiA) Winding Up by the Court with a Regulation Order

Rules and Fees

PART VI - RECEIVERS AND MANAGERS

PART VII - GENERAL PROVISIONS AS TO REGISTRATION

Part VIII - Application Of Ordinance To Companies Formed Or Registered Under Former Ordinances

PART IX - COMPANIES NOT FORMED UNDER THIS ORDINANCE AUTHORIZED TO REGISTER UNDER THIS ORDINANCE

PART X - WINDING UP OF UNREGISTERED COMPANIES

PART XI - COMPANIES INCORPORATED OUTSIDE HONG KONG

Provisions as to Establishment of Place of Business in Hong Kong

Part XII - Restrictions On Sale Of Shares And Offers Of Shares For Sale

PART XIIA - DORMANT COMPANIES

PART XIII - MISCELLANEOUS

Prohibition of Partnerships with more than Twenty Members

Provisions relating to Documents and Disposal thereof

Form of Registers etc.

Miscellaneous Offences

General Provisions as to Offences

PART XIIIA - PREVENTION OF EVASION OF THE SOCIETIES ORDINANCE

PART XIV - SAVINGS

First Schedule

Table A.

Part I: Regulations for Management of a Company Limited by Shares, not being a Private Company

Part II: Regulations for the Management of a Private Company Limited by Shares

Table B.

Form of Memorandum of Association of a Company Limited by Shares

Table C.

Form of Memorandum and Articles of Association of a Company Limited by Guarantee, and not having a Share Capital

Table D.

Memorandum and Articles of Association of a Company Limited by Guarantee and having a Share Capital

Table E.

Memorandum and Articles of Association of an Unlimited Company having a Share Capital

Second Schedule

Form of Statement in lieu of Prospectus to be delivered to Registrar by a Private Company on becoming a Public Company and Reports to be set out therein

Third Schedule

Matters to be Specified in Prospectus and Reports to be set out therein

Fourth Schedule

Form of Statement in lieu of Prospectus to be delivered to Registrar by a Company which does not issue a Prospectus or which does not go to Allotment on a Prospectus Issued, and Reports to be set out therein

Fifth Schedule

Contents and Form of Annual Return of a Company

Sixth Schedule

Form of Statement to be published by Banking and Insurance Companies and Deposit, Provident, or Benefit Societies

Seventh Schedule

Powers

Eighth Schedule

Table of Fees to be paid to the Registrar of Companies

Ninth Schedule

Provisions relating to acquisition of minority shares after successful take-over offer

Tenth Schedule

Accounts

Eleventh Schedule

Accounts of certain Private Companies under Section 141D

Twelfth Schedule

Punishment of offences under this Ordinance

Thirteenth Schedule

Provisions relating to acquisition of minority shares after successful buy out by share repurchase

Fourteenth Schedule

Table of fees to be paid to a company

Fifteenth Schedule

Matters for determining unfitness of directors.

To consolidate and amend the law relating to companies.

Short title

1.   This Ordinance may be cited as the Companies Ordinance.

Interpretation and Specification of Forms

2.(1)   In this Ordinance, unless the context otherwise requires-

"accounts" includes a company's group accounts, whether prepared in the form of accounts or not;

"agent" does not include a person's counsel acting as such;

"annual return" means the return required to be made, in the case of a company having a share capital, under section 107, and, in the case of a company not having a share capital, under section 108;

"articles" means the articles of association of a company, as originally framed or as altered by special resolution, including, so far as they apply to the company, the regulations contained in Table A in the First Schedule annexed to the Companies Ordinance 1865, or in that table as altered in pursuance of powers given under that Ordinance, or in Table A in the First Schedule to the Companies Ordinance 1911, or in that table as altered in pursuance of section 17 of the last mentioned Ordinance, or in Table A in the First Schedule to this Ordinance;

"authorized financial institution" means an authorized institution within the meaning of section 2 of the Banking Ordinance (Cap. 155);

"book and paper" and "book or paper" includes accounts, deeds, writings, and documents;

"Commission" means-

> (a)   subject to paragraph (b), the Securities and Futures Commission established by section 3 of the Securities and Futures Commission Ordinance (Cap. 24); or
>
> (b)   where any relevant transfer order made under section 47 of that Ordinance is in force, the Exchange Company or both the Securities and Futures Commission and the Exchange Company, in accordance with the provisions of that order;

"company" means a company formed and registered under this Ordinance or an existing company;

"company limited by guarantee" and "company limited by shares" have the meanings assigned to them respectively by section 4(2);

"contributory" has the meaning assigned to it by section 171;

"court" means the High Court;

"creditors' voluntary winding up" has the meaning assigned to it by section 233(4);

"debenture" includes debenture stock, bonds and any other securities of a company whether constituting a charge on the assets of the company or not;

"default fine" has the meaning assigned to it by section 351(1A)(d);

"director" includes any person occupying the position of director by whatever name called;

"document" includes summons, notice, order, and other legal process, and registers;

"Exchange Company" means the Exchange Company as defined in section 2(1) of the Stock Exchanges Unification Ordinance (Cap. 361);

"existing company" means a company formed and registered under the Companies Ordinance 1865, or the Companies Ordinance 1911;

"financial year", in relation to any body corporate, means the period in respect of which any profit and loss account of the body corporate laid before it in general meeting is made up, whether that period is a year or not;

"general rules" means general rules made under section 296 and includes forms;

"group accounts" has the meaning assigned to it by section 124(1);

"group of companies" means any 2 or more companies or bodies corporate one of which is the holding company of the other or others;

"issued generally", in relation to a prospectus, means issued to persons who not existing members or debenture holders of the company;

"listed company" means a company which has any of its shares listed on the Unified Exchange;

"members' voluntary winding up" has the meaning assigned to it by section 233(4);

"memorandum" means the memorandum of association of a company, as originally framed or as altered in pursuance of any enactment;

"the minimum subscription" has the meaning assigned to it by section 42(2);

"officer" in relation to a body corporate, includes a director, manager or secretary;

"officer who is in default" has the meaning assigned to it by section 351(2);

"oversees company" has the meaning assigned to it by section 332;

"prescribed" means as respects the provisions of this Ordinance relating to the winding-up of companies, prescribed by general rules, and as respects the other provisions of this Ordinance, prescribed by the Governor in Council;

"printed" means produced by ordinary letterpress or lithography or by such other process as the Registrar in his discretion may accept;

"private company" has the meaning assigned to it by section 29;

"prospectus" means any prospectus, notice, circular, brochure, advertisement, or other document,-

> *(a)* offering any shares or debentures of a company to the public for subscription or purchase for cash or other consideration; or

> *(b)* calculated to invite offers by the public to subscribe for or purchase for cash or other consideration any shares or debentures of a company;

"Registrar" means the Registrar of Companies appointed under section 303;

"Registrar's index of company names" means the index of names kept by the Registrar under section 22C;

"resolution for reducing share capital" has the meaning assigned to it by section 58(2);

"a resolution for voluntary winding up" has the meaning assigned to it by section 228(2);

"share" means share in the share capital of a company, and includes stock except where a distinction between stock and shares is expressed or implied;

"share warrant" has the meaning assigned to it by section 73;

"specified form", in relation to a particular provision of this Ordinance, means the appropriate form specified for the time being under section 2A, for the purposes of that provision;

"Table A" means Table A in the First Schedule;

"the time of the opening of the subscription lists" has the meaning assigned it by section 44A(1);

"Unified Exchange" means the Unified Exchange established under section 27 of the Stock Exchanges Unification Ordinance (Cap. 361);

"unlimited company" has the meaning assigned to it by section 4(2);

"unlisted company" means a company which does not have any of its shares listed on the Unified Exchange.

(2) A person shall not be deemed to be within the meaning of any provision in this Ordinance a person in accordance with whose directions or instructions the directors of a company are accustomed to act, by reason only that the directors of the company act on advice given by him in a professional capacity.

(3) References in this Ordinance to a body corporate or to a corporation shall be construed as not including a corporation sole but as including a company incorporated outside Hong Kong.

(4) For the purposes of this Ordinance, a company shall, subject to the provisions of subsection (6), be deemed to be a subsidiary of another company, if-

> *(a)* that other company-
>
>> **(i)** controls the composition of the board of directors of the first-mentioned company; or
>>
>> **(ii)** controls more than half of the voting power of the first mentioned company; or
>>
>> **(iii)** holds more than half of the issued share capital of the first-mentioned company (excluding any part of it which carries no right to participate beyond a specified amount in a distribution of either profits or capital); or
>
> *(b)* the first-mentioned company is a subsidiary of any company which is that other company's subsidiary.

(5) For the purposes of subsection (4), the composition of a company's board of directors shall be deemed to be controlled by another company if that other company by the exercise of some power exercisable by it, without the consent or concurrence of any other person, can appoint or remove all or a majority of the directors, and, for the purposes of this provision, that other company shall be deemed to have power to make such an appointment if-

> *(a)* a person cannot be appointed as a director without the exercise in his favour by that other company of such a power; or
>
> *(b)* a person's appointment as a director follows necessarily from his being a director or other officer of that other company.

(6) In determining whether one company is a subsidiary of another company-

> *(a)* any shares held or power exercisable by that other company in a fiduciary capacity shall be treated as not held or exercisable by it;
>
> *(b)* subject to paragraphs (c) and (d), any shares held or power exercisable-

(i)   by any person as a nominee for that other company (except where that other company is concerned only in a fiduciary capacity); or

(ii)   by, or by a nominee for, a subsidiary of that other company, not being a subsidiary which is concerned only in a fiduciary capacity,

shall be treated as held or exercisable by that other company;

(c)   any shares held or power exercisable by any person by virtue of the provisions of any debentures of the first-mentioned company or of a trust deed for securing any issue of such debentures shall be disregarded; and

(d)   any shares held or power exercisable by, or by a nominee for, that other company or its subsidiary (not being held or exercisable as mentioned in paragraph (c)) shall be treated as not held or exercisable by that other company if the ordinary business of that other company or its subsidiary, as the case may be, includes the lending of money and the shares are held or power is exercisable as aforesaid by way of security only for the purposes of a transaction entered into in the ordinary course of that business.

(7)   A reference in this Ordinance to the holding company of a company shall be read as a reference to a company of which that last-mentioned company is a subsidiary.

(8)   In subsections (4), (5), (6) and (7) the expression "company" includes any body corporate or corporation.

(9)   For the avoidance of doubt it is declared that a reference, in relation to any purpose of this Ordinance, to any form, matter, particular or information specified by the Registrar means, except where it is provided otherwise, specified by him for the time being for that purpose.

Registrar to specify forms

2A.(1) The Registrar may specify a form, for use in relation to any purpose of this Ordinance -

(a)   unless it is provided otherwise in this Ordinance; or

(b)   except where a form for that purpose may be or is prescribed,

and any such form may contain any particulars ancillary or incidental to that purpose.

(2)   In exercising, as regards any purpose of this Ordinance, the power conferred on him by subsection (1), the Registrar may, if he thinks fit, specify 2 or more different forms to be used in respect of that purpose, in different circumstances.

(3)   Where any form is specified under this section, deviations therefrom, not affecting the substance of such form, shall not invalidate it.

3.   *(Repealed)*

PART I - Incorporation Of Companies And Matters Incidental Thereto

Memorandum of Association

Mode of forming incorporated company

4.(1)   Any 2 or more persons, associated for any lawful purpose may, by subscribing their names to a memorandum of association (which must be printed in the English language) and otherwise complying with the requirements of this Ordinance in respect of registration, form an incorporated company, with or without limited liability.

(2)   Such a company may be either-

(a)   a company having, or deemed by virtue of subsection (3) to have, the liability of its members limited by the memorandum to the amount, if any, unpaid on the shares respectively held by them (in this Ordinance termed a company limited by shares); or

(b)   a company having the liability of its members limited by the memorandum to such amount as the members may respectively thereby undertake to contribute to the assets of the company in the event of its being wound up (in this Ordinance termed a company limited by guarantee); or

(c)   a company not having any limit on the liability of its members (in this Ordinance termed an unlimited company).

(3)   A company whose memorandum contains a condition in accordance with the fourth paragraph of the form set out in Table B in the First Schedule shall be deemed to be, and, in the case of such a company registered at the commencement of the Companies (Amendment) Ordinance 1984, always to have been, a company having the liability of its members limited by the memorandum to the amount, if any, unpaid on the shares respectively held by them.

Requirements with respect to memorandum

5.(1)   The memorandum of every company limited by shares or by guarantee must state the name of the company and -

(a)   if the name is in English, with "Limited" as the last word of the name;

(b)   if the name is in Chinese, with "   " as the last 4 Chinese characters of the name; and

(c)   if the name is both in English and Chinese, with "Limited" as the last word of the name in English and "   " as the last 4 Chinese characters of the name in Chinese respectively.

(1A)   The -

(a)   memorandum of -

> **(i)** an association referred to in section 21(1) must state the objects of the association; and
>
> **(ii)** a company which is authorized to change its name under section 21(2) must state the objects of the company; and

(b) memorandum of any other company may state the objects of the company.

(1B) Subsection (1A) does not affect any requirement relating to the memorandum of a company specified in or under any other enactment.

Powers of a company

5A.(1) A company has the capacity and the rights, powers and privileges of a natural person.

(2) Without limited subsection (1), a company may do anything which it is permitted or required to do by its memorandum or by any enactment or rule of law.

Power limited by memorandum, etc.

5B.(1) A company -

(a) whose objects are stated in its memorandum shall not carry on any business or do anything that it is not authorized by its memorandum to carry on or do; and

(b) shall not exercise any power which is expressly excluded or modified by its memorandum or articles, contrary to such exclusion or modification.

(2) A member of a company may bring proceedings to restrain the doing or an act in contravention of subsection (1); but no such proceedings shall lie in respect of an act to be done in fulfilment of any legal obligation arising under a previous act of the company.

(3) An act of a company (including a transfer of property to or by the company) is not invalid by reason only that it contravenes subsection (1).

Exclusion of deemed notice

5C. A person shall not be taken to have notice of any matter merely because of its being disclosed in the memorandum or articles kept by the Registrar or a return or resolution lodged with hi

Signature of memorandum

6. The memorandum shall be signed by each subscriber in the presence of a witness who shall attest the signature by signing his name and stating his occupation and address in legible form.

Restriction on alteration of memorandum

7. A company may not alter its memorandum except in the cases, in the mode and to the extent for which express provision is made in this Ordinance.

Mode in which and extent to which objects may be altered

8.(1) A company may, by special resolution of which notice has been duly given to all the members of the company (including, for the purposes of this section, members who are not entitled to such notice under the articles of the company), alter the conditions of its memorandum with respect to the objects of the company by abandoning or restricting any of those objects or by adopting any new object which could lawfully have been contained in the memorandum at the time of its registration:

Provided that, if an application is made to the court in accordance with this section for the alteration to be annulled, the alteration shall not have effect except in so far as it is confirmed by the court.

(2) An application under this section may be made-

> *(a)* by the holders of not less in the aggregate than 5 per cent in nominal value of the company's issued share capital or any class thereof or, if the company is not limited by shares, not less than 5 per cent of the company's members; or

> *(b)* by the holders of not less than 5 per cent of the company's debentures entitling the holders to object to alterations of its objects.

(3) An application under this section shall be made within 28 days after the date on which the resolution altering the company's objects was passed, and may be made on behalf of the persons entitled to make the application by such one or more of their number as they may appoint in writing for the purpose.

(4) On an application under this section the court may make an order confirming the alteration either wholly or in part and on such terms and conditions as it thinks fit, and may, if it thinks fit, adjourn the proceedings in order that an arrangement may be made to the satisfaction of the court for the purchase of the interests of dissentient members, and may give such directions and make such orders as it may think expedient for facilitating or carrying into effect any such arrangement.

(5) The debentures entitling the holders to object to alterations of a company's objects shall be any debentures secured by a floating charge that were issued or first issued before 15 February 1963, or form part of the same series as any debentures so issued, and a special resolution altering a company's objects shall require the same notice to the holders of any such debentures as to members of the company.

In default of any provisions regulating the giving of notice to any such debenture holders, the provisions of the company's articles regulating the giving of notice to members shall apply.

(6) *(Repealed)*

(7) Where a company passes a resolution altering its objects-

    (a) if no application is made with respect thereto under this section, it shall within 15 days after the end of the period for making such an application deliver to the Registrar a printed copy of its memorandum as altered and certified as correct by an officer of the company; and

    (b) if such an application is made it shall-

        (i) forthwith give notice of that fact to the Registrar; and

        (ii) within 15 days after the date of any order annulling or confirming the alteration, deliver to the Registrar an office copy of the order and, in the case of an order confirming the alteration, a printed copy of its memorandum as altered and certified as correct by an officer of the company.

The court may by order at any time extend the time for the delivery of documents to the Registrar under paragraph (b) of this subsection for such period as the court may think proper.

(8) If a company makes default in giving notice or delivering any document to the Registrar as required by subsection (7), the company and every officer of the company who is in default shall be liable to a fine and, for continued default, to a daily default fine.

(9) In relation to a resolution for altering the conditions of a company's memorandum with respect to the objects of the company passed before the commencement of the Companies (Amendment) Ordinance 1984, the provisions of this section in force immediately before such commencement shall continue to have effect as if that Ordinance had not been enacted.

Articles of Association

Articles prescribing regulations for companies

9. There may in the case of a company limited by shares, and there shall in the case of a company limited by guarantee or unlimited, be registered with the memorandum, articles of association signed by the subscribers to the memorandum and prescribing regulations for the company.

Regulations required in case of unlimited company or company limited by guarantee

10.(1) In the case of an unlimited company the articles shall state the number of members with which the company proposes to be registered and, if the company has a share capital, the amount of share capital with which the company proposes to be registered.

(2) In the case of a company limited by guarantee, the articles shall state the number of members with which the company proposes to be registered.

(3) Where a company not having a share capital has increased the number of its members beyond the registered number, it shall, within 15 days after the increase was resolved on or took place, give to the Registrar notice of the increase, and the Registrar shall record the increase. If default is made in complying with this subsection, the company and every officer of the company who is in default shall be liable to a fine and, for continued default, to a daily default fine.

Adoption and application of Table A

11.(1) Articles of association may adopt all or any of the regulations contained in Table A.

(2) In the case of a company limited by shares and registered after the commencement of this Ordinance, if articles are not registered, or, if articles are registered, in so far as the articles do not exclude or modify the regulations contained in Table A, those regulations shall, so far as applicable, be the regulations of the company in the same manner and to the same extent as if they were contained in duly registered articles.

Printing and signature of articles

12. Articles shall-

   (a)   be printed in the English language;

   (b)   be divided into paragraphs numbered consecutively;

   (c)   be signed by each subscriber of the memorandum of association in the presence of a witness who shall attest the signature by signing his name and stating his occupation and address in legible form.

Alteration of articles by special resolution

13.(1) Subject to the provisions of this Ordinance and to the conditions contained in its memorandum, a company may by special resolution alter or add to its articles.

(1A) Nothing in this section shall authorize a company to make any alteration or addition in its articles which is inconsistent with any special rights attached to a class of shares in the company.

(2) Any alteration or addition so made in the articles shall, subject to the provisions of this Ordinance, be as valid as if originally contained therein, and be subject in like manner to alteration by special resolution.

Form of Memorandum and Articles

Statutory forms of memorandum and articles

14. The form of-

   (a)   the memorandum of association of a company limited by shares;

(b)   the memorandum and articles of association of a company limited by guarantee and not having a share capital;

(c)   the memorandum and articles of association of a company limited by guarantee and having a share capital;

(d)   the memorandum and articles of association of an unlimited company having a share capital;

shall be respectively in accordance with the forms set out in Tables B, C, D and E in the First Schedule, or as near thereto as circumstances admit.

Registration

Registration of memorandum and articles

15.   The memorandum and the articles, if any, shall be delivered to the Registrar and the Registrar shall retain and register them.

Effect of registration

16.(1) On the registration of the memorandum of a company the Registrar shall certify under his hand that the company is incorporated and, in the case of a limited company, that the company is limited.

(2)   From the date of incorporation mentioned in the certificate of incorporation, the subscribers of the memorandum, together with such other persons as may from time to time become members of the company, shall be a body corporate by the name contained in the memorandum, capable forthwith of exercising all the functions of an incorporated company, and having perpetual succession and a common seal, but with such liability on the part of the members to contribute to the assets of the company in the event of its being wound up as is mentioned in this Ordinance.

Power of company to hold lands

17.(1) Every company incorporated under this Ordinance shall have power to acquire, hold and dispose of land.

(2)   For the purposes of this section, "land" includes any estate or interest in land, buildings, messuages and tenements of what nature or kind soever.

Conclusiveness of certificate of incorporation

18.(1) A certificate of incorporation given by the Registrar in respect of any association shall be conclusive evidence that all the requirements of this Ordinance in respect of registration and of matters precedent and incidental thereto have been complied with, and that the association is a company authorized to be registered and duly registered under this Ordinance.

(2)   A statutory declaration by a solicitor of the High Court, engaged in the formation of the company, or by a person named in the articles as a director or secretary of the company, of compliance with all or any of the said requirements shall be produced to the Registrar, and the Registrar may accept such a declaration as sufficient evidence of compliance.

Unlimited companies may be re-registered as limited

19.(1) A company which, at or after the commencement of the Companies (Amendment) Ordinance 1984, is registered as unlimited may be re-registered as limited if a special resolution that it should be so re-registered (complying with the requirement of subsection (2)) is passed and an application in that behalf, framed in the specified form and signed by a director or by the secretary of the company, is lodged with the Registrar together with the documents mentioned in subsection (3) not earlier than the day on which the copy of the resolution forwarded to him in pursuance of section 117 is received by him; and the Eighth Schedule shall have effect for the purposes of this section as if for references in that Schedule to the registration of a company there were substituted references to its re-registration under this section.

(2)   The said requirement is that the resolution-

(a)   shall state the manner in which the liability of the members of the company is to be limited and, if the company is to have a share capital, what that capital is to be; and

(b)   shall-

(i)   if the company is to be limited by guarantee, provide for the making of such alterations in its memorandum and such alterations in and additions to its articles as are requisite to bring the memorandum and articles, both in substance and in form, into conformity with the requirements of this Ordinance with respect to the substance and form of the memorandum and articles of a company to be formed thereunder whose condition as to mode of limitation of liability and possession of a share capital (or want of it) will be similar to the condition of the company as to those matters which will obtain upon its re-registration;

(ii)   if the company is to be limited by shares, provide for the making of such alterations in its memorandum as are requisite to bring it, both in substance and in form, into conformity with the requirements of this Ordinance with respect to the substance and form of the memorandum of a company to be formed thereunder as a company so limited, and such alterations in and additions to its articles as are requisite in the circumstances.

(3)   The documents referred to in subsection (1) are a printed copy of the memorandum as altered in pursuance of the resolution and a printed copy of the articles as so altered.

(4) The Registrar shall retain the application and other documents lodged with him under subsection (1) and shall issue to the company a certificate of incorporation appropriate to the status to be assumed by the company by virtue of this section; and upon the issue of the certificate-

> *(a)* the status of the company shall, by virtue of the issue, be changed from unlimited to limited; and

> *(b)* the alterations in the memorandum specified in the resolution and the alterations in, and additions to, the articles so specified shall, notwithstanding anything in this Ordinance, take effect.

(5) A certificate of incorporation issued by virtue of this section shall be conclusive evidence that the requirements of this section with respect to re-registration and of matters precedent and incidental thereto have been complied with, and that the company was authorized to be re-registered under this Ordinance in pursuance of this section and was duly so re-registered.

(6) In the event of the winding up of a company re-registered in pursuance of this section, the following provisions shall have effect-

> *(a)* notwithstanding section 170(1)(a), a past member of the company who was a member thereof at the time of re-registration shall, if the winding up commences within the period of 3 years beginning with the day on which the company is re-registered, be liable to contribute to the assets of the company in respect of debts and liabilities of its contracted before that time;

> *(b)* where no persons who were members of the company at that time are existing members of the company, a person who, at that time, was a present or past member thereof shall, subject to section 170(1)(a) and paragraph (a) of this subsection, but notwithstanding section 170(1)(c), be liable to contribute as aforesaid notwithstanding that the existing members have satisfied the contributions required to be made by them in pursuance of this Ordinance;

> *(c)* notwithstanding section 170(1)(d) and (e), there shall be no limit on the amount which a person who, at that time, was a past or present member of the company is liable to contribute as aforesaid.

Provisions with respect to Names of Companies

Restriction on registration of companies by certain names

20.(1) A company shall not be registered by a name-

> *(a)* which is the same as a name appearing in the Registrar's index of company names;

(b) which is the same as that of a body corporate incorporated or established under an Ordinance;

(c) the use of which by the company would, in the opinion of the Governor, constitute a criminal offence; or

(d) which, in the opinion of the Governor, is offensive or otherwise contrary to the public interest.

(2) Except with the consent of the Governor no company shall be registered by a name which-

(a) in the opinion of the Governor, would be likely to give the impression that the company is connected in any way with Her Majesty's Government or the Government of Hong Kong or any department of either Government; or

(b) includes any word or expression for the time being specified in an order made under section 22B.

(3) In determining for the purposes of subsection (1)(a) or (b) whether one name is the same as another-

(a) the following shall be disregarded-

 (i) the definite article, where it is the first word of the name;

 (ii) the following words and expressions where they appear at the end of the name, that is to say-

  (A) "company";

  (B) "and company";

  (C) "company limited";

  (D) "and company limited";

  (E) "limited";

  (F) "unlimited"; and

  (G) "public limited company";

 (iii) abbreviations of any of the words or expressions referred to in subparagraph (ii) where they appear at the end of the name; and

> > **(iv)** type and case of letters, accents, spaces between letters and punctuation marks;
>
> *(b)* "and" and "&", "Hong Kong", "Hongkong" and "HK", and "Far East" and "FE" are respectively to be taken as the same; and
>
> *(c)* two different Chinese characters shall be regarded as the same if the Registrar is satisfied that having regard to the usage of the two Chinese characters in Hong Kong, they can reasonably be used interchangeably.

20A. *(Repealed)*

Power to dispense with "limited" in name of charitable and other companies

21.(1) Where it is proved to the satisfaction of the Registrar that an association about to be formed as a limited company is to be formed for promoting commerce, art, science, religion, charity or any other useful object, and intends to apply its profits, if any, or other income in promoting its objects, and to prohibit the payment of any dividend to its members, the Registrar may by licence direct that the association may be registered as a company with limited liability, without the addition of -

> *(a)* if the name of the association is in English, the word "Limited" to its name;
>
> *(b)* if the name of the association is in Chinese, the expression in Chinese " " to its name; and
>
> *(c)* if the name of the association is both in English and Chinese, such word and expression to its name in English and Chinese respectively,

and the association may be registered accordingly and shall, on registration, enjoy all the privileges and (subject to the provisions of this section) be subject to all the obligations of limited companies.

(2) Where it is proved to the satisfaction of the Registrar-

> *(a)* that the objects of a company registered under this Ordinance as a limited company are restricted to those specified in subsection (1) and to objects incidental or conducive thereto; and
>
> *(b)* that by its constitution the company is required to apply its profits, if any, or other income in promoting its objects and is prohibited from paying any dividend to its members,

the Registrar may by licence authorize the company to make by special resolution a change in its name including or consisting of the omission of the word "Limited", or the expression in Chinese " " or both such word and expression, as the case may be and subsections (4) and (5) of section 22 shall apply to a change of name under this subsection as they apply to a change of name under that section.

(3) A licence by the Registrar under this section may be granted on such conditions and subject to such regulations as the Registrar thinks fit, and those conditions and regulations shall be binding on the body to which the licence is granted, and (where the grant is under subsection (1)) shall, if the Registrar so directs, be inserted in the memorandum and articles, or in one of those documents.

(4) A body to which a licence is granted under this section shall be exempted from the provisions of this Ordinance relating to the use of the word "Limited" or the expression in Chinese " " or both such word and expression, as the case may be, as any part of its name, the publishing of its name and the sending of lists of members to the Registrar.

(5) A licence under this section may at any time be revoked by the Registrar, and upon revocation the Registrar shall, where the name upon the register of the body to which it was granted is -

  (a) in English, enter the word "Limited" at the end of that name;

  (b) in Chinese, enter the expression in Chinese " " at the end of that name; or

  (c) both in English and Chinese, enter such word and expression at the end of its name in English and Chinese respectively,

and the body shall cease to enjoy the exemptions and privileges or, as the case may be, the exemptions granted by this section:

Provided that before a licence is so revoked, the Registrar shall give to the body notice in writing of his intention, and shall afford it an opportunity of being heard in opposition to the revocation.

(6) A body in respect of which a licence under this section is in force shall not have power to alter its memorandum or articles unless-

  (a) it gives to the Registrar the same notice of the resolution relating to the proposed alteration as it is required to give to the members of the body; and

  (b) the proposed alteration is approved in writing by the Registrar.

(7) Where a body in respect of which a licence under this section is in force alters its memorandum or articles, the Registrar may (unless he sees fit to revoke the licence) vary the licence by making it subject to such conditions and regulations as the Registrar thinks fit, in lieu of or in addition to the conditions and regulations, if any, to which the licence was formerly subject.

(8) Where a licence granted under this section to a body the name of which contains the words "Chamber of Commerce" or the expression in Chinese " " is revoked, the body shall within a period of 6 weeks from the date of revocation or such longer period as the Registrar may think fit to allow, change its name to a name which does not contain those words, and-

> (a) the notice to be given under the proviso to subsection (5) to that body shall include a statement to the effect of the foregoing provisions of this subsection; and
>
> (b) subsections (4) and (5) of section 22 shall apply to a change of name under this subsection as they apply to a change of name under that section.

(9) If a body referred to in subsection (8) makes default in complying with the requirements of that subsection, it shall be liable to a fine and, for continued default, to a daily default fine.

(10) Without prejudice to section 23 of the Interpretation and General Clauses Ordinance (Cap. 1), this section shall apply in relation to any body in respect of which a licence (being a licence granted under this Ordinance in respect of the registration of that body as a company with limited liability without the addition of the word "Limited" to its name) is in force at the commencement of the Companies (Amendment) Ordinance 1978 as if such licence had been granted under this section after the commencement of that Ordinance.

Change of name

22.(1) A company may by special resolution change its name.

(2) Where a company has been registered by a name which-

> (a) is the same as or, in the opinion of the Registrar, too like a name appearing at the time of the registration in the Registrar's index of company names;
>
> (b) is the same as or, in the opinion of the Registrar, too like a name which should have appeared in that index at that time; or
>
> (c) is the same as or, in the opinion of the Registrar, too like the name of a body corporate incorporated or established under any Ordinance at the time of the registration,

the Registrar may within 12 months of that time, in writing, direct the company to change its name within such period as he may specify.

(3) Section 20(3) applies in determining under subsection (2) whether a name is the same as or too like another.

(4) If it appears to the Registrar that misleading information has been given for the purpose of a company's registration by a particular name, or that undertakings or assurances have been given for that purpose and have not been fulfilled, he may within 5 years of the date of its registration by that name direct, in writing, the company to change its name within such period as he may specify.

(5) Where a direction is given under subsection (2) or (4), the Registrar may by a further direction in writing extend the period within which the company is to change its name, at any time before the end of that period.

(6) A company which fails to comply with a direction under this section and every officer of the company who is in default shall be liable to-

> *(a)* a fine and, in the case of an individual, imprisonment; and

> *(b)* for continued default, a daily default fine.

(7) Where a company changes its name under this section, the Registrar shall, subject to section 20-

> *(a)* enter the new name on the register in place of the former name; and

> *(b)* issue a certificate of incorporation altered to meet the circumstances of the case,

and the change of name shall have effect from the date on which the altered certificate is issued.

(8) A change of name by a company under this section does not affect any rights or obligations of the company or render defective any legal proceedings by or against it and any legal proceedings that could have been commenced or continued against it by its former name may be commenced or continued against it by its new name.

Power of Registrar to require company to abandon misleading name

22A.(1) If in the opinion of the Registrar the name by which a company is registered gives so misleading an indication of the nature of its activities as to be likely to cause harm to the public, he may direct it to change its name.

(2) A direction given under this section to a company shall, if not duly made the subject of an application under subsection (3) to the court, be complied with within a period of 6 weeks from the date of the direction or such longer period as the Registrar may think fit to allow.

(3) A company to which a direction is given under this section may, within a period of 3 weeks from the date of the direction, apply to the court to set the direction aside, and the court may set it aside or confirm it; and if it confirms it, it shall specify a period within which it shall be complied with.

(4) If a company makes default in complying with a direction under this section, it shall be liable to a fine and, for continued default, to a daily default fine.

(5) Subsections (4) and (5) of section 22 shall apply in relation to a change of name under this section as they apply in relation to a change of name under that section.

Specification of names by Governor

22B.(1) The Governor may by order-

(a) specify words or expressions for the registration of which as, or as part of, a company's name his approval is required under section 20(2)(b); and

(b) in relation to any such word or expression, specify a Government department or other body as the relevant body for the purposes of subsection (2).

(2) Where a company or the promoter of a proposed company proposes to have as, or as part of, its name any word or expression referred to in subsection (1), a request shall be made in writing by the company or the promoter to any body specified under subsection (1)(b) as the relevant body in relation to such word or expression, to indicate whether it has any objection to the proposed name and the reasons for any such objection.

(3) Where a company or a promoter makes a request under subsection (2) the company secretary or the promoter shall deliver in writing to the Registrar a statement that such request has been made to the body referred to in subsection (2) together with a copy of any written reply received from that body and, in the case of a change of name, a copy of the special resolution under section 22(1) changing the company's name.

(4) Section 305 (inspection, production and evidence of documents kept by Registrar) shall not apply to any document delivered under subsection (3).

(5) An order under this section may contain such transitional provisions and savings as the Governor may consider appropriate, and may make different provisions for different cases or different classes of cases.

Registrar's index of company names

22C.(1) The Registrar shall keep an index of the names of the following-

(a) every company; and

(b) every company incorporated outside Hong Kong which has complied with section 333.

(2) The Governor may by order amend subsection (1) so as to add to it any other body or class of body whether incorporated or unincorporated.

General Provisions with respect to Memorandum and Articles

Effect of memorandum and articles

23.(1) Subject to the provisions of this Ordinance the memorandum and articles shall, when registered, bind the company and the members thereof to the same extent as if they respectively had been signed and sealed by each member, and contained covenants on the part of each member to observe all the provisions of the memorandum and of the articles.

(2) All money payable by any member to the company under the memorandum or articles shall be a debt due from him to the company, and be of the nature of a specialty debt.

Provision as to memorandum and articles of companies limited by guarantee

24.(1) In the case of a company limited by guarantee and not having a share capital, and registered on or after 1 January 1912, every provision in the memorandum or articles or in any resolution of the company purporting to give any person a right to participate in the divisible profits of the company otherwise than as a member shall be void.

(2) For the purpose of the provisions of this Ordinance relating to the memorandum of a company limited by guarantee and of this section, every provision in the memorandum or articles, or in any resolution, of a company limited by guarantee and registered on or after the date aforesaid, purporting to divide the undertaking of the company into shares or interests shall be treated as a provision for a share capital, notwithstanding that the nominal amount or number of the shares or interests is not specified thereby.

Alterations in memorandum or articles increasing liability to contribute to share capital not to bind existing members without consent

25. Notwithstanding anything in the memorandum or articles of a company, no member of the company shall be bound by an alteration made in the memorandum or articles after the date on which he became a member, if and so far as the alteration requires him to take or subscribe for more shares than the number held by him at the date on which the alteration is made, or in any way increases his liability as at that date to contribute to the share capital of, or otherwise to pay money to, the company:

Provided that this section shall not apply in any case where the member agrees in writing, either before or after the alteration is made, to be bound thereby.

Power to alter conditions in memorandum which could have been contained in articles

25A.(1) Subject to the provisions of sections 25 and 168A, any condition contained in a company's memorandum which could lawfully have been contained in articles of association instead of in the memorandum may, subject to the provisions of this section, be altered by the company by special resolution:

Provided that if an application is made to the court for the alteration to be cancelled, it shall not have effect except in so far as it is confirmed by the court.

(2) This section shall not apply where the memorandum itself provides for or prohibits the alteration of all or any of the said conditions, and shall not authorize any variation or abrogation of the special rights of any class of members.

(3) Subsections (2)(a), (3), (4), (7) and (8) of section 8 shall apply in relation to any alteration and to any application made under this section as they apply in relation to alterations and to applications made under that section.

(4) This section shall apply to a company's memorandum whether registered before or after the commencement of the Companies (Amendment) Ordinance 1984.

Copies of memorandum and articles to be given to members

26.(1) A company shall, on being so required by any member, send to him a copy of the memorandum and of the articles, if any, and a copy of any Ordinance which alters the memorandum, subject to payment, in the case of a copy of the memorandum and of the articles, of $5 or such less sum as the company may prescribe, and, in the case of a copy of an Ordinance, of such sum not exceeding the published price thereof as the company may require.

(2) If a company makes default in complying with this section, the company and every officer of the company who is in default shall be liable for each offence to a fine.

Issued copies of memorandum to embody alterations

27.(1) Where an alteration is made in the memorandum of a company, every copy of the memorandum issued after the date of the alteration shall be in accordance with the alteration.

(2) If, where any such alteration has been made, the company at any time after the date of the alteration issues any copies of the memorandum which are not in accordance with the alteration, the company and every officer of the company who is in default shall be liable for each offence to a fine.

Membership of Company

Definition of member

28.(1) The subscribers of the memorandum of a company shall be deemed to have agreed to become members of the company, and on its registration shall be entered as members in its register of members.

(2) Every other person who agrees to become a member of a company, and whose name is entered in its register of members, shall be a member of the company.

Membership of holding company

28A.(1) Subject to the provisions of this section, a body corporate cannot be a member of a company which is its holding company, and any allotment or transfer of shares in a company to its subsidiary shall be void.

(2) Nothing in this section shall apply where the subsidiary is concerned as personal representative, or where it is concerned as trustee, unless the holding company or a subsidiary thereof is beneficially interested under the trust and is not so interested only by way of security for the purposes of a transaction entered into by it in the ordinary course of a business which includes the lending of money.

(3) This section shall not prevent a subsidiary which was, at the commencement of the Companies (Amendment) Ordinance 1984, a member of its holding company, from continuing to be a member.

(4) This section shall not prevent a company which at the date it becomes a subsidiary of another company is a member of that other company, from continuing to be a member.

(5) This section shall not prevent a subsidiary from becoming a member of its holding company, or prevent an allotment to a subsidiary of shares in its holding company, by or by virtue of the exercise by the subsidiary of any rights of conversion attached to any shares in its holding company or under any debentures thereof held by the subsidiary at the commencement of the Companies (Amendment) Ordinance 1984.

(6) This section shall not prevent a subsidiary which is a member of its holding company from accepting and holding further shares in its holding company if such further shares are allotted to it as fully paid up in consequence of a capitalization of reserves or profits by such holding company.

(7) Subject to subsection (2), a subsidiary which is a member of its holding company shall have no right to vote at meetings of the holding company or any class of members thereof.

(8) Subject to subsection (2), this section shall apply in relation to a nominee for a body corporate which is a subsidiary, as if references therein to such a body corporate included references to a nominee for it.

(9) Where a holding company makes an offer of shares to its members it may sell, on behalf of a subsidiary, any such shares which the subsidiary could, but for this section, have taken by virtue of shares already held by it in the holding company, and pay the proceeds of the sale to the subsidiary.

(10) In relation to a company limited by guarantee or unlimited which is a holding company, the reference in this section to shares, whether or not it has a share capital, shall be construed as including a reference to the interest of its members as such, whatever the form of that interest.

Private Companies

Meaning of private company

29(1) For the purposes of this Ordinance, the expression "private company" means a company which by its articles-

> *(a)* restricts the right to transfer its shares; and
>
> *(b)* limits the number of its members to 50, not including persons who are in the employment of the company and persons who, having been formerly in the

employment of the company, were while in that employment, and have continued after the determination of that employment to be, members of the company; and

  (c) prohibits any invitation to the public to subscribe for any shares or debentures of the company.

(2) Where 2 or more persons hold one or more shares in a company jointly, they shall, for the purposes of this section, be treated as a single member.

Circumstances in which company ceases to be or to enjoy privileges of a private company

30.(1) If a company, being a private company, alters its articles in such manner that they no longer include the provisions which, under section 29, are required to be included in the articles of a company in order to constitute it a private company, the company shall, as on the date of the alteration, cease to be a private company and shall, within a period of 14 days after the said date, deliver to the Registrar for registration a prospectus or a statement in lieu of prospectus in the form and containing the particulars set out in Part I of the Second Schedule and, in the cases mentioned in Part II of that Schedule setting out the reports specified therein, and the said Parts I and II shall have effect subject to the provisions contained in Part III of that Schedule.

(1A) Every statement in lieu of prospectus delivered under subsection (1) shall, where the persons making any report required by Part II of the Second Schedule have made therein or have, without giving the reasons, indicated therein any such adjustments as are mentioned in paragraph 5 of the Second Schedule, have endorsed thereon or attached thereto a written statement signed by those persons setting out the adjustments and giving the reasons therefor.

(2) If default is made in complying with subsection (1) or (1A), the company and every officer of the company who is in default shall be liable to a default fine.

(2A) Where a statement in lieu of prospectus delivered to the Registrar under subsection (1) includes any untrue statement, any person who authorized the delivery of the statement, in lieu of prospectus for registration shall be liable to imprisonment and a fine, unless he proves either that the untrue statement was immaterial or that he had reasonable ground to believe and did up to the time of the delivery for registration of the statement in lieu of prospectus believe that the untrue statement was true.

(2B) For the purposes of this section-

  (a) a statement included in a statement in lieu of prospectus shall be deemed to be untrue if it is misleading in the form and context in which it is included; and

  (b) a statement shall be deemed to be included in a statement in lieu of prospectus if it is contained therein or in any report or memorandum appearing on the face thereof or by reference incorporated therein.

(2C) The Governor in Council may by regulation amend the Second Schedule.

(3) Where the articles of a company include the provisions aforesaid but default is made in complying with any of those provisions, the company shall cease to be entitled to the privileges and exemptions conferred on private companies under the provisions contained in sections 109(3) and 141D, and thereupon the said provisions shall apply to the company as if it were not a private company:

Provided that the court, on being satisfied that the failure to comply with the conditions was accidental or due to inadvertence or to some other sufficient cause, or that on other grounds it is just and equitable to grant relief, may, on the application of the company or any other person interested and on such terms and conditions as seem to the court just and expedient, order that the company be relieved from such consequences as aforesaid.

Reduction of Number of Members below Legal Minimum

Liability for debts where business carried on without minimum number of members

31. If a company carries on business without having at least 2 members and does so for more than 6 months, a person who, for the whole or any part of the period that it so carries on business after those 6 months,-

> *(a)* is a member of the company; and

> *(b)* knows that it is carrying on business with only 1 member,

shall be liable (jointly and severally with the company) for the payment of the debts of the company contracted during the period or, as the case may be, that part of it.

Contracts, etc.

Form of contracts

32.(1) Contracts on behalf of a company may be made as follows 0

> *(a)* a contract which if made between private persons would be by law required to be in writing and under seal, may be made on behalf of the company in writing under the common seal of the company;

> *(b)* a contract which if made between private persons would be by law required to be in writing, signed by the parties to be charged therewith, may be made on behalf of the company in writing signed by any person acting under its authority, express or implied;

> *(c)* a contract which if made between private persons would by law be valid

although made by parol only, and not reduced into writing, may be made by parol on behalf of the company by any person acting under its authority, express or implied.

(2) A contract made according to this section shall be effectual in law, and shall bind the company and its successors and all other parties thereto.

(3) A contract made according to this section may be varied or discharged in the same manner in which it is authorized by this section to be made.

Pre-incorporation contracts

32A.(1) Where a contract purports to have been made in the name or on behalf of a company at a time when the company has not been incorporated-

> *(a)* subject to subsection (2) and any express agreement to the contrary, the contract shall have effect as a contract entered into by the person purporting to act for the company or as agent for it, and he shall be personally liable on and entitled to enforce the contract accordingly;
>
> *(b)* the company may, after incorporation, ratify the contract to the same extent as if it had already been incorporated at that time and as if the contract had been entered into on its behalf by an agent acting without its authority.

(2) Where a contract is ratified by virtue of this section, the person who purported to act for or on behalf of the company in making the contract shall not thereafter be under any greater liability than he would have been if he had entered into the contract on behalf of the company as an agent acting without its authority and after its incorporation.

Bills of exchange and promissory notes

33. A bill of exchange or promissory note shall be deemed to have been made, accepted, or endorsed on behalf of a company if made, accepted, or endorsed in the name of, or by or on behalf or on account of, the company by any person acting under its authority.

Execution of deeds abroad

34.(1) A company may, by writing under its common seal, empower any person, either generally or in respect of any specified matters, as its attorney, to execute deeds on its behalf in any place not situate in Hong Kong.

(2) A deed signed by such an attorney on behalf of the company and under his seal shall bind the company and have the same effect as if it were under its common seal.

Power for company to have official seal for use abroad

35.(1) A company whose objects require or comprise the transaction of business outside Hong Kong, may, if authorized by its articles, have for use in any territory, district, or place not situate in Hong Kong, an official seal, which shall be a facsimile of the common seal of the company, with the addition on its face of the name of every territory, district, or place where it is to be used.

(2) A deed or other document to which an official seal is duly affixed shall bind the company as if it had been sealed with the common seal of the company.

(3) A company having an official seal for use in any such territory, district or place may, by writing under its common seal, authorize any person appointed for the purpose in that territory, district or place, to affix the official seal to any deed or other document to which the company is party in that territory, district or place.

(4) The authority of any such agent shall, as between the company and any person dealing with the agent, continue during the period, if any, mentioned in the instrument conferring the authority, or if no period is there mentioned, then until notice of the revocation or determination of the agent's authority has been given to the person dealing with him.

(5) The person affixing any such official seal shall, by writing under his hand, certify on the deed or other instrument, to which the seal is affixed, the date on which and the place at which it is affixed.

Authentication of Documents

Authentication of documents

36. A document or proceeding requiring authentication by a company may be signed by a director, secretary, or other authorized officer of the company, and need not be under its common seal.

PART II - Share Capital And Debentures

Prospectus

Dating of prospectus

37.   A prospectus issued by or on behalf of a company shall be dated, and that date shall, unless the contrary is proved, be taken as the date of publication of the prospectus.

Specific requirements as to particulars in prospectus

38.(1)   Subject to the provisions of section 38A, every prospectus issued by or on behalf of a company must be in the English language and contain a Chinese translation and must state the matters specified in Part I of the Third Schedule and set out the reports specified in Part II of that Schedule, and the said Parts I and II shall have effect subject to the provisions contained in Part III of the said Schedule.

(1A)   Every prospectus to which subsection (1) applies must contain in a prominent position in the English version a statement in the following form-

"IMPORTANT

If you are in any doubt about this prospectus you should consult your stockbroker, bank manager, solicitor, professional accountant or other professional adviser.";

(1B)   If any prospectus is issued which does not comply with or contravenes the requirements of subsections (1) and (1A), the company and every person who is knowingly a party to the issue thereof shall be liable to a fine.

(2)   A condition requiring or binding an applicant for shares in or debentures of a company to waive compliance with any requirement of this section, or purporting to affect him with notice of any contract, document, or matter not specifically referred to in the prospectus, shall be void.

(3)   Subject to the provisions of section 38A, it shall not be lawful to issue any form of application for shares in or debentures of a company unless the form is issued with a prospectus which complies with the requirements of this section:

Provided that this subsection shall not apply if it is shown that the form of application was issued either-

> *(a)*   in connexion with a bona fide invitation to a person to enter into an underwriting agreement with respect to the shares or debentures; or

> *(b)*   in relation to shares or debentures which were not offered to the public.

If any person acts in contravention of the provisions of this subsection, he shall be liable to a fine.

(3A) This section shall not prevent the publication of the English version only of a prospectus in an English language newspaper or the Chinese version only in a Chinese language newspaper, nor the publication in such newspaper together with the prospectus of a form of application relating thereto.

(4) In the event of non-compliance with or contravention of any of the requirements of this section, a director or other person responsible for the prospectus shall not incur any liability by reason of the non-compliance or contravention, if-

(a) as regards any matter not disclosed, he proves that he was not cognisant thereof; or

(b) he proves that the non-compliance or contravention arose from an honest mistake of fact on his part; or

(c) the non-compliance or contravention was in respect of matters which in the opinion of the court dealing with the case were immaterial or was otherwise such as ought, in the opinion of that court, having regard to all the circumstances of the case, reasonably to be excused:

Provided that, in the event of failure to include in a prospectus a statement with respect to the matters specified in paragraph 19 of Part I of the Third Schedule, no director or other person shall incur any liability in respect of the failure unless it be proved that he had knowledge of the matters not disclosed.

(5) This section shall not apply-

(a) to the issue to existing members or debenture holders of a company of a prospectus or form of application relating to shares in or debentures of the company, whether an applicant for shares or debentures will or will not have the right to renounce in favour of other persons; or

(b) to the issue of a prospectus or form of application relating to shares or debentures which are or are to be in all respects uniform with shares or debentures previously issued and for the time being listed on the Unified Exchange;

but, subject as aforesaid, this section shall apply to a prospectus or a form of application whether issued on the formation of a company or subsequently.

(6) Nothing in this section shall limit or diminish any liability which any person may incur under the general law or this Ordinance apart from this section.

(7) The Governor in Council may by regulation amend the Third Schedule.

Exemption of certain persons and prospectuses from compliance with certain provisions

38A.(1) Where it is proposed to offer any shares in or debentures of a company to the public by a prospectus issued generally, there may, on the request of the applicant, and subject to such conditions (if any) as the Commission thinks fit, be issued by the Commission a certificate of exemption from compliance with any or all of the requirements of sections 38(1) and (3), 42(1) and (4) and 44A(2), that is to say, a certificate that, having regard to the circumstances of the case, compliance with any or all of those provisions would be either irrelevant or unduly burdensome.

(2)   Whether or not a request referred to in subsection (1) has been made, the Commission may, by notice in the Gazette, exempt any class of companies or any class of prospectuses issued by companies from any or all of the requirements of sections 38(1) and (3), 42(1) and (4) and 44A(2), if, having regard to the circumstances, the Commission considers that compliance with any or all of those requirements would be either irrelevant or unduly burdensome in the case of that class of companies or prospectuses, as the case may be.

(3)   Where exemption from compliance with section 38(1) and (3) in relation to the requirements of the Third Schedule is granted under this section, whether by the issue of a certificate of exemption or by a notice in the Gazette, the certificate or notice, as the case may be, shall be expressed to have effect with regard to all of the requirements of the Third Schedule or to such of them as are specified in the certificate or notice, as the case may be.

Advertisements concerning prospectuses

38B.(1) Subject to subsection (2), it shall not be lawful for any person to publish or cause to be published by way of advertisement in any manner, any extract from or abridged version of a prospectus whether in English or in any other language in relation to shares or debentures of a company whether incorporated in or outside Hong Kong.

(2)   Notwithstanding subsection (1)-

> *(a)*   the publication of an extract from or abridged version of a prospectus which is in accordance with such form and manner of publication as may have been specified by the Commission under subsection (2A)(a);

> *(b)*   the publication of the English version only of a prospectus in an English language newspaper or the Chinese version only in a Chinese language newspaper;

> *(c)*   the publication of an advertisement, invitation or document which has been authorized by the Commission under section 4(2)(g) of the Protection of Investors Ordinance (Cap. 335); or

> *(d)*   the publication of an extract from or abridged version of a prospectus which is in accordance with such form and manner of publication as may have been

authorized by the Commission under subsection (2A)(b) in that particular case,

shall not contravene this section.

(2A) The Commission may-

    (a) by notice in the Gazette, specify the form and manner of publication of an extract from or abridged version of a prospectus, or any class of prospectuses;

    (b) in any particular case, authorize the form and manner of publication of any extract from or abridged version of a prospectus.

(2B) A prospectus referred to in subsection (2A) means a prospectus relating to shares in or debentures of a company, whether incorporated in or outside Hong Kong.

(3) If any person acts in contravention of subsection (1), he shall be liable to a fine.

Expert's consent to issue of prospectus containing statement by him

38C.(1) A prospectus inviting persons to subscribe for shares in or debentures of a company and including a statement purporting to be made by an expert shall not be issued unless-

    (a) he has given and has not, before delivery of a copy of the prospectus for registration, withdrawn his written consent to the issue thereof with the statement included in the form and context in which it is included; and

    (b) a statement that he has given and has not withdrawn his consent as aforesaid appears in the prospectus.

(2) If any prospectus is issued in contravention of this section the company and every person who is knowingly a party to the issue thereof shall be liable to a fine.

(3) In this section the expression "expert" includes engineer, valuer, accountant, and any other person whose profession gives authority to a statement made by him.

Registration of prospectus

38D.(1) No prospectus shall be issued by or on behalf of a company unless the prospectus complies with the requirements of this Ordinance and, on or before the date of its publication, its registration has been authorized under this section and a copy thereof has been registered by the Registrar.

(2) Every prospectus shall-

    (a) on the face of it, state that a copy has been registered as required by this section and, immediately after such statement, state that neither the

Commission nor the Registrar takes any responsibility as to the contents of the prospectus or, where the prospectus is or is to be authorized for issue by the Exchange Company pursuant to a transfer order made under section 47 of the Securities and Futures Commission Ordinance (Cap. 24), state that neither the Commission nor the Exchange Company nor the Registrar takes any responsibility as to the contents of the prospectus;

(b)   on the face of it, specify or refer to statements included in the prospectus which specify, any documents required by this section to be endorsed on or attached to the copy so registered; and

(c)   conform with such requirements as are prescribed by the Governor in Council or specified by the Registrar under section 346 which are applicable to prospectuses to be registered under this Part.

(3)   An application for authorization for registration of a prospectus under this section shall be made in writing to the Commission and there shall be delivered to the Commission together with the application a copy of the prospectus proposed to be registered which has been signed by every person who is named therein as a director or proposed director of the company or by his agent authorized in writing and having endorsed thereon or attached thereto-

(a)   any consent to the issue of the prospectus required by section 38C from any person as an expert; and

(b)   in the case of a prospectus issued generally, also-

    (i)   a copy of any contract required by paragraph 17 of the Third Schedule to be stated in the prospectus or, in the case of a contract not reduced into writing, a memorandum giving full particulars thereof or, if in the case of a prospectus exempted under section 38A from compliance with the requirements of section 38(1), a contract or a copy thereof or a memorandum of a contract is required by the Commission to be available for inspection in connection with the request made under section 38A(1), a copy or, as the case may be, a memorandum of that contract;

    (ii)   where the prospectus offers shares in the company for sale to the public, a list of the names, addresses and descriptions of the vendor or vendors of the shares; and

    (iii)   where the persons making any report required by Part II of the Third Schedule have made therein, or have, without giving the reasons, indicated therein, any such adjustments as are mentioned in paragraph 42 of that Schedule, a written statement signed by those persons setting out the adjustments and giving the reasons therefor.

(4) The references in subsection (3)(b)(i) to the copy of a contract required thereby to be endorsed on or attached to a copy of the prospectus shall, in the case of a contract wholly or partly in a language other than English, be taken as references to a copy of a translation of the contract in English or a copy embodying a translation in English of the parts not in English, as the case may be, being a translation certified in the prescribed manner to be a correct translation, and the reference to a copy of a contract required to be available for inspection shall include a reference to a copy of a translation thereof or a copy embodying a translation of the parts thereof.

(5) The Commission may-

    (a) authorize the registration by the Registrar, of a prospectus to which this section applies and where the Commission so authorizes, the Commission shall issue a certificate-

        (i) certifying that the Commission has done so; and

        (ii) specifying the documents which are required to be endorsed on or attached to the copy of the prospectus to be registered; or

    (b) refuse to authorize such registration.

(6) The Commission shall not authorize the registration of a prospectus which relates to an intended company.

(7) The Registrar-

    (a) shall not register a prospectus under this section unless-

        (i) it is dated and the copy thereof to be registered has been signed in the manner required by this section;

        (ii) it is accompanied by a certificate issued under subsection (5);

        (iii) it has endorsed thereon or attached thereto all the documents specified in the certificate issued under subsection (5); and

        (iv) it conforms with such requirements as are prescribed by the Governor in Council or specified by the Registrar under section 346 which are applicable to prospectuses to be registered under this Part; and

    (b) shall register a prospectus if subparagraphs (i), (ii), (iii) and (iv) of paragraph (a) are complied with in respect of that prospectus.

(8) If a prospectus is issued without having endorsed thereon or attached thereto the required documents or without a copy thereof which has the required documents endorsed or attached having been registered under this section by the Registrar, the company, and every person who is knowingly a party to the issue of the prospectus, shall be liable to a fine and, for continued default, to a daily default fine from the date of the issue of the prospectus until a copy thereof is so registered or until the required documents are endorsed or attached, as the case may be.

(9) Any person aggrieved by the refusal to authorize the registration of a prospectus under this section may appeal to the court and the court may either dismiss the appeal or order that the registration of the prospectus be authorized by the Commission under this section.

39. *(Repealed)*

Civil liability for misstatements in prospectus

40.(1) Subject to the provisions of this section, where a prospectus invites persons to subscribe for shares in or debentures of a company, the following persons shall be liable to pay compensation to all persons who subscribe for any shares or debentures on the faith of the prospectus for the loss or damage they may have sustained by reason of any untrue statement included therein, that is to say-

> *(a)* every person who is a director of the company at the time of the issue of the prospectus
>
> *(b)* every person who has authorized himself to be named and is named in the prospectus as a director or as having agreed to become a director either immediately or after an interval of time;
>
> *(c)* every person being a promoter of the company; and
>
> *(d)* every person who has authorized the issue of the prospectus:

Provided that where under section 38C the consent of a person is required to the issue of a prospectus and he has given that consent, he shall not by reason of his having given it be liable under this subsection as a person who has authorized the issue of the prospectus except in respect of an untrue statement purporting to be made by him as an expert.

(1A) Subsection (1)(d) shall not apply to the Commission or, where the relevant prospectus is authorized by the Exchange Company pursuant to a transfer order made under section 47 of the Securities and Futures Commission Ordinance (Cap. 24), shall not apply to the Commission nor the Exchange Company.

(2) No person shall be liable under subsection (1) if he proves-

> *(a)* that, having consented to become a director of the company, he withdrew his consent before the issue of the prospectus, and that it was issued without his authority or consent; or
>
> *(b)* that the prospectus was issued without his knowledge or consent, and that on

becoming aware of its issue he forthwith gave reasonable public notice that it was issued without his knowledge or consent; or

(c) that, after the issue of the prospectus and before allotment thereunder, he, on becoming aware of any untrue statement therein, withdrew his consent thereto and gave reasonable public notice of the withdrawal and of the reason therefor; or

(d) that-

(i) as regards every untrue statement not purporting to be made on the authority of an expert or of a public official document or statement, he had reasonable ground to believe, and did up to the time of the allotment of the shares or debentures, as the case may be, believe, that the statement was true; and

(ii) as regards every untrue statement purporting to be a statement by an expert or contained in what purports to be a copy of or extract from a report or valuation of an expert, it fairly represented the statement, or was a correct and fair copy of or extract from the report or valuation, and he had reasonable ground to believe and did up to the time of the issue of the prospectus believe that the person making the statement was competent to make it and that person had given the consent required by section 38C to the issue of the prospectus and had not withdrawn that consent before delivery of a copy of the prospectus for registration or, to the defendant's knowledge, before allotment thereunder; and

(iii) as regards every untrue statement purporting to be a statement made by an official person or contained in what purports to be a copy of or extract from a public official document, it was a correct and fair representation of the statement or copy of or extract from the document:

Provided that this subsection shall not apply in the case of a person liable, by reason of his having given a consent required of him by the said section 38C, as a person who has authorized the issue of the prospectus in respect of an untrue statement purporting to be made by him as an expert.

(3) A person who, apart from this subsection would under subsection (1) be liable, by reason of his having given a consent required of him by section 38C, as a person who has authorized the issue of a prospectus in respect of an untrue statement purporting to be made by him as an expert, shall not be so liable if he proves-

(a) that, having given his consent under the said section 38C to the issue of the

prospectus, he withdrew it in writing before delivery of a copy of the prospectus for registration; or

(b)　　that, after delivery of a copy of the prospectus for registration and before allotment thereunder, he, on becoming aware of the untrue statement, withdrew his consent in writing and gave reasonable public notice of the withdrawal, and of the reason therefor; or

(c)　　that he was competent to make the statement and that he had reasonable ground to believe and did up to the time of the allotment of the shares or debentures, as the case may be, believe that the statement was true.

(4)　　Where-

(a)　　the prospectus contains the name of a person as a director of the company, or as having agreed to become a director thereof, and he has not consented to become a director, or has withdrawn his consent before the issue of the prospectus, and has not authorized or consented to the issue thereof; or

(b)　　the consent of a person is required under section 38C to the issue of the prospectus and he either has not given that consent or has withdrawn it before the issue of the prospectus,

the directors of the company, except any without whose knowledge or consent the prospectus was issued, and any other person who authorized the issue thereof shall be liable to indemnify the person named as aforesaid or whose consent was required as aforesaid, as the case may be, against all damages, costs and expenses to which he may be made liable by reason of his name having been inserted in the prospectus or of the inclusion therein of a statement purporting to be made by him as an expert, as the case may be, or in defending himself against any action or legal proceeding brought against him in respect thereof.

Provided that a person shall not be deemed for the purposes of this subsection to have authorized the issue of a prospectus by reason only of his having given the consent required by section 38C to the inclusion therein of a statement purporting to be made by him as an expert.

(5)　　For the purposes of this section-

(a)　　the expression "promoter" means a promoter who was a party to the preparation of the prospectus, or of the portion thereof containing the untrue statement, but does not include any person by reason of his acting in a professional capacity for persons engaged in procuring the formation of the company; and

(b)　　the expression "expert" has the same meaning as in section 38C.

Criminal liability for misstatements in prospectus

40A.(1) Where a prospectus issued after the commencement of the Companies (Amendment) Ordinance 1972 includes any untrue statements, any person who authorized the issue of the prospectus shall be liable to imprisonment and a fine, unless he proves either that the statement was immaterial or that he had reasonable grounds to believe and did up to the time of the issue of the prospectus believe that the statement was true.

(2) A person shall not be deemed for the purposes of this section to have authorized the issue of a prospectus by reason only of his having given the consent required by section 38C to the inclusion therein of a statement purporting to be made by him as an expert.

(3) Subsection (1) shall not apply to the Commission or, where the relevant prospectus is authorized by the Exchange Company pursuant to a transfer order made under section 47 of the Securities and Futures Commission Ordinance (Cap. 24), shall not apply to the Commission nor the Exchange Company.

Right to damages and compensation not affected

40B. A person is not debarred from obtaining damages or other compensation from a company by reason only of -

    (a)   his holding or having held shares in the company; or

    (b)   his having any right -

        (i)   to apply or subscribe for shares; or

        (ii)   to be included in the register of the company in respect of shares.

Document containing offer of shares or debentures for sale to be deemed prospectus

41.(1) Where a company allots or agrees to allot any shares in or debentures of the company with a view to all or any of those shares or debentures being offered for sale to the public, any document by which the offer for sale to the public is made shall for all purposes be deemed to be a prospectus issued by the company, and all enactments and rules of law as to the contents of prospectuses and to liability in respect of statements in and omissions from prospectuses, or otherwise relating to prospectuses, shall apply and have effect accordingly, as if the shares or debentures had been offered to the public for subscription and as if persons accepting the offer in respect of any shares or debentures were subscribers for those shares or debentures, but without prejudice to the liability, if any, of the persons by whom the offer is made, in respect of misstatements contained in the document or otherwise in respect thereof.

(2) For the purposes of this Ordinance, it shall, unless the contrary is proved, be evidence that an allotment of, or an agreement to allot, shares or debentures was made with a view to the shares or debentures being offered for sale to the public if it is shown-

> (a) that an offer of the shares or debentures or of any of them for sale to the public was made within 6 months after the allotment or agreement to allot; or
>
> (b) that at the date when the offer was made the whole consideration to be received by the company in respect of the shares or debentures had not been so received.

(3) Section 38D as applied by this section shall have effect as though the persons making the offer were persons named in a prospectus as directors of a company, and section 38 as applied by this section shall have effect as if it required a prospectus to state in addition to the matters required by that section to be stated in a prospectus-

> (a) the net amount of the consideration received or to be received by the company in respect of the shares or debentures to which the offer relates; and
>
> (b) the place and time at which the contract under which the said shares or debentures have been or are to be allotted, or a copy thereof, may be inspected.

(4) Where a person making an offer to which this section relates is a company or a firm, it shall be sufficient if the document aforesaid is signed on behalf of the company or firm by 2 directors of the company or not less than half of the partners, as the case may be, and any such director or partner may sign by his agent authorized in writing.

Interpretation of provisions relating to prospectuses

41A. For the purposes of the foregoing provisions of this Part-

> (a) a statement included in a prospectus shall be deemed to be untrue if it is misleading in the form and context in which it is included; and
>
> (b) a statement shall be deemed to be included in a prospectus if it is contained therein or in any report or memorandum appearing on the face thereof or by reference incorporated therein or issued therewith.

Allotment

Prohibition of allotment unless minimum subscription received

42.(1) Subject to section 38A, no allotment shall be made of any share capital of a company offered to the public for subscription unless the amount stated in the prospectus as the minimum amount which, in the opinion of the directors must be raised by the issue of share capital in order to provide for the matters specified in paragraph 7 in Part I of the Third Schedule has been subscribed, and the sum payable on application for the amount so stated has been paid to and received by the company. For the purposes of this subsection, a sum shall be deemed to have been paid to and received by the company if a cheque for that sum has been received in good faith by the company and the directors of the company have no reason for suspecting that the cheque will not be paid.

(2) The amount so stated in the prospectus shall be reckoned exclusively of any amount payable otherwise than in cash and is in this Ordinance referred to as the minimum subscription.

(3) The amount payable on application on each share shall not be less than 5 per cent of the nominal amount of the share.

(4) Subject to section 38A, if the conditions aforesaid have not been complied with on the expiration of 30 days after the first issue of the prospectus, all money received from applicants for shares shall be forthwith repaid to them without interest, and, if any such money is not so repaid within 38 days after the issue of the prospectus, the directors of the company shall be jointly and severally liable to repay that money with interest at the rate of 8 per cent per annum from the expiration of the 38th day:

Provided that a director shall not be liable if he proves that the default in the repayment of the money was not due to any misconduct or negligence on his part.

(5) Any condition requiring or binding any applicant for shares to waive compliance with any requirement of this section shall be void.

(6) This section, except subsection (3), shall not apply to any allotment of shares subsequent to the first allotment of shares offered to the public for subscription.

Prohibition of allotment in certain cases unless statement in lieu of prospectus delivered to Registrar

43.(1) A company having a share capital which does not issue a prospectus on its formation, or which has issued such a prospectus but has not proceeded to allot any of the shares offered to the public for subscription, shall not allot any of its shares or debentures unless at least 3 days before the first allotment of either shares or debentures there has been delivered to the Registrar for registration a statement in lieu of prospectus signed by every person who is named therein as a director or a proposed director of the company or by his agent authorized in writing, in the form and containing the particulars set out in Part I of the Fourth Schedule and, in the cases mentioned in Part II of that Schedule, setting out the reports specified therein, and the said Parts I and II shall have effect subject to the provisions contained in Part III of that Schedule.

(2) Every statement in lieu of prospectus delivered under subsection (1) shall, where the persons making any such report as aforesaid have made therein or have, without giving the reasons, indicated therein any such adjustments as are mentioned in paragraph 5 of the said Fourth Schedule, have endorsed thereon or attached thereto a written statement signed by those persons setting out the adjustments and giving the reasons therefor.

(3) This section shall not apply to a private company.

(4) If a company acts in contravention of subsection (1) or (2), the company and every director of the company who knowingly and wilfully authorizes or permits the contravention shall be liable to a fine.

(5) Where a statement in lieu of prospectus delivered to the Registrar under subsection (1) includes any untrue statement, any person who authorized the delivery of the statement in lieu of prospectus for registration shall be liable to imprisonment and a fine, unless he proves either that the untrue statement was immaterial or that he had reasonable ground to believe and did up to the time of the delivery for registration of the statement in lieu of prospectus believe that the untrue statement was true.

(6) For the purposes of this section-

        (a)   a statement included in a statement in lieu of prospectus shall be deemed to be untrue if it is misleading in the form and context in which it is included; and

        (b)   a statement shall be deemed to be included in a statement in lieu of prospectus if it is contained therein or in any report or memorandum appearing on the face thereof or by reference incorporated therein.

(7) The Governor in Council may by regulation amend the Fourth Schedule.

Effect of irregular allotment

44.(1) An allotment made by a company to an applicant in contravention of the provisions of sections 42 and 43, shall be voidable at the instance of the applicant within 1 month after the holding of the statutory meeting of the company and not later, or, in any case where the company is not required to hold a statutory meeting, or where the allotment is made after the holding of the statutory meeting, within 1 month after the date of the allotment, and not later, and shall be so voidable notwithstanding that the company is in course of being wound up.

(2) If any director of a company knowingly contravenes, or permits or authorizes the contravention of, any of the provisions of the said sections with respect to allotment, he shall be liable to compensate the company and the allottee respectively for any loss, damages, or costs which the company or the allottee may have sustained or incurred thereby:

Provided that proceedings to recover any such loss, damages, or costs shall not be commenced after the expiration of 2 years from the date of the allotment.

Applications for, and allotment of, shares and debentures

44A.(1) No allotment shall be made of any shares in or debentures of a company in pursuance of a prospectus issued generally and no proceedings shall be taken on applications made in pursuance of a prospectus so issued, until the beginning of the 3rd day after that on which the prospectus is first so issued or such later time (if any) as may be specified in the prospectus. The beginning of the said 3rd day or such later time as aforesaid is hereafter in this Ordinance referred to as "the time of the opening of the subscription lists".

(2) Subject to section 38A, no allotment shall be made of any shares in or debentures of a company in pursuance of a prospectus issued generally later than 30 days after the day on which the prospectus is first so issued.

(3) In subsections (1) and (2), the references to the day on which the prospectus is first issued generally shall be construed as referring to the day on which it is first so issued as a newspaper advertisement:

Provided that, if it is not so issued as a newspaper advertisement before the 3rd day after that on which it is first so issued in any other manner, the said reference shall be construed as referring to the day on which it is first so issued in any manner.

(4) The validity of an allotment shall not be affected by any contravention of the foregoing provisions of this section but, in the event of any such contravention, the company and every officer of the company who is in default shall be liable to a fine.

(5) In the application of this section to a prospectus offering shares or debentures for sale, the foregoing subsections shall have effect with the substitution of references to sale for references to allotment, and with the substitution for the reference to the company and every officer of the company who is in default of a reference to any person by or through whom the offer is made and who knowingly and wilfully authorizes or permits the contravention.

(6) An application for shares in or debentures of a company which is made in pursuance of a prospectus issued generally shall not be revocable until after the expiration of the 5th day after the time of the opening of the subscription lists, or the giving before the expiration of the said 5th day, by some person responsible under section 40 for the prospectus, of a public notice having the effect under that section of excluding or limiting the responsibility of the person giving it.

(7) In reckoning for the purposes of this section and section 44B the 3rd or 5th day after another day, any intervening day which is a Saturday or Sunday or which is a general holiday in Hong Kong shall be disregarded, and if the 3rd or 5th day (as so reckoned) is itself a Saturday or Sunday or such a holiday there shall for the said purposes be substituted the 1st day thereafter which is none of them.

Allotment of shares and debentures to be listed on stock exchange

44B.(1) Where a prospectus, whether issued generally or not, states that application has been or will be made for permission for the shares or debentures offered thereby to be listed on any stock exchange, any allotment made on an application in pursuance of the prospectus shall, whenever made, be void if the permission has not been applied for before the 3rd day after the first issue of the prospectus or if the permission has been refused before the expiration of 3 weeks from the date of the closing of the subscription lists or such longer period not exceeding 6 weeks as may, within the said 3 weeks, be notified to the applicant for permission by or on behalf of the stock exchange.

(2) Where the permission has not been applied for as aforesaid, or has been refused as aforesaid, the company shall forthwith repay without interest all money received from applicants in pursuance of the prospectus, and, if any such money is not repaid within 8 days after the company becomes liable to repay it, the directors of the company shall be jointly and severally liable to repay that money with interest at the rate of 8 per cent per annum from the expiration of the 8th day:

Provided that a director shall not be liable if he proves that the default in the repayment of the money was not due to any misconduct or negligence on his part.

(3) All money received as aforesaid shall be kept in a separate bank account so long as the company may become liable to repay it under subsection (2); and, if default is made in complying with this subsection, the company and every officer of the company who is in default shall be liable to a fine.

(4) Any condition requiring or binding any applicant for shares or debentures to waive compliance with any requirement of this section shall be void.

(5) For the purposes of this section, permission shall not be deemed to be refused if it is intimated that the application for it, though not at present granted, will be given further consideration.

(6) This section shall have effect-

> *(a)* in relation to any shares or debentures agreed to be taken by a person underwriting an offer thereof by a prospectus as if he had applied therefor in pursuance of the prospectus; and

> *(b)* in relation to a prospectus offering shares for sale with the following modifications, that is to say-

>> **(i)** references to sale shall be substituted for references to allotment;

>> **(ii)** the persons by whom the offer is made, and not the company, shall be liable under subsection (2) to repay money received from applicants, and references to the company's liability under that subsection shall be construed accordingly; and

>> **(iii)** for the reference in subsection (3) to the company and every officer of the company who is in default there shall be substituted a reference to any person by or through whom the offer is made and who knowingly and wilfully authorizes or permits the default.

Return as to allotments

45.(1) Whenever a company limited by shares or a company limited by guarantee and having a share capital makes any allotment of its shares, the company shall within 8 weeks thereafter deliver to the Registrar for registration-

> *(a)* a return of the allotments in the specified form stating the number and nominal amount of the shares comprised in the allotment, the names (and, in the case of a Chinese allottee who has signed in Chinese characters any document

relating to his allotment, or who has, by adding Chinese characters after his name on any such document or by other means, indicated that he wishes the Chinese characters to be entered on the register of members, his name both in English and in Chinese characters) addresses and the occupations or descriptions of the allottees, and the amount, if any, paid or due and payable on each share whether on account of the nominal value of the share or by way of premium; and

    (b)   in the case of shares allotted as fully or partly paid up otherwise than in cash, or allotted in consideration of a premium paid or payable wholly or partly otherwise than in cash, a contract in writing constituting the title of the allottee to the allotment together with any contract for sale, or for services or other consideration in respect of which that allotment was made, such contracts being duly stamped, and a return stating the number and nominal amount of shares so allotted, the extent to which they are to be treated as paid up, the extent to which premium paid or payable wholly or partly otherwise than in cash is to be treated as paid, and the consideration for which they have been allotted.

(1A)   Notwithstanding subsection (1)-

    (a)   where shares are allotted credited as fully or partly paid up otherwise than in cash in pursuance of a scheme of arrangement under section 166, the delivery to the Registrar under that section of an office copy of the order of the court sanctioning the scheme shall be a sufficient compliance with the requirements of subsection (1)(b);

    (b)   where shares are allotted credited as fully paid up on a capitalization, the delivery by the company to the Registrar of a copy of the resolution authorizing the allotment shall be a sufficient compliance with the requirements of subsection (1)(b).

(2) Where such a contract as mentioned in subsection (1)(b) is not reduced to writing, the company shall within 8 weeks after the allotment deliver to the Registrar for registration the particulars of the contract specified in that subsection, and the Registrar may, as a condition of filing the particulars, require that the duty payable thereon be adjudicated under section 13 of the Stamp Duty Ordinance (Cap.117).

(3) If default is made in complying with this section, the company and every officer of the company who is in default shall be liable to a default fine and, for continued default, to a daily default fine:

Provided that, in case of default in delivering to the Registrar any document within 8 weeks after the allotment any document required to be delivered by this section, the company, or any person liable for the default, may apply to the court for relief, and the court, if satisfied that the omission to deliver the document was accidental or due to inadvertence or that it is just and equitable to grant relief, may make an order extending the time for the delivery of the document for such period as the court may think proper.

Commissions and Discounts

Power to pay certain commissions, and prohibition of payment of all other commissions, discounts, &c.

46.(1) It shall be lawful for a company to pay a commission to any person in consideration of his subscribing or agreeing to subscribe, whether absolutely or conditionally, for any shares in the company, or procuring or agreeing to procure subscriptions, whether absolute or conditional, for any shares in the company if-

(a) the payment of the commission is authorized by the articles; and

(b) the commission paid or agreed to be paid does not exceed 10 per cent of the price at which the shares are issued or the amount or rate authorized by the articles, whichever is the less; and

(c) the amount or rate per cent of the commission paid or agreed to be paid is-

(i) in the case of shares offered to the public for subscription, disclosed in the prospectus; or

(ii) in the case of shares not offered to the public for subscription, disclosed in the statement in lieu of prospectus, or in a statement in the specified form signed in like manner as a statement in lieu of prospectus and delivered before the payment of the commission to the Registrar for registration, and, where a circular or notice, not being a prospectus, inviting subscription for the shares is issued, also disclosed in that circular or notice; and

(d) the number of shares which persons have agreed for a commission to subscribe absolutely is disclosed in manner aforesaid.

(2) Save as aforesaid, no company shall apply any of its shares or capital money either directly or indirectly in payment of any commission, discount, or allowance, to any person in consideration of his subscribing or agreeing to subscribe, whether absolutely or conditionally, for any shares of the company, or procuring or agreeing to procure subscriptions, whether absolute or conditional, for any shares in the company, whether the shares or money be so applied by being added to the purchase money of any property acquired by the company or to the contract price of any work to be executed for the company, or the money be paid out of the nominal purchase money or contract price, or otherwise.

(3) Nothing in this section shall affect the power of any company to pay such brokerage as it has heretofore been lawful for a company to pay.

(4) A vendor to, promoter of, or other person who receives payment in money or shares from, a company shall have and shall be deemed always to have had power to apply any part of the money or shares so received in payment of any commission, the payment of which, if made directly by the company, would have been legal under this section.

(5) If default is made in complying with the provisions of this section relating to the delivery to the Registrar of the statement in the specified form, the company and every officer of the company who is in default shall be liable to a fine.

47.   *(Repealed)*

Financial assistance by a company for acquisition of its own shares

Provisions applying to all companies

Financial assistance generally prohibited

47A.(1) Subject to sections 47B to 48, where a person is acquiring or is proposing to acquire shares in a company, it is not lawful for the company or any of its subsidiaries to give financial assistance directly or indirectly for the purpose of that acquisition before or at the same time as the acquisition takes place.

(2)   Subject to sections 47B to 48, where a person has acquired shares in a company and any liability has been incurred (by that or any other person), for the purpose of that acquisition, it is not lawful for the company or any of its subsidiaries to give financial assistance directly or indirectly for the purpose of reducing or discharging the liability so incurred.

(3)   If a company acts in contravention of this section, it is liable to a fine, and every officer who is in default is liable to imprisonment or a fine.

Definitions

47B.(1)   In sections 47A to 48-

"distributable profits", in relation to the giving of any financial assistance-

> *(a)*   means those profits out of which the company could lawfully make a distribution equal in value to that assistance; and

> *(b)*   includes, in a case where the financial assistance is or includes a non-cash asset, any profit which, if the company were to make a distribution of that asset, would under section 79L be available for that purpose;

"distribution" has the meaning given by section 79A;

"financial assistance" means-

(a)   financial assistance given by way of gift;

(b)   financial assistance given by way of guarantee, security or indemnity, other than an indemnity in respect of the indemnifier's own neglect or default, or by way of release or waiver;

(c)   financial assistance given by way of a loan or any other agreement under which any of the obligations of the person giving the assistance are to be fulfilled at a time when in accordance with the agreement any obligation of another party to the agreement remains unfulfilled, or by way of the novation of, or the assignment of rights arising under, a loan or such other agreement; or

(d)   any other financial assistance given by a company the net assets of which are thereby reduced to a material extent or which has no net assets.

(2)   In paragraph (d) of the definition of "financial assistance" in subsection (1), "net assets" has the same meaning as in section 157H(1).

(3)   In sections 47A to 48-

(a)   a reference to a person incurring a liability includes his changing his financial position by making an agreement or arrangement (whether enforceable or unenforceable, and whether made on his own account or with any other person) or by any other means; and

(b)   a reference to a company giving financial assistance for the purpose of reducing or discharging a liability incurred by a person for the purpose of the acquisition of shares includes its giving such assistance for the purpose of wholly or partly restoring his financial position to what it was before the acquisition took place.

Transactions not prohibited by section 47A

47C.(1) Section 47A(1) does not prohibit a company from giving financial assistance for the purpose of an acquisition of shares in it or its holding company if-

(a)   the company's principal purpose in giving that assistance is not to give it for the purpose of any such acquisition, or the giving of the assistance for that purpose is but an incidental part of some larger purpose of the company; and

(b)   the assistance is given in good faith in the interests of the company.

(2)   Section 47A(2) does not prohibit a company from giving financial assistance if-

(a) the company's principal purpose in giving the assistance is not to reduce or discharge any liability incurred by a person for the purpose of the acquisition of shares in the company or its holding company, or the reduction or discharge of any such liability is but an incidental part of some larger purpose of the company; and

(b) the assistance is given in good faith in the interests of the company.

(3) Section 47A does not prohibit-

(a) a distribution of a company's assets by way of dividend lawfully made or a distribution made in the course of the company's winding up;

(b) the allotment of bonus shares;

(c) a reduction of capital confirmed by order of the court under section 60;

(d) a redemption or purchase of shares made in accordance with sections 49 to 49S;

(e) anything done in pursuance of an order of the court under section 166;

(f) anything done under an arrangement made in pursuance of section 237; or

(g) anything done under an arrangement made between a company and its creditors which is binding on the creditors by virtue of section 254.

(4) Section 47A does not prohibit-

(a) where the lending of money is part of the ordinary business of the company, the lending of money by the company in the ordinary course of its business;

(b) the provision by a company in accordance with any scheme for the time being in force, of money for the purchase of, or subscription for, fully paid shares in the company or its holding company, being a purchase or subscription by trustees of or for shares to be held by or for the benefit of employees of the company or of any subsidiary of the company, including any director holding a salaried employment or office in the company or any subsidiary of the company;

(c) the making by a company of loans to persons (other than directors) employed in good faith by the company with a view to enabling those persons to acquire fully paid shares in the company or its holding company to be held by them by way of beneficial ownership.

(5) References in subsection (4)(c) to a director shall include references *(a)*   the spouse or any child or step-child of such director;

(b)   a person acting in his capacity as the trustee (other than as trustee under an employee's share scheme or a pension scheme) of any trust the beneficiaries of which include the director, his spouse or any of his children or step-children or the terms of which confer a power on the trustees that may be exercised for the benefit of the director, his spouse or any of his children or step-children; and

(c)   a person acting in his capacity as partner of that director or of his spouse, child or step-child, or of any trustee referred to in paragraph (b).

(6)   References in subsection (5) to the child or step-child of any person shall include a reference to any illegitimate child of that person, but shall not include a reference to any person who has attained the age of 18 years.

Listed Companies

Special restriction for listed companies

47D.(1) In the case of a listed company, section 47C(4) authorizes the giving of financial assistance only if the company has net assets which are not thereby reduced or, to the extent that those assets are thereby reduced, if the assistance is provided out of distributable profits.

(2)   For this purpose the following definitions apply-

(a)   "net assets" means the amount by which the aggregate of the company's assets exceeds the aggregate of its liabilities (taking the amount of both assets and liabilities to be as stated in the company's accounting records immediately before the financial assistance is given);

(b)   "liabilities" includes any amount retained as reasonably necessary for the purpose of providing for any liability or loss which is either likely to be incurred, or certain to be incurred but uncertain as to the amount or as to the date on which it will arise.

Unlisted Companies

Relaxation of section 47A for unlisted companies

47E.(1) Section 47A does not prohibit an unlisted company from giving financial assistance in a case where the acquisition of shares in question is or was an acquisition of shares in the company or, if it is a subsidiary of another unlisted company, in that other company if the following provisions of this section, and sections 47F to 48, are complied with as respects the giving of that assistance.

(2) The financial assistance may only be given if the company has net assets which are not thereby reduced or, to the extent that they are reduced, if the assistance is provided out of distributable profits and section 47D(2) applies for the interpretation of this subsection.

(3) This section does not permit financial assistance to be given by a subsidiary, in a case where the acquisition of shares in question is or was an acquisition of shares in its holding company, if it is also a subsidiary of a listed company which is itself a subsidiary of that holding company.

(4) Unless the company proposing to give the financial assistance is a wholly-owned subsidiary, the giving of assistance under this section shall be approved by special resolution of the company in general meeting.

(5) Where the financial assistance is to be given by the company in a case where the acquisition of shares in question is or was an acquisition of shares in its holding company, that holding company and any other company which is both the company's holding company and a subsidiary of that other holding company (except, in any case, a company which is a wholly-owned subsidiary) shall also approve by special resolution in general meeting the giving of the financial assistance.

(6) A majority of the directors of the company proposing to give the financial assistance and, where the shares acquired or to be acquired are shares in its holding company, a majority of the directors of that company and of any other company which is both the company's holding company and a subsidiary of that other holding company shall before the financial assistance is given make a statutory declaration in the specified form complying with section 47F.

Statutory declaration under section 47E

47F.(1) A statutory declaration made by a majority of a company's directors under section 47E(6) shall state-

> *(a)*   the form which such assistance is to take;

> *(b)*   the names, addresses and occupations of the persons to whom such assistance is to be given;

> *(c)*   the purpose for which the company intends those persons to use such assistance;

> *(d)*   that the directors making the declaration have formed the opinion, as regards the company's initial situation immediately following the date on which the assistance is proposed to be given, that there will be no ground on which it could then be found to be unable to pay its debts; and either-

>> **(i)**   if it is intended to commence the winding up of the company within 12 months of that date, that the company will be able to pay its debts in full within 12 months of the commencement of the winding up; or

(ii) in any other case, that the company will be able to pay its debts as they fall due during the year immediately following that date.

(2) In forming their opinion for purposes of subsection (1)(d), the directors shall take into account the same liabilities (including contingent and prospective liabilities) as would be relevant under section 177 to the question whether the company is unable to pay its debts.

(3) The statutory declaration shall be delivered to the Registrar-

(a) together with a copy of any special resolution passed by the company under section 47E and delivered to the Registrar in compliance with section 117; or

(b) where no such resolution is required to be passed, within 15 days after the making of the declaration.

(4) If a company fails to comply with subsection (3), the company and every officer who is in default is liable to a fine and, for continued default, to a daily default fine.

(5) A director of a company who makes a statutory declaration under section 47E without having reasonable grounds for the opinion expressed in it is liable to imprisonment or a fine.

Special resolution under section 47E

47G.(1) A special resolution required by section 47E to be passed by a company approving the giving of financial assistance shall be passed on the date on which the directors of that company make the statutory declaration required by that section in connection with the giving of that assistance, or within 30 days immediately following that date.

(2) Where such a resolution has been passed, an application may be made to the court for the cancellation of the resolution-

(a) by the holders of not less in the aggregate than 10% in nominal value of the company's issued share capital or any class of it; or

(b) if the company is not limited by shares, by not less than 10% of the company's members,

but the application shall not be made by a person who has consented to or voted in favour of the resolution.

(3) The application shall be made within 28 days after the passing of the resolution and may be made on behalf of the persons entitled to make the application by such one or more of their number as they may appoint in writing for the purpose.

(4) If such an application is made, the company shall forthwith give notice in the specified form of that fact to the Registrar.

(5) On the hearing of the application, the court shall make an order either cancelling or confirming the resolution and-

> *(a)* may make that order on such terms and conditions as it thinks fit, and may (if it thinks fit) adjourn the proceedings in order that an arrangement may be made to the satisfaction of the court for the purchase of the interests of dissentient members; and

> *(b)* may give such directions and make such orders as it thinks expedient for facilitating or carrying into effect any such arrangement.

(6) The court's order may, if the court thinks fit, provide for the purchase by the company of the shares of any of its members and for the reduction accordingly of the company's capital, and may make such alterations in the company's memorandum and articles as may be required in consequence of that provision.

(7) The company shall, within 15 days from the making of the court's order, or within such longer period as the court may at any time by order direct, deliver to the Registrar an office copy of the order.

(8) If the court's order requires the company not to make any, or any specified, alteration in its memorandum or articles, the company has not then power without the leave of the court to make any such alteration in breach of the requirement.

(9) An alteration in the memorandum or articles made by virtue of an order under this section, if not made by resolution of the company, is of the same effect as if duly made by resolution; and this Ordinance applies accordingly to the memorandum or articles as so altered.

(10) A company which fails to comply with subsection (4) or (7), and any officer who is in default, is liable to a fine and, for continued default, to a daily default fine.

(11) A special resolution passed by a company is not effective for purposes of section 47E-

> *(a)* unless the declaration made in compliance with section 47E(6) by the directors of the company is available for inspection by members of the company at the meeting at which the resolution is passed;

> *(b)* if it is cancelled by the court on an application under this section.

Time for giving financial assistance under section 47E

48.(1) This section applies as to the time before and after which financial assistance may not be given by a company in pursuance of section 47E.

(2) Where a special resolution is required by that section to be passed approving the giving of the assistance, the assistance shall not be given before the expiry of the period of 4 weeks beginning with-

> > (a)   the date on which the special resolution is passed; or
>
> > (b)   where more than one such resolution is passed, the date on which the last of them is passed,

unless for that resolution (or, if more than one, each of them), every member of the company which passed the resolution who is entitled to vote at general meetings of the company voted in favour of the resolution.

(3)   If application for the cancellation of any such resolution is made under section 47G, the financial assistance shall not be given before the final determination of the application unless the court otherwise orders.

(4)   The assistance shall not be given after the expiry of the period of 3 months beginning with-

> > (a)   the date on which the directors of the company proposing to give the assistance made their statutory declaration under section 47E; or
>
> > (b)   where that company is a subsidiary and both its directors and the directors of any of its holding companies made such a declaration, the date on which the earliest of the declarations is made,

unless the court, on an application under section 47G, otherwise orders.

Construction of References to offering Shares or Debentures to the Public

Construction of references to offering shares or debentures to the public

48A.(1)   Any reference in this Ordinance to offering shares or debentures to the public shall, subject to any provision to the contrary contained therein, be construed as including a reference to offering them to any section of the public, whether selected as members or debenture holders of the company concerned or as clients of the person issuing the prospectus or in any other manner, and references in this Ordinance or in a company's articles to invitations to the public to subscribe for shares or debentures shall, subject as aforesaid, be similarly construed.

(2)   Subsection (1) shall not be taken as requiring any offer or invitation to be treated as made to the public if it can properly be regarded, in all the circumstances, as not being calculated to result, directly or indirectly, in the shares or debentures becoming available for subscription or purchase by persons other than those receiving the offer or invitation, or otherwise as being a domestic concern of the persons making and receiving it, and in particular-

> > (a)   a provision in a company's articles prohibiting invitations to the public to subscribe for shares or debentures shall not be taken as prohibiting the making to members or debenture holders of an invitation which can properly be regarded as aforesaid; and

(b)   the provisions of this Ordinance relating to private companies shall be construed accordingly.

Issue of Shares at Premium, Redeemable Preference Shares, and Shares at Discount

Application of premiums received on issue of shares

48B.(1) Where a company issues shares at a premium, whether for cash or otherwise, a sum equal to the aggregate amount or value of the premiums on those shares shall be transferred to an account, to be called "the share premium account", and the provisions of this Ordinance relating to the reduction of the share capital of a company shall, except as provided in this section, apply as if the share premium account were paid-up share capital of the company.

(2)   Where shares are issued for a consideration other than cash and the value of the consideration, as estimated by the directors having regard to all relevant information, is in excess of the amount credited as paid up on the shares so issued, the shares shall be deemed to have been issued at a premium equal to the difference between the value so estimated and the amount credited as paid up on the shares so issued.

(3)   The share premium account may, notwithstanding anything in subsection (1), be applied by the company-

(a)   in paying up unissued shares of the company to be issued to members of the company as fully paid bonus shares;

(b)   in writing off-

    (i)   the preliminary expenses of the company; or

    (ii)   the expenses of, or the commission paid or discount allowed on, any issue of shares of the company; or

(c)   in providing for the premium payable on redemption of any redeemable preference shares of the company.

(4)   For the purposes of subsection (3), the expenses of the issue of any shares shall be deemed to include such portion of the ad valorem fee paid under the Eighth Schedule by the company upon its registration or upon any increase thereafter in its nominal share capital as is attributable to the nominal amount of the shares issued.

(5)   Where a company has before the commencement of the Companies (Amendment) (No. 4) Ordinance 1974 issued any shares at a premium, this section shall apply as if the shares had been issued after the commencement of that Ordinance:

Provided that any part of the premiums which has been so applied that it does not at the commencement of that Ordinance form an identifiable part of the company's reserves within the meaning of the Tenth Schedule shall be disregarded in determining the sum to be included in the share premium account.

Redeemable shares; Purchase by a company of its own shares

Redemption and purchase generally

Power to issue redeemable shares

49.(1) Subject to sections 49 to 49S, a company limited by shares or limited by guarantee and having a share capital may, if authorized to do so by its articles, issue shares which are to be redeemed or are liable to be redeemed at the option of the company or the shareholder.

(2) No redeemable shares may be issued at a time when there are no issued shares of the company which are not redeemable.

(3) Redeemable shares may not be redeemed unless they are fully paid; and the terms of redemption shall provide for payment on redemption.

Financing etc. of redemption

49A.(1) Subject to subsection (2) and to sections 49I and 49P(4)-

  (a) redeemable shares may only be redeemed out of distributable profits of the company or out of the proceeds of a fresh issue of shares made for the purposes of the redemption; and

  (b) any premium payable on redemption shall be paid out of distributable profits of the company.

(2) If the redeemable shares were issued at a premium, any premium payable on their redemption may be paid out of the proceeds of a fresh issue of shares made for the purposes of the redemption, up to an amount equal to-

  (a) the aggregate of the premiums received by the company on the issue of the shares redeemed; or

  (b) the current amount of the company's share premium account (including any sum transferred to that account in respect of premiums on the new shares),

whichever is the less; and in that case the amount of the company's share premium account shall be reduced by a sum corresponding (or by sums in the aggregate corresponding) to the amount of any payment made by virtue of this subsection out of the proceeds of the issue of the new shares.

(3) Subject to sections 49 to 49S, redemption of shares may be effected on such terms and in such manner as may be provided by the company's articles.

(4) Shares redeemed under this section shall be treated as cancelled on redemption, and the amount of the company's issued share capital shall be diminished by the nominal value of those shares accordingly; but the redemption of shares by a company is not to be taken as reducing the amount of the company's authorized share capital.

(5) Without prejudice to subsection (4) and subject to subsection (6), where a company is about to redeem shares, it has power to issue shares up to the nominal value of the shares to be redeemed as if those shares had never been issued.

(6) Where new shares are issued before the redemption of existing shares, the new shares shall be deemed, so far as relates to the Eighth Schedule, not to have been issued under subsection (5) unless the existing shares are redeemed within 1 month of the issue of the new shares.

Power of company to purchase own shares

49B.(1) Subject to sections 49, 49A, 49BA, 49C, 49E, 49F, 49G, 49H, 49P, 49Q, 49R and 49S, a listed company may, if authorized to do so by its articles, purchase its own shares (including any redeemable shares).

(2) Subject to sections 49 to 49S, an unlisted company limited by shares or limited by guarantee and having a share capital may, if authorized to do so by its articles, purchase its own shares (including any redeemable shares).

(3) Sections 49 and 49A apply to the purchase by a company under this section of its own shares as they apply to the redemption of redeemable shares, save that the terms and manner of purchase need not be determined by the articles as required by section 49A(3).

(4) Notwithstanding subsections (1) and (2) but subject to sections 49, 49A, 49F, 49G, 49H, 49I(4) and (5), 49P, 49Q, 49R and 49S, except that such purchases may be made either out of or otherwise than out of its distributable profits or the proceeds of a fresh issue of shares, a listed company and an unlisted company limited by shares or limited by guarantee and having a share capital may, if authorized to do so by its articles, purchase its own shares (including any redeemable shares) in order to-

> *(a)* settle or compromise a debt or claim;

> *(b)* eliminate a fractional share or fractional entitlement or in the case of a listed company, an odd lot of shares;

> *(c)* fulfil an agreement in which the company has an option or is obliged to purchase shares under an employee share scheme which had previously been approved by the company in general meeting; or

     (d)   comply with an order of the court under section 8(4), 47G(5) or 168A(2).

(5)   In subsection (4)(b), an "odd lot of shares" means a number of shares in the company less than the usual number authorized for trading on the Unified Exchange.

(6)   A company may not under this section purchase its shares if as a result of the purchase there would no longer be any member of the company holding shares other than redeemable shares.

Requirements for listed company to purchase own shares

49BA.(1) A listed company may purchase its own shares-

     (a)   subject to subsections (2), (3) and (7), under a general offer;

     (b)   subject to subsections (2), (3) and (4), on the Unified Exchange or on a recognized stock exchange;

     (c)   subject to subsections (5) and (6), otherwise than on the Unified Exchange or on a recognized stock exchange, and otherwise than under a general offer referred to in paragraph (a).

(2)   A listed company shall not-

     (a)   make a general offer under subsection (1)(a) unless the proposed general offer is authorized by the company in general meeting; or

     (b)   purchase any of its own shares on the Unified Exchange or on a recognized stock exchange under subsection (1)(b), unless the proposed purchase is authorized by the company in general meeting.

(3)   A listed company shall include together with the notice of any general meeting called for the purpose of subsection (2) -

     (a)   in the case of a general offer under subsection (1)(a)-

          (i)   a copy of the document containing the proposed general offer; and

          (ii)   a statement, signed by the directors of the company, containing such particulars as would enable a reasonable person to form as a result thereof a valid and justifiable opinion as to the merits of the proposed general offer; and

     (b)   in the case of a purchase under subsection (1)(b), a memorandum of the terms of the proposed purchase.

(4)   An authorization given by a company in general meeting under subsection (2)(b) shall be valid for the period expiring on the date of the next annual general meeting of the company and such period may be extended by the company at such annual general meeting until the date of the next annual general meeting of the company.

(5) A listed company shall not make a purchase of any of its shares under subsection (1)(c) unless the proposed purchase has been authorized by a special resolution of the company and section 49D(4) shall apply to such a resolution as it applies to a resolution under that subsection.

(6) A listed company shall include together with the notice of any meeting called for the purpose of subsection (5) -

> *(a)* where the proposed purchase agreement is in writing, a copy of the proposed purchase agreement; or

> *(b)* where the proposed purchase agreement is not in writing, a memorandum of the terms of the proposed purchase agreement; and

> *(c)* a statement, signed by the directors of the company, after having made due and diligent inquiry of the members of the company holding the shares to which the proposed purchase agreement relates, containing such particulars as would enable a reasonable person to form as a result thereof a valid and justifiable opinion as to the merits of the proposed purchase agreement.

(7) If, in the case of a general offer under subsection (1)(a), a member of the company may be compelled to dispose of his shares under section 168B-

> *(a)* the company shall appoint an independent investment adviser to advise members who may be affected by the compulsory disposal on the merits of the proposed general offer; and

> *(b)* the proposed general offer shall be authorized by a special resolution of the company, on which no relevant shareholder votes and for this purpose-

>> **(i)** a relevant shareholder shall be regarded as voting not only if he votes on a poll on the question whether the resolution shall be passed, but also if he votes on the resolution otherwise than on a poll;

>> **(ii)** notwithstanding anything in the company's articles, any member of the company may demand a poll on that question; and

>> **(iii)** a vote and a demand for a poll by a person as proxy for a relevant shareholder are the same (respectively) as a vote and demand by a relevant shareholder.

(8) A person shall not be appointed as an investment adviser under subsection (7) unless he is a registered or exempt investment adviser within the meaning of the Securities Ordinance (Cap. 333) and is neither-

(a)   a member, officer or employee of the company making the general offer or of a related company thereof; nor

(b)   a related company of the company making the general offer.

(9)   For the purposes of this section -

"general offer" means an offer to all members of a company or to all members holding shares of a particular class in a company, other than any members residing in a jurisdiction where such an offer is contrary to the laws of that jurisdiction, on terms which are the same in relation to all such shares or in relation to the shares of each class;

"recognized stock exchange" means a stock exchange recognized for the purposes of this section by the Commission and the Exchange Company by notice published in the Gazette;

"related company" in relation to a company, means any company that is the company's subsidiary or holding company or a subsidiary of that company's holding company;

"relevant shareholder" means a person to whom the description "relevant shareholder" in the Thirteenth Schedule applies.

(10)   In the application of the definition of "officer" in section 2(1) to subsection (8), "director" includes-

(a)   any person occupying the position of director, by whatever name called; and

(b)   any person in accordance with whose directions or instructions the directors of the company are accustomed to act.

(11)   The Commission may exempt any listed company from any of the provisions of this section, subject to such conditions as it thinks fit.

(12)   The Commission may-

(a)   suspend or withdraw an exemption granted under subsection (11) on the ground that the conditions subject to which the exemption was granted have not been complied with or on such other ground as the Commission thinks fit; or

(b)   vary any condition imposed under subsection (11).

Payments apart from purchase price to be made out of distributable profits

49C.   A payment made by a company in consideration of-

(a)   acquiring any right with respect to the purchase of its own shares permitted under section 49B;

(b) acquiring any right with respect to the purchase of its own shares in pursuance of a contract approved under section 49E;

(c) the variation of a contract permitted under section 49B or approved under section 49D or 49E; or

(d) the release of any of the company's obligations with respect to the purchase of any of its own shares under a contract permitted under section 49B or approved under section 49D or 49E,

shall be made out of the company's distributable profits.

Authority for purchase by unlisted company

49D.(1) An unlisted company may only purchase its own shares under a contract approved in advance in accordance with this section or under section 49E.

(2) The terms of the proposed contract shall be authorized by a special resolution of the company before the contract is entered into; and this section applies with respect to that authority and to resolutions conferring it.

(3) The authority to enter into a contract to purchase an unlisted company's own shares may be varied, revoked or from time to time renewed by special resolution of the company.

(4) A special resolution to confer, vary, revoke or renew authority under subsection (3) is not effective if any member of the company holding shares to which the resolution relates exercises the voting rights carried by any of those shares in voting on the resolution and the resolution would not have been passed if he had not done so and for this purpose-

(a) a member who holds shares to which the resolution relates is regarded as exercising the voting rights carried by those shares not only if he votes in respect of them on a poll on the question whether the resolution shall be passed, but also if he votes on the resolution otherwise than on a poll;

(b) notwithstanding anything in the company's articles, any member of the company may demand a poll on that question; and

(c) a vote and a demand for a poll by a person as proxy for a member are the same respectively as a vote and a demand by the member.

(5) A special resolution to confer, vary, revoke or renew authority under subsection (3) is not effective for the purposes of this section unless (if the proposed contract is in writing) a copy of the contract or (if not) a written memorandum of its terms is available for inspection by members of the company both-

(a) at the company's registered office for not less than 15 days ending with the date of the meeting at which the resolution is passed; and

(b)   at the meeting itself.

A memorandum of contract terms so made available shall include the names of any members holding shares to which the contract relates; and a copy of the contract so made available shall have annexed to it a written memorandum specifying any such names which do not appear in the contract itself.

(6)   An unlisted company may agree to a variation of an existing contract so approved, but only if the variation is authorized by a special resolution of the company before it is agreed to; and subsections (3), (4) and (5) apply to the authority for a proposed variation as they apply to the authority for a proposed contract, save that a copy of the original contract or (as the case may require) a memorandum of its terms, together with any variations previously made, shall also be available for inspection in accordance with subsection (5).

Authority for contingent purchase contract

49E.(1) A contingent purchase contract is a contract entered into by a company and relating to any of its shares-

(a)   which does not amount to a contract to purchase those shares; but

(b)   under which the company may (subject to any conditions) become entitled or obliged to purchase those shares.

(2)   A listed company may only make a purchase of its own shares in pursuance of a contingent purchase contract if the proposed contingent purchase contract is authorized in advance by a special resolution of the company before the contract is entered into, and section 49BA(5) and (6) applies to authorization for a proposed contingent purchase contract as to authorization for a proposed purchase agreement under section 49BA(1)(c).

(3)   An unlisted company may only make a purchase of its own shares in pursuance of a contingent purchase contract if the contract is approved in advance by a special resolution of the company before the contract is entered into; and section 49D(3), (4), (5) and (6) applies to the contract and its terms.

Assignment or release of company's right to purchase own shares

49F.(1) The rights of a company under a contract approved under section 49D or 49E or authorized under section 49BA or 49E are not capable of being assigned.

(2)   An agreement by an unlisted company to release its rights under a contract approved under section 49D or 49E is void unless the terms of the release agreement are approved in advance by a special resolution of the company before the agreement is entered into; and section 49D(3), (4), (5) and (6) applies to approval for a proposed release agreement as to authority for a proposed variation of an existing contract.

(3)   An agreement by a listed company to release its rights under a contract authorized under section 49BA(1)(a) or (c) or under section 49E is void unless the terms of the release agreement are authorized in advance by a special resolution of the company before the agreement is entered into; and section 49BA(5) and (6) applies to authorization for a proposed release agreement as to authorization for a proposed purchase agreement under section49BA(1)(c).

Disclosure by company of purchase of own shares

49G.(1) Within the period of 14 days beginning with the date on which any shares purchased by a company under this Ordinance are delivered to it, the company shall deliver to the Registrar for registration a return in the specified form stating with respect to shares of each class purchased the number and nominal value of those shares and the date on which they were delivered to the company.

(2)   In the case of a listed company, the return shall also state-

        (a)   the aggregate amount paid by the company for the shares; and

        (b)   the maximum and minimum prices paid in respect of shares of each class purchased

(3)   Particulars of shares delivered to the company on different dates and under different contracts may be included in a single return to the Registrar; and in such a case the amount required to be stated under subsection (2)(a) is the aggregate amount paid by the company for all the shares to which the return relates.

(4)   Where a company enters into a contract approved under section 49BA(1)(c), 49D or 49E, the company shall keep at its registered office-

        (a)   if the contract is in writing, a copy of it; and

        (b)   if not, a memorandum of its terms,

from the conclusion of the contract until the end of the period of 10 years beginning with the date on which the purchase of all the shares in pursuance of the contract is completed or (as the case may be) the date on which the contract otherwise determines.

(5)   Every copy and memorandum so required to be kept shall, during business hours (subject to such reasonable restrictions as the company may in general meeting impose, provided that not less than 2 hours in each day are allowed for inspection), be open to inspection without charge-

        (a)   by any member of the company; and

        (b)   if it is a listed company, by any other person.

(6)   If default is made in delivering to the Registrar any return required by this section, every officer of the company who is in default is liable to a fine and, for continued default, to a daily default fine.

(7) If default is made in complying with subsection (4), or if an inspection required under subsection

(5) is refused, the company and every officer who is in default is liable to a fine and, for continued default, to a daily default fine.

(8) In the case of a refusal of an inspection required under subsection (5) of a copy or memorandum, the court may by order compel an immediate inspection of it.

(9) The obligation of a company under subsection (4) to keep a copy of any contract or (as the case may be) a memorandum of its terms applies to any variation of the contract so long as it applies to the contract.

The capital redemption reserve

49H.(1) Where under this Ordinance shares of a company are redeemed or purchased wholly out of the company's profits, the amount by which the company's issued share capital is diminished in accordance with section 49A(4) on cancellation of the shares redeemed or purchased shall be transferred to a reserve, called "the capital redemption reserve".

(2) If the shares are redeemed or purchased wholly or partly out of the proceeds of a fresh issue and the aggregate amount of those proceeds is less than the aggregate nominal value of the shares redeemed or purchased, the amount of the difference shall be transferred to the capital redemption reserve.

(3) Subsection (2) does not apply if the proceeds of the fresh issue are applied by the company in making a redemption or purchase of its own shares in addition to a payment out of capital under section 49I.

(4) The provisions of this Ordinance relating to the reduction of a company's share capital apply as if the capital redemption reserve were paid-up share capital of the company, except that the reserve may be applied by the company in paying up its unissued shares to be allotted to members of the company as fully paid bonus shares.

Redemption or purchase of own shares out of capital (private companies only)

Power of private companies to redeem or purchase own shares out of capital

49I.(1) Subject to sections 49I to 49O, a private company limited by shares or limited by guarantee and having a share capital may, if so authorized by its articles, make a payment in respect of the redemption or purchase under section 49A or (as the case may be) section 49B, of its own shares otherwise than out of its distributable profits or the proceeds of a fresh issue of shares.

(2) References in this section to payment out of capital are (subject to subsection (6)) to any payment so made, whether or not it would be regarded apart from this section as a payment out of capital.

(3) The payment which may (if authorized in accordance with this Ordinance) be made by a company out of capital in respect of the redemption or purchase of its own shares is such an amount as, taken together with-

(a)   any available profits of the company; and

(b)   the proceeds of any fresh issue of shares made for the purposes of the redemption or purchase,

is equal to the price of redemption or purchase; and the payment permissible under this subsection is referred to in section 49S as the "permissible capital payment".

(4)   Subject to subsection (6), if the permissible capital payment for shares redeemed or purchased is less than their nominal amount, the amount of the difference shall be transferred to the company's capital redemption reserve.

(5)   Subject to subsection (6), if the permissible capital payment is greater than the nominal amount of the shares redeemed or purchased-

(a)   the amount of any capital redemption reserve, share premium account or fully paid share capital of the company; and

(b)   any amount representing unrealised profits of the company for the time being standing to the credit of any revaluation reserve maintained by the company,

may be reduced by a sum not exceeding (or by sums not in the aggregate exceeding) the amount by which the permissible capital payment exceeds the nominal amount of the shares.

(6)   Where the proceeds of a fresh issue are applied by a company in making any redemption or purchase of its own shares in addition to a payment out of capital under this section, the references in subsections (4) and (5) to the permissible capital payment are to be read as referring to the aggregate of that payment and those proceeds.

Availability of profits for purposes of section 49I

49J(1) The reference in section 49I(3)(a) to available profits of the company is to the company's profits which are available for distribution (within the meaning of Part IIA); but the question whether a company has any profits so available and the amount of any such profits are to be determined for purposes of that section in accordance with subsections (2), (3), (4), (5) and (6), instead of sections 79F, 79G, 79H, 79I, 79J and 79K.

(2)   Subject to subsection (3), that question is to be determined by reference to-

(a)   profits, losses, assets and liabilities;

(b)   provisions for depreciation, diminution in value of assets and retentions to meet liabilities; and

(c)   share capital and reserves (including undistributable reserves),

as stated in the relevant accounts for determining the permissible capital payment.

(3)   The relevant accounts for this purpose are such accounts, prepared as at any date within the period for determining the amount of the permissible capital payment, as are necessary to enable a reasonable judgment to be made as to the amounts of any of the items mentioned in subsection (2)(a) to (c).

(4)   For purposes of determining the amount of the permissible capital payment, the amount of the company's available profits (if any) determined in accordance with subsections (2) and (3) is treated as reduced by the amount of any distributions lawfully made by the company after the date of the relevant accounts and before the end of the period for determining the amount of that payment.

(5)   The reference in subsection (4) to distributions lawfully made by the company includes-

> *(a)*   financial assistance lawfully given out of distributable profits in a case falling within section 47D or 47E;

> *(b)*   any payment lawfully made by the company in respect of the purchase by it of any shares in the company (except a payment lawfully made otherwise than out of distributable profits); and

> *(c)*   a payment of any description specified in section 49C(1) lawfully made by the company.

(6)   Reference in this section to the period for determining the amount of the permissible capital payment is to the period of 3 months ending with the date on which the statutory declaration of the directors purporting to specify the amount of that payment is made in accordance with section 49K(3).

Conditions for payment out of capital

49K.(1) Subject to any order of the court under section 49O, a payment out of capital by a private company for the redemption or purchase of its own shares is not lawful unless the requirements of this section and sections 49L and 49M are satisfied.

(2)   The payment out of capital shall be approved by a special resolution of the company.

(3)   The company's directors shall make a statutory declaration specifying the amount of the permissible capital payment for the shares in question and stating that, having made full inquiry into the affairs and prospects of the company, they have formed the opinion-

> *(a)*   as regards its initial situation immediately following the date on which the payment out of capital is proposed to be made, that there will be no grounds on which the company could then be found unable to pay its debts; and

> *(b)*   as regards its prospects for the year immediately following that date, that, having regard to their intentions with respect to the management of the company's business during that year and to the amount and character of the

financial resources which will in their view be available to the company during that year, the company will be able to continue to carry on business as a going concern (and will accordingly be able to pay its debts as they fall due) throughout that year.

(4)   In forming their opinion for purposes of subsection (3)(a), the directors shall take into account the same liabilities (including prospective and contingent liabilities) as would be relevant under section 177 to the question whether a company is unable to pay its debts.

(5)   The directors' statutory declaration shall be in the specified form and contain such information with respect to the nature of the company's business as may be specified by the Registrar, and shall in addition have annexed to it a report addressed to the directors by the company's auditors stating that-

> *(a)*   they have inquired into the company's state of affairs;
>
> *(b)*   the amount specified in the declaration as the permissible capital payment for the shares in question is in their view properly determined in accordance with sections 49I and 49J; and
>
> *(c)*   they are not aware of anything to indicate that the opinion expressed by the directors in the declaration as to any of the matters mentioned in subsection (3) is unreasonable in all the circumstances.

(6)   A director who makes a declaration under this section without having reasonable grounds for the opinion expressed in the declaration is liable to imprisonment or a fine, or both.

Procedure for special resolution under section 49K

49L.(1) The resolution required by section 49K shall be passed on, or within the week immediately following, the date on which the directors make the statutory declaration required by that section; and the payment out of capital shall be made no earlier than 5 nor more than 7 weeks after the date of the resolution.

(2)   The resolution is ineffective if any member of the company holding shares to which the resolution relates exercises the voting rights carried by any of those shares in voting on the resolution and the resolution would not have been passed if he had not done so.

(3)   For purposes of subsection (2), a member who holds such shares is to be regarded as exercising the voting rights carried by them in voting on the resolution not only if he votes in respect of them on a poll on the question whether the resolution shall be passed, but also if he votes on the resolution otherwise than on a poll; and, notwithstanding anything in a company's articles, any member of the company may demand a poll on that question.

(4)   The resolution is ineffective unless the statutory declaration and auditors' report required by section 49K are available for inspection by members of the company at the meeting at which the resolution is passed.

(5) For purposes of this section a vote and a demand for a poll by a person as proxy for a member are the same (respectively) as a vote and demand by the member.

Publicity for proposed payment out of capital

49M.(1) Within the week immediately following the date of the resolution for payment out of capital the company shall cause to be published in the Gazette a notice-

> *(a)* stating that the company has approved a payment out of capital for the purpose of acquiring its own shares by redemption or purchase or both (as the case may be);
>
> *(b)* specifying the amount of the permissible capital payment for the shares in question and the date of the resolution under section 49L;
>
> *(c)* stating that the statutory declaration of the directors and the auditors' report required by that section are available for inspection at the company's registered office; and
>
> *(d)* stating that any creditor of the company may at any time within the 5 weeks immediately following the date of the resolution for payment out of capital apply to the court under section 49N for an order prohibiting the payment

(2) Within the week immediately following the date of the resolution the company shall also either cause a notice to the same effect as that required by subsection (1) to be published once in each of an English language newspaper and a Chinese language newspaper specified in the list issued for the purposes of section 71A or give notice in writing to that effect to each of its creditors.

(3) References in this section to the first notice date are to the day on which the company first publishes the notice required by subsection (1) or first publishes or gives the notice required by subsection (2) (whichever is the earlier).

(4) Not later than the first notice date the company shall deliver to the Registrar a copy of the statutory declaration of the directors and of the auditors' report required by section 49K.

(5) The statutory declaration and auditors' report-

> *(a)* shall be kept at the company's registered office throughout the period beginning with the first notice date and ending 5 weeks after the date of the resolution for payment out of capital; and
>
> *(b)* shall during business hours on any day during that period be open to the inspection of any member or creditor of the company without charge.

(6) If an inspection required under subsection (5) is refused, the company and every officer who is in default is liable to a fine and, for continued default, to a daily default fine.

(7) In the case of refusal of an inspection required under subsection (5) of a declaration or report, the court may by order compel an immediate inspection of that declaration or report.

Objections by company's members or creditors

49N.(1) Where a private company passes a special resolution approving for purposes of this Ordinance any payment out of capital for the redemption or purchase of any of its shares-

> *(a)* any member of the company other than one who consented to or voted in favour of the resolution; and
>
> *(b)* any creditor of the company,

may within 5 weeks of the date on which the resolution was passed apply to the court for cancellation of the resolution.

(2) The application may be made on behalf of the persons entitled to make it by such one or more of their number as they may appoint in writing for the purpose.

(3) If an application is made, the company shall-

> *(a)* forthwith give notice in the specified form of that fact to the Registrar; and
> *(b)* within 15 days from the making of any order of the court on the hearing of the application, or such longer period as the court may by order direct, deliver an office copy of the order to the Registrar.

(4) A company which fails to comply with subsection (3), and any officer who is in default, is liable to a fine and for continued default, to a daily default fine.

Powers of court on application under section 49N

49O(1) On the hearing of an application under section 49N the court may, if it thinks fit, adjourn the proceedings in order that an arrangement may be made to the court's satisfaction for the purchase of the interests of dissentient members or for the protection of dissentient creditors (as the case may be); and the court may give such directions and make such orders as it thinks expedient for facilitating or carrying into effect any such arrangement.

(2) Without prejudice to its powers under subsection (1), the court shall make an order on such terms and conditions as it thinks fit either confirming or cancelling the resolution; and, if the court confirms the resolution, it may in particular by order alter or extend any date or period of time specified in the resolution or in any provision in sections 49 to 49S which applies to the redemption or purchase of shares to which the resolution refers.

(3) The court's order may, if the court thinks fit, provide for the purchase by the company of the shares of any of its members and for the reduction accordingly of the company's capital, and may make such alterations in the company's memorandum and articles as may be required in consequence of that provision.

(4) If the court's order requires the company not to make any, or any specified, alteration in its memorandum or articles, the company has not then power without leave of the court to make any such alteration in breach of the requirement.

(5) An alteration in the memorandum or articles made by virtue of an order under this section, if not made by resolution of the company, is of the same effect as if duly made by resolution; and this Ordinance applies accordingly to the memorandum or articles as so altered.

Supplementary

Effect of company's failure to redeem or purchase

49P.(1) This section has effect where a company has, on or after the commencement of the Companies) (Amendment) Ordinance 1991-

> *(a)* issued shares on terms that they are or are liable to be redeemed; or

> *(b)* agreed to purchase any of its own shares.

(2) The company is not liable in damages in respect of any failure on its part to redeem or purchase any of the shares.

(3) Subsection (2) is without prejudice to any right of the holder of the shares other than his right to sue the company for damages in respect of its failure; but the court shall not grant an order for specific performance of the terms of redemption or purchase if the company shows that it is unable to meet the costs of redeeming or purchasing the shares in question out of distributable profits.

(4) If the company is wound up and at the commencement of the winding up any of the shares have not been redeemed or purchased, the terms of redemption or purchase may be enforced against the company; and when shares are redeemed or purchased under this subsection, they are treated as cancelled.

(5) Subsection (4) does not apply if-

> *(a)* the terms provided for the redemption or purchase to take place at a date later than that of the commencement of the winding up; or

> *(b)* during the period beginning with the date on which the redemption or purchase was to have taken place and ending with the commencement of the winding up the company could not at any time have lawfully made a distribution equal in value to the price at which the shares were to have been redeemed or purchased.

(6) There shall be paid in priority to any amount which the company is liable under subsection (4) to pay in respect of any shares-

(*a*) all other debts and liabilities of the company (other than any due to members in their character as such);

(*b*) if other shares carry rights (whether as to capital or as to income) which are preferred to the rights as to capital attaching to the first-mentioned shares, any amount due in satisfaction of those preferred rights,

but, subject to that, any such amount shall be paid in priority to any amounts due to members in satisfaction of their rights (whether as to capital or income) as members.

(**7**) Where by virtue of section 71 of the Bankruptcy Ordinance (Cap. 6) as applied by section 264, a creditor of a company is entitled to payment of any interest only after payment of all other debts of the company, the company's debts and liabilities for purposes of subsection (6) include the liability to pay that interest.

Power for Governor in Council to modify certain sections

49Q.(1) The Governor in Council may by regulations modify sections 49 to 49S with respect to any of the following matters-

(*a*) the authority required for a purchase by a company of its own shares;
(*b*) the authority required for the release by a company of its rights under a contract for the purchase of its own shares or a contract under which the company may (subject to any conditions) become entitled or obliged to purchase its own shares;

(*c*) the information to be included in a return delivered by a company to the Registrar in accordance with section 49G(1);

(*d*) the matters to be dealt with in the statutory declaration of the directors under section 49K with a view to indicating their opinion of their company's ability to make a proposed payment out of capital with due regard to its financial situation and prospects; and

(*e*) the contents of the auditors' report required by that section to be annexed to that declaration.

(**2**) The Governor in Council may also by regulations so made make such provision (including modification of sections 49 to 49S) as appears to him to be appropriate-

(*a*) for wholly or partly relieving companies from the requirement of section 49I(3)(a) that any available profits shall be taken into account in determining the amount of the permissible capital payment under that section; or

(*b*) for permitting a company's share premium account to be applied, to any extent appearing to the Governor in Council to be appropriate, in providing for the premiums payable on redemption or purchase by the company of any of its own shares.

(3) Regulations under this section-

(a) may make such further modification of sections 49 to 49S and sections 79J(2) and (3) and 79M as appears to the Governor in Council to be reasonably necessary in consequence of any provision made under such regulations by virtue of subsection (1) or (2);

(b) may make different provision for different cases or classes of case; and

(c) may contain such further consequential provisions, and such incidental and supplementary provisions, as the Governor in Council thinks fit.

(4) No regulations shall be made under this section unless a draft of them has been laid before and approved by resolution of the Legislative Council and section 34 of the Interpretation and General Clauses Ordinance (Cap. 1) shall not apply to such regulations.

Transitional cases arising under sections 49 to 49S; and savings

49R.(1) Any preference shares issued by a company before the commencement of the Companies (Amendment) Ordinance 1991 which could but for the repeal by that Ordinance of section 49 have been redeemed under that section are subject to redemption in accordance with the provisions of this Ordinance as amended by that Ordinance.

(2) In a case to which sections 49 and 49A apply by virtue of this section, any premium payable on redemption may, notwithstanding the repeal by the Companies (Amendment) Ordinance 1991 of any provision of this Ordinance, be paid out of the share premium account instead of out of profits, or partly out of that account and partly out of profits (but subject to the provisions of this Ordinance as amended by that Ordinance so far as payment is out of profits).

(3) Any capital redemption reserve fund established before the commencement of the Companies (Amendment) Ordinance 1991 by a company for the purposes of the repealed section 49 is to be known as the company's capital redemption reserve and be treated as if it had been established for the purposes of section 49H; and accordingly, a reference in any enactment or in the articles of any company, or in any other instrument, to a company's capital redemption reserve fund is to be construed as a reference to the company's capital redemption reserve.

Definitions for sections 49 to 49R

49S.(1) In sections 49 to 49R-

"distributable profits", in relation to the making of any payment by a company, means those profits out of which it could lawfully make a distribution (within the meaning given by section 79B(2)) equal in value to the payment;

"permissible capital payment" means the payment permitted by section 49I

(2) In sections 49 to 49R, references to "payment out of capital" are to be construed in accordance with section 49I.

Power to issue shares at a discount

50.(1) Subject as provided in this section, it shall be lawful for a company to issue at a discount shares in the company of a class already issued:

Provided that-

> *(a)* the issue of the shares at a discount must be authorized by resolution passed in general meeting of the company, and must be sanctioned by the court;
>
> *(b)* the resolution must specify the maximum rate of discount at which the shares are to be issued;
>
> *(c)* not less than 1 year must at the date of the issue have elapsed since the date on which the company was entitled to commence business;
>
> *(d)* the shares to be issued at a discount must be issued within 1 month after the date on which the issue is sanctioned by the court or within such extended time as the court may allow.

(2) Where a company has passed a resolution authorizing the issue of shares at a discount, it may apply to the court for an order sanctioning the issue, and on any such application the court, if, having regard to all the circumstances of the case, it thinks proper so to do, may make an order sanctioning the issue on such terms and conditions as it thinks fit.

(3) Every prospectus relating to the issue of the shares must contain particulars of the discount allowed on the issue of the shares or of so much of that discount as has not been written off at the date of the issue of the prospectus. If default is made in complying with this subsection, the company and every officer of the company who is in default shall be liable to a fine and, for continued default, to a daily default fine.

Miscellaneous Provisions as to Share Capital

Power of company to arrange for different amounts being paid on shares

51. A company, if so authorized by its articles, may do any one or more of the following things-

> *(a)* make arrangements on the issue of shares for a difference between the shareholders in the amounts and times of payment of calls on their shares;
>
> *(b)* accept from any member the whole or a part of the amount remaining unpaid on any shares held by him, although no part of that amount has been called up;

(c)   pay dividend in proportion to the amount paid up on each share where a larger amount is paid up on some shares than on others.

Reserve liability of limited company

52.   A limited company may by special resolution determine that any portion of its share capital which has not been already called up shall not be capable of being called up, except in the event and for the purposes of the company being wound up, and thereupon that portion of its share capital shall not be capable of being called up except in the event and for the purposes aforesaid.

Power of company limited by shares to alter its share capital

53.(1)   A company limited by shares or a company limited by guarantee and having a share capital, if so authorized by its articles, may alter the conditions of its memorandum as follows, that is to say, it may-

(a)   increase its share capital by new shares of such amount as it thinks expedient;

(b)   consolidate and divide all or any of its share capital into shares of larger amount than its existing shares;

(c)   convert all or any of its paid-up shares into stock, and re-convert that stock into paid-up shares of any denomination;

(d)   subdivide its shares, or any of them, into shares of smaller amount than is fixed by the memorandum, so, however, that in the subdivision the proportion between the amount paid and the amount, if any, unpaid on each reduced share shall be the same as it was in the case of the share from which the reduced share is derived;

(e)   cancel shares which, at the date of the passing of the resolution in that behalf, have not been taken or agreed to be taken by any person, and diminish the amount of its share capital by the amount of the shares so cancelled.

(2)   The powers conferred by this section must be exercised by the company in general meeting.

(3)   A cancellation of shares in pursuance of this section shall not be deemed to be a reduction of share capital within the meaning of this Ordinance.

Notice to Registrar of consolidation of share capital, conversion of shares into stock, &c.

54.(1)   If a company having a share capital has-

(a)   consolidated and divided its share capital into shares of larger amount than its existing shares; or *(b)*   converted any shares into stock; or

(c)   re-converted stock into shares; or

(d)   subdivided its shares or any of them; or

(e)   redeemed any redeemable preference shares; or

(f)   cancelled any shares, otherwise than in connexion with a reduction of share capital under section 58,

it shall within 1 month after so doing give notice thereof to the Registrar of Companies specifying, as the case may be, the shares consolidated, divided, converted, subdivided, redeemed or cancelled, or the stock re-converted.

(2) If default is made in complying with this section, the company and every officer of the company who is in default shall be liable to a fine and, for continued default, to a daily default fine.

Notice of increase of share capital

55.(1) Where a company having a share capital, whether its shares have or have not been converted into stock, has increased its share capital beyond the registered capital, it shall within 15 days after the passing of the resolution authorizing the increase, give to the Registrar notice of the increase, and the Registrar shall record the increase.

(2) The notice to be given as aforesaid shall be in the specified form and include such particulars as may be specified by the Registrar with respect to the classes of shares affected and the conditions subject to which the new shares have been or are to be issued, and there shall be forwarded to the Registrar together with the notice a printed copy of the resolution authorizing the increase.

(3) If default is made in complying with this section, the company and every officer of the company who is in default shall be liable to a fine and, for continued default, to a daily default fine.

Power of unlimited company to provide for reserve share capital on re-registration

56.   An unlimited company having a share capital may, by its resolution for re-registration as a limited company under section 19, do either or both of the following things, namely-

(a)   increase the nominal amount of its share capital by increasing the nominal amount of each of its shares, but subject to the condition that no part of the increased capital shall be capable of being called up except in the event and for the purposes of the company being wound up;

(b)   provide that a specified portion of its uncalled share capital shall not be capable of being called up except in the event and for the purposes of the company being wound up.

Power of company to pay interest out of capital in certain cases

57.   Where any shares of a company are issued for the purpose of raising money to defray the expenses of the construction of any works or buildings or the provision of any plant which cannot be made profitable for a lengthened period, the company may pay interest on so much of that share capital as is for the time being paid up for the period and subject to the conditions and restrictions in this section mentioned, and may charge the sum so paid by way of interest to capital as part of the cost of construction of the work or building, or the provision of plant:

Provided that-

> *(a)*   no such payment shall be made unless it is authorized by the articles or by special resolution;
>
> *(b)*   no such payment, whether authorized by the articles or by special resolution, shall be made without the previous sanction of the court;
>
> *(c)*   before sanctioning any such payment the court may, at the expense of the company, appoint a person to inquire and report to them as to the circumstances of the case, and may, before making the appointment, require the company to give security for the payment of the costs of the inquiry;
>
> *(d)*   the payment shall be made only for such period as may be determined by the court, and that period shall in no case extend beyond the close of the half year next after the half year during which the works or buildings have been actually completed or the plant provided;
>
> *(e)*   the rate of interest shall in no case exceed 8 per cent per annum;
>
> *(f)*   the payment of the interest shall not operate as a reduction of the amount paid up on the shares in respect of which it is paid.

Non voting shares and shares with different voting rights

57A.(1) In the case of a company the share capital of which is divided into different classes of shares and includes a class of shares (other than preference or preferred shares so described) the holders of which are not entitled to vote at general meetings of the company, the descriptive title of the shares of that class shall include the words "non voting" and those words shall appear legibly on any share certificate, prospectus or directors' report issued by the company.

(2)   In the case of a company the share capital of which is divided into different classes of shares, every share certificate issued by the company shall contain in a prominent position a statement that its share capital is divided into different classes of shares; and such statement shall specify in respect of the shares of each class the nominal value thereof and the voting rights attached thereto.

(3)   If default is made in complying with subsection (1) or (2), the company and every officer of

the company who is in default shall be liable to a fine and, for continued default, to a daily default fine.

(4) This section shall not apply to any share certificate, prospectus or report issued by a company before the commencement of the Companies (Amendment) Ordinance 1984.

Approval of company required for allotment of shares by directors

57B.(1) Notwithstanding anything in a company's memorandum or articles, the directors shall not without the prior approval of the company in general meeting exercise any power of the company to allot shares:

Provided that no such prior approval shall be required in relation to the allotment of shares in the company under an offer made pro rata by the company to the members of the company, excluding for that purpose any member whose address is in a place where such offer is not permitted under the law of that place.

(2) Approval for the purposes of this section may be confined to a particular exercise of that power or may apply to the exercise of that power generally; and any such approval may be unconditional or subject to conditions.

(3) Any approval for the purposes of this section shall continue in force until -

    (a)   the conclusion of the annual general meeting commencing next after the date on which the approval was given; or

    (b)   the expiration of the period within which the next annual general meeting after that date is required by law to be held,

whichever is the earlier; but any approval may be previously revoked or varied by the company in general meeting.

(4) The directors may allot shares notwithstanding that an approval for the purposes of this section has ceased to be in force if the shares are allotted in pursuance of an offer, agreement or option made or granted by them while the approval was in force and they were authorized by the approval to make or grant an offer, agreement or option which would or might require shares to be allotted after the expiration of the approval.

(5) Section 117 shall apply to any resolution whereby an approval is given for the purposes of this section or revoked or varied under subsection (3).

(6) Any director who knowingly and willfully contravenes, or permits or authorizes the contravention of, this section shall be liable to imprisonment and a fine.

(7) Nothing in this section shall affect the validity of any allotment of shares or require approval for the allotment to the subscribers of a company's memorandum of shares in the company which, by subscribing the memorandum, they have agreed to take.

(8) This section shall not apply to any allotment of shares made by a company before-

        (a)   the beginning of the annual general meeting commencing next after the commencement of the Companies (Amendment) Ordinance 1984; or

        (b)   the expiration of the period within which the next annual general meeting after the commencement of that Ordinance is required by law to be held,

whichever is the earlier.

(9) This section shall not apply to any allotment of shares made by a company in pursuance of an offer, agreement or option made or granted by the company before the commencement of the Companies (Amendment) Ordinance 1984.

Validation of shares improperly issued

57C. Where a company has purported to issue or allot shares and the creation, issue or allotment of those shares was invalid by reason of any provision of this or any other Ordinance, or of the memorandum or articles of the company or otherwise, or the terms of issue or allotment were inconsistent with or unauthorized by any such provision, the court may, upon application made by the company or by a holder or mortgagee of any of those shares or by a creditor of the company, and upon being satisfied that in all the circumstances it is just and equitable so to do, make an order validating the issue or allotment of those shares or confirming the terms of issue or allotment thereof, or both, and upon an office copy of the order being lodged with the Registrar those shares shall be deemed to have been validly issued or allotted upon the terms of the issue or allotment thereof.

Reduction of Share Capital

Special resolution for reduction of share capital

58.(1) Subject to confirmation by the court, a company limited by shares or a company limited by guarantee and having a share capital may, if so authorized by its articles, by special resolution reduce its share capital in any way, and in particular, without prejudice to the generality of the foregoing power, may-

        (a)   extinguish or reduce the liability on any of its shares in respect of share capital not paid up; or

        (b)   either with or without extinguishing or reducing liability on any of its shares, cancel any paid-up share capital which is lost or unrepresented by available assets; or

        (c)   either with or without extinguishing or reducing liability on any of its shares, pay off any paid-up share capital which is in excess of the wants of the company,

and may, if and so far as is necessary, alter its memorandum by reducing the amount of its share capital and of its shares accordingly.

(1A) Except as provided in this Ordinance, no company limited by shares or limited by guarantee and having a share capital shall purchase or subscribe for any shares in the company or reduce its share capital in any way; and this subsection shall apply as if any share premium account or capital redemption reserve fund of a company were paid up share capital of the company.

(1B) If a company purports to act in contravention of subsection (1A),-

> *(a)* the company is liable to a fine;

> *(b)* every officer who is in default is liable to imprisonment and a fine; and

> *(c)* a relevant shareholder within the meaning given in the Thirteenth Schedule who knowingly permits the contravention of subsection (1A) is liable to imprisonment and a fine.

(1C) Subject to section 168A and subsection (1D), if a company purchases any shares in itself under sections 49 to 49S, no such purchase shall be void by reason only of a failure to comply with any of those provisions.

(1D) Notwithstanding subsection (1C), a purchase which contravenes section 49B(6) is void.

(2) A special resolution under this section is in this Ordinance referred to as a resolution for reducing share capital.

Application to court for confirming order, objections by creditors and settlement of list of objecting creditors

59.(1) Where a company has passed a resolution for reducing share capital, it may apply by petition to the court for an order confirming the reduction.

(2) Where the proposed reduction of share capital involves either diminution of liability in respect of unpaid share capital or the payment to any shareholder of any paid-up share capital, and in any other case if the court so directs, the following provisions shall have effect, subject nevertheless to subsection (3)-

> *(a)* every creditor of the company who at the date fixed by the court is entitled to any debt or claim which, if that date were the commencement of the winding up of the company, would be admissible in proof against the company, shall be entitled to object to the reduction;

> *(b)* the court shall settle a list of creditors so entitled to object, and for that purpose shall ascertain, as far as possible without requiring an application from any creditor, the names of those creditors and the nature and amount of their

debts or claims, and may publish notices fixing a day or days within which creditors not entered on the list are to claim to be so entered or are to be excluded from the right of objecting to the reduction;

(c) where a creditor entered on the list whose debt or claim is not discharged or has not determined does not consent to the reduction, the court may, if it thinks fit, dispense with the consent of that creditor, on the company securing payment of his debt or claim by appropriating, as the court may direct, the following amount-

(i) if the company admits the full amount of the debt or claim, or, though not admitting it is willing to provide for it, then the full amount of the debt or claim;

(ii) if the company does not admit and is not willing to provide for the full amount of the debt or claim, or if the amount is contingent or not ascertained, then an amount fixed by the court after the like inquiry and adjudication as if the company were being wound up by the court.

(3) Where a proposed reduction of share capital involves either the diminution of any liability in respect of unpaid share capital or the payment to any shareholder of any paid-up share capital, the court may, if having regard to any special circumstances of the case it thinks proper so to do, direct that subsection (2) shall not apply as regards any class or any classes of creditors.

Order confirming reduction and powers of court on making such order

60.(1) The court, if satisfied, with respect to every creditor of the company who under section 59 is entitled to object to the reduction, that either his consent to the reduction has been obtained or his debt or claim has been discharged or has determined, or has been secured, may make an order confirming the reduction on such terms and conditions as it thinks fit.

(2)-(3) *(Repealed)*

Registration of order and minute of reduction

61.(1) The Registrar, on production to him of an order of the court confirming the reduction of the share capital of a company, and the delivery to him of a copy of the order and of a minute approved by the court, showing with respect to the share capital of the company, as altered by the order, the amount of the share capital, the number of shares into which it is to be divided, and the amount of each share, and the amount, if any, at the date of the registration deemed to be paid up on each share, shall register the order and minute.

(2) On the registration of the order and minute, and not before, the resolution for reducing share capital as confirmed by the order so registered shall take effect.

(3) Notice of the registration shall be published in such manner as the court may direct.

(4) The Registrar shall certify under his hand the registration of the order and minute, and his certificate shall be conclusive evidence that all the requirements of this Ordinance with respect to reduction of share capital have been complied with, and that the share capital of the company is such as is stated in the minute.

(5) The minute when registered shall be deemed to be substituted for the corresponding part of the memorandum, and shall be valid and alterable as if it had been originally contained therein.

(6) The substitution of any such minute as aforesaid for part of the memorandum of the company shall be deemed to be an alteration of the memorandum within the meaning of section 27.

Liability of members in respect of reduced shares

62.(1) In the case of a reduction of share capital, a member of the company, past or present, shall not be liable in respect of any share to any call or contribution exceeding in amount the difference, if any, between the amount of the share as fixed by the minute and the amount paid, or the reduced amount, if any, which is to be deemed to have been paid, on the share, as the case may be:

Provided that, if any creditor, entitled in respect of any debt or claim to object to the reduction of share capital, is, by reason of his ignorance of the proceedings for reduction, or of their nature and effect with respect to his claim, not entered on the list of creditors, and, after the reduction, the company is unable, within the meaning of the provisions of this Ordinance with respect to winding up by the court, to pay the amount of his debt or claim, then-

> *(a)* every person who was a member of the company at the date of the registration of the order for reduction and minute, shall be liable to contribute for the payment of that debt or claim an amount not exceeding the amount which he would have been liable to contribute if the company had commenced to be wound up on the day before the said date; and

> *(b)* if the company is wound up, the court, on the application of any such creditor and proof of his ignorance as aforesaid, may, if it thinks fit, settle accordingly a list of persons so liable to contribute, and make and enforce calls and orders on the contributories settled on the list, as if they were ordinary contributories in a winding up.

(2) Nothing in this section shall affect the rights of the contributories among themselves.

Penalty for concealing name of creditor

63. If any officer of the company

> *(a)* willfully conceals the name of any creditor entitled to object to the reduction; or

> *(b)* wilfully misrepresents the nature or amount of the debt or claim of any creditor; or

   (c) aids, abets or is privy to any such concealment or misrepresentation as aforesaid,

he shall be guilty of an offence and liable to imprisonment and a fine.

Variation of Shareholders' Rights

Variation of rights attached to special classes of shares

63A.(1) Where, in the case of a company the share capital of which is divided into different classes of shares, special rights are attached to any such class of shares otherwise than by the memorandum and the articles do not provide for the variation of those rights, the articles shall be deemed to contain provision that such rights shall not be varied except with the consent in writing of the holders of three-fourths in nominal value of the issued shares of the class in question or with the sanction of a special resolution passed at a separate general meeting of the holders of that class.

(2) Where, in the case of a company the share capital of which is divided into different classes of shares, special rights are attached to any such class of shares by the memorandum and provision for the variation of those rights is, at the time of the company's incorporation, contained in the articles, those rights shall be capable of variation in accordance with the articles as for the time being in force, even if no reference is made in the memorandum to their variation in that manner.

(3) Where, in the case of a company the share capital of which is divided into different classes of shares, special rights are attached to any such class of shares by the memorandum and the memorandum and articles do not contain provision with respect to the variation of the rights, those rights may be varied if all the members of the company agree to the variation.

(4) Where the articles of a company contain, or by virtue of this section are deemed to contain, a provision for the variation of the rights attached to any class of shares, those rights shall not be capable of variation otherwise than in accordance with that provision.

(5) Any provision deemed by virtue of this section to be contained in a company's articles shall be subject to alteration in like manner as a provision in fact contained therein; but any alteration of a provision for the variation of the rights attached to a class of shares which is, or by virtue of this section is deemed to be, contained in a company's articles or the insertion of any such provision into a company's articles shall itself be treated as a variation of those rights.

(6) Sections 114, 114A and 115A and the provisions of the articles relating to general meetings shall, so far as applicable, apply in relation to any meeting of shareholders required by virtue of this section or otherwise to take place in connexion with the variation of the rights attached to a class of shares, and shall so apply with the necessary modifications and subject to the following-

   (a) the necessary quorum at any such meeting other than an adjourned meeting shall be 2 persons holding or representing by proxy at least one-third in nominal value of the issued shares of the class in question, and at an adjourned meeting 1 person holding shares of the class in question or his proxy;

(b)   any holder of shares of the class in question present in person or by proxy may demand a poll.

(7)   Section 64 shall apply where a company's articles are by virtue of subsection (1) deemed to contain a provision for the variation of the rights attached to a class of shares as it applies where the articles in fact contain such a provision.

(8)   In this section and, except where the context otherwise requires, in any provision for the variation of the rights attached to a class of shares contained in a company's articles, references to the variation of those rights shall include references to their abrogation.

(9)   Nothing in subsection (4) shall be construed as derogating from the powers of the court under section 166, 167 or 168A.

Rights of holders of special classes of shares

64.(1) If in the case of a company, the share capital of which is divided into different classes of shares, provision is made by the memorandum or articles for authorizing the variation of the rights attached to any class of shares in the company, subject to the consent of any specified proportion of the holders of the issued shares of that class or the sanction of a resolution passed at a separate meeting of the holders of those shares, and in pursuance of the said provision the rights attached to any such class of shares are at any time varied, the holders of not less in the aggregate than 10 per cent in nominal value of the issued shares of that class may apply to the court to have the variation cancelled, and, where any such application is made, the variation shall not have effect unless and until it is confirmed by the court.

(1A)   Nothing in this section shall affect the right of any member of the company to apply to the court by petition under section 168A.

(2)   An application under this section must be made within 28 days after the date on which the consent was given or the resolution was passed, as the case may be, and may be made on behalf of the shareholders entitled to make the application by such one or more of their number as they may appoint in writing for the purpose.

(3)   On any such application the court, after hearing the applicant and any other persons who apply to the court to be heard and appear to the court to be interested in the application, may, if it is satisfied, having regard to all the circumstances of the case, that the variation would unfairly prejudice the shareholders of the class represented by the applicant, disallow the variation and shall, if not so satisfied, confirm the variation.

(4)   The decision of the court on any such application shall be final.

(5)   The company shall within 21 days after the making of an order by the court on any such application forward a copy of the order to the Registrar, and, if default is made in complying with this provision, the company and every officer of the company who is in default shall be liable to a fine and, for continued default, to a daily default fine.

(6)   In this section, "variation" includes abrogation and "varied" shall be construed accordingly.

Documents relating to rights of holders of special classes of shares to he filed with Registrar

64A.   Every company the share capital of which is divided into different classes of shares shall deliver to the Registrar for filing-

> *(a)*   a copy of any document or resolution attaching rights to any class of shares in the company which is not otherwise required by this Ordinance to be so filed;

> *(b)*   a return in respect of the classification of any unissued shares in the company;

> *(c)*   a return in respect of the conversion of shares of one class into shares of another class.

Transfer of Shares and Debentures, Evidence of Title

Nature of shares

65.   The shares or other interest of any member in a company shall be personal estate, transferable in manner provided by the articles of the company, and shall not be of the nature of real estate.

Numbering of shares

65A.(1) Subject to subsections (2) and (3), each share in a company having a share capital shall be distinguished by its appropriate number.

(2)   If at any time all the issued shares in a company, or all the issued shares therein of a particular class, are fully paid up and rank pari passu for all purposes, none of those shares need thereafter have a distinguishing number, so long as it remains fully paid up and ranks pari passu for all purposes with all shares of the same class for the time being issued and fully paid up.

(3)   Where new shares are issued by a company on the terms that, within a period not exceeding 12 months, they will rank pari passu for all purposes with all the existing shares, or all the existing shares of a particular class, in the company, neither the new shares nor the corresponding existing shares need have distinguishing numbers so long as all of them are fully paid up and rank pari passu but the share certificates of the new shares shall, if not numbered, be appropriately worded or enfaced.

Transfer not to be registered except on production of instrument of transfer

66.   Notwithstanding anything in the articles of a company, it shall not be lawful for the company to register a transfer of shares in or debentures of the company unless a proper instrument of transfer has been delivered to the company:

Provided that nothing in this section shall prejudice any power of the company to register as shareholder or debenture holder any person to whom the right to any shares in or debentures of the company has been trasmitted by operation of law.

Transfer by personal representative

67. A transfer of the share or other interest of a deceased member of a company made by his personal representative shall, although the personal representative is not himself a member of the company, be as valid as if he had been such a member at the time of the execution of the instrument of transfer.

Registration of transfer at request of transferor

68. On the application of the transferor of any share or interest in a company, the company shall enter in its register of members the name of the transferee in the same manner and subject to the same conditions as if the application for the entry were made by the transferee.

Notice of refusal to register transfer

69.(1) If a company refuses to register a transfer of any shares or debentures, the company shall, within 2 months after the date on which the transfer was lodged with the company, send to the transferor and the transferee notice of the refusal.

(1A) Where a company refuses to register any person as a member in respect of shares which have been transmitted to him by operation of law, that person shall be entitled to call on the company to furnish a statement of the reasons for the refusal, and, if the company fails to furnish such statement within a period of 28 days after the request therefor, the company shall, on the expiration of that period, register the transfer forthwith:

Provided that nothing in this subsection shall affect the rights of any member under the articles whereby he is entitled to any rights of pre-emption over, or rights of purchasing, the shares in question.

(1B) Where a company refuses to register a transfer of any shares, the transferee may apply to the court to have the transfer registered by the company; and the court may, if it is satisfied that the application is well founded, disallow the refusal and order that the transfer be registered forthwith by the company.

(2) If default is made in complying with this section or any order made thereunder, the company and every officer of the company who is in default shall be liable to a fine and, for continued default, to a daily default fine.

Certification of transfers

69A.(1) The certification by a company of any instrument of transfer of shares in or debentures of the company shall be taken as a representation by the company to any person acting on the faith of the certification that there have been produced to the company such documents as on the face of them show a prima facie title to the shares or debentures in the transferor named in the instrument of transfer, but not as a representation that the transferor has any title to the shares or debentures.

(2) Where any person acts on the faith of a false certification by a company made negligently, the company shall be under the same liability to him as if the certification had been made fraudulently.

(3) For the purposes of this section-

> *(a)* an instrument of transfer shall be deemed to be certificated if it bears the words "certificate lodged" or words in English or Chinese to the like effect;

> *(b)* the certification of an instrument of transfer shall be deemed to be made by a company if-

>> **(i)** the person issuing the instrument is a person authorized, or having apparent authority as agent, to issue certificated instruments of transfer on the company's behalf, and

>> **(ii)** the certification is signed by a person authorized, or having apparent authority as agent, to certificate transfers on the company's behalf or by any officer or servant either of the company or of a body corporate so authorized or having such apparent authority;

> *(c)* a certification shall be deemed to be signed by any person if-

>> **(i)** it purports to be authenticated by his signature or initials (whether handwritten or not); and

>> **(ii)** it is not shown that the signature or initials was or were placed there neither by himself nor by any person authorized, or having apparent authority as agent, to use the signature or initials for the purpose of certificating transfers on the company's behalf.

Duties of company with respect to issue of certificates

70.(1) Every company shall, within 2 months after the allotment of any of its shares, debentures, or debenture stock, and within 2 months after the date on which a transfer of any such shares, debentures, or debenture stock, is lodged with the company, complete and have ready for delivery the certificates of all shares, the debentures, and the certificates of all debenture stock allotted or transferred, unless the conditions of issue of the shares, debentures, or debenture stock otherwise provide. The expression transfer for the purpose of this subsection means a transfer duly stamped and otherwise valid, and does not include such a transfer as the company is for any reason entitled to refuse to register and does not register.

(2) If default is made in complying with this section, the company and every officer of the company who is in default shall be liable to a fine and, for continued default, to a daily default fine.

(3) If any company on whom a notice has been served requiring the company to make good any default in complying with the provisions of subsection (1) fails to make good the default within 10 days after the service of the notice, the court may, on the application of the person entitled to have the certificates or the debentures delivered to him, make an order directing the company and any officer of the company to make good the default within such time as may be specified in the order, and any such order may provide that all costs of and incidental to the application shall be borne by the company or by any officer of the company responsible for the default.

Certificate to be evidence of title

71. A certificate, under the common seal of the company or the seal kept by the company under section 73A, specifying any shares held by any member, shall be prima facie evidence of the title of the member to the shares.

Procedure for replacement of lost certificate

71A.(1) Any person who is a registered holder of shares in a company or who claims to be entitled to have his name entered in the register of members of a company in respect of shares in that company may, if it appears that the certificate (in this section referred to as the "original certificate") relating to the shares is lost, apply to the company in the specified form for a new certificate in respect of such shares (in this section referred to as the "relevant shares").

(2) An application to a company under this section for a new certificate shall be accompanied by a statutory declaration made by the applicant stating the grounds upon which the application is made and, in particular-

> *(a)* when the original certificate was last in the applicant's possession and how he ceased to have possession thereof;

> *(b)* whether the applicant has executed any transfer in respect of the relevant shares, in blank or otherwise;

> *(c)* that no other person is entitled to have his name entered in the register of members of the company in respect of the relevant shares; and

> *(d)* such other particulars as the case may require in order to verify the grounds upon which the application is made.

(3) Subject to subsection (4), where an application is made to a company under this section for a new certificate, the company shall, if it intends to issue such certificate under this section, publish a notice in the specified form advertising its intention to do so, as follows-

> *(a)* if the application is made by the registered holder of the relevant shares or by a person other than the registered holder with his consent and in either case the latest value of the relevant shares does not exceed $20,000, the notice shall be published once in, respectively, an English language newspaper and

a Chinese language newspaper specified in a list of newspapers issued for the purposes of this section by the Chief Secretary and published in the Gazette;

(b)   if the application is made by a person other than the registered holder of the relevant shares without his consent or the latest value of the relevant shares exceeds $20,000, the notice shall be published in the Gazette once in each of 3 consecutive months,

and for the purposes of this subsection "latest value" in relation to the relevant shares, means the value thereof calculated at the last recorded price paid for shares in the company of the same class, prior to the application, at the Unified Exchange.

(4)   A notice which it is proposed to publish under subsection (3) shall not be published until, and any publication thereof shall not be valid for the purposes of this section unless, the following requirements are first complied with-

(a)   the company has delivered a copy of the notice to the Unified Exchange and an authorized officer thereof has certified to the company in writing that such copy is being exhibited in accordance with subsection (5);

(b)   where the notice relates to an application made by a person other than the registered holder of the relevant shares without the consent of the registered holder-

(i)   the company has served a copy of the notice on the registered holder by sending it by registered post to his last address appearing in the register of members of the company; and

(ii)   a period of 3 months has expired since the date of service of such copy.

(5)   The Unified Exchange shall set aside a conspicuous place therein for posting and exhibiting all copies of notices delivered to the exchange under subsection (4)(a), and shall keep every such copy exhibited in such place for a period of not less than-

(a)   in the case of an application referred to in subsection (3)(a), 1 month;

(b)   in the case of an application referred to in subsection (3)(b), 3 months.

(6)   A company shall not issue a new certificate under this section unless-

(a)   the company has published a notice under subsection (3) advertising its intention to do so and-

> (i) in the case of a notice published under subsection (3)(a), a period of not less than 1 month from the latest valid publication thereof has expired; or
>
> (ii) in the case of a notice published under subsection (3)(b), a period of not less than 3 months from the first valid publication thereof has expired; and

(b) the company has not received notice of any other claim in respect of the relevant shares; and

(c) where the applicant for the new certificate is a person other than the registered holder of the relevant shares-

> (i) an instrument of transfer in respect of the relevant shares is delivered to the company under section 66; or
>
> (ii) if, in the case of an application made without the consent of the registered holder, such instrument has not been delivered, and the applicant is unable to procure its delivery, to the company under section 66, the company has caused an instrument of transfer in respect of the relevant shares to be executed on behalf of the registered holder by any person appointed by the company and on his own behalf by the applicant.

(7) Where a company issues a new certificate under this section, it shall forthwith cancel the original certificate and make such entry in the register of members of the company as the case may require in order to record such issue and cancellation and, where the new certificate is issued to a person other than the registered holder of the relevant shares, any instrument of transfer caused to be executed by the company under subsection (6)(c)(ii) shall, for the purpose of registering the relevant shares in the name of that person, be deemed to be an instrument of transfer duly delivered to the company under section 66.

(8) Every company which issues a new certificate under this section shall, not later than 14 days from the date of issue of the new certificate, give public notice of the issue thereof and of the cancellation of the original certificate by publishing a notice in the Gazette in the specified form and the company shall deliver a copy of the notice to the Unified Exchange.

(9) Where a company fails to publish a notice as required by subsection (8), the company and every officer of the company who is in default shall be liable to a fine and, for continued default, to a daily default fine.

(10) Where a new certificate is issued by a company under this section, the following shall apply-

(a)   save as otherwise provided in this subsection, nothing in this section shall affect the power of the court to make an order under section 100 in favour of any person claiming to be entitled to the relevant shares as against the person to whom the new certificate is issued or any person whose name is subsequently entered in the register of members of the company in respect of the relevant shares, but no such order shall be made as against a bona fide purchaser;

(b)   in any case where the court makes an order under section 100 as against the person to whom the new certificate is issued or any person whose name is subsequently entered in the register of members of the company in respect of the relevant shares, the court shall not order the payment of damages by the company and the company shall not otherwise be liable for any damage sustained by reason of the issue of the new certificate or the cancellation of the original certificate;

(c)   where any person (in this paragraph referred to as "the claimant") would have been entitled but for this subsection to have his name entered in the register of members of the company in respect of the relevant shares or any of them-

   (i)   except where the company is shown to have acted deceitfully, the company shall not be liable for any damage sustained by the claimant by reason of the issue of the new certificate or the cancellation of the original certificate;

   (ii)   the person to whom the new certificate is issued shall, where the relevant shares or any of them are purchased from him by a bona fide purchaser, be liable in damages to the claimant for the value of the shares so purchased as at the date of purchase;

   (iii)   the person to whom the new certificate is issued and any other person (other than a bona fide purchaser) whose name is subsequently entered in the register of members of the company in respect of the relevant shares or any of them shall, where the relevant shares or any of them are purchased from such other person by a bona fide purchaser, be jointly and severally liable in damages to the claimant for the value of the shares so purchased as at the date of purchase.

(11)   All expenses relating to an application under this section for the issue of a new certificate or the cancellation of an original certificate by any company shall be borne by the applicant, and the company may refuse to take any step in respect of the application until it is satisfied that reasonable provision for the payment of such expenses has been made.

(12) In this section-

"bona fide purchaser", in relation to any relevant shares, means any of the following-

> *(a)* a person who purchases such shares in good faith for value and without notice of any defect in the title of the seller;
>
> *(b)* a person who becomes entitled to such shares at any time after the purchase thereof by any other person in good faith for value and without notice of any defect in the title of the seller;

"company" means a company in the case of which shares are listed on the Unified Exchange;

"new certificate" means a certificate issued under this section in replacement of an original certificate;

"registered holder", in relation to shares in a company, means any person whose name is entered in the register of members of that company in respect of such shares.

Evidence of grant of probate

72. The production to a company of any document which is by law sufficient evidence of probate of the will, or letters of administration of the estate of a deceased person having been granted to some person shall be accepted by the company, notwithstanding anything in its articles, as sufficient evidence of the grant.

Issue and effect of share warrants to bearer

73.(1) A company limited by shares, if so authorized by its articles, may, with respect to any fully paid-up shares, issue under its common seal a warrant stating that the bearer of the warrant is entitled to the shares therein specified, and may provide, by coupons or otherwise, for the payment of the future dividends on the shares included in the warrant.

(2) Such a warrant as aforesaid is in this Ordinance termed a share warrant.

(3) A share warrant shall entitle the bearer thereof to the shares therein specified, and the shares may be transferred by delivery of the warrant.

Official seals for sealing share certificates etc.

73A.(1) A company may have, for use for sealing securities issued by the company and for sealing documents creating or evidencing securities so issued, an official seal which is a facsimile of the common seal of the company with the addition on its face of the word "securities" or the expression in Chinese "...." or both such word or expression.

(2) A company which was incorporated before the commencement of the Companies (Amendment) Ordinance 1984 and which has such an official seal as is mentioned in subsection (1) may use the seal for sealing such securities and documents as are there mentioned notwithstanding anything in any instrument constituting or regulating the company or in any instrument made before such commencement which relates to any securities or documents if they are sealed with that seal.

Power to make compensation for losses from forged transfers

74.(1) Every company having a share capital shall have power to make compensation by a cash payment out of its funds for any loss arising from a transfer of any shares in the company in pursuance of a forged transfer or of a transfer under a forged power of attorney, and, where the shares or stock of a company have by amalgamation or otherwise become the shares or stock of another company, that other company shall have the same power under this section as the original company would have had if it had continued.

(2) Every company may provide, by insurance or reservation of capital or accumulation of income, a fund to meet claims for such compensation.

(3) For the purpose of providing such compensation, any company may borrow on the security of its property.

(4) A company may, for the purposes of this section, impose such reasonable restrictions on the transfer of shares in the company, or with respect to powers of attorney for the transfer thereof, as it may deem necessary for guarding against losses arising from forgery.

(5) Where a company compensates any person under this section for any loss arising from forgery, the company shall, without prejudice to any other rights or remedies, have the same rights and remedies against the person liable for the loss as the person compensated would have had.

Special Provisions as to Debentures

Company's register of debenture holders

74A.(1) Any company which issues a series of debentures or debenture stock not transferable by delivery shall keep a register of the holders of such debentures or debenture stock, and shall enter therein the following particulars-

(a) the names and addresses, and the occupations or descriptions, of the holders (and in the case of a Chinese holder who has signed in Chinese characters any document relating to the debentures or debenture stock held by him, or who has, by adding Chinese characters after his name on such document or by other means, indicated that he wishes the Chinese characters to be entered in the register, his name both in English and in Chinese characters) and a statement of the amount of such debentures or debenture stock held by each holder;

(b) the date at which each person was entered in the register as the holder of such debentures or debenture stock;

(c)   the date at which any person ceased to be a holder of any such debentures or debenture stock.

(2)   The register of holders of debentures of a company shall be kept-

(a)   at the registered office of the company; or

(b)   if the work of making it up is done at an office of the company other than the registered office of the company, at that other office; or

(c)   if the company arranges with some other person for the making up of the register to be undertaken on behalf of the company by that other person, at the office of that other person at which the work is done,

so, however, that it shall not be kept at a place outside Hong Kong.

(3)   Every company shall send notice to the Registrar in the specified form of the place where the register required to be kept by the company under this section is kept, and of any change in that place.

(4)   Where a company makes default in complying with subsection (1) or (2) or makes default for 14 days in complying with subsection (3), the company and every officer of the company who is in default shall be liable to a fine and, for continued default, to a daily default fine.

Construction of provision of instrument relating to form of register of debenture holders

74B.   Any provision of an instrument made by a company which requires a register of holders of debentures of the company to be kept in a legible form shall be construed as requiring the register to be kept either-

(a)   in a legible form; or

(b)   in a non-legible form capable of being reproduced in a legible form.

Rights of inspection of register of debenture holders and to copies of register and trust deed or other document

75.(1)   Every register of holders of debentures of a company shall, except when duly closed (but subject to such reasonable restrictions as the company may in general meeting impose, so that no less than 2 hours in each day shall be allowed for inspection), be open to the inspection of the registered holder of any such debentures or any holder of shares in the company without fee, and of any other person on payment of $1 or such less sum as may be prescribed by the company.

(2)   Any person may require a copy of the register of the holders of debentures of the company or any part thereof on payment of $2 or such less sum as may be prescribed by the company for every 100 words or fractional part thereof required to be copied, and such copy shall be forwarded by the company to the person requiring it within 20 days of the receipt by the company of the request.

(3) A copy of any trust deed or other document for securing any issue of debentures shall be forwarded to any person requiring it within 20 days of the receipt by the company of the request, on payment in the case of a printed trust deed or other document of the sum of $4 or such less sum as may be prescribed by the company, or where the trust deed or other document has not been printed, on payment of $2 for every 100 words or fractional part thereof required to be copied.

(4) If inspection is refused, or a copy is refused or not forwarded within 20 days after the request therefor is received, the company and every officer of the company who is in default shall be liable to a fine and, for continued default, to a daily default fine.

(5) Where a company is in default as aforesaid, the court may by order compel an immediate inspection of the register or direct that the copies required shall be sent to the person requiring them.

(6) For the purposes of this section, a register shall be deemed to be duly closed if it is closed under section 99.

Meetings of debenture holders

75A.(1) Where in the case of-

> *(a)* debentures forming part of a series issued by a company and ranking pari passu with the other debentures of that series; or
>
> *(b)* debenture stock,

the debentures or the trust deed or other document securing the debentures or stock provide for the holding of meetings of holders of debentures or stock, then subject to any provision so made, sections 113, 114B, 114C, 114D(2) and 114E shall apply in relation to such meetings and to the holders of the debentures or stock as they apply in relation to meetings of the company and members of the company.

(2) The sections mentioned in subsection (1) shall, in their application by virtue of that subsection, have effect with the necessary modifications and as if for the reference in section 113(1) to the members there mentioned there were substituted a reference to holders of the debentures or stock entitled to exercise not less than one-tenth of the total voting rights of all holders having the right to vote at the meeting.

Liability of trustees for debenture holders

75B.(1) Subject to this section, any provision contained in a trust deed for securing an issue of debentures, or in any contract with the holders of debentures secured by a trust deed, shall be void in so far as it would have the effect of exempting a trustee thereof from or indemnifying him against liability for breach of trust where he fails to show the degree of care and diligence required of him as trustee, having regard to the provisions of the trust deed conferring on him any powers, authorities or discretions.

(2)   Subsection (1) shall not invalidate-

        (a)   any release otherwise validly given in respect of anything done or omitted to be done by a trustee before the giving of the release; or

        (b)   any provision enabling such a release to be given-

                (i)   on the agreement thereto of a majority of not less than three-fourths in value of the debenture holders present and voting in person or, where proxies are permitted, by proxy at a meeting summoned for the purpose; and

                (ii)   either with respect to specific acts or omissions or on the trustee dying or ceasing to act.

(3)   Subsection (1) shall not operate-

        (a)   to invalidate any provision in force at the commencement of the Companies (Amendment) Ordinance 1984 so long as any person then entitled to the benefit of that provision or afterwards given the benefit thereof under subsection (4) remains a trustee of the deed in question; or

        (b)   to deprive any person of any exemption or right to be indemnified in respect of anything done or omitted to be done by him while any such provision was in force.

(4)   While any trustee of a trust deed remains entitled to the benefit of a provision saved by subsection (3), the benefit of that provision may be given either-

        (a)   to all trustees of the deed, present and future; or

        (b)   to any named trustees or proposed trustees thereof,

by a resolution passed by a majority of not less than three-fourths in value of the debenture holders present in person or, where proxies are permitted, by proxy at a meeting summoned for the purpose in accordance with the provisions of the deed or, if the deed makes no provision for summoning meetings, a meeting summoned for the purpose in any manner approved by the court.

Perpetual debentures

76.   A condition contained in any debentures or in any deed for securing any debentures, whether issued or executed before or after the commencement of this Ordinance shall not be invalid by reason only that the debentures are thereby made irredeemable or redeemable only on the happening of a contingency, however remote, or on the expiration of a period, however long, any rule of equity to the contrary notwithstanding.

Power to re-issue redeemed debentures on certain cases

77.(1) Where either before or after the commencement of this Ordinance a company has redeemed any debentures previously issued, then-

> *(a)* unless any provision to the contrary, whether express or implied, is contained in the articles or in any contract entered into by the company; or

> *(b)* unless the company has, by passing a resolution to that effect or by some other act, manifested its intention that the debentures shall be cancelled,

the company shall have, and shall be deemed always to have had, power to re-issue the debentures, either by re-issuing the same debentures or by issuing other debentures in their place.

(2) Subject to subsection (6), on a re-issue of redeemed debentures the person entitled to the debentures shall have, and shall be deemed always to have had, the same priorities as if the debentures had never been redeemed.

(3) *(Repealed)*

(4) Where a company has either before or after the commencement of this Ordinance deposited any of its debentures to secure advances from time to time on current account or otherwise, the debentures shall not be deemed to have been redeemed by reason only of the account of the company having ceased to be in debit whilst the debentures remained so deposited.

(5) The re-issue of a debenture or the issue of another debenture in its place under the power by this section given to, or deemed to have been possessed by, a company, whether the re-issue or issue was made before or after the commencement of this Ordinance, shall be treated as the issue of a new debenture for the purposes of stamp duty, but it shall not be so treated for the purposes of any provision limiting the amount or number of debentures to be issued:

Provided that any person lending money on the security of a debenture re-issued under this section which appears to be duly stamped may give the debenture in evidence in any proceedings for enforcing his security without payment of the stamp duty or any penalty in respect thereof, unless he had notice or, but for his negligence, might have discovered, that the debenture was not duly stamped, but in any such case the company shall be liable to pay the proper stamp duty and penalty.

(6) Where any debentures which have been redeemed before the commencement of this Ordinance are re-issued subsequently to that date, the re-issue of the debentures shall not prejudice and shall be deemed never to have prejudiced any right or priority which any person would have had under or by virtue of any mortgage or charge created before the commencement of this Ordinance, if section 106 of the Companies Ordinance 1911, as originally enacted, had been enacted in this Ordinance instead of this section.

Specific performance of contracts to subscribe for debentures

78. A contract with a company to take up and pay for any debentures of the company may be enforced by an order for specific performance.

Payment of certain debts out of assets subject to floating charge in priority to claims under the charge

79.(1) Where a receiver is appointed on behalf of the holders of any debentures of a company secured by a charge which, as created, was a floating charge, or possession is taken by or on behalf of those debenture holders of any property comprised in or subject to the charge, then, if the company is not at the time in course of being wound up, the debts, which in every winding-up are under the provisions of Part V relating to preferential payments to be paid in priority to all other debts, shall, according to their respective priorities under section 265, be paid out of any assets coming to the hands of the receiver or other person taking possession as aforesaid in priority to any claim for principal or interest in respect of the debentures.

(1A) In the application of the provisions of Part V, section 265 shall be construed as if the provision for payment of accrued holiday remuneration becoming payable on the termination of employment before or by the effect of the winding-up order or resolution were a provision for payment of such remuneration becoming payable on the termination of employment before or by the effect of the appointment of the receiver or possession being taken as aforesaid.

(2) The periods of time mentioned in the said provisions of Part V shall be reckoned from the date of the appointment of the receiver or of possession being taken as aforesaid, as the case may be.

(2A) Where the date referred to in subsection (2) occurred before the commencement* of the Companies (Amendment) Ordinance 1984, subsections (1) and (2) shall have effect with the substitution, for references to the provisions of Part V, of references to the provisions which, by virtue of section 265(7) are deemed to remain in force in the case therein mentioned, and subsection (1A) shall not apply.

(3) Any payments made under this section shall be recouped as far as may be out of the assets of the company available for payment of general creditors.

PART II A - Distribution Of Profits And Assets

Interpretation

79A.(1) In this Part-

"appointed day" means the date of commencement of this Part under the Companies (Amendment) Ordinance 1991;

"called up share capital", in relation to a company, means so much of its share capital as equals the aggregate amount of the calls made on its shares (whether or not those calls have been paid), together with any share capital paid up without being called and any share capital to be paid on a specified future date under the articles, the terms of allotment of the relevant shares or any other arrangements for payment of those shares and "uncalled share capital" is to be construed accordingly;

"capitalisation", in relation to a company's profits, means any of the following operations (whenever carried out)-

    (a)   applying the profits in wholly or partly paying up unissued shares in the company to be allotted to members of the company as fully or partly paid bonus shares; or

    (b)   transferring the profits to capital redemption reserve;

"distribution" means every description of distribution of a company's assets to its members, whether in cash or otherwise, except distribution by way of-

    (a)   an issue of shares as fully or partly paid bonus shares;

    (b)   the redemption or purchase of any of the company's own shares out of capital (including the proceeds of any fresh issue of shares) or out of unrealised profits in accordance with sections 49 to 49S;

    (c)   the reduction of share capital by extinguishing or reducing the liability of any of the members on any of the company's shares in respect of share capital not paid up, or by paying off paid up share capital; and

    (d)   a distribution of assets to members of the company on its winding up;

"net assets", in relation to a company, has the same meaning as in section 157H (1).

(2)   References to profits and losses of any description are (respectively) to profits and losses of that description made at any time.

(3)   Without prejudice to-

(a)　　the construction of any other expression (where appropriate) by reference to accepted accounting principles or practice; or

(b)　　any specific provision for the treatment of profits of any description as realised,

it is declared that references in this Part to realised profits, in relation to a company's accounts, are to such profits of the company as fall to be treated as realised profits for the purposes of those accounts in accordance with principles generally accepted with respect to the determination for accounting purposes of realised profits at the time when those accounts are prepared.

Certain distributions prohibited

79B.(1) A company shall not make a distribution except out of profits available for the purpose.

(2) For the purposes of this Part, a company's profits available for distribution are its accumulated, realised profits, so far as not previously utilised by distribution or capitalisation, less its accumulated, realised losses, so far as not previously written off in a reduction or reorganisation of capital duly made.

(3) A company shall not apply an unrealised profit in paying up debentures, or any amounts unpaid on its issued shares.

(4) Where the directors of a company are, after making all reasonable enquiries, unable to determine whether a particular profit made before the appointed day is realised or unrealised, they may treat the profit as realised; and where after making such enquiries they are unable to determine whether a particular loss so made is realised or unrealised, they may treat the loss as unrealised.

Restriction on distribution of assets

79C.(1) A listed company may only make a distribution at any time-

(a)　　if at that time the amount of its net assets is not less than the aggregate of its called up share capital and undistributable reserves; and

(b)　　if, and to the extent that, the distribution does not reduce the amount of those assets to less than that aggregate.

(2)　　A listed company's undistributable reserves are-

(a)　　the share premium account;

(b)　　the capital redemption reserve;

(c)　　the amount by which the company's accumulated, unrealised profits, so far as not previously utilised by capitalisation of a description to which this paragraph applies, exceed its accumulated, unrealised losses (so far as not

previously written off in a reduction or reorganisation of capital duly made); and

    (d)   any other reserve which the company is prohibited from distributing by any enactment (other than one contained in this Part) or by its memorandum or articles,

and paragraph (c) applies to every description of capitalisation except a transfer of profits of the company to its capital redemption reserve on or after the appointed day.

(3)   A listed company shall not include any uncalled share capital as an asset in any accounts relevant for the purposes of this section.

Exemption of certain companies

79D.   The Financial Secretary may, on the application of any listed company whose principal business consists of investing its funds in securities, land or other assets with the aim of spreading investment risk and giving its members the benefit of the results of the management of the assets, modify or exempt in relation to that company any of the requirements of sections 79B and 79C, subject to such terms and conditions as he may consider appropriate.

Realised profits of insurance company with long term business

79E.(1) Where an insurance company to which Parts III to VI of the Insurance Companies Ordinance (Cap. 41) apply carries on long term business-

    (a)   any amount properly transferred to the profit and loss account of the company from a surplus in the fund or funds maintained by it in respect of that business; and

    (b)   any deficit in that fund or those funds,

are to be (respectively) treated, for the purposes of this Part, as a realised profit and a realised loss; and, subject to this, any profit or loss arising in that business is to be left out of account for those purposes.

(2)   In subsection (1)-

    (a)   the reference to a surplus in any fund or funds of an insurance company is to an excess of the assets representing that fund or those funds over that liabilities of the company attributable to its long term business, as shown by an actuarial investigation; and

    (b)   the reference to a deficit in any such fund or funds is to the excess of those liabilities over those assets, as so shown.

(3) In this section -

"actuarial investigation" means an investigation to which section 18 of the Insurance Companies Ordinance (Cap. 41) applies or which is made in pursuance of a requirement imposed by section 32 of that Ordinance;

"long term business" has the same meaning as in the Insurance Companies Ordinance (Cap. 41).

Relevant Accounts

Distribution to be justified by reference to company's accounts

79F.(1) This section and sections 79G to 79L are for determining the question whether a distribution may be made by a company without contravening section 79B or 79C.

(2) The amount of a distribution which may be made is determined by reference to the following items as stated in the company's accounts-

        (a) profits, losses, assets and liabilities;

        (b) provisions within the meaning of paragraph 30(1) of the Tenth Schedule (depreciation, renewals, diminution in value of assets, retentions to meet liabilities, etc.); and

        (c) share capital and reserves (including undistributable reserves).

(3) Except in a case falling within subsection (4), the company's accounts which are relevant for this purpose are its last annual accounts, that is to say, those prepared under Part IV which were laid in respect of the last preceding financial year in respect of which accounts so prepared were laid; and for this purpose accounts are laid if section 122 has been complied with in relation to them.

(4) In the following 2 cases-

        (a) where the distribution would be found to contravene the relevant section if reference were made only to the company's last annual accounts; or

        (b) where the distribution is proposed to be declared before any accounts are laid in compliance with section 122,

the accounts relevant under this section (called "interim accounts" in the first case, and "initial accounts" in the second) are those necessary to enable a reasonable judgment to be made as to the amounts of the items mentioned in subsection (2).

(5) The relevant section is treated as contravened in the case of a distribution unless the statutory requirement about the relevant accounts (that is, the requirement of this section and sections 79G, 79H and 79I, as and where applicable) are complied with in relation to that distribution.

Requirement for last annual accounts

79G.(1) If the company's last annual accounts constitute the only accounts relevant under section 79F, the statutory requirements in respect of them are as follows.

(2) The accounts shall have been properly prepared in accordance with this Ordinance, or have been so prepared subject only to matters which are not material for determining, by reference to items mentioned in section 79F(2), whether the distribution would contravene that relevant section; and, without prejudice to the foregoing-

> *(a)* in the case of a company where the shareholders have agreed to apply the provisions of section 141D, so much of the accounts as consists of a balance sheet shall give a true and correct view of the state of the company's affairs; and

> *(b)* in the case of any other company-

>> **(i)** so much of the accounts as consists of a balance sheet shall give a true and fair view of the state of the company's affairs as at the balance sheet date; and

>> **(ii)** so much of the accounts as consists of a profit and loss account shall give a true and fair view of the company's profit or loss for the period in respect of which the accounts were prepared.

(3) The auditors shall have made their report on the accounts under section 141 or 141D as appropriate; and subsection (4) applies if the report is a qualified report, that is to say, it is not a report without qualification to the effect that in the auditors' opinion the accounts have been properly prepared in accordance with this Ordinance.

(4) The auditors shall in that case also have stated in writing (either at the time of their report or subsequently) whether, in their opinion, the matter in respect of which their report is qualified is material for determining, by reference to items mentioned in section 79F(2), whether the distribution would contravene the relevant section; and a copy of the statement shall have been laid before the company in general meeting.

(5) A statement under subsection (4) suffices for the purposes of a particular distribution not only if it relates to a distribution which has been proposed but also if it relates to distributions of any description which includes that particular distribution, notwithstanding that at the time of the statement it has not been proposed.

Requirement for interim accounts

79H.(1) The following are the statutory requirements in respect of interim accounts prepared for a proposed distribution by a listed company.

(2) The accounts shall have been properly prepared, or have been so prepared subject only to matters which are not material for determining, by reference to items mentioned in section 79F(2), whether the proposed distribution would contravene the relevant section.

(3) "Properly prepared" means that the accounts shall comply with section 123 (applying that section and the Tenth Schedule with such modifications as are necessary because the accounts are prepared otherwise than in respect of a financial year) and any balance sheet comprised in the accounts shall have been signed in accordance with section 129B; and, without prejudice to the foregoing-

> *(a)* so much of the accounts as consists of a balance sheet shall give a true and fair view of the state of the company's affairs as at the balance sheet date; and

> *(b)* so much of the accounts as consists of a profit and loss account shall give a true and fair view of the company's profit or loss for the period in respect of which the accounts were prepared.

(4) A copy of the accounts shall have been delivered to the Registrar.

(5) If the accounts are not in the English language, a translation into English of the accounts, certified in the prescribed manner to be a correct translation, shall also have been delivered to the Registrar.

Requirements for initial accounts

79I(1) The following are the statutory requirements in respect of initial accounts prepared for a proposed distribution by a listed company.

(2) The accounts shall have been properly prepared, or they shall have been so prepared subject only to matters which are not material for determining, by reference to items mentioned in section 79F(2), whether the proposed distribution would contravene the relevant section.

(3) Section 79H(3) applies as respects the meaning of "properly prepared".

(4) The company's auditors shall have made a report stating whether, in their opinion, the accounts have been properly prepared; and subsection (5) applies if their report is a qualified report, that is to say, it is not a report without qualification to the effect that in the auditors' opinion the accounts have been so prepared.

(5) The auditors shall in that case also have stated in writing whether, in their opinion, the matter in respect of which their report is qualified is material for determining, by reference to items mentioned in section 79F(2), whether the distribution would contravene the relevant section.

(6) A copy of the accounts, of the auditors' report under subsection (4) and of the auditors' statement (if any) under subsection (5) shall have been delivered to the Registrar.

(7) If the accounts are, or the auditors' report under subsection (4) or the statement (if any) under subsection (5) is, in a language other than English, a translation into English of the accounts, the report or the statement (as the case may be) certified in the prescribed manner to be a correct translation, shall also have been delivered to the Registrar.

Method of applying section 79F to successive distributions

79J.(1) For the purpose of determining by reference to particular accounts whether a proposed distribution may be made by a company, section 79F has effect, in a case where one or more distributions have already been made in pursuance of determinations made by reference to those same accounts, as if the amount of the proposed distribution was increased by the amount of the distributions so made.

(2) Subsection (1) applies (if it would not otherwise do so) to-

> *(a)* financial assistance lawfully given by a listed company out of its distributable profits in a case where the assistance is required to be so given by section 47D;

> *(b)* financial assistance lawfully given by an unlisted company out of its distributable profits in a case where the assistance is required to be so given by section 47E(2);

> *(c)* financial assistance given by a company in contravention of section 47A, in a case where the giving of that assistance reduces the company's net assets or increases its net liabilities;

> *(d)* a payment made by a company in respect of the purchase by it of shares in the company (except a payment lawfully made otherwise than out of distributable profits); and

> *(e)* a payment of any description specified in section 49F (company's purchase of right to acquire its own shares, etc.),

being financial assistance given or payment made since the relevant accounts were prepared, as if any such financial assistance or payment were a distribution already made in pursuance of a determination made by reference to those accounts.

(3)   In this section-

"financial assistance" has the same meaning as in sections 47A to 48;

"net liabilities", in relation to the giving of financial assistance by a company, means the amount by which the aggregate amount of the company's liabilities (within the meaning of section 47D(2)(b)) exceeds the aggregate amount of its assets, taking the amount of the assets and liabilities to be as stated in the company's books of account immediately before the financial assistance is given.

Treatment of assets in the relevant accounts

79K.(1) For the purposes of sections 79B and 79C, a provision of any kind mentioned in paragraph 30(1) of the Tenth Schedule, other than one in respect of a diminution in value of a fixed asset appearing on a revaluation of all the fixed assets of the company, or of all of its fixed assets other than goodwill, is treated as a realised loss.

(2) If, on the revaluation of a fixed asset, an unrealised profit is shown to have been made and, on or after the revaluation, a sum is written off or retained for depreciation of that asset over a period, then an amount equal to the amount by which that sum exceeds the sum which would have been so written off or retained for the depreciation of that asset over that period, if that profit had not been made, is treated for purposes of sections 79B and 79C as a realised profit made over that period.

(3) Where there is no record of the original cost of an asset, or a record cannot be obtained without unreasonable expense or delay, then for the purpose of determining whether the company has made a profit or loss in respect of that asset, its cost is taken to be the value ascribed to it in the earliest available record of its value made on or after its acquisition by the company.

(4) Subject to subsection (6), any consideration by the directors of the value at a particular time of a fixed asset is treated as a revaluation of the asset for the purposes of determining whether any such revaluation of the company's fixed assets as is required for purposes of the exception from subsection (1) has taken place at that time.

(5) But where any such assets which have not actually been revalued are treated as revalued for those purposes under subsection (4), that exception applies only if the directors are satisfied that their aggregate value at the time in question is not less than the aggregate amount at which they are for the time being stated in the company's accounts.

(6) Where section 79G(2), 79H(2) or 79I(2) applies to the relevant accounts, subsections (4) and (5) do not apply for the purpose of determining whether a revaluation of the company's fixed assets affecting the amount of the relevant items (that is, the items mentioned in section 79F(2)) as stated in those accounts has taken place, unless it is stated in a note to the accounts-

        (a)   that the directors have considered the value at any time of any fixed assets of the company, without actually revaluing those assets;

(b) that they are satisfied that the aggregate value of those assets at the time in question is or was not less than the aggregate amount at which they are or were for the time being stated in the company's accounts; and

(c) that the relevant items in question are accordingly stated in the relevant accounts on the basis that a revaluation of the company's fixed assets which by virtue of subsections (4) and (5) included the assets in question took place at that time.

(7) For the purposes of this section, assets of a company are taken to be fixed assets if they are intended for use or otherwise to be held on a continuing basis in the company's activities.

Distributions in kind

79L. Where a company makes a distribution of or including a non-cash asset, and any part of the amount at which that asset is stated in the accounts relevant for the purposes of the distribution in accordance with sections 79F to 79K represents an unrealised profit, that profit is to be treated as a realised profit for the purpose of determining the lawfulness of the distribution in accordance with this Part (whether before or after the distribution takes place).

Supplementary

Consequences of unlawful distribution

79M.(1) Where a distribution, or part of one, made by a company to one of its members is made in contravention of this Part and, at the time of the distribution, he knows or has reasonable grounds for believing that it is so made, he is liable to repay it (or that part of it, as the case may be) to the company or (in the case of a distribution made otherwise than in cash) to pay the company a sum equal to the value of the distribution (or part) at that time.

(2) Subsection (1) is without prejudice to any obligation imposed apart from this section on a member of a company to repay a distribution unlawfully made to him; but this section does not apply in relation to-

(a) financial assistance given by a company in contravention of section 47A; or

(b) any payment made by a company in respect of the redemption or purchase by the company of shares in itself.

Saving for provision in articles operative before the appointed day

79N. Where immediately before the appointed day a company was authorized by a provision of its articles to apply its unrealised profits in paying up in full or in part unissued shares to be allotted to members of the company as fully or partly paid bonus shares, that provision continues (subject to any alteration of the articles) as authority for those profits to be so applied after the date.

Application to certain companies

79O. Where a company is-

> (*a*)   a banking company as defined in paragraph 26 of the Tenth Schedule;

> (*b*)   an insurance company authorized to carry on business under the Insurance Companies Ordinance (Cap. 41); or

> (*c*)   a shipping company as defined in paragraph 28 of the Tenth Schedule,

sections 79G to 79K shall apply with the following modifications-

> **(i)**   section 79G applies as if in subsection 79G(2)(b), immediately after the words "in the case of any other company" there were inserted ", except where the company is entitled to avail itself, and has availed itself, of any of the provisions of Part III of the Tenth Schedule,";

> **(ii)**   sections 79H and 79I apply as if in section 79H(3), immediately after the words "without prejudice to the foregoing" there were inserted ", except where the company is entitled to avail itself, and has availed itself, of any of the provisions of Part III of the Tenth Schedule,".

Saving for other restraints on distribution

79P.   The provisions of this Part are without prejudice to any enactment or rule of law, or any provision of a company's memorandum or articles, restricting the sums out of which, or the cases in which, a distribution may be made.

PART III

REGISTRATION OF CHARGES

Registration of Charges with Registrar of Companies

Registration of charges created by companies

80.(1) Subject to the provisions of this Part of this Ordinance, every charge created after the fixed date by a company and being a charge to which this section applies shall, so far as any security on the company's property or undertaking is conferred thereby, be void against the liquidator and any creditor of the company, unless the particulars of the charge (which must include those specified in subsection (1A) and be in the specified form), together with the instrument, if any, by which the charge is created or evidenced, are delivered to or received by the Registrar for registration in manner required by this Ordinance within 5 weeks after the date of its creation, but without prejudice to any contract or obligation for repayment of the money thereby secured, and when a charge becomes void under this section the money secured thereby shall immediately become payable.

(1A) The particulars referred to in subsection (1) are, the date and description of the instrument creating the charge, the amount secured, short particulars of the property mortgaged or charged, names, addresses and description of mortgagees or persons entitled to the charge, details of any commission, discount or allowance payable to any person in consideration of his agreeing to subscribe to any debenture.

(2) This section applies to the following charges-

> *(a)* a charge for the purpose of securing any issue of debentures;

> *(b)* a charge on uncalled share capital of the company;

> *(c)* a charge created or evidenced by an instrument which, if executed by an individual, would require registration as a bill of sale;

> *(d)* a charge on land, wherever situate, or any interest therein, but not including a charge for any rent or other periodical sum issuing out of land;

> *(e)* a charge on book debts of the company;

> *(f)* a floating charge on the undertaking or property of the company;

> *(g)* a charge on calls made but not paid;

> *(h)* a charge on a ship or any share in a ship;

> *(i)* a charge on goodwill, on a patent or a licence under a patent, on a trademark or on a copyright or a licence under a copyright.

(3) In the case of a charge created out of Hong Kong comprising property situate outside Hong Kong the delivery to and the receipt by the Registrar of a copy verified in the prescribed manner of the instrument by which the charge is created or evidenced, shall have the same effect for the purposes of this section as the delivery and receipt of the instrument itself, and 5 weeks after the date on which the instrument or copy could, in due course of post, and if dispatched with due diligence, have been received in Hong Kong shall be substituted for 5 weeks after the date of the creation of the charge, as the time within which the particulars and instrument or copy are to be delivered to the Registrar.

(4) Where a charge is created in Hong Kong but comprises property outside Hong Kong the instrument creating or purporting to create the charge may be sent for registration under this section notwithstanding that further proceedings may be necessary to make the charge valid or effectual according to the law of the country in which the property is situate.

(5) Where a negotiable instrument has been given to secure the payment of any book debts of a company the deposit of the instrument for the purpose of securing an advance to the company shall not for the purposes of this section be treated as a charge on those book debts.

(6) The holding of debentures entitling the holder to a charge on land shall not for the purposes of this section be deemed to be an interest in land.

(7) Where a series of debentures containing, or giving by reference to any other instrument, any charge to the benefit of which the debenture holders of that series are entitled pari passu is created by a company, it shall for the purposes of this section be sufficient if there are delivered to or received by the Registrar within 5weeks after the execution of the deed containing the charge or, if there is no such deed, after the execution of any debentures of the series, the following particulars-

  (a) the total amount secured by the whole series; and

  (b) the dates of the resolutions authorizing the issue of the series and the date of the covering deed, if any, by which the security is created or defined; and

  (c) a general description of the property charged; and

  (d) the names of the trustees, if any, for the debenture holders,

together with the deed containing the charge, or, if there is no such deed, one of the debentures of the series:

  Provided that, where more than one issue is made of debentures in the series, there shall be sent to the Registrar for entry in the register particulars of the date and amount of each issue, but an omission to do this shall not affect the validity of the debentures issued.

(8) Where any commission, allowance, or discount has been paid or made either directly or indirectly by a company to any person in consideration of his subscribing or agreeing to subscribe, whether absolutely or conditionally, for any debentures of the company, or procuring or agreeing to procure subscriptions, whether absolute or conditional, for any such debentures, the particulars required to be sent for registration under this section shall include particulars as to the amount or rate per cent of the commission, discount, or allowance so paid or made, but omission to do this shall not affect the validity of the debentures issued:

Provided that the deposit of any debentures as security for any debt of the company shall not for the purposes of this subsection be treated as the issue of the debentures at a discount.

(9) In this Part-

"charge" includes mortgage;

"the fixed date" means in relation to the charges specified in paragraphs (a) to (f), both inclusive, of subsection (2), 1 January 1912, and in relation to the charges specified in paragraphs (g) to (i), both inclusive, of the said subsection, the commencement of this Ordinance.

Duty of company to register charges created by company

81.(1) It shall be the duty of a company to send to the Registrar for registration the particulars of every charge created by the company and of the issues of debentures of a series, requiring registration under section 80, but registration of any such charge may be effected on the application of any person interested therein.

(2) Where registration is effected on the application of some person other than the company, that person shall be entitled to recover from the company the amount of any fees properly paid by him to the Registrar on the registration.

(3) If any company makes default in sending to the Registrar for registration the particulars of any charge created by the company, or of the issues of debentures of a series, requiring registration as aforesaid, then, unless the registration has been effected on the application of some other person, the company and every officer of the company who is in default shall be liable to a fine and, for continued default, to a daily default fine.

Duty of company to register charges existing on property acquired

82.(1) Where a company acquires any property which is subject to a charge of any such kind as would, if it had been created by the company after the acquisition of the property, have been required to be registered under this Part, the company shall cause the particulars of the charge (which must include those specified in section 80(1A) and be in the specified form), together with a copy (certified in the prescribed manner to be a correct copy) of the instrument, if any, by which the charge was created or is evidenced, to be delivered to the Registrar for registration in manner required by this Ordinance within 5 weeks after the date on which the acquisition is completed:

Provided that, if the property is situate and the charge was created outside Hong Kong, 5 weeks after the date on which the copy of the instrument could in due course of post, and if dispatched with due diligence, have been received in Hong Kong shall be substituted for 5 weeks after the completion of the acquisition as the time within which the particulars and the copy of the instrument are to be delivered to the Registrar.

(1A) The requirement in subsection (1) to register a charge referred to in that subsection shall apply in relation to any property of an existing company acquired by the company before the date of commencement of the Companies (Amendment) Ordinance 1984 as if that property was so acquired on that date, except that, for the purposes of this subsection-

      (a)   subsection (1) shall be read and construed as if for "5 weeks after the date on which the acquisition is completed" there were substituted "6 months after the date of commencement of the Companies (Amendment) Ordinance 1984, unless the property ceased to be so charged, or the charge was registered, prior to that date";

      (b)   the proviso to subsection (1) shall not apply.

(2)   If default is made in complying with this section, the company and every officer of the company who is in default shall be liable to a fine and, for continued default, to a daily default fine.

Register of charges to be kept by Registrar

83.(1) The Registrar of Companies shall keep, with respect to each company, a register in a form determined by him of all the charges requiring registration under this Part, and shall, on payment of the prescribed fee, enter in the register with respect to such charges the following particulars-

      (a)   in the case of a charge to the benefit of which the holders of a series of debentures are entitled, such particulars as are specified in section 80(7);

      (b)   in the case of any other charge-

            (i)   if the charge is a charge created by the company, the date of its creation, and if the charge was a charge existing on property acquired by the company, the date of the acquisition of the property; and

            (ii)   the amount secured by the charge; and

            (iii)   short particulars of the property charged; and

            (iv)   the persons entitled to the charge.

(2)   The Registrar shall give a certificate under his hand of the registration of any charge registered in pursuance of this Part stating the amount thereby secured, and the certificate shall be conclusive evidence that the requirements of this Part as to registration have been complied with.

(3)   The register kept in pursuance of this section shall be open to inspection by any person on payment of the prescribed fee.

(4)   (*Repealed*)

84.   (*Repealed*)

Entries of satisfaction and release of property from charge

85.   The Registrar, on evidence being given to his satisfaction with respect to any registered charge-

        (a)   that the debt for which the charge was given has been paid or satisfied in whole or in part; or

        (b)   that part of the property or undertaking charged has been released from the charge or has ceased to form part of the company's property or undertaking,

may enter on the register a memorandum of satisfaction in whole or in part, or of the fact that part of the property or undertaking has been released from the charge or has ceased to form part of the company's property or undertaking, as the case may be; and where he enters a memorandum of satisfaction in whole he shall, if required and upon payment of the prescribed fee, endorse the words "satisfaction entered" or the expression in Chinese "...." upon the instrument creating the charge or furnish the company with a copy of the memorandum, as required.

Extension of time for registration, and rectification of register of charges

86.(1) The court, on being satisfied that the omission to register a charge within the time required by this Ordinance or that the omission or mis-statement of any particular with respect to any such charge or in a memorandum of satisfaction was accidental, or due to inadvertence or to some other sufficient cause, or is not of a nature to prejudice the position of creditors or shareholders of the company, or that on other grounds it is just and equitable to grant relief, may, on the application of the company or any person interested, and on such terms and conditions as seem to the court just and expedient, order that the time for registration shall be extended, or, as the case may be, that the omission or mis-statement shall be rectified.

(2)   The grant of relief by the court under this section shall, if the court so directs, not have the effect of relieving the company or its officers of any liability already incurred under section 81.

Notice to Registrar of appointment of receiver or manager, or of mortgagee taking possession

87.(1) If any person obtains an order for the appointment of a receiver or manager of the property of a company, or appoints such a receiver or manager under any powers contained in any instrument, or as mortgagee enters into possession of the property, he shall, within 7 days from the date of the order or of the appointment under the said powers or of his entering into possession of the property, as the case may be, give notice of the fact to the Registrar, and the Registrar shall, on payment of the prescribed fee, enter the notice in the register of charges.

(2)　　Where-

　　　　(a)　　any person appointed receiver or manager of the property of a company under the powers contained in any instrument ceases to act as such receiver or manager; or

　　　　(b)　　any person who is in possession of the property of a company as mortgagee goes out of possession of the property,

he shall, on ceasing so to act or on going out of possession, as the case may be, give the Registrar notice to that effect, and the Registrar shall enter the notice in the register of charges.

(3)　　If any person makes default in complying with the requirements of this section, he shall be liable to a fine and, for continued default, to a daily default fine.

(4)　　This section shall, in relation to any mortgagee in possession of the property of any company who entered into possession thereof as mortgagee prior to the date on which the provisions of this section in force at the commencement of the Companies (Amendment) Ordinance 1984 ceased to have effect, be read and construed as if for the reference to the date of entering into possession there were substituted a reference to the date aforesaid.

Provisions as to Company's Register of Charges and as to Copies of Instruments creating Charges

Copies of instruments creating charges to be kept by company

88.(1) Every company shall cause a copy of every instrument creating any charge requiring registration under this Part to be kept-

　　　　(a)　　at the registered office of the company; or

　　　　(b)　　if the work in connexion with the keeping of copies of such instruments is done at an office of the company other than the registered office of the company, at that other office; or

　　　　(c)　　if the company arranges with some other person for the keeping of such copies to be undertaken on behalf of the company by that other person, at the office of that other person at which the work in connexion with the keeping thereof is done,

so, however, that such copies shall not be kept at a place outside Hong Kong.

(2) In the case of a series of uniform debentures, the keeping of a copy of one debenture of the series shall be sufficient for the purposes of subsection (1).

(3) Every company shall send notice to the Registrar in the specified form of the place where copies of instruments required to be kept under subsection (1) are so kept and of any change in that place:

Provided that a company shall not be bound to send such notice where such copies have, at all times since they came into existence or, in the case of copies in existence at the commencement of the Companies (Amendment) Ordinance 1984, at all times since then, been kept at the registered office of the company.

(4) Where a company makes default in complying with subsection (1) or makes default for 14 days in complying with subsection (3), the company and every officer of the company who is in default shall be liable to a fine and, for continued default, to a daily default fine.

Company's register of charges

89.(1) Every company shall keep a register of charges and enter therein all charges specifically affecting property of the company and all floating charges on the undertaking or any property of the company, giving in each case a short description of the property charged, the amount of the charge, and, except in the case of securities to bearer, the names of the persons entitled thereto.

(2) The register of charges of a company shall be kept-

> *(a)* at the registered office of the company; or

> *(b)* if the work of making it up is done at an office of the company other than the registered office of the company, at that other office; or

> *(c)* if the company arranges with some other person for the making up of the register to be undertaken on behalf of the company by that other person, at the office of that other person at which the work is done,

so, however, that it shall not be kept at a place outside Hong Kong.

(3) Every company shall send notice to the Registrar in the specified form of the place where its register of charges is kept and of any change in that place:

Provided that a company shall not be bound to send such notice where the register has, at all times since it came into existence or, in the case of a register in existence at the commencement of the Companies (Amendment) Ordinance 1984, at all times since then, been kept at the registered office of the company.

(4) Where a company makes default in complying with subsection (1) or (2) or makes default for 14 days in complying with subsection (3), the company and every officer of the company who is in default shall be liable to a fine and, for continued default, to a daily default fine.

(5) If any officer of the company knowingly and wilfully authorizes or permits the omission of any entry required to be made under this section, he shall be liable to imprisonment and a fine.

Right to inspect copies of instruments creating mortgages and charges and company's register of charges

90.(1) The copies of instruments creating any charge requiring registration under this Part with the Registrar, and the register of charges kept in pursuance of section 89, shall be open during business hours (but subject to such reasonable restrictions as the company in general meeting may impose, so that not less than 2 hours in each day shall be allowed for inspection) to the inspection of any creditor or member of the company without fee, and the register of charges shall also be open to the inspection of any other person on payment of such fee, not exceeding $2 for each inspection, as the company may prescribe.

(2) If inspection of the said copies or register is refused-

> *(a)* every officer of the company who is in default shall be liable to a fine and, for continued default, to a daily default fine;

> *(b)* without prejudice to any proceedings under paragraph (a), the court may by order compel an immediate inspection of the copies or register.

(3) *(Repealed)*

Application of Part III to Companies incorporated outside Hong Kong

Application of Part III to company incorporated outside Hong Kong

91.(1) This Part shall extend to charges on property in Hong Kong which are created, and to charges on property in Hong Kong which is acquired, by a company (whether a company within the meaning of this Ordinance or not) incorporated outside Hong Kong which has a place of business in Hong Kong.

(2) In the application of sections 88 and 89 to a company referred to in subsection (1)-

> *(a)* references in those sections to the registered office of a company shall be construed as references to the principal place of business of the company in Hong Kong;

> *(b)* references in section 89 to charges shall be construed as references to charges of any kind mentioned in subsection (1).

(3) Where a company (whether a company within the meaning of this Ordinance or not) incorporated outside Hong Kong has, when it establishes a place of business in Hong Kong, property in Hong Kong which is subject to a charge created by the company or subsisting when the property was acquired, being a charge of any such kind as would, if it had been created by the company or the property had been acquired after the establishment of that place of business, have been required to be registered under this Part, the company shall, within 5 weeks after the date on which it establishes the place of business, send to the Registrar for registration the particulars (including any instrument or copy of any instrument) mentioned in this Part as requiring registration in respect of a charge of that kind.

(4) If default is made in complying with subsection (3), the company and every officer of the company who is in default shall be liable to a fine and, for continued default, to a daily default fine.

PART IV - MANAGEMENT AND ADMINISTRATION

Registered Office and Name

Registered office of company

92.(1) A company shall, as from the day on which it begins to carry on business or as from the 14th day after the date of its incorporation, whichever is the earlier, have a registered office in Hong Kong to which all communications and notices may be addressed.

(1A) Notwithstanding that the memorandum of a company provides that its registered office shall be situated in a particular place in Hong Kong, the company may have its registered office in that place or in any other place in Hong Kong.

(2) Notice of the situation of the registered office, and of any change therein, shall be given within 14 days after the date of the incorporation of the company or of the change, as the case may be, to the Registrar, who shall record the same. The inclusion in the annual return of a company of a statement as to the address of its registered office shall not be taken to satisfy the obligation imposed by this subsection.

(3) If default is made in complying with this section, the company and every officer of the company who is in default shall be liable to a fine and, for continued default, to a daily default fine.

Publication of name by company

93.(1) Every company-

> *(a)* shall paint or affix, and keep painted or affixed, its name on the outside of every office or place in which its business is carried on, in a conspicuous position, in legible characters;

> *(b)* shall have as its common seal a metallic seal on which it shall have its name engraves in legible characters;

> *(c)* shall have its name mentioned in legible characters in all business letters of the company and in all notices and other official publications of the company, and in all contracts, deeds, bills of exchange, promissory notes, endorsements, cheques and orders for money or goods purporting to be signed by or on behalf of the company, and in all consignment notes, invoices, receipts and letters of credit of the company;

> *(d)* shall mention in legible characters in all documents in which the company is required under paragraph (c) to have its name mentioned-

> > **(i)** in the case of a limited company exempt from the obligation to use the word "Limited" or the expression in Chinese "....." or both such

word and expression, as the case may be, as part of its name, the fact that it is incorporated with limited liability;

(ii) in the case of an unlimited company, the fact that it is incorporated without limited liability.

(2) Every limited company registered by a name in English only (other than a company licensed to be registered without the addition of the word "Limited" to its name)-

(a) which exhibits outside or inside its registered office or outside or inside any office or place in which its business is carried on; or

(b) which uses on its seal; or

(c) which uses in any business letter of the company or in any notice or other official publication of the company, or in any contract, deed, bill of exchange, promissory note, endorsement, cheque, or order for money or goods purporting to be signed by or on behalf of the company, or in any consignment note, invoice, receipt or letter of credit of the company,

any name of or for the company in Chinese characters, whether such name be a transliteration or translation of its name in the memorandum or not, shall append to such name so used in Chinese characters:

Provided that it shall be lawful for the Registrar by licence to direct that such company shall be exempted, wholly or in part, from the requirements of this subsection, and to revoke any such licence.

(2A) Every limited company registered by a name in Chinese only (other than a company licensed to be registered without the addition of the expression in Chinese "…" to its name) -

(a) which exhibits outside or inside its registered office or outside or inside any office or place in which its business is carried on; or

(b) which uses on its seal; or

(c) which uses in any business letter of the company or in any notice or other official publication of the company, or in any contract, deed, bill of exchange, promissory note, endorsement, cheque, or order for money or goods purporting to be signed by or on behalf of the company, or in any consignment note, invoice, receipt or letter of credit of the company,

any name of or for the company in English, whether such name be a transliteration or translation of its name in the memorandum or not, shall append to such name so used in English the word "Limited".

(2B) Notwithstanding subsection (2A), it shall be lawful for the Registrar by licence to direct that such company shall be exempted, wholly or in part, from the requirements of that subsection, and to revoke any such licence.

(3) If a company does not paint or affix its name in manner directed by this Ordinance, the company and every officer of the company who is in default shall be liable to a fine and if a company does not keep its name painted or affixed in manner so directed, the company and every officer of the company who is in default shall be liable to a default fine.

(4) If a company fails to comply with any of the provisions of subsection (1), other than paragraph (a) thereof, and subsection (2) the company shall be liable to a fine.

(5) If any officer of a company, or any person on its behalf-

> *(a)* uses or authorizes the use of any seal purporting to be a seal of the company which is not a metallic seal or whereon its name is not so engraven as aforesaid; or

> *(b)* issues or authorizes the issue of any business letter of the company or any notice or other official publication of the company, or signs or authorizes to be signed on behalf of the company any contract, deed, bill of exchange, promissory note, endorsement, cheque or order for money or goods, wherein its name is not mentioned in manner aforesaid; or

> *(c)* issues or authorizes the issue of any consignment note, invoice, receipt, or letter of credit of the company, wherein its name is not mentioned in manner aforesaid,

he shall be liable to a fine and shall further be personally liable to the holder of the bill of exchange, promissory note, cheque, or order for money or goods, for the amount thereof, unless it is duly paid by the company.

(6) Until the expiration of a period of 12 months from the date of commencement of the Companies (Amendment) Ordinance 1984, subsections (1)(b) and (5)(a) as amended by that Ordinance shall have effect in relation to any company registered at that date as if-

> *(a)* in subsection (1)(b), for the words "metallic seal" there were substituted the word "seal";

> *(b)* in subsection (5)(a), the words "which is not a metallic seal or" were omitted.

Adequacy of certain descriptions of companies

94. No description of a company shall be inadequate or incorrect by reason of the use of-

(a)   the abbreviation "Co." or "Coy." in lieu of the word "Company" contained in the name of the company;

(b)   the abbreviation "Ltd." in lieu of the word "Limited" contained in the name of the company;

(c)   the abbreviation "HK" or "H.K." in lieu of the words "Hong Kong" contained in the name of the company;

(d)   the symbol "&" in lieu of the word "and" contained in the name of the company;

(e)   any of such words in lieu of the corresponding abbreviation or symbol contained in the name of the company;

(f)   any type or case of letters, spaces between letters, accents or punctuation marks which are not the same as those appearing in the name of the company, or by reason of the use or omission of the definite article as the first word in the description.

Register of Members

Register of members

95.(1) Every company shall keep in the English language a register of its members, and enter therein the following particulars-

(a)   the names and addresses, and the occupations or descriptions, of the members (and, in the case of a Chinese member of a company having a share capital who has signed in Chinese characters any instrument of transfer relating to the shares held by him, or who has, by adding Chinese characters after his name on such instrument or by other means, indicated that he wishes the Chinese characters to be entered in the register, his name both in English and Chinese characters), and in the case of a company having a share capital a statement of the shares held by each member, distinguishing each share by its number so long as the share has a number, and of the amount paid or agreed to be considered as paid on the shares of each member;

(b)   the date at which each person was entered in the register as a member;

(c)   the date at which any person ceased to be a member:

Provided that-

(i)   where the company has converted any of its shares into stock and given notice of the conversion to the Registrar, the register shall show the amount of stock held by each member instead of the amount of shares and the particulars relating to shares specified in paragraph (a);

(ii)   in the case of a person referred to in paragraph (c), all entries in the register relating to such person at the date when he ceased to be a member may be destroyed after the expiry of a period of 30 years from that date.

(2)   The register of members shall be kept at the registered office of the company and may be kept by the use of any method or means, mechanical or electrical or otherwise, which does not restrict the availability for public inspection in a legible form of the information contained in the register:

Provided that-

(a)   if the work of making it up is done at an office of the company other than the registered office of the company, it may be kept at that other office; and

(b)   if the company arranges with some other person for the making up of the register to be undertaken on behalf of the company by that other person, it may be kept at the office of that other person at which the work is done,

so, however, that it shall not be kept at a place outside Hong Kong.

(3)   Every company shall send notice to the Registrar in the specified form of the place where its register of members is kept and of any change in that place:

Provided that a company shall not be bound to send such notice where the register has, at all times since it came into existence or, in the case of a register in existence at the commencement of the Companies (Amendment) Ordinance 1984, at all times since then, been kept at the registered office of the company.

(4)   Where a company makes default in complying with subsection (1) or (2) or makes default for 14 days in complying with subsection (3), the company and every officer of the company who is in default shall be liable to a fine and, for continued default, to a daily default fine.

Index of members of company

96.(1) Every company having more than 50 members shall, unless the register of members is in such a form as to constitute in itself an index, keep an index of the names of the members of the company and shall, within 14 days after the date on which any alteration is made in the register of members, make any necessary alteration in the index.

(2)   The index shall in respect of each member contain a sufficient indication to enable the account of that member in the register to be readily found.

(2A)   The index shall at all times be kept at the same place as the register of members.

(3) If default is made in complying with this section, the company and every officer of the company who is in default shall be liable to a fine and, for continued default, to a daily default fine.

Provisions as to entries in register in relation to share warrants

97.(1) On the issue of a share warrant the company shall strike out of its register of members the name of the member then entered therein as holding the shares specified in the warrant as if he had ceased to be a member, and shall enter in the register the following particulars, namely-

> *(a)* the fact of the issue of the warrant;

> *(b)* a statement of the shares included in the warrant, distinguishing each share by its number so long as the share has a number, and

> *(c)* the date of the issue of the warrant.

(2) The bearer of a share warrant shall, subject to the articles of the company, be entitled, on surrendering it for cancellation, to have his name entered as a member in the register of members.

(3) The company shall be responsible for any loss incurred by any person by reason of the company entering in the register the name of a bearer of a share warrant in respect of the shares therein specified without the warrant being surrendered and cancelled.

(4) Until the warrant is surrendered, the particulars specified in subsection (1) shall be deemed to be the particulars required by this Ordinance to be entered in the register of members, and, on the surrender, the date of the surrender must be entered.

(5) Subject to the provisions of this Ordinance, the bearer of a share warrant may, if the articles of the company so provide, be deemed to be a member of the company within the meaning of this Ordinance, either to the full extent or for any purposes defined in the articles.

Inspection of register of members

98.(1) Except when the register of members is closed under the provisions of this Ordinance, the register, and the index of names, of the members of a company shall during business hours (subject to such reasonable restrictions as the company in general meeting may impose, so that not less than 2 hours in each day be allowed for inspection) be open to the inspection of any member without charge and of any other person on payment of the appropriate fee specified in the Fourteenth Schedule, or such less sum as the company may prescribe, for each inspection.

(2) Any member or other person may require a copy of the register, or of any part thereof, on payment of the appropriate fee specified in the Fourteenth Schedule, or such less sum as the company may prescribe. The company shall cause any copy so required by any person to be sent to that person within a period of 10 days commencing on the day next after the day on which the requirement is received by the company.

(3) If any inspection required under this section is refused of if any copy required under this section is not sent within the proper period, the company and every officer of the company who is in default shall be liable in respect of each offence to a fine and, for continued default, to a daily default fine.

(4) In the case of any such refusal or default, the court may by order compel an immediate inspection of the register and index or direct that the copies required shall be sent to the persons requiring them.

Consequences of failure to comply with requirements as to register owing to agent's default

98A. Where, by virtue of proviso (b) to section 95(2), the register is kept at the office of some person other than the company, and by reason of any default of his the company fails to comply with subsection (3) of that section, section 96(2A) or section 98 or with any requirements of this Ordinance as to the production of the register, that other person shall be liable to the same penalties as if he were an officer of the company who was in default, and the power of the court under section 98(4) shall extend to the making of orders against that other person and his officers and servants.

Power to close register of members and register of debenture holders

99.(1) A company may, on giving notice by advertisement in a newspaper circulating generally in Hong Kong, close for any time or times not exceeding in the whole 30 days in each year-

    (a) the register of members of the company or the part thereof relating to members holding shares of any class;

    (b) any register of debenture holders of the company.

(2) The period of 30 days referred to in subsection (1) may be extended in respect of any year-

    (a) in relation to the register (or any part of the register) of members of a company, by an ordinary resolution passed at a general meeting of the company in that year; or

    (b) in relation to the register of debenture holders of a company, by a resolution passed in that year by a majority in value of the debenture holders present in person or, where proxies are permitted, by proxy at a meeting summoned for the purpose or otherwise in accordance with the trust deed or other document securing the debentures:

Provided that the said period shall not be extended beyond 60 days in any year.

(3) A company shall, on demand, furnish any person seeking to inspect a register or part of a register which is closed by virtue of this section with a certificate under the hand of the secretary of the company stating the period for which, and by whose authority, it is closed.

(4) If a company makes default in complying with subsection (3), the company and every officer of the company who is in default shall be liable to a fine.

Power of court to rectify register

100. If -

> *(a)* the name of any person is, without sufficient cause, entered in or omitted from the register of members of a company; or

> *(b)* default is made or unnecessary delay takes place in entering on the register the fact of any person having ceased to be a member;

the person aggrieved, or any member of the company, or the company, may apply to the court for rectification of the register.

(2) Where an application is made under this section, the court may either refuse the application or may, subject to section 71A, order rectification of the register and payment by the company of any damages sustained by any party aggrieved.

(3) Subject to section 71A, on an application under this section the court may decide any question relating to the title of any person who is a party to the application to have his name entered in or omitted from the register, whether the question arises between members or alleged members, or between members or alleged members on the one hand and the company on the other hand, and generally may decide any question necessary or expedient to be decided for rectification of the register.

(4) In the case of a company required by this Ordinance to send a list of its members to the Registrar, the court, when making an order for rectification of the register, shall by its order direct notice of the rectification to be given to the Registrar.

Trusts not to be entered on register

101. No notice of any trust, expressed, implied, or constructive, shall be entered on the register, or be receivable by the Registrar.

Register to be evidence

102.(1) The register of members shall be prima facie evidence of any matters by this Ordinance directed or authorized to be inserted therein.

(2) Where in any proceedings under this Ordinance it is sought to challenge the accuracy of any entry in the register of members by evidence of any transaction, such evidence shall not be admissible for that purpose unless the transaction occurred not more than 30 years prior to the proceedings.

Branch Register

Power of company to keep branch register

103.(1) The Governor may issue an annual licence to any company whose objects comprise the transaction of business outside Hong Kong, empowering such company, if it is authorized so to do by its articles, to keep a register of members in any place at or near which it transacts business:

Provided that-

(a) a company applying for such licence shall satisfy the Governor by a statutory declaration to be filed with the Registrar that a substantial part of the business of the company is transacted at or near the place where it desires to keep such register;

(b) every such licence shall be valid only until the 31 December next following the date on which it is issued.

(2) There shall be paid to the Registrar in respect of a licence issued to a company under this section, prior to the issue thereof, a fee calculated at the rate of 4 cents for every $100 of the paid-up capital of such company or, in the case of a company whose share capital is expressed in any other currency, at the equivalent rate in that currency according to the rate of exchange prevailing at the date of the application for such licence:

Provided that where the period between the date of issue of the first licence issued to a company under this section and the 31 December next following is less than a year, a proportionate part only of such fee shall be charged.

(3) When the Registrar has reasonable cause to believe that a company is keeping a register of members at any place outside Hong Kong without having a valid licence under this Ordinance, he shall publish in the Gazette and send to the company by post a notice that at the expiration of 3 months from the date of that notice the name of the company mentioned therein will, unless cause is shown to the contrary, be struck off the register and the company will be dissolved.

(4) At the expiration of the time specified in the notice referred to in subsection (3) the Registrar may, unless cause to the contrary is previously shown by the company, strike its name off the register, and shall publish notice thereof in the Gazette and, on the publication in the Gazette of this notice, the company shall be dissolved:

Provided that-

(a) the liability, if any, of every director, managing officer and member of the company shall continue and may be enforced as if the company had not been dissolved; and

(b) nothing in this subsection shall affect the power of the court to wind up a company the name of which has been struck off the register.

(5) If a company or any member or creditor thereof feels aggrieved by the company having been struck off the register, the court on an application made by the company or member or creditor before the expiration of 20 years from the publication in the Gazette of the notice aforesaid may, if satisfied that it is just that the company be restored to the register, order the name of the company to be restored to the register, and upon an office copy of the order being delivered to the Registrar for registration the company shall be deemed to have continued in existence as if its name had not been struck off; and the court may by the order give such directions and make such provisions as seem just for placing the company and all other persons in the same position as nearly as may be as if the name of the company had not been struck off.

(6) A notice to be sent under this section to a company may be addressed to the company at its registered office, or, if no office has been registered, to the care of some officer of the company or, if there is no officer of the company whose name and address are known to the Registrar, may be sent to each of the persons who subscribed the memorandum, addressed to him at the address mentioned in the memorandum.

(7) No company shall keep a register of members at any place outside Hong Kong unless it is empowered to do so by virtue of a licence issued to the company under this section and, if default is made in complying with this subsection, the company and every officer of the company who is in default shall be liable to a fine and, for continued default, to a daily default fine.

Regulations as to branch register

104.(1) A branch register shall be deemed to be part of the company's register of members (in this section called the principal register).

(2) It shall be kept in the same manner in which the principal register is by this Ordinance required to be kept, except that the advertisement before closing the register shall be inserted in some newspaper circulating in the district where the branch register is kept.

(3) The company shall-

> *(a)* transmit to its registered office a copy of every entry in its branch register as soon as may be after the entry is made; and

> *(b)* cause to be kept at the place where the company's principal register is kept a duplicate of its branch register duly entered up from time to time.

Every duplicate shall for all the purposes of this Ordinance be deemed to be part of the principal register.

(4) Subject to the provisions of this section with respect to the duplicate register, the shares registered in a branch register shall be distinguished from the shares registered in the principal register, and no transaction with respect to any shares registered in a branch register shall, during the continuance of that registration, be registered in any other register.

(5) A company may discontinue to keep a branch register, and thereupon all entries in that register shall be transferred to some other branch register kept by the company or to the principal register.

(6) Subject to the provisions of this Ordinance, any company may, by its articles, make such provisions as it may think fit respecting the keeping of branch registers.

(7) If default is made in complying with subsection (3), the company and every officer of the company who is in default shall be liable to a fine and, for continued default, to a daily default fine; and where, by virtue of proviso (b) to section 95(2), the principal register is kept at the office of some person other than the company and by reason of any default of his the company fails to comply with subsection (3)(b), he shall be liable to the same penalty as if he were an officer of the company who was in default.

105. *(Repealed)*

Provisions as to branch registers of oversea companies kept in Hong Kong

106. If by virtue of the law in force in any place outside Hong Kong companies incorporated under that law have power to keep in Hong Kong branch registers of their members resident in Hong Kong, the Governor in Council may by order direct that-

> *(a)* every such branch register shall be kept at such place in Hong Kong as may be specified in the order in respect thereof;

> *(b)* sections 98 and 100 shall, subject to any modifications and adaptations specified in the order, apply to and in relation to any such branch registers kept in Hong Kong as they apply to and in relation to the registers of companies within the meaning of this Ordinance.

Annual Return

Annual return to be made by company

107.(1) Subject to this section and section 109, every company shall once in every year make a return which shall contain, with respect to the company, such particulars as specified therein.

(2) Without prejudice to the generality of subsection (1), a return under that subsection shall state -

> *(a)* the company name, its registered number and business name (if any);

> *(b)* the type of company;

> *(c)* the address of the registered office of the company;

> *(d)* the date of the return;

> (e)   particulars of the total amount of the indebtedness of the company in respect of all mortgages and charges which are required to be registered with the Registrar under this Ordinance, or which would have been required so to be registered if created after 1 January 1912;

> (f)   in the case of a company having a share capital -

>> **(i)**   particulars relating to members and share capital of the company; and

>> **(ii)**   where the company has converted any of its shares into stock and given notice of it to the Registrar, the amount of stock held by each of the existing members;

> (g)   in the case of a company not having a share capital, except in the case of a company registered with an unlimited number of members, the number of members of the company;

> (h)   in a case in which the register of members is, under the provisions of this Ordinance, kept elsewhere than at the registered office, the address of the place where it is kept;

> (i)   all such particulars with respect to the persons who at the date of the return are the directors of the company and any person who at that date is the secretary of the company as are by this Ordinance required to be contained with respect to directors and the secretary respectively in the register of directors and secretaries of a company;

> (j)   if any register of holders of debentures or any duplicate of any such register or part of any such register is, under the provisions of this Ordinance, kept elsewhere than at the registered office of the company, the address of the place where it is kept.

(3) A company need not make a return under subsection (1) in the year of its incorporation or, if it is not required by section 111 to hold an annual general meeting during the following year, in that year.

(4) In the case of a company which keeps a branch register, the particulars of the entries in that register shall, so far as they relate to matters which are required to be contained in the return, be included in the return made next after copies of those entries are received at the registered office of the company.

(5) In the case of a company having a share capital if there has been no change in the matters required to be contained in a return, since the date of the last return, the company may in lieu of the return required by subsection (1), make a return by certificate in the specified form, signed by a director and the secretary of the company stating -

> (a) the date at which the last return under subsection (1) was made up; and

> (b) that, as at the day of the annual general meeting for the year there has been no change since that date, in the information contained in that return.

(6) In the case of a private company having a share capital subsection (5)(b) shall be read as if "the most recent anniversary of the date of incorporation of the company" were substituted for "the annual general meeting for the year".

(7) Without affecting the generality of section 2A, the Registrar may, for the purposes of this section, specify different forms or particulars in relation to companies having a share capital, companies not having a share capital or companies which are private companies.

108. *(Repealed)*

General provisions as to annual returns

109.(1) Except where the company is a private company having a share capital, the annual return shall be completed within 42 days after the annual general meeting for the year, whether or not that meeting is the first or only ordinary general meeting, or the first or only general meeting, of the company in the year, and the company shall forthwith forward to the Registrar a copy of the return signed both by a director and the secretary of the company.

(1A) In the case of a private company having a share capital, the annual return shall, subject to subsection (1B), be completed within 42 days after the most recent anniversary of the date of incorporation of the company and the company shall forthwith forward to the Registrar a copy of the return signed both by a director and the secretary of the company.

(1B) As regards a private company having a share capital which was incorporated before the commencement of section 5 of the Companies (Amendment) (No. 2) Ordinance 1993 -

> (a) if the next anniversary of the date of incorporation falls within 6 months of the date on which the last annual return was or ought to have been filed, the next annual return shall be filed not later than 42 days after the anniversary following the next anniversary of the date of incorporation;

> (b) if the next anniversary of the date of incorporation falls after 6 months of the date on which the last annual return was or ought to have been filed, the next annual return shall be filed not later than 42 days after that anniversary.

(2) *(Repealed)*

(3) Except where the company is a private company, the annual return shall include-

(a)   a copy, certified by a director or the manager or the secretary of the company to be a true copy, of every balance sheet laid before the company in general meeting during the period to which the return relates (including every document required by law to be annexed to the balance sheet); and

(b)   a copy, certified as aforesaid, of the report of the auditors on, and of the report of the directors accompanying, each such balance sheet;

and where any such balance sheet, document or report is not in the English language, there shall be annexed to that balance sheet a translation in English of the balance sheet, document or report, certified in the prescribed manner to be a correct translation.

(3A)   If any such balance sheet as aforesaid or document required by law to be annexed thereto did not comply with the requirements of the law as in force at the date of the audit with respect to the form of balance sheets or documents aforesaid, as the case may be, there shall be made such additions to and corrections in the copy as would have been required to be made in the balance sheet or document in order to make it comply with the said requirements, and the fact that the copy has been so amended shall be stated thereon.

(4) If a company fails to comply with this section or section 107, the company and every officer of the company who is in default shall be liable to a fine and, for continued default, to a daily default fine.

(5) For the purposes of subsection (4), the expression "officer", and for the purposes of section 107 the expression "director", shall include any person in accordance with whose directions or instructions the directors of the company are accustomed to act.

Certificates to be sent by private company with annual return

110.   A private company shall send with the annual return required by section 107 a certificate signed by a director and the secretary of the company that the company has not, since the date of the last return, or, in the case of a first return, since the date of the incorporation of the company, issued any invitation to the public to subscribe for any shares or debentures of the company, and, where the annual return discloses the fact that the number of members of the company exceeds 50, also a certificate so signed that the excess consists wholly of persons who, under section 29(1)(b), are not to be included in reckoning the number of 50.

Meetings and Proceedings

Annual general meeting

111.(1) Every company shall in each year hold a general meeting as its annual general meeting in addition to any other meetings in that year, and shall specify the meeting as such in the notices calling it; and not more than 15 months, or such longer period as the Registrar may in any particular case authorize in writing, shall elapse between the date of one annual general meeting of the company and the next:

Provided that, so long as the company holds its first annual general meeting within 18 months of its incorporation, it need not hold it in the year of its incorporation or in the following year.

(2) If default is made in holding a meeting of the company in accordance with subsection (1), the court may, on the application of any member of the company, call, or direct the calling of, a general meeting of the company and give such ancillary or consequential directions as the court thinks expedient, including directions modifying or supplementing, in relation to the calling, holding and conducting of the meeting, the operation of the company's articles, and including a direction that 1 member of the company present in person or by proxy shall be deemed to constitute a meeting.

(3) A general meeting held in pursuance of subsection (2) shall, subject to any directions of the court, be deemed to be an annual general meeting of the company; but, where a meeting so held is not held in the year in which the default in holding the company's annual general meeting occurred, the meeting so held shall not be treated as the annual general meeting for the year in which it is held unless at that meeting the company resolves that it shall be so treated.

(4) Where a company resolves that a meeting shall be so treated, a copy of the resolution shall, within 15 days after the passing thereof, be forwarded to the Registrar and recorded by him.

(5) If default is made in holding a meeting of the company in accordance with subsection (1), or in complying with any direction under subsection (2), the company and every officer of the company who is in default shall be liable to a fine; and if default is made in complying with subsection (4), the company and every officer of the company who is in default shall be liable to a fine and, for continued default, to a daily default fine.

112. *(Repealed)*

Convening of extraordinary general meeting on requisition

113.(1) The directors of a company, notwithstanding anything in its articles shall, on the requisition of members of the company holding at the date of the deposit of the requisition not less than one-tenth of such of the paid-up capital of the company as at the date of the deposit carries the right of voting at general meetings of the company, or, in the case of a company not having a share capital, members of the company representing not less than one-tenth of the total voting rights of all the members having at the said date a right to vote at general meetings of the company, forthwith proceed duly to convene an extraordinary general meeting of the company.

(2) The requisition must state the objects of the meeting, and must be signed by the requisitionists and deposited at the registered office of the company, and may consist of several documents in like form, each signed by one or more requisitionists.

(3) If the directors do not within 21 days from the date of the deposit of the requisition proceed duly to convene a meeting for a day not more than 28 days after the date on which the notice convening the meeting is given, the requisitionists, or any of them representing more than one-half of the total voting rights of all of them, may themselves convene a meeting, but any meeting so convened shall not be held after the expiration of 3 months from the said date.

(4) A meeting convened under this section by the requisitionists shall be convened in the same manner, as nearly as possible, as that in which meetings are to be convened by directors.

(5) Any reasonable expenses incurred by the requisitionists by reason of the failure of the directors duly to convene a meeting shall be repaid to the requisitionists by the company, and any sum so repaid shall be retained by the company out of any sums due or to become due from the company by way of fees or other remuneration in respect of their services to such of the directors as were in default.

(6) For the purposes of this section, the directors shall, in the case of a meeting at which a resolution is to be proposed as a special resolution, be deemed not to have duly convened the meeting if they do not give such notice thereof as is required by section 116.

Length of notice for calling meetings

114.(1) Any provision of a company's articles shall be void in so far as it provides for the calling of a meeting of the company (other than an adjourned meeting) by a shorter notice than-

> *(a)* in the case of the annual general meeting, 21 days' notice in writing; and

> *(b)* in the case of a meeting other than an annual general meeting or a meeting for the passing of a special resolution, 14 days' notice in writing in the case of a company other than an unlimited company and 7 days' notice in writing in the case of an unlimited company.

(2) Save in so far as the articles of a company make other provision in that behalf (not being a provision avoided by subsection (1)) a meeting of the company (other than an adjourned meeting) may be called-

> *(a)* in the case of the annual general meeting, by 21 days' notice in writing; and

> *(b)* in the case of a meeting other than an annual general meeting or a meeting for the passing of a special resolution, by 14 days' notice in writing in the case of a company other than an unlimited company and by 7 days' notice in writing in the case of an unlimited company.

(3) A meeting of a company shall, notwithstanding that it is called by shorter notice than that specified in subsection (2) or in the company's articles, as the case may be, be deemed to have been duly called if it is so agreed-

> *(a)* in the case of a meeting called as the annual general meeting, by all the members entitled to attend and vote threat; and

> *(b)* in the case of any other meeting, by a majority in number of the members having the right to attend and vote at the meeting, being a majority together holding not less than 95 per cent in nominal value of the shares giving a right

to attend and vote at the meeting, or, in the case of a company not having a share capital, together representing not less than 95 per cent of the total voting rights at the meeting of all the members.

General provisions as to meetings and votes

114A.(1) Subject to sections 155B and 163D, the following provisions shall have effect in so far as the articles of the company do not make other provision in that behalf-

(a) notice of the meeting of a company shall be served on every member of the company in the manner in which notices are required to be served by Table A, and for the purpose of this paragraph the expression "Table A" means that Table as for the time being in force;

(b) 2 or more members holding not less than one-tenth in nominal value of the issued share capital or, if the company has not a share capital, not less than 5 per cent in number of the members of the company may call a meeting;

(c) 2 members personally present shall be a quorum;

(d) any member elected by the members present at a meeting may be chairman thereof;

(e) in the case of a company originally having a share capital, every member shall have 1 vote in respect of each share or each $100 of stock held by him, and in any other case every member shall have 1 vote.

(2) Notwithstanding anything to the contrary in the articles of a company-

(a) in the case of a company the capital of which is divided into shares which are listed on the Unified Exchange, notice of every general meeting of the company shall be served on any member not entitled to vote thereat at the same time as notice of the meeting is served on members who are so entitled:

Provided that where a meeting is called at any time by shorter notice than that specified in section 114(2) or in the company's articles, service of the notice required by this paragraph shall be deemed to be in compliance with this paragraph if such notice is served as soon as practicable after that time;

(b) where any shares in a company are held in trust for that company, such shares shall not, for so long as they are so held, confer any right to vote at meetings of the company.

(3) The articles of a company shall, if the articles so provide, apply in relation to the service by the company of notices under subsection (2)(a) and in determining the time at which such service shall be deemed to be effected.

Power of court to order meeting

114B.(1) If for any reason it is impracticable to call a meeting of a company in any manner in which meetings of that company may be called, or to conduct the meeting of the company in manner prescribed by the articles or this Ordinance, the court may, either of its own motion or on the application of any director of the company or of any member of the company who would be entitled to vote at the meeting, order a meeting of the company to be called, held and conducted in such manner as the court thinks fit, and where any such order is made may give such ancillary or consequential directions as it thinks expedient, including a direction that 1 member of the company present in person or by proxy shall be deemed to constitute a meeting.

(2) Any meeting called, held and conducted in accordance with an order under subsection (1) shall for all purposes be deemed to be a meeting of the company duly called, held and conducted.

(3) The legal personal representative of a deceased member of a company shall, for the purposes of this section, be treated in all respects as a member of the company having the same rights with respect to attending and voting at a meeting of the company as such deceased member would, if living, have had.

Proxies

114C.(1) Subject to subsection (1A), any member of a company entitled to attend and vote at a meeting of the company shall be entitled to appoint another person (whether a member or not) as his proxy to attend and vote instead of him, and a proxy so appointed shall also have the same right as the member to speak at the meeting.

(1A) Unless the articles otherwise provide-

> *(a)* a proxy shall not be entitled to vote except on a poll; and

> *(b)* subsection (1) shall not apply in the case of a company not having a share capital.

(2) The right of a member of a company having a share capital to appoint a proxy shall include the right to appoint separate proxies to represent respectively such number of the shares held by him as may be specified in their instruments of appointment; but (without prejudice to the appointment of alternates) the number of proxies so appointed by any person to attend on the same occasion shall not, unless the articles otherwise provide, exceed 2.

(3) In every notice calling a meeting of a company having a share capital there shall appear with reasonable prominence a statement that a member entitled to attend and vote is entitled to appoint a proxy or, where that is allowed, 1 or more proxies to attend and vote instead of him, and that a proxy need not also be a member; and if default is made in complying with this subsection as respects any meeting, every officer of the company who is in default shall be liable to a fine.

(4) Any provision contained in a company's articles shall be void in so far as it would have the effect of requiring the instrument appointing a proxy, or any other document necessary to show the validity or otherwise relating to the appointment of a proxy, to be received by the company or any other person more than 48 hours before a meeting or adjourned meeting in order that the appointment may be effective thereat.

(5) If, for the purpose of any meeting of a company, invitations to appoint as proxy a person or 1 of a number of persons specified in the invitations are issued at the company's expense to some only of the members entitled to be sent a notice of the meeting and to vote thereat by proxy, every officer of the company who knowingly and wilfully authorizes or permits their issue as aforesaid shall be liable to a fine:

Provided that an officer shall not be liable under this subsection by reason only of the issue to a member at his request in writing of a forth of appointment naming the proxy or of a list of persons willing to act as proxy if the form or list is available on request in writing to every member entitled to vote at the meeting by proxy.

(6) Notwithstanding anything to the contrary in the articles of a company, any form issued to a member of the company by the directors for use by him for appointing a proxy to attend and vote at a meeting of the company shall be such as to enable the member, according to his intention, to instruct the proxy to vote in favour of or against (or, in default of instructions, to exercise his discretion in respect of) each resolution dealing with any special business to be transacted at the meeting.

(7) In subsection (6) "special business" means-

> *(a)* all business transacted at an extraordinary general meeting; and

> *(b)* all business transacted at an annual general meeting except the declaration of a dividend, the consideration of the accounts and the reports of the directors and auditors, the election of directors in place of those retiring and the appointment of, and the fixing of the remuneration of, the auditors.

(8) This section shall apply to meetings of any class of members of a company as it applies to general meetings of the company.

Right to demand a poll

114D.(1) Any provision contained in a company's articles shall be void in so far as it would have the effect either-

> *(a)* of excluding the right to demand a poll at a general meeting on any question other than the election of the chairman of the meeting or the adjournment of the meeting; or

> *(b)* of making ineffective a demand for a poll on any such question which is made either-
> > **(i)** by not less than 5 members having the right to vote at the meeting; or

(ii)   by a member or members representing not less than one-tenth of the total voting rights of all the members having the right to vote at the meeting; or

(iii)   by a member or members holding shares in the company conferring a right to vote at the meeting, being shares on which an aggregate sum has been paid up equal to not less than one-tenth of the total sum paid up on all the shares conferring that right.

(2) The instrument appointing a proxy to vote at a meeting of a company shall be deemed also to confer authority to demand or join in demanding a poll, and for the purposes of subsection (1) a demand by a person as proxy for a member shall be the same as a demand by the member.

Voting on a poll

114E. On a poll taken at a meeting of a company or a meeting of any class of members of a company, a member entitled to more than 1 vote need not, if he votes, use all his votes or cast all the votes he uses in the same way.

Representation of companies at meetings of other companies and of creditors

115.(1) A corporation may by resolution of its directors or other governing body-

(a)   if it is a member of a company, authorize such person as it thinks fit to act as its representative at any meeting of the company or at any meeting of any class of members of the company;

(b)   if it is a creditor (including a holder of debentures) of a company, authorize such person as it thinks fit to act as its representative at any meeting of any creditors of the company held in pursuance of this Ordinance or of any rules made thereunder, or in pursuance of the provisions contained in any debenture or trust deed or other instrument, as the case may be.

(1A)   A recognized clearing house within the meaning of section 2 of the Securities and Futures (Clearing Houses) Ordinance (Cap. 420) may, if it or its nominee is a member of a company, authorize such person or persons as it thinks fit to act as its representative or representatives, as the case may be, at any meeting of the company or at any meeting of any class of members of the company provided that, if more than one person is so authorized, the authorization shall specify the number and class of shares in respect of which each such person is so authorized.

(2) A person authorized under subsection (1) shall be entitled to exercise the same powers on behalf of the corporation which he represents as that corporation could exercise if it were an individual shareholder, creditor, or holder of debentures, of the company.

(3) A person authorized under subsection (1A) shall be entitled to exercise the same powers on behalf of the recognized clearing house (or its nominee) which he represents as that clearing house (or its nominee) could exercise if it were an individual shareholder of the company.

Circulation of members' resolutions, etc.

115A.(1) Subject to this section, it shall be the duty of a company, on the requisition in writing of such number of members as is hereinafter specified and (unless the company otherwise resolves) at the expense of the requisitionists-

(a)   to give to members of the company entitled to receive notice of the next annual general meeting notice of any resolution which may properly be moved and is intended to be moved at that meeting;

(b)   to circulate to members entitled to have notice of any general meeting sent to them any statement of not more than 1000 words with respect to the matter referred to in any proposed resolution or the business to be dealt with at that meeting.

(2)   The number of members necessary for a requisition under subsection (1) shall be-

(a)   any number of members representing not less than one-twentieth of the total voting rights of all members having at the date of the requisition a right to vote at the meeting to which the requisition relates; or

(b)   not less than 100 members holding shares in the company on which there has been paid up an average sum, per member, of not less than $2,000.

(3) Notice of any such resolution shall be given, and any such statement shall be circulated, to members of the company entitled to have notice of the meeting sent to them by serving a copy of the resolution or statement on each such member in any manner permitted for service of notice of the meeting, and notice of any such resolution shall be given to any other member of the company by giving notice of the general effect of the resolution in any manner permitted for giving him notice of meetings of the company:

Provided that the copy shall be served, or notice of the effect of the resolution shall be given, as the case may be, in the same manner and, so far as practicable, at the same time as notice of the meeting and, where it is not practicable for it to be served or given at that time, it shall be served or given as soon as practicable thereafter.

(4) A company shall not be bound under this section to give notice of any resolution or to circulate any statement unless-

(a)   a copy of the requisition signed by the requisitionists (or 2 or more copies which between them contain the signatures of all the requisitionists) is deposited at the registered office of the company-

> **(i)** in the case of a requisition requiring notice of a resolution, not less than 6 weeks before the meeting; and
>
> **(ii)** in the case of any other requisition, not less than 1 week before the meeting; and

> *(b)* there is deposited or tendered with the requisition a sum reasonably sufficient to meet the company's expenses in giving effect thereto:

Provided that if, after a copy of a requisition requiring notice of a resolution has been deposited at the registered office of the company, an annual general meeting is called for a date 6 weeks or less after the copy has been deposited, the copy though not deposited within the time required by this subsection shall be deemed to have been properly deposited for the purposes thereof.

(5) The company shall also not be bound under this section to circulate any statement if, on the application either of the company or of any other person who claims to be aggrieved, the court is satisfied that the rights conferred by this section are being abused to secure needless publicity for defamatory matter; and the court may order the company's costs on an application under this section to be paid in whole or in part by the requisitionists, notwithstanding that they are not parties to the application.

(6) Notwithstanding anything in the company's articles, the business which may be dealt with at an annual general meeting shall include any resolution of which notice is given in accordance with this section, and for the purposes of this subsection notice shall be deemed to have been so given notwithstanding the accidental omission, in giving it, of 1 or more members.

(7) In the event of any default in complying with the provisions of this section, every officer of the company who is in default shall be liable to a fine.

Special resolutions

116.(1) A resolution shall be a special resolution when it has been passed by not less than three-fourths of the votes cast by such members as, being entitled so to do, vote in person or, where proxies are allowed, by proxy, at a general meeting of which not less than 21 days' notice, specifying the intention to propose the resolution as a special resolution, has been duly given:

Provided that, if it is so agreed by a majority in number of the members having the right to attend and vote at any such meeting, being a majority together holding not less than 95 per cent in nominal value of the shares giving that right, or, in the case of a company not having a share capital, together representing not less than 95 per cent of the total voting rights at that meeting of all the members, a resolution may be proposed and passed as a special resolution-

> *(a)* in the case of a resolution for voluntary winding up pursuant to section 228(1)(b) in circumstances other than a members' voluntary winding up, at a meeting of which less than 21 days' notice but not less than 7 days' notice has been given;

(b)   in any other case, at a meeting of which less than 21 days' notice has been given.

(2) At any meeting at which a special resolution is submitted to be passed, a declaration of the chairman that the resolution is carried shall, unless a poll is demanded, be conclusive evidence of the fact without proof of the number or proportion of the votes recorded in favour of or against the resolution.

(3) In computing the majority on a poll demanded on the question that a special resolution be passed, reference shall be had to the number of votes cast for and against the resolution.

(4) For the purposes of this section, notice of a meeting shall be deemed to be duly given and the meeting to be duly held when the notice is given and the meeting held in manner provided by this Ordinance or the articles.

(5) Any reference to an extraordinary resolution of a company or of a meeting of any class of members of a company contained in any Ordinance which was enacted or document which existed before the date of commencement of the Companies (Amendment) Ordinance 1984 shall, in relation to a resolution passed or to be passed on or after that date, be deemed to be a reference to a special resolution of the company or meeting.

(6) Where before the date of commencement of the Companies (Amendment) Ordinance 1984 a meeting had been convened for the purpose of passing a resolution as an extraordinary resolution, and at that meeting that resolution has after that date been passed in the manner required by the law in force before that date relating to the passing of an extraordinary resolution and such resolution would under that law have been effective for its purpose, such resolution shall be as effective as if it had been a special resolution.

Restriction on alteration of articles to improve director's emoluments

116A.(1) A company shall not at any meeting alter or add to its articles so as to provide emoluments or improved emoluments for a director of the company in respect of his office as such unless-

(a)   there is set out in the notice convening the meeting or in a document attached thereto an adequate explanation of the provision; and

(b)   the provision is approved by a resolution not relating also to other matters.

(2) In this section "emoluments", in relation to a director, includes fees and percentages, any sums paid by way of expenses allowance, any contribution paid in respect of him under any pension scheme and any benefits received by him otherwise than in cash in respect of his services as director.

Resolutions signed by all members deemed to have been passed at meeting

116B.(1) Notwithstanding anything to the contrary in this Ordinance, a resolution in writing signed by or on behalf of all persons for the time being entitled to receive notice of and to attend and vote at general meetings of a company shall, for the purposes of this Ordinance and the articles of the company, be treated as a resolution duly passed at a general meeting of the company and, where relevant, as a special resolution so passed.

(2) Any such resolution shall be deemed to have been passed at a meeting held on the date on which it was signed by the last member to sign, and where the resolution states a date as being the date of his signature thereof by any member the statement shall be prima facie evidence that it was signed by him on that date.

(3) This section shall not be construed as requiring that persons signing a resolution under this section shall sign the same document containing the resolution; but where 2 or more documents are used for the purpose of obtaining signatures under this section in respect of any resolution, each such document shall be certified in advance by the secretary of the company to contain the correct version of the proposed resolution.

Resolutions requiring special notice

116C. Where by any provision hereafter contained in this Ordinance special notice is required of a resolution, the resolution shall not be effective unless notice of the intention to move it has been given to the company not less than 28 days before the meeting at which it is moved, and the company shall give its members notice of any such resolution at the same time and in the same manner as it gives notice of the meeting or, if that is not practicable, shall give them notice thereof, either by advertisement in a newspaper having an appropriate circulation or in any other mode allowed by the articles, not less than 21 days before the meeting:

Provided that if, after notice of the intention to move such a resolution has been given to the company, a meeting is called for a date 28 days or less after the notice has been given, the notice though not given within the time required by this section shall be deemed to have been properly given for the purposes thereof.

Registration and copies of certain resolutions and agreements

117.(1) A printed copy of every resolution or agreement to which this section applies shall, within 15 days after the passing or making thereof, be forwarded to the Registrar and recorded by him.

(2) Where articles have been registered, a copy of every such resolution or agreement for the time being in force shall be embodied in or annexed to every copy of the articles issued after the passing of the resolution or the making of the agreement.

(3) Where articles have not been registered, a printed copy of every such resolution or agreement shall be forwarded to any member at his request, on payment of $1 or such less sum as the company may direct.

(4)   This section shall apply to-

        (a)   special resolutions;

     (b)   *(Repealed)*

     (c)   resolutions which have been agreed to by all the members of a company, but which, if not so agreed to, would not have been effective for their purpose unless they had been passed as special resolutions;

     (d)   resolutions or agreements which have been agreed to by all the members of some class of shareholders, but which, if not so agreed to, would not have been effective for their purpose unless they had been passed by some particular majority or otherwise in some particular manner, and all resolutions or agreements which effectively bind all the members of any class of shareholders though not agreed to by all those members;

     (e)   resolutions requiring a company to be wound up voluntarily, passed under section 228(1)(a);

     (f)   resolutions varying any matter or provision in the articles of a company which is expressly authorized by the articles to be varied by ordinary resolution.

(5)   If a company fails to comply with subsection (1), the company and every officer of the company who is in default shall be liable to a fine and, for continued default, to a daily default fine.

(6)   If a company fails to comply with subsection (2) or (3), the company and every officer of the company who is in default shall be liable to a fine for each copy in respect of which default is made.

(7)   For the purposes of subsections (5) and (6), a liquidator of the company shall be deemed to be an officer of the company.

Resolutions passed at adjourned meetings

118.   Where a resolution is passed at an adjourned meeting of-

     (a)   a company;

     (b)   the holders of any class of shares in a company;

     (c)   the directors of a company,

the resolution shall for all purposes be treated as having been passed on the date on which it was in fact passed, and shall not be deemed to have been passed on any earlier date.

Minutes of proceedings of meetings and directors

119.(1) Every company shall cause minutes of all proceedings at general meetings and at meetings of its directors to be entered in books kept for that purpose.

(2) Any such minute if purporting to be signed by the chairman of the meeting at which the proceedings were had, or by the chairman of the next succeeding meeting, shall be evidence of the proceedings.

(3) Where minutes have been made in accordance with the provisions of this section of the proceedings at any general meeting of the company or meeting of directors or managers, then, until the contrary is proved, the meeting shall be deemed to have been duly held and convened, and all proceedings had thereat to have been duly had, and all appointments of directors, managers, or liquidators, shall be deemed to be valid.

(4) If a company fails to comply with subsection (1), the company and every officer of the company who is in default shall be liable to a fine and, for continued default, to a daily default fine.

Place where minute books to be kept and notice of change of place

119A.(1) The books containing the minutes of proceedings of any general meeting of a company, any meeting of directors or any meeting of managers, shall be kept at the registered office of the company:

Provided that-

> *(a)* if the work of making up the books is done at an office of the company other than the registered office of the company, they may be kept at that other office; and

> *(b)* if the company arranges with some other person for the making up of the books to be undertaken on behalf of the company by that other person, they may be kept at the office of that other person at which the work is done,

so, however, that they shall not be kept at a place outside Hong Kong.

(2) Every company shall send notice to the Registrar in the specified form of the place where the books containing the minutes of proceedings of any meeting referred to in subsection (1) are kept and of any change in that place:

Provided that a company shall not be bound to send such notice where the said books have, at all times since they came into existence or, in the case of any such books in existence at the commencement of the Companies (Amendment) Ordinance 1984, at all times since then, been kept at the registered office of the company.

(3) Where a company makes default in complying with subsection (1) or makes default for 14 days in complying with subsection (2), the company and every officer of the company who is in default shall be liable to a fine and, for continued default, to a daily default fine.

Inspection of minute books

120.(1) The books containing the minutes of proceedings of any general meeting of a company shall during business hours (subject to such reasonable restrictions as the company may by its articles or in general meeting impose, so that no less than 2 hours in each day be allowed for inspection) be open to the inspection of any member without charge.

(2) Any member shall be entitled to be furnished, within 7 days after he has made a request in that behalf to the company, with a copy of any such minutes as aforesaid at a charge not exceeding $1 for every 100 words.

(3) If any inspection required under this section is refused or if any copy required under this section is not sent within the proper time, the company and every officer of the company who is in default shall be liable in respect of each offence to a fine and, for continued default, to a daily default fine.

(4) In the case of any such refusal or default, the court may by order compel an immediate inspection of the books in respect of all proceedings of general meetings or direct that the copies required shall be sent to the persons requiring them.

Accounts and Audit

Keeping of books of account

121.(1) Every company shall cause to be kept proper books of account with respect to-

    (a)   all sums of money received and expended by the company and the matters in respect of which the receipt and expenditure takes place;

    (b)   all sales and purchases of goods by the company;

    (c)   the assets and liabilities of the company.

(2) For the purposes of subsection (1), proper books of account shall not be deemed to be kept with respect to the matters aforesaid if there are not kept such books as are necessary to give a true and fair view of the state of the company's affairs and to explain its transactions.

(3) The books of account shall be kept at the registered office of the company or at such other place as the directors think fit, and shall at all times be open to inspection by the directors:

Provided that if books of account are kept at a place outside Hong Kong there shall be sent to, and kept at a place in, Hong Kong and be at all times open to inspection by the directors such accounts and returns with respect to the business dealt with in the books of account so kept as will disclose with reasonable accuracy the financial position of that business at intervals not exceeding 6 months and will enable to be prepared in accordance with this Ordinance the company's balance sheet, its profit and loss account or income and expenditure account, and any document annexed to any of those documents giving information which is required by this Ordinance and is thereby allowed to be so given.

(3A) Any books of account which a company is required by this section to keep shall be preserved by it for 7 years from the end of the financial year to which the last entry made or matter recorded therein relates.

(4) If any person being a director of a company fails to take all reasonable steps to secure compliance by the company with the requirements of this section, or has by his own wilful act been the cause of any default by the company thereunder, he shall, in respect of each offence, be liable to imprisonment and a fine:

Provided that-

> *(a)* in any proceedings against a person in respect of an offence under this section consisting of a failure to take reasonable steps to secure compliance by the company with the requirements of this section, it shall be a defence to prove that he had reasonable ground to believe and did believe that a competent and reliable person was charged with the duty of seeing that those requirements were complied with and was in a position to discharge that duty; and

> *(b)* a person shall not be sentenced to imprisonment for such an offence unless, in the opinion of the court dealing with the case, the offence was committed wilfully.

Profit and loss account and balance sheet

122.(1) Subject to subsection (1B), the directors of every company shall lay before the company at its annual general meeting a profit and loss account or, in the case of a company not trading for profit, an income and expenditure account for the period, in the case of the first account, since the incorporation of the company, and, in any other case, since the preceding account.

(1A) The accounts referred to in subsection (1) shall be made up to a date falling not more than 6 months, or, in the case of a private company (other than a private company which at any time during the period to which the said accounts relate was a member of a group of companies of which a company other than a private company was a member) and a company limited by guarantee not more than 9 months, before the date of the meeting.

(1B) The court, if for any reason it thinks fit so to do, may in the case of any company and with respect to any year-

> *(a)* substitute for the requirement in subsection (1) to lay a profit and loss account or (as the case may be) an income and expenditure account before the company at its annual general meeting a requirement to lay such account before the company at such other general meeting of the company as the court may specify; and

> *(b)* extend the periods of 6 and 9 months referred to in subsection (1A).

(2) The directors shall cause to be made out in every calendar year, and to be laid before the company at its annual general meeting or at such other general meeting of the company as may be specified by the court under subsection (1B), a balance sheet as at the date to which the profit and loss account, or the income and expenditure account, as the case may be, is made up.

(3) If any person being a director of a company fails to take all reasonable steps to comply with the provisions of this section he shall, in respect of each offence, be liable to imprisonment and a fine:

Provided that-

(a)   in any proceedings against a person in respect of an offence under this section, it shall be a defence to prove that he had reasonable ground to believe and did believe that a competent and reliable person was charged with the duty of seeing that the provisions of this section were complied with and was in a position to discharge that duty; and

(b)   a person shall not be sentenced to imprisonment for such an offence unless, in the opinion of the court dealing with the case, the offence was committed wilfully.

General provisions as to contents and form of accounts

123.(1) Every balance sheet of a company shall give a true and fair view of the state of affairs of the company as at the end of its financial year, and every profit and loss account of a company shall give a true and fair view of the profit or loss of the company for the financial year.

(2) A company's balance sheet and profit and loss account shall comply with the requirements of the Tenth Schedule, so far as applicable thereto.

(3) Save as expressly provided in the following provisions of this section or in Part III of the Tenth Schedule, the requirements of subsection (2) and the said Schedule shall be without prejudice either to the general requirements of subsection (1) or to any other requirements of this Ordinance.

(4) The Financial Secretary may, on the application or with the consent of a company's directors, modify in relation to that company any of the requirements of this Ordinance as to the matters to be stated in a company's balance sheet or profit and loss account (except the requirements of subsection (1)) for the purpose of adapting them to the circumstances of the company.

(5) Subsections (1) and (2) shall not apply to a company's profit and loss account if-

(a)   the company has subsidiaries; and

(b)   the profit and loss account is framed as a consolidated profit and loss account dealing with all or any of the company's subsidiaries as well as the company and-

(i) complies with the requirements of this Ordinance relating to consolidated profit and loss accounts; and

(ii) shows how much of the consolidated profit or loss for the financial year is dealt with in the accounts of the company.

(6) If any person being a director of a company fails to take all reasonable steps to secure compliance as respects any accounts laid before the company in general meeting with the provisions of this section and with the other requirements of this Ordinance as to the matters to be stated in accounts, he shall, in respect of each offence, be liable to imprisonment and a fine:

Provided that-

(a) in any proceedings against a person in respect of an offence under this section, it shall be a defence to prove that he had reasonable ground to believe and did believe that a competent and reliable person was charged with the duty of seeing that the said provisions or the said other requirements, as the case may be, were complied with and was in a position to discharge that duty; and

(b) a person shall not be sentenced to imprisonment for any such offence unless, in the opinion of the court dealing with the case, the offence was committed wilfully.

(7) For the purposes of this section and the following provisions of this Ordinance, except where the context otherwise requires,-

(a) any reference to a balance sheet or profit and loss account shall include any notes thereon or document annexed thereto giving information which is required by this Ordinance and is thereby allowed to be so given; and

(b) any reference to a profit and loss account shall be taken, in the case of a company not trading for profit, as referring to its income and expenditure account, and references to profit or to loss and, if the company has subsidiaries, references to a consolidated profit and loss account shall be construed accordingly.

Obligation to lay group accounts before holding company

124.(1) Where at the end of its financial year a company has subsidiaries, accounts or statements (in this Ordinance referred to as "group accounts") dealing as hereinafter mentioned with the state of affairs and profit or loss of the company and the subsidiaries shall, subject to subsection (2), be laid before the company in general meeting when the company's own balance sheet and profit and loss account are so laid.

(2) Notwithstanding anything in subsection (1)-

(a)   group accounts shall not be required where the company is at the end of its financial year the wholly owned subsidiary of another body corporate; and

(b)   group accounts need not deal with a subsidiary of the company if the company's directors are of opinion that-

       (i)   it is impracticable, or would be of no real value to members of the company, in view of the insignificant amount involved, or would involve expense or delay out of proportion to the value to members of the company; or

       (ii)   the result would be misleading, or harmful to the business of the company or any of its subsidiaries; or

       (iii)   the business of the holding company and that of the subsidiary are so different that they cannot reasonably be treated as a single undertaking; and, if the directors are of such an opinion about each of the company's subsidiaries, group accounts shall not be required:

Provided that the approval of the Financial Secretary shall be required for not dealing in group accounts with a subsidiary on the ground that the result would be harmful or on the ground of the difference between the business of the holding company and that of the subsidiary.

(3) If any person being a director of a company fails to take all reasonable steps to secure compliance as respects the company with the provisions of this section, he shall, in respect of each offense, be liable to imprisonment and a fine:

Provided that-

(a)   in any proceedings against a person in respect of an offence under this section, it shall be a defence to prove that he had reasonable ground to believe and did believe that a competent and reliable person was charged with the duty of seeing that the requirements of this section were complied with and was in a position to discharge that duty; and

(b)   a person shall not be sentenced to imprisonment for an offence under this section unless, in the opinion of the court dealing with the case, the offence was committed wilfully.

(4) For the purposes of this section a body corporate shall be deemed to be the wholly owned subsidiary of another if it has no members except that other and that other's wholly owned subsidiaries and its or their nominees.

Form of group accounts

125.(1) Subject to subsection (2), the group accounts laid before a holding company shall be consolidated accounts comprising-

> *(a)* a consolidated balance sheet dealing with the state of affairs of the company and all the subsidiaries to be dealt with in group accounts;

> *(b)* a consolidated profit and loss account dealing with the profit or loss of the company and those subsidiaries.

(2) If the company's directors are of opinion that it is better for the purpose-

> *(a)* of presenting the same or equivalent information about the state of affairs and profit or loss of the company and those subsidiaries; and

> *(b)* of so presenting it that it may be readily appreciated by the company's members,

the group accounts may be prepared in a form other than that required by subsection (1), and in particular may consist of more than one set of consolidated accounts dealing respectively with the company and one group of subsidiaries and with other groups of subsidiaries, or of separate accounts dealing with each of the subsidiaries, or of statements expanding the information about the subsidiaries in the company's own accounts, or any combination of those forms.

(3) The group accounts may be wholly or partly incorporated in the company's own balance sheet and profit and loss account.

Contents of group accounts

126.(1) The group accounts laid before a company shall give a true and fair view of the state of affairs and profit or loss of the company and the subsidiaries dealt with thereby as a whole, so far as concerns members of the company.

(2) Where the financial year of a subsidiary does not coincide with that of the holding company, the group accounts shall, unless the Financial Secretary on the application or with the consent of the holding company's directors otherwise directs, deal with the subsidiary's state of affairs as at the end of its financial year ending with or last before that of the holding company, and with the subsidiary's profit or loss for that financial year.

(3) Without prejudice to subsection (1), the group accounts, if prepared as consolidated accounts, shall comply with the requirements of the Tenth Schedule, so far as applicable thereto, and if not so prepared shall give the same or equivalent information:

Provided that the Financial Secretary may, on the application or with the consent of a company's directors, modify the said requirements in relation to that company for the purpose of adapting them to the circumstances of the company.

Financial year of holding company and subsidiary

127.(1) A holding company's directors shall secure that except where in their opinion there are good reasons against it, the financial year of each of its subsidiaries shall coincide with the company's own financial year.

(2) Where a holding company or a holding company's subsidiary wishes to extend its financial year so that the subsidiary's financial year may end with that of the holding company, and for that purpose to postpone the submission of the relevant accounts to a general meeting from one calendar year to the next, the Registrar may on the application of the directors of the company whose financial year is to be extended direct that, in the case of that company, the submission of accounts to a general meeting, the holding of a general meeting in order to comply with section 111(1), or the making of an annual return shall not be required in the earlier of the said calendar years.

Statement in holding company's accounts of identities and places of incorporation of subsidiaries, and particulars of share-holdings therein

128.(1) Subject to the provisions of this section, where, at the end of its financial year, a company has subsidiaries, there shall, in the case of each subsidiary, be stated in, or in a note on, or statement annexed to, the company's accounts laid before it in general meeting-

    (a)   the subsidiary's name;

    (b)   the country in which it is incorporated; and

    (c)   in relation to shares of each class of the subsidiary held by the company, the identity of the class and the proportion of the nominal value of the issue shares of that class represented by the shares held.

(2)   For the purposes of subsection (1)-

    (a)   shares of a body corporate shall be treated as being held, or as not being held, by another such body if they would, by virtue of section 2(4) to (7), be treated as being held or, as the case may be, as not being held by that other body for the purpose of determining whether the first-mentioned body is its subsidiary;

    (b)   the proportion of the nominal value of the issued shares of any class represented by the shares held by the company shall be stated by way of a percentage, and any such percentage may be stated to the nearest whole number per cent except where it is between 49% and 50% or between 50% and 51%, in either of which events it shall be stated to as many decimal

places as would be required to indicate the percentage, to one significant figure, of the proportion of the nominal value of the issued shares of that class represented by one share; and

    (c)   to the particulars required by subsection (1) there shall be added, with reference to the proportion of the nominal value of the issued shares of a class represented by shares held by a company, a statement of the extent (if any) to which it consists in shares held by, or by a nominee for, a subsidiary of the company and the extent (if any) to which it consists in shares held by, or by a nominee for, the company itself.

(3)   Subsection (1) shall not require the disclosure of information with respect to a body corporate which is the subsidiary of another and is incorporated outside Hong Kong or, being incorporated in Hong Kong, carries on business outside Hong Kong if the disclosure would, in the opinion of the directors of that other, be harmful to the business of that other or of any of its subsidiaries and the Financial Secretary agrees that the information need not be disclosed.

(4)   If, in the opinion of the directors of a company having, at the end of its financial year, subsidiaries, the number of them is such that compliance with subsection (1) would result in particulars of excessive length being given, compliance with that subsection shall not be requisite except in the case of the subsidiaries carrying on the businesses the results of the carrying on of which, in the opinion of the directors, principally affected the amount of the profit or loss of the company and its subsidiaries or the amount of the assets of the company and its subsidiaries.

(5)   Where, in the case of a company not being a private company having a share capital, advantage is taken of subsection (4), -

    (a)   there must be included in the statement required by this section the information that it deals only with the subsidiaries carrying on such businesses as are referred to in that subsection; and

    (b)   the particulars given in compliance with subsection (1), together with those which, but for the fact that advantage is so taken, would have to be so given, shall be annexed to the annual return first made by the company after its accounts have been laid before it in general meeting.

(5A)   Where, in the case of a private company having a share capital, advantage is taken of subsection (4)-

    (a)   there must be included in the statement required by this section the information that it deals only with the subsidiaries carrying on such businesses as are referred to in that subsection; and

    (b)   the particulars given in compliance with subsection (1), together with those which, but for the fact that advantage is so taken, would have to be so given,

shall be forwarded to the Registrar within 42 days after its accounts have been laid before it in general meeting.

(6) If a company fails to satisfy an obligation imposed on it by subsection (5) to annex particulars to a return, the company and every officer of the company who is in default shall be liable to a fine and, for continued default, to a daily default fine.

Statement in company's accounts of identities and places of incorporation of companies not subsidiaries whose shares it holds, and particulars of those shares

129.(1) Subject to the provisions of this section, where, at the end of its financial year, a company holds shares of any class comprised in the equity share capital of another body corporate (not being its subsidiary) exceeding in nominal value one fifth of the nominal value of the issued shares of that class, there shall be stated in, or in a note on, or statement annexed to, the accounts of the company laid before it in general meeting-

> *(a)* the name of that other body corporate;

> *(b)* the country in which it is incorporated;

> *(c)* the identity of the class and the proportion of the nominal value of the issued shares of that class represented by the shares held; and

> *(d)* if the company also holds shares in that other body corporate of another class (whether or not comprised in its equity share capital), or of other classes (whether or not so comprised), the like particulars as respects that other class or, as the case may be, each of those other classes.

(2) If, at the end of its financial year, a company holds shares in another body corporate (not being its subsidiary) and the amount of all the shares therein which it holds (as stated or included in its accounts laid before it in general meeting) exceeds one tenth of the amount of its assets (as so stated), there shall be stated in, or in a note on, or statement annexed to, those accounts-

> *(a)* the name of that other body corporate;

> *(b)* the country in which it is incorporated; and

> *(c)* in relation to shares in that other body corporate of each class held, the identity of the class and the proportion of the nominal value of the issued shares of that class represented by the shares held.

(3) Neither subsection (1) nor subsection (2) shall require the disclosure by a company of information with respect to another body corporate if that other body is incorporated outside Hong Kong or, being incorporated in Hong Kong, carries on business outside Hong Kong if the disclosure would, in the opinion of the directors of the company, be harmful to the business of the company or of that other body and the Financial Secretary agrees that the information need not be disclosed.

(4) If, at the end of its financial year, a company falls within subsection (1) in relation to more bodies corporate than one, and the number of them is such that, in the opinion of the directors, compliance with that subsection would result in particulars of excessive length being given, compliance with that subsection shall not be requisite except in the case of the bodies, carrying on the businesses the results of the carrying on of which, in the opinion of the directors, principally affected the amount of the profit or loss of the company or the amount of its assets.

(5) Where, in the case of a company not being a private company having a share capital, advantage is taken of subsection (4) -

(a) there must be included in the statement dealing with the bodies last mentioned in that subsection the information that it deals only with them; and

(b) the particulars given in compliance with subsection (1), together with those which, but for the fact that advantage is so taken, would have to be so given, shall be annexed to the annual return first made by the company after its accounts have been laid before it in general meeting.

(5A) Where, in the case of a private company having a share capital, advantage is taken of subsection (4)-

(a) there must be included in the statement dealing with the bodies last mentioned in that subsection the information that it deals only with them; and

(b) the particulars given in compliance with subsection (1), together with those which, but for the fact that advantage is so taken, would have to be so given, shall be forwarded to the Registrar within 42 days after its accounts have been laid before it in general meeting.

(6) If a company fails to satisfy an obligation imposed on it by subsection (5) to annex particulars to a return, the company and every officer of the company who is in default shall be liable to a fine and, for continued default, to a daily default fine.

(7) For the purposes of this section-

(a) shares of a body corporate shall be treated as being held, or as not being held, by another such body if they would, by virtue of section 2(4) to (7) (but on the assumption that paragraph (b)(ii) of subsection (6) had been omitted therefrom), be treated as being held or, as the case may be, as not being held by that other body for the purpose of determining whether the first-mentioned body is its subsidiary; and

(b) the proportion of the nominal value of the issued shares of any class

represented by the shares held by the company shall be stated by way of a percentage, and any such percentage may be stated to the nearest whole number per cent except where it is between 49% and 50%, in which event it shall be stated to as many decimal places as would be required to indicate the percentage, to one significant figure, of the proportion of the nominal value of the issued shares of that class represented by one share.

(8) In this section "equity share capital" means, in relation to a company, its issued share capital excluding any part thereof which does not, either as respects dividends or as respects capital, carry any right to participate beyond a specified amount in a distribution.

Statement in subsidiary company's accounts of name and place of incorporation of its ultimate holding company

129A.(1) Subject to subsection (2), where, at the end of its financial year, a company is the subsidiary of another body corporate, there shall be stated in, or in a note on, or statement annexed to, the company's accounts laid before it in general meeting the name of the body corporate regarded by the directors as being the company's ultimate holding company and, if known to them, the country in which it is incorporated.

(2) Subsection (1) shall not require the disclosure by a company which carries on business outside Hong Kong of information with respect to the body corporate regarded by the directors as being its ultimate holding company if the disclosure would, in their opinion, be harmful to the business of that holding company or of the first-mentioned company or any other of that holding company's subsidiaries and the Financial Secretary agrees that the information need not be disclosed.

Signing of balance sheet

129B.(1) Every balance sheet of a company shall be approved by the board of directors of the company and signed on behalf of the board by 2 of the directors.

(2) In the case of a company carrying on banking business, the balance sheet shall be signed by the secretary or manager, if any, and where there are more than 3 directors of the company by at least 3 of those directors, and where there are not more than 3 directors by all the directors.

(3) If any copy of a balance sheet which has not been signed as required by this section is issued, circulated or published, the company and every officer of the company who is in default shall be liable to a fine.

Accounts to be annexed, and auditors' report to be attached, to balance sheet

129C.(1) The profit and loss account and, so far as not incorporated in the balance sheet or profit and loss account, any group accounts laid before the company in general meeting, shall be annexed to the balance sheet, and the auditors' report shall be attached thereto.

(2) Any accounts so annexed shall be approved by the board of directors before the balance sheet is signed on their behalf.

(3) If any copy of a balance sheet is issued, circulated or published without having annexed thereto a copy of the profit and loss account or any group accounts required by this section to be so annexed, or without having attached thereto a copy of the auditors' report, the company and every officer of the company who is in default shall be liable to a fine.

Directors' report to be attached to balance sheet

129D.(1) There shall be attached to every balance sheet laid before a company in general meeting a report by the directors with respect to the profit or loss of the company for the financial year and the state of the company's affairs as at the end thereof.

(2) Every directors' report so attached shall be approved by the board of directors and signed on behalf of the board either by the chairman of the meeting at which it was approved or by the secretary of the company.

(3) The report shall-

(a) state the principal activities of the company and of its subsidiaries in the course of the financial year and any significant change in those activities in that year;

(b) state the amount, if any, which the directors recommend should be paid by way of dividend;

(c) state the amount, if any, which the directors propose to carry to reserves within the meaning of the Tenth Schedule;

(d) if the company (not being the wholly owned subsidiary of a company incorporated in Hong Kong) has no subsidiaries and has in the financial year made donations for charitable or other purposes to a total amount of not less than $10,000, state the total amount of such donations;

(e) if the company (not being the wholly owned subsidiary of a company incorporated in Hong Kong) has subsidiaries and the company and its subsidiaries have between them made donations for charitable or other purposes to a total amount of not less than $1,000, state the total amount of such donations;

(f) if significant changes in the fixed assets of the company or of any of its subsidiaries have occurred in the financial year, contain particulars of the changes;

(g) if, in the financial year, the company has issued any shares, state the reason for making the issue, the classes of shares issued and, as respects each class of shares, the number issued and the consideration received by the company for the issue;

(h)   if, in the financial year, it has issued any debentures, state the reason for making the issue, the classes of debentures issued and, as respects each class of debentures, the amount issued and the consideration received by the company for the issue;

(i)   state the names of the persons who, at any time during the financial year, were directors of the company;

(ia)   contain in respect of any contract referred to in section 162A(1)(a) the information required to be included in the report by that section;

(j)   if, at the end of the financial year, there subsists a contract with the company or the company's subsidiary or holding company or a subsidiary of the company's holding company in which a director of the company has, or at any time in that year had, in any way, whether directly or indirectly, an interest, or there has, at any time in that year, subsisted a contract with the company or the company's subsidiary or holding company or a subsidiary of the company's holding company in which a director of the company had, at any time in that year, in any way, whether directly or indirectly, an interest (being, in either case, in the opinion of the directors, a contract of significance in relation to the company's business and in which the director's interest is or was material), contain-

     (i)   a statement of the fact of the contract's subsisting or, as the case may be, having subsisted;

     (ii)   the names of the parties to the contract (other than the company);

     (iii)   the name of the director (if not a party to the contract);

     (iv)   an indication of the nature of the contract; and

     (v)   an indication of the nature of the director's interest in the contract;

(k)   if, at the end of the financial year, there subsist arrangements to which the company or the company's subsidiary or holding company or a subsidiary of the company's holding company is a party, being arrangements whose objects are, or one of whose objects is, to enable directors of the company to acquire benefits by means of the acquisition of shares in, or debentures of, the company or any other body corporate, or there have, at any time in that year, subsisted such arrangements as aforesaid to which the company or the company's subsidiary or holding company or a subsidiary of the company's holding company was a party, contain a statement explaining the effect of the arrangements and giving the names of the persons who at any time in that

year were directors of the company and held, or whose nominees held, shares or debentures acquired in pursuance of the arrangements;

    (l)   contain particulars of any other matters so far as they are material for the appreciation of the state of the company's affairs by its members, being matters the disclosure of which will not, in the opinion of the directors, be harmful to the business of the company or of any of its subsidiaries.

(4) As respect a company entitled to the benefit of any provision contained in Part III (exceptions for special classes of company) of the Tenth Schedule, subsection (3) shall have effect as if paragraph (f) were omitted.

(5) For the purposes of subsection (3)(d) and (e), "wholly owned subsidiary" shall be construed in accordance with section 124(4).

(6) The references in subsection (3)(j) to a contract do not include references to a director's contract of service or to a contract between the company and another body corporate, being a contract in which a director of the company has or had an interest by virtue only of his being a director of that other body.

Directors' report to show, for items included under authority of proviso to section 141C corresponding amounts for preceding financial year

129E. Where advantage is taken of the proviso to section 141C to show an item in the directors' report instead of in the accounts, the report shall also show the corresponding amount of that item for (or, as the case may require, as at the end of) the immediately preceding financial year, except where that amount would not have had to be shown had the item been shown in the accounts.

Penalization of failure by directors to secure compliance with requirements of sections 129D and 129E

129F. If any person being a director of a company fails to take all reasonable steps to secure compliance with the requirements of sections 129D and 129E, he shall, in respect of each offence, be liable to imprisonment and a fine:

Provided that-

    (a)   in any proceedings against a person in respect of an offence under this section, it shall be a defence to prove that he had reasonable ground to believe, and did believe, that a competent and reliable person was charged with the duty of seeing that the said sections were complied with and was in a position to discharge that duty; and

    (b)   a person shall not be sentenced to imprisonment for any such offence unless, in the opinion of the court dealing with the case, the offence was committed wilfully.

Right to receive copies of balance sheets and directors' and auditors' reports

129G.(1) A copy of every balance sheet, including every document required by law to be annexed thereto, which is to be laid before a company in general meeting, together with a copy of the directors' report and a copy of the auditors' report, shall, not less than 21 days before the date of the meeting, be sent to every member of the company (whether he is or is not entitled to receive notices of general meetings of the company), every holder of debentures of the company (whether he is or is not so entitled) and all persons other than members or holders of debentures of the company, being persons so entitled:

Provided that-

(a) in the case of a company not having a share capital this subsection shall not require the sending of a copy of the documents aforesaid to a member of the company who is not entitled to receive notices of general meetings of the company or to a holder of debentures of the company who is not so entitled;

(b) this subsection shall not require a copy of those documents to be sent-

    (i) to a member of the company or a holder of debentures of the company, being in either case a person who is not entitled to receive notices of general meetings of the company and of whose address the company is unaware;

    (ii) to more than one of the joint holders of any shares or debentures none of whom are entitled to receive such notices; or

    (iii) in the case of joint holders of any shares or debentures some of whom are and some of whom are not entitled to receive such notices, to those who are not so entitled; and

(c) if the copies of the documents aforesaid are sent less than 21 days before the date of the meeting, they shall, notwithstanding that fact, be deemed to have been duly sent if it is so agreed by all the members entitled to attend and vote at the meeting.

(2) Any member of a company, whether he is or is not entitled to have sent to him copies of the company's balance sheets, the personal representatives of any such member who has died, and any holder of debentures of the company, whether he is or is not so entitled, shall be entitled to be furnished on demand without charge with a copy of the last balance sheet of the company, including every document required by law to be annexed thereto, together with a copy of the directors' report and a copy of the auditors' report.

(2A) Any member of a company who is not entitled to vote at a general meeting of the company shall, notwithstanding subsection (1), be furnished with a copy of any statement issued by the company as a chairman's statement, and of any other document intended for the purpose of providing information about the affairs of the company, which is circulated by the company with the documents required to be sent to members under subsection (l).

(3) If default is made in complying with subsection (1) or (2A), the company and every officer of the company who is in default shall be liable to a fine, and if, when any person makes a demand for any document with which he is by virtue of subsection (2) entitled to be furnished, default is made in complying with the demand within 7 days after the making thereof, the company and every officer of the company who is in default shall be liable to a fine and, for continued default, to a daily default fine, unless it is proved that that person has already made a demand for and been furnished with a copy of the document.

(4) Subsections (1), (2) and (3) shall not have effect in relation to a balance sheet of a private company laid before it before 1 October 1975, but the provisions of this Ordinance which were in force immediately before the said date shall apply in relation to-

(a) the right of any person to be furnished with a copy of any such balance sheet, and

(b) the liability of the company and any officer thereof in respect of a failure to satisfy that right.

130. *(Repealed)*

Appointment and removal of auditors

131.(1) Every company shall at each annual general meeting of the company appoint an auditor or auditors to hold office from the conclusion of that meeting until the conclusion of the next annual general meeting of the company.

(2) Where at an annual general meeting of a company no auditors are appointed or reappointed, the court may, on the application of any member of the company, appoint a person to fill the vacancy.

(3) The first auditors of a company may be appointed by the directors at any time before the first annual general meeting of the company, and auditors so appointed shall hold office until the conclusion of that meeting.

(4) If the directors fail to exercise their powers under subsection (3), those powers may be exercised by the company in general meeting.

(5) The directors, or the company in general meeting, may fill any casual vacancy in the office of auditor, but while any such vacancy continues, the surviving or continuing auditor or auditors, if any, may act.

(6) A company may by ordinary resolution remove an auditor before the expiration of his term of office, notwithstanding anything in any agreement between it and him; and, except in the case of a private company, where a resolution removing an auditor is passed at a general meeting of a company, the company shall within 14 days give notice of that fact in the specified form to the Registrar.

(7)   If a company fails to give notice as required by subsection (6), the company and every officer of the company who is in default shall be guilty of an offence and liable to a fine and, for continued default, to a daily default fine.

(8)   The remuneration of the auditor of a company-

> *(a)*   in the case of an auditor appointed by the directors or by the court, may be fixed by the directors or by the court, as the case may be;

> *(b)*   subject to paragraph (a), shall be fixed by the company in general meeting or in such manner as the company in general meeting may determine.

For the purpose of this subsection "remuneration" includes any sums paid by the company in respect of the auditor's expenses.

(9) The appointment of a firm by its firm name to be the auditors of a company shall be deemed to be an appointment of those persons who shall from time to time during the currency of the appointment be the partners in that firm as from time to time constituted and who are qualified for appointment as auditors of that company:

Provided that any such appointment shall lapse, and thereby create a casual vacancy in the office of auditor, if all those persons who were partners in the firm and qualified as aforesaid at the date of the appointment cease to be partners or so qualified before the period of the appointment expires.

(10)   Nothing in subsection (6) shall be taken as depriving a person removed thereunder of compensation or damages payable to him in respect of the termination of his appointment as auditor or of any appointment terminating with that as auditor.

(11)   Where a company's auditor or auditors are holding office at the date of commencement of the Companies (Amendment) Ordinance 1984, nothing in this section as amended by that Ordinance shall be taken as terminating their appointment, or as requiring either their reappointment or the appointment of other auditors, before the conclusion of the annual general meeting of the company held next after that date.

Supplementary provisions relating to appointment and removal of auditors

132.(1) Special notice shall be required for a resolution at a general meeting of a company-

> *(a)*   appointing as auditor a person other than a retiring auditor; or

> *(b)*   filling a casual vacancy in the office of auditor; or

> (c)   reappointing as auditor a retiring auditor who was appointed by the directors to fill a casual vacancy; or
>
> (d)   removing an auditor before the expiration of his term of office.

(2)   On receipt of notice of such an intended resolution as aforesaid the company shall forthwith send a copy thereof-

> (a)   to the person proposed to be appointed or removed, as the case may be;
>
> (b)   in a case within subsection (1)(a), to the retiring auditor; and
>
> (c)   where, in a case within subsection (1)(b) or (c), the casual vacancy was caused by the resignation of an auditor, to the auditor who resigned.

(3)   Where notice is given of such a resolution as is mentioned in subsection (1)(a) or (d) and the retiring auditor or, as the case may be, the auditor proposed to be removed makes with respect to the intended resolution representations in writing to the company (not exceeding a reasonable length) and requests their notification to members of the company, the company shall (unless the representations are received by it too late for it to do so)-

> (a)   in any notice of the resolution given to members of the company state the fact of the representations having been made; and
>
> (b)   send a copy of the representations to every member of the company to whom notice of the meeting is or has been sent.

(4)   If a copy of any such representations as are mentioned in subsection (3) is not sent out as required by that subsection because received too late or because of the company's default, the auditor may (without prejudice to his right to be heard orally) require that the representations shall be read out at the meeting.

(5)   Copies of the representations need not be sent out and the representations need not be read out at the meeting if, on the application either of the company or of any other person who claims to be aggrieved, the court is satisfied that the rights conferred by this section are being abused to secure needless publicity for defamatory matter; and the court may order the company's costs on an application under this subsection to be paid in whole or in part by the auditor, notwithstanding that he is not a party to the application.

(6)   An auditor of a company who has been removed shall be entitled to attend-

> (a)   the general meeting at which his term of office would otherwise have expired; and
>
> (b)   any general meeting at which it is proposed to fill the vacancy caused by his removal,

and to receive all notices of, and other communications relating to, any such meeting which any member of the company is entitled to receive, and to be heard at any such meeting which he attends on any part of the business of the meeting which concerns him as former auditor of the company.

Powers of auditors in relation to subsidiaries

133.(1) Where a company ("the holding company") has a subsidiary, then-

    (a)   if the subsidiary is a body corporate incorporated in Hong Kong, it shall be the duty of the subsidiary and its auditors to give to the auditors of the holding company such information and explanation as those auditors may reasonably require for the purposes of their duties as auditors of the holding company;

    (b)   in any other case, it shall be the duty of the holding company, if required by its auditors to do so, to take all such steps as are reasonably open to it to obtain from the subsidiary such information and explanation as aforesaid.

(2)   If a subsidiary or holding company fails to comply with subsection (1) the subsidiary or holding company and every officer thereof who is in default shall be guilty of an offence; and if an auditor fails without reasonable excuse to comply with paragraph (a) of that subsection he shall be guilty of an offence.

(3)   A person guilty of an offence under this section shall be liable to a fine.

False statements etc. to auditors

134.(1) An officer of a company who knowingly or recklessly makes a statement which-

    (a)   is misleading, false or deceptive in a material particular; and

    (b)   is a statement to which this section applies,

shall be guilty of an offence and liable to imprisonment and a fine.

(2)   This section applies to any statement made to the auditors of the company (whether orally or in writing) which conveys, or purports to convey, any information or explanation which they require, or are entitled to require, as auditors of the company.

135-139.   *(Repealed)*

Disqualifications for appointment as auditor

140.(1) A person shall not be appointed as auditor of a company unless-

    (a)   he is qualified for appointment as such auditor under the Professional Accountants Ordinance (Cap. 50); and

(b)   he is not disqualified under subsection (2).

(2)   None of the following persons shall be qualified for appointment as auditor of a company-

(a)   an officer or servant of the company;

(b)   a person who is a partner of or in the employment of an officer or servant of the company;

(c)   a body corporate;

(d)   a person who is, by virtue of paragraph (a), (b) or (c), disqualified for appointment as auditor of any other body corporate which is the company's subsidiary or holding company or a subsidiary of the company's holding company, or would be so disqualified if the body corporate were a company,

and references in this subsection to an officer or servant shall be construed as not including references to an auditor.

(3)   A person shall not be disqualified by virtue of subsection (2)(b) or (d) for appointment as auditor of a company at any time during the period of 3 years beginning on the day on which the Companies (Amendment) Ordinance 1984 comes into operation if-

(a)   on that day, the company is a private company and he is a duly appointed auditor thereof,

(b)   at the time of his appointment, no shares or debentures of the company, or of a body corporate of which it is a subsidiary, have been listed on a stock exchange (whether in Hong Kong or elsewhere) or offered (whether in Hong Kong or elsewhere) to the public for subscription or purchase; and

(c)   he would not, but for subsection (2)(b), be disqualified for appointment as such auditor by virtue of subsection (2)(d).

(4)   Any person appointed as auditor of a company who ceases to be qualified, or who becomes disqualified, for appointment as auditor of the company before the period of his appointment expires shall forthwith vacate his office as such auditor.

(5)   Any body corporate which acts as auditor of a company shall be liable to a fine.

Resignation of auditor

140.(1) An auditor of a company may resign his office by depositing a notice in writing to that effect at the registered office of the company; and any such notice shall operate to bring his term of office to an end on the date on which the notice is deposited or on such later date as may be specified therein.

(2)   An auditor's notice of resignation shall not be effective unless it contains either-

> *(a)*   a statement to the effect that there are no circumstances connected with his resignation which he considers should be brought to the notice of the members or creditors of the company; or

> *(b)*   a statement of any such circumstances as aforesaid.

(3)   Where a notice having effect under this section is deposited at a company's registered office the company shall within 14 days send a copy of the notice-

> *(a)*   except in the case of a private company, to the Registrar; and

> *(b)*   if the notice contained a statement under subsection (2)(b), to every person who under section 129G(1) is entitled to be sent copies of the documents there mentioned.

(4)   The company or any person who claims to be aggrieved may, within 14 days of the receipt by the company of a notice containing a statement under subsection (2)(b), apply to the court for an order under subsection (5).

(5)   If the court, on an application under subsection (4), is satisfied that the auditor is using the notice to secure needless publicity for defamatory matter, it may by order direct that copies of the notice need not be sent out; and the court may further order the company's costs on the application to be paid in whole or in part by the auditor, notwithstanding that he is not a party to the application.

(6)   The company shall, within 14 days of the court's decision, send to the persons mentioned in subsection (3)-

> *(a)*   if the court makes an order under subsection (5), a statement setting out the effect of the order;

> *(b)*   if the court does not make an order under that subsection, a copy of the notice containing the statement under subsection (2)(b).

(7)   If default is made in complying with subsection (3) or (6), the company and every officer of the company who is in default shall be guilty of an offence and liable to a fine and in the case of an individual to imprisonment.

Right of auditor who resigns to requisition meeting of company, etc.

140B.(1) Where an auditor's notice of resignation contains a statement under section 140A(2)(b), there may be deposited with the notice a requisition signed by the auditor calling on the directors of the company forthwith duly to convene an extraordinary general meeting of the company for the purpose of receiving and considering such explanation of the circumstances connected with his resignation as he may wish to place before the meeting.

(2) Where an auditor's notice of resignation contains any such statement as aforesaid and the auditor requests the company to circulate to its members-

> *(a)* before the general meeting at which his term of office would otherwise have expired; or
>
> *(b)* before any general meeting at which it is proposed to fill the vacancy caused by his resignation or convened on his requisition,

a statement in writing (not exceeding a reasonable length) of the circumstances connected with his resignation, the company shall (unless the statement is received by it too late for it to do so)-

> **(i)** in any notice of the meeting given to members of the company state the fact of the statement having been made; and
>
> **(ii)** send a copy of the statement to every member of the company to whom notice of the meeting is or has been sent.

(3) If the directors do not within 21 days from the date of the deposit of a requisition under this section proceed duly to convene a meeting for a day not more than 28 days after the date on which the notice convening the meeting is given, every director who failed to take all reasonable steps to secure that a meeting was convened as mentioned above shall be guilty of an offence and liable to imprisonment and a fine, and if a copy of any such statement as is mentioned in subsection (2) is not sent out as required by that subsection because received too late or because of the company's default, the auditor may (without prejudice to his right to be heard orally) require that the statement shall be read out at the meeting.

(4) Copies of a statement need not be sent out and the statement need not be read out at the meeting if, on the application either of the company or of any other person who claims to be aggrieved, the court is satisfied that the rights conferred by this section are being abused to secure needless publicity for defamatory matter; and the court may order the company's costs on an application under this subsection to be paid in whole or in part by the auditor, notwithstanding that he is not a party to the application.

(5) An auditor of a company who has resigned his office shall be entitled to attend any such meeting as is mentioned in subsection (2)(a) or (b) and to receive all notices of, and other communications relating to, any such meeting which any member of the company is entitled to receive, and to be heard at any such meeting which he attends on any part of the business of the meeting which concerns him as former auditor of the company.

Auditors' report and rights of access to books and to attend and be heard at meetings

141.(1) The auditors of a company shall make a report to the members on the accounts examined by them, and on every balance sheet, every profit and loss account and all group accounts laid before the company in general meeting during their tenure of office.

(2) The auditors' report shall be read before the company in general meeting and shall be open to inspection by any member.

(3) The report shall-

    (a) except in the case of a company that is entitled to avail itself, and has availed itself, of the benefit of any of the provisions of Part III of the Tenth Schedule, state whether in the auditors' opinion the company's balance sheet and profit and loss account and (if it is a holding company submitting group accounts) the group accounts have been properly prepared in accordance with the provisions of this Ordinance and whether in their opinion a true and fair view is given-

        (i) in the case of the balance sheet, of the state of the company's affairs as at the end of its financial year;

        (ii) in the case of the profit and loss account (if it is not framed as a consolidated profit and loss account), of the company's profit or loss for its financial year;

        (iii) in the case of group accounts submitted by a holding company, of the state of affairs and profit or loss of the company and its subsidiaries dealt with thereby, so far as concerns members of the company;

    (b) in the said excepted case, state whether in the auditors' opinion the company's balance sheet and profit and loss account and (if it is a holding company submitting group accounts) the group accounts have been properly prepared in accordance with the provisions of this Ordinance applicable to such companies and whether in their opinion, on the basis aforesaid, a true and fair view is given-

        (i) in the case of the balance sheet, of the state of the company's affairs as at the end of its financial year;

        (ii) in the case of the profit and loss account (if it is not framed as a consolidated profit and loss account), of the company's profit or loss for its financial year;

        (iii) in the case of group accounts submitted by a holding company, of the state of affairs and profit or loss of the company and its subsidiaries dealt with thereby, so far as concerns members of the company.

(4) It shall be the duty of the auditors of a company, in preparing their report under this section, to carry out such investigations as will enable them to form an opinion as to the following matters, that is to say,-

(a)   whether proper books of account have been kept by the company and proper returns adequate for their audit have been received from branches not visited by them; and

(b)   whether the company's balance sheet and (unless it is framed as a consolidated profit and loss account) profit and loss account are in agreement with the books of account and returns;

and if the auditors are of opinion that proper books of account have not been kept by the company or that proper returns adequate for their audit have not been received from branches not visited by them, or if the balance sheet and (unless it is framed as a consolidated profit and loss account) profit and loss account are not in agreement with the books of account and returns, the auditors shall state that fact in their report.

(5) Every auditor of a company shall have a right of access at all times to the books and accounts and vouchers of the company, and shall be entitled to require from the officers of the company such information and explanations as he thinks necessary for the performance of the duties of the auditors:

Provided that, in the case of a banking company which has branch banks beyond the limits of Hong Kong, it shall be sufficient (subject to the powers of the auditors under subsections (4) and (6)) if the auditor is allowed access to such copies and extracts from such books and accounts of any such branch as have been transmitted to the head office of the company in Hong Kong.

(6) If the auditors fail to obtain all the information and explanations which, to the best of their knowledge and belief, are necessary for the purposes of their audit, they shall state that fact in their report.

(7) The auditors of a company shall be entitled to attend any general meeting of the company and to receive all notices of, and other communications relating to, any general meeting which any member of the company is entitled to receive, and to be heard at any general meeting which they attend on any part of the business of the meeting which concerns them as auditors.

Special provisions in respect of financial years ending before 30.9.75

141A.(1) Sections 123, 128, 129 and 129A shall not apply to a balance sheet or profit and loss account of a company laid before it in general meeting in respect of a financial year ending before 30 September 1975, but all the provisions of this Ordinance which were in force at the end of the financial year in relation to a balance sheet or profit and loss account required to be laid before a company in general meeting shall apply in relation to any balance sheet or profit and loss account laid before a company in general meeting in respect of a financial year ending before 30 September 1975.

(2) Section 124 shall not operate so as to require group accounts to be laid before a company in general meeting along with the company's own balance sheet and profit and loss account in any case where the company's own balance sheet and profit and loss account which are being laid before the company in general meeting are in respect of a financial year ending before 30 September 1975, and sections 125, 126 and 127 shall accordingly not apply in any such case.

(3) Section 129D shall not apply to a directors' report in respect of a financial year ending before 30 September 1975, but all the provisions of this Ordinance which were in force at the end of the financial year in relation to the attaching of a directors' report to every balance sheet of a company laid before it in general meeting and to the contents of such a report shall apply in relation to a directors' report in respect of a financial year ending before 30 September 1975.

(4) Section 141(3) and (6) shall not apply in relation to an auditors' report on a balance sheet or other accounts of a company laid before it in general meeting in respect of a financial year ending before 30 September 1975, but the provisions of this Ordinance which were in force at the end of the financial year in relation to the auditors' report on accounts examined by them and on every balance sheet laid before a company in general meeting during their tenure of office shall apply in relation to the auditors' report on any such balance sheet or other accounts laid before a company in general meeting in respect of a financial year ending before 30 September 1975.

Special provisions in respect of first financial year ending after 29.9.75

141B.(1) In relation to the first balance sheet of a company laid before it in general meeting in respect of a financial year ending after 29 September 1975, paragraph 12(16) of the Tenth Schedule shall not have effect so as to require there to be shown corresponding amounts at the end of the immediately preceding financial year of items which would not have had to be shown in the balance sheet if it had been a balance sheet in respect of a financial year ending before 30 September 1975.

(2) In relation to the first profit and loss account of a company laid before it in general meeting in respect of a financial year ending after 29 September 1975, paragraph 17(5) of the Tenth Schedule shall not have effect so as to require there to be shown corresponding amounts for the immediately preceding financial year of items which would not have had to be shown in the profit and loss account if it had been a profit and loss account in respect of a financial year ending before 30 September 1975.

Construction of references to documents annexed to accounts

141C. References in this Ordinance to a document annexed or required to be annexed to a company's accounts or any of them shall not include the directors' report or the auditors' report:

Provided that any information which is required by this Ordinance to be given in accounts, and is thereby allowed to be given in a statement annexed, may be given in the directors' report instead of in the accounts and, if any such information is so given, the report shall be annexed to the accounts and this Ordinance shall apply in relation thereto accordingly, except that the auditors shall report thereon only so far as it gives the said information.

Accounts of certain private companies

Power of shareholders of certain private companies to waive compliance with requirements as to accounts

141D.(1) Where all the shareholders of a private company agree in writing that this section shall apply with respect to a financial year of that company-

(a) the following provisions of this Ordinance shall not apply with respect to that financial year, that is to say, sections 121(2), 123, 129, 129A, 129D, 129E and 141(3);

(b) the company's balance sheet as at the end of that financial year shall comply with the requirements of the Eleventh Schedule;

(c) there shall be attached to the balance sheet a report by the directors with respect to-

   (i) the state of the company's affairs;

   (ii) the amount (if any) which they recommend should be paid by way of dividend;

   (iii) the amount of (if any) which they propose to carry to the reserve fund, general reserve or reserve account shown specifically on the balance sheet or to a reserve fund, general reserve or reserve account to be shown specifically on a subsequent balance sheet;

(d) the directors' report so attached shall be approved by the board of directors and signed on behalf of the board either by the chairman of the meeting at which it was approved or by the secretary of the company;

(e) the auditors' report shall state-

   (i) whether or not the auditors have obtained all the information and explanations which they have required; and

   (ii) whether, in their opinion, the balance sheet referred to in the report is properly drawn up so as to exhibit a true and correct view of the state of the company's affairs according to the best of their information and the explanations given to them, and as shown by the books of the company.

(2) The shareholders shall not in any financial year of the company enter into an agreement for the purposes of subsection (1) with respect to more than one such financial year.

(3) This section does not apply to a private company which-

    (a) has any subsidiary or is a subsidiary of another company formed and registered under this Ordinance or an existing company; or

    (b) carries on banking business and holds a valid banking licence granted under the Banking Ordinance (Cap. 155); or

    (c) is a dealer registered under the Securities Ordinance (Cap. 333); or either solely or in common with any other business,

    (d) carries on any insurance business otherwise than solely as an agent; or

    (e) by way of trade or business, other than banking business, accepts loans of money at interest, or repayable at a premium, otherwise than on terms involving the issue of debentures or other securities; or

    (f) owns and operates ships or aircraft engaged in the carriage of cargo between Hong Kong and places outside Hong Kong.

(4) Without prejudice to any other provision of this Ordinance, if any person being a director of a company fails to take all reasonable steps to secure compliance with the requirements of subsection (1)(c) and (d), he shall, in respect of each offence, be liable to imprisonment and a fine:

Provided that-

    (a) in any proceedings against the person in respect of an offence under this subsection, it shall be a defence to prove that he had reasonable ground to believe, and did believe, that a competent and reliable person was charged with the duty of seeing that the said paragraphs were complied with and was in a position to discharge that duty; and

    (b) a person shall not be sentenced to imprisonment for any such offence unless, in the opinion of the court dealing with the case, the offence was committed wilfully.

Inspection

Investigation of the affairs of a company on application of members

142.(1) The Financial Secretary may appoint one or more competent inspectors to investigate the affairs of a company and to report thereon in such manner as the Financial Secretary may direct-

    (a) in the case of a company having a share capital, on the application either of not less than 100 members or of members holding not less than one-tenth of the shares issued;

(b)   in the case of a company not having a share capital, on the application of not less than one-tenth in number of the persons on the company's register of members.

(2)   The application shall be supported by such evidence as the Financial Secretary may require for the purpose of showing that the applicants have good reason for requiring the investigation, and the Financial Secretary may, before appointing an inspector, require the applicants to give security in such amount as he may require for payment of the costs of the investigation.

Investigation of the affairs of a company in other cases

143.(1) Without prejudice to his powers under section 142, the Financial Secretary-

(a)   shall appoint one or more competent inspectors to investigate the affairs of a company and to report thereon in such manner as the Financial Secretary may direct, if the court by order declares that its affairs ought to be investigated by an inspector appointed by the Financial Secretary; and

(b)   may do so if the company by special resolution declares that its affairs ought to be investigated by an inspector appointed by the Financial Secretary and the company gives security in such amount as the Financial Secretary may require; and

(c)   may also do so if it appears to the Financial Secretary that there are circumstances suggesting-

     (i)   that the business of the company has been or is being conducted with intent to defraud its creditors or the creditors of any other person or otherwise for a fraudulent or unlawful purpose or in a manner oppressive of any part of its members or that it was formed for any fraudulent or unlawful purpose; or

     (ii)   that persons concerned with its formation or the management of its affairs have in connexion therewith been guilty of fraud, misfeasance or other misconduct towards it or towards its members; or

     (iii)   that its members have not been given all the information with respect to its affairs that they might reasonably expect.

(2)   The power of the Financial Secretary under subsection (1)(c) shall be exercisable with respect to a body corporate notwithstanding that it is in course of being voluntarily wound up.

Power of an inspector to investigate affairs of related company

144.   If an inspector appointed under section 142 or 143 to investigate the affairs of a company thinks it necessary for the purposes of his investigation to investigate also the affairs of any other body corporate that is or has at any relevant time been-

(a)   a subsidiary or a holding company of the company,

(b)   a subsidiary of its holding company,

(c)   a holding company of its subsidiary, or

(d)   substantially under the control of the same person as the first mentioned company,

he shall have power so to do, and shall report on the affairs of the other body corporate so far as he thinks the results of his investigation thereof are relevant to the investigation of the affairs of the first-mentioned company.

Production of documents, and evidence, on investigation

145.(1) It shall be the duty of all officers and agents of the company and of all officers and agents of any other body corporate whose affairs are investigated by virtue of section 144 to produce to the inspector all books and documents of or relating to the company or, as the case may be, the other body corporate that are in their custody or power, to attend before the inspector when required so to do and otherwise to give to the inspector all assistance in connexion with the investigation that they are reasonably able to give.

(1A) If an inspector considers that a person other than an officer or agent of the company or other body corporate is or may be in possession of any information concerning its affairs, he may require that person to produce to him any books or documents in his custody or power relating to the company or other body corporate, to attend before him and otherwise to give him all assistance in connexion with the investigation which he is reasonably able to give; and it shall be the duty of that person to comply with the requirement.

(2) An inspector may examine on oath the officers and agents of the company or other body corporate, and any such person as is mentioned in subsection (1A), in relation to the affairs of the company or other body, and may administer an oath accordingly.

(3) If any officer or agent of the company or other body corporate, or any such person as is mentioned in subsection (1A), refuses to produce to the inspector any book or document which it is his duty under this section so to produce, refuses to attend before the inspector when required so to do, or refuses to answer any question that is put to him by the inspector with respect to the affairs of the company or other body corporate, as the case may be, the inspector may certify the fact under his hand to the court, and the court may thereupon inquire into the case, and, after hearing any witnesses who may be produced against or on behalf of the alleged offender and after hearing any statement that may be offered in defence, punish the offender in like manner as if he had been guilty of contempt of the court.

(3A) A person is not excused from answering a question put to him under this section by an inspector on the ground that the answer might tend to incriminate him but, where such person claims, before answering the question, that the answer might tend to incriminate him, neither the question nor the answer shall be admissible in evidence against him in criminal proceedings other than proceedings in relation to a charge of perjury or proceedings for an offence under section 36 of the Crimes Ordinance (Cap. 200) in respect of the answer.

(3AA) If a claim of tendency to incriminate is not made in advance under subsection (3A), an answer given by a person to a question put to him in exercise of powers conferred by this section may be used in evidence against him.

(3B)   A person who complies with any requirement under this section of an inspector investigating the affairs of a company or other body corporate shall not incur any liability to any person by reason only of that compliance, and a certificate by the inspector under his hand stating that he is investigating the affairs of the company or other body corporate and that the person to whom the requirement is made is an officer or agent, as the case may be, of the company or other body corporate, or person whom he considers may be in possession of any information concerning its affairs, shall be conclusive evidence of those facts.

(4)-(4A) (*Repealed*)

(5)   In this section, any reference to officers or to agents shall include past, as well as present, officers or agents, as the case may be, and for the purposes of this section the expression "agents", in relation to a company or other body corporate, shall include the bankers and solicitors of the company or other body corporate and any person employed by the company or other body corporate as auditor, whether any such person is or is not an officer of the company or other body corporate.

Delegation of powers by inspector

145A.(1) An inspector appointed under section 142 or 143 to investigate the affairs of a company may, by instrument in writing, delegate to any person the powers conferred by section 145 and where he does so, references to an inspector in section 145 shall be deemed to include the person so delegated.

(2)   Where 2 or more inspectors are appointed as aforesaid in respect of the same investigation, the power conferred by this section may be exercised by any of them.

Power of inspector to call for director's accounts

145B. If an inspector has reasonable grounds for believing that a director or past director of the company or other body corporate whose affairs he is investigating maintains or has maintained an account of any description with a bank, deposit-taking company or similar financial institution (whether alone or jointly with any other person and whether in Hong Kong or elsewhere), into or out of which there has been paid-

> *(a)*   any emolument, pension or compensation, or any part thereof, in respect of his office as such director particulars of which have not been shown in the accounts, or in any statement annexed thereto, of the company or other body corporate, contrary to section 161;

(b)   any money which has resulted from or been used in the financing of any transaction particulars of which are not contained in the accounts of any company for any financial year, contrary to section 161B(1), (2) or (4);

(c)   any money which has been in any way connected with an act or omission, or series of acts or omissions, which on the part of that director constituted misconduct (whether fraudulent or not) towards the company or body corporate or its members,

the inspector may require the director to produce to him all documents in the director's possession, or under his control, relating to that account.

Inspector's report

146.(1) The inspector may, and, if so directed by the Financial Secretary, shall, make interim reports to the Financial Secretary, and on the conclusion of the investigation shall make a final report to the Financial Secretary.

(2)   Any such report shall be written or printed, as the Financial Secretary directs.

(3)   The Financial Secretary-

     (a)   shall-

         (i)   forward a copy of any report made by the inspector to the company at its registered office;

         (ii)   if he thinks fit, furnish a copy thereof, on request and on payment of the fee appointed under section 305 for a certified copy of a document where the copy has been prepared in the office of the Registrar, to any person who is a member of the company or of any other body corporate dealt with in the report by virtue of section 144 or whose interests as a creditor of the company or of any such other body corporate appear to the Financial Secretary to be affected;

         (iii)   where the inspector is appointed under section 142, furnish, at the request of the applicants for the investigation, a copy to them; and

         (iv)   where the inspector is appointed under section 143 in pursuance of an order of the court, file a copy in the court;

     (b)   may cause the report or any part thereof to be printed and published;

     (c)   may, or if such report or any part thereof is printed and published shall, cause a copy to be delivered to the Registrar.

(4) The inspector may at any time in the course of his investigation, without the necessity of making an interim report, inform the Financial Secretary of matters coming to his knowledge as a result of the investigation tending to show that an offence has been committed or that civil proceedings ought in the public interest to be brought by any body corporate.

Extension of Financial Secretary's powers of investigation to certain bodies incorporated outside Hong Kong

146A. Sections 143 to 149 and section 150 shall apply to all bodies corporate incorporated outside Hong Kong which have a place of business in Hong Kong or have at any time had a place of business therein as if they were companies registered under this Ordinance, but subject to such (if any) adaptations and modifications as may be specified by regulations made by the Financial Secretary.

Proceedings on inspector's report

147.(1) In relation to any prosecution arising from any report made or information supplied under section 146 or from any information or document obtained under section 152A or 152B, it shall be the duty of all officers and agents of the company or other body corporate whose affairs have been investigated by virtue of section 144, other than the defendant in the proceedings, to give to the Attorney General all assistance in connexion with the prosecution that they are reasonably able to give, and section 145(5) shall apply for the purposes of this subsection as it applies for the purposes of that section.

(2) If, in the case of any body corporate liable to be wound up under this Ordinance, it appears to the Financial Secretary from any report made under section 146 or from any information or document obtained under section 152A or 152B-

> *(a)* that it is expedient in the public interest that the body should be wound up, he may present a petition for it to be wound up if the court thinks it just and equitable for it to be so wound up;

> *(b)* that the business of such body corporate is being or has been conducted in a manner unfairly prejudicial to the interests of the members generally or of any part of its members, he may (in addition to, or instead of, presenting a petition under paragraph (a)) present a petition for an order under section 168A.

(3) If from any report made or information supplied under section 146 or from any information or document obtained under section 152A or 152B it appears to the Financial Secretary that any civil proceedings ought in the public interest to be brought by any body corporate, he may himself bring such proceedings in the name of and on behalf of the body corporate.

(4) The Government shall indemnify the body corporate against any costs or expenses incurred by it in or in connexion with any proceedings brought by virtue of subsection (3).

Expenses of investigation of the affairs of a company

148.(1) The expenses of and incidental to an investigation by an inspector appointed by the Financial Secretary under section 142 or 143 shall be defrayed in the first instance out of the general revenue of Hong Kong, but the following persons shall, to the extent mentioned, be liable to repay such expenses to the Government-

(a) any person who is convicted by a court or magistrate on a prosecution instituted as a result of the investigation, or who is ordered by a court or magistrate to pay damages or restore any property in proceedings brought by virtue of section 147(3) or to pay the whole or any part of the costs of any such proceedings, to such extent as may be ordered by such court or magistrate;

(b) any body corporate in whose name proceedings are brought as aforesaid, to the amount or value of any sums or property recovered by it as a result of those proceedings;

(c) any body corporate dealt with by the report, where the inspector was appointed otherwise than of the Financial Secretary's own motion, shall be liable, except so far as the Financial Secretary otherwise directs; and

(d) the applicants for the investigation, where the inspector was appointed under section 142, shall be liable to such extent (if any) as the Financial Secretary may direct;

and any amount for which a body corporate is liable by virtue of paragraph (b) shall be a first charge on the sums or property mentioned in that paragraph.

(2) The report of an inspector appointed otherwise than of the motion of the Financial Secretary may, if he thinks fit, and shall, if the Financial Secretary so directs, include a recommendation as to the directions, if any, that he thinks appropriate, in the light of his investigation, to be given under subsection (1)(c) and (d).

(3) For the purposes of this section, any costs or expenses incurred by the Financial Secretary in or in connexion with proceedings brought by virtue of section 147(3), including expenses incurred by virtue of subsection (4) thereof, shall be treated as expenses of the investigation giving rise to the proceedings.

(4) Any liability to repay the Government imposed by paragraphs (a) and(b) of subsection (1) shall, subject to the satisfaction of the right of Government to repayment, be a liability also to indemnify all persons against liability under paragraphs (c) and (d) thereof, and any such liability imposed by the said paragraph (a) shall, subject as aforesaid, be a liability also to indemnify all persons against liability under the said paragraph (b); and any person liable under any of the said paragraphs shall be entitled to contribution from any other person liable under the same paragraph, according to the amount of their respective liabilities thereunder.

Inspector's report to be evidence

149. A copy of any report of an inspector appointed under section 142 or 143, signed by the inspector and counter-signed by the Financial Secretary, shall be admissible in any legal proceedings as evidence of the opinion of the inspector in relation to any matter contained in the report and, in proceedings on an application under section 168J, as evidence of any fact stated therein.

149A. (*Repealed*)

Saving for solicitors and bankers

150. Nothing in sections 142 to 149 shall require disclosure to the Financial Secretary or to an inspector appointed by him-

    (a)   by a solicitor of any privileged communication made to him in that capacity, except as respects the name and address of his client; or

    (b)   by a body corporate's bankers as such of any information as to the affairs of any of their customers other than the body corporate.

Notice to Registrar

151. Upon the appointment of an inspector under section 142 or 143 and upon the submission of his final report, the inspector shall forward to the Registrar a notice in writing under his hand of such appointment or of such submission, as the case may be.

Power of company to appoint inspector

152.(1) A company may, by special resolution, appoint an inspector to investigate its affairs.

(2) It shall be the duty of all officers and agents of the company to produce to the inspector all books and documents in their custody or power.

(3) An inspector may examine on oath the officers and agents of the company in relation to its business, and may administer an oath accordingly.

(4) If any officer or agent of the company refuses to produce to the inspector any book or document which it is his duty under this section so to produce, refuses to attend before the inspector when required so to do, or refuses to answer any question that is put to him by the inspector with respect to the affairs of the company, the inspector may certify the fact under his hand to the court, and the court may thereupon inquire into the case, and, after hearing any witnesses who may be produced against or on behalf of the alleged offender and after hearing any statement that may be offered in defence, punish the offender in like manner as if he had been guilty of contempt of the court.

(5) On the conclusion of the investigation the inspector shall report his opinion in such manner and to such persons as the company in general meeting may direct.

(6) A copy of the report of an inspector appointed under this section, signed by the inspector and sealed with the seal of the company to which the report relates, shall be admissible in any legal proceedings as evidence of the opinion of the inspector in relation to any matter contained in the report.

Inspection of Companies' Books and Papers

Power of Financial Secretary to require production of documents

152A.(1) Where-

(a) an application is made to the Financial Secretary under section 142 to appoint an inspector to investigate the affairs of a company;

(b) in the case of any company, or in the case of any body corporate incorporated outside Hong Kong which is carrying on business in Hong Kong or has at any time carried on business therein, it appears to the Financial Secretary that there is good reason to do so,

the Financial Secretary may give directions to the company or body corporate, as the case may be, requiring it, at such time and place as may be specified in the directions, to produce such books or papers as may be so specified, or may at any time, if the Financial Secretary thinks there is good reason so to do, authorize any person, on producing (if required to do so) evidence of his authority, to require any such company or body corporate as aforesaid to produce to him forthwith any books or papers which the authorized person may specify.

(2) Where by virtue of subsection (1) the Financial Secretary or any authorized person has power to require the production of any books or papers from any company or body corporate, the Financial Secretary or authorized person shall have the like power to require production of those books or papers from any person who appears to the Financial Secretary or such authorized person to be in possession of them; but where any such person claims a lien on books or papers produced by him, the production shall be without prejudice to the lien.

(3) Any power conferred by or by virtue of this section to require a company or body corporate or other person to produce books or papers shall include power-

(a) if the books or papers are produced-

(i) to take copies of them or extracts from them; and

(ii) to require that person, or any other person who is a present or past officer of, or is or was at any time employed by, the company or body corporate in question, to provide an explanation of any of them;

(b) if the books or papers are not produced, to require the person who was required to produce them to state, to the best of his knowledge and belief, where they are.

(4)   If a requirement to produce books or papers or provide an explanation or make a statement which is imposed by virtue of this section is not complied with, the company or body corporate or other person on whom the requirement was so imposed shall be guilty of an offence and liable to a fine and, in the case of an individual, to imprisonment; but where a person is charged with an offence under this subsection in respect of a requirement to produce any books or papers, it shall be a defence to prove that they were not in his possession or under his control and that it was not reasonably practicable for him to comply with the requirement.

(5)   A person is not excused from providing an explanation or making a statement under this section on the ground that providing the explanation or making the statement might tend to incriminate him but, where the person claims, before providing the explanation or making the statement that the explanation or statement might tend to incriminate him, neither the requirement to provide the explanation or make the statement nor the explanation or statement is admissible in evidence against him in criminal proceedings other than proceedings for an offence under section 36 of the Crimes Ordinance (Cap. 200) in respect of the explanation or statement.

(6)   If a claim of tendency to incriminate is not made in advance under subsection (5), an explanation provided or statement made by a person to an authorized person in exercise of powers conferred by this section may be used in evidence against him.

Entry and search of premises

152B.(1) If a magistrate is satisfied on information on oath laid by an inspector appointed by the Financial Secretary, or by any person acting under the authority of the Financial Secretary, that there are reasonable grounds for suspecting that there are on any premises any books or papers of which production ought to be made but has not been made under section 145 or of which production has been required by virtue of section 152A and which have not been produced in compliance with that requirement, the magistrate may issue a warrant authorizing any police officer, together with other persons named in the warrant and any other police officer, to enter the premises specified in the information (using such force as is reasonably necessary for the purpose) and to search the premises and take possession of any books or papers appearing to be such books or papers as aforesaid, or to take, in relation to any books or papers so appearing, any other steps which may appear necessary for preserving them and preventing interference with them.

(2)   Every warrant issued under this section shall continue in force until the end of the period of 1 month after the date on which it is issued.

(3)   Any books or papers of which possession is taken under this section may be retained for a period of 3 months or, if within that period any criminal proceedings to which the books and papers are relevant are commenced, until the conclusion of those proceedings.

(4)   A person who obstructs the exercise of a right of entry or search conferred by virtue of a warrant issued under this section, or who obstructs the exercise of a right so conferred to take possession of any books or papers, shall be guilty of an offence and liable on conviction to a fine and imprisonment.

Provision for security of information

152C.(1) No information or document relating to a company or body corporate which has been obtained under section 152A or 152B shall, without the previous consent in writing of the company or body corporate, as the case may be, be published or disclosed, except to a competent authority, unless the publication or disclosure is required with a view to the institution of, or otherwise for the purposes of, any criminal proceedings.

(2) Any person who publishes or discloses any information or document in contravention of subsection (1) shall be guilty of an offence and liable to imprisonment and a fine.

(3) For the purposes of this section, "competent authority" means any of the following-

      (a)   the Financial Secretary;

      (b)   an inspector appointed under this Ordinance by the Financial Secretary;

      (c)   any person acting under the authority of the Financial Secretary.

Penalization of destruction, mutilation, etc. of company documents

152D.(1) A person who-

      (a)   conceals, destroys, mutilates or falsifies, or is privy to the concealment, destruction, mutilation or falsification of a book or paper affecting or relating to the property or affairs of any company or body corporate mentioned in section 152A(1); or

      (b)   parts with, alters or makes an omission in any such book or paper, or who is privy to parting with, altering or making an omission in any such book or paper; or

      (c)   sends, causes to be sent or conspires with another person to send, out of Hong Kong such a book or paper or any property belonging to or under the control of the company,

shall be guilty of an offence and liable to imprisonment and a fine.

(2) In a prosecution for an offence under subsection (1), it shall be a defence if the person charged with the offence proves that he did not act with intent to defeat the purposes of sections 142 to 152B.

Penalization of furnishing false information under section 152A

152E. A person who, in purported compliance with a requirement imposed under section 152A to provide an explanation or make a statement, provides or makes an explanation or statement which he knows to be false in a material particular or recklessly provides or makes an explanation or statement which is so false shall be guilty of an offence and liable to imprisonment and a fine.

Saving for solicitors and bankers

152F.(1) Nothing in section 152A, 152B, 152C, 152D or 152E shall compel the production by a solicitor of a document containing a privileged communication made by or to him in that capacity or authorize the taking of possession of any such document which is in his possession.

(2)   The Financial Secretary shall not, under section 152A, require, or authorize any person to require, the production by a person carrying on the business of banking of a document relating to the affairs of a customer of his unless either it appears to the Financial Secretary that it is necessary so to do for the purpose of investigating the affairs of the first-mentioned person or the customer is a person on whom a requirement has been imposed by virtue of that section.

Directors and other Officers

Directors

153.(1) Every company shall have at least 2 directors.

(2)   In the case of a company referred to in paragraph (a) or (b) which has not at any time (whether before or after the commencement of the Companies (Amendment) Ordinance 1984) sent to the Registrar under section 158 a return containing the names of at least 2 directors of the company, each of the following shall, until such return is so sent, be deemed to be a director of the company-

> *(a)*   if the company is a private company which is not a member of a group of companies of which a listed company is a member, the persons whose names appear first and second in order in the list of subscribers to the memorandum of the company;

> *(b)*   if paragraph (a) does not apply to the company and one or more individuals are named as subscribers in the list of subscribers to the memorandum of the company-

>> **(i)**   where one individual only is so named in the memorandum, that individual;

>> **(ii)**   where 2 or more individuals are so named in the memorandum, the first 2 individuals so named in the order in which the names appear therein,

and for the purposes of this section "listed company" means a company in the case of which shares are listed on the Unified Exchange.

(3)   Subject to subsection (4), if any company makes default in complying with subsection (1) at any time after the expiration of 6 months from the commencement of the Companies (Amendment) Ordinance 1984, the company and every officer of the company who is in default shall be liable to a fine and, for continued default, to a daily default fine.

(4) Where the number of directors of a company is reduced below 2 by reason of the office of any director being vacated, the company or any officer of the company shall not be liable for any default in respect thereof under this section unless the default continues for a period of 2 months beginning on the day on which the office is vacated.

(5) Any power exercisable by a director under the articles of a company in a case where the number of directors is reduced below the number fixed as the necessary quorum of directors, being a power to act for the purpose of increasing the number of directors or of summoning a general meeting of the company but not for any other purpose, shall be exercisable also in a case where the number of directors is reduced below the number required by subsection (1).

Secretary

154.(1) Every company shall have a secretary, who may be one of the directors.

(2)   The secretary of a company shall-

> *(a)*   if an individual, ordinarily reside in Hong Kong;

> *(b)*   if a body corporate, have its registered office or a place of business in Hong Kong.

(3)   Anything required or authorized to be done by or to the secretary may, if the office is vacant or there is for any other reason no secretary capable of acting, be done by or to any assistant or deputy secretary or, if there is no assistant or deputy secretary capable of acting, by or to any officer of the company authorized generally or specially in that behalf by the directors.

Restriction on body corporate being director

154A.(1) A company shall not, after the expiration of 6 months from the commencement of the Companies (Amendment) Ordinance 1984, have as director of the company a body corporate.

(2) This section shall not apply to a private company excepted under subsection (3).

(3) A private company is excepted under this subsection if, but only if, it is not a member of a group of companies of which a listed company is a member; and for the purposes of this subsection "listed company" means a company in the case of which shares are listed on the Unified Exchange.

(4) A body corporate which, at the commencement of the Companies (Amendment) Ordinance 1984, is a director of a company other than a private company excepted under subsection (3) shall, if it has not vacated its office as such director within a period of 6 months thereafter, be deemed to have done so upon the expiration of that period, and all acts or things purporting to be made or done after the expiration of that period by a body corporate as director of any such company shall be null and void.

Avoidance of acts done by person in dual capacity as director and secretary

154B. A provision requiring or authorizing a thing to be done by or to a director and the secretary shall not be satisfied by its being done by or to the same person acting both as director and as, or in place of, the secretary.

Qualification of director

155.(1) It shall be the duty of every director who is by the articles of the company required to hold a specified share qualification, and who is not already qualified, to obtain his qualification within 2 months after his appointment, or such shorter time as may be fixed by the articles.

(2) For the purpose of any provision in the articles requiring a director to hold a specified share qualification, the bearer of a share warrant shall not be deemed to be the holder of the shares specified in the warrant.

(3) The office of director of a company shall be vacated if the director does not within 2 months from the date of his appointment, or within such shorter time as may be fixed by the articles, obtain his qualification, or if after the expiration of the said period or shorter time he ceases at any time to hold his qualification.

(4) A person vacating office under this section shall be incapable of being reappointed director of the company until he has obtained his qualification.

(5) If after the expiration of the said period or shorter time any unqualified person acts as a director of the company, he shall be liable to a fine, and a daily fine for every day between the expiration of the said period or shorter time or the day on which he ceased to be qualified, as the case may be, and the last day on which it is proved that he acted as a director.

Approval of company required for disposal by directors of company's fixed assets

155A.(1) Notwithstanding anything in the memorandum or articles of-

      (a)   a company in the case of which shares are listed on the Unified Exchange; or

      (b)   a company which is a member of a group of companies of which a company referred to in paragraph (a) is a member,

the directors of such a company shall not carry into effect any proposals to which this section applies unless those proposals have been approved by the company in general meeting.

(2) This section applies to proposals for disposing of any fixed assets of a company referred to in subsection (1)(a) or (b) if, but only if, the aggregate of-

> *(a)* the amount or value of the consideration for the proposed disposal; and
>
> *(b)* where any fixed assets of the company have been disposed of in the period of 4 months immediately preceding the proposed disposal, the amount or value of the consideration for any such disposal in that period,

exceeds 33 per cent of the value of the company's fixed assets as shown in the latest balance sheet laid before the company in general meeting.

(3) The court may, on the application of any member or holder of debentures of a company referred to in subsection (1)(a) or (b), restrain the directors from entering into a transaction in contravention of subsection (1).

(4) A transaction entered into in contravention of subsection (1) shall be as valid as if that subsection had been complied with.

(5) If any person being a director of a company referred to in subsection (1)(a) or (b) fails to take all reasonable steps to comply with subsection (1) he shall, in respect of each offence, be liable to a fine and imprisonment.

(6) In this section a reference to proposals for disposing of any fixed assets does not include a reference to proposals for charging such fixed assets or granting any interest therein by way of security.

Notices of resolutions to contain explanation of their effect and particulars of relevant interests of directors

155B.(1) Subject to subsection (2), where a company (not being a company which is a wholly owned subsidiary) gives notice of the intention to move a resolution at a general meeting of the company or a meeting of any class of members of the company the notice shall include or be accompanied by a statement-

> *(a)* containing such information and explanation, if any, as is reasonably necessary to indicate the purpose of the resolution; and
>
> *(b)* disclosing any material interests of any director in the matter dealt with by the resolution so far as the resolution affects those interests differently from the interests of other members of the company.

(2) Subsection (1)(a) shall not apply in relation to any resolution of which notice is given by the company under section 115A.

(3) It shall be the duty of any director of the company to give notice to the company of such matters relating to himself as may be necessary for the purposes of this section; and any person who makes default in complying with this subsection shall be liable to a fine.

(4) If a company makes default in complying with subsection (1) the company and every officer of the company who is in default shall be liable to a fine.

(5) Nothing in this section shall affect the validity of a resolution passed at a general meeting of a company.

(6) For the purposes of this section "wholly owned subsidiary" has the same meaning as it has for the purposes of section 124.

Directors' duty to shareholders regarding prospectus or statement in lieu

155C.(1) Where any company delivers a prospectus or statement in lieu of prospectus to the Registrar for registration, the company shall, at the same time or, if it is not practicable to do so at that time, as soon as practicable thereafter but not later than 3 weeks from the date of delivery of such prospectus or statement in lieu of prospectus, send a copy thereof to every person who is a member of the company.

(2) The reference in subsection (1) to a member of a company is a reference to any person who is a member on the date referred to in that subsection or, if another date is specified in that respect in the prospectus or statement in lieu of prospectus, the date so specified.

Provisions as to undischarged bankrupts acting as directors

156.(1) If any person being an undischarged bankrupt acts as director of, or directly or indirectly takes part in or is concerned in the management of, any company except with the leave of the court by which he was adjudged bankrupt, he shall be guilty of an offence and liable to imprisonment and a fine:

Provided that a person shall not be guilty of an offence under this section by reason that he, being an undischarged bankrupt, has acted as director of, or taken part or been concerned in the management of, a company, if at the commencement of this Ordinance he was acting as director of, or taking part or being concerned in the management of, that company and has continuously so acted, taken part, or been concerned since that date and the bankruptcy was prior to that date.

(2) The leave of the court for the purpose of this section shall not be given unless notice of intention to apply therefor has been served on the Official Receiver and it shall be the duty of the Official Receiver, if he is of opinion that it is contrary to the public interest that any such application should be granted, to attend on the hearing of and oppose the granting of the application.

(3) In this section, the expression "company" has the meaning assigned to it by section 168C, and the expression "Official Receiver" means the Official Receiver appointed under the Bankruptcy Ordinance (Cap.6).

Validity of acts of directors

157. The acts of a director or manager shall be valid notwithstanding any defect that may afterwards be discovered in his appointment or qualification.

Appointment of directors to be voted on individually

157A.(1) At a general meeting of a company other than a private company or a company not having a share capital, a motion for the appointment of 2 or more persons as directors of the company by a single resolution shall not be made, unless a resolution that it shall be so made has first been agreed to by the meeting without any vote being given against it.

(2) A resolution moved in contravention of this section shall be void, whether or not its being so moved was objected to at the time:

Provided that-

(a)   this subsection shall not be taken as excluding the operation of section 157; and

(b)   where a resolution so moved is passed, no provision for the automatic reappointment of retiring directors in default of another appointment shall apply.

(3) For the purposes of this section, a motion for approving a person's appointment or for nominating a person for appointment shall be treated as a motion for his appointment.

(4) Nothing in this section shall apply to a resolution altering the company's articles.

Removal of directors

157B.(1) A company may by special resolution remove a director before the expiration of his period of office, notwithstanding anything in its memorandum or articles or in any agreement between it and him:

Provided that this subsection shall not, in the case of a private company, authorize the removal of a director holding office for life on the commencement of the Companies (Amendment) Ordinance 1984.

(2) On receipt of notice of an intended resolution to remove a director under this section the company shall forthwith send a copy thereof to the director concerned, and the director (whether or not he is a member of the company) shall be entitled to be heard on the resolution at the meeting.

(3) Where notice is given of an intended resolution to remove a director under this section and the director concerned makes with respect thereto representations in writing to the company (not exceeding a reasonable length) and requests their notification to members of the company, the company shall, unless the representations are received by it too late for it to do so-

(a)   in any notice of the resolution given to members of the company state the fact of the representations having been made; and

(b)   send a copy of the representations to every member of the company to whom notice of the meeting is sent (whether before or after receipt of the representations by the company),

and if a copy of the representations is not sent as aforesaid because received too late or because of the company's default, the director may (without prejudice to his right to be heard orally) require that the representations shall be read out at the meeting.

(4) Copies of the representations need not be sent out and the representations need not be read out at the meeting if, on the application either of the company or of any other person who claims to be aggrieved, the court is satisfied that the rights conferred by this section are being abused to secure needless publicity for defamatory matter; and the court may order the company's costs on an application under this section to be paid in whole or in part by the director, notwithstanding that he is not a party to the application.

(5) On a resolution to remove a director before the expiration of his term of office no share shall, on a poll, carry a greater number of votes than it would carry in relation to the generality of matters to be voted on at a general meeting; and where a share carries special voting rights (that is to say, rights different from those carried by other shares of the same nominal value) in relation to some matters but not others, the reference in this subsection to the generality of matters to be voted on at a general meeting of the company shall be construed as a reference to the matters in relation to which the share carries no special voting rights.

(6) A vacancy created by the removal of a director under this section, if not filled at the meeting at which he is removed, may be filled as a casual vacancy.

(7) A person appointed director in place of a person removed under this section shall be treated, for the purpose of determining the time at which he or any other director is to retire, as if he had become director on the day on which the person in whose place he is appointed was last appointed a director.

(8) Nothing in this section shall be taken as depriving a person removed thereunder of compensation or damages payable to him in respect of the termination of his appointment as director or of any appointment terminating with that as director or as derogating from any power to remove a director which may exist apart from this section.

Minimum age limit for directors

157C. No person shall be capable of being appointed a director of a company on or after the commencement of the Companies (Amendment) Ordinance 1984 unless at the time of his appointment he has attained the age of 18 years.

Resignation of director or secretary

157D.(1) A director or secretary of a company may, unless it is otherwise provided in the articles of the company or by any agreement with the company, resign his office at any time.

(2)   Notification of the resignation of a director or secretary of a company shall, subject to subsection (3)(c), be given by the company to the Registrar in like manner as a notification of any change among its directors is required to be given by section 158(4):

Provided that where there are reasonable grounds for believing that the company will not give such notification, such notification shall be given in the specified form by the person resigning and shall state whether the person resigning is required by the articles of the company or by any agreement with the company to give notice of his resignation to the company, and, if such notice is so required, whether such notice has been given in accordance with such requirement.

(3)　　Where notice of the resignation of a director or secretary of a company is required to be given by the articles of the company or by any agreement with the company, the following shall apply to the person resigning-

> *(a)*　　the resignation shall not have effect unless he gives notice in writing thereof either in accordance with such requirement or by sending it by post to, or by leaving it at, the registered office of the company;

> *(b)*　　he shall deliver a copy of such notice to the Registrar not later than 3 days after it is given to the company and shall endorse thereon a certificate stating whether the original has been posted to, or, as the case may be, left at, the registered office of the company and specifying the date on which it was so posted or left;

> *(c)*　　any notification required by subsection (2) to be given to the Registrar shall be given not later than 7 days after the expiration of such notice.

157E-157F.　　*(Repealed)*

157G.　*(Repealed)*

Prohibition of loans to directors, etc.

157H.(1) In this section-

"company" means any of the following-

> *(a)*　　a company;

> *(b)*　　any other body corporate-
> **(i)**　　incorporated in Hong Kong under an Ordinance; and

> **(ii)**　　in the case of which shares are listed on the Unified Exchange,

but does not include an authorized institution within the meaning of section 2 of the Banking Ordinance (Cap. 155);

"net assets", in relation to a company, means the aggregate of the company's assets less the aggregate of its liabilities, and for the purposes of this definition "liabilities" includes any provision within the meaning of the Tenth Schedule except to the extent that that provision is taken into account in calculating the value of any asset of the company.

(2) Subject to this section, a company shall not, directly or indirectly-

> *(a)* make a loan to a director of the company or of its holding company;

> *(b)* enter into any guarantee or provide any security in connexion with a loan made by any person to such a director;

> *(c)* if any one or more of the directors of the company hold jointly or severally or directly or indirectly) a controlling interest in another company, make a loan to that other company or enter into any guarantee or provide any security in connexion with a loan made by any person to that other company.

(3) Subject to subsections (4), (5), (6), (7) and (8), each of the following transactions is excepted from the prohibitions in subsection (2)-

> *(a)* a loan by a company which is a member of a group of companies to another company which is a member of the same group of companies or such a company's entering into a guarantee or providing any security in connexion with a loan made by any person to that other company;

> *(b)* in the case of a private company other than a private company which is a member of a group of companies of which a company referred to in subsection (9)(a) is a member, anything done by the company which has been approved by the company in general meeting;

> *(c)* a company's doing anything to provide any of its directors with funds to meet expenditure incurred or to be incurred by him for the purposes of the company or for the purpose of enabling him properly to perform his duties as an officer of the company;

> *(d)* a loan by a company to a director of the company-

>> **(i)** for the purpose of facilitating the purchase, for use as that director's only or main residence, of the whole or part of any residential premises together with any land to be occupied and enjoyed therewith;

>> **(ii)** for the purpose of improving any residential premises so used or any land occupied and enjoyed therewith; or

>> **(iii)** in substitution for any loan made by any person and falling within sub-paragraph (i) or (ii);

        (e)   in the case of a company the ordinary business of which includes the lending of money or the giving of guarantees in connexion with loans made by other persons, a loan by any such company to any person or such a company's entering into a guarantee in connexion with a loan by one person to another.

(4)   Subject to subsection (7), the exception specified in subsection (3)(c) operates only if either of the following conditions is satisfied-

        (a)   the thing in question is done with the prior approval of the company given at a general meeting at which the purpose of any expenditure and the amount of any loan to be made by the company or the extent of the company's liability under any guarantee to be given by the company or, as the case may be, in respect of any security to be provided by the company are disclosed; or

        (b)   that thing is done on condition that, if the approval of the company is not so given at or before the next following annual general meeting, the loan shall be repaid or that liability discharged within 6 months from the conclusion of that meeting.

(5)   Subject to subsection (7), the exception specified in subsection (3)(d) operates in respect of a loan referred to therein only if the following conditions are satisfied-

        (a)   the company ordinarily makes loans of that description to its employees on terms no less favourable than those on which the loan itself is made; and

        (b)   the loan does not exceed 80 per cent of the value of the residential premises, or the part thereof, in question and any land to be occupied and enjoyed therewith as stated in a valuation report which complies with the following requirements-

                (i)   the valuation report shall be made by a professionally qualified valuation surveyor who is subject to the discipline of a professional body; and

                (ii)   the valuation report shall be made and signed by the valuation surveyor not earlier than 3 months prior to the date on which the loan is made; and

        (c)   the loan is secured by a legal mortgage on the land comprising the residential premises, or the part thereof, in question and any land to be occupied and enjoyed therewith.

(6)   Subject to subsections (7) and (8), the exception specified in subsection (3)(e) operates only if the following conditions are satisfied-

     (a)   the loan in question is made by the company or it enters into the guarantee in question in the ordinary course of the company's business; and

     (b)   the amount of the loan or the amount guaranteed is not greater, and the terms of the loan or guarantee are not more favourable, in the case of the person to whom the loan is made or in respect of whom the guarantee is entered into than that or those which it is reasonable to expect that company to have offered to or in respect of a person of the same financial standing as that person but unconnected with the company.

(7)   The exception specified in subsection (3)(c), (d) or (e) does not authorize a company to enter into a transaction if at the time that the transaction is entered into the aggregate of the following amounts-

     (a)   the amount outstanding at that time on all loans made by the company to any of its directors otherwise than under subsection (3)(a) or (b);

     (b)   the amount representing the maximum liability of the company at that time under all guarantees entered into, and in respect of any security provided, by the company in connexion with loans made by any person to any of its directors; and

     (c)   if the transaction in question is-

          (i)   a loan, the amount of such loan;

          (ii)   a guarantee, the amount representing the maximum liability of the company under such guarantee; or

          (iii)   the provision of a security, the amount representing the maximum liability of the company in respect of such security,

exceeds 5 per cent of the amount of the company's net assets as shown in the latest balance sheet laid before the company in general meeting.

(8)   The exception specified in subsection (3)(e) does not authorize a company to make a loan to any director of the company or of its holding company or, where any one or more of the directors of the company hold (jointly or severally or directly or indirectly) a controlling interest in another company, to that other company, or to enter into a guarantee in connexion with a loan made by any person to any such director or other company, if at the time that the loan is made or, as the case may be, that guarantee is given the aggregate of the following amounts exceeds $500,000-

     (a)   the principal of the loan to be made or guaranteed by the company or, if the case so requires, so much of that principal as is so guaranteed;

(b)   any amount outstanding at that time by way of principal on any other loan made by the company by virtue of that exception to such director or other company; and

(c)   where at that time the company is or may be made liable in pursuance of any guarantee entered into by virtue of that exception, the amount for which the company is or may be so made liable in respect of the principal of any other loan to such director or other company.

(9)   In the application of this section to-

(a)   a company in the case of which shares are listed on the Unified Exchange;

(b)   a company which is a member of a group of companies of which a company referred to in paragraph (a) is a member,

references in this section, except in subsection (3)(c) or (d), to a director shall include references to-

(i)   the spouse or any child or step-child of such director;

(ii)   a person acting in his capacity as the trustee (other than as trustee under an employees' share scheme or a pension scheme) of any trust the beneficiaries of which include the director, his spouse or any of his children or step-children or the terms of which confer a power on the trustees that may be exercised for the benefit of the director, his spouse or any of his children or step-children; and

(iii)   a person acting in his capacity as partner of that director or of his spouse, child or step-child, or of any trustee referred to in paragraph (ii).

(10)   References in subsection (9) to the child or step-child of any person shall include a reference to. any illegitimate child of that person, but shall not include a reference to any person who has attained the age of 18 years.

Civil consequences of transactions contravening section 157H

157I.(1) A person who receives from a company a sum paid in pursuance of a loan made in contravention of section 157H(2) shall be liable to repay that sum to the company forthwith, except where he is not a director of the company or of its holding company and he shows that, at the time the loan was made, he did not know the relevant circumstances.

(2)   Subject to subsection (3), a guarantee entered into or any security provided by a company in contravention of section 157H(2) shall be unenforceable against the company.

(3)   Subsection (2)-

(a)   shall not apply to a guarantee entered into or any security provided in connexion with a loan to a person who is not a director of the company or of its holding company if it is shown that, at the time the guarantee was entered into or the security provided, the person to whom the guarantee was given or the security provided, as the case may be, did not know the relevant circumstances; and

(b)   shall not affect an interest in any property which has been passed by the company to any person by way of security provided in connexion with any loan.

(4)   Without prejudice to any liability imposed on directors of companies otherwise than by this subsection, a director of a company which has entered into a transaction (whether the making of a loan, the giving of a guarantee or the provision of a security) in contravention of section 157H(2) shall be liable -

(a)   to account to the company for any gain which he has made directly or indirectly by the transaction; and

(b)   jointly and severally with any other director liable under this subsection, to indemnify the company for any loss or damage resulting from that transaction,

if-

(i)   he knowingly and wilfully authorized or permitted the transaction to be entered into; or

(ii)   the transaction consists in the making of a loan to that director or a person connected with him; or

(iii)   the transaction consists in the giving of a guarantee or the provision of any security in connexion with a loan made by any person to that director or a person connected with him.

(5)   Without prejudice to the foregoing provisions of this section, section 157H(2) shall not of itself invalidate any transaction entered into in contravention thereof.

(6)   In this section and in section 157J, "the relevant circumstances" means, in relation to a contravention of section 157H(2), all the facts and other circumstances constituting that contravention including, in the case of a transaction which but for any fact or circumstance would be authorized by any provision of section 157H, that fact or circumstance.

(7)   For the purposes of this section a person is connected with a director of a company if, but only if, he is-

(a)   the spouse, child or step-child of that director; or

(b)   a person acting in his capacity as the trustee (other than as trustee under an employees' share scheme or a pension scheme) of any trust the beneficiaries of which include the director, his spouse or any of his children or step-children or the terms of which confer a power on the trustees that may be exercised for the benefit of the director, his spouse or any of his children or step-children; or

(c) a person acting in his capacity as partner of that director or of any person who by virtue of paragraph (a) or (b) is connected with that director; or

(d) a company in which that director or his spouse or any of his children or step-children, or any person to whom paragraph (b) or (c) applies, holds (jointly or severally or directly or indirectly) a controlling interest,

and in this subsection a reference to the child or step-child of any person shall include a reference to any illegitimate child of that person, but shall not include a reference to any person who has attained the age of 18 years.

Criminal penalties for contravention of section 157H

157J.(1) Where a company enters into a transaction (whether the making of a loan, the giving of a guarantee or the provision of a security) in contravention of section 157H(2), the following persons shall, subject to subsection (2), be guilty of an offence-

(a) if the transaction is entered into in contravention of section 157H(2)(a) or (b), the company;

(b) any director of the company who wilfully authorized or permitted the transaction to be entered into; and

(c) any person who knowingly procured the company to enter into the transaction.

(2) A person shall not be guilty of an offence under this section if he shows that, at the time the transaction was entered into, he did not know the relevant circumstances.

(3) A person guilty of an offence under this section shall be liable to imprisonment and a fine.

Register of directors and secretaries

158.(1) Every company shall keep a register of its directors and secretaries.

(2) Where the company is an unlisted company, the register shall contain the particulars with respect to each director-

(a) in the case of an individual, his present forename and surname and any former forename or surname (including, in the case of a Chinese director, the Chinese characters for any such forename or surname if they are used by such director),

any alias, his usual residential address, his nationality and the number of his identity card (if any) or, in the absence of such number, the number and issuing country of any passport held by him; and

(b)   in the case of a body corporate, its corporate name and registered or principal office.

(2A)   Where the company is a listed company, the register shall contain the following particulars with respect to each director-

(a)   his present forename and surname and any former forename or surname (including, in the case of a Chinese director, the Chinese characters for any such forename or surname if they are used by such director);

(b)   any alias;

(c)   his usual residential address;

(d)   his nationality;

(e)   the number of his identity card (if any) or, in the absence of such number, the number and issuing country of any passport held by him; and

(f)   if he holds other directorships in companies incorporated in Hong Kong or registered under Part XI, particulars of each of those directorships.

(3)   The said register shall contain the following particulars with respect to the secretary or, where there are joint secretaries, with respect to each of them-

(a)   in the case of an individual, his present forename and surname and any former forename or surname (including, in the case of a Chinese secretary, the Chinese characters for any such forename or surname if they are used by such secretary), any alias, his usual residential address, his nationality and the number of his identity card (if any) or, in the absence of such number, the number and issuing country of any passport held by him; and

(b)   in the case of a body corporate, its corporate name and registered or principal office:

Provided that, where all the partners in a firm are joint secretaries, the name and principal office of the firm may be stated instead of the said particulars.

(4)   The company shall, within the periods respectively mentioned in subsection (6), send to the Registrar a return in the specified form containing the particulars specified in the said register and a notification in the specified form of any change among its directors or in its secretary or in any of the particulars contained in the register, specifying the date of the change.

(4A) Any listed company formed and registered before the commencement of section 11 of the Companies (Amendment) (No. 2) Ordinance 1993 shall, within 3 months after the commencement of that section, send to the Registrar a return in the specified form containing the particulars mentioned in subsection (2A) with respect to each of its directors.

(5) On the first appointment of a person as director of a company, the company shall send with the said return or notification, as the case may be, a statement in writing, signed by such person, that he has accepted his appointment as such director and that he has attained the age of 18 years; and for the purposes of this subsection "director" does not include a person deemed to be a director under section 153 (2).

(6) The periods referred to in subsection (4) are the following-

    (a)   the period within which the said return is to be sent shall be a period of 14 days from the appointment of the first directors of the company otherwise than by virtue of section 153(2); and

    (b)   the period within which the said notification of a change is to be sent shall be 14 days from the happening thereof.

Provided that, in the case of a company registered before the commencement of the Companies (Amendment) Ordinance 1984, the period within which the said return is to be sent shall be 30 days from that date.

(7) The register to be kept under this section shall during business hours (subject to such reasonable restrictions as the company may by its articles or in general meeting impose, so that not less than 2 hours in each day be allowed for inspection) be open to the inspection of any member of the company without charge and of any other person on payment of $1, or such less sum as the company may prescribe, for each inspection.

(8) If any inspection required under this section is refused or if default is made in complying with subsection (1), (2), (2A), (3), (4), (4A) or (5), the company and every officer of the company who is in default shall be liable to a fine and, for continued default, to a daily default fine.

(9) In the case of any such refusal, the court may by order compel an immediate inspection of the register.

(10) For the purposes of this section-

    (a)   a person in accordance with whose directions or instructions the directors of a company are accustomed to act shall be deemed to be a director and officer of the company;

    (b)   the expression "forename" includes a Christian or given name;

(c)   the expression "identity card" means an identity card issued under the Registration of Persons Ordinance (Cap. 177);

(d)   the expression "residential address" does not include an address at a hotel unless the person to whom it relates is stated, for the purposes of this section, to have no other permanent address, nor does it include a post office box number unless coupled with a residential address;

(e)   in the case of a person usually known by a title different from his surname, the expression "surname" means that title;

(f)   references to a former forename or surname do not include-

   (i)   in the case of a person usually known by a title different from his surname, the name by which he was known previous to the adoption of or succession to the title; or

   (ii)   in the case of any person, a former forename or surname where that forename or surname was changed or disused before the person bearing the name attained the age of 18 years or has been changed or disused for a period of not less than 20 years; or

   (iii)   in the case of a married woman, the name or surname by which she was known previous to the marriage.

Place where register of directors and secretaries may be kept

158A.(1) The register of directors and secretaries of a company shall be kept at its registered office:

Provided that-

(a)   if the work of making it up is done at an office of the company other than the registered office of the company, it may be kept at that other office; and

(b)   if the company arranges with some other person for the making up of the register to be undertaken on behalf of the company by that other person, it may be kept at the office of that other person at which the work is done,

so, however, that it shall not be kept at a place outside Hong Kong.

(2) Every company shall send notice to the Registrar in the specified form of the place where its register of directors and secretaries is kept and of any change in that place:

Provided that a company shall not be bound to send such notice where the register has, at all times since it came into existence or, in the case of a register in existence at the commencement of the

Companies (Amendment) Ordinance 1984, at all times since then, been kept at the registered office of the company.

(3) Where a company makes default in complying with subsection (1) or makes default for 14 days in complying with subsection (2), the company and every officer of the company who is in default shall be liable to a fine and, for continued default, to a daily default fine.

Duty to make disclosure for purposes of section 158

158B.(1) It shall be the duty of any director or secretary of a company to give notice to the company of such matters relating to himself as may be necessary for the purposes of section 158.

(2)   Any person who makes default in complying with subsection (1) shall be liable to a fine.

Registrar to keep an index of directors

158C.(1)   *(a)*   The Registrar shall, as from a date to be appointed by the Registrar by notice in the Gazette, keep and maintain an index of every person who is a director of a company.

(b)   The particulars contained in the index shall, in respect of each director, include his name and address and the latest particulars sent in respect of him to the Registrar, together with the name of each company of which he is a director, whether it is a company incorporated in Hong Kong or registered under Part XI.

(2) The index kept in pursuance of this section shall be open to inspection by any person on payment of the prescribed fee.

Limited company may have directors with unlimited liability

159.(1) In a limited company the liability of the directors or managers, or of the managing director, may, if so provided by the memorandum, be unlimited.

(2) In a limited company in which the liability of a director or manager is unlimited, the directors or managers of the company, if any, and the member who proposes a person for election or appointment to the office of director or manager, shall add to that proposal a statement that the liability of the person holding that office will be unlimited, and the promoters, directors, managers, and secretary, if any, of the company, or one of them, shall, before the person accepts the office or acts therein, give him notice in writing that his liability will be unlimited.

(3) If any director, manager, or proposer makes default in adding such a statement, or if any promoter, director, manager, or secretary makes default in giving such a notice, he shall be liable to a fine, and shall also be liable for any damage which the person so elected or appointed may sustain from the default, but the liability of the person elected or appointed shall not be affected by the default.

Special resolution of limited company making liability of directors unlimited

160.(1) A limited company, if so authorized by its articles, may, by special resolution, alter its memorandum so as to render unlimited the liability of its directors, or managers, or of any managing director.

(2) Upon the passing of any such special resolution the provisions thereof shall be as valid as if they had been originally contained in the memorandum.

Particulars in accounts of directors' emoluments, pensions, etc.

161.(1) In any accounts of a company laid before it in general meeting, or in statement annexed thereto, there shall, subject to and in accordance with the provisions of this section, be shown so far as the information is contained in the company's books and papers or the company has the right to obtain it from the persons concerned-

> *(a)* the aggregate amount of the directors' emoluments;

> *(b)* the aggregate amount of directors' or past directors' pensions; and

> *(c)* the aggregate amount of any compensation to directors or past directors in respect of loss of office.

(2) The amount to be shown under subsection (1)(a)-

> *(a)* shall include any emoluments paid to or receivable by any person in respect of his services as director of the company or in respect of his services, while director of the company, as director of any subsidiary thereof or otherwise in connexion with the management of the affairs of the company or any subsidiary thereof; and

> *(b)* shall distinguish between emoluments in respect of services as director, whether of the company or its subsidiary, and other emoluments;

and for the purposes of this section the expression "emoluments", in relation to a director, includes fees and percentages, any sums paid by way of expenses allowance less amounts actually spent on the expenses for which the allowance was made, any contribution paid in respect of him under any pension scheme and the estimated money value of any other benefits received by him otherwise than in cash.

(3) The amount to be shown under subsection (1)(b)-

> *(a)* shall not include any pension paid or receivable under a pension scheme if the scheme is such that the contributions thereunder are substantially adequate for the maintenance of the scheme, but save as aforesaid shall include any pension paid or receivable in respect of any such services of a director or

past director of the company as are mentioned in subsection (1), whether to or by him or, on his nomination or by virtue of dependence on or other connexion with him, to or by any other person; and

(b) shall distinguish between pensions in respect of services as director, whether of the company or its subsidiary, and other pensions;

and for the purposes of this section the expression "pension" includes any superannuation allowance, superannuation gratuity or similar payment, and the expression "pension scheme" means a scheme for the provision of pensions in respect of services as director or otherwise which is maintained in whole or in part by means of contributions, and the expression "contribution" in relation to a pension scheme means any payment (including an insurance premium) paid for the purposes of the scheme by or in respect of persons rendering services in respect of which pensions will or may become payable under the scheme, except that it does not include any payment in respect of 2 or more persons if the amount paid in respect of each of them is not ascertainable.

(4) The amount to be shown under subsection (1)(c)-

(a) shall include any sums paid to or receivable by a director or past director by way of compensation for the loss of office as director of the company or for the loss, while director of the company or on or in connexion with his ceasing to be a director of the company, of any other office in connexion with the management of the company's affairs or of any office as director or otherwise in connexion with the management of the affairs of any subsidiary thereof; and

(b) shall distinguish between compensation in respect of the office of director, whether of the company or its subsidiary, and compensation in respect of other offices;

and for the purposes of this section references to compensation for loss of office shall include sums paid as consideration for or in connexion with a person's retirement from office.

(5) The amounts to be shown under each paragraph of subsection (1)-

(a) shall include all relevant sums paid by or receivable from-

(i) the company; and

(ii) the company's subsidiaries; and

(iii) any other person;

except sums to be accounted for to the company or any of its subsidiaries or, by virtue of section 163B(3), to past or present members of the company or any of its subsidiaries or any class of those members; and

(b) shall distinguish, in the case of the amount to be shown under subsection (1)(c), between the sums respectively paid by or receivable from the company, the company's subsidiaries and persons other than the company and its subsidiaries.

(6) The amounts to be shown under this section for any financial year shall be the sum receivable in respect of that year, whenever paid, or, in the case of sums not receivable in respect of a period, the sums paid during that year, so, however, that where any sums are not shown in the accounts for the relevant financial year on the ground that the person receiving them is liable to account therefor as mentioned in subsection (5)(a), but the liability is thereafter wholly or partly released or is not enforced within a period of 2 years, those sums shall, to the extent to which the liability is released or not enforced, be shown in the first accounts in which it is practicable to show them or in a statement annexed thereto, and shall be distinguished from the amounts to be shown therein apart from this provision.

(7) Where it is necessary so to do for the purpose of making any distinction required by this section in any amount to be shown thereunder, the directors may apportion any payments between the matters in respect of which they have been paid or are receivable in such manner as they think appropriate.

(8) If in the case of any accounts the requirements of this section are not complied with, it shall be the duty of the auditors of the company by whom the accounts are examined to include in their report thereon, so far as they are reasonably able to do so, a statement giving the required particulars.

(9) In this section any reference to a company's subsidiary-

(a) in relation to a person who is or was, while a director of the company, a director also, by virtue of the company's nomination, direct or indirect, of any other body corporate, shall, subject to paragraph (b), include that body corporate, whether or not it is or was in fact the company's subsidiary; and

(b) shall for the purposes of subsections (2) and (3) be taken as referring to a subsidiary at the time the services were rendered, and for the purposes of subsection (4) be taken as referring to a subsidiary immediately before the loss of office as director of the company.

Statements annexed to accounts showing certain items to include corresponding amounts for preceding financial year

161A.(1) Where an item required by section 161 to be shown in a company's accounts or in a statement annexed is, in the case of a financial year, shown in such a statement, the corresponding amount for the immediately preceding financial year shall be included in that statement.

(2) If any person being a director of a company fails to take all reasonable steps to secure compliance with the provisions of subsection (1), he shall, in respect of each offence, be liable to imprisonment and a fine:

Provided that-

(a)   in any proceedings against a person in respect of an offence under this section, it shall be a defence to prove that he had reasonable ground to believe and did believe that a competent and reliable person was charged with the duty of seeing that the provisions of subsection (1) were complied with and was in a position to discharge that duty; and

(b)   a person shall not be sentenced to imprisonment for any such offence unless, in the opinion of the court dealing with the case, the offence was committed wilfully.

Particulars in accounts of loans to officers, etc.

161B.(1) The accounts which, under this Ordinance, are to be laid before a company in general meeting shall, subject to this section, contain the following particulars of every relevant loan made by the company after the commencement of the Companies (Amendment) Ordinance 1984 -

(a)   the name of the borrower and, if this subsection applies to a loan-

   (i)   by reason of the borrower's being connected with a director of the company or of its holding company; or

   (ii)   where the borrower is a body corporate, by reason of the fact that a director of the company or a person connected with him has held (jointly or severally or directly or indirectly) a controlling interest therein,

   the name of that director;

(b)   the terms of the loan, including the rate of interest and the security therefor, if any;

(c)   the amount outstanding on the loan, in respect of principal and interest, at the beginning and at the end of the company's financial year and the maximum amount so outstanding during that financial year; and

(d)   the amount of interest which, having fallen due, has not been paid and the amount of any provision (within the meaning of the Tenth Schedule) made in respect of any failure or anticipated failure by the borrower to repay the whole or part of the loan or to pay the whole or part of any interest thereon.

(2)   The accounts referred to in subsection (1) shall contain the particulars specified in subsection (3) of every guarantee entered into and of every security provided by the company in respect of which the following conditions are satisfied-

> *(a)*   the guarantee was entered into, or the security provided, by the company in connexion with a relevant loan made by any person after the commencement of the Companies (Amendment) Ordinance 1984; and

> *(b)*   the liability of the company in respect of the guarantee or security has not been discharged before the beginning of the financial year.

(3)   The particulars referred to in subsection (2) are-

> *(a)*   in respect of the relevant loan in connexion with which the guarantee is entered into or the security provided, the name of the borrower and, if subsection (2) applies to the guarantee or security-

>> **(i)**   by reason of the borrower's being connected with a director of the company or of its holding company; or

>> **(ii)**   where the borrower is a body corporate, by reason of the fact that a director of the company or a person connected with him has held (jointly or severally or directly or indirectly) a controlling interest therein,

> the name of that director;

> *(b)*   the maximum liability of the company under the guarantee or in respect of the security both at the beginning and at the end of the financial year;

> *(c)*   any amount paid and any liability incurred by the company for the purpose of fulfilling the guarantee or discharging the security (including any loss incurred by the company by reason of the enforcement of the guarantee or security).

(4)   As respects any transaction referred to in this subsection which is entered into after the commencement of the Companies (Amendment) Ordinance 1984 by a subsidiary of a company to which section 124 applies, group accounts prepared by the company under that section (or, where group accounts are not so prepared by virtue of subsection (2) of that section, the accounts of the company prepared under section 122) shall contain particulars showing-

> *(a)*   the amount of any loan made to an officer of the company (whether or not he was an officer of the company at the time the loan was made) by the subsidiary, and-

(i)   the name of the officer;

(ii)   the terms of the loan including the rate of interest and the security therefor;

(iii)   the amount outstanding on the loan, in respect of principal and interest, at the beginning and at the end of the company's financial year and the maximum amount so outstanding during that financial year; and

(iv)   the amount of interest which, having fallen due, has not been paid and the amount of any provision (within the meaning of the Tenth Schedule) made in respect of any failure or anticipated failure by the officer to repay the whole or part of the loan or to pay the whole or part of any interest therein; and

(b)   the amount of any loan made by any other person to an officer of the company (whether or not he was an officer of the company at the time the loan was made) under a guarantee from or on a security provided by the subsidiary in respect of which the liability of the subsidiary has not been discharged before the beginning of the company's financial year, and-

(i)   the name of the officer;

(ii)   the maximum liability of the subsidiary under the guarantee or in respect of the security both at the beginning and at the end of the financial year; and

(iii)   any amount paid and any liability incurred by the subsidiary for the purpose of fulfilling the guarantee or discharging the security (including any loss incurred by the subsidiary by reason of the enforcement of the guarantee or security),

being a loan which either is made during the company's financial year or, if made before it, is outstanding at any time during that financial year.

(4A)   Except as provided in subsections (4B) and (4C), this section shall not require the inclusion in accounts prepared by a company which is, or is the holding company of, an authorized financial institution of particulars of any loan made to any person by the authorized financial institution or of any guarantee entered into or security provided by the authorized financial institution in connection with a loan made to any person if, but only if, either of the following conditions is satisfied-

(a)   the amount of the loan or the amount guaranteed or secured is not greater, and the terms of the transaction are not more favourable in the case of that person than that or those which it is reasonable to expect the authorized financial institution to have offered to or in respect of a person of the same financial standing as that person but unconnected with the authorized financial institution; or

(b)   where the transaction in question does not fall within paragraph (a), the aggregate of the following amounts does not exceed $10,000,000 or an amount equivalent to 10 per cent of the paid up capital and reserves of the authorized financial institution, whichever is the lower-

    (i)   the maximum amount outstanding, in respect of principal and interest, during the financial year on all loans (other than loans falling within paragraph (a)) made by the authorized financial institution to that person; and

    (ii)   the amount representing the maximum liability of the authorized financial institution during the financial year under all guarantees entered into and in respect of every security provided by the authorized financial institution (not being transactions falling within paragraph (a)) in connection with loans made to that person.

(4B)   In the case of a company which is an authorized financial institution, the accounts of the company shall contain a statement showing-

(a)   the aggregate of the following amounts as at the end of the financial year-

    (i)   the amount outstanding, in respect of principal and interest, on every relevant load made after 31 August 1984 by the company; and

    (ii)   the amount representing the maximum liability of the company under all guarantees entered into, and in respect of any security provided, by that company in connection with any relevant loan made after 31 August 1984 by any person; and

(b)   the maximum aggregate of the amounts referred to in paragraph (a) that obtained at any time during the financial year.

(4C)   In the case of a company which is the holding company of an authorized financial institution the accounts (or, if group accounts are required to be prepared under section 124 dealing with the authorized financial institution, the group accounts) of the company shall contain a statement showing-

(a)   the aggregate of the following amounts as at the end of the financial year-

    (i)   the amount outstanding, in respect of principal and interest, on every loan made to an officer of the company (whether or not he was an officer of the company at the time the loan was made) after 31 August 1984 by the authorized financial institution; and

   (ii) the amount representing the maximum liability of the authorized financial institution under all guarantees entered into, and in respect of any security provided, by that authorized financial institution in connection with any loan made to an officer of the company (whether or not he was an officer of the company at the time the loan was made) after 31 August 1984 by any person; and

  (b) the maximum aggregate of the amounts referred to in paragraph (a) that obtained during the financial year.

(5) This section shall not require the inclusion in accounts of particulars of any loan made by a company or a subsidiary thereof to an employee of the company or subsidiary, as the case may be, if the loan-

  (a) does not exceed $100,000 and is certified by the directors of the company or subsidiary, as the case may be, to have been made in accordance with any practice adopted or about to be adopted by the company or subsidiary with respect to loans to its employees; and

  (b) is not a loan made by the company under a guarantee from or on a security provided by a subsidiary thereof or a loan made by a subsidiary of the company under a guarantee from or on a security provided by the company or any other subsidiary thereof.

(6) If in the case of any such accounts as aforesaid the requirements of this section are not complied with, it shall be the duty of the auditors of the company by whom the accounts are examined to include in their report thereon, so far as they are reasonably able to do so, a statement giving the required particulars.

(7) In this section "relevant loan" means any loan made to-

  (a) a person who, whether or not he was an officer of the company or a director of its holding company at the time the loan was made, is such an officer or director at any time during the financial year in respect of which the accounts are made up; or

  (b) a body corporate in which a director of the company, at any time during the financial year, held (jointly or severally or directly or indirectly) a controlling interest, whether or not such controlling interest was so held at the time the loan was made; or

  (c) in the case of a loan made by a company referred to in section 157H(9)(a) or (b), a person who is-

    (i) a person connected with a director of the company at any time during the financial year when the loan is outstanding; or

225

(ii) a person connected with a director of the company's holding company at any such time; or

(iii) a body corporate in which a person referred to in sub-paragraph (i), at any time during the financial year, held (jointly or severally or directly or indirectly) a controlling interest,

whether or not he was such a person or such controlling interest was so held at the time the loan was made,

being a loan which either is made during that financial year or, if made before it, is outstanding at any time during that financial year.

(7A) In this section and in sections 161BA and 161C "company" means-

(a) a company; or

(b) any other body corporate incorporated in Hong Kong under an Ordinance.

(8) For the purposes of this section, a person is connected with a director of a company if, but only if, he is-

(a) that director's spouse, child or step-child; or

(b) a person acting in his capacity as the trustee (other than as trustee under an employees' share scheme or a pension scheme) of any trust the beneficiaries of which include the director, his spouse or any of his children or step-children or the terms of which confer a power on the trustees that may be exercised for the benefit of the director, his spouse or any of his children or step-children; or

(c) a person acting in his capacity as partner of that director or of any person who by virtue of paragraph (a) or (b) is connected with that director;

and in this subsection a reference to the child or step-child of any person shall include a reference to any illegitimate child of that person, but shall not include a reference to any person who has attained the age of 18 years.

(9) References in subsections (4) and (5) to a subsidiary shall be taken as referring to a subsidiary at the end of the company's financial year (whether or not a subsidiary at the date of the loan).

(10) In the case of any loans made before the commencement of the Companies (Amendment) Ordinance 1984, the accounts for any financial year of a company shall contain in respect of any such loan outstanding at the end of the financial year the particulars which, but for that Ordinance, would have had to be contained in the accounts under the provisions of this section in force immediately before the commencement of that Ordinance.

Further provisions relating to loans to officers, etc. of authorized financial institutions

161BA.(1) A Company which is, or is the holding company of, an authorized financial institution shall maintain a register containing a copy of every agreement in writing relating to any transaction (or if no such document exists, a written memorandum setting out the terms of any transaction) of which particulars would, but for section 161B(4A), be required by section 161B to be shown in the accounts of the company (including group accounts) in respect of each financial year, and such copies (or memoranda) shall be retained in the register for a period of 10 years.

(2) A company which is an authorized financial institution shall before its annual general meeting make available, at the place where its register of members is kept, for a period of not less than 14 days ending on the date of the meeting and for a period of 7 days thereafter, for inspection by members of the public a statement containing the particulars of transactions which the company would, but for section 161B(4A), be required by section 161B to include in its accounts for the financial year preceding that annual general meeting (or if there are no such transactions, a statement to that effect), and such a statement shall also be made available for inspection by members of the company at the annual general meeting.

(3) It shall be the duty of the auditors of the company by whom the accounts are examined to examine the statement referred to in subsection (2) before it is made available for inspection and to make a report on the statement; and a copy of the report shall be annexed to the statement before it is so made available.

(4) A report under subsection (3) shall state whether in the opinion of the auditors the statement contains the particulars required by subsection (2) and where their opinion is that it does not, they shall include in the report, so far as they are reasonably able to do so, a statement giving the required particulars.

(5) A company which is an authorized financial institution shall give public notice of the date of its annual general meeting in, respectively, an English language newspaper and a Chinese language newspaper specified in a list of newspapers issued for the purposes of section 71A by the Secretary for Administrative Services and Information and published in the Gazette.

(6) The notice referred to in subsection (5) shall be published not less than 28 days before the date of the meeting.

(7) If any person being a director of a company fails to take all reasonable steps to secure compliance by the company with the requirements of this section, or has by his own willful act been the cause of any default by the company thereunder, he shall be liable on conviction to imprisonment and a fine.

(8) As respects an offence under this section-

    (a)   in any proceedings against a person in respect of such an offence consisting of a failure to take reasonable steps to secure compliance by the company

with the requirements of this section, it shall be a defence to prove that he had reasonable ground to believe and did believe that a competent and reliable person was charged with the duty of seeing that those requirements were complied with and was in a position to discharge that duty; and

(b)   a person shall not be sentenced to imprisonment for such an offence unless, in the opinion of the court dealing with the case, the offence was committed wilfully.

(9)   The statement referred to in subsection (2) shall be made available for inspection during business hours (subject to such reasonable restrictions as the company may by its articles or in general meeting impose, so that not less than 2 hours in each day be allowed for inspection) by any member of the company, without charge and by any other person on payment of $5, or such less sum as the company may prescribe, for each inspection.

(10)   Any member of the company or other person may require a copy of the statement referred to in subsection (2), or any part thereof, on payment of 25 cents, or such less sum as the company may prescribe, for every 100 words or fractional part thereof required to be copied. The company shall cause any copy so required by any person to be sent to that person within a period of 10 days commencing on the day next after the day on which the requirement is received by the company.

(11)   If any inspection required under this section is refused or if any copy required under this section is not sent within the proper period, the company and every officer of the company who is in default shall be liable to a fine and, for continued default, to a daily default fine.

(12)   In the case of any such refusal or default, the court may by order compel an immediate inspection of the statement or direct that the copies required shall be sent to the person requiring them.

General duty to make disclosure for purposes of sections 161 and 161B

161C.(1) It shall be the duty of any director of a company to give notice in writing to the company of such matters relating to himself as may be necessary for the purposes of section 161 and of section 161B except so far as it relates to loans made, by the company or by any other person under a guarantee from or on a security provided by the company, to an officer thereof.

(2)   Subsection (1) shall apply-

(a)   for the purposes of section 161B, in relation to officers other than directors; and

(b)   for the purposes of sections 161 and 161B, in relation to persons who are or have at any time during the preceding 5 years been officers,

as it applies in relation to directors.

(3) Any person who makes default in complying with this section shall be liable to a fine.

Disclosure by directors of material interests in contracts

162.(1) Any director of a company who is in any way, directly or indirectly, interested in a contract or proposed contract with the company shall, if his interest in such contract or proposed contract is material, declare the nature of his interest at the earliest meeting of the directors at which it is practicable for him so to do notwithstanding that the question of entering into the contract is not taken into consideration at that meeting.

(2) Where a director gives to the directors of a company a general notice stating that, by reason of facts specified in the notice, he is to be regarded as interested in contracts of any description which may subsequently be made by the company, that notice shall be deemed for the purposes of this section to be a sufficient declaration of his interest, so far as attributable to those facts, in relation to any contract of that description which may subsequently be made by the company; but no such general notice shall have effect in relation to any contract unless it is given before the date on which the question of entering into the contract is first taken into consideration on behalf of the company.

(3) Any director who fails to comply with the provisions of this section shall be liable to a fine:

Provided that in a prosecution for an offence under this section in relation to any contract, it shall be a defence if the person charged with the offence proves that he had no knowledge of the contract and that he could not reasonably have been expected to have had such knowledge.

(4) In the foregoing provisions of this section "contract", in relation to a company, means a contract which is of significance in relation to the company's business.

(5) Nothing in this section shall be taken to prejudice the operation of any rule of law restricting directors of a company from having any interest in contracts with the company.

Special provision relating to management contracts

162A.(1) Where a company enters into any contract, other than a contract of service with any director or any person engaged in the full-time employment of the company, whereby any individual, firm or body corporate undertakes the management and administration of the whole or any substantial part of any business of the company-

    (a) there shall be included in the directors' report for any year in which the contract is in force a statement of the existence and duration of the contract and the name of any director interested therein; and

    (b) a copy of the contract shall be made available for inspection by the members of the company at each annual general meeting held during the period of the contract.

(2) If default is made in complying with this section, the company and every officer of the company who is in default shall be liable to a fine and, for continued default, to a daily default fine.

Approval of company requisite for payment by it to director or past director for loss of office etc.

163. It shall not be lawful for a company to make to any director or past director of the company any payment by way of compensation for loss of office, or as consideration for or in connexion with his retirement from office, without particulars with respect to the proposed payment (including the amount thereof) being disclosed to the members of the company and the proposal being approved by the company.

Approval of company requisite for any payment, in connexion with transfer of its property, to director or past director for loss of office etc.

163A.(1) It is hereby declared that it is not lawful in connexion with the transfer of the whole or any part of the undertaking or property of a company for any payment to be made to any director or past director of the company by way of compensation for loss of office, or as consideration for or in connexion with his retirement from office, without particulars with respect to the proposed payment (including the amount thereof) being disclosed to the members of the company and the proposal being approved by the company.

(2) Where a payment which is hereby declared to be illegal is made to a director or past director of the company, the amount received shall be deemed to have been received by him in trust for the company.

Duty of director or past director to disclose payment for loss of office, etc., made in connexion with transfer of shares in company

163B.(1) Where, in connexion with the transfer to any persons of all or any of the shares in a company, being a transfer resulting from-

    (a) an offer made to the general body of shareholders;

    (b) an offer made by or on behalf of some other body corporate with a view to the company becoming its subsidiary or a subsidiary of its holding company;

    (c) an offer made by or on behalf of an individual with a view to his obtaining the right to exercise or control the exercise of not less than one-third of the voting power at any general meeting of the company; or

    (d) any other offer which is conditional on acceptance to a given extent,

a payment is to be made to a director or past director of the company by way of compensation for loss of office, or as consideration for or in connexion with his retirement from office, it shall be the duty of that director or past director to take all reasonable steps to secure that particulars with respect to the proposed payment (including the amount thereof) shall be included in or sent with any notice of the offer made for their shares which is given to any shareholders.

(2)   If-

        (a)   any such director or past director fails to take reasonable steps as aforesaid; or

        (b)   any person who has been properly required by any such director or past director to include the said particulars in or send them with any such notice as aforesaid fails so to do,

he shall be liable to a fine.

(3)   If-

        (a)   the requirements of subsection (1) are not complied with in relation to any such payment as is therein mentioned; or

        (b)   the making of the proposed payment is not, before the transfer of any shares in pursuance of the offer, approved by a meeting summoned for the purpose of the holders of the shares to which the offer relates and of other holders of shares of the same class as any of the said shares,

any sum received by the director or past director on account of the payment shall be deemed to have been received by him in trust for any persons who have sold their shares as a result of the offer made, and the expenses incurred by him in distributing that sum amongst those persons shall be borne by him and not retained out of that sum.

(4)   Subject to section 163D(4), where the shareholders referred to in subsection (3)(b) are not all the members of the company and no provision is made by the articles for summoning or regulating such a meeting as is mentioned in that paragraph, the provisions of this Ordinance and of the company's articles relating to general meetings of the company shall, for that purpose, apply to the meeting either without modification or with such modifications as the court on the application of any person concerned may direct for the purpose of adapting them to the circumstances of the meeting.

(5)   If at a meeting summoned for the purpose of approving any payment as required by subsection (3)(b) a quorum is not present and, after the meeting has been adjourned to a later date, a quorum is again not present, the payment shall be deemed for the purposes of that subsection to have been approved.

Approval of company requisite for payment of damages or pension to director or past director in certain cases

163C.(1) It shall not be lawful for a company to make to any director or past director of the company any payment by way of damages or pension referred to in section 163D(3)(b) if the company makes or has made to that director any payment to which section 163, 163A or 163B applies, without particulars with respect to the proposed payment of damages or pension (including the amount thereof) being disclosed to the members of the company and the proposal being approved by the company; and for the purposes of this section "pension" has the same meaning as it has for the purposes of section 163D(3)(b).

(2) Where a payment which is hereby declared to be illegal is made to a director or past director of the company, the amount received shall be deemed to have been received by him in trust for the company.

Provisions supplementary to sections 163, 163A, 163B and 163C

163D.(1) Where in proceedings for the recovery of any payment as having, by virtue of subsections (1) and (2) of section 163A or subsections (1) and (3) of section 163B, been received by any person in trust, it is shown that-

> *(a)* the payment was made in pursuance of any arrangement entered into as part of the agreement for the transfer in question or within 1 year before or 2 years after that agreement or the offer leading thereto; and

> *(b)* the company or any person to whom the transfer was made was privy to that arrangement,

the payment shall be deemed, except in so far as the contrary is shown, to be one to which the subsections apply.

(2) If in connexion with any such transfer as is mentioned in section 163A or 163B-

> *(a)* the price to be paid to a director of the company whose office is to be abolished or who is to retire from office for any shares in the company held by him is in excess of the price which could at the time have been obtained by other holders of the like shares; or

> *(b)* any valuable consideration is given to any such director,

the excess or the money value of the consideration, as the case may be, shall, for the purposes of that section, be deemed to have been a payment made to him by way of compensation for loss of office or as consideration for or in connexion with his retirement from office.

(3) References in sections 163, 163A and 163B to payments to any director of a company by way of compensation for loss of office, or as consideration for or in connexion with his retirement from office-

    (a)   include any such payments to him in respect of the loss of or retirement from his office as director of the company or in respect of the loss or retirement, while a director of the company or on or in connexion with his ceasing to be a director of the company, of or from-

        (i)   any other office in connexion with the management of the company's affairs; or

        (ii)   any office as director or otherwise in connexion with the management of the affairs of any subsidiary of the company; but

    (b)   do not include any bona fide payment by way of damages for breach of contract or by way of pension in respect of past services; and for the purposes of this paragraph "pension" includes any superannuation allowance, superannuation gratuity or similar payment.

(4)   The following provisions shall apply in relation to any meeting of a company and any meeting referred to in section 163B(3)(b) summoned for the purpose of approving any payment as required by section 163, 163A, 163B or163C-

    (a)   the notice convening the meeting shall give full particulars with respect to such payment, including the amount thereof;

    (b)   the approval of the company for any such payment shall be given by ordinary resolution;

    (c)   any director to whom it is proposed to make any such payment, and any person who holds any shares in the company in trust for him, shall not be entitled to vote on any resolution to approve such payment or any other payment in respect of which approval is required by section 163, 163A, 163B or 163C, nor shall the director or such person, if any, be counted in determining whether a quorum is present at the meeting.

(5)   Nothing in sections 163A, 163B and 163C shall be taken to prejudice the operation of any rule of law requiring disclosure to be made with respect to any such payments as are therein mentioned or with respect to any other like payments made or to be made to the directors of a company.

(6)   References in this section to a director include references to a past director.

Provisions as to assignment of office by directors

164.(1) If in the case of any company provision is made by the articles or by any agreement entered into between any person and the company for empowering a director or managing agent of the company to assign his office as such to another person, any assignment of office made in pursuance of the said provision shall, notwithstanding anything to the contrary contained in the said provision, be of no effect unless and until it is approved by a special resolution of the company.

(2) It shall be the duty of a company which is the managing agent of another company to notify forthwith to that other company-

> *(a)* any change in the control of such first-mentioned company;
>
> *(b)* any material change in the composition of the board of directors of such first-mentioned company.

(3) Notwithstanding anything in any agreement providing for the appointment of a company as the managing agent of another company, where that other company is notified under subsection (2)(a) that a change in the control of such first-mentioned company has occurred and, at the same time or thereafter, is notified under subsection (2)(b) that a material change in the composition of the board of directors of such first-mentioned company has also occurred, such agreement may be terminated by that other company at any time within 1 month after being so notified under subsection (2)(b).

(4) For the purposes of this section "material change", in relation to the composition of the board of directors of a company, means any change whereby more than half of the number of directors of the company cease to be directors.

Avoidance of Provisions in Articles or Contracts relieving Officers from Liability

Provisions as to liability of officers and auditors

165. Subject as hereinafter provided, any provision, whether contained in the articles of a company or in any contract with a company or otherwise, for exempting any officer of the company, or any person employed by the company as auditor from, or indemnifying him against, any liability which by virtue of any rule of law would otherwise attach to him in respect of any negligence, default, breach of duty or breach of trust of which he may be guilty in relation to the company shall be void:

Provided that-

> *(a)* *(Repealed)*
>
> *(b)* nothing in this section shall operate to deprive any person of any exemption or right to be indemnified in respect of anything done or omitted to be done by him while any such provision was in force; and
>
> *(c)* notwithstanding anything in this section, a company may, in pursuance of any such provision as aforesaid, indemnify any such officer or auditor against any liability incurred by him in defending any proceedings, whether civil or criminal, in which judgment is given in his favour or in which he is acquitted or in connexion with any application under section 358 in which relief is granted to him by the court.

Companies Ordinance

Arrangements and Reconstructions

Power to compromise with creditors and members

166.(1) Where a compromise or arrangement is proposed between a company and its creditors or any class of them, or between the company and its members or any class of them, the court may, on the application in a summary way of the company or of any creditor or member of the company, or, in the case of a company being wound up, of the liquidator, order a meeting of the creditors or class of creditors, or of the members of the company or class of members, as the case may be, to be summoned in such manner as the court directs.

(2) If a majority in number representing three-fourths in value of the creditors or class of creditors, or members or class of members, as the case may be, present and voting either in person or by proxy at the meeting, agree to any compromise or arrangement, the compromise or arrangement shall, if sanctioned by the court, be binding on all the creditors or the class of creditors, or on the members or class of members, as the case may be, and also on the company or, in the case of a company in the course of being wound up, on the liquidator and contributories of the company.

(3) An order made under subsection (2) shall have no effect until an office copy of the order has been delivered to the Registrar for registration, and a copy of every such order shall be annexed to every copy of the memorandum of the company issued after the order has been made, or, in the case of a company not having a memorandum, of every copy so issued of the instrument constituting or defining the constitution of the company.

(4) If a company makes default in complying with subsection (3), the company and every officer of the company who is in default shall be liable to a fine for each copy in respect of which default is made.

(5) In this section and in section 166A, the expression "company" means any company liable to be wound up under this Ordinance, and the expression "arrangement" includes a re-organization of the share capital of the company by the consolidation of shares of different classes or by the division of shares into shares of different classes or by both those methods.

Information as to compromises with creditors and members

166A.(1) Where a meeting of creditors or any class of creditors or of members or any class of members is summoned under section 166 there shall-

    (a)   with every notice summoning the meeting which is sent to a creditor or member, be sent also a statement explaining the effect of the compromise or arrangement and in particular stating any material interests of the directors of the company, whether as directors or as members or as creditors of the company or otherwise, and the effect thereon of the compromise or arrangement, in so far as it is different from the effect on the like interests of other persons; and

(b)   in every notice summoning the meeting which is given by advertisement, be included either such a statement as aforesaid or a notification of the place at which and the manner in which creditors or members entitled to attend the meeting may obtain copies of such a statement as aforesaid.

(2)   Where the compromise or arrangement affects the rights of debenture holders of the company, the said statement shall give the like explanation as respects the trustees of any deed for securing the issue of the debentures as it is required to give as respects the company's directors.

(3)   Where a notice given by advertisement includes a notification that copies of a statement explaining the effect of the compromise or arrangement proposed can be obtained by creditors or members entitled to attend the meeting, every such creditor or member shall, on making application in the manner indicated by the notice, be furnished by the company free of charge with a copy of the statement.

(4)   Where a company makes default in complying with any requirement of this section, the company and every officer of the company who is in default shall be liable to a fine, and for the purpose of this subsection any liquidator of the company and any trustee of a deed for securing the issue of debentures of the company shall be deemed to be an officer of the company:

Provided that a person shall not be liable under this subsection if that person shows that the default was due to the refusal of any other person, being a director or trustee for debenture holders, to supply the necessary particulars as to his interests.

(5)   It shall be the duty of any director of the company and of any trustee for debenture holders of the company to give notice to the company of such matters relating to himself as may be necessary for the purposes of this section, and any person who makes default in complying with this subsection shall be liable to a fine.

Provisions for facilitating reconstruction and amalgamation of companies

(1)   Where an application is made to the court under section 166 for the sanctioning of a compromise or arrangement proposed between a company and any such persons as are mentioned in that section, and it is shown to the court that the compromise or arrangement has been proposed for the purposes of or in connexion with a scheme for the reconstruction of any company or companies or the amalgamation of any 2 or more companies, and that under the scheme the whole or any part of the undertaking or the property of any company concerned in the scheme (in this section referred to as a transferor company) is to be transferred to another company (in this section referred to as the transferee company), the court may, either by the order sanctioning the compromise or arrangement or by any subsequent order, make provision for all or any of the following matters-

(a)   the transfer to the transferee company of the whole or any part of the undertaking and of the property or liabilities of any transferor company;

(b)   the allotting or appropriation by the transferee company of any shares, debentures, policies, or other like interests in that company which under the compromise or arrangement are to be allotted or appropriated by that company to or for any person;

(c)   the continuation by or against the transferee company of any legal proceedings pending by or against any transferor company;

(d)   the dissolution, without winding up, of any transferor company;

(e)   the provision to be made for any persons, who within such time and in such manner as the court may direct, dissent from the compromise or arrangement;

(f)   such incidental, consequential and supplemental matters as are necessary to secure that the reconstruction or amalgamation shall be fully and effectively carried out.

(2)   Where an order under this section provides for the transfer of property or liabilities, that property shall, by virtue of the order, be transferred to and vest in, and those liabilities shall, by virtue of the order, be transferred to and become the liabilities of, the transferee company, and in the case of any property, if the order so directs, freed from any charge which is by virtue of the compromise or arrangement to cease to have effect.

(3)   Where an order is made under this section, every company in relation to which the order is made shall cause an office copy thereof to be delivered to the Registrar for registration within 7 days after the making of the order, and if default is made in complying with this subsection, the company and every officer of the company who is in default shall be liable to a fine and, for continued default, to a daily default fine.

(4)   In this section, the expression "property" includes property, rights and powers of every description, and the expression "liabilities" includes duties.

(5)   Notwithstanding the provisions of section 166(5), the expression company in this section does not include any company other than a company within the meaning of this Ordinance.

Rights of company and minority shareholders in case of successful take-over offer

168.(1) This section and the Ninth Schedule shall apply where a company (in this section and the Ninth Schedule referred to as "the transferee company"), whether a company within the meaning of this Ordinance or not, makes an offer to acquire all the shares, or all the shares of any class or classes, not already held by it in another company (in the Ninth Schedule referred to as "the transferor company") on terms which are the same in relation to all the shares to which the offer relates or, where those shares include shares of different classes, in relation to all the shares of each class.

(2)   This section and the Ninth Schedule shall apply in relation to debentures convertible into shares or any rights to subscribe for shares as if those debentures or rights were shares of a separate class, and references to shares, the shareholder and a share warrant shall be construed accordingly.

(3)   For the purposes of this section and the Ninth Schedule-

(a)   shares held or acquired-

(i)   by a nominee on behalf of the transferee company; or

(ii)   where the transferee company is a member of a group of companies, by, or by a nominee on behalf of, a company which is a member of the same group of companies,

shall be treated as held or acquired by the transferee company;

(b)   where an offer referred to in subsection (1) relates to debentures convertible into shares, such debentures shall be treated as so convertible whether or not any rights of conversion thereunder are exercisable at the time of the offer or at any time thereafter, and whether or not they are contingent upon the happening of any event; and such debentures shall, if such rights are exercisable at the time of the offer, be treated as shares to which such rights relate;

(c)   references to value are references to nominal value or, in relation to debentures convertible into shares, the amount payable on such debentures.

(4)   In relation to a case where an offer in respect of any scheme or contract involving the transfer of shares in a company to another company was made before the commencement of the Companies (Amendment) Ordinance 1984, the provisions of this section in force immediately before the commencement of that Ordinance shall continue to have effect as if that Ordinance had not been enacted.

Minorities

Alternative remedy to winding up in cases of unfair prejudice

168A.(1) Any member of a company who complains that the affairs of the company are being or have been conducted in a manner unfairly prejudicial to the interests of the members generally or of some part of the members (including himself) or, in a case falling within section 147(2)(b), the Financial Secretary, may make an application to the court by petition for an order under this section.

(2)   If on any petition under this section the court is of opinion that the company's affairs are being or have been conducted in a manner unfairly prejudicial to the interests of the members generally or of some part of the members, whether or not such conduct consists of an isolated act or a series of acts, the court may, with a view to bringing to an end the matters complained of-

(a)   make an order restraining the commission of any such act or the continuance of such conduct;

(b)   order that such proceedings as the court may think fit shall be brought in the name of the company against such person and on such terms as the court may so order;

(ba)   appoint a receiver or manager of the whole or a part of a company's property

or business and may specify the powers and duties of the receiver or manager and fix his remuneration;

    (c)   make such other order as it thinks fit, whether for regulating the conduct of the company's affairs in future, or for the purchase of the shares of any members of the company by other members of the company or by the company and, in the case of a purchase by the company, for the reduction accordingly of the company's capital, or otherwise.

(3) Where an order under this section makes any alteration in or addition to the memorandum or articles of a company, then, notwithstanding anything in any other provision of this Ordinance but subject to the provisions of the order, the company shall not have power without the leave of the court to make any further alteration in or addition to the memorandum or articles inconsistent with the provisions of the order; but, subject to the provisions of this subsection, the alterations or additions made by the order shall be of the same effect as if duly made by resolution of the company and the provisions of this Ordinance shall apply to the memorandum or articles as so altered or added to accordingly.

(4) An office copy of any order under this section altering or adding to, or giving leave to alter or add to, a company's memorandum or articles shall, within 14 days after the making thereof, be delivered by the company to the Registrar for registration; and if a company makes default in complying with this subsection, the company and every officer of the company who is in default shall be liable to a fine and, for continued default, to a daily default fine.

(5) The personal representative of a person who, at the date of his death, was a member of a company, or any trustee of, or person beneficially interested in, the shares of a company by virtue of the will or intestacy of any such person, may apply to the court under subsection (1) for an order under this section and, accordingly, any reference in that subsection to a member of a company shall be construed as including a reference to any such personal representative, trustee or person beneficially interested.

(6) Section 296 shall apply in relation to a petition under this section as it applies in relation to a winding-up petition.

Rights of company and minority shareholders in case of successful buy out by share repurchase

168B. The Thirteenth Schedule shall apply where a company (in that Schedule referred to as the "repurchasing company") makes a general offer to purchase all of its shares, or all of its shares of a particular class.

PART IVA - DISQUALIFICATION OF DIRECTORS

Interpretation

168C.(1)   In this Part-

"company" means -

> *(a)*   a company within the meaning of section 2; or

> *(b)*   an unregistered company within the meaning of Part X (other than a partnership, whether limited or not or an association) -

>> **(i)**   wherever incorporated;

>> **(ii)**   carrying on business in Hong Kong or which has carried on business in Hong Kong; and

>> **(iii)**   which is capable of being wound up under this Ordinance;

"Official Receiver" means the Official Receiver appointed under the Bankruptcy Ordinance (Cap. 6);

"shadow director" in relation to a company, means a person in accordance with whose directions or instructions the directors of a company are accustomed to act but a person shall not be considered to be a shadow director by reason only that the directors act on advice given by him in a professional capacity.

(2)   *Repealed*

Disqualification orders: general

168D.(1) In the circumstances specified in this Part, a court may, and under section 168H shall, make against a person a disqualification order, that is to say an order that he shall not, without leave of the court-

> *(a)*   be a director of a company;

> *(b)*   be a liquidator of a company;

> *(c)*   be a receiver or manager of a company's property; or

> *(d)*   in any way, whether directly or indirectly, be concerned or take part in the promotion, formation or management of a company,
> for a specified period beginning with the date of the order.

(2) In each section which gives to a court power or, as the case may be, imposes on it the duty to make a disqualification order there is specified the maximum (and, in section 168H, the minimum) period of disqualification which may or, as the case may be, shall be imposed by means of the order.

(3) Where a disqualification order is made against a person who is already subject to such an order, the periods specified in those orders shall run concurrently.

(4) A disqualification order may be made on grounds which are or include matters other than criminal convictions, notwithstanding that the person in respect of whom it is to be made may be criminally liable in respect of those matters.

Disqualification on conviction of indictable offence

168E.(1) The court may make a disqualification order against a person where he is convicted of an indictable offence (whether on indictment or summarily)-

> *(a)* in connection with the promotion, formation, management or liquidation of a company; or

> *(b)* in connection with the receivership or management of a company's property,

or any other indictable offence his conviction for which necessarily involves a finding that he acted fraudulently or dishonestly.

(2) In subsection (1) "the court" means the High Court or the court by or before which the person is convicted of the offence.

(3) The maximum period of disqualification under this section is, where the disqualification order is made-

> *(a)* by a judge of the High Court, 15 years;

> *(b)* by a judge of the District Court, 10 years;

> *(c)* by a magistrate, 5 years.

(4) Where a disqualification order is made by a magistrate and the Official Receiver or-

> *(a)* the liquidator;

> *(b)* a past or present member; or

> *(c)* a creditor,

of the company affected believes that the facts would justify a disqualification order for a longer period, he may apply to the High Court for such a disqualification order and it may, if it considers it appropriate in the circumstances, make an order for such longer period as it determines.

Disqualification for persistent breaches of Ordinance

168F.(1) The court may make a disqualification order against a person where it appears to it that he has been persistently in default in relation to provisions of this Ordinance requiring any return, account or other document to be filed with, delivered or sent, or notice of any matter to be given, to the Registrar.

(2) On an application to the court for an order to be made under this section, the fact that a person has been persistently in default in relation to such provisions may (without prejudice to its proof in any other manner) be conclusively proved by showing that in the 5 years ending with the date of the application he has been adjudged guilty (whether or not on the same occasion) of 3 or more defaults in relation to those provisions.

(3) A person is to be treated under subsection (2) as being adjudged guilty of a default in relation to any provision if-

    (a) he is convicted of an offence consisting in a contravention of that provision (whether on his own part or on the part of any company); or

    (b) an order of the court is made against him under section 279, 302 or 306.

(4) For the purposes of this section, "court" includes a magistrate where the application under this section is made in the course of a prosecution in which the person is adjudged guilty of a default referred to in subsection (1) and, as a result, subsection (2) applies to him.

(5) The maximum period of disqualification under this section is 5 years.

Disqualification for fraud, etc., in winding up

168G.(1) The court may make a disqualification order against a person if, in the course of the winding up of a company, it appears that he-

    (a) has been guilty of an offence for which he is liable (whether he has been convicted or not) under section 275; or

    (b) has otherwise been guilty, while an officer or liquidator of the company or receiver or manager of its property, of any fraud in relation to the company or of any breach of his duty as such officer, liquidator, receiver or manager.

(2) The maximum period of disqualification under this section is 15 years.

(3) In this section, "officer" includes a shadow director.

Duty of court to disqualify unfit directors of insolvent companies

168H.(1) The court shall make a disqualification order against a person in any case where, on an application under this section, it is satisfied-

> *(a)* that he is or has been a director of a company which has at any time become insolvent whether while he was a director or subsequently; and

> *(b)* that his conduct as a director of that company, either taken alone or taken together with his conduct as a director of any other company or companies, makes him unfit to be concerned in the management of a company.

(2) For the purposes of this section, a company becomes insolvent if-

> *(a)* the company goes into liquidation at a time when its assets are insufficient for the payment of its debts and other liabilities and the expenses of the winding up; or

> *(b)* a receiver of the company is appointed,

and references to a person's conduct as a director of any company or companies include, where that company or any of those companies has become insolvent, that person's conduct in relation to any matter connected with or arising out of the insolvency of that company.

(3) In this section and section 168I, "director" includes a shadow director.

(4) Under this section the minimum period of disqualification is 1 year, and the maximum period is 15 years.

Applications to court under section 168H reporting provisions

(1) If it appears to-

> *(a)* the Financial Secretary in any case; or

> *(b)* the Official Receiver in the case of a person who is or has been a director of a company that is being wound up,

that it is in the public interest that a disqualification order under section 168H should be made, an application for the making of such an order may be made by the Financial Secretary or the Official Receiver.

(2) Except with the leave of the court, an application for the making under section 168H of a disqualification order against any person shall not be made after the end of the period of 4 years beginning, in the case of a company-

> *(a)* that is wound up, with the day on which the winding up of the company, of

which that person is or has been a director, is deemed, under section 184, 228A or 230, as the case may be, to have commenced; or

(b) that goes into receivership, with the day on which the receiver vacated his office.

(3) If it appears to-

(a) the liquidator of a company that is being wound up by him; or

(b) the receiver in respect of a company for which he has been so appointed,

that the matters listed in section 168H(1)(a) and (b) may apply to a person who is or has been a director of that company, he shall forthwith report the matter to the Official Receiver who may, or in cases not involving the winding-up of the company shall, report the matter to the Financial Secretary.

(4) The Financial Secretary or the Official Receiver may require the liquidator or receiver of a company, or the former liquidator or receiver of a company-

(a) to furnish him with such information with respect to any person's conduct as a director of the company; and

(b) to produce and permit inspection of such books, papers and other records relevant to that person's conduct as such a director,

as the Financial Secretary or the Official Receiver, as the case may be, may reasonably require for the purpose of determining whether to exercise, or of exercising, any of his functions under this section.

Disqualification after investigation of company

168J.(1) If it appears to the Financial Secretary from a report made by inspectors under section 146 or information or documents obtained under section 152A or 152B, that it is expedient in the public interest that a disqualification order should be made against any person who is or has been a director or shadow director of any company, he may apply to the court for such an order to be made against that person.

(2) The court may make a disqualification order against a person where, on an application under this section, it is satisfied that his conduct in relation to the company makes him unfit to be concerned in the management of a company.

(3) The maximum period of disqualification under this section is 15 years.

Matters for determining unfitness of directors

168K.(1) Where it falls to a court to determine whether a person's conduct as a director of any particular company or companies makes him unfit to be concerned in the management of a company, the court shall, as respects his conduct as a director of that company or, as the case may be, each of those companies, have regard in particular-

> *(a)* to the matters mentioned in Part I of the Fifteenth Schedule; and

> *(b)* where the company has become insolvent, to the matters mentioned in Part II of that Schedule,

and references in that Schedule to the director and the company are to be read accordingly.

(2) Section 168H(2) applies for the purposes of this section and the Fifteenth Schedule as it applies for the purposes of section 168H.

(3) The Financial Secretary may by order modify any of the provisions of the Fifteenth Schedule; and such an order may contain such transitional provisions as may appear to the Financial Secretary necessary or expedient.

(4) In this section and the Fifteenth Schedule, "director" includes a shadow director.

Fraudulent trading

168L.(1) Where the court makes a declaration under section 275 that a person is liable for all or any of the debts or other liabilities of a company, the court may, if it thinks fit and whether or not any person applies for such an order, make a disqualification order against the person to whom the declaration relates.

(2) The maximum period of a disqualification order under this section is 15 years.

Criminal penalties

168M. If a person acts in contravention of a disqualification order, he is guilty of an offence and is liable to imprisonment and a fine.

Offences by body corporate

168N.(1) Where a body corporate is guilty of an offence of acting in contravention of a disqualification order, and it is proved that the offense occurred with the consent or connivance of, or was attributable to any neglect on the part of, any director, manager, secretary or other similar officer of the body corporate, or any person who was purporting to act in any such capacity he, as well as the body corporate, is guilty of the offence and liable to be proceeded against and punished accordingly.

(2) Where the affairs of a body corporate are managed by its members, subsection (1) applies in relation to the acts and defaults of a member in connection with his functions of management as if he were a director of the body corporate.

Personal liability for company's debts where person acts while disqualified

168O.(1) A person is personally responsible for all the relevant debts of a company if at any time-

> *(a)* in contravention of a disqualification order or of section 156 he is involved in the management of the company; or

> *(b)* as a person who is involved in the management of the company, he acts or is willing to act on instructions given without the leave of the court by a person whom he knows at that time to be the subject of a disqualification order or to be an undischarged bankrupt.

(2) Where a person is personally responsible under this section for the relevant debts of a company, he is jointly and severally liable in respect of those debts with the company and any other person who, whether under this section or otherwise, is so liable.

(3) For the purposes of this section the relevant debts of a company are-

> *(a)* in relation to a person who is personally responsible under subsection (1)(a), such debts and other liabilities of the company as are incurred at a time when that person was involved in the management of the company; and

> *(b)* in relation to a person who is personally responsible under subsection (1)(b), such debts and other liabilities of the company as are incurred at a time when that person was acting or was willing to act on instructions given as mentioned in subsection (1)(b).

(4) For the purposes of this section, a person is involved in the management of a company if he is a director of the company or if he is concerned, whether directly or indirectly, or takes part, in the management of the company.

(5) For the purposes of this section a person who, as a person involved in the management of a company, has at any time acted on instructions given without the leave of the court by a person whom he knew at that time to be the subject of a disqualification order or to be an undischarged bankrupt is presumed, unless the contrary is shown, to have been willing at any time thereafter to act on any instructions given by that person.

Application for disqualification order

168P.(1) A person intending to apply for the making of a disqualification order by the court, other than an application made in the course of a proceeding for the prosecution of an offence, shall give not less than 10 days' notice of his intention to the person against whom the order is sought; and on the hearing of the application the last-mentioned person may appear and himself give evidence or call witnesses.

(2) An application to a court for the making against any person of a disqualification order under-

> *(a)*   section 168F may be made by the Registrar; and
>
> *(b)*   any of sections 168E to 168G may be made by the Official Receiver, the Financial Secretary or by the liquidator or any past or present member or creditor of any company in relation to which that person has committed or is alleged to have committed an offence or other default.

(3)   On the hearing of any application under this Part made by the Registrar, the Official Receiver, the Financial Secretary or the liquidator, the applicant shall appear and call the attention of the court to any matters which seem to him to be relevant, and may himself give evidence or call witnesses.

(4)   Where, under this Part, a court may make a disqualification order in the course of a proceeding for the prosecution of an offence, it may make such an order if it thinks fit and whether or not any person applies for such an order.

Application for leave under an order

168Q. Where-

> *(a)*   a person who is the subject of a disqualification order made under this Part applies for leave of the court to participate in a company in one of the ways prohibited under section 168D(1); and
>
> *(b)*   the disqualification order to which the application relates was made as a result of an application by the Financial Secretary, the Registrar, the Official Receiver or a liquidator,

the Financial Secretary, Registrar, Official Receiver or liquidator, as the case may be, shall appear and call the attention of the court to any matters which seem to him to be relevant, and may himself give evidence or call witnesses.

Register of disqualification orders

168R.(1) The Financial Secretary may make regulations requiring officers of courts to furnish the Registrar with such particulars as the regulations may specify of cases in which-

> *(a)*   a disqualification order is made; or
>
> *(b)*   any action is taken by a court in consequence of which such an order is varied or ceases to be in force; or
>
> *(c)*   leave is granted by a court for a person subject to such an order to do anything which otherwise the order prohibits him from doing,

and the regulations may specify the time within which, and the form and manner in which, such particulars are to be furnished.

(2) The Registrar shall, from the particulars so furnished, maintain a register of orders and of cases in which leave has been granted as mentioned in subsection (1)(c).

(3) When an order of which entry is made in the register ceases to be in force, the Registrar shall delete the entry from the register and all particulars relating to it which have been furnished to him under this section.

(4) The register shall be open to inspection on payment of such fee as may be specified in the Eighth Schedule.

Regulations

168S.(1) The Chief Justice may make regulations respecting proceedings in the High Court for a disqualification order under this Part.

(2) The Financial Secretary may make regulations respecting the reporting to the Official Receiver of the conduct of persons as directors under section 168I(3).

Transitional

168T.(1) Sections 168E and 168G do not apply in relation to anything done before this Part comes into operation by a person in his capacity as liquidator of a company or as receiver or manager of a company's property.

(2) Subject to subsection (1), sections 168E and 168G apply in a case where a person is convicted of an offence, referred to in the relevant section, which he committed (and, in the case of a continuing offence, has ceased to commit) before this Part comes into operation; but in such a case a disqualification order under the relevant section shall not be made for a period in excess of 5 years.

(3) Section 168F applies in respect of matters that took place before or after this Part comes into operation.

PART V - Winding Up

(i)   Preliminary

Modes of Winding Up

Modes of winding up

169.(1) The winding up of a company may be either-

(a)   by the court; or

(b)   voluntary.

(2)   The provisions of this Ordinance with respect to winding up apply, unless the contrary appears, to the winding up of a company in any of those modes.

Contributories

Liability as contributories of present and past members

170.(1) In the event of a company being wound up, every present and past member shall be liable to contribute to the assets of the company to an amount sufficient for payment of its debts and liabilities, and the costs, charges, and expenses of the winding up, and for the adjustment of the rights of the contributories among themselves, subject to the provisions of subsection (2) and the following qualifications-

(a)   a past member shall not be liable to contribute if he has ceased to be a member for 1 year or upwards before the commencement of the winding up;

(b)   a past member shall not be liable to contribute in respect of any debt or liability of the company contracted after he ceased to be a member;

(c)   a past member shall not be liable to contribute unless it appears to the court that the existing members are unable to satisfy the contribution required to be made by them in pursuance of this Ordinance;

(d)   in the case of a company limited by shares no contribution shall be required from any member exceeding the amount, if any, unpaid on the shares in respect of which he is liable as a present or past member;

(e)   in the case of a company limited by guarantee, no contribution shall, subject to the provisions of subsection (3), be required from any member exceeding the amount undertaken to be contributed by him to the assets of the company in the event of its being wound up;

(f)   nothing in this Ordinance shall invalidate any provision contained in any policy of insurance or other contract whereby the liability of individual members on the policy or contract is restricted, or whereby the funds of the company are alone made liable in respect of the policy or contract;

(g)   a sum due to any member of a company, in his character of a member, by way of dividends, profits or otherwise, shall not be deemed to be a debt of the company, payable to that member in a case of competition between himself and any other creditor not a member of the company, but any such sum may be taken into account for the purpose of the final adjustment of the rights of the Contributories among themselves.

(2)   In the winding up of a limited company, any director, whether past or present, whose liability is, under the provisions of this Ordinance, unlimited, shall, in addition to his liability (if any) to contribute as an ordinary member, be liable to make a further contribution as if he were at the commencement of the winding up a member of an unlimited company:

Provided that-

(a)   a past director shall not be liable to make such further contribution if he has ceased to hold office for a year or upwards before the commencement of the winding up;

(b)   a past director shall not be liable to make such further contribution in respect of any debt or liability of the company contracted after he ceased to hold office;

(c)   subject to the articles of the company, a director shall not be liable to make such further contribution unless the court deems it necessary to require that contribution in order to satisfy the debts and liabilities of the company, and the costs, charges, and expenses of the winding up.

(3)   In the winding up of a company limited by guarantee which has a share capital, every member of the company shall be liable, in addition to the amount undertaken to be contributed by him to the assets of the company in the event of its being wound up, to contribute to the extent of any sums unpaid on any shares held by him.

Definition of contributory

171.   The term "contributory" means every person liable to contribute to the assets of a company in the event of its being wound up, and for the purposes of all proceedings for determining, and all proceedings prior to the final determination of, the persons who are to be deemed contributories, includes any person alleged to be a contributory.

Nature of liability of contributory

172. The liability of a contributory shall create a debt of the nature of a specially accruing due from him at the time when his liability commenced, but payable at the times when calls are made for enforcing the liability.

Contributories in case of death of member

173.(1) If a contributory dies either before or after he has been placed on the list of contributories, his personal representatives shall be liable in due course of administration to contribute to the assets of the company in discharge of his liability and shall be Contributories accordingly.

(2) *(Repealed)*

(3) If the personal representatives make default in paying any money ordered to be paid by them, proceedings may be taken for administering the estate of the deceased contributory, and for compelling payment thereout of the money due.

Contributories in case of bankruptcy of member

174. If a contributory becomes bankrupt, either before or after he has been placed on the list of contributories-

> *(a)* his trustee in bankruptcy shall represent him for all the purposes of the winding up, and shall be a contributory accordingly, and may be called on to admit to proof against the estate of the bankrupt, or otherwise to allow to be paid out of his assets in due course of law, any money due from the bankrupt in respect of his liability to contribute to the assets of the company; and

> *(b)* there may be proved against the estate of the bankrupt the estimated value of his liability to future calls as well as calls already made.

175. *(Repealed)*

(ii) **WINDING UP BY THE COURT**

Jurisdiction

Jurisdiction to wind up companies

176. The High Court shall have jurisdiction to wind up any company.

Cases in which Company may be wound up by Court

Circumstances in which company may be wound up by court

177.(1) A company may be wound up by the court if-

(a)   the company has by special resolution resolved that the company be wound up by the court;

(b)   the company does not commence its business within a year from its incorporation, or suspends its business for a whole year;

(c)   the number of members is reduced below 2;

(d)   the company is unable to pay its debts;

(e)   the event, if any, occurs on the occurrence of which the memorandum or articles provide that the company is to be dissolved;

(f)   the court is of opinion that it is just and equitable that the company should be wound up.

(2)   On the application of the Registrar for the winding up of a company, the company may be wound up by the court if it appears to the court-

(a)   that the company is being carried on for an unlawful purpose or any purpose lawful in itself but one which cannot be carried out by a company; or

(b)   that throughout a period of not less than 6 months ending on the date of the winding-up petition the company has not had at least 2 directors; or

(c)   that throughout the period referred to in paragraph (b) the company has not had a secretary; or

(d)   that the company has failed to pay the annual registration fee payable under the Eighth Schedule; or

(e)   without prejudice to paragraphs (a) to (d), that the company has been persistently in breach of its obligations under this Ordinance.

(3)   A company registered before the commencement of the Companies (Amendment) Ordinance 1984 may by special resolution alter the conditions contained in its memorandum by adding a condition to the effect that the company shall be dissolved on the occurrence of a specified event, with or without a provision providing for or prohibiting the alteration of that condition:

Provided that, if an application is made to the court for any such alteration to be cancelled, the alteration shall not have effect except in so far as it is confirmed by the court.

(4) Subsections (2)(a), (3), (4), (7) and (8) of section 8 shall apply in relation to any such alteration and to any application under subsection (3) as they apply in relation to alterations and to applications made under that section.

Definition of inability to pay debts

178.(1) A company shall be deemed to be unable to pay its debts-

    (a)   if a creditor, by assignment or otherwise, to whom the company is indebted in a sum exceeding $5,000 then due, has served on the company, by leaving it at the registered office of the company, a demand under his hand requiring the company to pay the sum so due, and the company has for 3 weeks thereafter neglected to pay the sum, or to secure or compound for it to the reasonable satisfaction of the creditor; or

    (b)   if execution or other process issued on a judgment, decree or order of any court in favour of a creditor of the company is returned unsatisfied in whole or in part; or

    (c)   if it is proved to the satisfaction of the court that the company is unable to pay its debts, and, in determining whether a company is unable to pay its debts, the court shall take into account the contingent and prospective liabilities of the company.

(2) Subsection (1)(a) shall apply to 2 or more creditors to whom the company is indebted in respect of unpaid wages, wages in lieu of notice or severance payments, as the case may be, or all or any of them if the total of that indebtedness exceeds the sum referred to in that subsection, as if those creditors were a single creditor, and a demand under that subsection shall be valid if signed by any one or more of those creditors.

Petition for Winding Up and Effects thereof

Provisions as to applications for winding up

179.(1) An application to the court for the winding up of a company shall be by petition, presented subject to the provisions of this section either by the company, or by any creditor or creditors (including any contingent or prospective creditor or creditors), contributory or contributories or the trustee in bankruptcy or the personal representative of a contributory, or by all or any of those parties, together or separately:

Provided that-

    (a)   a contributory shall not be entitled to present a winding-up petition unless-

        (i)   the number of members is reduced below 2; or

        (ii)   the shares in respect of which he is a contributory, or some of them, either were originally allotted to him or have been held by him, and registered in his name, for at least 6 months during the 18 months before the commencement of the winding up, or have devolved on him through the death of a former holder; and *(b)*　*(Repealed)*

(c)　the court shall not give a hearing to a winding-up petition presented by contingent or prospective creditor until such security for costs has been given as the court thinks reasonable and until a prima facie case for winding up has been established to the satisfaction of the court; and

(d)　in a case falling within section 147(2)(a), a winding-up petition may be presented by the Financial Secretary; and

(e)　in a case referred to in section 177(1)(c) or (2), a winding-up petition may be presented by the Registrar.

(2)　Where a company is being wound up voluntarily, a winding-up petition may be presented by the Official Receiver as well as by any other person authorized in that behalf under the other provisions of this section, but the court shall not make a winding-up order on the petition unless it is satisfied that the voluntary winding up cannot be continued with due regard to the interests of the creditors or contributories.

(3)　*(Repealed)*

Appearance of Official Receiver

179A.　On the hearing of a winding-up petition by the court, the Official Receiver may appear and call, examine and cross-examine any witness and, if he so thinks fit, support or oppose the making of a winding-up order.

Powers of court on bearing petition

180.(1)　On hearing a winding-up petition the court may dismiss it, or adjourn the hearing conditionally or unconditionally, or make any interim order, or any other order that it thinks fit, but the court shall not refuse to make a winding-up order on the ground only that the assets of the company have been mortgaged to an amount equal to or in excess of those assets, or that the company has no assets.

(1A)　Where the petition is presented by members of the company as contributories on the ground that it is just and equitable that the company should be wound up, the court shall not refuse to make a winding-up order on the ground only that some other remedy is available to the petitioners unless it is also of opinion that they are acting unreasonably in seeking to have the company wound up instead of pursuing that other remedy.

(2)　*(Repealed)*

Hearing of unopposed petition by Registrar of Supreme Court

180A.(1)　Subject to general rules limiting the power conferred by this section, the jurisdiction of the court under this Part may, in the case of an unopposed petition for winding-up by the court, be exercised by the Registrar of the Supreme Court.

(2)　　Any hearing of a petition in pursuance of the jurisdiction conferred on the Registrar of the Supreme Court by this section shall be in open court.

Power to stay or restrain proceedings against company

181.　　At any time after the presentation of a winding-up petition and before a winding-up order has been made, the company or any creditor or contributory may-

> *(a)*　　where any action or proceeding against the company is pending in the High Court or the Court of Appeal, apply to the court in which the action or proceeding is pending for a stay of proceedings therein;

> *(b)*　　where any action or proceeding against the company is pending in any court or tribunal other than the High Court or the Court of Appeal, apply to the High Court to restrain further proceedings in the action or proceeding,

and the court to which application is so made may, as the case may be, stay or restrain the proceedings accordingly on such terms as it thinks fit.

Avoidance of dispositions of property, &c. after commencement of winding up

182.　　In a winding up by the court, any disposition of the property of the company, including things in action, and any transfer of shares, or alteration in the status of the members of the company, made after the commencement of the winding up, shall, unless the court otherwise orders, be void.

Avoidance of attachments, &c.

183.　　Where any company is being wound up by the court, any attachment, sequestration, distress, or execution put in force against the estate or effects of the company after the commencement of the winding up shall be void to all intents.

Commencement of Winding Up

Commencement of winding up by the court

184.(1)　　Where before the presentation of a petition for the winding up of a company by the court a resolution has been passed by the company for voluntary winding up, the winding up of the company shall be deemed to have commenced at the time of the passing of the resolution, and unless the court, on proof of fraud or mistake, thinks fit otherwise to direct, all proceedings taken in the voluntary winding up shall be deemed to have been validly taken.

(2)　　In any other case, the winding up of a company by the court shall be deemed to commence at the time of the presentation of the petition for the winding up.

Consequences of Winding-up Order

Copy of order to be delivered to Registrar

185. On the making of a winding-up order, a copy of the order shall forthwith be delivered by the company, or otherwise as may be prescribed, to the Registrar for registration.

Actions stayed on winding-up order

186. When a winding-up order has been made, or a provisional liquidator has been appointed, no action or proceeding shall be proceeded with or commenced against the company except by leave of the court, and subject to such terms as the court may impose.

Effect of winding-up order

187. An order for winding up a company shall operate in favour of all the creditors and of all the contributories of the company as if made on the joint petition of a creditor and of a contributory.

Official Receiver in Winding Up

Official Receiver appointed under Bankruptcy Ordinance to he official receiver for winding-up purposes

188. For the purposes of this Ordinance so far as it relates to the winding up of companies by the court the term "Official Receiver" means the Official Receiver appointed under the Bankruptcy Ordinance (Cap. 6).

189. *(Repealed)*

Statement of company's affairs to be submitted to Official Receiver

190.(1) Where the court has made a winding-up order or appointed a provisional liquidator, there shall, unless the court thinks fit to order otherwise and so orders, be made out and submitted to the Official Receiver a statement as to the affairs of the company in the prescribed form, verified by affidavit, and showing the particulars of its assets, debts, and liabilities, the names, addresses, and occupations of its creditors, the securities held by them respectively, the dates when the securities were respectively given, and such further or other information as may be prescribed or as the Official Receiver may require.

(2) The statement shall be submitted and verified by one or more of the persons who are at the relevant date the directors and by the person who is at that date the secretary of the company, or by such of the persons hereinafter in this subsection mentioned as the Official Receiver, subject to the direction of the court, may require to submit and verify the statement, that is to say, persons -

 (a) who are or have been directors or officers of the company;

 (b) who have taken part in the formation of the company at any time within 1 year before the relevant date;

(c)   who are in the employment of the company, or have been in the employment of the company within the said year, and are in the opinion of the Official Receiver capable of giving the information required;

(d)   who are or have been within the said year officers of or in the employment of a company, which is, or within the said year was, an officer of the company to which the statement relates.

(3)   The statement shall be submitted within 28 days from the relevant date, or within such extended time as the Official Receiver or the court may for special reasons appoint.

(4)   Any person making or concurring in making the statement and affidavit required by this section shall be allowed, and shall be paid by the Official Receiver or provisional liquidator, as the case may be, out of the assets of the company, such costs and expenses incurred in and about the preparation and making of the statement and affidavit as the Official Receiver may consider reasonable, subject to an appeal to the court.

(5)   If any person, without reasonable excuse, makes default in complying with the requirements of this section, he shall be liable to a fine and, for continued default, to a daily default fine.

(5A)   A statement required by this section may be used in evidence against any person making or concurring in making the statement.

(6)   Any person stating himself in writing to be a creditor or contributory of the company shall be entitled by himself or by his agent at all reasonable times, on payment of the prescribed fee, to inspect the statement submitted in pursuance of this section, and to a copy thereof or extract therefrom.

(7)   Any person untruthfully so stating himself to be a creditor or contributory shall be guilty of a contempt of court and shall, on the application of the liquidator or of the Official Receiver, be punishable accordingly.

(8)   In this section, the expression "the relevant date" means in a case where a provisional liquidator is appointed, the date of his appointment, and, in a case where no such appointment is made, the date of the winding-up order.

Report by Official Receiver

191.(1) In a case where a winding-up order is made, the Official Receiver shall, as soon as practicable after receipt of the statement to be submitted under section 190, or, in a case where the court orders that no statement shall be submitted, as soon as practicable after the date of the order, submit a preliminary report to the court-

(a)   as to the amount of capital issued, subscribed, and paid up, and the estimated amount of assets and liabilities; and

(b)   if the company has failed, as to the causes of the failure; and

(c)   whether in his opinion further inquiry is desirable as to any matter relating to the promotion, formation or failure of the company, or the conduct of the business thereof.

(2) The Official Receiver may also, if he thinks fit, make a further report, or further reports, stating the manner in which the company was formed and whether in his opinion any fraud has been committed by any person in its promotion or formation, or by any officer of the company in relation to the company since the formation thereof, and any other matters which in his opinion it is desirable to bring to the notice of the court.

(3) If the Official Receiver states in any such further report as aforesaid that in his opinion a fraud has been committed as aforesaid, the court shall have the further powers provided in section 222.

Liquidators

Power of court to appoint liquidators

192. For the purpose of conducting the proceedings in winding up a company and performing such duties in reference thereto as the court may impose, the court may appoint a liquidator or liquidators in accordance with sections 193 and 194.

Appointment and powers of provisional liquidator

193.(1) Subject to the provisions of this section, the court may appoint a liquidator provisionally at any time after the presentation of a winding-up petition.

(2) The appointment of a provisional liquidator may be made at any time before the making of a winding-up order, and either the Official Receiver or any other fit person may be appointed.

(3) Where a liquidator is provisionally appointed by the court, the court may limit and restrict his powers by the order appointing him.

Appointment, style, &c. of liquidators

194.(1) The following provisions with respect to liquidators shall have effect on a winding-up order being made-

  (a) subject to paragraph (aa) the Official Receiver shall by virtue of his office become the provisional liquidator and shall continue to act as such until he or another person becomes liquidator and is capable of acting as such;

  (aa) where under section 193 a person other than the Official Receiver is appointed as provisional liquidator, he shall continue to act as the provisional liquidator until he or another person becomes the liquidator and is capable of acting as such;

  (b) the provisional liquidator shall summon separate meetings of the creditors

and contributories of the company for the purpose of determining whether or not an application is to be made to the court for appointing a liquidator in the place of the provisional liquidator;

(c)   the court may make any appointment and order required to give effect to any such determination, and, if there is a difference between the determinations of the meetings of the creditors and contributories in respect of the matter aforesaid, the court shall decide the difference and make such order thereon as the court may think fit;

(d)   where a liquidator is not appointed by the court, the provisional liquidator shall be the liquidator of the company;

(e)   the Official Receiver shall by virtue of his office be the liquidator during any vacancy;

(f)   a liquidator shall be described, where a person other than the Official Receiver is liquidator, by the style of the liquidator, and, where the Official Receiver is liquidator, by the style of the Official Receiver and liquidator, of the particular company in respect of which he is appointed, and not by his individual name.

(2) Where the Official Receiver is the liquidator of the company, he may, at any time, apply to the court for the appointment of a person as a liquidator in his place.

(3) On an application under subsection (2) the court shall either made an appointment or decline to make one.

(4) Where a liquidator is appointed by the court under subsection (3), the liquidator shall give notice of his appointment to the company's creditors and contributories in accordance with the directions of the court.

(5) In a notice under subsection (4), the liquidator shall state his intention to summon meetings of the company's creditors and contributories, in accordance with section 206, for the purpose of determining -

(a)   whether or not an application is to be made to the court for the appointment of a committee of inspection to act with the liquidator; and

(b)   who are to be the members of the committee, if appointed.

Provisions where person other than Official Receiver is appointed liquidator

195.   Where in the winding up of a company by the court a person other than the Official Receiver is appointed liquidator, that person-

(a) shall not be capable of acting as liquidator until he has notified his appointment to the Registrar and given security in the prescribed manner to the satisfaction of the Official Receiver;

(b) shall give the Official Receiver such information and such access to and facilities for inspecting the books and documents of the company, and generally such aid as may be requisite for enabling that officer to perform his duties under this Ordinance.

General provisions as to liquidators

196.(1) A liquidator appointed by the court may resign or, on cause shown, be removed by the court.

(2) Where a person other than the Official Receiver is appointed liquidator, he shall receive such remuneration by way of percentage or otherwise as is determined -

(a) where there is a committee of inspection, by agreement between the liquidator and the committee of inspection; or

(b) where there is no committee of inspection or the liquidator and the committee of inspection fail to agree, by the court,

and if two or more persons are appointed liquidators, their remuneration shall be distributed among them in such proportions as may be determined by the committee of inspection or the court, as the case may be.

(2A) If the Official Receiver is of the opinion that the remuneration of a liquidator as determined under subsection (2)(a) should be reviewed the Official Receiver may apply to the court, and the court may make an order confirming, increasing or reducing the remuneration of the liquidator.

(3) A vacancy in the office of a liquidator appointed by the court shall be filled by the court.

(4) If more than one liquidator is appointed by the court, the court shall declare whether any act by this Ordinance required or authorized to be done by the liquidator is to be done by all or any one or more of the persons appointed.

(5) Subject to the provisions of section 278, the acts of a liquidator shall be valid notwithstanding any defects that may afterwards be discovered in his appointment or qualification.

Custody of company's property

197. Where a winding-up order has been made or where a provisional liquidator has been appointed, the liquidator, or the provisional liquidator, as the case may be, shall take into his custody, or under his control, all the property and things in action to which the company is or appears to be entitled.

Vesting of property of company in liquidator

198. Where a company is being wound up by the court, the court may on the application of the liquidator by order direct that all or any part of the property of whatsoever description belonging to the company or held by trustees on its behalf shall vest in the liquidator by his official name, and thereupon the property to which the order relates shall vest accordingly, and the liquidator may, after giving such indemnity, if any, as the court may direct, bring or defend in his official name any action or other legal proceeding which relates to that property or which it is necessary to bring or defend for the purpose of effectually winding up the company and recovering its property.

Powers of liquidator

199.(1) The liquidator in a winding up by the court shall have power with the sanction either of the court or of the committee of inspection-

    (a)   to bring or defend any action or other legal proceeding in the name and on behalf of the company;

    (b)   to carry on the business of the company, so far as may be necessary for the beneficial winding up thereof;

    (c)   to appoint a solicitor to assist him in the performance of his duties;

    (d)   to pay any classes of creditors in full;

    (e)   to make any compromise or arrangement with creditors or persons claiming to be creditors, or having or alleging themselves to have any claim, present or future, certain or contingent, ascertained or sounding only in damages against the company, or whereby the company may be rendered liable;

    (f)   to compromise all calls and liabilities to calls, debts, and liabilities capable of resulting in debts, and all claims, present or future, certain or contingent, ascertained or sounding only in damages, subsisting or supposed to subsist between the company and a contributory, or alleged contributory, or other debtor or person apprehending liability to the company, and all questions in any way relating to or affecting the assets or the winding up of the company, on such terms as may be agreed, and take any security for the discharge of any such call, debt, liability or claim, and give a complete discharge in respect thereof.

(2)   The liquidator in a winding up by the court shall have power-

    (a)   to sell the real and personal property and things in action of the company by public auction or private contract, with power to transfer the whole thereof to any person or company, or to sell the same in parcels;

(b)   to do all acts and to execute, in the name and on behalf of the company, all deeds, receipts, and other documents, and for that purpose to use, when necessary, the company's seal;

(c)   to prove, rank, and claim in the bankruptcy, insolvency, or sequestration of any contributory, for any balance against his estate, and to receive dividends in the bankruptcy, insolvency, or sequestration in respect of that balance, as a separate debt due from the bankrupt or insolvent, and rateably with the other separate creditors;

(d)   to draw, accept, make, and endorse any bill of exchange or promissory note in the name and on behalf of the company, with the same effect with respect to the liability of the company as if the bill or note had been drawn, accepted, made, or endorsed by or on behalf of the company in the course of its business;

(e)   to raise on the security of the assets of the company any money requisite;

(f)   to take out in his official name letters of administration to any deceased contributory, and to do in his official name any other act necessary for obtaining payment of any money due from a contributory or his estate which cannot be conveniently done in the name of the company, and in all such cases the money due shall, for the purpose of enabling the liquidator to take out the letters of administration or recover the money, be deemed to be due to the liquidator himself;

(g)   to appoint an agent to do any business which the liquidator is unable to do himself;

(h)   to do all such other things as may be necessary for winding up the affairs of the company and distributing its assets.

(3) The exercise by the liquidator in a winding up by the court of the powers conferred by this section shall be subject to the control of the court, and any creditor or contributory may apply to the court with respect to any exercise or proposed exercise of any of those powers.

Exercise and control of liquidator's powers

200.(1) Subject to the provisions of this Ordinance, the liquidator of a company which is being wound up by the court shall, in the administration of the assets of the company and in the distribution thereof among its creditors, have regard to any directions that may be given by resolution of the creditors or contributories at any general meeting, or by the committee of inspection, and any directions given by the creditors or contributories at any general meeting shall in case of conflict be deemed to override any directions given by the committee of inspection.

(2) The liquidator may summon general meetings of the creditors or contributories for the purpose of ascertaining their wishes, and it shall be his duty to summon meetings at such times as the creditors or contributories, by resolution, either at the meeting appointing the liquidator or otherwise, may direct, or whenever requested in writing to do so by one-tenth in value of the creditors or contributories as the case may be.

(3) The liquidator may apply to the court in manner prescribed for directions in relation to any particular matter arising under the winding up.

(4) Subject to the provisions of this Ordinance, the liquidator shall use his own discretion in the administration of the assets and the distribution thereof among the creditors.

(5) If any person is aggrieved by any act or decision of the liquidator, that person may apply to the court, and the court may confirm, reverse, or modify the act or decision complained of, and make such order in the premises as it thinks just.

Books to be kept by liquidator

201. Every liquidator of a company which is being wound up by the court shall keep, in manner prescribed, proper books in which he shall cause to be made entries or minutes of proceedings at meetings, and of such other matters as may be prescribed, and any creditor or contributory may, subject to the control of the court, personally or by his agent inspect any such books.

Payments of liquidator into bank or Treasury

202.(1) Every liquidator other than the Official Receiver of a company which is being wound up by the court shall, in such manner and at such times as the Official Receiver directs, pay the money received by him to the Companies Liquidation Account at the bank where such account is kept, and when the Official Receiver is the liquidator of such company he shall pay all moneys received by him in such capacity into the Companies Liquidation Account:

Provided that the Official Receiver may, on the application of the committee of inspection, authorize the liquidator to make his payments into and out of any other bank specified by the committee in such application, and thereupon those payments shall be made in the prescribed manner.

(2) If any such liquidator at any time retains for more than 10 days a sum exceeding $2,000, or such other amount as the Official Receiver in any particular case may authorize him to retain, then, unless he explains the retention to the satisfaction of the court, he shall pay interest on the amount so retained in excess at the rate of 20 per cent per annum, and shall be liable to disallowance of all or such part of his remuneration as the court may think just, and to be removed from his office by the court, and shall be liable to pay any expenses occasioned by reason of his default.

(3) A liquidator of a company which is being wound up by the court shall not pay any sums received by him as liquidator into his private banking account.

Audit of liquidator's accounts

203.(1) Every liquidator (other than the Official Receiver) of a company which is being wound up by the court shall, at such times as may be prescribed but not less than twice in each year during his tenure of office, send to the Official Receiver, an account of his receipts and payments as liquidator.

(2) The account shall be in a prescribed form and shall be made in duplicate.

(3) The liquidator shall furnish the Official Receiver with such vouchers and information relating to the account as he requires, and the Official Receiver may at any time require the production of, and inspect, any books or accounts kept by the liquidator.

(3A) The Official Receiver may at any time cause the account to be audited.

(4) When the account has been audited (or, as the case may be, forthwith if the Official Receiver decides that the account need not be audited), one copy thereof shall be filed and kept by the Official Receiver, and the other copy shall be delivered to the court for filing, and each copy shall be open, upon payment of the prescribed fee, to the inspection of any creditor or any person having an interest.

(5) The liquidator shall, when the account has been audited or, when he has been notified that the Official Receiver has decided that the account need not be audited, cause the account or a summary thereof to be printed, and shall send a printed copy of the account or summary by post to every creditor and contributory:

Provided that the Official Receiver may in any case dispense with compliance with this subsection.

(6) Notwithstanding the fact that a liquidator has been notified that the Official Receiver has decided that the account need not be audited, the Official Receiver may subsequently cause the account to be audited, and in that event-

> *(a)* a copy of the audited account shall be filed and kept by the Official Receiver, and a further copy shall be delivered to the court for filing, and each copy shall be open, upon payment of the prescribed fee, to the inspection of any creditor or any person having an interest; and

> *(b)* the liquidator shall cause the audited account or a summary thereof to be printed, and shall send a printed copy of the account or summary by post to every creditor and contributory:

> Provided that the Official Receiver may in any case dispense with compliance with this paragraph.

Control of Official Receiver over liquidators

204.(1) The Official Receiver shall take cognizance of the conduct of liquidators of companies which are being wound up by the court, and, if a liquidator does not faithfully perform his duties and duly observe all the requirements imposed on him by statute, rules, or otherwise with respect to the performance of his duties, or if any complaint is made to the Official Receiver by any creditor or contributory in regard thereto, the Official Receiver shall inquire into the matter, and take such action thereon as he may think expedient.

(2) The Official Receiver may at any time require any liquidator of a company which is being wound up by the court to answer any inquiry in relation to any winding up in which he is engaged, and may, if he thinks fit, apply to the court to examine him or any other person on oath concerning the winding up.

(3) The Official Receiver may also direct an investigation to be made of the books and vouchers of the liquidator.

Release of liquidators

205.(1) When the liquidator of a company which is being wound up by the court has realized all the property of the company, or so much thereof as can, in his opinion, be realized without needlessly protracting the liquidation, and has distributed a final dividend, if any, to the creditors, and adjusted the rights of the contributories among themselves, and made a final return, if any, to the contributories, or has resigned, or has been removed from his office, the court shall, on his application, cause a report on his accounts to be prepared, and, on his complying with all the requirements of the court, shall take into consideration the report, and any objection which may be urged by any creditor or contributory, or person interested against the release of the liquidator, and shall either grant or withhold the release accordingly.

(2) Where the release of a liquidator is withheld, the court may, on the application of any creditor or contributory, or person interested, make such order as it thinks just, charging the liquidator with the consequences of any act or default which he may have done or made contrary to his duty.

(3) An order of the court releasing the liquidator shall discharge him from all liability in respect of any act done or default made by him in the administration of the affairs of the company, or otherwise in relation to his conduct as liquidator, but any such order may be revoked on proof that it was obtained by fraud or by suppression or concealment of any material fact.

(4) Where the liquidator has not previously resigned or been removed, his release shall operate as a removal of him from his office.

Committees of Inspection

Meetings of creditors and contributories to determine whether committee of inspection shall be appointed

206.(1) When a winding-up order has been made by the court, it shall be the business of the separate meetings of creditors and contributories summoned for the purpose of determining whether or not an application should be made to the court for appointing a liquidator in place of the provisional liquidator, to determine further whether or not an application is to be made to the court for the appointment of a committee of inspection to act with the liquidator and who are to be members of the committee if appointed.

(2) The court may make any appointment and order required to give effect to any such determination, and if there is a difference between the determinations of the meetings of the creditors and contributories in respect of the matters aforesaid the court shall decide the difference and make such order thereon as the court may think fit.

Constitution and proceedings of committee of inspection

207.(1) A committee of inspection appointed in pursuance of this Ordinance shall consist of creditors and contributories of the company or persons holding general powers of attorney from creditors or contributories in such proportions as may be agreed on by the meetings of creditors and contributories, or as, in case of difference, may be determined by the court.

(2) The committee shall meet at such times as they from time to time appoint, and, failing such appointment, at least once a month, and the liquidator or any member of the committee may also call a meeting of the committee as and when he thinks necessary.

(3) The committee may act by a majority of their members present at a meeting, but shall not act unless a majority of the committee are present.

(4) A member of the committee may resign by notice in writing signed by him and delivered to the liquidator.

(5) If a member of the committee becomes bankrupt, or compounds or arranges with his creditors, or is absent from 5 consecutive meetings of the committee without the leave of those members who together with himself represent the creditors or contributories, as the case may be, his office shall thereupon become vacant.

(6) A member of the committee may be removed by an ordinary resolution at a meeting of creditors, if he represents creditors, or of contributories, if he represents contributories, of which 7 days' notice has been given, stating the object of the meeting.

(7) On a vacancy occurring in the committee the liquidator shall forthwith summon a meeting of creditors or of contributories, as the case may require, to fill the vacancy, and the meeting may, by resolution, re-appoint the same or appoint another creditor or contributory to fill the vacancy:

Provided that if the liquidator, having regard to the position in the winding up, is of the opinion that it is unnecessary for the vacancy to be filled he may apply to the court and the court may make an order that the vacancy shall not be filled, or shall not be filled except in such circumstances as may be specified in the order.

(8) The continuing members of the committee, if not less than 2, may act notwithstanding any vacancy in the committee.

Powers of court where no committee of inspection

208. Where in the case of a winding up there is no committee of inspection, the court may, on the application of the liquidator, do any act or thing or give any direction or permission which is by this Ordinance authorized or required to be done or given by the committee.

General Powers of Court in case of Winding Up by Court

Power to stay winding up

209.(1) The court may at any time after an order for winding up, on the application either of the liquidator, or the Official Receiver, or any creditor or contributory, and on proof to the satisfaction of the court that all proceedings in relation to the winding up ought to be stayed, make an order staying the proceedings, either altogether or for a limited time, on such terms and conditions as the court thinks fit.

(2) On any application under this section the court may, before making an order, require the Official Receiver to furnish to the court a report with respect to any facts or matters which are in his opinion relevant to the application.

(3) A copy of every order made under this section shall forthwith be delivered by the company, or otherwise as may be prescribed, to the Registrar.

Power of court to order winding up to be conducted as creditors' voluntary winding up

209A.(1) The court may on the application of the liquidator or any creditor made-

> *(a)* in the case of a company in respect of which an order has been made under section 227F, not later than 3 months from the date of such order; and
>
> *(b)* in any other case, not later than 3 months from the date of a resolution to make such an application passed at any of the meetings (including an adjourned meeting) of creditors and of contributories held pursuant to section 194 or such further time as the court may permit,

order that the winding up of a company ordered to be wound up by the court shall, from the date of the order made on such application, be conducted as if the winding up were a creditors' voluntary winding up.

(2) Where an application is made under subsection (1), the court shall have regard to-

> *(a)* the wishes of the creditors and contributories of the company, as proved to it by sufficient evidence;
>
> *(b)* the progress of the winding up (including in particular assets realized, proofs of debts submitted by creditors and whether a statement of affairs has been submitted under section 190);
>
> *(c)* whether any report has been made to the court under-
>
> > **(i)** section 191(1); or

> **(ii)** section 191(2) that in the liquidator's opinion a fraud has been committed;

(d) whether any director, former director or other officer of the company has been convicted under this Ordinance or any other law for any offence involving fraud, dishonesty, fraudulent trading, misfeasance or breach of duty in relation to the affairs of the company;

(e) whether any criminal proceedings in respect of any offence referred to in paragraph (d) are contemplated or have been instituted against any person referred to in that paragraph;

(f) whether the company forms part of a group of companies the affairs of which are proposed to be investigated or are being investigated under this Ordinance or any other law;

(g) whether there has been a failure on the part of the directors to provide a statement of affairs which the court considers satisfactory or to co-operate with the Official Receiver or liquidator or to comply with any requirement under this Ordinance in relation to the winding up of the company;

(h) whether any director or former director of any other company which has gone into liquidation within 5 years of the date when the company went into liquidation, has been directly or indirectly concerned in the management of the company;

(i) the fact that the insolvency of the company is a matter of public concern; and

(j) any other matter which the court considers appropriate in the particular circumstances.

(3) Where an application has been made under subsection (1) in relation to a company in respect of which an order had been made under section 227F then, without affecting the generality of subsection (2)(a) and subject to subsection (4), the court shall before hearing the application direct that meetings of the creditors and contributories be called, held and conducted in such manner as the court may direct for the purpose of ascertaining the wishes of the creditors and contributories and may appoint a person to act as the chairman of any such meeting and to report the result of the meeting to the court.

(4) Where the court is of the opinion that it is impractical to hold meetings of the creditors or of the contributories, the court may order that such other course of action as directed by the court be taken to ascertain the wishes of the creditors and contributories.

(5) In an order made under this section, notwithstanding any other provision of this Ordinance, the court may, after taking into consideration the wishes of the creditors and Contributories, direct either that the liquidator of the winding up by the court appointed under section 192 continue to act as the liquidator or appoint any other person to act as the liquidator.

(6) Where an application is made under subsection (1)-

> *(a)* the Official Receiver, if he is the liquidator in the winding up by the court; or

> *(b)* the liquidator and the Official Receiver, if the Official Receiver is not the liquidator in such winding up,

shall submit to the court a report with regard to the application.

(7) On the hearing of any application made under subsection (1), the Official Receiver may appear and call, examine or cross-examine any witness if he so thinks fit and may support or oppose the application.

Consequences of an order under section 209A

209B. Where an order is made under section 209A that the winding up of a company shall be conducted as if it were a creditors' voluntary winding up-

> *(a)* the date of-

> > **(i)** the commencement of the winding up shall be the date deemed under section 184 to be the date of the commencement of the winding up by the court;

> > **(ii)** the appointment of the liquidator shall be the date of the appointment (or first appointment) of a provisional liquidator in the winding up by the court; and

> > **(iii)** the order for winding up shall be the date on which the order for winding up by the court is made,

> > for any purpose for which the date of the commencement of the winding up, the date of the appointment of a liquidator or the date of the winding-up order respectively is relevant under this Ordinance;

> *(b)* sections 182, 183 and 186 shall continue to apply;

> *(c)* the rights of a creditor or a contributory under section 257 shall not be affected;

> *(d)* the fees of the liquidator and any charges or expenses due and payable under section 296 or under any other provision in this Ordinance up to the date of the order made under section 209A shall be paid forthwith out of the assets of the company in priority to all the other claims;

(e)   the statement of the affairs of the company required to be submitted under section 190 and the accounts of the liquidator up to the date of the order made under section 209A may be inspected by the creditors;

(f)   any creditor is entitled to have a copy of any document referred to in paragraph (e) on payment of reasonable photocopy charges (if any);

(g)   the court shall make such other orders as it considers appropriate to safeguard the books, records and documents of the company in the custody of the liquidator or the Official Receiver, and notwithstanding section 283 or any other provision of this Ordinance they shall not be disposed of otherwise than as specified in such order.

Transitional

209C.(1) Any application for an order that the winding up of a company ordered to be wound up by the court be conducted as if it were a creditors' voluntary winding up made before the commencement of the Companies (Amendment) (No. 4) Ordinance 1990 (in this section referred to as "the amending Ordinance") shall be considered or continued with as if the amending Ordinance had not been enacted.

(2) The liquidator or any creditor of any company in respect of which an order for winding up by the court was made after 30 August 1984 and before the commencement of the amending Ordinance may, before the expiration of 3 months from that commencement, apply to the court for an order that such winding up be conducted as if it were a creditors' voluntary winding up and the provisions of section 209A in force immediately be fire the commencement of the amending Ordinance shall apply to that application as if the amending Ordinance had not been enacted.

Settlement of list of contributories and application of assets

210.(1) As soon as may be after making a winding-up order, the court shall settle a list of contributories, with power to rectify the register of members in all cases where rectification is required in pursuance of this Ordinance, and shall cause the assets of the company to be collected, and applied in discharge of its liabilities:

Provided that, where it appears to the court that it will not be necessary to make calls on or adjust the rights of contributories, the court may dispense with the settlement of a list of contributories.

(2) In settling the list of contributories, the court shall distinguish between persons who are contributories in their own right and persons who are contributories as being representatives of or liable for the debts of others.

Delivery of property to liquidator

211. The court may, at any time after making a winding-up order, require any contributory for the time being on the list of contributories, and any trustee, receiver, banker, agent or officer of the company to pay, deliver, convey, surrender, or transfer forthwith, or within such time as the court directs, to the liquidator any money, property, or books and papers in his hands to which the company is prima facie entitled.

Payment of debts due by contributory to company and extent to which set-off allowed

212.(1) The court may, at any time after making a winding-up order, make an order on any contributory for the time being on the list of contributories to pay, in manner directed by the order, any money due from him or from the estate of the person whom he represents to the company, exclusive of any money payable by him or the estate by virtue of any call in pursuance of this Ordinance.

(2) The court in making such an order may-

  (a) in the case of an unlimited company, allow to the contributory by way of set-off any money due to him or to the estate which he represents from the company on any independent dealing or contract with the company, but not any money due to him as a member of the company in respect of any dividend or profit; and

  (b) in the case of a limited company, make to any director or manager whose liability is unlimited or to his estate the like allowance.

(3) In the case of any company, whether limited or unlimited, when all the creditors are paid in full, any money due on any account whatever to a contributory from the company may be allowed to him by way of set-off against any subsequent call.

Power of court to make calls

213.(1) The court may, at any time after making a winding-up order, and either before or after it has ascertained the sufficiency of the assets of the company, make calls on all or any of the contributories for the time being settled on the list of the contributories to the extent of their liability, for payment of any money which the court considers necessary to satisfy the debts and liabilities of the company, and the costs, charges, and expenses of winding up, and for the adjustment of the rights of the contributories among themselves, and make an order for payment of any calls so made.

(2) In making a call the court may take into consideration the probability that some of the contributories may partly or wholly fail to pay the call.

Payment into bank of moneys due to company

214.(1) The court may order any contributory, purchaser or other person from whom money is due to the company to pay the amount due into such bank as the court may direct to the account of the liquidator instead of to the liquidator, and any such order may be enforced in the same manner as if it had directed payment to the liquidator.

(2) All moneys and securities paid or delivered into any bank pursuant to this Part in the event of a winding up by the court shall be subject in all respects to the orders of the court.

Order on contributory conclusive evidence

215.(1) An order made by the court on a contributory shall, subject to any right of appeal, be conclusive evidence that the money, if any, thereby appearing to be due or ordered to be paid is due.

(2) All other pertinent matters stated in the order shall be taken to be truly stated as against all persons and in all proceedings.

Appointment of special manager

216.(1) Where the Official Receiver becomes the liquidator of a company, whether provisionally or otherwise, he may, if satisfied that the nature of the estate or business of the company, or the interests of the creditors or contributories generally, require the appointment of a special manager of the estate or business of the company other than himself, apply to the court, and the court may on such application, appoint a special manager of the said estate or business to act during such time as the court may direct, with such powers, including any of the powers of a receiver or manager, as may be entrusted to him by the court.

(2) The special manager shall give such security and account in such manner as the court may direct.

(3) The special manager shall receive such remuneration as may be fixed by the court.

Exclusion of creditors not proving in time

217.(1) The court may fix a date on or before which creditors are to prove their debts or claims.

(2) Any creditor who has not proved his debt or claim on or before the date fixed under subsection (1) shall be excluded from the benefit of the distribution made next after that date and from the benefit of any previous distribution.

Adjustment of rights of contributories

218. The court shall adjust the rights of the contributories among themselves, and distribute any surplus among the persons entitled thereto.

Inspection of books by creditors and contributories

219.(1) The court may, at any time after making a winding-up order, make such order for inspection of the books and papers of the company by creditors and contributories as the court thinks just, and any books and papers in the possession of the company may be inspected by creditors or contributories accordingly, but not further or otherwise.

(2) Nothing in this section shall be taken as excluding or restricting any rights or powers conferred on a public officer by any enactment.

Power to order costs of winding up to be paid out of assets

220. The court may, in the event of the assets being insufficient to meet the costs, charges and expenses incurred in the winding up, make an order as to the payment thereof out of the assets in such order of priority as the court thinks just.

Power to summon persons suspected of having property of company

221.(1) The court may, at any time after the appointment of a provisional liquidator or the making of a winding-up order, summon before it any officer of the company or person known or suspected to have in his possession any property of the company or supposed to be indebted to the company, or any person whom the court deems capable of giving information concerning the promotion, formation, trade, dealings, affairs, or property of the company.

(2) The court may examine him on oath concerning the matters aforesaid, either by word of mouth or on written interrogatories, and may reduce his answers to writing and require him to sign them.

(3) The court may require him to produce any books and papers in his custody or power relating to the company, but, where be claims any lien on books or papers produced by him, the production shall be without prejudice to that lien, and the court shall have jurisdiction in the winding up to determine all questions relating to that lien.

(4) If any person so summoned, after being tendered a reasonable sum for his expenses, refuses to come before the court at the time appointed, not having a lawful impediment (made known to the court at the time of its sitting, and allowed by it), the court may cause him to be apprehended and brought before the court for examination.

Power to order public examination of promoters, directors, &c.

222.(1) Where an order has been made for winding up a company by the court, and the Official Receiver has made a further report under this Ordinance stating that in his opinion-

> *(a)* a fraud has been committed by any person in the promotion or formation of the company or by any officer of the company in relation to the company since its formation; or

> *(b)* in the case of an insolvent company, a prima facie case exists against any person that would render him liable to a disqualification order under Part IVA in relation to the affairs of the company,

the court may, after consideration of the report, direct that that person or officer shall attend before the court on a day appointed by the court for that purpose and be publicly examined as to the promotion or formation or the conduct of the business of the company or as to his conduct and dealings as officer thereof.

(2) The Official Receiver shall take part in the examination, and for that purpose may, if specially authorized by the court in that behalf, employ a solicitor with or without counsel.

(3) The liquidator, where the Official Receiver is not the liquidator, and any creditor or contributory, may also take part in the examination either personally or by solicitor or counsel.

(4) The court may put such questions to the person examined as the court thinks fit.

(5) The person examined shall be examined on oath, and shall answer all such questions as the court may put or allow to be put to him.

(6) A person ordered to be examined under this section shall, before his examination, be furnished with a copy of the Official Receiver's report, and may at his own cost employ a solicitor with or without counsel, who shall be at liberty to put to him such questions as the court may deem just for the purpose of enabling him to explain or qualify any answers given by him:

Provided that, if any such person applies to the court to be exculpated from any charges made or suggested against him, it shall be the duty of the Official Receiver to appear on the hearing of the application and call the attention of the court to any matters which appear to the Official Receiver to be relevant, and if the court, after hearing any evidence given or witnesses called by the Official Receiver, grants the application, the court may allow the applicant such costs as in its discretion it may think fit.

(7) Notes of the examination shall be taken down in writing, and shall be read over to or by, and signed by, the person examined, and may thereafter be used in evidence against him, and shall be open to the inspection of any creditor or contributory at all reasonable times.

(8) The court may, if it thinks fit, adjourn the examination from time to time.

Jurisdiction of Registrar

222A.(1) Unless otherwise ordered by the court in a particular case, the Registrar may exercise and perform the powers and duties conferred or imposed upon the court by sections 221 and 222.

(2) The Registrar may, if he exercises the jurisdiction conferred on him by this section-

      (a) refer any examination for hearing by a judge;

      (b) at any time adjourn an examination for further hearing before a judge.

(3) A judge may, if an examination is referred to him under subsection (2)(a), hear it himself, or refer it back to the Registrar for hearing by him.

(4) A judge may, if an examination is adjourned under subsection (2)(b) for further hearing before a judge-

      (a) continue the examination;

<ol type="b" start="2">
<li>at any time direct that the examination be continued before the Registrar; and</li>
</ol>

<ol type="c" start="3">
<li>make such other order the give such directions as he may consider proper
.</li>
</ol>

(5)   Any reference in this Ordinance to the court shall include a reference to the Registrar exercising the jurisdiction conferred on him by this section.

(6)   Notwithstanding subsection (5), the Registrar, when exercising the jurisdiction conferred by this section, shall not have power to make an order for the committal of a person for contempt of court.

(7)   In this section-

"Registrar" means-

<ol type="a">
<li>the registrar of the Supreme Court;</li>
</ol>

<ol type="b" start="2">
<li>any Deputy Registrar of the Supreme Court; and</li>
</ol>

<ol type="c" start="3">
<li>any Assistant Registrar of the Supreme Court appointed by the Chief Justice for the purposes of this section.</li>
</ol>

223.   *(Repealed)*

Power to arrest absconding contributory or officer

224.   The court, at any time either before or after making a winding-up order, on proof of probable cause for believing that a contributory or any past or present officer of the company has absconded or is about to quit Hong Kong or otherwise to abscond or to remove or conceal any of his property for the purpose of evading payment of calls or debts due to the company or of avoiding examination respecting the affairs of the company, may order that the contributory or officer be arrested and his books and papers and movable personal property seized and him and them safely kept until such time as the court may order.

Powers of court cumulative

225.   Any powers by this Ordinance conferred on the court shall be in addition to and not in restriction of any existing powers of instituting proceedings against any contributory or officer or debtor of the company, or the estate of any contributory or officer or debtor, for the recovery of any call or other sums.

Delegation to liquidator of certain powers of court

226.   Provision may be made by general rules for enabling or requiring all or any of the powers and duties conferred and imposed on the court by this Ordinance in respect of the following matters-

(a)   the holding and conducting of meetings to ascertain the wishes of creditors and contributories;

(b)   the settling of lists of contributories and the rectifying of the register of members where required, and the collecting and applying of the assets;

(c)   the paying, delivery, conveyance, surrender or transfer of money, property, books or papers to the liquidator;

(d)   the making of calls;

(e)   the fixing of a date on or before which creditors are to prove their debts or claims,

to be exercised or performed by the liquidator as an officer of the court, and subject to the control of the court:

Provided that the liquidator shall not, without the special leave of the court, rectify the register of members, and shall not make any call without either the special leave of the court or the sanction of the committee of inspection.

Dissolution of company otherwise than by order of court

226A.(1) In the case of a company in respect of which the following conditions are satisfied-

(a)   the affairs of the company have been completely wound up; and

(b)   the liquidator has been granted his release by order of the court under section 205,

the Official Receiver may deliver to the Registrar a certificate, signed by the Official Receiver, stating that the company is a company in respect of which those conditions are satisfied.

(2) The Registrar shall forthwith register any certificate delivered under subsection (1), and on the expiration of 2 years from the registration thereof the company shall be dissolved:

Provided that the court may, on the application of the Official Receiver, make an order deferring the date at which the dissolution of the company is to take effect for such time as the court may think fit.

(3) The Official Receiver shall, within 7 days after the making of an order of the court under subsection (2), deliver an office copy thereof to the Registrar for registration.

Dissolution of company by order of court

227.(1) When the affairs of a company have been completely wound up, the court, if the liquidator makes an application in that behalf, shall make an order that the company be dissolved from the date of the order, and the company shall be dissolved accordingly.

(2) A copy of the order shall within 14 days from the date thereof be delivered by the liquidator to the Registrar for registration.

(3) If the liquidator makes default in complying with the requirements of this section, he shall be liable to a fine and, for continued default, to a daily default fine.

(iiA) Winding Up By The Court With A Regulation Order

Court may make a regulating order

227A.(1) Where it appears to the court on application being made by the Official Receiver, liquidator or by any creditor at any time after the presentation of a winding up petition that by reason of the large number of creditors or contributories or for any other reason the interest of the creditors so requires, it may, on or after the making of a winding-up order, order that the winding up of the company by the court shall be regulated specially by the court, and such order shall be known as a regulating order.

(2) Where a regulating order is made it shall be published in such manner as the court may direct, and sections 227B to 227E inclusive shall apply to the winding up.

(3) Where a regulating order is made the Companies (Winding-up) Rules (Cap. 32 sub. leg.) shall apply mutatis mutandis to the Official Receiver, liquidator and committee of inspection appointed or acting after the making of a regulating order, and to the conduct of any ballot or other proceedings ordered by the court under section 227C or 227D.

(4) Where any order made under section 227B, 227C or 227D prescribes any procedure it shall be deemed to be in substitution for the procedure which would be required by this Ordinance but for the making of such order, and in particular where any such order prescribes a procedure for doing something which would otherwise be done at a meeting of creditors or Contributories no such meeting shall be required to be held.

Appointment of liquidator and committee of inspection

227B.(1) The court may on the application of the Official Receiver by order-

(a) dispense with the summoning of first meetings of creditors and contributories as required under sections 194 and 206 for the purpose of considering the appointment of a liquidator and a committee of inspection;

(b) appoint the Official Receiver or such other person or persons recommended by him as liquidator or liquidators; and

(c) appoint such qualified persons as it thinks fit as a committee of inspection, and may remove any member thereof and fill any vacancy therein.

(2) Where under subsection (1) the court makes any appointment of a liquidator or a committee

of inspection, or where it removes any member of such committee of inspection or fills any vacancy therein, it shall not be necessary to ascertain the wishes of the creditors or contributories, and the provisions of section 194(b) or 206(1) and (2) or 207(6) and (7), as the case may be, shall cease to apply and any action taken under such provisions in respect of any appointment of a liquidator or committee of inspection or any removal therefrom or any filling of any vacancy therein shall cease to have effect.

Informing creditors and contributories and ascertaining their wishes and directions

227C.   The court may vary the procedure for ascertaining the wishes and directions of creditors and contributories, and for keeping such creditors and contributories informed as to any matter relating to the winding up, and for such purposes the court may-

(a)   order that the Official Receiver or liquidator inform the creditors and contributories of such matters in such manner as it may direct;

(b)   for the purposes of sections 200 and 287 order that the wishes of creditors and contributories be ascertained by the Official Receiver or liquidator in such manner as it may direct;

(c)   for the purposes of section 200 order that the wishes of the creditors and contributories ascertained pursuant to paragraph *(b)* be reported by the Official Receiver or liquidator to the court, which may thereupon give such directions as it sees fit, and that notwithstanding section 200(2) the liquidator shall not be required to summon any meetings of creditors or contributories:

Provided that nothing in section 227A(4) or in this paragraph shall operate to prevent any person making application to the court under section 200(5);

(d)   order that instead of the same being sent by post as required under section 203(5) the account of the liquidator or a summary thereof be communicated by the Official Receiver to the creditors and contributories in such manner as it may direct.

Compromises and arrangements with creditors

227D.(1) The court may for the purposes of section 166 and notwithstanding subsection (1) thereof order that the wishes of creditors or contributories concerning agreement to or rejection of any compromise or arrangement be ascertained by the liquidator in such manner as it may direct including the conduct of a ballot and the use of voting letters and without holding meetings.

(2)   Where a majority in number and three-fourths in value of the creditors, or a class of creditors, as the case may be, who have proved their debt, or who by virtue of section 227E are deemed for voting purposes to have proved a debt exceeding $250, agree to any compromise, such agreement shall, for the purposes of section 166, have the same effect as if a meeting of the creditors or class of creditors had been summoned under section 166(1) and a majority in number representing three-fourths in value of the creditors or class of creditors, as the case may be, had been present and voted either in person or by proxy at the meeting and agreed to the compromise.

(3) In the event of the court ordering the holding of any meetings it may order that the provisions of this Ordinance relating to the holding of meetings be varied, abrogated or added to for the purpose of such meetings.

(4) In subsection (1) "arrangement" has the meaning assigned to it by section 166(5).

Proof of debts

227E.(1) In the case of a bank, any creditor who is a depositor, whether on current, savings, deposit, fixed deposit or other account, shall, unless and until the Official Receiver or liquidator by notice in writing requires him to make a formal proof of debt, be deemed to have proved his debt-

> *(a)* for voting purposes, for the net balance to his credit in the books of the bank on all his accounts taken together, at the relevant date,

> *(b)* for dividend purposes, for the said balance plus or minus, as the case may be, the net amount of interest accrued due by or to the bank on the said accounts at the relevant date.

(2) Any debt which is deemed to have been proved by virtue of subsection (1) shall be treated as if a proof thereof had been duly lodged in due time with the Official Receiver or liquidator, and had been admitted for voting and dividend purposes respectively for the said amounts stated in subsection (1).

(3) In subsection (1), the expression "the relevant date" shall have the meaning assigned to it by section 265(6).

(iiB) Winding Up By Court By Way Of Summary Procedure

Application of Ordinance to small winding-ups

227F.(1) Where after the presentation of a winding-up petition-

> *(a)* the court is satisfied; or

> *(b)* the Official Receiver reports to the court,

that the property of the company is not likely to exceed in value $200,000, the court may make an order that the company be wound up in a summary manner, and thereupon the provisions of this Ordinance shall apply subject to the following modifications-

> **(i)** the Official Receiver shall be the liquidator but there shall be no meetings of creditors and contributories under section 194 or 206;

      (ii)   there shall be no committee of inspection, and the Official Receiver may do all things which may be done by a liquidator with the sanction of a committee of inspection;

      (iii)   such other modifications as may be prescribed with a view to saying expense and simplifying procedure.

(2)   The court may, upon the application of the Official Receiver, at any time before the dissolution of the company rescind an order made under subsection (1) and thereupon the winding up shall proceed as if the order had not been made.

(iii) Voluntary Winding Up

Resolutions for, and commencement of Voluntary Winding Up

Circumstances in which company may be wound up voluntarily

228.(1) A company may be wound up voluntarily-

      (a)   when the period, if any, fixed for the duration of the company by the articles expires, or the event, if any, occurs on the occurrence of which the memorandum or articles provide that the company is to be dissolved, and the company in general meeting has passed a resolution requiring the company to be wound up voluntarily;

      (b)   if the company resolves by special resolution that the company be wound up voluntarily;

      (c)   if the company resolves by special resolution to the effect that it cannot by reason of its liabilities continue its business, and that it is advisable to wind up;

      (d)   if the directors of the company or, in the case of a company having more than 2 directors, the majority of the directors, make and deliver to the Registrar a statutory declaration under section 228A(1).

(2)   In this Ordinance, the expression "a resolution for voluntary winding up" means a resolution passed under subsection (1)(a), (b) or (c).

Special procedure for voluntary winding up in case of inability to continue its business

228A.(1) The directors of a company or, in the case of a company having more than 2 directors, the majority of the directors, may, if they have formed the opinion that the company cannot by reason of its liabilities continue its business, resolve at a meeting of the directors and deliver to the Registrar a statutory declaration by one of the directors verifying written statements signed by the directors recording the resolution that-

(a)   the company cannot by reason of its liabilities continue its business; and

(b)   they consider it is necessary that the company be wound up and that there are good and sufficient reasons for the winding up to be commenced under this section; and

(c)   meetings of the company and of its creditors will be summoned for a date not later than 28 days after the delivery of the declaration to the Registrar.

(1A)   A statutory declaration made under subsection (1) shall have no effect for the purposes of this Ordinance unless it is delivered to the Registrar for registration within 7 days after the date on which it was made.

(2)   Any director of a company making a declaration under subsection (1) without having reasonable grounds for the opinion that the company cannot by reason of its liabilities continue in business, shall be liable to a fine and imprisonment.

(3)   Where a statutory declaration made by a director of a company under subsection (1) is delivered to the Registrar-

(a)   the winding up of the company shall commence at the time of the delivery of such declaration;

(b)   the directors shall forthwith appoint a person to be provisional liquidator in the winding up and deliver evidence of the appointment to the Registrar with the statutory declaration;

(c)   the directors shall cause meetings of the company and the creditors of the company to be summoned for a date not later than 28 days after the delivery of such declaration.

(3A)   A director who fails to comply with subsection (3)(b) or (c) shall be liable to a fine.

(3B)   Where the directors of a company fail to comply with the requirements of subsection (3)(c) the provisional liquidator appointed under subsection (3)(b) may summon such meetings.

(3C)   No person shall be appointed to be a provisional liquidator under subsection (3)(b) unless-

(a)   he has consented in writing to such appointment; and

(b)   he is a solicitor, or a professional accountant under the Professional Accountants Ordinance (Cap. 50).

(4)   Not later than 14 days after the appointment of a provisional liquidator by the directors of a company under this section, the directors shall give public notice in the Gazette of-

> *(a)* the commencement of the winding up of the company by the delivery to the Registrar of a statutory declaration made under this section, and the date of such delivery; and
>
> *(b)* the appointment of the provisional liquidator and his name and address.

(4A) A provisional liquidator appointed by the directors of a company under this section shall, within 14 days after the date of his appointment, deliver to the Registrar for registration a notice of his appointment.

(4B) If a provisional liquidator fails to comply with subsection (4A) he shall be liable to a daily default fine.

(5) *(Repealed)*

(6) A provisional liquidator appointed by the directors of a company under this section shall-

> *(a)* unless the liquidator is sooner appointed, hold office until a meeting of creditors of the company summoned under subsection (3)(c) or, if that meeting is adjourned, any adjourned meeting, may allow;
>
> *(b)* take into his custody or under his control all the property and things in action to which the company is or appears to be entitled;
>
> *(c)* be entitled, out of the funds of the company, to such remuneration as the committee of inspection or, if there is no such committee, the creditors, may fix and to reimbursement of expenses properly incurred by him, but he shall not be liable, and no civil action or other proceedings shall lie against him, in respect of acts properly done by him.

(7) A provisional liquidator appointed by the directors of a company under this section shall, for the period of his appointment, have the like powers and be subject to the like duties as a liquidator in a creditors' voluntary winding up, and, accordingly, all the powers of the directors shall cease during that period except so far as may be necessary for the purpose of enabling the directors to comply with this section or the provisional liquidator sanctions the continuance thereof for any other purpose.

(7A) Notwithstanding subsection (7), a provisional liquidator appointed by the directors of a company under this section shall not have power to sell any property to which the company is or appears to be entitled, except where such sale is made in the course of carrying on business in accordance with section 231, unless-

> *(a)* the property is of a perishable nature or likely to deteriorate if kept; or
>
> *(b)* the court, on the application of the provisional liquidator, orders the sale of the property.

(8)   In relation to every winding up commenced under this section-

    (a)   section 241 shall apply to a meeting of the creditors of the company summoned under this section as it applies to a meeting of the creditors of a company summoned under that section except that-

        (i)   for the words "at which the resolution for voluntary winding up is to be proposed" in subsection (1) of that section there shall be substituted the words "of the company";

        (ia)   the sending of the notices by post and the advertisement of the meeting of creditors required by subsections (1) and (2) of that section respectively shall occur at least 7 days before the meeting of creditors, and the requirement in subsection (1) of that section as to simultaneous sending of notices shall not apply;

        (ii)   subsection (5) of that section shall be omitted;

    (b)   subject to paragraph (a), sections 241 to 248 shall apply as they apply in relation to a creditors' voluntary winding up.

Notice of resolution to wind up voluntarily

229.(1) When a company has passed a resolution for voluntary winding up, it shall, within 14 days after the passing of the resolution, give notice of the resolution by advertisement in the Gazette.

(2)   If default is made in complying with this section, the company and every officer of the company who is in default shall be liable to a fine and, for continued default, to a daily default fine, and for the purposes of this subsection the liquidator of the company shall be deemed to be an officer of the company.

Commencement of voluntary winding up

230.   Except as provided in section 228A(3)(a), a voluntary winding up shall be deemed to commence at the time of the passing of the resolution for voluntary winding up.

Consequences of Voluntary Winding Up

Effect of voluntary winding up on business and status of company

231.   In case of a voluntary winding up, the company shall, from the commencement of the winding up, cease to carry on its business, except so far as may be required for the beneficial winding up thereof.

Provided that the corporate state and corporate powers of the company shall, notwithstanding anything to the contrary in its articles, continue until it is dissolved.

Avoidance of transfers, &c., after commencement of voluntary winding up

232.   Any transfer of shares, not being a transfer made to or with the sanction of the liquidator, and any alteration in the status of the members of the company, made after the commencement of a voluntary winding up, shall be void.

Declaration of Solvency

Statutory declaration of solvency in case of proposal to wind up voluntarily

233.(1) Where it is proposed to wind up a company voluntarily, the directors of the company or, in the case of a company having more than 2 directors, the majority of the directors, may at a meeting of the directors make a statutory declaration to the effect that they have made a full inquiry into the affairs of the company, and that, having so done, they have formed the opinion that the company will be able to pay its debts in full within such period not exceeding 12 months from the commencement of the winding up as may be specified in the declaration.

(2)   A declaration made as aforesaid shall have no effect for the purposes of this Ordinance unless-

> *(a)*   it is made within the 5 weeks immediately preceding the date of the passing of the resolution for winding up the company or on that date but before the passing of the resolution and is delivered to the Registrar for registration not later than the date of delivery to the Registrar of a copy of the resolution; and

> *(b)*   it embodies a statement of the company's assets and liabilities as at the latest practicable date before the making of the declaration.

(3) Any director of a company making a declaration under this section without having reasonable grounds for the opinion that the company will be able to pay its debts in full within the period specified in the declaration, shall be liable to a fine and imprisonment; and if the company is wound up in pursuance of a resolution passed within the period of 5 weeks after the making of the declaration, but its debts are not paid or provided for in full within the period stated in the declaration, it shall be presumed until the contrary is shown that the director did not have reasonable grounds for his opinion.

(4) A winding up in the case of which a declaration has been made and delivered under this section is in this Ordinance referred to as "a members' voluntary winding up", and a winding up in the case of which a declaration has not been made and delivered as aforesaid is in this Ordinance referred to as "a creditors' voluntary winding up".

(5) Notwithstanding subsections (1) and (2), any declaration of solvency made in connexion with a winding up commenced but not completed before the date of commencement of the Companies (Amendment) Ordinance 1984 (6 of 1984) shall, if it has been effective for the purposes of this Ordinance before that date, continue to have effect for those purposes on and after that date, and-

(a)   such winding up shall be deemed to be a members' voluntary winding up within the meaning of this section;

(b)   subsection (3) shall not apply in relation to any such declaration or winding up.

Provisions applicable to a Members' Voluntary Winding Up

Provisions applicable to members' winding up

234.   The provisions contained in sections 235 to 239A shall apply in relation to members' voluntary winding up.

Power of company to appoint and fix remuneration of liquidators

235.(1) The company in general meeting shall appoint one or more liquidators for the purpose of winding up the affairs and distributing the assets of the company, and may fix the remuneration to be paid to him or them.

(2)   On the appointment of a liquidator all the powers of the directors shall cease, except so far as the company in general meeting, or the liquidator, sanctions the continuance thereof.

Power to remove liquidator

235A.(1) The company may by special resolution remove a liquidator from office at a general meeting of which notice specifying the intention to propose such resolution has been duly given to the creditors and the liquidator.

(2)   The court may, on the application of any creditor or contributory, order that a liquidator whom it is proposed to remove from office under this section shall not be so removed.

(3)   A general meeting for the purpose of this section may be convened by any contributory.

Power to fill vacancy in office of liquidators

236.(1) If a vacancy occurs by death, resignation, or otherwise in the office of liquidator appointed by the company, the company in general meeting may, subject to any arrangement with its creditors, fill the vacancy.

(2) For that purpose a general meeting may be convened by any contributory or, if there were more liquidators than one, by the continuing liquidators.

(3) The meeting shall be held in manner provided by this Ordinance or by the articles, or in such manner as may, on application by any contributory or by the continuing liquidators, be determined by the court.

Power of Liquidator to accept shares, &c. as consideration for sale of property of company

237.(1) Where a company is proposed to be, or is in course of being, wound up voluntarily, and the whole or part of its business or property is proposed to be transferred or sold to another company, whether a company within the meaning of this Ordinance or not (in this section called the transferee company) the liquidator of the first-mentioned company (in this section called the transferor company) may, with the sanction of a special resolution of that company, conferring either a general authority on the liquidator or an authority in respect of any particular arrangement, receive in compensation or part compensation for the transfer or sale, shares, policies, or other like interests in the transferee company, for distribution among the members of the transferor company, or may enter into any other arrangement whereby the members of the transferor company may, in lieu of receiving cash, shares, policies, or other like interests, or in addition thereto, participate in the profits of or receive any other benefit from the transferee company.

(2) Any sale or arrangement in pursuance of this section shall be binding on the members of the transferor company.

(3) If any member of the transferor company, whether he voted in favour of the special resolution or not, expresses his dissent therefrom in writing addressed to the liquidator, and left at the registered office of the company within 7 days after the passing of the resolution, he may require the liquidator either to abstain from carrying the resolution into effect, or to purchase his interest at a price to be determined by agreement or by arbitration in manner provided by this section.

(4) If the liquidator elects to purchase the member's interest, the purchase money must be paid before the company is dissolved, and be raised by the liquidator in such manner as may be determined by special resolution.

(5) A special resolution shall not be invalid for the purposes of this section by reason that it is passed before or concurrently with a resolution for voluntary winding up or for appointing liquidators, but, if an order is made within a year for winding up the company by the court, the special resolution shall not be valid unless sanctioned by the court.

(6) For the purposes of an arbitration under this section, the provisions of the Companies Clauses Consolidation Act 1845 (1845 c. 16), with respect to the settlement of disputes by arbitration, shall be incorporated with this Ordinance, and in the construction of those provisions this Ordinance shall be deemed to be the special Act, and the company shall mean the transferor company, and any appointment by the said incorporated provisions directed to be made under the hand of the secretary, or any 2 of the directors, may be made under the hand of the liquidator, or, if there is more than one liquidator, then of any 2 or more of the liquidators.

Duty of liquidator to call creditors' meeting in case of insolvency

237A.(1) If, in the case of a winding up commenced after the commencement of the Companies (Amendment) Ordinance 1984 (6 of 1984), the liquidator is at any time of opinion that the company will not be able to pay its debts in full within the period stated in the declaration under section 233, he shall forthwith summon a meeting of the creditors, and shall lay before the meeting a statement of the assets and liabilities of the company.

(2) The creditors may, at a meeting called by the liquidator under this section, appoint another liquidator in his place and fix the remuneration of the liquidator so appointed, and may, if they think fit, appoint a committee of inspection.

(3) If the liquidator fails to comply with subsection (1), he shall be liable to a fine.

Duty of liquidator to call general meeting at end of each year

238.(1) Subject to section 239A, in the event of the winding up continuing for more than 1 year, the liquidator shall summon a general meeting of the company at the end of the first year from the commencement of the winding up, and of each succeeding year, or at the first convenient date within 3 months from the end of the year or such longer period as the Official Receiver may allow, and shall lay before the meeting an account of his acts and dealings and of the conduct of the winding up during the preceding year.

(2) If the liquidator fails to comply with this section, he shall be liable to a fine.

Final meeting and dissolution

239.(1) Subject to section 239A, as soon as the affairs of the company are fully wound up, the liquidator shall make up an account of the winding up, showing how the winding up has been conducted and the property of the company has been disposed of, and thereupon shall call a general meeting of the company for the purpose of laying before it the account, and giving any explanation thereof.

(2) The meeting shall be called by advertisement in the Gazette, specifying the time, place, and object thereof, and published 1 month at least before the meeting.

(3) Within 1 week after the meeting, the liquidator shall send to the Registrar a copy of the account, and shall make a return to him of the holding of the meeting and of its date, and if the copy is not sent or the return is not made in accordance with this subsection the liquidator shall be liable to a fine and, for continued default, to a daily default fine:

Provided that, if a quorum is not present at the meeting, the liquidator shall, in lieu of the return herein before mentioned, make a return that the meeting was duly summoned and that no quorum was present thereat, and upon such a return being made the provisions of the subsection as to the making of the return shall be deemed to have been complied with.

(4) The Registrar on receiving the account and either of the returns hereinbefore mentioned shall forthwith register them, and on the expiration of 3 months from the registration of the return the company shall be dissolved:

Provided that the court may, on the application of the liquidator or of any other person who appears to the court to be interested, make an order deferring the date at which the dissolution of the company is to take effect for such time as the court thinks fit.

(5) It shall be the duty of the person on whose application an order of the court under this section is made, within 7 days after the making of the order, to deliver to the Registrar an office copy of the order for registration, and if that person fails so to do he shall be liable to a fine and, for continued default, to a daily default fine.

(6) If the liquidator fails to call a general meeting of the company as required by this section, he shall be liable to a fine.

Alternative provisions as to annual and final meetings in case of insolvency

239A. Where section 237A has effect, sections 247 and 248 shall apply to the winding up to the exclusion of sections 238 and 239, as if the winding up were a creditors' voluntary winding up and not a members' voluntary winding up:

Provided that the liquidator shall not be required to summon a meeting of creditors under section 247 at the end of the first year from the commencement of the winding up, unless the meeting held under section 237A is held more than 3 months before the end of that year.

Provisions applicable to a Creditors' Voluntary Winding Up

Provisions applicable to creditors' winding up

240. The provisions contained in sections 241 to 248 shall apply in relation to a creditors' voluntary winding up.

Meeting of creditors

241.(1) The company shall cause a meeting of the creditors of the company to be summoned for the day, or the day next following the day, on which there is to be held the meeting at which the resolution for voluntary winding up is to be proposed, and shall cause the notices of the said meeting of creditors to be sent by post to the creditors simultaneously with the sending of the notices of the said meeting of the company.

(2) The company shall cause notice of the meeting of the creditors to be advertised once in the Gazette and once at least in, respectively, an English language newspaper and a Chinese language newspaper circulating in Hong Kong.

(3) The directors of the company shall-

> *(a)* cause a full statement of the position of the company's affairs together with a list of the creditors of the company and the estimated amount of their claims to be laid before the meeting of creditors to be held as aforesaid; and

> *(b)* appoint one of their number to preside at the said meeting.

(4) It shall be the duty of the director appointed to preside at the meeting of creditors to attend the meeting and preside thereat.

(5) If the meeting of the company at which the resolution for voluntary winding up is to be proposed is adjourned and the resolution is passed at an adjourned meeting, any resolution passed at the meeting of the creditors held in pursuance of subsection (1) shall have effect as if it had been passed immediately after the passing of the resolution for winding up the company.

(6)   If default is made-

        (a)   by the company in complying with subsections (1) and (2);

        (b)   by the directors of the company in complying with subsection (3);

        (c)   by any director of the company in complying with subsection (4),

the company, directors or director, as the case may be, shall be liable to a fine, and, in the case of default by the company, every officer of the company who is in default shall be liable to the like penalty.

Appointment of liquidator

242.   The creditors and the company at their respective meetings mentioned in section 241 may nominate a person to be liquidator for the purpose of winding up the affairs and distributing the assets of the company, and if the creditors and the company nominate different persons, the person nominated by the creditors shall be liquidator, and if no person is nominated by the creditors the person, if any, nominated by the company shall be liquidator:

Provided that in the case of different persons being nominated any director, member, or creditor of the company may, within 7 days after the date on which the nomination was made by the creditors, apply to the court for an order either directing that the person nominated as liquidator by the company shall be liquidator instead of or jointly with the person nominated by the creditors, or appointing some other person to be liquidator instead of the person appointed by the creditors.

Appointment of committee of inspection

243.(1)   The creditors at the meeting to be held in pursuance of section 241 or at any subsequent meeting, may, if they think fit, appoint a committee of inspection consisting of not more than 5 persons, and if such a committee is appointed the company may, either at the meeting at which the resolution for voluntary winding up is passed or at any time subsequently in general meeting, appoint such number of persons as they think fit to act as members of the committee not exceeding 5 in number:

Provided that the creditors may, if they think fit, resolve that all or any of the persons so appointed by the company ought not to be members of the committee of inspection, and, if the creditors so resolve, the persons mentioned in the resolution shall not, unless the court otherwise directs, be qualified to act as members of the committee, and on any application to the court under this provision the court may, if it thinks fit, appoint other persons to act as such members in place of the persons mentioned in the resolution.

(2) Subject to the provisions of this section and to general rules, section 207 (except subsection (1)) shall apply with respect to a committee of inspection appointed under this section as they apply with respect to a committee of inspection appointed in a winding up by the court.

Fixing of liquidators' remuneration and cesser of directors' powers

244.(1) The committee of inspection, or if there is no such committee, the creditors, may fix the remuneration to be paid to the liquidator or liquidators.

(2) On the appointment of a liquidator, all the powers of the directors shall cease, except so far as the committee of inspection, or if there is no such committee, the creditors, sanction the continuance thereof.

Power to fill vacancy in office of liquidator

245. If a vacancy occurs, by death, resignation or otherwise, in the office of a liquidator, other than a liquidator appointed by, or by the direction of, the court, the creditors may fill the vacancy.

Application of section 237 to a creditors' voluntary winding up

246. Section 237 shall apply in the case of a creditors' voluntary winding up as in the case of a members' voluntary winding up, with the modification that the powers of the liquidator under the said section shall not be exercised except with the sanction either of the court or of the committee of inspection.

Duty of liquidator to call meetings of company and of creditors at end of each year

247.(1) In the event of the winding up continuing for more than 1 year, the liquidator shall summon a general meeting of the company and a meeting of creditors at the end of the first year from the commencement of the winding up, and of each succeeding year, or at the first convenient date within 3 months from the end of the year or such longer period as the Official Receiver may allow, and shall lay before the meetings an account of his acts and dealings and of the conduct of the winding up during the preceding year.

(2) If the liquidator fails to comply with this section, he shall be liable to a fine.

Final meeting and dissolution

248.(1) As soon as the affairs of the company are fully wound up, the liquidator shall make up an account of the winding up, showing how the winding up has been conducted and the property of the company has been disposed of, and thereupon shall call a general meeting of the company and a meeting of the creditors, for the purpose of laying the account before the meetings, and giving any explanation thereof.

(2) Each such meeting shall be called by advertisement in the Gazette, specifying the time, place, and object thereof, and published 1 month at least before the meeting.

(3) Within 1 week after the date of the meetings, or, if the meetings are not held on the same date, after the date of the later meeting, the liquidator shall send to the Registrar a copy of the account, and shall make a return to him of the holding of the meetings and of their dates, and if the copy is not sent or the return is not made in accordance with this subsection the liquidator shall be liable to a fine and, for continued default, to a daily default fine:

Provided that, if a quorum is not present at either such meeting, the liquidator shall, in lieu of the return hereinbefore mentioned, make a return that the meeting was duly summoned and that no quorum was present thereat, and upon such a return being made the provisions of this subsection as to the making of the return shall, in respect of that meeting, be deemed to have been complied with.

(4) The Registrar on receiving the account and in respect of each such meeting either of the returns herein before mentioned shall forthwith register them, and on the expiration of 3 months from the registration thereof the company shall be dissolved:

Provided that the court may, on the application of the liquidator or of any other person who appears to the court to be interested, make an order deferring the date at which the dissolution of the company is to take effect for such time as the court thinks fit.

(5) It shall be the duty of the person on whose application an order of the court under this section is made, within 7 days after the making of the order, to deliver to the Registrar an office copy of the order for registration, and if that person fails so to do he shall be liable to a fine and, for continued default, to a daily default fine.

(6) If the liquidator fails to call a general meeting of the company or a meeting of the creditors as required by this section, he shall be liable to a fine.

Provisions applicable to every Voluntary Winding Up

Provisions applicable to every voluntary winding up

249. The provisions contained in sections 250 to 257 shall apply to every voluntary winding up.

Distribution of property of company

250. Subject to the provisions of this Ordinance as to preferential payments, the property of a company shall, on its winding up, be applied in satisfaction of its liabilities *pari passu*, and, subject to such application, shall, unless the articles otherwise provide, be distributed among the members according to their rights and interests in the company.

Powers and duties of liquidator in voluntary winding up

251.(1) The liquidator may-

    (a)   in the case of a members' voluntary winding up, with the sanction of a special resolution of the company, and, in the case of a creditors' voluntary winding up, with the sanction of the court or the committee of inspection or (if there

is no such committee) a meeting of the creditors, exercise any of the powers given by paragraphs (d), (e) and (f) of section 199(1) to a liquidator in a winding up by the court;

(b)   without sanction, exercise any of the other powers by this Ordinance given to the liquidator in a winding up by the court;

(c)   exercise the power of the court under this Ordinance of settling a list of contributories, and the list of contributories shall be prima facie evidence of the liability of the persons named therein to be contributories;

(d)   exercise the power of the court of making calls;

(e)   summon general meetings of the company for the purpose of obtaining the sanction of the company by special resolution or for any other purpose he may think fit.

(2)   The liquidator shall pay the debts of the company and shall adjust the rights of the contributories among themselves.

(3)   When several liquidators are appointed, any power given by this Ordinance may be exercised by such one or more of them as may be determined at the time of their appointment, or, in default of such determination, by any number not less than 2.

Court may appoint and remove liquidator in voluntary winding up

252.(1)   If from any cause whatever there is no liquidator acting, the court may appoint a liquidator.

(2)   The court may, on cause shown, remove a liquidator and appoint another liquidator.

Notice by liquidator of his appointment

253.(1)   The liquidator shall, within 21 days after his appointment, publish in the Gazette and deliver to the Registrar for registration a notice of his appointment in the form prescribed.

(2)   If the liquidator fails to comply with the requirements of this section he shall be liable to a fine and, for continued default, to a daily default fine.

(3)   This section shall not apply to the appointment of a provisional liquidator by the directors of a company under section 228A(3)(b).

Arrangement, when binding on creditors

254.(1)   Any arrangement entered into between a company about to be, or in the course of being, wound up and its creditors shall, subject to the right of appeal under this section, be binding on the company if sanctioned by a special resolution, and on the creditors if acceded to by three-fourths in number and value of the creditors.

(2) Any creditor or contributory may, within 3 weeks from the completion of the arrangement, appeal to the court against it, and the court may thereupon, as it thinks just, amend, vary, or confirm the arrangement.

Power to apply to court to have questions determined or powers exercised

255.(1) The liquidator or any contributory or creditor may apply to the court to determine any question arising in the winding up of a company, or to exercise, as respects the enforcing of calls, or any other matter, all or any of the powers which the court might exercise if the company were being wound up by the court.

(2) The court, if satisfied that the determination of the question or the required exercise of power will be just and beneficial, may accede wholly or partially to the application on such terms and conditions as it thinks fit, or may make such other order on the application as it thinks just.

(3) A copy of an order made by virtue of this section staying the proceedings in the winding up shall forthwith be delivered by the company, or otherwise as may be prescribed, to the Registrar for registration.

Audit of liquidator's accounts in voluntary winding up

255A.(1) The liquidator shall keep an account of his receipts and payments as liquidator and, subject to subsection (2), shall cause the account to be audited.

(2) An audit under this section shall not be required if the committee of inspection or, as the case may be, the company by ordinary resolution so determines.

Costs of voluntary winding up

256. All costs, charges, and expenses properly incurred in the winding up, including the remuneration of the liquidator, shall be payable out of the assets of the company in priority to all other claims.

Saving for rights of creditors and contributories

257. The winding up of a company shall not bar the right of any creditor or contributory to have it wound up by the court, but in the case of an application by a contributory, the court must be satisfied that the rights of the contributories will be prejudiced by a voluntary winding up.

(iv) *(Repealed)*

258-262. *(Repealed)*

(v) **Provisions Applicable To Every Mode Of Winding Up**

Proof and Ranking of Claims

Debts of all descriptions to be proved

263.   In every winding up (subject in the case of insolvent companies to the application in accordance with the provisions of this Ordinance of the law of bankruptcy) all debts payable on a contingency, and all claims against the company, present or future, certain or contingent, ascertained or sounding only in damages, shall be admissible to proof against the company, a just estimate being made, so far as possible, of the value of such debts or claims as may be subject to any contingency or sound only in damages, or for some other reason do not bear a certain value.

Application of bankruptcy rules in winding up of insolvent companies

264.   In the winding up of an insolvent company the same rules shall prevail and be observed with regard to the respective rights of secured and unsecured creditors and to debts provable and to the valuation of annuities and future and contingent liabilities as are in force for the time being under the law of bankruptcy with respect to the estates of persons adjudged bankrupt, and all persons who in any such case would be entitled to prove for and receive dividends out of the assets of the company may come in under the winding up, and make such claims against the company as they respectively are entitled to by virtue of this section.

Interest on debts

264A.(1) In the winding up of a company, not being an insolvent company, interest is payable in accordance with this section on any debt proved in the winding up, including so much of any such debt as represents interest on the remainder.

(2)   Any surplus remaining after the payment of debts proved in a winding up referred to in subsection (1) shall, before being applied for any other purpose, be applied in paying interest on those debts in respect of the period during which the debt has been outstanding, in the case of -

      (a)   a winding up by court -

            (i)   where the company has by special resolution resolved that the company be wound up, since the date of the resolution; and

            (ii)   in any other case, since the date of the winding-up order; and

      (b)   a voluntary winding up, since the commencement of the winding up (which must be construed having regard to section 228A(3)(a) or 230, as may be appropriate).

(3)   All interest under this section ranks equally, whether or not the debts on which it is payable rank equally.

(4)   The rate of interest payable under this section in respect of any debt is whichever is the greater of the following -

(a)   the rate specified under section 49(1) of the Supreme Court Ordinance (Cap.4); and

(b)   the rate applicable to that debt apart from the winding up.

Extortionate credit transactions

264B.(1) This section applies, in relation to a company being wound up where the company is, or has been, a party to a transaction for, or involving, the provision of credit to the company.

(2)   The court may, on the application of the liquidator, make an order with respect to the transaction if the transaction is or was extortionate and was entered into in the period of 3 years ending on, in the case of -

(a)   a winding up by court -

(i)   where the company has by special resolution resolved that the company be wound up, the date of the resolution; and

(ii)   in any other case, the date of the winding-up order; and

(b)   a voluntary winding up, the commencement of the winding up (which must be construed having regard to section 228A(3)(a) or 230, as may be appropriate).

(3)   For the purposes of this section a transaction is extortionate if, having regard to the risk accepted by the person providing the credit -

(a)   the terms of it are or were such as to require grossly exorbitant payments to be made (whether unconditionally or in certain contingencie) in respect of the provision of credit; or

(b)   it otherwise grossly contravenes ordinary principles of fair dealing,

and it shall be presumed, unless the contrary is proved, that a transaction with respect to which an application is made under this section is or, as the case may be, was extortionate.

(4)   An order under this section with respect to any transaction may contain such one or more of the following as the court thinks fit, that is to say -

(a)   provision setting aside the whole or part of any obligation created by the transaction;

(b)   provision otherwise varying the terms of the transaction or varying the terms on which any security for the purposes of the transaction is held;

(c)   provision requiring any person who is or was a party to the transaction to pay to the liquidator any sums paid to that person, by virtue of the transaction, by the company;

(d)   provision requiring any person to surrender to the liquidator any property held by him as security for the purposes of the transaction; or

(e)   provision directing accounts to be taken between any persons.

Preferential payments

265.(1) In a winding up there shall be paid in priority to all other debts-

(a)   (*Repealed*)

(b)   any-

 (i) payment from the Protection of Wages on Insolvency Fund under section 18 of the Protection of Wages on Insolvency Ordinance (Cap. 380) to any clerk or servant in respect of wages or salary or both in respect of services rendered to the company if such payment was made during a period of 4 months before the commencement of the winding up; and

 (ii) wages and salary (including commission provided that the amount thereof is fixed or ascertainable at the relevant date) of any clerk or servant in respect of services rendered to the company during the relevant period not exceeding, together with any payment under sub-paragraph (i), $3,000;

(c)   any-

 (i) payment from the Protection of Wages on Insolvency Fund under section 18 of the Protection of Wages on Insolvency Ordinance (Cap. 380) to any labourer or workman in respect of wages, whether payable for time or for piece work, in respect of services rendered to the company if such payment was made during a period of 4 months before the commencement of the winding up; and

 (ii) wages of any labourer or workman, whether payable for time or for piece work, in respect of services rendered to the company during the relevant period not exceeding, together with any payment under sub-paragraph (i), $3,000;

(ca)   any severance payment payable to an employee under the Employment Ordinance (Cap. 57), not exceeding in respect of each employee $6,000;

(caa) any long service payment payable to an employee under the Employment Ordinance (Cap. 57), not exceeding in respect of each employee $8,000;

(cb) any amount due in respect of compensation or liability for compensation under the Employees' Compensation Ordinance (Cap. 282) accrued before the relevant date and, where the compensation is a periodical payment, the amount due in respect thereof shall be taken to be the amount of the lump sum for which the periodical payment could, if redeemable, be redeemed on an application being made for that purpose under the Employees' Compensation Ordinance (Cap. 282), but this paragraph shall not apply to any amount due in respect of compensation or liability for compensation where the company has entered into a contract with a person carrying on accident insurance business in Hong Kong in respect of its liability under the Employees' Compensation Ordinance (Cap. 282) for personal injury by accident to the employee to whom the compensation or liability for compensation is due or where the company is wound up voluntarily merely for the purposes of reconstruction or of amalgamation with another company;

(cc) any wages in lieu of notice payable to an employee under the Employment Ordinance (Cap. 57), not exceeding in respect of each employee one month's wages or $2,000 whichever is the lesser;

(cd) all accrued holiday remuneration becoming payable to any clerk, servant, workman or labourer (or in the case of his death to any other person in his right) on the termination of his employment before or by the effect of the winding-up order or resolution;

(ce) any payment from the Employees Compensation Assistance Fund under Part IV of the Employees Compensation Assistance Ordinance (Cap. 365) representing an amount due by the company in respect of compensation or liability for compensation under the Employees' Compensation Ordinance (Cap. 282) accrued before the relevant date;

(cf) any amount of unpaid contribution or any amount deemed to be unpaid contribution calculated in accordance with rules made under section 73(1)(n) of the Occupational Retirement Schemes Ordinance (Cap. 426) which should have been paid by the company being wound up in accordance with the terms of an occupational retirement scheme within the meaning of that Ordinance before the commencement of the winding up:

Provided that where such amount exceeds $50,000 in respect of an employee, 50% of such part of the amount that exceeds $50,000 shall not be paid in priority to all other debts under this subsection;

(cg) (without prejudice to any right or liability under a trust) any amount of salaries deducted by the company being wound up from its employees' salaries for

the purpose of making contributions in respect of such employees to the funds of an occupational retirement scheme within the meaning of the Occupational Retirement Schemes Ordinance (Cap. 426) which have not been paid into such funds;

(d)   all statutory debts due from the company to the Crown at the relevant date and which became due and payable within 12 months next before that date;

(da)   where the company is revived under section 290A(6), the fee payable under that section;

(db)   where the company being wound up is or was a bank and, at the commencement of the winding up, held deposits, the aggregate amount held on deposit, up to a maximum of $100,000, to each depositor, regardless of the number of his deposits;

(e)   where the company being wound up is an insurer, any sum payable to a person in respect of any claim (other than a claim for a refund of premium) made under or in accordance with a contract of insurance (but not a contract of reinsurance) effected by the insurer as part of its general business carried on in or from Hong Kong, unless-

    (i)   such sum is, under the contract or in the ordinary course of business, payable in a place outside Hong Kong where assets of the company are maintained and under the law of that place the claim in respect of which the sum is payable is, in the event of a winding up, accorded priority with respect to those assets over claims which under the contract or in the ordinary course of business are payable at any other place; or

    (ii)   the person to whom the sum is payable is entitled with respect to the claim to claim compensation under any scheme designed to secure compensation to persons in circumstances where the insurer becomes insolvent;

(ea)   where the company being wound up is an insurer, any payment from the Employees Compensation Assistance Fund under Part IV of the Employees Compensation Assistance Ordinance (Cap. 365) representing a sum payable by the company to a person in respect of any claim (other than a claim for refund of premium) made under or in accordance with a contract of insurance issued for the purposes of Part IV of the Employees' Compensation Ordinance (Cap. 282) effected by the insurer as part of its general business carried on in or from Hong Kong; unless such sum is, under the contract or in the ordinary course of business, payable in a place outside Hong Kong where assets of the company are maintained and under the law of that place the claim in respect of which the sum is payable is, in the event of a winding up, accorded

priority with respect to those assets over claims which under the contract or in the ordinary course of business are payable at any other place;

     (f)   where the company being wound up is an insurer, any sum payable (after offsetting the amount of any sums owing from the claimant) to a person in respect of any claim (other than a claim for a refund of premium) made under or in accordance with a contract of reinsurance effected by the insurer, as reinsurer, as part of its general business carried on in or from Hong Kong, unless such sum is, under the contract or in the ordinary course of business, payable in a place outside Hong Kong where assets of the company are maintained and under the law of that place the claim in respect of which the sum is payable is, in the event of a winding up, accorded priority with respect to those assets over claims which under the contract or in the ordinary course of business are payable at any other place.

(1A)   Where the relevant date is on or after 1 June 1970 but before 1 April 1977, the sum of $6,000 shall be deemed to be substituted in each case for the sums of $3,000 referred to in paragraphs (b) and (c) respectively of subsection (1).

(1B)   Where the relevant date is on or after the 1 April 1977, the sum of $8,000 shall be deemed to be substituted in each case for the sums of $3,000 referred to in paragraphs (b) and (c) respectively, and for the sum of $6,000 referred to in paragraph (ca), of subsection (1).

(2)   Subject to subsection (1)(b) and (c), where any payment on account of wages or salary, or severance payment, or long service payment or wages in lieu of notice payable under the Employment Ordinance (Cap. 57), or accrued holiday remuneration, has been made to any clerk, servant, workman or labourer in the employment of a company out of money advanced by some person for that purpose, that person shall in a winding up have a right of priority in respect of the money so advanced and paid up to the amount by which the sum in respect of which that clerk, servant, workman or labourer would have been entitled to priority in the winding up has been diminished by reason of the payment having been made.

(3)   The debts specified in subsection (1)(b), (c), (ca), (caa), (cb), (cc), (cd), (ce), (cf) and (cg)-

     (a)   shall have priority over the debts specified in subsection (1)(d);

     (b)   shall rank equally among themselves; and

     (c)   shall be paid in full unless the assets are insufficient to meet them, in which case they shall abate in equal proportions among themselves.

(3A)   The debts specified in subsection (1)(d) shall have priority over the debts specified in subsection (1)(da), (db), (e), (ea) and (f).

(3AAA) The debts specified in subsection (1)(da) shall have priority over the debts specified in subsection (1)(db), (e), (ea) and (f).

(3AAAA)   The debts specified in subsection (1)(db)-

> *(a)*   shall have priority over the debts in subsection (1)(e), (ea) and (f);
>
> *(b)*   shall rank equally among themselves; and
>
> *(c)*   shall be paid in full unless the assets are insufficient to meet them, in which case they shall abate in equal proportions among themselves.

(3AA) The debts specified in subsection (1)(e) and (ea)-

> *(a)*   shall have priority over the debts specified in subsection (1)(f);
>
> *(b)*   shall rank equally among themselves; and
>
> *(c)*   shall be paid in full unless the assets are insufficient to meet them, in which case they shall abate in equal proportions among themselves.

(3AB) The debts specified in subsection (1)(f)-

> *(a)*   shall rank equally among themselves; and
>
> *(b)*   shall be paid in full unless the assets are insufficient to meet them, in which case they shall abate in equal proportions among themselves.

(3B)   The debts specified in subsection (1) shall, so far as the assets of the company available for payment of general creditors are insufficient to meet those debts, have priority over the claims of holders of debentures under any charge created as a floating charge by the company, and shall be paid accordingly out of any property comprised in or subject to the charge.

(4) Subject to the retention of such sums as may be necessary for the costs and expenses of the winding up, the foregoing debts shall be discharged forthwith so far as the assets are sufficient to meet them.

(5) In the event of a landlord or other person distraining or having distrained on any goods or effects of the company within 3 months next before the date of a winding-up order, the debts to which priority is given by this section shall be a first charge on the goods or effects so distrained on, or the proceeds of the sale thereof.

(5A)   Any money paid under a charge under subsection (5) shall be a debt due from the company to the landlord or other person having distrained, and such debt shall be discharged so far as the assets are sufficient to meet it after payment of the debts specified in subsection (1) but before payment of the other debts proved in the winding up.

(5B)   Where in any winding up assets have been recovered under an indemnity for costs of litigation given by certain creditors, or have been protected or preserved by the payment of moneys or the giving of indemnity by creditors, or where expenses in relation to which a creditor has indemnified a liquidator have been recovered, the court may, on the application of the Official Receiver or the liquidator or any such creditor, make such order as it deems just with respect to the distribution of those assets and the amount of those expenses so recovered with a view to giving those creditors an advantage over others in consideration of the risk run by them in so doing.

(5C)   Any remuneration in respect of a period of holiday or of absence from work through sickness or other good cause shall be deemed to be wages in respect of services rendered to the company during that period.

(5D)   The deposits given priority under subsection (1)(db) do not include the following-

> *(a)*   terms deposits where the current term agreed to by the depositor at the most recent time it was negotiated exceeds 5 years;

> *(b)*   deposits made after the date of publication of a notice in the Gazette under section 28(2)(b) of the Banking Ordinance (Cap. 155) that the company has been removed from the register and has ceased to be a bank.

(5E)   The priority given under subsection (1)(db) does not apply to money held on deposit where a depositor, after a bank ceases carrying on banking business and whether or not winding up proceedings have commenced at that time, assigns to another person his rights to a portion of the money on deposit in the depositor's name, if the effect of such an assignment is to increase the amount of money that will be eligible for priority under subsection (1)(db).

(5F)   Deposits given priority under subsection (1)(db) do not include deposits made in the name of-

> *(a)*   the Exchange Fund established under the Exchange Fund Ordinance (Cap. 66);

> *(b)*   a multilateral development bank as defined in paragraph 1 of the Third Schedule to the Banking Ordinance (Cap. 155);

> *(c)*   a holding company that holds all of the shares of the company being wound up, a subsidiary of the company being wound up or a subsidiary of the holding company;

> *(d)*   a person who, at the commencement of the winding up, was a director, controller or manager of-

> > **(i)**   the company being wound up;

> > **(ii)**   a subsidiary of the company being wound up;

301

> **(iii)** a holding company that holds all of the shares of the company being wound up or a subsidiary of the holding company;

> *(e)* an authorized institution as defined in the Banking Ordinance (Cap.155).

(6) In this section-

"accrued holiday remuneration" includes, in relation to any person, all sums which, by virtue either of his contract of employment or of any enactment (including any order made or direction given under any Ordinance), are payable on account of the remuneration which would, in the ordinary course, have become payable to him in respect of a period of holiday had his employment with the company continued until he became entitled to be allowed the holiday;

"bank" has the same meaning as in the Banking Ordinance (Cap. 155);

"controller" has the same meaning as in the Banking Ordinance (Cap. 155);

"deposit" and "depositor" have the same meaning as in the Banking Ordinance (Cap.155);

"Employees Compensation Assistance Fund" means the fund established by section 7 of the Employees Compensation Assistance Ordinance (Cap. 365);

"general business" means insurance business not being long term business as defined in section 2(1) of the Insurance Companies Ordinance (Cap. 41);

"insurer" means a person carrying on insurance business;

"manager" has the same meaning as in the Banking Ordinance (Cap. 155);

"Protection of Wages on Insolvency Fund" means the fund deemed to be established and continued in existence under section 6 of the Protection of Wages on Insolvency Ordinance (Cap. 380);

"the relevant date" means-

> *(a)* in the case of a company ordered to be wound up compulsorily, the date of the appointment (or first appointment) of a provisional liquidator or, if no such appointment was made, the date of the winding-up order, unless in either case the company had commenced to be wound up voluntarily before that date; and

> *(b)* in any case where paragraph (a) does not apply, the date of the commencement of the winding up;

"the relevant period" means-

(a) in a case where a company is being wound up by the court and the relevant date in the case of that company is a date other than the date of the commencement of the winding up, the period-

(i) beginning 4 months next before the commencement of the winding up and ending on the relevant date; or

(ii) beginning 4 months next before the date of application for an ex gratia payment, under section 16 of the Protection of Wages on Insolvency Ordinance (Cap. 380), from the Protection of Wages on Insolvency Fund, and ending on that date of application,

whichever is the earlier;

(b) in any case where paragraph (a) does not apply, the period-

(i) of 4 months next before the relevant date; or

(ii) beginning 4 months next before the date of application for an ex gratia payment, under section 16 of the Protection of Wages on Insolvency Ordinance (Cap. 380), from the Protection of Wages on Insolvency Fund,

whichever is the earlier;

"statutory debt" means a debt the liability for which and the amount of which are determined by or under any provision in any Ordinance or imperial enactment;

"wages" includes, in relation to any person, any sum which, by virtue of his contract of employment, is payable to him as a Lunar New Year bonus, but does not include any accrued holiday remuneration.

(7) The Companies (Amendment) Ordinance 1984 (6 of 1984) shall not apply in the case of a winding up where the relevant date occurred before the commencement of that Ordinance, and, in such a case, the provisions relating to preferential payments which would have applied if that Ordinance had not been enacted shall be deemed to remain in full force.

(8) The Fourth Schedule to the Protection of Wages on Insolvency Ordinance 1985 (12 of 1985) shall not apply in the case of a winding up where the date of the commencement of the winding up occurred before the commencement of that Ordinance, and, in such case, the provisions relating to preferential payments which would have applied if that Ordinance had not been enacted shall be deemed to remain in full force.

(9) The Companies (Amendment) (No. 3) Ordinance 1988 (79 of 1988) shall not apply in the case of a winding up where the date of the commencement of the winding up occurred before the

commencement of that Ordinance, and, in such a case, the provisions relating to preferential payments which would have applied if that Ordinance had not been enacted shall be deemed to remain in full force.

Effect of Winding Up on antecedent and other Transactions

Fraudulent preference

266.(1) Any conveyance, mortgage, delivery of goods, payment, execution or other act relating to property made or done by or against a company within 6 months before the commencement of its winding up which, had it been made or done by or against an individual within 6 months before the presentation of a bankruptcy petition on which he is adjudged bankrupt, would be deemed in his bankruptcy a fraudulent preference, shall in the event of the company being wound up be deemed a fraudulent preference of its creditors and be invalid accordingly:

Provided that, in relation to things made or done before the commencement of the Companies (Amendment) Ordinance 1984 (6 of 1984), this subsection shall have effect with the substitution, for references to 6 months, of references to 3 months.

(2) Any conveyance or assignment by a company of all its property to trustees for the benefit of all its creditors shall be void to all intents.

Liabilities and rights of certain fraudulently preferred persons

267.(1) Where anything made or done after the commencement of the Companies (Amendment) Ordinance 1984 (6 of 1984) is void under section 266 as a fraudulent preference of a person interested in property mortgaged or charged to secure the company's debt, then (without prejudice to any rights or liabilities arising apart from this provision) the person preferred shall be subject to the same liabilities, and shall have the same rights, as if he had undertaken to be personally liable as surety for the debt to the extent of the charge on the property or the value of his interest, whichever is the less.

(2) The value of the said person's interest shall be determined as at the date of the transaction constituting the fraudulent preference, and shall be determined as if the interest were free of all encumbrances other than those to which the charge for the company's debt was then subject.

(3) On any application made to the court with respect to any payment on the ground that the payment was a fraudulent preference of a surety or guarantor, the court shall have jurisdiction to determine any questions with respect to the payment arising between the person to whom payment was made and the surety or guarantor and to grant relief in respect thereof, notwithstanding that it is not necessary so to do for the purposes of the winding up and for that purpose may give leave to bring in the surety or guarantor as a third party as in the case of an action for the recovery of the sum paid.

(4) Subsection (3) shall apply, with the necessary modifications, in relation to transactions other than the payment of money as it applies in relation to payments.

Effect of floating charge

267. Where a company is being wound up, a floating charge on the undertaking or property of the company created within 12 months of the commencement of the winding up shall, unless it is proved that the company immediately after the creation of the charge was solvent, be invalid, except to the amount of any cash paid to the company at the time of or subsequently to the creation of, and in consideration for, the charge, together with interest on that amount at the rate specified in the charge or at the rate 12 per cent per annum whichever is the less.

Disclaimer of onerous property in case of company wound up

268.(1) Where any part of the property of a company which is being wound up consists of land of any tenure burdened with onerous covenants, of shares or stock in companies, of unprofitable contracts, or of any other property that is unassailable, or not readily saleable, by reason of its binding the possessor thereof to the performance of any onerous act, or to the payment of any sum of money, the liquidator of the company, notwithstanding that he has endeavoured to sell or has taken possession of the property, or exercised any act of ownership in relation thereto, may, with the leave of the court and subject to the provisions of this section, by writing signed by him, at any time within 12 months after the commencement of the winding up or such extended period as may be allowed by the court, disclaim the property:

Provided that, where any such property has not come to the knowledge of the liquidator within 1 month after the commencement of the winding up, the power under this section of disclaiming the property may be exercised at any time within 12 months after he has become aware thereof or such extended period as may be allowed by the court.

(2) The disclaimer shall operate to determine, as from the date of disclaimer, the rights, interest, and liabilities of the company, and the property of the company, in or in respect of the property disclaimed, but shall not, except so far as is necessary for the purpose of releasing the company and the property of the company from liability, affect the rights or liabilities of any other person.

(3) The court, before or on granting leave to disclaim, may require such notices to be given to persons interested, and impose such terms as a condition of granting leave, and make such other order in the matter as the court thinks just.

(4) The liquidator shall not be entitled to disclaim any property under this section in any case where an application in writing has been made to him by any persons interested in the property requiring him to decide whether he will or will not disclaim, and the liquidator has not, within a period of 28 days after the receipt of the application or such further period as may be allowed by the court, given notice to the applicant that he intends to apply to the court for leave to disclaim, and, in the case of a contract, if the liquidator, after such an application as aforesaid, does not within the said period or further period disclaim the contract, the company shall be deemed to have adopted it.

(5) The court may, on the application of any person who is, as against the liquidator, entitled to the benefit or subject to the burden of a contract made with the company, make an order rescinding the contract on such terms as to payment by or to either party of damages for the non-performance of the contract, or otherwise as the court thinks just, and any damages payable under the order to any such person may be proved by him as a debt in the winding up.

(6) The court may, on an application by any person who either claims any interest in any disclaimed property or is under any liability not discharged by this Ordinance in respect of any disclaimed property and on hearing any such persons as it thinks fit, make an order for the vesting of the property in or the delivery of the property to any persons entitled thereto, or to whom it may seem just that the property should be delivered by way of compensation for such liability as aforesaid, or a trustee for him, and on such terms as the court thinks just, and on any such vesting order being made, the property comprised therein shall vest accordingly in the person therein named in that behalf without any conveyance or assignment for the purpose:

Provided that, where the property disclaimed is of a leasehold nature, the court shall not make a vesting order in favour of any person claiming under the company, whether as under-lessee or as a person entitled to a mortgage or charge, except upon the terms of making that person-

> *(a)* subject to the same liabilities and obligations as those to which the company was subject under the lease in respect of the property at the commencement of the winding up; or

> *(b)* if the court thinks fit, subject only to the same liabilities and obligations as if the lease had been assigned to that person at that date,

and in either event (if the case so requires) as if the lease had comprised only the property comprised in the vesting order, and any under-lessee or person entitled to a mortgage or charge who declines to accept a vesting order upon such terms shall be excluded from all interest in and security upon the property, and, if there is no person claiming under the company who is willing to accept an order upon such terms, the court shall have power to vest the estate and interest of the company in the property in any person liable either personally or in a representative character, and either alone or jointly with the company to perform the lessee's covenants in the lease, freed and discharged from all estates, incumbrances and interests created therein by the company.

(7) Any person injured by the operation of a disclaimer under this section shall be deemed to be a creditor of the company to the amount of the injury, and may accordingly prove the amount as a debt in the winding up.

Restriction of rights of creditor as to execution or attachment in case of company being wound up

269.(1) Where a creditor has issued execution against the goods or lands of a company or has attached any debt due to the company, and the company is subsequently wound up, he shall not be entitled to retain the benefit of the execution or attachment against the liquidator in the winding up of the company unless he has completed the execution or attachment before the commencement of the winding up:

Provided that-

(a) where any creditor has had notice of a meeting having been called at which a resolution for voluntary winding up is to be proposed, the date on which the creditor so had notice shall for the purposes of the foregoing provision be substituted for the date of the commencement of the winding up; and

(b) a person who purchases in good faith under a sale by the bailiff any goods of a company on which an execution has been levied shall in all cases acquire a good title to them against the liquidator; and

(c) the rights conferred by this subsection on the liquidator may be set aside by the court in favour of the creditor to such extent and subject to such terms as the court may think fit.

(2) For the purposes of this Ordinance-

(a) an execution against goods is completed by seizure and sale or by the making of a charging order under section 20 of the Supreme Court Ordinance (Cap. 4);

(b) attachment of a debt is completed by the receipt of the debt; and

(c) an execution against land is completed by seizure, by the appointment of a receiver, or by the making of a charging order under the said section 20.

(3) In this section, "goods" includes all chattels personal, and "bailiff" includes any officer charged with the execution of a writ or other process.

Duties of bailiff as to goods taken in execution

270.(1) Subject to subsection (2A), where any goods of a company are taken in execution, and, before the sale thereof or the completion of the execution by the receipt or recovery of the full amount of the levy, notice is served on the bailiff that a provisional liquidator has been appointed or that a winding-up order has been made or that a resolution for voluntary winding up has been passed, the bailiff shall, on being so required, deliver the goods and any money seized or received in part satisfaction of the execution to the liquidator, but the costs of the execution shall be a first charge on the goods or money so delivered, and the liquidator may sell the goods, or a sufficient part thereof, for the purpose of satisfying that charge.

(2) Subject to subsection (2A), where under an execution the goods of a company are sold or money is paid in order to avoid sale, the bailiff shall deduct the costs of the execution from the proceeds of the sale or the money paid and retain the balance for 14 days, and if within that time notice is served on him of a petition for the winding up of the company having been presented or of a meeting having been called at which there is to be proposed a resolution for the voluntary winding up of the company and an order is made or a resolution is passed, as the case may be, for the winding up of the company, the bailiff shall pay the balance to the liquidator, who shall be entitled to retain it as against the execution creditor.

(2A) The rights conferred by this section on the liquidator may be set aside by the court in favour of the creditor to such extent and subject to such terms as the court thinks fit.

(3) In this section, "goods" includes all chattels personal, and "bailiff" includes any officer charged with the execution of a writ or other process.

Offences antecedent to or in course of Winding Up

Offences by officers of companies in liquidation

271.(1) If any person, being a past or present officer of a company which is at the time of the commission of the alleged offence being wound up, whether by the court or voluntarily, or which, subsequently to that time, is ordered to be wound up by the court or passes a resolution for voluntary winding up-

> *(a)* does not to the best of his knowledge and belief fully and truly discover to the liquidator all the property, real and personal, of the company, and how and to whom and for what consideration and when the company disposed of any part thereof, except such part as has been disposed of in the ordinary way of the business of the company; or

> *(b)* does not deliver up to the liquidator, or as he directs, all such part of the real and personal property of the company as is in his custody or under his control, and which he is required by law to deliver up; or

> *(c)* does not deliver up to the liquidator, or as he directs, all books and papers in his custody or under his control belonging to the company and which he is required by law to deliver up; or

> *(d)* within 12 months next before the commencement of the winding up or at any time thereafter conceals any part of the property of the company to the value of $100 or upwards, or conceals any debt due to or from the company; or

> *(e)* within 12 months next before the commencement of the winding up or at any time thereafter fraudulently removes any part of the property of the company to the value of $100 or upwards;

> *(f)* or makes any material omission in any statement relating to the affairs of the company; or

> *(g)* knowing or believing that a false debt has been proved by any person under the winding up, fails for the period of a month to inform the liquidator thereof; or

(h)   after the commencement of the winding up prevents the production of any book or paper affecting or relating to the property or affairs of the company; or

(i)   within 12 months next before the commencement of the winding up or at any time thereafter, conceals, destroys, mutilates, or falsifies, or is privy to the concealment, destruction, mutilation, or falsification of, any book or paper affecting or relating to the property or affairs of the company; or

(j)   within 12 months next before the commencement of the winding up or at any time thereafter makes or is privy to the making of any false entry in any book or paper affecting or relating to the property or affairs of the company; or

(k)   within 12 months next before the commencement of the winding up or at any time thereafter fraudulently parts with, alters, or makes any omission in, or is privy to the fraudulent relating to the property or affairs of the company; or

(l)   after the commencement of the winding up or at any meeting of the creditors of the company within 12 months next before the commencement of the winding up attempts to account for any part of the property of the company by fictitious losses or expenses; or

(m)-(n) *(Repealed)*

(o)   within 12 months next before the commencement of the winding up or at any time thereafter pawns, pledges, or disposes of any property of the company which has been obtained on credit and has not been paid for, unless such pawning, pledging, or disposing is in the ordinary way of the business of the company; or

(p)   is guilty of any false representation or other fraud for the purpose of obtaining the consent of the creditors of the company or any of them to an agreement with reference to the affairs of the company or to the winding up,

he shall, in the case of the offence mentioned in paragraph (o), be liable to imprisonment, and in the case of any other offence shall be liable to imprisonment and a fine:

Provided that it shall be a good defence to a charge under any of paragraphs (a), (b), (c), (d), (f) and (o), if the accused proves that he had no intent to defraud, and to a charge under any of paragraphs (h), (i) and (j), if he proves that he had no intent to conceal the state of affairs of the company or to defeat the law.

(2)   Where any person pawns, pledges or disposes of any property in circumstances which amount to an offense under subsection (1)(o), any person who takes in pawn or pledge or otherwise receives the property knowing it to be pawned, pledged, or disposed of in such circumstances as aforesaid shall be guilty of an offence, and on conviction thereof liable to be punished in the same way as if he had received the property knowing it to have been obtained in circumstances amounting to an offence.

(3) For the purposes of this section, "officer" includes any person in accordance with whose directions or instructions the directors of a company have been accustomed to act.

Penalty for falsification of books

272. If any person, being a past or present officer or a contributory of any company being wound up, before or after the commencement of the winding up destroys, mutilates, alters or falsifies any books, papers or securities, or makes or is privy to the making of any false or fraudulent entry in any register, book of account or document belonging to the company with intent to defraud or deceive any person, he shall be guilty of an offence and liable to imprisonment and a fine.

Frauds by officers of companies which have gone into liquidation

273. If any person, being at the time of the commission of the alleged offence an officer of a company which is subsequently ordered to be wound up by the court or subsequently passes a resolution for voluntary winding up-

  (a) *(Repealed)*

  (b) with intent to defraud creditors of the company, has made or caused to be made any gift or transfer of or charge on, or has caused or connived at the levying of any execution against, the property of the company;

  (c) with intent to defraud creditors of the company, has concealed or removed any part of the property of the company since, or within 2 months before, the date of any unsatisfied judgment or order for payment of money obtained against the company,

he shall be guilty of an offence and liable to imprisonment and a fine.

Liability where proper accounts not kept

274.(1) If where a company is wound up it is shown that proper books of account were not kept by the company throughout the period of 2 years immediately preceding the commencement of the winding up, or the period between the incorporation of the company and the commencement of the winding up, whichever is the shorter, every officer of the company who is in default shall, unless he shows that he acted honestly and that in the circumstances in which the business of the company was carried on the default was excusable, be guilty of an offence and liable to imprisonment and a fine.

(2) For the purposes of this section, proper books of account shall be deemed not to have been kept in the case of any company if there have not been kept such books or accounts as are necessary, to exhibit and explain the transactions and financial position of the trade or business of the company, including books containing entries from day to day in sufficient detail of all cash received and cash paid, and, where the trade or business has involved dealings in goods, statements of the annual stocktakings and (except in the case of goods sold by way of ordinary retail trade) of all goods sold and purchased, showing the goods and the buyers and sellers thereof in sufficient detail to enable those goods and those buyers and sellers to be identified.

Responsibility of directors for fraudulent trading

275(1) If in the course of the winding up of a company it appears that any business of the company has been carried on with intent to defraud creditors of the company or creditors of any other person or for any fraudulent purpose, the court, on the application of the Official Receiver, or the liquidator or any creditor or contributory of the company, may, if it thinks proper so to do, declare that any persons who were knowingly parties to the carrying on of the business in manner aforesaid shall be personally responsible, without any limitation of liability, for all or any of the debts or other liabilities of the company as the court may direct.

(1A) On the hearing of an application under subsection (1) the Official Receiver or the liquidator, as the case may be, may himself give evidence or call witnesses.

(2) Where the court makes any such declaration, it may give such further directions as it thinks proper for the purpose of giving effect to that declaration, and in particular may make provision for making the liability of any person under the declaration a charge on any debt or obligation due from the company to him, or on any mortgage or charge or any interest in any mortgage or charge on any assets of the company held by or vested in him, or any company or person on his behalf, or any person claiming as assignee from or through the person liable or any such company or person, and may from time to time make such further order as may be necessary for the purpose of enforcing any charge imposed under this subsection.

For the purpose of this subsection, "assignee" includes any person to whom or in whose favour, by the directions of the person liable under the declaration, the debt, obligation, mortgage or charge was created, issued or transferred or the interest created, but does not include an assignee for valuable consideration (not including consideration by way of marriage) given in good faith and without notice of any of the matters on the ground of which the declaration is made.

(3) Where any business of a company is carried on with such intent or for such purpose as is mentioned in subsection (1), every person who was knowingly a party to the carrying on of the business in manner aforesaid shall, whether or not the company has been or is in course of being wound up, be guilty of an offence and liable to imprisonment and a fine.

(4)-(5) (*Repealed*)

(6) The provisions of this section shall have effect notwithstanding that the person concerned may be criminally liable in respect of the matters on the ground of which the declaration is to be made, and where the declaration under subsection (1) is made the declaration shall be deemed to be a final judgment within the meaning of section 3(1)(g) of the Bankruptcy Ordinance (Cap. 6).

(7) *(Repealed)*

Power of court to assess damages against delinquent officer, etc.

276.(1) If in the course of winding up a company it appears that any person who has taken part in the formation or promotion of the company, or any past or present officer or liquidator or receiver of the company, has misapplied or retained or become liable or accountable for any money or property of the company, or been guilty of any misfeasance or breach of duty in relation to the company which is actionable at the suit of the company, the court may, on the application of the Official Receiver, or of the liquidator, or of any creditor or contributory, examine into the conduct of the promoter, officer, liquidator or receiver, and compel him to repay or restore the money or property or any part thereof respectively with interest at such rate as the court thinks just, or to contribute such sum to the assets of the company by way of compensation in respect of the misapplication, retainer, misfeasance, or breach of trust as the court thinks just.

(2) The provisions of this section shall have effect notwithstanding that the offence is one for which the offender may be criminally liable.

(3) Where an order for payment of money is made under this section, the order shall be deemed to be a final judgment within the meaning of section 3(1)(g) of the Bankruptcy Ordinance (Cap. 6).

Prosecution of delinquent officers and members of company

277.(1) If it appears to the court in the course of a winding up by the court that any past or present officer or member of the company has been guilty of any offence in relation to the company for which he is criminally liable, the court may, either on the application of any person interested in the winding up or of its own motion, direct the liquidator to refer the matter to the Attorney General.

(2) If it appears to the liquidator in the course of a voluntary winding up that any past or present officer or member of the company has been guilty of any offence in relation to the company for which he is criminally liable, he shall forthwith report the matter to the Attorney General, and shall furnish to the Attorney General such information and give to him such access to and facilities for inspecting and taking copies of any documents, being information or documents in the possession or under the control of the liquidator and relating to the matter in question, as he may require.

(3) If it appears to the court in the course of a voluntary winding up that any past or present officer or member of the company has been guilty as aforesaid, and that no report with respect to the matter has been made by the liquidator to the Attorney General under subsection (2), the court may, on the application of any person interested in the winding up or of its own motion, direct the liquidator to make such a report, and on a report being made accordingly the provisions of this section shall have effect as though the report had been made in pursuance of the provisions of subsection (2).

(4) If, where any matter is reported or referred to the Attorney General under this section, he considers that the case is one in which a prosecution ought to be instituted, he shall institute proceedings accordingly, and it shall be the duty of the liquidator and of every officer and agent of the company past and present (other than the defendant in the proceedings) to give him all assistance in connexion with the prosecution which he is reasonably able to give.

For the purposes of this subsection, the expression "agent" in relation to a company shall be deemed to include any banker or solicitor of the company and any person employed by the company as auditor, whether that person is or is not an officer of the company.

(5) If any person fails or neglects to give assistance in manner required by subsection (4), the court may, on the application of the Attorney General, direct that person to comply with the requirements of the said subsection, and where any such application is made with respect to a liquidator the court may, unless it appears that the failure or neglect to comply was due to the liquidator not having in his hands sufficient assets of the company to enable him so to do, direct that costs of the application shall be borne by the liquidator personally.

Supplement Provisions as to Winding Up

Disqualification for appointment as liquidator

278. No person being an undischarged bankrupt and no body corporate shall be qualified for appointment as liquidator of a company, whether in a winding up by the court or in a voluntary winding up, and-

> *(a)* any appointment made in contravention of this section shall be void; and

> *(b)* where any such person or any body corporate acts as a liquidator of a company, such person or body corporate shall be liable to a fine.

Corrupt inducement affecting appointment as liquidator

278A. Any person who gives or agrees or offers to give to any member or creditor of a company any valuable consideration with a view to securing his own appointment or nomination, or to securing or preventing the appointment or nomination of some person other than himself, as the company's liquidator shall be liable to a fine.

Enforcement of duty of liquidator to make returns, &c.

279.(1) If any liquidator, who has made any default in filing, delivering or making any return, account or other document, or in giving any notice which he is by law required to file, deliver, make or give, fails to make good the default within 14 days after the service on him of a notice requiring him to do so, the court may, on an application made to the court by any contributory or creditor of the company or by the Registrar, make an order directing the liquidator to make good the default within such time as may be specified in the order.

(2) Any such order may provide that all costs of and incidental to the application shall be borne by the liquidator.

(3)   Nothing in this section shall be taken to prejudice the operation of any enactment imposing penalties on a liquidator in respect of any such default as aforesaid.

Notification that a company is in liquidation

280.(1) Where a company is being wound up, whether by the court or voluntarily, every invoice, order for goods or business letter issued by or on behalf of the company or a liquidator of the company, or a receiver or manager of the property of the company, being a document on or in which the name of the company appears, shall contain a statement that the company is being wound up.

(2)   If default is made in complying with this section, the company and any of the following persons who knowingly and wilfully authorizes or permits the default, namely, any officer of the company, any liquidator of the company and any receiver or manager, shall be liable to a fine.

Exemption of certain documents from stamp duty on winding up of companies

281.(1) In the case of a winding up by the court or a creditors' voluntary winding up of a company, stamp duty shall not be payable in respect of

> *(a)*   any assurance relating solely to immovable property or personal property which forms part of the assets of the company and which, after the execution of the assurance, either at law or in equity, is or remains part of the assets of the company; or

> *(b)*   any other instrument relating solely to the property of any company which is being so wound up.

(2)   In this section, "assurance" includes deed, conveyance, assignment and surrender.

Books of company to be evidence

282.   Where a company is being wound up, all books and papers of the company and of the liquidators shall, as between the contributories of the company, be prima facie evidence of the truth of all matters purporting to be therein recorded.

Disposal of books and papers of company

283.(1) When a company has been wound up and is about to be dissolved, the books and papers of the company and of the liquidators may be disposed of as follows, that is to say-

> *(a)*   in the case of a winding up by the court in such way as the court directs;

> *(b)*   in the case of a members' voluntary winding up, in such way as the company by special resolution directs, and, in the case of a creditors' voluntary winding up, in such way as the committee of inspection or, if there is no such committee, as the creditors of the company, may direct.

(2) After 5 years from the dissolution of the company no responsibility shall rest on the company, the liquidators, or any person to whom the custody of the books and papers has been committed, by reason of any book or paper not being forthcoming to any person claiming to be interested therein.

(3) Provision may be made by general rules for enabling the Official Receiver to prevent, for such period (not exceeding 5 years from the dissolution of the company) as he thinks proper, the destruction of the books and papers of a company which has been wound up, and for enabling any creditor or contributory of the company to make representations to him, and to appeal to the court from any direction which may be given by him in the matter.

(4) If any person acts in contravention of any general rules made for the purposes of this section or of any direction of the Official Receiver thereunder, he shall be liable to a fine.

Information as to pending liquidation

284.(1) If where a company is being wound up the winding up is not concluded within 1 year after its commencement, the liquidator shall, at such intervals as may be prescribed, until the winding up is concluded, send to the Registrar a statement in the prescribed form and containing the prescribed particulars with respect to the proceedings in and position of the liquidation.

(2) Any person stating himself in writing to be a creditor or contributory of the company shall be entitled, by himself or by his agent, at all reasonable times, on payment of the prescribed fee, to inspect the statement, and to receive a copy thereof or extract therefrom.

(3) If a liquidator fails to comply with this section, he shall be liable to a fine and, for continued default, to a daily default fine, and any person untruthfully stating himself as aforesaid to be a creditor or contributory shall be guilty of a contempt of court, and shall, on the application of the liquidator or of the Official Receiver, be punishable accordingly.

Unclaimed assets to be paid to companies liquidation account

285.(1) If it appears either from any statement sent to the Registrar under section 284 or otherwise that a liquidator has in his hands or under his control any money representing unclaimed or undistributed assets of the company which have remained unclaimed or undistributed for 6 months after the date of their receipt, or any money held by the company in trust in respect of dividends or other sums due to any person as a member of the company, the liquidator shall forthwith pay the said money to the companies liquidation account, and shall be entitled to the prescribed certificate of receipt for the money so paid, and that certificate shall be an effectual discharge to him in respect thereof.

(2) *(Repealed)*

(3) Any person claiming to be entitled to any money paid in pursuance of this section may, within 5 years of the date when the money was so paid, apply to the Official Receiver for payment thereof, and the Official Receiver may, on a certificate by the liquidator that the person claiming is entitled, make an order for the payment to that person of the sum due.

(4)   Any person dissatisfied with the decision of the Official Receiver in respect of a claim made in pursuance of this section may appeal to the court.

(5)   Any money paid in pursuance of this section which remains unclaimed for a period of 5 years shall be transferred to the general revenue of Hong Kong.

Resolutions passed at adjourned meetings of creditors and contributories

286.   Where a resolution is passed at an adjourned meeting of any creditors or contributories of a company, the resolution shall, for all purposes, be treated as having been passed on the date on which it was in fact passed, and shall not be deemed to have been passed on any earlier date.

Supplementary Powers of Court

Meetings to ascertain wishes of creditors or contributories

287.(1) The court may, as to all matters relating to the winding up of a company, have regard to the wishes of the creditors or contributories of the company, as proved to it by any sufficient evidence, and may, if it thinks fit, for the purpose of ascertaining those wishes, direct meetings of the creditors or contributories to be called, held, and conducted in such manner as the court directs, and may appoint a person to act as chairman of any such meeting and to report the result thereof to the court.

(2)   In the case of creditors, regard shall be had to the value of each creditor's debt.

(3)   In the case of contributories, regard shall be had to the number of votes conferred on each contributory by this Ordinance or the articles.

288.   (*Repealed*)

Affidavits, &c. in Hong Kong and Commonwealth

289.(1) Any affidavit required to be sworn under the provisions or for the purposes of this Part may be sworn in Hong Kong, or elsewhere within the Commonwealth, before any court, judge, or person lawfully authorized to take and receive affidavits or before any of Her Majesty's consuls or vice-consuls in any place outside the Commonwealth.

(2)   All courts, judges, justices, commissioners, and persons acting judicially shall take judicial notice of the seal or stamp or signature, as the case may be, of any such court, judge, person, consul, or vice-consul attached, appended, or subscribed to any such affidavit, or to any other document to be used for the purposes of this Part.

Provisions as to Dissolution

Power of court to declare dissolution of company void

290.(1) Subject to subsection (1A), in the case of a company which has been dissolved under section 226A, 227, 239 or 248, the court may at any time within 2 years of the date of the dissolution, on an application being made for the purpose by the liquidator of the company or by any other person who appears to the court to be interested, make an order, upon such terms as the court thinks fit, declaring the dissolution to have been void, and thereupon such proceedings may be taken as might have been taken if the company had not been dissolved.

(1A) The liquidator of the company or any other person who appears to the court to be interested may at any time apply to extend the period of 2 years referred to in subsection (1) and the court may so extend, on such terms and conditions as seem to it just and expedient, if it is satisfied that there are exceptional circumstances justifying the extension.

(2) It shall be the duty of the person on whose application the order was made, within 7 days after the making of the order, or such further time as the court may allow, to deliver to the Registrar for registration an office copy of the order, and if that person fails so to do he shall be liable to a fine and, for continued default, to a daily default fine.

Registrar may strike off company for failure to forward annual returns

290A.(1) Where a company has for 2 consecutive years failed to forward to the Registrar the annual return required by this Ordinance to be forwarded by it, the Registrar may send by post to the company and each of its directors and secretaries named in the last annual return forwarded to him, if any, as amended by any subsequent notice of change of particulars sent under section 158(4), a registered letter notifying them of its failure and of his powers under subsection (2).

(2) Where, within 1 month after the Registrar sends by post the letter referred to in subsection (1), he does not receive-

> *(a)*   all overdue annual returns;

> *(b)*   the annual registration fee payable on delivery of such annual return under the Eighth Schedule; and

> *(c)*   an additional fee of $500,

the Registrar may publish in the Gazette and send by post to the company and each of its directors and secretaries referred to in subsection (1), a notice that at the expiration of 3 months from the date of that notice the name of the company mentioned therein will, unless the returns and fees referred to in paragraphs (a), (b) and (c), together with the penalty specified in subsection (3), have been received by him, be struck off the register and the company will be dissolved.

(3) At the expiration of the time specified in the notice referred to in subsection (2), the Registrar may, unless he has received the returns and fees referred to in subsection (2)(a), (b) and (c), together with a penalty of $5,000, strike its name off the register, and shall publish notice thereof in the Gazette and on the publication in the Gazette of this notice the company shall be dissolved.

(4) Notwithstanding subsection (3), the liability, if any, of every director, managing officer, and member of the company shall continue and may be enforced as if the company had not been dissolved.

(5) Nothing in this section shall affect the power of the court to wind up a company the name of which has been struck off the register.

(6) If a company or any member or creditor thereof feels aggrieved by the company having been struck off the register, the Registrar on an application made by the company or member or creditor before the expiration of 20 years from the publication in the Gazette of the notice under subsection (3) may, if satisfied that it is just that the company be restored to the register and a fee of not more than $20,000 as may be decided by the Registrar having regard to the circumstances of the case has been paid, publish a notice to that effect in the Gazette and upon the notice being published the company shall be deemed to have continued in existence as if its name had not been struck off, and the Registrar may in the notice give such directions and make such provisions as seem just for placing the company and all other persons in the same position as nearly as may be as if the name of the company had not been struck off.

(7) A letter or notice to be sent under this section to a company may be addressed to the company at its registered office, or, if no office has been registered, to the care of some officer of the company or, if there is no officer of the company whose name and address are known to the Registrar, may be sent to each of the persons who subscribed the memorandum, addressed to him at the address mentioned in the memorandum.

(8) A letter or notice to be sent under this section to a director or secretary of a company shall be addressed to him at the address given in the last annual return filed with the Registrar, if any, or in any subsequent notice of change of particulars sent to the Registrar under section 158(4).

(9) Where an application is made under subsection (6) by a member or creditor of the company, the company shall be liable to pay such member or creditor the amount of fee paid by him to the Registrar in respect of publication of a notice under subsection (6) within 3 months from the date of the publication of such notice.

(10)   Any fee paid to the Registrar in respect of publication of a notice under subsection (6) shall be deemed to be a debt owed by the company named in the notice, to the member or creditor of the company who made the application to the Registrar and shall be recoverable as a civil debt.

Bona vacantia

290B.(1) Where a company is dissolved under section 290A, all property and rights whatsoever vested in or held on trust for the company immediately before its dissolution (including leasehold property but not including property held by the company on trust for any other person) shall, subject and without prejudice to any notice which may be published by the Registrar under section 290A, be deemed to be bona vacantia and shall accordingly belong to the Crown, and shall vest and may be dealt with in the same manner as other bona vacantia accruing to the Crown.

(2) A person claiming to be a creditor of the company dissolved under section 290A(3) or any other person who claims an interest in the bona vacantia may, within a period of 4 months from the date of dissolution of the company, apply to the Registrar for the payment of the debt owed by the company out of the bona vacantia.

(3) The Registrar may reject any application made under subsection (2) or accept the application and pay the creditor or any other person who claims an interest in the bona vacantia such amount that the Registrar thinks fit.

(4) The amount paid by the Registrar under subsection (3) shall not exceed the total amount of the net value of the bona vacantia.

(5) The Registrar may, if he thinks appropriate, refer the application made by the creditor or any other person who claims an interest in the bona vacantia under subsection (2) to the court.

(6) In respect of an application referred to it under subsection (5), the court may reject any application made under subsection (2) or accept the application and order the Registrar to pay the creditor or any other person who claims an interest in the bona vacantia such amount that the court thinks fit.

(7) Any creditor or any other person who claims an interest in the bona vacantia under subsection (2) dissatisfied with a decision of the Registrar in respect of an application made under subsection (2) may appeal to the court.

(8) On an appeal under subsection (7), the court may confirm or reverse any decision made by the Registrar in respect of an application made under subsection (2) and may order the Registrar to pay the creditor or any other person who claims an interest in the bona vacantia such amount that the court thinks fit.

Crown disclaimer of property other than immovable property vesting as bona vacantia

290C.(1) Where any property other than immovable property vests in the Crown as bona vacantia under section 290B or 292, the Crown's title to it may be disclaimed by a notice signed by the Registrar.

(2) The right to execute a notice of disclaimer under this section may be waived by or on behalf of the Crown either expressly, or by taking possession or other act evincing that intention.

(3) A notice of disclaimer under this section is of no effect unless it is executed within 12 months from the date on which the vesting of the property under section 290B or 292 came to the Registrar's notice, or, if an application in writing is made to him by any person interested in the property requiring him to decide whether or not he will disclaim, within 3 months after the receipt of the application.

(4) A statement in a notice of disclaimer under this section that the vesting of the property came to the Registrar's notice on a specified date, or that no such application under subsection (3) was received by him with respect to the property before a specified date, is sufficient evidence of the fact stated, until the contrary is proved.

(5) A notice of disclaimer under this section shall be registered by the Registrar; and copies of it shall be published in the Gazette and sent to any persons who have given the Registrar notice that they claim to be interested in the property.

Effect of Crown disclaimer under section 290C

290D.(1) Where notice of disclaimer is executed under section 290C as respects any property, that property is deemed not to have vested in the Crown under section 290B or 292.

(2)   A disclaimer under section 290C-

      (a)   operates so as to determine, as from the date of the disclaimer, the rights, interests and liabilities of the company in or in respect of the property disclaimed; but

      (b)   does not, except so far as is necessary for the purpose of releasing the company from any liability, affect the rights, interests or liabilities of any other person.

Effect on section 290B of company's revival after dissolution

290E.(1) Where any property or right is vested in the Crown by section 290B, the Registrar may dispose of, or of an interest in, that property or right notwithstanding that a notice may be or has been published under section 290A(6).

(2)   Where such notice is published-

      (a)   it does not affect the disposition (but without prejudice to the notice so far as it relates to any other property or right previously vested in or held on trust for the company); and

      (b)   the Registrar shall pay to the company an amount equal to-

            (i)   the amount of any consideration received for the property or right, or interest therein; or

            (ii)   the value of any such consideration at the time of the disposition, or, if no consideration was received, an amount equal to the value of the property, right or interest disposed of, as at the date of the disposition.

(3)   Nothing in this section shall affect the validity of any payment by the Registrar under section 290B(3), (6) or (8) and the Registrar shall not be liable to make any payment to the company in refund of, or otherwise in connection with, any payment made under that section.

Registrar may strike defunct company off register

291.(1) Where the Registrar has reasonable cause to believe that a company is not carrying on business or in operation, he may send to the company by post a letter inquiring whether the company is carrying on business or in operation.

(2) If the Registrar does not within 1 month of sending the letter receive any answer thereto, he shall within 14 days after the expiration of the month send to the company by post a registered letter referring to the first letter, and stating that no answer thereto has been received, and that if an answer is not received to the second letter within 1 month from the date thereof, a notice will be published in the Gazette with a view to striking the name of the company off the register.

(3) If the Registrar either receives an answer to the effect that the company is not carrying on business or in operation, or does not within 1 month after sending the second letter receive any answer, he may publish in the Gazette and send to the company by post, a notice that at the expiration of 3 months from the date of that notice the name of the company mentioned therein will, unless cause is shown to the contrary, be struck off the register and the company will be dissolved.

(4) If, in any case where a company is being wound up, the Registrar has reasonable cause to believe either that no liquidator is acting, or that the affairs of the company are fully wound up, and the returns required to be made by the liquidator have not been made for a period of 6 consecutive months, the Registrar shall publish in the Gazette and send to the company or the liquidator, if any, a like notice as is provided in subsection (3).

(5) Where the Registrar is of the opinion that the registered office of a company or the name and address of a liquidator or subscriber to the memorandum of association of a company cannot be ascertained, or the Registrar is of the opinion that a letter or notice to be sent under subsection (1), (2), (3) or (4) is unlikely to be received by the person to whom it would be directed, it shall be sufficient compliance with the provisions of the said subsections if the Registrar shall publish in the Gazette a notice stating that at the expiration of 3 months from the date of the publication of such notice the name of the company mentioned therein will, unless cause is shown to the contrary, be struck off the register and the company will be dissolved.

(6) At the expiration of the time specified in any notice referred to in subsection (3), (4) or (5) the Registrar may, unless cause to the contrary is previously shown, strike its name off the register, and shall publish notice thereof in the Gazette and on the publication in the Gazette of this notice the company shall be dissolved:

Provided that-

    (a)   the liability, if any, of every director, managing officer, and member of the company shall continue and may be enforced as if the company had not been dissolved; and

    (b)   nothing in this subsection shall affect the power of the court to wind up a company the name of which has been struck off the register.

(7) If a company or any member or creditor thereof feels aggrieved by the company having been struck off the register, the court on an application made by the company or member or creditor before the expiration of 20 years from the publication in the Gazette of the notice aforesaid may, if satisfied that the company was at the time of the striking off carrying on business or in operation, or otherwise that it is just that the company be restored to the register, order the name of the company to be restored to the register, and upon an office copy of the order being delivered to the Registrar for registration the company shall be deemed to have continued in existence as if its name had not been struck off; and the court may by the order give such directions and make such provisions as seem just for placing the company and all other persons in the same position as nearly as may be as if the name of the company had not been struck off.

(8) A notice to be sent under this section to a liquidator may be addressed to the liquidator at his last known place of business, and a letter or notice to be sent under this section to a company may be addressed to the company at its registered office, or, if no office has been registered, to the care of some officer of the company or, if there is no officer of the company whose name and address are known to the Registrar, may be sent to each of the persons who subscribed the memorandum, addressed to him at the address mentioned in the memorandum.

Power of court to order company to be struck off and dissolved

291A.(1) If, on the application of the Registrar, it appears to the court that, having regard to the assets (if any) of a company or for other reason, it would not be appropriate to wind up the company, the court may order that the company be struck off the register and dissolved, and the company shall, as from the date of the order, be dissolved accordingly.

(2) Section 291(7) shall apply in relation to a company dissolved under this section as it applies to a company dissolved under that section.

Registrar to act as representative of defunct company in certain events

291B.(1) Where after a company has been dissolved it is proved to the satisfaction of the Registrar-

    (a) that the company if still existing would be legally or equitably bound to carry out, complete or give effect to some dealing, transaction or matter; and

    (b) that in order to carry out, complete or give effect thereto, some purely administrative act, not discretionary, should have been done by or on behalf of the company, or should be done by or on behalf of the company if still existing,

the Registrar may, as representing the company or its liquidator under this section, do or cause to be done any such act.

(2) The Registrar may execute or sign any relevant instrument or document, adding a memorandum stating that he has done so in pursuance of this section, and such execution or signature shall have the same force, validity and effect as if the company, if existing, had duly executed such instrument or document.

(3)   In the exercise of his functions under this section, the Registrar shall not be liable, and no civil action or other proceedings shall lie against him, in respect of acts properly done by him.

Property of dissolved company to be bona vacantia

292.   Where a company is dissolved otherwise than under section 290A, all property and rights whatsoever vested in or held on trust for the company immediately before its dissolution (including leasehold property but not including property held by the company on trust for any other person) shall, subject and without prejudice to any order which may at any time be made by the court under sections 290 and 291, be deemed to be bona vacantia and shall accordingly belong to the Crown, and shall vest and may be dealt with in the same manner as other bona vacantia accruing to the Crown.

Effect on section 292 of company's revival after dissolution

292A.(1)   Where any property or right is vested in the Crown by section 292, the Registrar may dispose of, or of an interest in, that property or right notwithstanding that an order may be made under section 290 or 291(7).

(2)   Where such an order is made -

    (a)   it does not affect the disposition (but without prejudice to the order so far as it relates to any other property or right previously vested in or held on trust for the company); and

    (b)   the Registrar shall pay to the company an amount equal to-

        (i)   the amount of any consideration received for the property or right, or interest therein; or

        (ii)   the value of any such consideration at the time of the disposition, or, if no consideration was received, an amount equal to the value of the property, right or interest disposed of, as at the date of the disposition.

Central Accounts

Companies liquidation account

293.(1)   An account, to be called the Companies Liquidation Account, shall be kept by the Official Receiver at such bank as the Governor may from time to time direct, and all moneys received by the Official Receiver in respect of proceedings under this Ordinance in connexion with the winding up of companies shall be paid to that account.

(2) All payments out of money standing to the credit of the Official Receiver in the Companies Liquidation Account shall be made in the prescribed manner.

Investment of surplus funds on general account

294.(1) Whenever the cash balance standing to the credit of the Companies Liquidation Account is in excess of the amount which in the opinion of the Official Receiver is required for the time being to answer demands in respect of companies' estates, he may invest in his name the whole or any part of such excess on fixed deposit or deposit at call with such bank as he thinks fit or in Government securities (including securities issued by the Government of the United Kingdom).

(2) When any part of the money placed on deposit or otherwise invested under subsection (1) is, in the opinion of the Official Receiver, required to answer any demands in respect of companies' estates, he shall raise such sum as may be required by the withdrawal of such part of any money placed on deposit or by sale of such part of the securities referred to in subsection (1), as may be necessary.

(3) The interest on investments or deposits made under this section, any profits realized on the sale of such investments and any bank interest received shall be paid into the Companies Liquidation Account, and the Official Receiver shall on or before 31 March in each year transfer to the general revenue the accumulated balance of such income, profits and bank interest, after deducting therefrom any losses on the realization of such investments.

Separate accounts of particular estates

295.(1) The Official Receiver shall keep an account of the receipts and payments in the winding up of each company.

(2) When the cash balance standing to the credit of the account of any company exceeds by $100,000 or more the amount which, in the opinion of the committee of inspection or where there is no committee of inspection in the opinion of the liquidator, is required for the time being to answer demands in respect of the company's estate, the Official Receiver shall, on the request of the committee of inspection or where there is no committee of inspection on the request of the liquidator, invest the amount of such excess on fixed deposit or on deposit at call with such bank as the Official Receiver thinks fit or in Government securities (including securities issued by the Government of the United Kingdom), to be placed to the credit of the account of the company.

(3) When any part of the money so invested is, in the opinion of the committee of inspection or where there is no committee of inspection in the opinion of the liquidator, required to answer any demands in respect of the estate of the company, the Official Receiver shall, on the request of the committee of inspection or where there is no committee of inspection on the request of the liquidator, raise such sum as may be required by the withdrawal of such part of any money placed on deposit or by the sale of such part of the securities referred to in subsection (2), as may be necessary.

(4) Out of the interest paid on the investments made under this section, an amount equal to 1½% per annum (or such other rate as may be fixed by the Financial Secretary for the purposes of this section by notice published in the Gazette) of the money invested shall be paid to the credit of the Official Receiver and the balance shall be paid to the credit of the company.

(5) The Official Receiver shall on or before 31 March in each year transfer to the general revenue the accumulated amount paid to his credit under subsection (4).

Rules and Fees

General rules and fees

296.(1) The Chief Justice may, with the approval of the Legislative Council, make general rules for carrying into effect the objects of this Ordinance so far as relates to the winding up of companies.

(2) All rules and orders made under this section shall be judicially noticed, and shall have effect as if enacted by this Ordinance.

(2A) An answer given by a person to a question put to him in exercise of powers conferred by rules made under this section may be used in evidence against him.

(3) There shall be paid in respect of proceedings under this Ordinance, where no fee is otherwise fixed, such fees as the Chief Justice may, with the approval of the Legislative Council, by order direct, and he may direct by whom and in what manner the same are to be collected and accounted for.

(4) The amount of any fees prescribed under this section shall not be limited by reference to the amount of administrative or other costs incurred or likely to be incurred by the Official Receiver in the winding up of companies or of any particular company.

(5) Without prejudice to the generality of subsection (4), fees referred to in that subsection may be fixed by reference to a scale of fees and percentages.

(6) Rules or orders made under this section may authorize the court to fix any fee or to vary the amount of any fee otherwise prescribed.

(7) No fee prescribed under this section shall be invalid by reason only of the amount of that fee.

(8) Fees required to be paid under rules or orders made under this section shall be recoverable as debts.

(9) Rules or orders made under this section before the commencement of the Companies (Amendment) (No. 2) Ordinance 1987 (38 of 1987) and in force immediately before such commencement shall have effect as from the commencement of that Ordinance as if made under this section as amended by that Ordinance.

PART VI - Receivers And Managers

Disqualification for appointment as receiver

297.(1) A body corporate shall not be qualified for appointment as receiver of the property of a company.

(2)   Any body corporate which acts as receiver as aforesaid shall be liable to a fine.

Disqualification of undischarged bankrupts

297A. No person being an undischarged bankrupt shall be qualified for appointment as receiver or manager of the property of a company on behalf of debenture holders, and if such person acts as such receiver or manager, he shall be guilty of an offence and liable to imprisonment and a fine.

Power to appoint Official Receiver as receiver for debenture holders or creditors

298.   Where an application is made to the court to appoint a receiver on behalf of the debenture holders or other creditors of a company which is being wound up by the court, the Official Receiver may be so appointed.

Receivers and managers appointed out of court

298A.(1) A receiver or manager of the property of a company appointed under the powers contained in any instrument, or a holder of debentures of the company, may apply to the court for directions in relation to any particular matter arising in connexion with the performance of the functions of such receiver or manager, and on any such application the court may give such directions, or may make such order declaring the rights of persons before the court or otherwise, as the court thinks just.

(2) A receiver or manager of the property of a company appointed as aforesaid shall, to the same extent as if he had been appointed by order of a court, be personally liable on any contract entered into by him in the performance of his functions, except in so far as the contract otherwise provides, and entitled in respect of that liability to indemnity out of the assets; but nothing in this subsection shall be taken as limiting any right to indemnity which he would have apart from this subsection, or as limiting his liability on contracts entered into without authority or as conferring any right to indemnity in respect of that liability.

(3) This section shall apply whether the receiver or manager was appointed before or after the commencement of the Companies (Amendment) Ordinance 1984 (6 of 1984) but subsection (2) shall not apply to contracts entered into before the commencement of that Ordinance.

Notification that receiver or manager appointed

299.(1)   Where a receiver or manager of the property of a company has been appointed, every invoice, order for goods or business letter issued by or on behalf of the company or the receiver or manager or the liquidator of the company, being a document on or in which the name of the company appears, shall contain a statement that a receiver or manager has been appointed.

(2) If default is made in complying with the requirements of this section, the company and any of the following persons who knowingly and wilfully authorizes or permits the default, namely, any officer of the company, any liquidator of the company and any receiver or manager, shall be liable to a fine.

Power of court to fix remuneration on application of liquidator

300.(1) The court may, on an application made to the court by the liquidator of a company, by order fix the amount to be paid by way of remuneration to any person who, under the powers contained in any instrument, has been appointed as receiver or manager of the property of the company, and may from time to time, on an application made either by the liquidator, or by the receiver or manager, vary or amend any order so made.

(2) The power of the court under subsection (1) shall, where no previous order has been made with respect thereto under that subsection,-

> *(a)* extend to fixing the remuneration for any period before the making of the order or the application therefor; and
>
> *(b)* be exercisable notwithstanding that the receiver or manager has died or ceased to act before the making of the order or the application therefor; and
>
> *(c)* where the receiver or manager has been paid or has retained for his remuneration for any period before the making of the order any amount in excess of that so fixed for that period, extend to requiring him or his personal representatives to account for the excess or such part thereof as may be specified in the order:

Provided that the power conferred by paragraph (c) shall not be exercised as respects any period before the making of the application for the order unless in the opinion of the court there are special circumstances making it proper for the power to be so exercised.

(3) This section shall apply whether the receiver or manager was appointed before or after the commencement of the Companies (Amendment) Ordinance 1984 (6 of 1984), and to periods before, as well as to periods after, the commencement of that Ordinance.

Provisions as to information where receiver or manager appointed

300A.(1) Where a receiver or manager of the whole or substantially the whole of the property of the company (in this section and in section 300B referred to as "the receiver") is appointed on behalf of the holders of any debentures of the company secured by a floating charge, then subject to the provisions of this section and section 300B-

> *(a)* the receiver shall forthwith send to the company notice of his appointment in the specified form; and

(b)   there shall, within 14 days after receipt of the notice, or such longer period as may be allowed by the court or by the receiver, be made out and submitted to the receiver in accordance with section 300B a statement in the specified form as to the affairs of the company; and

(c)   the receiver shall within 2 months after receipt of the said statement send-

    (i)   to the Registrar and to the court, a copy of the statement and of any comments he sees fit to make thereon and in the case of the Registrar also a summary of the statement and of his comments (if any) thereon; and

    (ii)   to the company, a copy of any such comments as aforesaid or, if he does not see fit to make any comment, a notice to that effect; and

    (iii)   to any trustees for the debenture holders on whose behalf he was appointed and, so far as he is aware of their addresses, to all such debenture holders a copy of the said summary.

(2)   The receiver shall within 2 months, or such longer period as the court may allow after the expiration of the period of 12 months from the date of his appointment and of every subsequent period of 12 months, and within 2 months or such longer period as the court may allow after he ceases to act as receiver or manager of the property of the company, send to the Registrar, to any trustees for the debenture holders of the company on whose behalf he was appointed, to the company and (so far as he is aware of their addresses) to all such debenture holders an abstract in the specified form showing his receipts and payments during that period of 12 months or, where he ceases to act as aforesaid, during the period from the end of the period to which the last preceding abstract related up to the date of his so ceasing, and the aggregate amounts of his receipts and of his payments during all preceding periods since his appointment.

(3)   Where the receiver is appointed under the powers contained in any instrument, this section shall have effect-

(a)   with the omission of the references to the court in subsection (1); and

(b)   with the substitution for the references to the court in subsection (2) of references to the Official Receiver.

(4)   Subsection (1) shall not apply in relation to the appointment of a receiver or manager to act with an existing receiver or manager or in place of a receiver or manager dying or ceasing to act, except that, where that subsection applies to a receiver or manager who dies or ceases to act before it has been fully complied with, the references in paragraphs (b) and (c) thereof to the receiver shall, subject to subsection (5), include references to his successor and to any continuing receiver or manager.

Nothing in this subsection shall be taken as limiting the meaning of the expression "the receiver" where used in, or in relation to, subsection (2).

(5) This section and section 300B, where the company is being wound up, shall apply notwithstanding that the receiver or manager and the liquidator are the same person, but with any necessary modifications arising from that fact.

(6) Nothing in subsection (2) shall be taken to prejudice the duty of the receiver to render proper accounts of his receipts and payments to the persons to whom, and at the times at which, he may be required to do so apart from that subsection.

(7) If the receiver makes default in complying with the requirements of this section, he shall be liable to a fine and, for continued default, to a daily default fine.

(8) This section shall not apply where the receiver or manager was appointed before the commencement of the Companies (Amendment) Ordinance 1984 (6 of 1984).

Special provisions as to statement submitted to receiver

300B.(1) The statement as to the affairs of a company required by section 300A to be submitted to the receiver (or his successor) shall show as at the date of the receiver's appointment the particulars of the company's assets, debts and liabilities, the names, addresses and occupations of its creditors, the securities held by them respectively, the dates when the securities were respectively given and such further or other information as may be prescribed.

(2) The said statement shall be submitted by, and be verified by affidavit of, one or more of the persons who are at the date of the receiver's appointment the directors and by the person who is at that date the secretary of the company, or by such of the persons hereafter in this subsection mentioned as the receiver (or his successor), subject to the direction of the court, may require to submit and verify the statement, that is to say, persons-

(a) who are or have been officers of the company;

(b) who have taken part in the formation of the company at any time within 1 year before the date of the receiver's appointment;

(c) who are in the employment of the company, or have been in the employment of the company within the said year, and are in the opinion of the receiver capable of giving the information required;

(d) who are or have been within the said year officers of or in the employment of a company which is, or within the said year was, an officer of the company to which the statement relates.

(3) Any person making the statement and affidavit shall be allowed, and shall be paid by the receiver (or his successor) out of his receipts, such costs and expenses incurred in and about the preparation and making of the statement and affidavit as the receiver (or his successor) may consider reasonable, subject to an appeal to the court.

(4) Where the receiver is appointed under the powers contained in any instrument, this section shall have effect with the substitution for references to the court of references to the Official Receiver and for references to an affidavit of references to a statutory declaration.

(5) If any person without reasonable excuse makes default in complying with the requirements of this section, he shall be liable to a fine and, for continued default, to a daily default fine.

(6) References in this section to a receiver's successor shall include a continuing receiver or manager.

(7) This section shall not apply where the receiver or manager was appointed before the commencement of the Companies (Amendment) Ordinance 1984 (6 of 1984).

Delivery to Registrar of accounts of receivers and managers

301.(1) Except where section 300A(2) applies, every receiver or manager of the property of a company who has been appointed under the powers contained in any instrument shall, within 1 month, or such longer period as the Registrar may allow, after the expiration of the period of 6 months from the date of his appointment and of every subsequent period of 6 months and within 1 month after he ceases to act as receiver or manager, deliver to the Registrar for registration an abstract in the specified form showing his receipts and his payments during that period of 6 months, or, where he ceases to act as aforesaid, during the period from the end of the period to which the last preceding abstract related up to the date of his so ceasing, and the aggregate amount of his receipts and of his payments during all preceding periods since his appointment.

(2) Any receiver or manager who makes default in complying with the provisions of this section shall be liable to a fine and, for continued default, to a daily default fine.

Enforcement of duty of receiver to make returns, &c.

302.(1) If-

> *(a)* any receiver or manager of the property of a company, who has made default in filing, delivering or making any return, account or other document or in giving any notice, which a receiver or manager is by law required to file, deliver, make or give, fails to make good the default within 14 days after the service on him of a notice requiring him to do so; or

> *(b)* any receiver or manager of the property of a company who has been appointed under the powers contained in any instrument, has, after being required at any time by the liquidator of the company so to do, failed to render proper accounts of his receipts and payments and to vouch the same and to pay over to the liquidator the amount properly payable to him;

the court may, on an application made for the purpose, make an order directing the receiver or manager, as the case may be, to make good the default within such time as may be specified in the order.

(2) In the case of any such default as is mentioned in subsection (1)(a), an application for the purposes of this section may be made by any member or creditor of the company or by the Registrar, and in the case of any such default as is mentioned in subsection (1)(b), the application shall be made by the liquidator, and in either case the order may provide that all costs of and incidental to the application shall be borne by the receiver or manager, as the case may be.

(3) Nothing in this section shall be taken to prejudice the operation of any enactment imposing penalties on receivers or managers in respect of such default as is mentioned in subsection (1).

Construction of references to receivers and managers

302A. Except where the context otherwise requires-

(a) any reference in this Ordinance to a receiver or manager of the property of a company, or to a receiver thereof, includes a reference to a receiver or manager, or (as the case may be) to a receiver, of part only of that property and to a receiver only of the income arising from that property or from part thereof; and

(b) any reference in this Ordinance to the appointment of a receiver or manager under powers contained in any instrument includes a reference to an appointment made under powers conferred by any enactment including powers which, by virtue of any enactment, are implied in and have effect as if contained in an instrument.

PART VII - General Provisions As To Registration

Registration offices and appointment of officers for purposes of this Ordinance

303.(1) For the purposes of the registration of companies under this Ordinance, there shall be an office at such place as the Governor directs.

(2) The Governor may appoint a Registrar of Companies and such other officers as he may think necessary for the purposes of this Ordinance, and may make regulations with respect to their duties, and may remove any persons so appointed.

(3) (*Repealed*)

(4) The Governor may direct a seal or seals to be prepared for the authentication of documents required for or connected with the registration of companies.

(5) (*Repealed*)

Taking of affidavits, etc.

303A.(1) The Registrar and a person holding or acting in an office authorized by him by notice in the Gazette may take an affidavit, affirmation or statutory or other declaration required to be made before or produced or delivered to or filed with the Registrar under an Ordinance notwithstanding any Ordinance requiring the taking of the affidavit, affirmation or statutory or other declaration by or before another person.

(2) The Registrar may charge and recover the fee approved by the Financial Secretary and published in the Gazette for the taking of an affidavit, affirmation or statutory or other declaration under subsection (1).

Fees

304.(1) There shall be paid to the Registrar in respect of the several matters mentioned in the table set out in the Eighth Schedule the several fees therein specified.

(1A) (*Repealed*)

(2) All fees paid to the Registrar in pursuance of this Ordinance shall be paid into the general revenue.

(3) (*Repealed*)

(4) The Registrar may charge in respect of any service provided by him under this Ordinance otherwise than in pursuance of an obligation imposed by this Ordinance and for which a fee is not specified under this Ordinance such reasonable fee as the Financial Secretary may approve.

Inspection, production and evidence of documents kept by Registrar

305.(1) Any person may, on payment of the fee required to be paid under section 304(1)-

    (a)   inspect-

        (i)   a copy of any document kept by the Registrar; or

        (ii)   the document itself if a copy is unavailable; or

    (b)   require-

        (i)   a certificate of the incorporation of any company; or

        (ii)   a copy or extract of any other document or part of any other document, to be certified by the Registrar.

(2) No process for compelling the production of any document kept by the Registrar shall issue from any court except with the leave of that court, and any such process if issued shall bear thereon a statement that it is issued with the leave of the court.

(3) A copy of or extract from any document kept and registered at the office for the registration of companies, certified to be a true copy under the hand of the Registrar (whose official position it shall not be necessary to prove), shall in all legal proceedings be admissible in evidence-

    (a)   as of equal validity with the original document; and

    (b)   on its production without further proof,

and, until the contrary is proved, the court before which such copy or extract is produced shall presume-

        (i)   that the document is certified by the Registrar; and

        (ii)   that the document is a true copy of or extract from the original document.

(4)   For the purpose of this section-

    (a)   a copy of a document, notwithstanding that it is taken from a copy or other reproduction of the original document, shall be treated for all purposes as a copy of the original document; and

    (b)   a copy of a document includes a copy of part of the document.

Enforcement of duties under Ordinance by court order

306.(1) If a company or any officer of a company, having made default in complying with any requirement of this Ordinance, fails to make good the default within 14 days after the service of a notice on the company or officer requiring the company or officer to comply with that requirement, the court may, on an application made to it by any member or creditor of the company or by the Registrar, make an order -

> *(a)* where the default was that of the company, directing the company and any officer thereof;
>
> *(b)* where the default was that of an officer, directing that officer,

to make good the default within such time as may be specified in the order.

(2) Any such order may provide that all costs of and incidental to the application shall be borne-

> *(a)* where the default was that of a company, by the company or by any officer of the company responsible for the default;
>
> *(b)* where the default was that of an officer, by that officer.

(3) Nothing in this section shall be taken to prejudice the operation of any enactment imposing penalties on a company or any officer of a company in respect of any such default as aforesaid.

PART VIII - Application Of Ordinance To Companies Formed Or Registered Under Former Ordinances

Application of Ordinance to companies formed under former Companies Ordinance

307.   In the application of this Ordinance to existing companies, it shall apply in the same manner-

      (a)   in the case of a limited company, other than a company limited by guarantee, as if the company had been formed and registered under this Ordinance as a company limited by shares;

      (b)   in the case of a company limited by guarantee, as if the company had been formed and registered under this Ordinance as a company limited by guarantee; and

      (c)   in the case of a company other than a limited company, as if the company had been formed and registered under this Ordinance as an unlimited company:

Provided that reference, express or implied, to the date of registration shall be construed as a reference to the date at which the company was registered under the Companies Ordinance 1865 (1 of 1865), or the Companies Ordinance 1911 (58 of 1911), as the case may be.

Application of Ordinance to companies registered under former Companies Ordinances

308.   This Ordinance shall apply to every company registered but not formed under the Companies Ordinance 1865 (1 of 1865), or the Companies Ordinance 1911 (58 of 1911), in the same manner as it is in Part IX of this Ordinance declared to apply to companies registered but not formed under this Ordinance:

Provided that reference, express or implied, to the date of registration shall be construed as a reference to the date at which the company was registered under the Companies Ordinance 1865 (1 of 1865), or the Companies Ordinance 1911 (58 of 1911), as the case may be.

Application of Ordinance to companies re-registered under former Companies Ordinance

309.   The Ordinance shall apply to every unlimited company registered as a limited company in pursuance of section 58 of the Companies Ordinance 1911 (58 of 1911), in the same manner as it applies to an unlimited company registered in pursuance of this Ordinance as a limited company:

Provided that reference, express or implied, to the date of registration shall be construed as a reference to the date at which the company was registered as a limited company under the said section of the Companies Ordinance 1911 (58 of 1911).

PART IX - Companies Not Formed Under This Ordinance Authorized To Register Under This Ordinance

Companies capable of being registered

310.(1) With the exceptions and subject to the provisions contained in this section, any company formed whether before or after the commencement of this Ordinance, in pursuance of any Ordinance other than this Ordinance, or of letters patent, or being otherwise duly constituted according to law, and consisting of 2 or more members, may at any time register under this Ordinance as an unlimited company, or as a company limited by shares, or as a company limited by guarantee; and the registration shall not be invalid by reason that it has taken place with a view to the company being wound up:

Provided that-

(a)   a company registered under the Companies Ordinance 1865 (1 of 1865), or the Companies Ordinance 1911 (58 of 1911), shall not register in pursuance of this section;

(b)   a company having the liability of its members limited by Ordinance, Act of Parliament or letters patent, and not being a joint stock company as hereinafter defined, shall not register in pursuance of this section;

(c)   a company having the liability of its members limited by Ordinance, Act of Parliament or letters patent shall not register in pursuance of this section as an unlimited company or as a company limited by guarantee;

(d)   a company that is not a joint stock company as hereinafter defined shall not register in pursuance of this section as a company limited by shares;

(e)   a company shall not register in pursuance of this section without the assent of a majority of such of its members as are present in person or by proxy (in cases where proxies are allowed by the regulations of the company) at a general meeting summoned for the purpose;

(f)   where a company not having the liability of its members limited by Ordinance, Act of Parliament or letters patent is about to register as a limited company, the majority required to assent as aforesaid shall consist of not less than three-fourths of the members present in person or by proxy at the meeting;

(g)   where a company is about to register as a company limited by guarantee, the assent to its being so registered shall be accompanied by a resolution declaring that each member undertakes to contribute to the assets of the company, in the event of its being wound up while he is a member, or within 1 year after he ceases to be a member, for payment of the debts and liabilities of the company contracted before he ceased to be a member, and of the costs and expenses of winding up, and for the adjustment of the rights of the contributories among themselves, such amount as may be required, not exceeding a specified amount.

(2) In computing any majority under this section when a poll is demanded regard shall be had to the number of votes to which each member is entitled according to the regulations of the company.

Definition of joint stock company

311. For the purposes of this Part, as far as relates to registration of companies as companies limited by shares, a joint stock company means a company having a permanent paid-up or nominal share capital of fixed amount divided into shares, also of fixed amount, or held and transferable as stock, or divided and held partly in one way and partly in the other, and formed on the principle of having for its members the holders of those shares or that stock, and no other persons, and such a company when registered with limited liability under this Ordinance shall be deemed to be a company limited by shares.

Requirements for registration by joint stock companies

312. Before the registration in pursuance of this Part of a joint stock company, there shall be delivered to the Registrar the following documents-

    (a) a list showing the names, addresses, and occupations of all persons who on a day named in the list, not being more than 6 clear days before the day of registration, were members of the company, with the addition of the shares or stock held by them respectively, distinguishing, in cases where the shares are numbered, each share by its number;

    (b) a copy of any Ordinance, Act of Parliament, royal charter, letters patent, deed of settlement, contract of copartnery, cost book regulations, or other instrument constituting or regulating the company; and

    (c) if the company is intended to be registered as a limited company, a statement specifying the following particulars-

        (i) the nominal share capital of the company and the number of shares into which it is divided, or the amount of stock of which it consists;

        (ii) the number of shares taken and the amount paid on each share;

        (iii) the name of the company, and

            (A) if the name is in English, with the addition of the word "Limited" as the last word thereof;

> *(B)* if the name is in Chinese, with the addition of "...." As the last 4 Chinese characters thereof; and
>
> *(C)* if the name is both in English and Chinese, with the addition of the word "Limited" as the last word of the name in English and of "...." as the last 4 Chinese characters of the name in Chinese respectively; and
>
> **(iv)** in the case of a company intended to be registered as a company limited by guarantee, the resolution declaring the amount of the guarantee.

Requirements for registration by other than joint stock companies

313. Before the registration in pursuance of this Part of any company not being a joint stock company, there shall be delivered to the Registrar-

> *(a)* a list showing the names, addresses, and occupations of the directors or other managers (if any) of the company; and
>
> *(b)* a copy of any Ordinance, Act of Parliament, letters patent, deed of settlement, contract of copartnery, cost book regulations, or other instrument constituting or regulating the company; and
>
> *(c)* in the case of a company intended to be registered as a company limited by guarantee, a copy of the resolution declaring the amount of the guarantee.

Authentication of statements of existing companies

314. The lists of members and directors and any other particulars relating to the company required to be delivered to the Registrar shall be versified by a statutory declaration of any 2 or more directors or other principal officers of the company.

Registrar may require evidence as to nature of company

315. The Registrar may require such evidence as he thinks necessary for the purpose of satisfying himself whether any company proposing to be registered is or is not a joint stock company as hereinbefore defined.

Exemption of certain companies from payment of fees

316. No fees shall be charged in respect of the registration in pursuance of this Part of a company if it is not registered as a limited company, or if before its registration as a limited company the liability of the shareholders was limited by some other Ordinance or Act of Parliament or by letters patent.

Addition of "Limited" etc., to name

317. When a company registers in pursuance of this Part with limited liability -

    (a)   if the name of the company is in English, the word "Limited" shall form, and be registered as, part of its name and any Chinese equivalent of its name which the company may use shall contain the expression in Chinese "....";

    (b)   if the name of the company is in Chinese, the expression in Chinese "..." shall form, and be registered as, part of its name and any English equivalent of its name which the company may use shall contain the word "Limited"; and

    (c)   if the name of the company is both in English and Chinese, the word "Limited" and the expression in Chinese "...." shall form, and be registered as, part of its name in English and Chinese respectively.

Certificate of registration of existing companies

318. On compliance with the requirements of this Part with respect to registration, and on payment of such fees, if any, as are payable under the Eighth Schedule the Registrar shall certify under his hand that the company applying for registration is incorporated as a company under this Ordinance, and in the case of a limited company that it is limited, and thereupon the company shall be so incorporated.

Vesting of property on registration

319. All property, real and personal (including things in action), belonging to or vested in a company at the date of its registration in pursuance of this Part shall on registration pass to and vest in the company as incorporated under this Ordinance for all the estate and interest of the company therein.

Saving for existing liabilities

320. Registration of a company in pursuance of this Part shall not affect the rights or liabilities of the company in respect of any debt or obligation incurred, or any contract entered into, by, to, with, or on behalf of, the company before registration.

Continuation of existing actions

321. All actions and other legal proceedings which at the time of the registration of a company in pursuance of this Part are pending by or against the company, or the public officer or any member thereof, may be continued in the same manner as if the registration had not taken place:

Provided that execution shall not issue against the effects of any individual member of the company on any judgment, decree, or order obtained in any such action or proceeding, but, in the event of the property and effects of the company being insufficient to satisfy the judgment, decree, or order, an order may be obtained for winding up the company.

Effect of registration under Ordinance

322.(1) When a company is registered in pursuance of this Part the following provisions of this section shall have effect.

(2) All provisions contained in any Ordinance, Act or other instrument constituting or regulating the company, including, in the case of a company registered as a company limited by guarantee, the resolution declaring the amount of the guarantee, shall be deemed to be conditions and regulations of the company, in the same manner and with the same incidents as if so much thereof as would, if the company had been formed under this Ordinance, have been required to be inserted in the memorandum, were contained in a registered memorandum, and the residue thereof were contained in registered articles.

(3) All the provisions of this Ordinance shall apply to the company, and the members, contributories, and creditors thereof, in the same manner in all respects as if it had been formed under this Ordinance, subject as follows-

(a) Table A shall not apply unless adopted by special resolution;

(b) the provisions of this Ordinance relating to the numbering of shares shall not apply to any joint stock company whose shares are not numbered;

(c) subject to the provisions of this section the company shall not have power to alter any provision contained in any Ordinance or Act of Parliament relating to the company;

(d) subject to the provisions of this section the company shall not have power, without the sanction of the Governor, to alter any provision contained in any letters patent relating to the company;

(e) the company shall not have power to alter any provision contained in a royal charter or letters patent with respect to the objects of the company;

(f) in the event of the company being wound up, every person shall be a contributory, in respect of the debts and liabilities of the company contracted before registration, who is liable to pay or contribute to the payment of any debt or liability of the company contracted before registration, or to pay or contribute to the payment of any sum for the adjustment of the rights of the members among themselves in respect of any such debt or liability, or to pay or contribute to the payment of the costs and expenses of winding up the company, so far as relates to such debts or liabilities as aforesaid;

(g)   in the event of the company being wound up, every contributory shall be liable to contribute to the assets of the company, in the course of the winding up, all sums due from him in respect of any such liability as aforesaid, and, in the event of the death, bankruptcy, or insolvency, of any contributory, or marriage of any female contributory, the provisions of this Ordinance with respect to the personal representatives, to the trustees of bankrupt or insolvent contributories, and to the liabilities of husbands and wives respectively, shall apply.

(4)   The provisions of this Ordinance with respect to-

(a)   the registration of an unlimited company as limited;

(b)   the powers of an unlimited company on registration as a limited company to increase the nominal amount of its share capital and to provide that a portion of its share capital shall not be capable of being called up except in the event of winding up;

(c)   the power of a limited company to determine that a portion of its share capital shall not be capable of being called up except in the event of winding up,

shall apply notwithstanding any provisions contained in any Ordinance, Act of Parliament, royal charter, or other instrument constituting or regulating the company.

(5) Nothing in this section shall authorize the company to alter any such provisions contained in any instrument constituting or regulating the company, as would, if the company had originally been formed under this Ordinance, have been required to be contained in the memorandum and are not authorized to be altered by this Ordinance.

(6) Nothing in this Ordinance shall derogate from any power of altering its constitution or regulations which may, by virtue of any Ordinance, Act of Parliament or other instrument constituting or regulating the company, be vested in the company.

(7) In this section, "instrument" includes deed of settlement, contract of copartnery, cost book regulations and letters patent.

Power to substitute memorandum and articles for deed of settlement

323.(1) Subject to the provisions of this section, a company registered in pursuance of this Part may by special resolution alter the form of its constitution by substituting a memorandum and articles for a deed of settlement.

(2) The provisions of section 8 with respect to applications to the court for cancellation of alterations of the objects of a company and matters consequential on the passing of resolutions for such alterations shall so far as applicable apply to an alteration under this section with the following modifications-

(a)   there shall be substituted for the printed copy of the altered memorandum required to be delivered to the Registrar a printed copy of the substituted memorandum and articles; and

(b)   on the delivery to the Registrar of a printed copy of the substituted memorandum and articles or the date when the alteration is no longer liable to be cancelled by order of the court, whichever last occurs, the substituted memorandum and articles shall apply to the company in the same manner as if it were a company registered under this Ordinance with that memorandum and those articles, and the company's deed of settlement shall cease to apply to the company.

(3)   An alteration under this section may be made either with or without any alteration of the objects of the company under this Ordinance.

(4)   In this section, "deed of settlement" includes any contract of copartnery or other instrument constituting or regulating the company, not being an Ordinance, Act of Parliament, a royal charter, or letters patent.

Power of court to stay or restrain proceedings

324.   The provisions of this Ordinance with respect to staying and restraining actions and proceedings against a company at any time after the presentation of a petition for winding up and before the making of a winding-up order shall, in the case of a company registered in pursuance of this Part where the application to stay or restrain is by a creditor, extend to actions and proceedings against any contributory of the company.

Actions stayed on winding-up order

325.   Where an order has been made for winding up a company registered in pursuance of this Part no action or proceeding shall be commenced or proceeded with against the company or any contributory of the company in respect of any debt of the company, except by leave of the court, and subject to such terms as the court may impose.

PART X - Winding Up Of Unregistered Companies

Meaning of unregistered company

326.(1) For the purposes of this Part, "unregistered company" includes any partnership, whether limited or not, any association and any company with the following exceptions-

(a)   a company registered under the Companies Ordinance 1865 (1 of 1865), or under the Companies Ordinance 1911 (58 of 1911), or under this Ordinance;

(b)   a partnership, association or company which consists of less than 8 members and is not a foreign partnership, association or company;

(c)   a partnership registered in Hong Kong under the Limited Partnerships Ordinance(Cap. 37).

(2)   For the avoidance of doubt it is declared that in subsection (1) "unregistered company" includes an oversea company which is certified under section 333(3) as being registered under Part XI.

Winding up of unregistered companies

327.(1) Subject to the provisions of this Part, any unregistered company may be wound up under this Ordinance, and all the provisions of this Ordinance with respect to winding up shall apply to an unregistered company, with the exceptions and additions mentioned in this section.

(2)   No unregistered company shall be wound up voluntarily under this Ordinance.

(3)   The circumstances in which an unregistered company may be wound up are as follows-

(a)   if the company is dissolved, or has ceased to carry on business, or is carrying on business only for the purpose of winding up its affairs;

(b)   if the company is unable to pay its debts;

(c)   if the court is of opinion that it is just and equitable that the company should be wound up.

(4)   An unregistered company shall, for the purposes of this Ordinance, be deemed to be unable to pay its debts-

(a)   if a creditor, by assignment or otherwise, to whom the company is indebted in a sum exceeding $5,000 then due, has served on the company, by leaving at its principal place of business, or by delivering to any officer of the company, or by otherwise serving in such manner as the court may approve or direct, a demand under his hand requiring the company to pay the sum so due, and the company has for 3 weeks after the service of the demand neglected to pay the sum or to secure or compound for it to the satisfaction of the creditor;

(b) if any action or other proceeding has been instituted against any member for any debt or demand due, or claimed to be due, from the company, or from him in his character of member, and notice in writing of the institution of the action or proceeding having been served on the company by leaving the same at its principal place of business, or by delivering it to any officer of the company, or by otherwise serving the same in such manner as the court may approve or direct, the company has not within 10 days after service of the notice paid, secured or compounded for the debt or demand, or procured the action or proceeding to be stayed, or indemnified the defendant to his reasonable satisfaction against the action or proceeding, and against all costs, damages and expenses to be incurred by him by reason of the same;

(c) if execution or other process issued on a judgment, decree or order obtained in any court in favour of a creditor against the company, or any member thereof as such, or any person authorized to be sued as nominal defendant on behalf of the company, is returned unsatisfied;

(d) if it is otherwise proved to the satisfaction of the court that the company is unable to pay its debts.

Oversea companies may be wound up although dissolved

327A. Where a company incorporated outside Hong Kong which has been carrying on business in Hong Kong ceases to carry on business in Hong Kong, it may be wound up as an unregistered company under this Part, notwithstanding that it has been dissolved or otherwise ceased to exist as a company under or by virtue of the laws of the place of its incorporation.

Contributories in winding up of unregistered company

328.(1) In the event of an unregistered company being wound up, every person shall be deemed to be a contributory who is liable to pay or contribute to the payment of any debt or liability of the company, or to pay or contribute to the payment of any sum for the adjustment of the rights of the members among themselves, or to pay or contribute to the payment of the costs and expenses of winding up the company, and every contributory shall be liable to contribute to the assets of the company all sums due from him in respect of any such liability as aforesaid.

(2) In the event of the death, bankruptcy, or insolvency, of any contributory, or marriage of any female contributory, the provisions of this Ordinance with respect to the personal representatives of deceased contributories, to the trustees of bankrupt or insolvent contributories, and to the liabilities of husbands and wives respectively, shall apply.

Power of court to stay or restrain proceeding

329. The provisions of this Ordinance with respect to staying and restraining actions and proceedings against a company at any time after the presentation of a petition for winding up and before the making of a winding-up order shall, in the case of an unregistered company, where the application to stay or restrain is by a creditor, extend to actions and proceedings against any contributory of the company.

Actions stayed on winding-up order

330. Where an order has been made for winding up an unregistered company, no action or proceeding shall be proceeded with or commenced against any contributory of the company in respect of any debt of the company, except by leave of the court, and subject to such terms as the court may impose.

Provisions of Part X cumulative

331. The provisions of this Part with respect to unregistered companies shall be in addition to and not in restriction of any provisions herein before in this Ordinance contained with respect to winding up companies by the court, and the court or liquidator may exercise any powers or do any act in the case of unregistered companies which might be exercised or done by it or him in winding up companies formed and registered under this Ordinance:

Provided that an unregistered company shall not, except in the event of its being wound up, be deemed to be a company under this Ordinance, and then only to the extent provided by this Part.

Saving for enactments providing for winding up under former Companies Ordinances

331A. Nothing in this Part shall affect the operation of any enactment which provides for any partnership, association or company being wound up, or being wound up as a company or as an unregistered company, under any enactment repealed by this Ordinance.

PART XI - Companies Incorporated Outside Hong Kong

Provisions as to Establishment of Place of Business in Hong Kong

Application of Part XI

332.   This Part shall apply to all oversea companies, that is to say, companies incorporated outside Hong Kong which, after the commencement of this Ordinance, establish a place of business in Hong Kong, and companies incorporated outside Hong Kong which have, before the commencement of this Ordinance, established a place of business in Hong Kong and continue to have a place of business in Hong Kong at the commencement of this Ordinance.

Documents etc. to he delivered to Registrar by oversea companies which establish a place of business in Hong Kong

333.(1)   Any oversea company which, on or after the commencement of the Companies (Amendment) Ordinance 1984 (6 of 1984), establishes a place of business in Hong Kong shall, within 1 month of the establishment of the place of business, deliver to the Registrar for registration-

(a)   a certified copy of the charter, statutes or memorandum and articles of the company or other instrument constituting or defining the constitution of the company, and, if the instrument is not written in the English language, a certified translation thereof,

(b)   a list in the specified form of the directors and secretary of the company containing the particulars mentioned in subsection (2);

(c)   a list in the specified form of the names and addresses of some one or more persons resident in Hong Kong authorized to accept on behalf of the company service of process and any notices required to be served on the company, and also-

(i)   the address of the principal place of business of the company in Hong Kong; and

(ii)   the respective addresses of the principal place of business, if any, and the registered office (or its equivalent) of the company in the place of its incorporation;

(d)   a memorandum of appointment or power of attorney or other document under the seal of the company or executed on its behalf in such manner as to be binding on the company authorizing any person named under paragraph (c) to accept service of process and any notices on behalf of the company, together with a certified translation thereof if such memorandum or power of attorney or other document is in a language other than English;

(e) subject to subsection (1A), a certified copy of the company's certificate of incorporation, together with a certified translation thereof if the certificate is in a language other than English; and

(f) except in the case of a company referred to in section 336(6), a certified copy of the latest accounts of the company in the form required by the law of the place of its incorporation, or, if no such requirement is in force under the law of that place, in the form in which the accounts of the company are submitted to the members of the company, together with a certified translation thereof if the accounts are in a language other than English:

Provided that-

(i) a body corporate or a firm other than a firm of solicitors or professional accountants shall not be authorized to accept on behalf of any oversea company service of process or any notices required to be served on the company;

(ii) in the case of a firm of solicitors or professional accountants so authorized, it shall be sufficient for the purpose of paragraph (c) to deliver the name of the firm and its business address in Hong Kong.

(1A) Where it is shown to the satisfaction of the Registrar that it is not the practice under the law of the place where an oversea company purports to be incorporated to issue a certificate of incorporation, the company may, instead of delivering a copy of its certificate of incorporation as required by subsection (1)(e), within 1 month of the establishment of its place of business in Hong Kong, deliver to the Registrar for registration such other evidence of incorporation as the Registrar deems sufficient.

(2) The list referred to in subsection (1)(b) shall contain the following particulars-

(a) with respect to each director of an oversea company not having any of its shares listed on the Unified Exchange-

(i) in the case of an individual, his present forename and surname and any former forename or surname (including, in the case of a Chinese director, the Chinese characters for any such forename or surname if they are used by such director), any alias, his usual residential address, his nationality and the number of his identity card (if any) or, in the absence of such number, the number and issuing country of any passport held by him;

(ii) in the case of a body corporate, its corporate name and registered or principal office;

(aa) with respect to each director of an oversea company having any of its shares listed on the Unified Exchange-

(i) his present forename and surname and any former forename or surname (including, in the case of a Chinese director, the Chinese characters for any such forename or surname if they are used by such director);

(ii) any alias;

(iii) his usual residential address;

(iv) his nationality;

(v) the number of his identity card (if any) or, in the absence of such number, the number and issuing country of any passport held by him; and

(vi) if he holds other directorships in companies incorporated in Hong Kong or registered under Part XI, particulars of each of those directorships;

(b) with respect to the secretary or, where there are joint secretaries, with respect to each of them-

(i) in the case of an individual, his present forename and surname and any former forename or surname (including, in the case of a Chinese secretary, the Chinese characters for any such forename or surname if they are used by such secretary), any alias, his usual residential address, his nationality and the number of his identity card (if any) or, in the absence of such number, the number and issuing country of any passport held by him; and

(ii) in the case of a body corporate, its corporate name and registered or principal office:

Provided that where all the partners in a firm are joint secretaries of the company, the name and principal office of the firm may be stated instead of the particulars mentioned in paragraph (b).

(2A) Any listed oversea company registered before the commencement of section 18 of the Companies (Amendment) (No. 2) Ordinance 1993 (75 of 1993) shall, within 3 months after the commencement of that section, deliver to the Registrar a list in the specified form of the directors of the company containing the particulars mentioned in subsection (2)(aa).

(3) The Registrar shall keep a register of oversea companies complying with this section and shall, upon registration of the documents required by subsection (1) to be delivered by an oversea company for registration, enter the name of the oversea company in the register and certify under his hand that such company is a company registered under this Part; and where any change is made in the corporate name of an oversea company, the Registrar shall, upon registration of a return delivered by the company under section 335(2), issue a fresh certificate containing the name of the company as so changed.

(4) In this section-

    (a) references to solicitors are references to persons who are solicitors qualified to act as such under the Legal Practitioners Ordinance (Cap. 159);

    (b) references to professional accountants are references to persons who are registered as professional accountants and hold practising certificates under the Professional Accountants Ordinance (Cap. 50);

    (c) the expressions "forename" , "residential address" and "surname" have the meanings respectively assigned thereto by section 158(10);

    (ca) the expression "identity card" has the meaning assigned to it by section 158(10)(c);

    (d) references to a former forename or surname shall be construed in accordance with section 158(10)(f).

(5) Any oversea company which had, before the commencement of the Companies (Amendment) Ordinance 1984 (6 of 1984), complied with the provisions of this section in force immediately before such commencement shall be deemed to be an oversea company complying with this section, and the Registrar shall enter the name of every such company in the register of oversea companies and certify under his hand that the company is a company registered under this Part; and for the purposes of this subsection and subsection (6), any oversea company which, before the commencement of that Ordinance, delivered to the Registrar for registration the documents and other information required to be so delivered under the provisions of this section in force immediately before such commencement shall be deemed to have complied with those provisions.

(6) Subject to subsection (5), this section shall apply to an oversea company which-

    (a) at the commencement of the Companies (Amendment) Ordinance 1984 (6 of 1984), has a place of business in Hong Kong established before such commencement; and

    (b) had not complied with the provisions of this section in force immediately before such commencement,

as it applies to an oversea company referred to in subsection (1) with the substitution for "1 month of the establishment of the place of business" in that subsection of "3 months after the commencement of that Ordinance".

Continuing obligation in respect of authorized representative

333A.(1) Any oversea company registered under this Part shall at all times, until the expiration of a period of 3 years from the date on which it ceases to have a place of business in Hong Kong, keep registered under section 333(1) the name and address of a person resident in Hong Kong who is authorized to accept service of process and notices on its behalf.

(2) Where a person registered as so authorized at any time ceases to be able to act on behalf of the company whether by reason of death or incapacity or other unforeseen reason, the company shall be deemed to comply with this section if, not later than 6 weeks from that time, the company delivers to the Registrar in respect of some other person so authorized the particulars and documents specified in section 333(1)(c) and (d) for registration under that section.

Termination of registration of authorized representative

333B.(1) Where any person registered under section 333(1) as a person authorized to accept service of process and notices on behalf of an oversea company notifies the company by registered post addressed to its registered office (or its equivalent) in the place of its incorporation that he no longer wishes to act on behalf of the company as a person so authorized, such person may file with the Registrar a statutory declaration that-

(a) the company has been so notified; and

(b) such notice would have been delivered to the company in due course of post not less than 6 weeks before the date of the statutory declaration,

and such person shall, unless earlier replaced by the company, cease to be registered as a person so authorized on the expiration of a period of 6 weeks from the date of the filing of the statutory declaration.

(2) The Registrar shall, on the application of any oversea company which has not had a place of business in Hong Kong for a period of not less than 3 years preceding the application, remove from the register the particulars of any person registered under section 333(1) as a person authorized to accept service of process and notices on behalf of the company.

Registrar to keep an index of directors of oversea companies

333C.(1) *(a)* The Registrar shall, as from a date to be appointed by the Governor in Council by notice in the Gazette, keep and maintain an index of every person who is a director of an oversea company registered under this Part.

(b) The particulars contained in the index shall, in respect of each director, include his name and address and the latest particulars delivered in respect of him to the Registrar, together with the name of each company of which he is a director, whether it is a company incorporated in Hong Kong or registered under Part XI.

(2) The index kept in pursuance of this section shall be open to inspection by any person on payment of the prescribed fee.

334. (*Repealed*)

Return to be delivered to Registrar where documents, &c. altered

335.(1) If in the case of any oversea company any alteration is made in-

(a) the charter, statutes or memorandum and articles of the company or any such instrument as is mentioned in section 333(1)(a); or

(b) the directors or secretary of the company or the particulars contained in the list of directors and secretary of the company; or

(c) the names or addresses of the persons authorized to accept service on behalf of the company; or

(d) the address of the company's principal place of business in Hong Kong or of its registered office (or its equivalent), or of its principal place of business, in the place of its incorporation,

the company shall, within the prescribed time, deliver to the Registrar for registration a return in the specified form, containing the particulars of the alteration and, in respect of any change of the persons referred to in paragraph (c), a document complying with section 333(1)(d).

(2) If any change is made in the corporate name of an oversea company, the company shall, within the prescribed time, deliver to the Registrar a return in the specified form, containing particulars of the change.

Accounts of oversea company

336.(1) Subject to subsection (6), every oversea company shall, at least once in every calendar year and at intervals of not more than 15 months, deliver to the Registrar for registration a return, which shall be signed on behalf of the company by a director or the secretary or a person authorized to accept service on behalf of the company or the manager or principal officer of the company in Hong Kong, confirming that there has been no alteration in the documents and particulars delivered under section 333 other than the alterations, if any, notified under section 335, and copies, certified in the prescribed manner, of

(a) (i) its balance sheet as at the end of its last financial year,

(ii) its profit and loss account for the said year,

(iii) its group accounts, if any, in respect of the said year, and

(iv) its directors' report, if any, in respect of the said year,

all in such form and containing such particulars and including copies of such documents as the company is required to prepare by the law for the time being applicable to the company in the place of its incorporation or origin; and

(b) its auditors' report, if any, on the said balance sheet and accounts.

(2) The Registrar may, if he is of the opinion that the balance sheet, profit and loss account and documents referred to in subsection (1) do not sufficiently disclose the company's financial position, require the company to deliver to him for registration a balance sheet and profit and loss account within such period, in such form and, subject to subsection (3), containing such particulars and including such documents as he by notice in writing given to the company requires, and the company shall comply with the requirements set out in the notice.

(3) Subsection (2) does not authorize the Registrar to require a balance sheet or profit and loss account to contain any particulars or include any documents that would not be required to be furnished if the company were a company incorporated under this Ordinance.

(4) Where an oversea company is not required by the law of the place of its incorporation or origin to prepare a balance sheet and profit and loss account, the company shall prepare and deliver to the Registrar for registration-

(a) a balance sheet and profit and loss account within such period, in such form and containing such particulars and including such documents as the company would have been required to prepare if it were a company incorporated under this Ordinance, and

(b) a report by qualified auditors on the said balance sheet and profit and loss account.

(5) If any return, balance sheet, profit and loss account, group accounts or document delivered to the Registrar for registration under this section is not written in the English language, there shall be annexed to it a certified translation thereof in English.

(6) This section shall not apply to a company which-

(a) if it were incorporated under this Ordinance would be a private company within the meaning of section 29, or

(b) in the opinion of the Registrar has substantially the same general characteristics as such a private company,

and which is not required by the law of the place of its incorporation or origin to publish its accounts or to deliver copies to any person in whose office they may be inspected as of right by members of the public.

Obligation to state name of oversea company, whether limited and country where incorporated

337. Every oversea company shall-

(a) in every prospectus inviting subscriptions for its shares or debentures in Hong Kong state the country in which the company is incorporated; and

(b) conspicuously exhibit on every place where it carries on business in Hong Kong the name of the company and the country in which the company is incorporated; and

(c) cause the name of the company and of the country in which the company is incorporated to be stated in legible characters in all bill-heads and letter paper, and in all notices and other official publications of the company, and, if the company is in liquidation in that country, in all advertisements of the company; and

(ca) where the company is in liquidation in the country in which it is incorporated -

    (i) if the name of the company is in a language other than Chinese, add the words and parentheses "(in liquidation)" after its name as exhibited under paragraph (b) and as stated in documents of the company under paragraph (c);

    (ii) if the name of the company is in Chinese, add the expression in Chinese and parentheses "(.....)" after its name so exhibited and stated; and

    (iii) if the name of the company is both in Chinese and in a language other than Chinese, add the expression in Chinese and parentheses "(.....)" and the words and parentheses "(in liquidation)" respectively after its name in Chinese and in that other language so exhibited and stated; and

(d) if the liability of the members of the company is limited, cause notice of that fact to be stated in legible characters in every such prospectus as aforesaid and in all bill-heads, letter paper, notices and other official publications of the company in Hong Kong and, if the company is in liquidation in the country in which it is incorporated, in all advertisements of the company in Hong Kong, and to be affixed on every place where it carries on its business.

Notice of commencement of liquidation and of appointment of liquidator

337A.(1) Where any proceedings for the liquidation of an oversea company are commenced in the country in which it is incorporated, the company and the officers of the company in Hong Kong shall deliver to the Registrar notice of the commencement of such liquidation and, when a liquidator is appointed, notice of such appointment.

(2) Any notice required by subsection (1) to be delivered to the Registrar shall be so delivered within 7 days after the date on which such notice could, in due course of post and if despatched with due diligence from the country in which the company is incorporated, have been received in Hong Kong.

(3) The Registrar shall register every notice delivered under this section.

Regulation of use of corporate name by oversea company in Hong Kong

337B.(1) Subject to subsection (2), where the Registrar is satisfied that in the case of an oversea company registered under this Part and carrying on business in Hong Kong under its corporate name, its corporate name-

    (a)   is the same as or is too like-

        (i)   a name appearing, or which should have appeared, in the Registrar's index of company names on the relevant date; or

        (ii)   the name of a body corporate incorporated or established under an Ordinance before the relevant date; or

    (b)   gives so misleading an indication of the nature of its activities in Hong Kong as to be likely to cause harm to the public,

he may serve a notice to that effect on the oversea company.

(2) A notice shall not be served on an oversea company under subsection (1)(a) later than 6 months beginning on the relevant date.

(2A) In subsections (1) and (2), "relevant date" means the date on which the oversea company complies with section 333 or, where there has been a change in its corporate name, section 335.

(3) An oversea company on which a notice is served under subsection (1) may deliver to the Registrar for registration under section 333 a statement in the specified form specifying a name approved by the Financial Secretary other than its corporate name under which it proposes to carry on business in Hong Kong and may, after that name has been so registered, at any time deliver to the Registrar for registration under that section a statement in the specified form specifying a name approved by the Financial Secretary other than its corporate name in substitution for the name previously registered under that section.

(4) The name by which an oversea company is, by virtue of subsection (3), for the time being registered under section 333 shall for all purposes of the law applying in Hong Kong (including the Business Registration Ordinance (Cap. 310)) be deemed to be the corporate name of the company; but this subsection shall not affect references to the corporate name of the company in this section or any rights or obligations of the company, or render defective any legal proceedings by or against the company, and any legal proceedings that might have been continued or commenced against it by its corporate name or its name previously registered under that section may be continued or commenced against it by its name for the time being so registered.

(5) Subject to subsection (6), an oversea company on which a notice is served under subsection (1) shall not at any time after the expiration of 2 months from the service of that notice carry on business in Hong Kong under its corporate name.

(6) An oversea company on which a notice is served under subsection (1)(b) may, within a period of 3 weeks from the service of that notice, apply to the court to set aside the notice, and the court may set it aside or confirm it.

(7) If subsection (5) is contravened, the oversea company and every officer or agent of the company who knowingly and wilfully authorizes or permits the contravention shall be liable to-

> *(a)* a fine and, in the case of an individual, imprisonment; and

> *(b)* for continued default, a daily default fine,

but nothing in subsection (5) or this subsection shall invalidate any transaction entered into by the company.

Service of documents on oversea companies

338.(1) Subject to subsection (2), any process or notice required to be served on an oversea company shall be sufficiently served if addressed to any person whose name has been delivered to the Registrar under this Part and left at or sent by post to his address as so delivered.

(2) Where any oversea company makes default in delivering to the Registrar the name and address of a person resident in Hong Kong authorized to accept on behalf of the company service of process or notices, or if at any time all the persons whose names and addresses have been so delivered are dead or have ceased so to reside or refuse to accept service on behalf of the company or for any reason cannot be served, a document may be served on the company-

> *(a)* by leaving it at or sending it by post to any place of business established by the company in Hong Kong; or

> *(b)* if the company no longer has a place of business in Hong Kong-

>> **(i)** by sending it by registered post to its registered office, and a copy thereof by registered post to its principal place of business (if any), in

the place of its incorporation at the respective addresses thereof registered under section 333(1)(c); or

(ii) if no such addresses have been registered, by leaving it at or sending it by post to any place in Hong Kong at which the company has had a place of business within the previous 3 years.

Notice to be given when oversea company ceases to have a place of business in Hong Kong

339. If any oversea company ceases to have a place of business in Hong Kong, it shall forthwith give notice of the fact to the Registrar, and as from the date on which notice is so given, the obligation of the company to deliver any document to the Registrar shall cease.

Removal etc. of name of oversea company from register

339A.(1) The Registrar shall, on receipt of notice from an agent of an oversea company registered under this Part that the company has been dissolved, remove the name of the company from the register of oversea companies.

(2) Where the Registrar has reasonable cause to believe that an oversea company registered under this Part has ceased to have a place of business in Hong Kong, the provisions of this Ordinance relating to the striking off the register of companies of the names of defunct companies shall, with such adaptations as are necessary, extend and apply accordingly.

Penalties

340. If any oversea company fails to comply with any of the provisions of this Part the company, and every officer or agent of the company who authorizes or permits the default, shall be liable to a fine and, for continued default, to a daily default fine.

Interpretation of Part XI

341. For the purposes of this Part -

"certified" means certified in the prescribed manner to be a true copy or a correct translation;

"director" in relation to a company includes any person in accordance with whose directions or instructions the directors of the company are accustomed to act;

"place of business" includes a share transfer or share registration office and any place used for the manufacture or warehousing of any goods, but does not include a place not used by the company to transact any business which creates legal obligations;

"prospectus" has the same meaning as when used in relation to a company incorporated under this Ordinance;

"secretary" includes any person occupying the position of secretary by whatever name called.

PART XII - Restrictions On Sale Of Shares And Offers Of Shares For Sale

Dating of prospectus and particulars to be contained therein

342.(1) Subject to section 342A, it shall not be lawful for any person to issue, circulate or distribute in Hong Kong any prospectus offering for subscription shares in or debentures of a company incorporated outside Hong Kong, whether the company has or has not established a place of business in Hong Kong unless the prospectus is dated and-

> *(a)*   contains particulars with respect to the following matters-
>
> > **(i)**   the instrument constituting or defining the constitution of the company;
> >
> > **(ii)**   the enactments, or provisions having the force of an enactment, by or under which the incorporation of the company was effected;
> >
> > **(iii)**   an address in Hong Kong where the said instrument, enactments or provisions, or copies thereof, and if the same are in a language other than English a translation thereof certified in the prescribed manner, can be inspected;
> >
> > **(iv)**   the date on which and the country in which the company was incorporated;
> >
> > **(v)**   whether the company has established a place of business in Hong Kong, and, if so, the address of its principal office in Hong Kong;
>
> *(b)*   subject to the provisions of this section, is in the English language and contains a Chinese translation and states the matters specified in Part I of the Third Schedule and sets out the reports specified in Part II of that Schedule, subject always to the provisions contained in Part III of that Schedule:

Provided that the provisions of paragraph (a)(i), (ii) and (iii) shall not apply in the case of a prospectus issued more than 2 years after the date at which the company is entitled to commence business, and, in the application of Part I of the Third Schedule for the purposes of this subsection, paragraph 5 thereof shall have effect with the substitution, for the reference to the articles, of a reference to the constitution of the company.

(2) Any condition requiring or binding an applicant for shares or debentures to waive compliance with any requirement imposed by virtue of subsection (1)(a) or (b), or purporting to affect him with notice of any contract, document or matter not specifically referred to in the prospectus, shall be void.

(3) Subject to section 342A, it shall not be lawful for any person to issue to any person in Hong Kong a form of application for shares in or debentures of such a company as is mentioned in subsection (1) unless the form is issued with a prospectus which complies with this Part and the issue whereof in Hong Kong does not contravene the provisions of section 342B:

Provided that this subsection shall not apply if it is shown that the form of application was issued either-

> *(a)* in connexion with a bona fide invitation to a person to enter into an underwriting agreement with respect to the shares or debentures; or
>
> *(b)* in relation to shares or debentures which were not offered to the public.

(4) In the event of non-compliance with or contravention of any of the requirements imposed by subsection (1)(a) and (b), a director or other person responsible for the prospectus shall not incur any liability by reason of the non-compliance or contravention, if-

> *(a)* as regards any matter not disclosed, he proves that he was not cognisant thereof, or
>
> *(b)* he proves that the non-compliance or contravention arose from an honest mistake of fact on his part; or
>
> *(c)* the non-compliance or contravention was in respect of matters which, in the opinion of the court dealing with the case, were immaterial or were otherwise such as ought, in the opinion of that court, having regard to all the circumstances of the case, reasonably to be excused:

Provided that, in the event of failure to include in a prospectus a statement with respect to the matters contained in paragraph 19 of the Third Schedule, no director or other person shall incur any liability in respect of the failure unless it be proved that he had knowledge of the matters not disclosed.

(5) This section shall not apply-

> *(a)* to the issue to existing members or debenture holders of a company of a prospectus or form of application relating to shares in or debentures of the company, whether an applicant for shares or debentures will or will not have the right to renounce in favour of other persons; or
>
> *(b)* to the issue of a prospectus or a form of application relating to shares or debentures which are or are to be in all respects uniform with shares or debentures previously issued and for the time being listed on the Unified Exchange;

but, subject as aforesaid, this section shall apply to a prospectus or form of application whether issued on the formation of a company or subsequently.

(6) Nothing in this section shall limit or diminish any liability which any person may incur under the general law or this Ordinance apart from this section.

Exemption of certain persons and prospectuses from compliance with certain provisions

342A.(1) Where it is proposed to offer to the public by a prospectus issued generally any shares in or debentures of a company incorporated outside Hong Kong, whether the company has or has not established a place of business in Hong Kong, there may, on the request of the applicant, and subject to such conditions (if any) as the Commission thinks fit, be issued by the Commission a certificate of exemption from compliance with any or all of the requirements of sections 44A(2) and 342(1) and (3), that is to say, a certificate that, having regard to the circumstances of the case, compliance with any or all of those provisions would be either irrelevant or unduly burdensome.

(2) Whether or not a request referred to in subsection (1) has been made, the Commission may, by notice in the Gazette, exempt any class of companies or any class of prospectuses issued by companies from any or all of the requirements of sections 44A(2) and 342(1) and (3), if, having regard to the circumstances, the Commission considers that compliance with any or all of those requirements would be either irrelevant or unduly burdensome in the case of that class of companies or prospectuses, as the case may be.

(3) Where exemption from compliance with section 342(1) and (3) in relation to the requirements of the Third Schedule is granted under this section, whether by the issue of a certificate of exemption or by a notice in the Gazette, the certificate or notice, as the case may be, shall be expressed to have effect with regard to all of the requirements of the Third Schedule or to such of them as are specified in the certificate or notice, as the case may be.

Provisions as to expert's consent, and allotment

342B.(1) It shall not be lawful for any person to issue, circulate or distribute in Hong Kong any prospectus offering for subscription shares in or debentures of a company incorporated outside Hong Kong, whether the company has or has not established a place of business in Hong Kong-

    (a) if, where the prospectus includes a statement purporting to be made by an expert, he has not given, or has before delivery of the prospectus for registration withdrawn, his written consent to the issue of the prospectus with the statement included in the forth and context in which it is included or there does not appear in the prospectus a statement that he has given and has not withdrawn his consent as aforesaid; or

    (b) if the prospectus does not have the effect, where an application is made in pursuance thereof, of rendering all persons concerned bound by all the provisions (other than penal provisions) of sections 44A (except insofar as exemption from compliance has been granted under section 342A) and 44B so far as applicable.

(1A) Subsection (1)(b)-

(a)   shall apply in relation to a prospectus offering for subscription shares in a body corporate authorized as a mutual fund corporation under section 15 of the Securities Ordinance (Cap. 333) as if the reference to section 44A were a reference to that section excluding subsection (2) thereof,

(b)   shall not apply in relation to a prospectus offering for subscription debentures of a company incorporated outside Hong Kong.

(2)   In this section the expression "expert" includes engineer, valuer, accountant and any other person whose profession gives authority to a statement made by him, and for the purposes of this section a statement shall be deemed to be included in a prospectus if it is contained therein or in any report or memorandum appearing on the face thereof or by reference incorporated therein or issued therewith.

Registration of prospectus

342C.(1) No prospectus offering for subscription shares in or debentures of a company incorporated outside Hong Kong (whether the company has or has not established a place of business in Hong Kong) shall be issued, circulated or distributed in Hong Kong unless the prospectus complies with the requirements of this Ordinance and, on or before the date of its publication, circulation or distribution in Hong Kong, its registration has been authorized under this section and a copy thereof has been registered by the Registrar.

(2)   Every prospectus shall-

(a)   on the face of it, state that a copy has been registered as required by this section and, immediately after such statement, state that neither the Commission nor the Registrar takes any responsibility as to the contents of the prospectus;

(b)   on the face of it, specify or refer to statements included in the prospectus which specify, any documents required by this section to be endorsed on or attached to the copy so registered; and

(c)   conform with such requirements as are prescribed by the Governor in Council or specified by the Registrar under section 346 which are applicable to prospectuses to be registered under this Part.

(3)   An application for authorization for registration of a prospectus under this section shall be made in writing to the Commission and there shall be delivered to the Commission together with the application a copy of the prospectus proposed to be registered which has been certified by 2 members of the governing body of the company or by their agents authorized in writing as having been approved by resolution of the governing body and having endorsed thereon or attached thereto-

(a)   any consent to the issue of the prospectus required by section 342B from any person as an expert; and

(b) in the case of a prospectus issued generally, also-

(i) a copy of any contract required by paragraph 17 of the Third Schedule to be stated in the prospectus or, in the case of a contract not reduced into writing, a memorandum giving full particulars thereof or, if in the case of a prospectus exempted under section 342A from compliance with the requirements of section 342(1), a contract or a copy thereof or a memorandum of a contract is required by the Commission to be available for inspection in connection with the request made under section 342A(1), a copy or, as the case may be, a memorandum of that contract;

(ii) where the prospectus offers shares in the company for sale to the public, a list of the names, addresses and descriptions of the vendor or vendors of the shares; and

(iii) where the persons making any report required by Part II of the Third Schedule have made therein, or have, without giving the reasons, indicated therein, any such adjustments as are mentioned in paragraph 42 of that Schedule, a written statement signed by those persons setting out the adjustments and giving the reasons therefor.

(4) The references in subsection (3)(b)(i) to the copy of a contract required thereby to be endorsed on or attached to a copy of the prospectus shall, in the case of a contract wholly or partly in a language other than English, be taken as references to a copy of a translation of the contract in English or a copy embodying a translation in English of the parts not in English, as the case may be, being a translation certified in the prescribed manner to be a correct translation, and the reference to a copy of a contract required to be available for inspection shall include a reference to a copy of a translation thereof or a copy embodying a translation of the parts thereof.

(5) The Commission may-

(a) authorize the registration by the Registrar, of a prospectus to which this section applies and where the Commission so authorizes, the Commission shall issue a certificate-

(i) certifying that the Commission has done so; and

(ii) specifying the documents which are required to be endorsed on or attached to the copy of the prospectus to be registered; or

(b) refuse to authorize such registration.

(6) The Commission shall not authorize the registration of a prospectus which relates to an intended company.

(7) The Registrar-

    (a) shall not register a prospectus under this section unless-

        (i) it is dated and the copy thereof to be registered has been certified in the manner required by this section;

        (ii) it is accompanied by a certificate issued under subsection (5);

        (iii) it has endorsed thereon or attached thereto all the documents specified in the certificate granted under subsection (5); and

        (iv) it conforms with such requirements as are prescribed by the Governor in Council or specified by the Registrar under section 346 which are applicable to prospectuses to be registered under this Part; and

    (b) shall register a prospectus if subparagraphs (i), (ii), (iii) and (iv) of paragraph (a) are complied with in respect of that prospectus.

(8) Any person aggrieved by the refusal to authorize the registration of a prospectus under this section may appeal to the court and the court may either dismiss the appeal or order that the registration of the prospectus be authorized by the Commission under this section.

Penalty for contravention of sections 342 to 342C

342D. Any person who is knowingly responsible for the issue, circulation or distribution of a prospectus, or for the issue of a form of application for shares or debentures, in contravention of any of the provisions of sections 342 to 342C shall be liable to a fine.

Civil liability for misstatements in prospectus

342E. Section 40 shall extend to every prospectus offering for subscription shares in or debentures of a company incorporated outside Hong Kong, whether the company has or has not established a place of business in Hong Kong, with the substitution, for references to section 38C, of references to section 342B.

Criminal liability for misstatements in prospectus

342F.(1) Where a prospectus relating to shares in or debentures of a company incorporated outside Hong Kong (whether the company has or has not established a place of business in Hong Kong) which is issued, circulated or distributed in Hong Kong after the commencement of the Companies (Amendment) Ordinance 1992 (86 of 1992) includes any untrue statements, any person who authorized the issue, circulation or distribution of the prospectus in Hong Kong shall be liable to imprisonment and a fine, unless he proves either that the statement was immaterial or that he had reasonable grounds to believe and did up to the time of the issue, circulation or distribution of the prospectus in Hong Kong believe that the statement was true.

(2) A person shall not be deemed for the purposes of this section to have authorized the issue of a prospectus by reason only of his having given the consent required by section 342B to the inclusion therein of a statement purporting to be made by him as an expert.

(3) Subsection (1) shall not apply to the Commission or, where the prospectus is authorized by the Exchange Company pursuant to a transfer order made under section 47 of the Securities and Futures Commission Ordinance (Cap. 24), shall not apply to the Commission nor the Exchange Company.

Interpretation of provisions as to prospectuses

343.(1) Where any document by which any shares in or debentures of a company incorporated outside Hong Kong are offered for sale to the public would, if the company concerned had been a company within the meaning of this Ordinance, have been deemed by virtue of section 41 to be a prospectus issued by the company, that document shall be deemed to be, for the purposes of this Part of this Ordinance, a prospectus issued by the company.

(2) An offer of shares or debentures for subscription or sale to any person whose ordinary business it is to buy or sell shares or debentures, whether as principal or agent, shall not be deemed an offer to the public for the purposes of this Part of this Ordinance.

(3) In this Part the expressions "prospectus" "shares" and "debentures" have the same meanings as when used in relation to a company incorporated under this Ordinance.

344. *(Repealed)*

PART XIIA - Dormant Companies

Dormant companies

344A.(1) A company may pass a special resolution authorizing its directors-

    (a)   to make a statutory declaration that-

        (i)   the company will become dormant either as from the date of delivery of the statutory declaration to the Registrar or as from a later date as specified in the statutory declaration; an

        (ii)   prior to the company ceasing to be dormant, the directors of the company shall deliver to the Registrar a further statutory declaration that the company intends to enter into a relevant accounting transaction; and

    (b)   to deliver a copy of the statutory declaration to the Registrar.

(2) If the statutory declaration referred to in subsection (1) is made and delivered within 3 months from the date of the company's incorporation, the special resolution referred to in subsection (1) is not required before such declaration is made and delivered.

(3) Upon delivery of the statutory declaration made under sub-section (1), the company shall be deemed to be a dormant company for the purposes of this section as from the date of such delivery or, if the declaration specifies a later date for commencement of the company becoming dormant, as from that later date.

(4) A company which is deemed to be a dormant company under subsection (3) is exempt from complying with the requirements of sections 107 to 111, 122 to 134, 140A to 141 and 141B to 141D.

(5) A company shall cease to be deemed to be dormant under subsection (3) upon delivery to the Registrar of the further statutory declaration referred to in subsection (1)(a)(ii).

(6) If, during the period between the date on which a company is deemed under subsection (3) to have become a dormant company and the date on which the further statutory declaration referred to in subsection (1)(a)(ii) is delivered to the Registrar, a company enters into a relevant accounting transaction then-

> *(a)* the exemption conferred by subsection (4) shall cease as from the date of the relevant accounting transaction; and

> *(b)* any shareholder of the company who knew or ought to have known about the relevant accounting transaction and all directors of the company shall be personally liable for any debt or liability of the company arising out of the relevant accounting transaction.

(7) In subsection (6), "director", in relation to a company, includes any person in accordance with whose directions or instructions the directors of the company have been accustomed to act.

(8) This section shall not apply to-

> *(a)* a company which is not a private company;

> *(b)* an authorized institution as defined in the Banking Ordinance (Cap. 155);

> *(c)* a company of which an authorized institution as defined in the Banking Ordinance (Cap. 155) is a subsidiary;

> *(d)* an insurer as defined in the Insurance Companies Ordinance (Cap. 41);

> *(e)* a company of which an insurer as defined in the Insurance Companies Ordinance (Cap. 41) is a subsidiary;

(f)   a dealer registered under the Securities Ordinance (Cap. 333);

(g)   a company of which a dealer registered under the Securities Ordinance (Cap. 333) is a subsidiary;

(h)   an investment adviser registered under the Securities Ordinance (Cap. 333);

(i)   a company of which an investment adviser registered under the Securities Ordinance (Cap. 333) is a subsidiary;

(j)   a dealer registered under the Commodities Trading Ordinance (Cap. 250);

(k)   a company of which a dealer registered under the Commodities Trading Ordinance (Cap. 250) is a subsidiary;

(l)   a commodity trading adviser registered under the Commodities Trading Ordinance (Cap. 250);

(m)   a company of which a commodity trading adviser registered under the Commodities Trading Ordinance (Cap. 250) is a subsidiary; or

(n)   a company which at any time during the preceding 5 years has been a company which falls within any of the categories specified in paragraphs (a) to (m).

(9)   In this section-

(a)   a company is dormant during any period in which no transaction occurs which is, for the company, a relevant accounting transaction;

(b)   "relevant accounting transaction" means a transaction which is required by section 121 to be entered in the company's books of account (disregarding any transaction which arises from the payment of any fee which the company is required to pay by any Ordinance).

PART XIII - Miscellaneous

Prohibition of Partnerships with more than Twenty Members

Prohibition of partnerships with more than 20 members

345.(1) No company, association, or partnership consisting of more than 20 persons shall be formed for the purpose of carrying on any business that has for its object the acquisition of gain by the company, association or partnership, or by the individual members thereof, unless it is registered as a company under this Ordinance, or is formed in pursuance of some other Ordinance, Act of Parliament, or of letters patent.

(2)   This section shall not apply to a partnership formed-

> *(a)*   for the purpose of carrying on practice as solicitors and consisting of persons each of whom is a solicitor qualified to act as such under the Legal Practitioners Ordinance (Cap. 159);

> *(b)*   for the purpose of carrying on practice as accountants and consisting of persons each of whom is registered as a professional accountant and holds a practising certificate under the Professional Accountants Ordinance (Cap. 50);

> *(c)*   for the purpose of carrying on business as a member of the Unified Exchange and consisting of persons each of whom is a member of that exchange;

> *(d)*   for the purpose of carrying on a profession, vocation or business specified in regulations made by the Governor in Council and consisting of persons who satisfy any conditions imposed by those regulations.

(3)   For the purposes of this section, a body corporate shall be treated as a single person and any body unincorporate shall be treated as being the same number of persons as those who comprise it.

Provisions relating to Documents and Disposal thereof

Documents delivered to Registrar to conform to certain requirements

346.(1) Subject to this Ordinance, all documents delivered to the Registrar under this Ordinance shall, except for names in Chinese characters, be in the English language or accompanied by a translation certified in the specified manner to be a correct translation thereof but need not be printed, and for the purpose of securing that such documents are of standard size, durable and easily legible the Registrar may specify such requirements (whether as to size, weight, quality or colour of paper, size, type or colouring of lettering, or otherwise) as he may consider appropriate; and different requirements may be so specified for different documents or classes of documents.

(2)   If under any provision of this Ordinance there is delivered to the Registrar a document (whether being an original document or a copy) which in the opinion of the Registrar does not comply with such requirements specified by him under this section as are applicable to it, the

Registrar may serve on any person by whom under that provision the document was required to be delivered (or, if there are 2 or more such persons, may serve on any of them) a notice stating his opinion to that effect and indicating the requirements so specified with which in his opinion the document does not comply; and any such notice shall be served by registered post.

(3) Where the Registrar serves a notice under subsection (2) with respect to a document delivered under any such provision, then, for the purposes of any enactment which enables a penalty to be imposed in respect of any omission to deliver to the Registrar a document required to be delivered under that provision (and, in particular, for the purposes of any such enactment whereby such a penalty may be imposed by reference to each day during which the omission continues)-

> *(a)* any duty imposed by that provision to deliver such a document to the Registrar shall be treated as not having been discharged by the delivery of that document; but

> *(b)* no account shall be taken of any days falling within the period mentioned in subsection (4).

(4) The period referred to in subsection (3)(b) is the period beginning with the day on which the document was delivered to the Registrar as mentioned in subsection (2) and ending with the fourteenth day after the date of service of the notice under subsection (2) by virtue of which subsection (3) applies.

(5) In this section any reference to delivering a document shall be construed as including a reference to sending, forwarding, producing or (in the case of a notice) giving it.

(6) The Registrar may, by notice in the Gazette, specify requirements in relation to print size of prospectuses for the purpose of sections 38D(2)(c) and 342C(2)(c).

Power of Registrar to accept information on microfilm, etc.

347.(1) The Registrar may, if he thinks fit, accept under any provision of this Ordinance requiring a document to be delivered to him any material other than a document which contains the information in question and is of a kind approved by him.

(2) The delivery to the Registrar of material accepted by him as aforesaid shall be a sufficient compliance with the provision in question.

(3) Section 305 shall have effect as if any material so accepted were a document kept by the Registrar.

(4) In this section any reference to delivering a document shall be construed as including a reference to sending, forwarding, producing or (in the case of a notice) giving it.

Power of Registrar to refuse to register unlawful or ineffective documents

348. The Registrar may refuse to register or accept any document delivered to him for registration if it appears to him to be manifestly unlawful or ineffective; and any person aggrieved by the refusal of the Registrar to accept any document under this section may, within 42 days of the refusal, appeal to the court against the refusal and the court may make such order thereon as it may deem just, including an order as to costs:

Provided that where an order as to costs is made against the Registrar, such costs shall be payable out of the general revenue and the Registrar shall not be liable personally therefor.

Registrar not responsible for statements in documents

348A. The Registrar shall not be responsible for verifying the truth of any statement made in any document delivered to him for registration.

Disposal of documents

348B. The Registrar may, if in his opinion it is no longer necessary or desirable to maintain it, destroy or dispose of any document of a company which has been-

> *(a)* lodged, filed or registered for not less than 7 years; o

> *(b)* microfilmed.

Form of registers etc.

348C.(1) Any register, index, minute book or book of account required by this Ordinance to be kept by a company may be kept either by making entries in bound books or by recording the matters in question in any other manner.

(2) The power conferred on a company by subsection (1) includes power to keep the register or other record by recording the matters in question otherwise than in a legible form so long as the recording is capable of being reproduced in a legible form.

(3) If any register, index, minute book or book of account required by this Ordinance to be kept by a company is kept by the company by recording the matters in question otherwise than in a legible form, any duty imposed on the company by virtue of this Ordinance to allow inspection of, or to furnish a copy of, the register, index, minute book or book of account or any part of it shall be treated as a duty to allow inspection of, or to furnish, a reproduction of the recording or of the relevant part of it in a legible form.

(4) Where any such register, index, minute book or book of account is not kept by making entries in a bound book, but by some other means, adequate precautions shall be taken for guarding against falsification and facilitating its discovery, and where default is made in complying with this subsection, the company and every officer of the company who is in default shall be liable to a fine and, for continued default, to a daily default fine.

Power of Registrar to keep records in non-documentary form

348D. The records kept by the Registrar may be kept in a form other than documentary form.

Miscellaneous Offences

Penalty for false statements

349. If any person in any return, report, certificate, balance sheet or other document, required by or for the purposes of any of the provisions of this Ordinance, wilfully makes a statement false in any material particular, knowing it to be false, he shall be guilty of an offence and shall be liable on conviction to a fine and imprisonment:

Provided that nothing in this section shall affect the provisions of Part V (perjury) of the Crimes Ordinance (Cap. 200) or section 19, 20 or 21 of the Theft Ordinance (Cap. 210).

Penalty for dishonest destruction etc., of registers, books or documents

349A.(1) Any person who dishonestly, with a view to gain for himself or another, or with intent to cause loss to another, destroys, removes, alters, defaces or conceals any register, book or document belonging to, or filed or deposited in, the office of the Registrar shall be guilty of an offence and liable to imprisonment.

(2) Any person who wilfully or maliciously destroys, removes, alters, defaces or conceals any register, book or document belonging to, or filed or deposited in, the office of the Registrar shall be guilty of an offence and liable to imprisonment and a fine.

Penalty for improper use of "Limited", "Corporation" or "Incorporated"

350. If any person or persons use or trade or carry on business under any name or title of which "Limited" or "Corporation" or "Incorporated", or any contraction or imitation of any of those words or the Chinese version thereof, is the last word, or under any name or title of which the Chinese characters form part, that person or those persons shall, unless duly incorporated with limited liability, be liable to a fine and a daily fine for every day during which that name or title is used.

Obligation to give notice of paid-up capital

350A. If any company includes or permits to be included a statement of the authorized or issued capital of the company in any notice, circular, advertisement or other official publication of the company which is issued, circulated or distributed in Hong Kong, the company and an officer who is in default shall, unless a statement of the paid-up capital of the company is also stated not less prominently, be liable to a fine.

General Provisions as to Offences

Provision for punishment and offence

351.(1) The Twelfth Schedule has effect with respect to the way in which offences under this Ordinance are punishable on conviction.

(1A) As respects an offence under a provision of this Ordinance set out in column 1 of the Twelfth Schedule-

> *(a)* column 2 gives a description of the general nature of the offence only and shall not be used to interpret the provision;

> *(b)* column 3 shows whether the offence is punishable on conviction on indictment or on summary conviction;

> *(c)* column 4 shows, subject to paragraph (d), the maximum punishment by way of fine or imprisonment under this Ordinance which may be imposed on a person convicted of the offence;

> *(d)* column 5 shows in the case of an offence for which there is an entry in that column that a person convicted of the offence after continued default, refusal or contravention is liable to a default fine: that is to say, he is liable, in addition to the punishment that may be imposed under paragraph (c), to the fine set out in that column for each day on which the default, refusal or contravention is continued.

(1B) *(Repealed)*

(2) For the purpose of any provision in this Ordinance which provides that an officer of a company who is in default shall be liable to a fine or penalty, "officer who is in default" means any officer of the company, or any person in accordance with whose directions or instructions the directors of the company are accustomed to act, who knowingly and wilfully authorizes or permits the default, refusal or contravention mentioned in such provision.

Limitation on commencement of proceedings

351A.(1) Notwithstanding section 26 of the Magistrates Ordinance (Cap. 227), an information or complaint relating to an offence under this Ordinance may be tried if it is laid or made, as the case may be, at any time within 3 years after the commission of the offence and within 12 months after the date on which evidence sufficient in the opinion of the Attorney General to justify the proceedings comes to his knowledge.

(2) For the purposes of this section, a certificate of the Attorney General as to the date on which evidence sufficient to justify proceedings came to his knowledge shall be conclusive evidence.

(3) This section shall not apply in relation to an offence committed before the coming into operation of the Companies (Amendment) Ordinance 1972 (78 of 1972).

Production and inspection of books where offence suspected

351B.(1) If on the application of the Attorney General it is shown to the court that there is reasonable cause to believe that any person has, while an officer of the company, committed an offence in connexion with the management of the company's affairs and that evidence of the commission of the offence is to be found in any books or papers of or under the control of the company, the court may make an order-

> *(a)* authorizing any person named therein to inspect the said books or papers or any of them for the purpose of investigating and obtaining evidence of the offence; or

> *(b)* requiring the secretary of the company or such other officer thereof as may be named in the order to produce the said books or papers or any of them to a person named in the order at a place so named.

(2) Subsection (1) shall apply also in relation to any books or papers of a person carrying on the business of banking so far as they relate to the company's affairs, as it applies to any books or papers of or under the control of the company, except that no such order as is referred to in subsection (1)(b) shall be made by virtue of this subsection.

(3) The decision of the court on an application under this section shall be final.

Application of fines

352. The court or magistrate imposing any fine under this Ordinance may direct that the whole or any part thereof shall be applied in or towards payment of the costs of the proceedings, or in or towards rewarding the person on whose information or at whose suit the fine is recovered, and subject to any such direction all fines under this Ordinance shall, notwithstanding anything in any other Ordinance, be paid into the general revenue.

353. (*Repealed*)

Saving as to private prosecutors

354. Nothing in this Ordinance relating to the institution of criminal proceedings by the Attorney General shall be taken to preclude any person from instituting or carrying on any such proceedings.

Saving for privileged communications

355. Where proceedings are instituted under this Ordinance against any person by the Attorney General nothing in this Ordinance shall be taken to require any person who has acted as solicitor for the defendant to disclose any privileged communication made to him in that capacity.

Service of Documents and Legal Proceedings

Service of documents on company

356. A document may be served on a company by leaving it at or sending it by post to the registered office of the company.

Costs in actions by certain limited companies

357. Where a limited company is plaintiff in any action or other legal proceeding, any judge having jurisdiction in the matter may, if it appears by credible testimony that there is reason to believe that the company will be unable to pay the costs of the defendant if successful in his defence, require sufficient security to be given for those costs, and may stay all proceedings until the security is given.

Power of court to grant relief in certain cases

358.(1) If in any proceeding for negligence, default, breach of duty, or breach of trust against a person to whom this section applies it appears to the court hearing the case that that person is or may be liable in respect of the negligence, default, breach of duty or breach of trust, but that he has acted honestly and reasonably, and that, having regard to all the circumstances of the case, including those connected with his appointment, he ought fairly to be excused for the negligence, default, breach of duty or breach of trust, that court may relieve him, either wholly or partly, from his liability on such terms as the court may think fit.

(2) Where any person to whom this section applies has reason to apprehend that any claim will or might be made against him in respect of any negligence, default, breach of duty or breach of trust, he may apply to the court for relief, and the court on any such application shall have the same power to relieve him as under this section it would have had if it had been a court before which proceedings against that person for negligence, default, breach of duty or breach of trust had been brought.

(3) Where any case to which subsection (1) applies is being tried by a judge with a jury, the judge, after hearing the evidence, may, if he is satisfied that the defendant ought in pursuance of that subsection to be relieved either in whole or in part from the liability sought to be enforced against him, withdraw the case in whole or in part from the jury and forthwith direct judgment to be entered for the defendant on such terms as to costs or otherwise as the judge may think proper.

(4) The persons to whom this section applies are-

      (a)   officers of a company;

      (b)   persons employed by a company as auditors.

Power to enforce orders

359. Orders made by the court under this Ordinance may be enforced in the same manner as orders made in an action pending therein.

General provisions as to Governor in Council

Power to make regulations

359A. The Governor in Council may make regulations in respect of any matter required or permitted to be prescribed by the Governor in Council under this Ordinance.

Power to amend requirements as to accounts, Schedules, tables, forms and fees

360.(1) The Governor in Council may by order amend the requirements of this Ordinance as to the matters to be stated in a company's balance sheet, profit and loss account and group accounts, and in particular those of the Tenth and Eleventh Schedules; and any reference in this Ordinance to the Tenth or Eleventh Schedule shall be construed as a reference to that Schedule with any amendments made by an order for the time being in force under this subsection.

(2) The Governor in Council may by order amend Tables A, B, C, D and E in the First Schedule but no amendment made by the Governor in Council in Table A shall affect any company registered before the amendment comes into operation, or repeal as respects that company any portion of that Table.

(3) The Governor in Council may by order amend-

> *(a)* *(Repealed)*

> *(b)* *(Repealed)*

> *(c)* *(Repealed)*

(3A) The Financial Secretary may, by order published in the Gazette, amend the table of fees in the Eighth Schedule and the Fourteenth Schedule.

(4) The amount of any fee prescribed under this section shall not be limited by reference to the amount of administrative or other costs incurred or likely to be incurred in relation to providing the service to which such fee relates.

PART XIII A - Prevention Of Evasion Of The Societies Ordinance

Interpretation

360A. In this Part, unless the context otherwise requires -

"Official Receiver" means the Official Receiver appointed under the Bankruptcy Ordinance (Cap. 6).

Power of Governor in Council to order Registrar to refuse registration if satisfied that a company is being formed to evade the Societies Ordinance

360B. If the Registrar suspects that the memorandum and articles of association of a company delivered to him in accordance with section 15 relate to a company which is being formed with the object of circumventing the prohibition of the operation or continued operation of a society by the Secretary for Security under section 8 of the Societies Ordinance (Cap. 151) or for the purpose of otherwise evading or defeating the provisions of the Societies Ordinance (Cap. 151) or anything done thereunder, it shall be lawful for him to withhold registration of the same pending the receipt of the instructions of the Governor in Council with respect thereto. In the event of the Governor in Council being satisfied that the company is being formed with any such object or for any such purpose, he may order the Registrar to refuse registration of the memorandum and articles, and upon receipt of such order, the Registrar shall, notwithstanding the provisions of section 15, refuse registration of the memorandum and articles.

Power of Governor in Council to order company engaging in undesirable activities to be struck off

360C.(1) If the Governor in Council is satisfied that a company formed and registered under this Ordinance or any former Companies Ordinance would, if it were a society in respect of which the Societies Ordinance (Cap. 151) applied, be liable to have its operation or continued operation prohibited by the Secretary for Security under section 8 of that Ordinance, the Governor in Council may order the Registrar of Companies to strike such company off the register of companies.

(2) The Registrar shall thereupon strike the name of the company off the register, and shall publish notice thereof in the Gazette, and on such publication the company shall be dissolved:

Provided that the liability, if any, of every director, officer and member of the company shall continue and may be enforced as if the company had not been dissolved.

(3) A copy of such notice shall be sent to such company, and may either be sent by post or be delivered by hand addressed to the company at its registered office, or if no office has been registered, addressed to the care of some director or officer of the company, or if there is no director or officer of the company whose name and address are known to the Registrar, the notice may be sent or delivered to each of the persons who subscribed the memorandum of association, addressed to him at the address mentioned in that memorandum, but if none of such addresses is available or if for any other reason the Registrar considers it unlikely that any notice sent in pursuance of this subsection will come to the knowledge of the addressee, it shall be sufficient compliance with this subsection that notice in the Gazette shall have been published in accordance with subsection (2).

Certain sections not to apply

360D. Sections 290, 291(7) and 292 shall not apply in the case of a company struck off the register under section 360C.

Vesting and disposal of property of company struck off

360E.(1) Where a company is struck off the register and dissolved under section 360C, all property and rights whatsoever vested in or held on trust for the company immediately before its dissolution (including leasehold property but not including property held by the company on trust for any other person) shall vest in the Official Receiver.

(2)　　The Official Receiver shall with all due dispatch wind up the affairs of the company, and after realizing the said property and rights shall apply the sum so realized-

> **First**, in paying all fees, costs, charges and expenses properly incurred in preserving, realizing or getting in the said property and rights.

> **Next**, in paying all necessary fees, costs, charges and expenses incurred by the Official Receiver in and upon the winding up of the affairs of the company.

> **Next**, in paying to the Government a sum equal to the fees which the Official Receiver could lawfully have charged if he had acted as liquidator of the company in a winding up thereof by the court.

> **Next**, in paying the creditors of the company who shall have proved their debts within such time as shall have been limited by him not being less than 1 month from the date of publication of notice thereof in the Gazette and 2 or more local newspapers of which at least 1 shall be a Chinese newspaper, according to their respective rankings and priorities as if the company had been a company being wound up by the court by virtue of a winding up order dated the day of its dissolution under section 360C.

> **Next**, in paying or distributing the surplus to or among the persons entitled thereto under the company's memorandum and articles of association.

Provisions applicable to winding up of company struck off under section 360C

360F.　The provisions contained in sections 360G to 360M shall apply to the winding up by the Official Receiver of the affairs of a company struck off the register of companies under section 360C.

Certain sections to apply

360G.　Sections 170 to 175, 190, 211, 221, 263 to 277, 281 to 283 and 285 shall apply mutatis mutandis as if on the day of the dissolution of the company under section 360C an order had been made for the winding up of the company by the court and as if the Official Receiver were the liquidator thereof.

Calls on contributories

360H.　The Official Receiver shall have the same rights and powers to settle a list of the contributories of the company, to make and enforce calls on the contributories on the list so settled, and to compromise calls and liabilities to calls, as if the company were being wound up by the court and he were the liquidator thereof.

Continuation of pending legal proceedings

360I.　Where any legal proceeding instituted by or against a company is pending at the date of its dissolution, such proceeding may be continued by or against the Official Receiver as representing such company.

Obstruction of Official Receiver

360J. Every person who-

(a)   without lawful excuse refuses to hand over to the Official Receiver or any person authorized by him in that behalf any key, safe, document, account book, or other thing of any nature whatsoever belonging to the company of which he may have the custody or possession; or

(b)   without lawful excuse in any way obstructs the Official Receiver or any person authorized by him in that behalf in taking possession of any premises occupied by the company prior to its dissolution,

shall be guilty of an offence and shall be liable on conviction to a fine and imprisonment.

Control of Official Receiver

360K.(1) Subject to the provisions of this Part, the Official Receiver shall conform to any directions which may be given to him by the Governor for the purposes of this Part.

(2)   The Official Receiver shall with the permission of the Governor be entitled to apply by originating summons to the court for directions on any matter arising out of the winding up.

(3)   Any such application shall be heard and determined in such manner as the court may direct, and it shall be lawful for the court to hear such parties and persons as it may think fit.

(4)   Without prejudice to the generality of subsection (3) the court may if it sees fit direct that the proceedings or any part thereof be heard in camera.

(5)   If any person is aggrieved by any act or decision of the Official Receiver, that person may apply by originating summons to the court, and the court may confirm, reverse or modify the act or decision complained of, and make such order in the premises as it thinks just.

Audit of Official Receiver's accounts

360L.(1) The accounts of the Official Receiver with respect to the winding up shall be audited in such manner as the Governor may direct, and the cost of such audit shall be charged as an expense of the winding up.

(2)   In the event of the accounts being audited by a public servant there shall be paid to the Government in respect of such audit a sum equal to the fee which would have been chargeable on the audit of the Official Receiver's accounts if the winding up had been a winding up by the court.

Protection of Official Receiver

360M.(1) The Official Receiver shall not incur any personal liability in respect of the winding up of any company under this Part.

(2) No legal proceeding of any kind whatsoever, civil or criminal, shall without the permission of the Governor be brought against the Official Receiver in respect of any act or omission connected in any manner whatsoever with any winding up under this Part.

Companies to which Part XI applies

360N. If the Governor in Council is satisfied that a company to which Part XI applies would, if it were a society in respect of which the Societies Ordinance (Cap. 151) applied, be liable to have its operation or continued operation prohibited by the Secretary for Security under section 8 of that Ordinance, the Governor in Council may order the company to cease to carry on business within Hong Kong, and such company shall thereupon cease to carry on business within Hong Kong and shall be deemed to be an unlawful society within the meaning of and for the purposes of the Societies Ordinance (Cap. 151):

Provided that a person shall not be liable to prosecution for an offence against the Societies Ordinance (Cap. 151) by reason only that he is a member of a company which has been ordered to cease to carry on business under this section.

PART XIV - Savings

Saving

361.(1) Without prejudice to the provisions of section 23 of the Interpretation and General Clauses Ordinance (Cap. 1)-

(a) nothing in the repeal of the Companies Ordinance 1911 (58 of 1911), shall affect any order in council, order, rule, regulation, scale of fees, appointment, conveyance, mortgage, deed or agreement made, resolution passed, direction given, proceeding taken, instrument issued or thing done under any former enactment relating to companies, but any such order in council, order, rule, regulation, scale of fees, appointment, conveyance, mortgage, deed, agreement, resolution, direction, proceeding, instrument or thing shall, if in force at the commencement of this Ordinance, continue in force, and so far as it could have been made, passed, given, taken, issued or done under this Ordinance shall have effect as if made, passed, given, taken, issued or done under this Ordinance;

(b) any person appointed to any office under or by virtue of any former enactment relating to companies shall be deemed to have been appointed to that office under or by virtue of this Ordinance;

(c) any register kept under any former enactment relating to companies shall be deemed part of the register to be kept under the corresponding provisions of this Ordinance;

(d) all funds and accounts constituted under this Ordinance shall be deemed to be in continuation of the corresponding funds and accounts constituted under the former enactments relating to companies.

(2) In this section, "former enactment relating to companies" means the Companies Ordinance 1911 (58 of 1911), and any enactment repealed thereby.

Saving

362. Nothing in this Ordinance shall affect-

(a) the incorporation of any company registered under the Companies Ordinance 1911 (58 of 1911);

(b) Table A in the First Schedule annexed to the Companies Ordinance 1865 (1 of 1865), or any part thereof, either as originally contained in that schedule or as altered in pursuance of that Ordinance, so far as the same applies to any company existing at the commencement of this Ordinance;

    (c)   Table A in the First Schedule to the Companies Ordinance 1911 (58 of 1911), or any part thereof, either as originally contained in that schedule or as altered in pursuance of section 119 of that Ordinance, so far as the same applies to any company existing at the commencement of this Ordinance.

363.   *(Repealed)*

Saving

364.   Nothing in this Ordinance shall affect the provisions of the Insurance Companies Ordinance (Cap. 41).

Savings and transitional

365.(1) Any amendment made by the Companies (Amendment) Ordinance 1984 (6 of 1984) ("the amending Ordinance") to this Ordinance relating to the appointment of proxies, or to the rights of persons appointed as proxies, by members of a company shall not, as respects any company, apply in relation to any meeting of the company or any class of members of the company held within 3 months after the commencement of the amending Ordinance.

(2)   Any amendment made by the amending Ordinance to any provision of this Ordinance, except section 161B, relating to the form or contents of companies' accounts or annual returns or directors' reports shall not, as respects any company, affect any such accounts, returns or reports in respect of any period prior to the financial year of that company which begins next after the commencement of the amending Ordinance, and such provision shall continue to apply to such accounts, returns or reports in respect of any such period as if it had not been so amended.

(3)   *(Repealed)*

(4)   The repeal of sections 258 to 262 of this Ordinance and any amendment made by the amending Ordinance to any other provision of this Ordinance relating to winding up under the supervision of the court shall not affect any case in which an order was made under the said section 258 before the commencement of the amending Ordinance, and such sections and other provision shall continue to apply to such case as if they had not been so repealed or amended.

(5)   Section 253 and the First Schedule of the amending Ordinance shall not affect any company registered under this Ordinance before the commencement of the amending Ordinance.

(6)   Nothing in the amending Ordinance shall affect any proceedings commenced under the repealed Companies (Prevention of Evasion of the Societies Ordinance) Ordinance (Cap. 312, 1964 Ed.) which have not been finally disposed of before the commencement of the amending Ordinance, and any such proceedings may be continued and disposed of thereafter under this Ordinance.

Transitional

366.(1) Notwithstanding -

(a) the commencement of sections 58, 65 and 67 of the Companies (Amendment) Ordinance 1997 (3 of 1997) (referred to in this section and section 367 as "the Amending Ordinance");

(b) the repeal by the Amending Ordinance of any form in use immediately before the commencement of this section; or

(c) any provision in this Ordinance or the Amending Ordinance requiring, in relation to any purpose of this Ordinance, the use of a form specified by the Registrar under section 2A,

any form which was in force and which was required or permitted to be used for that purpose immediately before the commencement of this section, may be used for that purpose, until the Registrar determines that the specified form must be used for that purpose, until the Registrar determines that the specified form must be used.

(2) Notwithstanding any provision in this Ordinance or the Amending Ordinance requiring any person, in relation to a particular purpose of the Ordinance, to state or furnish any matter, particulars or information specified by the Registrar, any requirement in relation to that purpose -

(a) to state or furnish any matter or particulars prescribed by the Governor in Council; and

(b) in force immediately before the commencement of this section,

applies, until the Registrar determines that matters, particulars or information specified by him for that purpose must be stated or furnished.

Application of the Amending Ordinance

367.(1) For the avoidance of doubt it is declared that sections 5A and 5B apply in relation to a company notwithstanding that it was registered before the commencement of those sections.

(2) Subsection (1) shall not be construed as -

(a) limiting the application of any other provision in the Amending Ordinance; or

(b) validating any transaction, entered into before the commencement of sections 5A and 5B, which would have been void if not for the enactment of those sections.

Companies Ordinance

FIRST SCHEDULE

TABLE A

[ss. 11, 114A & 360]

PART I

Regulations For Management Of A Company Limited By Shares, Not Being A Private Company

Interpretation

1.   In these regulations-

"Ordinance" means the Companies Ordinance, Chapter 32;

"seal" means the common seal of the company;

"Secretary" means any person appointed to perform the duties of the secretary of the company.

Expressions referring to writing shall, unless the contrary intention appears, be construed as including references to printing, lithography, photography, and other modes of representing or reproducing words in a visible form.

Unless the context otherwise requires, words or expressions contained in these regulations shall bear the same meaning as in the Ordinance or any statutory modification thereof in force at the date at which these regulations become binding on the company.

Share Capital and Variation of Rights

2.   Without prejudice to any special rights previously conferred on the holders of any existing shares or class of shares, any share in the company may be issued with such preferred, deferred or other special rights or such restrictions, whether in regard to dividend, voting, return of capital or otherwise as the company may from time to time by ordinary resolution determine.

3.   Subject to the sections 49 to 49S of the Ordinance, the company may issue shares on the terms that they are, or at the option of the company or the holder of the shares are liable, to be redeemed on such terms and in such manner as may be provided by the company's articles of association.

4.   If at any time the share capital is divided into different classes of shares, the rights attached to any class may, whether or not the company is being wound up, be varied with the consent in writing of the holders of three-fourths in nominal value of the issued shares of that class, or with the sanction of a special resolution passed at a separate general meeting of the holders of the shares of the class.

5.   The rights conferred upon the holders of the shares of any class issued with preferred or other rights shall not, unless otherwise expressly provided by the terms of issue of the shares of that class, be deemed to be varied by the creation or issue of further shares ranking pari passu therewith.

6. The company may exercise the powers of paying commissions conferred by section 46 of the Ordinance, provided that the rate per cent or the amount of the commission paid or agreed to be paid shall be disclosed in the manner required by the said section and the rate of the commission shall not exceed the rate of 10 per cent of the price at which the shares in respect whereof the same is paid are issued or an amount equal to 10 per cent of such price (as the case may be). Such commission may be satisfied by the payment of cash or the allotment of fully or partly paid shares or partly in one way and partly in the other. The company may also on any issue of shares pay such brokerage as may be lawful.

7. Except as required by law, no person shall be recognized by the company as holding any share upon any trust, and the company shall not be bound by or be compelled in any way to recognize (even when having notice thereof) any equitable, contingent, future or partial interest in any share or any interest in any fractional part of a share or (except only as by these regulations or by law otherwise provided) any other rights in respect of any share except an absolute right to the entirety thereof in the registered holder.

8. Every person whose name is entered as a member in the register of members shall be entitled without payment to receive within 2 months after allotment or lodgment of transfer (or within such other period as the conditions of issue shall provide) one certificate for all his shares or several certificates each for 1 or more of his shares upon payment of $5 for every certificate after the first or such less sum as the directors shall from time to time determine. Every certificate shall be under the seal, or under the official seal kept by the company under section 73A of the Ordinance, and shall specify the shares to which it relates and the amount paid up thereon. Provided that in respect of a share or shares held jointly by several persons the company shall not be bound to issue more than 1 certificate, and delivery of a certificate for a share to 1 of several joint holders shall be sufficient delivery to all such holders.

9. If a share certificate be defaced, lost or destroyed, it may be renewed on payment of a fee of $5 or such less sum and on such terms (if any) as to evidence and indemnity and the payment of out-of-pocket expenses of the company of investigating evidence as the directors think fit.

10. (*Repealed*)

Lien

11. The company shall have a first and paramount lien on every share (not being a fully paid share) for all moneys (whether presently payable or not) called or payable at a fixed time in respect of that share, and the company shall also have a first and paramount lien on all shares (other than fully paid shares) standing registered in the name of a single person for all moneys presently payable by him or his estate to the company; but the directors may at any time declare any share to be wholly or in part exempt from the provisions of this regulation. The company's lien, if any, on a share shall extend to all dividends payable thereon.

12. The company may sell, in such manner as the directors think fit, any shares on which the company has a lien, but no sale shall be made unless a sum in respect of which the lien exists is presently payable, nor until the expiration of 14 days after a notice in writing, stating and demanding payment of such part of the amount in respect of which the lien exists as is presently payable, has been given to the registered holder for the time being of the share, or the person entitled thereto by reason of his death or bankruptcy.

13. To give effect to any such sale the directors may authorize some person to transfer the shares sold to the purchaser thereof. The purchaser shall be registered as the holder of the shares comprised in any such transfer, and he shall not be bound to see to the application of the purchase money, nor shall his title to the shares be affected by any irregularity or invalidity in the proceedings in reference to the sale.

14. The proceeds of the sale shall be received by the company and applied in payment of such part of the amount in respect of which the lien exists as is presently payable, and the residue, if any, shall (subject to a like lien for sums not presently payable as existed upon the shares before the sale) be paid to the person entitled to the shares at the date of the sale.

Calls on Shares

15. The directors may from time to time make calls upon the members in respect of any moneys unpaid on their shares (whether on account of the nominal value of the shares or by way of premium) and not by the conditions of allotment thereof made payable at fixed times, provided that no call shall exceed one-fourth of the nominal value of the share or be payable at less than 1 month from the date fixed for the payment of the last preceding call, and each member shall (subject to receiving at least 14 days' notice specifying the time or times and place of payment) pay to the company at the time or times and place so specified the amount called on his shares. A call may be revoked or postponed as the directors may determine.

16. A call shall be deemed to have been made at the time when the resolution of the directors authorizing the call was passed and may be required to be paid by instalments.

17. The joint holders of a share shall be jointly and severally liable to pay all calls in respect thereof.

18. If a sum called in respect of a share is not paid before or on the day appointed for payment thereof, the person from whom the sum is due shall pay interest on the sum from the day appointed for payment thereof to the time of actual payment at such rate not exceeding 10 per cent per annum as the directors may determine, but the directors shall be at liberty to waive payment of such interest wholly or in part.

19. Any sum which by the terms of issue of a share becomes payable on allotment or at any fixed date, whether on account of the nominal value of the share or by way of premium, shall for the purposes of these regulations be deemed to be a call duly made and payable on the date on which by the terms of issue the same becomes payable, and in case of non-payment all the relevant provisions of these regulations as to payment of interest and expenses, forfeiture or otherwise shall apply as if such sum had become payable by virtue of a call duly made and notified.

20. The directors may, on the issue of shares, differentiate between the holders as to the amount of calls to be paid and the times of payment.

21.   The directors may, if they think fit, receive from any member willing to advance the same, all or any part of the moneys uncalled and unpaid upon any shares held by him, and upon all or any of the moneys so advanced may (until the same would, but for such advance, become payable) pay interest at such rate not exceeding (unless the company in general meeting shall otherwise direct) 8 per cent per annum, as may be agreed upon between the directors and the member paying such sum in advance.

Transfer of Shares

22. The instrument of transfer of any share shall be executed by or on behalf of the transferor and transferee, and the transferor shall be deemed to remain a holder of the share until the name of the transferee is entered in the register of members in respect thereof.

23. Subject to such of the restrictions of these regulations as may be applicable, any member may transfer all or any of his shares by instrument in writing in any usual or common form or any other form which the directors may approve.

24. The directors may decline to register the transfer of a share (not being a fully paid share) to a person of whom they shall not approve, and they may also decline to register the transfer of a share on which the company has a lien.

25. The directors may also decline to recognize any instrument of transfer unless-

> *(a)*   a fee of $5 or such lesser sum as the directors may from time to time require is paid to the company in respect thereof;

> *(b)*   the instrument of transfer is accompanied by the certificate of the shares to which it relates, and such other evidence as the directors may reasonably require to show the right of the transferor to make the transfer; and

> *(c)*   the instrument of transfer is in respect of only one class of share.

26. If the directors refuse to register a transfer they shall within 2 months after the date on which the transfer was lodged with the company send to the transferor and transferee notice of the refusal.

27. The registration of transfers may be suspended at such times and for such periods as the directors may from time to time determine, provided always that such registration shall not be suspended in any year for more than 30 days or, where the period for closing the register of members is extended in respect of that year under section 99(2)(a) of the Ordinance, for more than that extended period.

28. The company shall be entitled to charge a fee not exceeding $5 on the registration of every probate, letters of administration, certificate of death or marriage, power of attorney, or other instrument.

Transmission of Shares

29. In case of the death of a member the survivor or survivors where the deceased was a joint holder, and the legal personal representatives of the deceased where he was a sole holder, shall be the only persons recognized by the company as having any title to his interest in the shares; but nothing herein contained shall release the estate of a deceased joint holder from any liability in respect of any share which had been jointly held by him with other persons.

30. Any person becoming entitled to a share in consequence of the death or bankruptcy of a member may, upon such evidence being produced as may from time to time properly be required by the directors and subject as hereinafter provided, elect either to be registered himself as holder of the share or to have some person nominated by him registered as the transferee thereof, but the directors shall, in either case, have the same right to decline or suspend registration as they would have had in the case of a transfer of the share by that member before his death or bankruptcy, as the case may be.

31. If the person so becoming entitled shall elect to be registered himself he shall deliver or send to the company a notice in writing signed by him stating that he so elects. If he shall elect to have another person registered he shall testify his election by executing to that person a transfer of the share. All the limitations, restrictions and provisions of these regulations relating to the right to transfer and the registration of transfers of shares shall be applicable to any such notice or transfer as aforesaid as if the death or bankruptcy of the member had not occurred and the notice or transfer were a transfer signed by that member.

32. A person becoming entitled to a share by reason of the death or bankruptcy of the holder shall be entitled to the same dividends and other advantages to which he would be entitled if he were the registered holder of the share, except that he shall not before being registered as a member in respect of the share, be entitled in respect of it to exercise any right conferred by membership in relation to meetings of the company:

Provided always that the directors may at any time give notice requiring any such person to elect either to be registered himself or to transfer the share, and if the notice is not complied with within 90 days the directors may thereafter withhold payment of all dividends, bonuses or other moneys payable in respect of the share until the requirements of the notice have been complied with.

33. Any person to whom the right to any shares in the company has been transmitted by operation of law shall, if the directors refuse to register the transfer, be entitled to call on the directors to furnish within 28 days a statement of the reasons for the refusal.

Forfeiture of Shares

34. If a member fails to pay any call or instalment of a call on the day appointed for payment thereof, the directors may, at any time thereafter during such time as any part of the call or instalment remains unpaid, serve a notice on him requiring payment of so much of the call or instalment as is unpaid, together with any interest which may have accrued.

35. The notice shall name a further day (not earlier than the expiration of 14 days from the date of service of the notice) on or before which the payment required by the notice is to be made, and shall state that in the event of non-payment at or before the time appointed the shares in respect of which the call was made will be liable to be forfeited.

36. If the requirements of any such notice as aforesaid are not complied with, any share in respect of which the notice has been given may at any time thereafter, before the payment required by the notice has been made, be forfeited by a resolution of the directors to that effect.

37. A forfeited share may be sold or otherwise disposed of on such terms and in such manner as the directors think fit, and at any time before a sale or disposition the forfeiture may be cancelled on such terms as the directors think fit.

38. A person whose shares have been forfeited shall cease to be a member in respect of the forfeited shares, but shall, notwithstanding, remain liable to pay to the company all moneys which, at the date of forfeiture, were payable by him to the company in respect of the shares, but his liability shall cease if and when the company shall have received payment in full of all such moneys in respect of the shares.

39. A statutory declaration in writing that the declarant is a director or the secretary of the company, and that a share in the company has been duly forfeited on a date stated in the declaration, shall be conclusive evidence of the facts therein stated as against all persons claiming to be entitled to the share. The company may receive the consideration, if any, given for the share on any sale or disposition thereof and may execute a transfer of the share in favour of the person to whom the share is sold or disposed of and he shall thereupon be registered as the holder of the share, and shall not be bound to see to the application of the purchase money, if any, nor shall his title to the share be affected by any irregularity or invalidity in the proceedings in reference to the forfeiture, sale or disposal of the share.

40. The provisions of these regulations as to forfeiture shall apply in the case of non-payment of any sum which, by the terms of issue of a share, becomes payable at a fixed time, whether on account of the nominal value of the share or by way of premium, as if the same had been payable by virtue of a call duly made and notified.

Conversion of Shares into Stock

41. The company may by ordinary resolution convert any paid-up shares into stock, and reconvert any stock into paid-up shares of any denomination.

42. The holders of stock may transfer the same, or any part thereof, in the same manner, and subject to the same regulations, as and subject to which the shares from which the stock arose might previously to conversion have been transferred, or as near thereto as circumstances admit; and the directors may from time to time fix the minimum amount of stock transferable but so that such minimum shall not exceed the nominal amount of the shares from which the stock arose.

43. The holders of stock shall, according to the amount of stock held by them, have the same rights, privileges and advantages as regards dividends, voting at meetings of the company and other matters as if they held the shares from which the stock arose, but no such privilege or advantage (except participation in the dividends and profits of the company and in the assets on winding up) shall be conferred by an amount of stock which would not, if existing in shares, have conferred that privilege or advantage.

44. Such of the regulations of the company as are applicable to paid-up shares shall apply to stock, and the words "share" and "shareholder" therein shall include "stock" and "stockholder".

Alteration of Capital

45. The company may from time to time by ordinary resolution increase the share capital by such sum, to be divided into shares of such amount, as the resolution shall prescribe.

46. The company may by ordinary resolution-

    (a)   consolidate and divide all or any of its share capital into shares of larger amount than its existing shares;

    (b)   sub-divide its existing shares, or any of them, into shares of smaller amount than is fixed by the memorandum of association subject, nevertheless, to the provisions of section 53(1)(d) of the Ordinance;

    (c)   cancel any shares which, at the date of the passing of the resolution, have not been taken or agreed to be taken by any person.

47. The company may by special resolution reduce its share capital, any capital redemption reserve fund or any share premium account in any manner and with, and subject to, any incident authorized, and consent required, by law.

Purchase of own Shares

47A. At any time while the company is a listed company within the meaning of the Ordinance, it may, subject to sections 49, 49A, 49B(6), 49BA, 49C, 49E, 49F, 49G, 49H, 49P, 49Q, 49R and 49S of the Ordinance, purchase its own shares (including any redeemable shares).

47B. At any time while the company is an unlisted company within the meaning of the Ordinance, it may, subject to sections 49 to 49S of the Ordinance, purchase its own shares (including any redeemable shares).

47C. Notwithstanding section 49B(I) and (2) but subject to sections 49, 49A, 49B(6), 49F, 49G, 49H, 491(4) and (5), 49P, 49Q, 49R and 49S of the Ordinance (except that such purchases may be made either out of or otherwise than out of the distributable profits of the company or the proceeds of a fresh issue of shares), the company may purchase its own shares (including any redeemable shares) in order to-

(a)   settle or compromise a debt or claim;

(b)   eliminate a fractional share or fractional entitlement or an odd lot of shares (as defined in section 49B(5) of the Ordinance);

(c)   fulfil an agreement in which the company has an option, or under which the company is obliged, to purchase shares under an employee share scheme which had previously been approved by the company in general meeting; or

(d)   comply with an order of the court under-

     (i)   section 8(4);

     (ii)   section 47G(5), where such order provides for the matters referred to in section 47G(6); or

     (iii)   section 168A(2),
                 of the Ordinance.

Allotment of Shares

48. The directors shall not exercise any power conferred on them to allot shares in the company without the prior approval of the company in general meeting where such approval is required by section 57B of the Ordinance.

General Meetings

49. The Company shall in each year hold a general meeting as its annual general meeting in addition to any other meetings in that year, and shall specify the meeting as such in the notices calling it; and not more than 15 months shall elapse between the date of one annual general meeting of the company and that of the next. Provided that so long as the company holds its first annual general meeting within 18 months of its incorporation, it need not hold it in the year of its incorporation or in the following year. The annual general meeting shall be held at such time and place as the directors shall appoint.

50. All general meetings other than annual general meetings shall be called extraordinary general meetings.

51. The directors may, whenever they think fit, convene an extraordinary general meeting, and extraordinary general meetings shall also be convened on such requisition, or in default, may be convened by such requisitionists, as provided by section 113 of the Ordinance. If at any time there are not within Hong Kong sufficient directors capable of acting to form a quorum, any director or any 2 members of the company may convene an extraordinary general meeting in the same manner as nearly as possible as that in which meetings may be convened by the directors.

Notice of General Meetings

52. An annual general meeting and a meeting called for the passing of a special resolution shall be called by 21 days' notice in writing at the least, and a meeting of the company other than an annual general meeting or a meeting for the passing of a special resolution shall be called by 14 days' notice in writing at the least. The notice shall be exclusive of the day on which it is served or deemed to be served and of the day for which it is given, and shall specify the place, the day and the hour of meeting and, in case of special business, the general nature of that business, and shall be given, in manner hereinafter mentioned or in such other manner, if any, as may be prescribed by the company in general meeting, to such persons as are, under the regulations of the company, entitled to receive such notices from the company:

Provided that a meeting of the company shall, notwithstanding that it is called by shorter notice than that specified in this regulation, be deemed to have been duly called if it is so agreed-

> *(a)* in the case of a meeting called as the annual general meeting, by all the members entitled to attend and vote thereat; and

> *(b)* in the case of any other meeting, by a majority in number of the members having a right to attend and vote at the meeting, being a majority together holding not less than 95 per cent in nominal value of the shares giving that right.

53. The accidental omission to give notice of a meeting to, or the non-receipt of notice of a meeting by, any person entitled to receive notice shall not invalidate the proceedings at that meeting.

Proceedings at General Meetings

54. All business shall be deemed special that is transacted at an extraordinary general meeting, and also all that is transacted at an annual general meeting, with the exception of declaring a dividend, the consideration of the accounts, balance sheets, and the reports of the directors and auditors, the election of directors in the place of those retiring and the appointment of, and the fixing of the remuneration of, the auditors.

55. No business shall be transacted at any general meeting unless a quorum of members is present at the time when the meeting proceeds to business and continues to be present until the conclusion of the meeting; save as herein otherwise provided, 2 members present in person or by proxy shall be a quorum.

56. If within half an hour from the time appointed for the meeting a quorum is not present, the meeting, if convened upon the requisition of members, shall be dissolved; in any other case it shall stand adjourned to the same day in the next week, at the same time and place or to such other day and at such other time and place as the directors may determine, and if at the adjourned meeting a quorum is not present within half an hour from the time appointed for the meeting, the members present shall be a quorum.

57. The chairman, if any, of the board of directors shall preside as chairman at every general meeting of the company, or if there is no such chairman, or if he shall not be present within 15 minutes after the time appointed for the holding of the meeting or is unwilling to act or is absent from Hong Kong or has given notice to the company of his intention not to attend the meeting, the directors present shall elect one of their number to be chairman of the meeting.

58. If at any meeting no director is willing to act as chairman or if no director is present within 15 minutes after the time appointed for holding the meeting, the members present shall choose one of their number to be chairman of the meeting.

59. The chairman may, with the consent of any meeting at which a quorum is present (and shall if so directed by the meeting), adjourn the meeting from time to time and from place to place, but no business shall be transacted at any adjourned meeting other than the business left unfinished at the meeting from which the adjournment took place. When a meeting is adjourned for 30 days or more, notice of the adjourned meeting shall be given as in the case of an original meeting. Save as aforesaid it shall not be necessary to give any notice of an adjournment or of the business to be transacted at an adjourned meeting.

60. At any general meeting a resolution put to the vote of the meeting shall be decided on a show of hands unless a poll is (before or on the declaration of the result of the show of hands) demanded-

        (a)   by the chairman; or

        (b)   by at least 2 members present in person or by proxy; or

        (c)   by any member or members present in person or by proxy and representing not less than one-tenth of the total voting rights of all the members having the right to vote at the meeting; or

        (d)   by a member or members holding shares in the company conferring a right to vote at the meeting being shares on which an aggregate sum has been paid up equal to not less than one-tenth of the total sum paid up on all the shares conferring that right.

Unless a poll be so demanded a declaration by the chairman that a resolution has on a show of hands been carried or carried unanimously, or by a particular majority, or lost and an entry to that effect in the book containing the minutes of the proceedings of the company shall be conclusive evidence of the fact without proof of the number or proportion of the votes recorded in favour of or against such resolution.

The demand for a poll may be withdrawn.

61. Except as provided in regulation 63, if a poll is duly demanded it shall be taken in such manner as the chairman directs, and the result of the poll shall be deemed to be the resolution of the meeting at which the poll was demanded.

62. In the case of an equality of votes, whether on a show of hands or on a poll, the chairman of the meeting at which the show of hands takes place or at which the poll is demanded, shall be entitled to a second or casting vote.

63. A poll demanded on the election of a chairman or on a question of adjournment shall be taken forthwith. A poll demanded on any other question shall be taken at such time as the chairman of the meeting directs, and any business other than that upon which a poll has been demanded may be proceeded with pending the taking of the poll.

Votes of Members

64. Subject to any rights or restrictions for the time being attached to any class or classes of shares, on a show of hands every member present in person shall have 1 vote, and on a poll every member shall have 1 vote for each share of which he is the holder.

65. In the case of joint holders the vote of the senior who tenders a vote, whether in person or by proxy, shall be accepted to the exclusion of the votes of the other joint holders; and for this purpose seniority shall be determined by the order in which the names stand in the register of members.

66. A member of unsound mind, or in respect of whom an order has been made by any court having jurisdiction in lunacy, may vote, whether on a show of hands or on a poll, by his committee, receiver, curator bonis, or other person in the nature of a committee, receiver or curator bonis appointed by that court, and any such committee, receiver, curator bonis or other person may, on a poll, vote by proxy.

67. No member shall be entitled to vote at any general meeting unless all calls or other sums presently payable by him in respect of shares in the company have been paid.

68. No objection shall be raised to the qualification of any voter except at the meeting or adjourned meeting at which the vote objected to is given or tendered, and every vote not disallowed at such meeting shall be valid for all purposes. Any such objection made in due time shall be referred to the chairman of the meeting, whose decision shall be final and conclusive.

69. On a poll votes may be given either personally or by proxy.

70. The instrument appointing a proxy shall be in writing under the hand of the appointer or of his attorney duly authorized in writing, or, if the appointer is a corporation, either under seal, or under the hand of an officer or attorney duly authorized. A proxy need not be a member of the company.

71. The instrument appointing a proxy and the power of attorney or other authority, if any, under which it is signed, or a notarially certified copy of that power or authority shall be deposited at the registered office of the company or at such other place within Hong Kong as is specified for that purpose in the notice convening the meeting, not less than 48 hours before the time for holding the meeting or adjourned meeting, at which the person named in the instrument proposes to vote, or, in the case of a poll, not less than 24 hours before the time appointed for the taking of the poll, and in default the instrument of proxy shall not be treated as valid.

72. An instrument appointing a proxy shall be in the following form or a form as near thereto as circumstances admit-

"   Limited

I/We   , of

, being a member/members of the above-named company, hereby appoint
of   , or failing him,
of   , as my/our proxy to vote for me/us on my/our behalf at the
[annual or extraordinary, as the case may be] general meeting of the company to be held on the
day of   19   , and at any adjournment thereof.

Signed this   day of   19   .".

73.   Where it is desired to afford members an opportunity of voting for or against a resolution
the instrument appointing a proxy shall be in the following form or a form as near thereto as
circumstances admit-

"   Limited

I/We,   , of   , being a member/members of the
above-named company, hereby appoint   of
, or failing him,   of   as my/our proxy to vote for me/us on my/our behalf
at the [annual or extraordinary, as the case may be] general meeting of the company, to be held on
the   day of   19   , and at any adjournment thereof.

Signed this   day of   19

This form is to be used *in favour of/against the resolution.

Unless otherwise instructed, the proxy will vote as he thinks fit.

*Strike out whichever is not desired.".

74. The instrument appointing a proxy shall be deemed to confer authority to demand or join in
demanding a poll.

75.   A vote given in accordance with the terms of an instrument of proxy shall be valid
notwithstanding the previous death or insanity of the principal or revocation of the proxy or of the
authority under which the proxy was executed, or the transfer of the share in respect of which the
proxy is given, provided that no intimation in writing of such death, insanity, revocation or transfer
as aforesaid shall have been received by the company at the office before the commencement of the
meeting or adjourned meeting at which the proxy is used.

Corporations acting by Representatives at Meetings

76.   Any corporation which is a member of the company may by resolution of its directors or
other governing body authorize such person as it thinks fit to act as its representative at any meeting
of the company or of any class of members of the company, and the person so authorized shall be

entitled to exercise the same powers on behalf of the corporation which he represents as that corporation could exercise if it were an individual member of the company.

Directors

77. The number of the directors and the names of the first directors shall be determined in writing by the subscribers of the memorandum of association or a majority of them.

78. The remuneration of the directors shall from time to time be determined by the company in general meeting. Such remuneration shall be deemed to accrue from day to day. The directors may also be paid all travelling, hotel and other expenses properly incurred by them in attending and returning from meetings of the directors or any committee of the directors or general meetings of the company or in connexion with the business of the company.

79. The shareholding qualification for directors may be fixed by the company in general meeting, and unless and until so fixed no qualification shall be required.

80. A director of the company may be or become a director or other officer of, or otherwise interested in, any company promoted by the company or in which the company may be interested as shareholder or otherwise, and, subject to the Ordinance, no such director shall be accountable to the company for any remuneration or other benefits received by him as a director or officer of, or from his interest in, such other company unless the company otherwise direct.

Borrowing Powers

81. The directors may exercise all the powers of the company to borrow money, and to mortgage or charge its undertaking, property and uncalled capital, or any part thereof, and to issue debentures, debenture stock, and, subject to section 57B of the Ordinance, convertible debentures and convertible debenture stock, and other securities whether outright or as security for any debt, liability or obligation of the company or of any third party:

Provided that the amount for the time being remaining undischarged of moneys borrowed or secured by the directors as aforesaid (apart from temporary loans obtained from the company's bankers in the ordinary course of business) shall not at any time, without the previous sanction of the company in general meeting, exceed the nominal amount of the share capital of the company for the time being issued, but nevertheless no lender or other person dealing with the company shall be concerned to see or inquire whether this limit is observed. No debt incurred or security given in excess of such limit shall be invalid or ineffectual except in the case of express notice to the lender or the recipient of the security at the time when the debt was incurred or security given that the limit hereby imposed had been or was thereby exceeded.

Powers and Duties of Directors

82. The business of the company shall be managed by the directors, who may pay all expenses incurred in promoting and registering the company, and may exercise all such powers of the company as are not, by the Ordinance or by these regulations, required to be exercised by the company in general meeting, subject, nevertheless, to any of these regulations, to the provisions of the Ordinance and to such regulations, being not inconsistent with the aforesaid regulations or provisions, as may be prescribed by the company in general meeting; but no regulation made by the company in general meeting shall invalidate any prior act of the directors which would have been valid if that regulation had not been made.

83. The directors may from time to time and at any time by power of attorney appoint any company, firm or person or body of persons, whether nominated directly or indirectly by the directors, to be the attorney or attorneys of the company for such purposes and with such powers, authorities and discretions (not exceeding those vested in or exercisable by the directors under these regulations) and for such period and subject to such conditions as they may think fit, and any such powers of attorney may contain such provisions for the protection and convenience of persons dealing with any such attorney as the directors may think fit and may also authorize any such attorney to delegate all or any of the powers, authorities and discretions vested in him.

84. The company may exercise the powers conferred by section 35 of the Ordinance with regard to having an official seal for use abroad, and such powers shall be vested in the directors.

85. The company may exercise the powers conferred upon the company by sections 103, 104 and 106 of the Ordinance with regard to the keeping of a branch register, and the directors may (subject to the provisions of those sections) make and vary such regulations as they may think fit respecting the keeping of any such register.

86.(1) A director who is in any way, whether directly or indirectly, interested in a contract or proposed contract (being a contract of significance in relation to the company's business) with the company shall, if his interest in the contract or proposed contract is material, declare the nature of his interest at a meeting of the directors in accordance with section 162 of the Ordinance.

(2) A director shall not vote in respect of any such contract or arrangement in which he is so interested, and if he shall do so his vote shall not be counted, nor shall he be counted in the quorum present at the meeting, but neither of these prohibitions shall apply to-

> *(a)* any arrangement for giving any director any security or indemnity in respect of money lent by him to or obligations undertaken by him for the benefit of the company; or
>
> *(b)* any arrangement for the giving by the company of any security to a third party in respect of a debt or obligation of the company for which the director himself has assumed responsibility in whole or in part under a guarantee or indemnity or by the deposit of a security; or
>
> *(c)* any contract by a director to subscribe for or underwrite shares or debentures of the company; or
>
> *(d)* any contract or arrangement with any other company in which he is interested only as an officer of the company or as holder of shares or other securities,

and these prohibitions may at any time be suspended or relaxed to any extent, and either generally or in respect of any particular contract, arrangement or transaction, by the company in general meeting.

(3) A director may hold any other office or place of profit under the company (other than the office of auditor) in conjunction with his office of director for such period and on such terms (as to remuneration and otherwise) as the directors may determine and no director or intending director shall be disqualified by his office from contracting with the company either with regard to his tenure of any such other office or place of profit or as vendor, purchaser or otherwise, nor shall any such contract, or any contract or arrangement entered into by or on behalf of the company in which any director is in any way interested, be liable to be avoided, nor shall any director so contracting or being so interested be liable to account to the company for any profit realized by any such contract or arrangement by reason of such director holding that office or of the fiduciary relation thereby established.

(4) A director, notwithstanding his interest, may be counted in the quorum present at any meeting whereas he or any other director is appointed to hold any such office or place of profit under the company or whereas the terms of any such appointment are arranged, and he may vote on any such appointment or arrangement other than his own appointment or the arrangement of the terms thereof.

(5) Any director may act by himself or his firm in a professional capacity for the company, and he or his firm shall be entitled to remuneration for professional services as if he were not a director; provided that nothing herein contained shall authorize a director or his firm to act as auditor to the company.

87. All cheques, promissory notes, drafts, bills of exchange and other negotiable instruments, and all receipts for moneys paid to the company, shall be signed, drawn, accepted, endorsed, or otherwise executed, as the case may be, in such manner as the directors shall from time to time by resolution determine.

88. The directors shall cause minutes to be made in books provided for the purpose-

> *(a)* of all appointments of officers made by the directors;
>
> *(b)* of the names of the directors present at each meeting of the directors and of any committee of the directors;
>
> *(c)* of all resolutions and proceedings at all meetings of the company, and of the directors, and of committees of directors,

and every director present at any meeting of directors or committee of directors shall sign his name in a book to be kept for that purpose.

89. The directors on behalf of the company may pay a gratuity or pension or allowance on retirement to any director who has held any other salaried office or place of profit with the company or to his widow or dependants and may make contributions to any fund and pay premiums for the purchase or provision of any such gratuity, pension or allowance.

Disqualification of Directors

90. The office of director shall be vacated if the director-

> *(a)* ceases to be a director by virtue of section 155 of the Ordinance; or

> *(b)* becomes bankrupt or makes any arrangement or composition with his creditors generally; or

> *(c)* becomes prohibited from being a director by reason of any disqualification order made under Part IVA of the Ordinance; or

> *(d)* becomes of unsound mind; or

> *(e)* resigns his office by notice in writing to the company given in accordance with section 157D(3)(a) of the Ordinance; or

> *(f)* shall for more than 6 months have been absent without permission of the directors from meetings of the directors held during that period.

Rotation of Directors

91. At the first annual general meeting of the company all the directors shall retire from office, and at the annual general meeting in every subsequent year one-third of the directors for the time being, or, if their number is not 3 or a multiple of 3, then the number nearest one-third, shall retire from office.

92. The directors to retire in every year shall be those who have been longest in office since their last election, but as between persons who became directors on the same day those to retire shall (unless they otherwise agree among themselves) be determined by lot.

93. A retiring director shall be eligible for re-election.

94. The company at the meeting at which a director retires in manner aforesaid may fill the vacated office by electing a person thereto, and in default the retiring director shall if offering himself for re-election be deemed to have been re-elected, unless at such meeting it is expressly resolved not to fill such vacated office or unless a resolution for the re-election of such director shall have been put to the meeting and lost.

95. No person other than a director retiring at the meeting shall unless recommended by the directors be eligible for election to the office of director at any general meeting unless not less than 3 nor more than 21 days before the date appointed for the meeting there shall have been left at the registered office of the company notice in writing, signed by a member duly qualified to attend and vote at the meeting for which such notice is given, of his intention to propose such person for election, and also notice in writing signed by that person of his willingness to be elected.

96. The company may from time to time by ordinary resolution increase or reduce the number of directors, and may also determine in what rotation the increased or reduced number is to go out of office.

97. The directors shall have power at any time, and from time to time, to appoint any person to be a director, either to fill a casual vacancy or as an addition to the existing directors, but so that the total number of directors shall not at any time exceed the number fixed in accordance with these regulations. Any director so appointed shall hold office only until the next following annual general meeting, and shall then be eligible for re-election but shall not be taken into account in determining the directors who are to retire by rotation at such meeting.

98. The company may by special resolution remove any director before the expiration of his period of office notwithstanding anything in these regulations or in any agreement between the company and such director. Such removal shall be without prejudice to any claim such director may have for damages for breach of any contract of service between him and the company.

99. The company may by ordinary resolution appoint another person in place of a director removed from office under the immediately preceding regulation, and without prejudice to the powers of the directors under regulation 97 the company in general meeting may appoint any person to be a director either to fill a casual vacancy or as an additional director. A person appointed in place of a director so removed or to fill such a vacancy shall be subject to retirement at the same time as if he had become a director on the day on which the director in whose place he is appointed was last elected a director.

Proceedings of Directors

100. The directors may meet together for the despatch of business, adjourn, and otherwise regulate their meetings, as they think fit. Questions arising at any meeting shall be decided by a majority of votes. In case of an equality of votes, the chairman shall have a second or casting vote. A director may, and the secretary on the requisition of a director shall, at any time summon a meeting of the directors. It shall not be necessary to give notice of a meeting of directors to any director for the time being absent from Hong Kong.

101. The quorum necessary for the transaction of the business of the directors may be fixed by the directors, and unless so fixed shall be 2.

102. The continuing directors may act notwithstanding any vacancy in their body, but, if and so long as their number is reduced below the number fixed by or pursuant to the regulations of the company as the necessary quorum of directors, the continuing directors or director may act for the purpose of increasing the number of directors to that number, or of summoning a general meeting of the company, but for no other purpose.

103. The directors may elect a chairman of their meetings and determine the period for which he is to hold office; but if no such chairman is elected, or if at any meeting the chairman is not present within 5 minutes after the time appointed for holding the same, the directors present may choose one of their number to be chairman of the meeting.

104.   The directors may delegate any of their powers to committees consisting of such member or members of their body as they think fit; any committee so formed shall in the exercise of the powers so delegated conform to any regulations that may be imposed on it by the directors.

105.   A committee may elect a chairman of its meetings; if no such chairman is elected, or if at any meeting the chairman is not present within 5 minutes after the time appointed for holding the same, the members present may choose one of their number to be chairman of the meeting.

106.   A committee may meet and adjourn as it thinks proper. Questions arising at any meeting shall be determined by a majority of votes of the members present, and in the case of an equality of votes the chairman shall have a second or casting vote.

107.   All acts done by any meeting of the directors or of a committee of directors or by any person acting as a director shall, notwithstanding that it be afterwards discovered that there was some defect in the appointment of any such director or person acting as aforesaid, or that they or any of them were disqualified, be as valid as if every such person had been duly appointed and was qualified to be a director.

108.   A resolution in writing, signed by all the directors for the time being entitled to receive notice of a meeting of the directors, shall be as valid and effectual as if it had been passed at a meeting of the directors duly convened and held:

Provided that this regulation shall not apply in relation to any contract or arrangement (not being one of the types specified in regulation 86(2)) in which a director or directors are interested, unless the number of directors signing the resolution who are not interested in the contract or arrangement would have constituted a quorum of directors if a meeting had been held for the purpose of considering the contract or arrangement.

Managing Director

109.   The directors may from time to time appoint one or more of their body to the office of managing director for such period and on such terms as they think fit, and, subject to the terms of any agreement entered into in any particular case, may revoke such appointment. A director so appointed shall not, whilst holding that office, be subject to retirement by rotation or be taken into account in determining the rotation of retirement of directors, but his appointment shall be automatically determined if he cease from any cause to be a director.

110.   A managing director shall receive such remuneration (whether by way of salary, commission or participation in profits, or partly in one way and partly in another) as the directors may determine.

111.   The directors may entrust to and confer upon a managing director any of the powers exercisable by them upon such terms and conditions and with such restrictions as they may think fit, and either collaterally with or to the exclusion of their own powers and may from time to time revoke, withdraw, alter or vary all or any of such powers.

Secretary

112. The secretary shall be appointed by the directors for such term, at such remuneration and upon such conditions as they may think fit; and any secretary so appointed may be removed by them.

113. A provision of the Ordinance or these regulations requiring or authorizing a thing to be done by or to a director and the secretary shall not be satisfied by its being done by or to the same person acting both as director and as, or in place of, the secretary.

The Seal

114. The directors shall provide for the safe custody of the seal, which shall only be used by the authority of the directors or of a committee of the directors authorized by the directors in that behalf, and every instrument to which the seal shall be affixed shall be signed by a director and shall be countersigned by the secretary or by a second director or by some other person appointed by the directors for the purpose.

Dividends and Reserve

115. The company in general meeting may declare dividends, but no dividend shall exceed the amount recommended by the directors.

116. The directors may from time to time pay to the members such interim dividends as appear to the directors to be justified by the profits of the company.

117. No dividend shall be paid otherwise than out of profits in accordance with the provisions of Part IIA of the Ordinance.

118. The directors may, before recommending any dividend, set aside out of the profits of the company such sums as they think proper as a reserve or reserves which shall, at the discretion of the directors, be applicable for any purpose to which the profits of the company may be properly applied, and pending such application may, at the like discretion, either be employed in the business of the company or be invested in such investments (other than shares of the company) as the directors may from time to time think fit. The directors may also without placing the same to reserve carry forward any profits which they may think prudent not to divide.

119. Subject to the rights of persons, if any, entitled to shares with special rights as to dividend, all dividends shall be declared and paid according to the amounts paid or credited as paid on the shares in respect whereof the dividend is paid, but no amount paid or credited as paid on a share in advance of calls shall be treated for the purposes of this regulation as paid on the share. All dividends shall be apportioned and paid proportionately to the amounts paid or credited as paid on the shares during any portion or portions of the period in respect of which the dividend is paid; but if any share is issued on terms providing that it shall rank for dividend as from a particular date such share shall rank for dividend accordingly.

120. The directors may deduct from any dividend payable to any member all sums of money (if any) presently payable by him to the company on account of calls or otherwise in relation to the shares of the company.

121. Any general meeting declaring a dividend or bonus may direct payment of such dividend or bonus wholly or partly by the distribution of specific assets and in particular of paid up shares, debentures or debenture stock of any other company or in any one or more of such ways, and the directors shall give effect to such resolution, and where any difficulty arises in regard to such distribution, the directors may settle the same as they think expedient, and in particular may issue fractional certificates and fix the value for distribution of such specific assets or any part thereof and may determine that cash payments shall be made to any members upon the footing of the value so fixed in order to adjust the rights of all parties, and may vest any such specific assets in trustees as may seem expedient to the directors.

122. Any dividend, bonus, interest or other moneys payable in cash in respect of shares may be paid by cheque or warrant sent through the post directed to the registered address of the holder or, in the case of joint holders, to the registered address of that one of the joint holders who is first named on the register of members or to such person and to such address as the holder or joint holders may in writing direct. Every such cheque or warrant shall be made payable to the order of the person to whom it is sent. Any one of 2 or more joint holders may give effectual receipts for any dividends, bonuses, interest or other moneys payable in respect of the shares held by them as joint holders.

123. No dividend shall bear interest against the company.

Accounts

124. The directors shall cause proper books of account to be kept with respect to-

> *(a)* all sums of money received and expended by the company and the matters in respect of which the receipt and expenditure takes place;

> *(b)* all sales and purchases of goods by the company; and

> *(c)* the assets and liabilities of the company.

Proper books shall not be deemed to be kept if there are not kept such books of account as are necessary to give a true and fair view of the state of the company's affairs and to explain its transactions.

125. The books of account shall be kept at the registered office of the company, or, subject to section 121(3) of the Ordinance, at such other place or places as the directors think fit, and shall always be open to the inspection of the directors.

126. The directors shall from time to time determine whether and to what extent and at what times and places and under what conditions or regulations the accounts and books of the company or any of them shall be open to the inspection of members not being directors, and no member (not being a director) shall have any right of inspecting any account or book or document of the company except as conferred by statue or authorized by the directors or by the company in general meeting.

127. The directors shall from time to time, in accordance with sections 122, 124 and 129D of the Ordinance, cause to be prepared and to be laid before the company in general meeting such profit and loss accounts, balance sheets, group accounts (if any) and reports as are referred to in those sections.

128. A copy of every balance sheet (including every document required by law to be annexed thereto) which is to be laid before the company in general meeting, together with a copy of the directors' report and a copy of the auditors' report, shall not less than 21 days before the date of the meeting be sent to every member of, and every holder of debentures of, the company and to all persons other than members or holders of debentures of the company, being persons entitled to receive notices of general meetings of the company:

Provided that this regulation shall not require a copy of those documents to be sent to any person of whose address the company is not aware or to more than one of the joint holders of any shares or debentures.

Capitalization of Profits

129. The company in general meeting may upon the recommendation of the directors resolve that it is desirable to capitalize any part of the amount for the time being standing to the credit of any of the company's reserve accounts or to the credit of the profit and loss account or otherwise available for distribution, and accordingly that such sum be set free for distribution amongst the members who would have been entitled thereto if distributed by way of dividend and in the same proportions on condition that the same be not paid in cash but be applied either in or towards paying up any amounts for the time being unpaid on any shares held by such members respectively or paying up in full unissued shares or debentures of the company to be allotted and distributed credited as fully paid up to and amongst such members in the proportion aforesaid, or partly in the one way and partly in the other, and the directors shall give effect to such resolution:

Provided that a share premium account and a capital redemption reserve fund may, for the purposes of this regulation, only be applied in the paying up of unissued shares to be allotted to members of the company as fully paid bonus shares.

130. Whenever such a resolution as aforesaid shall have been passed the directors shall make all appropriations and applications of the undivided profits resolved to be capitalized thereby, and all allotments and issues of fully-paid shares or debentures, if any, and generally shall do all acts and things required to give effect thereto, with full power to the directors to make such provision by the issue of fractional certificates or by payment in cash or otherwise as they think fit for the of shares or debentures becoming distributable in fractions, and also to authorize any person to enter on behalf of all the members entitled thereto into an agreement with the company providing for the allotment to them respectively, credited as fully paid up, of any further shares or debentures to which they may be entitled upon such capitalization, or (as the case may require) for the payment up by the company on their behalf, by the application thereto of their respective proportions of the profits resolved to be capitalized, of the amounts or any part of the amounts remaining unpaid on their existing shares, and any agreement made under such authority shall be effective and binding on all such members.

Audit

131. Auditors shall be appointed and their duties regulated in accordance with sections 131, 132, 133, 140, 140A, 140B and 141 of the Ordinance.

Notices

132. A notice may be given by the company to any member either personally or by sending it by post to him or to his registered address, or (if he has no registered address within Hong Kong) to the address, if any, within Hong Kong supplied by him to the company for the giving of notice to him. Where a notice is sent by post, service of the notice shall be deemed to be effected by properly addressing, prepaying, and posting a letter containing the notice, and to have been effected in the case of a notice of a meeting at the expiration of 48 hours after the letter containing the same is posted, and in any other case at the time at which the letter would be delivered in the ordinary course of post.

133. A notice may be given by the company to the joint holders of a share by giving the notice to the joint holder first named in the register of members in respect of the share.

134. A notice may be given by the company to the persons entitled to a share in consequence of the death or bankruptcy of a member by sending it through the post in a prepaid letter addressed to them by name, or by the title of representatives of the deceased, or trustee of the bankrupt, or by any like description, at the address, if any, within Hong Kong supplied for the purpose by the persons claiming to be so entitled, or (until such an address has been so supplied) by giving the notice in any manner in which the same might have been given if the death or bankruptcy had not occurred.

135. Notice of every general meeting shall be given in any manner herein before authorized to-

    (a)   every member except those members who (having no registered address within Hong Kong) have not supplied to the company an address within Hong Kong for the giving of notices to them;

    (b)   every person entitled to a share in consequence of the death or bankruptcy of a member who, but for his death or bankruptcy, would be entitled to receive notice of the meeting; and

    (c)   the auditor for the time being of the company.

No other person shall be entitled to receive notices of general meetings.

Winding up

136. If the company shall be wound up the liquidator may, with the sanction of a special resolution of the company and any other sanction required by the Ordinance, divide amongst the members in specie or kind the whole or any part of the assets of the company (whether they shall consist of property of the same kind or not) and may, for such purpose, set such value as he deems fair upon any property to be divided as aforesaid and may determine how such division shall be carried out as between the members or different classes of members. The liquidator may, with the like sanction, vest the whole or any part of such assets in trustees upon such trusts for the benefit of the contributories as the liquidator, with the like sanction, shall think fit, but so that no member shall be compelled to accept any shares or other securities whereon there is any liability.

Indemnity

137. Every director, managing director, agent, auditor, secretary and other officer for the time being of the company shall be indemnified out of the assets of the company against any liability incurred by him in relation to the company in defending any proceedings, whether civil or criminal, in which judgment is given in his favour or in which he is acquitted or in connexion with any application under section 358 of the Ordinance in which relief is granted to him by the court.

PART II

Regulations For The Management Of A Private Company Limited By Shares

1. The regulations contained in Part I of Table A (with the exception of regulations 24, 47A and 47B) shall apply.

2. The company is a private company and accordingly-

    (a) the right to transfer shares is restricted in manner hereinafter prescribed;

    (b) the number of members of the company (exclusive of persons who are in the employment of the company and of persons who having been formerly in the employment of the company were while in such employment and have continued after the determination of such employment to be members of the company) is limited to 50. Provided that where 2 or more persons hold one or more shares in the company jointly they shall for the purpose of this regulation be treated as a single member;

    (c) any invitation to the public to subscribe for any shares or debentures of the company is prohibited;

    (d) the company shall not have power to issue share warrants to bearer.

2A. Subject to sections 49 to 49S of the Ordinance, the company may purchase its own shares (including any redeemable shares).

2B. Subject to sections 49I to 49O of the Ordinance, the company may make a payment in respect of the redemption or purchase of its own shares otherwise than out of the distributable profits of the company or the proceeds of a fresh issue of shares.

3. The directors may, in their absolute discretion and without assigning any reason therefor, decline to register any transfer of any share, whether or not it is a fully paid share.

Note: Regulations 2A and 2B of this Part are alternative to regulations 47A and 47B of Part I, and regulation 3 of this Part is alternative to regulation 24 of Part I.

TABLE B

[ss. 14 & 360]

Form Of Memorandum Of Association Of A Company Limited By Shares

1st. The name of the company is "The Kwun Tong Electronics Manufacturing Company Limited".

2nd. The registered office of the company will be situated in Hong Kong.

3rd. The objects for which the company is established are [*If the objects are being stated, they should be set out here*].

Note: The 3rd paragraph applies only if the objects are being stated but that paragraph can be adapted or modified to contain any statement restricting or excluding objects.

4th. The liability of the members is limited.

5th. The share capital of the company is $15,000,000 divided into 150,000 shares of $100 each.

WE, the several persons whose names and addresses are subscribed, are desirous of being formed into a company, in pursuance of this memorandum of association, and we respectively agree to take the number of shares in the capital of the company set opposite our respective names.

Names, Addresses and Descriptions of Subscribers		Number of Shares taken by each Subscriber
1. Wong Tai-kwong of,	Electronics Engineer.	1
2. John Smith of,	Banker	1
		—

Total shares taken   2

Dated the   day of   19

Witness to the above signatures,

John Jones,

No. 13, Chater Road, Victoria, Hong Kong.

Solicitor.

TABLE C

[ss. 14 & 360]

Form Of Memorandum And Articles Of Association Of A Company Limited By Guarantee, And Not Having A Share Capital

Memorandum of Association

1st.   The name of the company is "The Yaumati District Elderly Residents Benevolent Association Limited

2nd.   The registered office of the company will be situated in Hong Kong.

3rd.   The objects for which the company is established are [*in the case of an association referred to in section 21(1) or a company referred to in section 21(2), the objects should be set out here; in any other case if the objects are being stated they should be set out here*]

4th.   The liability of the members is limited.

5th.   Every member of the company undertakes to contribute to the assets of the company in the event of its being wound up while he is a member, or within 1 year afterwards, for payment of the debts and liabilities of the company contracted before he ceases to be a member, and the costs, charges and expenses of winding up, and for the adjustment of the rights of the contributories among themselves, such amount as may be required not exceeding $100.

WE,   the several persons whose names and addresses are subscribed, are desirous of being formed into a company, in pursuance of this memorandum of association.

Names, Addresses and Descriptions of Subscribers

1.   Chan Kwok-wah of   , Headmaster.

2.   Lee Wing-tak of   , Stockbroker.

Dated the   day of   19

Witness to the above signatures,

John Jones,

No. 13, Chater Road, Victoria, Hong Kong.

Solicitor.

Articles Of Association To Accompany Preceding Memorandum Of Association

Interpretation

1.   In these articles-

"Ordinance" means the Companies Ordinance, Chapter 32.

"seal " means the common seal of the company.

"Secretary" means any person appointed to perform the duties of the secretary of the company.

Expressions referring to writing shall, unless the contrary intention appears, be construed as including references to printing, lithography, photography, and other modes of representing or reproducing words in a visible form.

Unless the context otherwise requires, words or expressions contained in these articles shall bear the same meaning as in the Ordinance or any statutory modification thereof in force at the date at which these articles become binding on the company.

Members

2.   The number of members with which the company proposes to be registered is 500, but the directors may from time to time register an increase of members.

3.   The subscribers to the memorandum of association and such other persons as the directors shall admit to membership shall be members of the company.

General Meetings

4.   The company shall in each year hold a general meeting as its annual general meeting in addition to any other meetings in that year, and shall specify the meeting as such in the notices calling it; and not more than 15 months shall elapse between the date of one annual general meeting of the company and that of the next. Provided that so long as the company holds its first annual general meeting within 18 months of its incorporation, it need not hold it in the year of its incorporation or in the following year. The annual general meeting shall be held at such time and place as the directors shall appoint.

5.   All general meetings other than annual general meetings shall be called extraordinary general meetings.

6.   The directors may, whenever they think fit, convene an extraordinary general meeting, and extraordinary general meetings shall also be convened on such requisition, or, in default, may be convened by such requisitionists, as provided by section 113 of the Ordinance. If at any time there are not within Hong Kong sufficient directors capable of acting to form a quorum, any director or any 2 members of the company may convene an extraordinary general meeting in the same manner as nearly as possible as that in which meetings may be convened by the directors.

Notice of General Meetings

7. An annual general meeting and a meeting called for the passing of a special resolution shall be called by 21 days' notice in writing at the least, and a meeting of the company other than an annual general meeting or a meeting for the passing of a special resolution shall be called by 14 days' notice in writing at the least. The notice shall be exclusive of the day on which it is served or deemed to be served and of the day for which it is given, and shall specify the place, the day and the hour of meeting and, in case of special business, the general nature of that business and shall be given, in manner hereinafter mentioned or in such other manner, if any, as may be prescribed by the company in general meeting, to such persons as are, under the articles of the company, entitled to receive such notices from the company:

Provided that a meeting of the company shall, notwithstanding that it is called by shorter notice than that specified in this article be deemed to have been duly called if it is so agreed-

> *(a)* in the case of a meeting called as the annual general meeting, by all the members entitled to attend and vote thereat; and

> *(b)* in the case of any other meeting, by a majority in number of the members having a right to attend and vote at the meeting, being a majority together representing not less than 95 per cent of the total voting rights of all the members entitled to attend and vote at that meeting.

8. The accidental omission to give notice of a meeting to, or the non-receipt of notice of a meeting by, any person entitled to receive notice shall not invalidate the proceedings at that meeting.

Proceedings at General Meetings

9. All business shall be deemed special that is transacted at an extraordinary general meeting, and also all that is transacted at an annual general meeting, with the exception of declaring a dividend, the consideration of the accounts, balance sheets, and the reports of the directors and auditors, the election of directors in the place of those retiring and the appointment of, and the fixing of the remuneration of, the auditors.

10. No business shall be transacted at any general meeting unless a quorum of members is present at the time when the meeting proceeds to business and continues to be present until the conclusion of the meeting; save as herein otherwise provided, 2 members present in person shall be a quorum.

11. If within half an hour from the time appointed for the meeting a quorum is not present, the meeting, if convened upon the requisition of members, shall be dissolved; in any other case it shall stand adjourned to the same day in the next week, at the same time and place, or to such other day and at such other time and place as the directors may determine, and if at the adjourned meeting a quorum is not present within half an hour from the time appointed for the meeting the members present shall be a quorum.

12. The chairman, if any, of the board of directors shall preside as chairman at every general meeting of the company, or if there is no such chairman, or if he shall not be present within 15 minutes after the time appointed for the holding of the meeting or is unwilling to act or is absent from Hong Kong or has given notice to the company of his intention not to attend the meeting, the directors present shall elect one of their number to be chairman of the meeting.

13. If at any meeting no director is willing to act as chairman or if no director is present within 15 minutes after the time appointed for holding the meeting, the members present shall choose one of their number to be chairman of the meeting.

14. The chairman may, with the consent of any meeting at which a quorum is present (and shall if so directed by the meeting), adjourn the meeting from time to time and from place to place, but no business shall be transacted at any adjourned meeting other than the business left unfinished at the meeting from which the adjournment took place. When a meeting is adjourned for 30 days or more, notice of the adjourned meeting shall be given as in the case of an original meeting. Save as aforesaid it shall not be necessary to give any notice of an adjournment or of the business to be transacted at an adjourned meeting.

15. At any general meeting a resolution put to the vote of the meeting shall be decided on a show of hands unless a poll is (before or on the declaration of the result of the show of hands) demanded-

> *(a)*   by the chairman; or
>
> *(b)*   by at least 2 members present in person or by proxy; or
>
> *(c)*   by any member or members present in person or by proxy and representing not less than one-tenth of the total voting rights of all the members having the right to vote at the meeting.

Unless a poll be so demanded a declaration by the chairman that a resolution has on a show of hands been carried or carried unanimously, or by a particular majority, or lost and an entry to that effect in the book containing the minutes of proceedings of the company shall be conclusive evidence of the fact without proof of the number or proportion of the votes recorded in favour of or against such resolution.

The demand for a poll may be withdrawn.

16. Except as provided in article 18, if a poll is duly demanded it shall be taken in such manner as the chairman directs, and the result of the poll shall be deemed to be the resolution of the meeting at which the poll was demanded.

17. In the case of an equality of votes, whether on a show of hands or on a poll, the chairman of the meeting at which the show of hands takes place or at which the poll is demanded, shall be entitled to a second or casting vote.

18. A poll demanded on the election of a chairman, or on a question of adjournment, shall be taken forthwith. A poll demanded on any other question shall be taken at such time as the chairman of the meeting directs, and any business other than that upon which a poll has been demanded may be proceeded with pending the taking of the poll.

Votes of Members

19. Every member shall have 1 vote.

20. A member of unsound mind, or in respect of whom an order has been made by any court having jurisdiction in lunacy, may vote, whether on a show of hands or on a poll, by his committee, receiver, curator bonis or other person in the nature of a committee, receiver or curator bonis appointed by that court, and any such committee, receiver, curator bonis or other person may, in a poll, vote by proxy.

21. No member shall be entitled to vote at any general meeting unless all moneys payable by him to the company in his capacity as member, and which have been outstanding for more than 1 month after they fell due for payment, have been paid.

22. On a poll votes may be given either personally or by proxy.

23. The instrument appointing a proxy shall be in writing under the hand of the appointer or of his attorney duly authorized in writing or, if the appointer is a corporation, either under seal or under the hand of an officer or attorney duly authorized. A proxy need not be a member of the company.

24. The instrument appointing a proxy and the power of attorney or other authority, if any, under which it is signed or a notarially certified copy of that power or authority shall be deposited at the registered office of the company or at such other place within Hong Kong as is specified for that purpose in the notice convening the meeting, not less than 48 hours before the time for holding the meeting or adjourned meeting at which the person named in the instrument proposes to vote, or, in the case of a poll, not less than 24 hours before the time appointed for the taking of the poll, and in default the instrument of proxy shall not be treated as valid.

25. An instrument appointing a proxy shall be in the following form or a form as near thereto as circumstances admit-

"   Limited. I/We
of   , being a member/members of the
above named company, hereby appoint   of

or failing him   of

as my/our proxy to vote for me/us on my/our behalf at the [annual or extraordinary, as the case may be] general meeting of the company to be held on the   day of   19
and at any adjournment thereof.

Signed this   day of   19

26.   Where it is desired to afford members an opportunity of voting for or against a resolution the instrument appointing a proxy shall be in the following form or a form as near thereto as circumstances admit-

"   Limited.

I/We   , of   , being a member/members of the above named company, hereby appoint

of   or failing him   of

as my/our proxy to vote for me/us on my/our behalf at the [annual or extraordinary, as the case may be] general meeting of the company to be held on the   day of   19   and at any adjournment thereof.

Signed this   day of   19

This form is to be used *in favour of/against the resolution. Unless otherwise instructed, the proxy will vote as he thinks fit.

*Strike out whichever is not desired.".

27.   The instrument appointing a proxy shall be deemed to confer authority to demand or join in demanding a poll.

28.   A vote given in accordance with the terms of an instrument of proxy shall be valid notwithstanding the previous death or insanity of the principal or revocation of the proxy or of the authority under which the proxy was executed, provided that no intimation in writing of such death, insanity or revocation as aforesaid shall have been received by the company at the office before the commencement of the meeting or adjourned meeting at which the proxy is used.

Corporations acting by Representatives at Meetings

29.   Any corporation which is a member of the company may by resolution of its directors or other governing body authorize such person as it thinks fit to act as its representative at any meeting of the company, and the person so authorized shall be entitled to exercise the same powers on behalf of the corporation which he represents as that corporation could exercise if it were an individual member of the company.

Directors

30.   The number of the directors and the names of the first directors shall be determined in writing by the subscribers of the memorandum of association or a majority of them.

31.   The remuneration of the directors shall from time to time be determined by the company in general meeting. Such remuneration shall be deemed to accrue from day to day. The directors shall also be paid all travelling, hotel and other expenses properly incurred by them in attending and returning from meetings of the directors or any committee of the directors or general meetings of the company or in connexion with the business of the company.

Borrowing Powers

32. The directors may exercise all the powers of the company to borrow money, and to mortgage or charge its undertaking and property, or any part thereof, and to issue debentures, debenture stock and other securities, whether outright or as security for any debt, liability or obligation of the company or of any third party.

Powers and Duties of Directors

33. The business of the company shall be managed by the directors, who may pay all expenses incurred in promoting and registering the company, and may exercise all such powers of the company as are not, by the Ordinance or by these articles, required to be exercised by the company in general meeting, subject nevertheless to the provisions of the Ordinance or these articles and to such regulations, being not inconsistent with the aforesaid provisions, as may be prescribed by the company in general meeting; but no regulation made by the company in general meeting shall invalidate any prior act of the directors which would have been valid if that regulation had not been made.

34. The directors may from time to time and at any time by power of attorney appoint any company, firm or person or body of persons, whether nominated directly or indirectly by the directors, to be the attorney or attorneys of the company for such purposes and with such powers, authorities and discretions (not exceeding those vested in or exercisable by the directors under these articles) and for such period and subject to such conditions as they may think fit, and any such powers of attorney may contain such provisions for the protection and convenience of persons dealing with any such attorney as the directors may think fit and may also authorize any such attorney to delegate all or any of the powers, authorities and discretions vested in him.

35. All cheques, promissory notes, drafts, bills of exchange and other negotiable instruments, and all receipts for moneys paid to the company, shall be signed, drawn, accepted, endorsed, or otherwise executed, as the case may be, in such manner as the directors shall from time to time by resolution determine.

36. The directors shall cause minutes to be made in books provided for the purpose-

  (a)   of all appointments of officers made by the directors;

  (b)   of the names of the directors present at each meeting of the directors and of any committee of the directors;

  (c)   of all resolutions and proceedings at all meetings of the company, and of the directors, and of committees of directors,

and every director present at any meeting of directors or committee of directors shall sign his name in a book to be kept for that purpose.

Disqualification of Directors

37.   The office of director shall be vacated if the director-

  (a)   without the consent of the company in general meeting holds any other office of profit under the company; or

  (b)   becomes bankrupt or makes any arrangement or composition with his creditors generally; or

  (c)   becomes prohibited from being a director by reason of any disqualification order made under Part IVA of the Ordinance; or

  (d)   becomes of unsound mind; or

  (e)   resigns his office by notice in writing to the company given in accordance with section 157D(3)(a) of the Ordinance; or

  (f)   shall for more than 6 months have been absent without permission of the directors from meetings of the directors held during that period; or

  (g)   is directly or indirectly interested in any contract (being a contract of significance in relation to the company's business) with the company and, if his interest in the contract is material, fails to declare the nature of his interest in manner required by section 162 of the Ordinance.

A director shall not vote in respect of any contract in which he is interested or any matter arising thereout, and if he does so vote his vote shall not be counted.

Rotation of Directors

38. At the first annual general meeting of the company all the directors shall retire from office, and at the annual general meeting in every subsequent year one-third of the directors for the time being, or, if their number is not 3 or a multiple of 3, then the number nearest one-third, shall retire from office.

39. The directors to retire in every year shall be those who have been longest in office since their last election, but as between persons who became directors on the same day those to retire shall (unless they otherwise agree among themselves) be determined by lot.

40. A retiring director shall be eligible for re-election.

41. The company at the meeting at which a director retires in manner aforesaid may fill the vacated office by electing a person thereto, and in default the retiring director shall, if offering himself for re-election, be deemed to have been re-elected, unless at such meeting it is expressly resolved not to fill such vacated office or unless a resolution for the re-election of such director shall have been put to the meeting and lost.

42. No person other than a director retiring at the meeting shall unless recommended by the directors be eligible for election to the office of director at any general meeting unless, not less than 3 nor more than 21 days before the date appointed for the meeting, there shall have been left at the registered office of the company notice in writing, signed by a member duly qualified to attend and vote at the meeting for which such notice is given, of his intention to propose such person for election, and also notice in writing signed by that person of his willingness to be elected.

43. The company may from time to time by ordinary resolution increase or reduce the number of directors, and may also determine in what rotation the increased or reduced number is to go out of office.

44. The directors shall have power at any time, and from time to time, to appoint any person to be a director, either to fill a casual vacancy or as an addition to the existing directors, but so that the total number of directors shall not at any time exceed the number fixed in accordance with these articles. Any director so appointed shall hold office only until the next following annual general meeting, and shall then be eligible for re-election, but shall not be taken into account in determining the directors who are to retire by rotation at such meeting.

45. The company may by special resolution remove any director before the expiration of his period of office notwithstanding anything in these articles or in any agreement between the company and such director. Such removal shall be without prejudice to any claim such director may have for damages for breach of any contract of service between him and the company.

46. The company may by ordinary resolution appoint another person in place of a director removed from office under the immediately preceding article. Without prejudice to the powers of the directors under article 44 the company in general meeting may appoint any person to be a director either to fill a casual vacancy or as an additional director. The person appointed to fill such a vacancy shall be subject to retirement at the same time as if he had become a director on the day on which the director in whose place he is appointed was last elected a director.

Proceedings of Directors

47. The directors may meet together for the despatch of business, adjourn, and otherwise regulate their meetings, as they think fit. Questions arising at any meeting shall be decided by a majority of votes. In the case of an equality of votes the chairman shall have a second or casting vote. A director may, and the secretary on the requisition of a director shall, at any time summon a meeting of the directors. It shall not be necessary to give notice of a meeting of directors to any director for the time being absent from Hong Kong.

48. The quorum necessary for the transaction of the business of the directors may be fixed by the directors, and unless so fixed shall be 2.

49. The continuing directors may act notwithstanding any vacancy in their body, but, if and so long as their number is reduced below the number fixed by or pursuant to the articles of the company as the necessary quorum of directors, the continuing directors or director may act for the purpose of increasing the number of directors to that number, or of summoning a general meeting of the company, but for no other purpose.

50. The directors may elect a chairman of their meetings and determine the period for which he is to hold office; but, if no such chairman is elected, or if at any meeting the chairman is not present within 5 minutes after the time appointed for holding the same, the directors present may choose one of their number to be chairman of the meeting.

51. The directors may delegate any of their powers to committees consisting of such member or members of their body as they think fit; any committee so formed shall in the exercise of the powers so delegated conform to any regulations that may be imposed on it by the directors.

52. A committee may elect a chairman of its meetings; if no such chairman is elected, or if at any meeting the chairman is not present within 5 minutes after the time appointed for holding the same, the members present may choose one of their number to be chairman of the meeting.

53. A committee may meet and adjourn as it thinks proper. Questions arising at any meeting shall be determined by a majority of votes of the members present, and in the case of an equality of votes the chairman shall have a second or casting vote.

54. All acts done by any meeting of the directors or of a committee of directors, or by any person acting as a director, shall notwithstanding that it be afterwards discovered that there was some defect in the appointment of any such director or person acting as aforesaid, or that they or any of them were disqualified, be as valid as if every such person had been duly appointed and was qualified to be a director.

55. A resolution in writing, signed by all the directors for the time being entitled to receive notice of a meeting of the directors, shall be as valid and effectual as if it had been passed at a meeting of the directors duly convened and held.

Secretary

56. The secretary shall be appointed by the directors for such term, at such remuneration and upon such conditions as they may think fit; and any secretary so appointed may be removed by them.

57. A provision of the Ordinance or these articles requiring or authorizing a thing to be done by or to a director and the secretary shall not be satisfied by its being done by or to the same person acting both as director and as, or in place of, the secretary.

The Seal

58. The directors shall provide for the safe custody of the seal, which shall only be used by the authority of the directors or of a committee of the directors authorized by the directors in that behalf, and every instrument to which the seal shall be affixed shall be signed by a director and shall be countersigned by the secretary or by a second director or by some other person appointed by the directors for the purpose.

Accounts

59. The directors shall cause proper books of account to be kept with respect to-

(a)   all sums of money received and expended by the company and the matters in respect of which the receipt and expenditure takes place;

(b)   all sales and purchases of goods by the company; and

(c)   the assets and liabilities of the company.

Proper books shall not be deemed to be kept if there are not kept such books of account as are necessary to give a true and fair view of the state of the company's affairs and to explain its transactions.

60. The books of account shall be kept at the registered office of the company, or, subject to section 121(3) of the Ordinance, at such other place or places as the directors think fit, and shall always be open to the inspection of the directors.

61. The directors shall from time to time determine whether and to what extent and at what times and places and under what conditions or regulations the accounts and books of the company or any of them shall be open to the inspection of members not being directors, and no member (not being a director) shall have any right of inspecting any account or book or document of the company except as conferred by statute or authorized by the directors or by the company in general meeting.

62. The directors shall from time to time in accordance with sections 122, 124 and 129D of the Ordinance, cause to be prepared and to be laid before the company in general meeting such profit and loss accounts, balance sheets, group accounts (if any) and reports as are referred to in those sections.

63. A copy of every balance sheet (including every document required by law to be annexed thereto) which is to be laid before the company in general meeting, together with a copy of the directors' report and a copy of the auditor's report, shall not less than 14 days before the date of the meeting be sent to every member of, and every holder of debentures of, the company:

Provided that this article shall not require a copy of those documents to be sent to any person of whose address the company is not aware or to more than one of the joint holders of any debentures.

Audit

64.   Auditors shall be appointed and their duties regulated in accordance with sections 131, 132, 133, 140, 140A, 140B and 141 of the Ordinance.

Notices

65.   A notice may be given by the company to any member either personally or by sending it by post to him or to his registered address, or (if he has no registered address within Hong Kong) to the

address, if any, within Hong Kong supplied by him to the company for the giving of notice to him. Where a notice is sent by post, service of the notice shall be deemed to be effected by properly addressing, prepaying and posting a letter containing the notice, and to have been effected in the case of a notice of a meeting at the expiration of 48 hours after the letter containing the same is posted, and in any other case at the time at which the letter would be delivered in the ordinary course of post.

66. Notice of every general meeting shall be given in any manner hereinbefore authorized to-

> *(a)* every member except those members who (having no registered address within Hong Kong) have not supplied to the company an address within Hong Kong for the giving of notices to them; and

> *(b)* the auditors for the time being of the company.

No other person shall be entitled to receive notices of general meetings.

67. Every director, managing director, agent, auditor, secretary and other officer for the time being of the company shall be indemnified out of the assets of the company against any liability incurred by him in relation to the company in defending any proceedings, whether civil or criminal, in which judgment is given in his favour or in which he is acquitted or in connexion with any application under section 358 of the Ordinance in which relief is granted to him by the court.

Names, Addresses and Descriptions of Subscribers
1. Chan Kwok-wah of , Headmaster.

2. Lee Wing-tak of , Stockbroker.
   Dated the   day of   19
Witness to the above signatures,
John Jones,
No. 13, Chater Road, Victoria, Hong Kong.
Solicitor.

Companies Ordinance

TABLE D

[ss. 14 & 360]

Memorandum And Articles Of Association Of A Company Limited By Guarantee And Having A Share Capital

Memorandum Of Association

1st. The name of the company is "The Yuen Long Motel Company Limited

2nd. The registered office of the company will be situated in Hong Kong.

3rd. The objects for which the company is established are [*If the objects are being stated, they should be set out here*].

Note: The 3rd paragraph applies only if the objects are being stated but that paragraph can be adapted or modified to contain any statement restricting or excluding objects.

4th. The liability of the members is limited.

5th. Every member of the company undertakes to contribute to the assets of the company in the event of its being wound up while he is a member, or within 1 year afterwards, for payment of the debts and liabilities of the company contracted before he ceases to be a member, and the costs, charges and expenses of winding up, and for the adjustment of the rights of the contributories among themselves, such amount as may be required not exceeding $500.

6th. The share capital of the company shall consist of $10,000,000 divided into 10,000 shares of $1,000 each.

WE, the several persons whose names and addresses are subscribed, are desirous of being formed into a company, in pursuance of this memorandum of association, and we respectively agree to take the number of shares in the capital of the company set opposite our respective names.

Names, Addresses and Descriptions of Subscribers	Number of shares taken by each Subscriber
1. Chow Tak-kwong of , Hotel Executive.	1
2. Hamish MacDonald of , Banker.	1
Total shares taken	2

Dated the   day of   19
Witness to the above signatures,
John Jones,
No. 13, Chater Road, Victoria, Hong Kong.
Solicitor.

Articles Of Association To Accompany Preceding Memorandum Of Association

1. The number of members with which the company proposes to be registered is 50, but the directors may from time to time register an increase of members.

2. The regulations of Table A, Part I, set out in the First Schedule to the Companies Ordinance, Chapter 32 (in these articles called "the Ordinance"), shall (with the exception of regulations 47A and 47B) be deemed to be incorporated with these articles and shall apply to the company.

3. Subject to sections 49 to 49S of the Ordinance, the company may purchase its own shares (including any redeemable shares).

4. Subject to sections 49I to 49O of the Ordinance, the company may make a payment in respect of the redemption or purchase of its own shares otherwise than out of the distributable profits of the company or the proceeds of a fresh issue of shares.

Note: Articles 3 and 4 of these articles are alternative to regulations 47A and 47B of Table A, Part I.

Names, Addresses and Descriptions of Subscribers

1. Chow Tak-kwong of   , Hotel Executive.

2. Hamish MacDonald of   , Banker
Dated the   day of   19
Witness to the above signatures,
John Jones,
No. 13, Chater Road, Victoria, Hong Kong.
Solicitor.

TABLE E

[ss. 14 & 360]

Memorandum And Articles Of Association Of An Unlimited Company Having A Share Capital

Memorandum of Association

1st. The name of the company is "Chan and Ma Consulting Civil Engineers Company

2nd. The registered office of the company will be situated in Hong Kong.

3rd. The objects for which the company is established are [*If the objects are being stated, they should be set out here*].

Note: The 3rd paragraph applies only if the objects are being stated but that paragraph can be adapted or modified to contain any statement restricting or excluding objects.

WE, the several persons whose names are subscribed, are desirous of being formed into a company, in pursuance of this memorandum of association, and we respectively agree to take the number of shares in the capital of the company set opposite our respective names.

Names, Addresses and Descriptions of Subscribers	Number of Shares taken by each Subscriber
1. Chan Tai-wai of , Consulting Civil Engineer	1
2. Ma Wai-tong .Consulting Civil Engineer	1
Total shares taken	2

Dated the   day of   19
Witness to the above signatures,
John Jones,
No. 13, Chater Road, Victoria, Hong Kong.
Solicitor.

Articles Of Association To Accompany The Preceding Memorandum Of Association

1.   The number of members with which the company proposes to be registered is 20, but the directors may from time to time register an increase of members.

2.   The share capital of the company is $ divided into shares of $ each.

3.   The company may by special resolution-

    (a)   increase the s are capital by such sum to be divided into shares of such amount as the resolution may prescribe;

    (b)   consolidate its shares into shares of a larger amount than its existing shares;

    (c)   sub-divide its shares into shares of a smaller amount than its existing shares;

    (d)   cancel any shares which at the date of the passing of the resolution have not been taken or agreed to be taken by any person;

(e)   reduce its share capital in any way.

4.   The regulations of Table A, Part I, set out in the First Schedule to the Companies Ordinance, Chapter 32 (other than regulations 41 to 48 inclusive) shall be deemed to be incorporated with these articles and shall apply to the company.

Names, Addresses and Descriptions of Subscribers

1.   Chan Tai-wai of   , Consulting Civil Engineer.

2.   Ma Wai-tong of   , Consulting Civil Engineer.

Dated the   day of   19

Witness to the above signatures,

John Jones,

No. 13, Chater Road, Victoria, Hong Kong.

Solicitor.

SECOND SCHEDULE

[s.30]

Form Of Statement In Lieu Of Prospectus To Be Delivered To Registrar By A Private Company On Becoming A Public Company And Reports To Be Set Out Therein

PART I

Form Of Statement And Particulars To Be Contained Therein

THE COMPANIES ORDINANCE

Statement in lieu of Prospectus delivered for registration by

[Insert the name of the company]

Pursuant to section 30 of the Companies Ordinance

Delivery for registration duly authorized by
(Insert the name of every director who has
authorized and signed this Statement).

The nominal share capital of the company........	$	
Divided into	Shares of $	each.
	Shares of $	each.
	Shares of $	each.
Amount (if any) of the above capital which	Shares of $	each.

consists of redeemable shares.
The earliest date on which the company has
power to redeem these shares.
Names, descriptions and addresses of directors
or proposed directors.

Amount of shares issued................................. Shares

Amount of commissions paid in connexion
therewith.
Amount of discount, if any, allowed on the
issue of any shares, or so much thereof as has
not been written off at the date of the statement.
Unless more than 1 year has elapsed since the
date on which the company began to carry on
business‑

     Amount of preliminary expenses.................... $
     By whom those expenses have been paid or

are payable.

Amount paid to any promoter..........................	Name of promoter
	Amount $
Consideration for the payment..........................	Consideration-
Any other benefit given to any promoter...........	Name of promoter-
	Name and value of benefit-
Consideration for giving of benefit..................	Consideration-

If the share capital of the company is divided into different classes of shares, the right of voting at meetings of the company conferred by, and the rights in respect of capital and dividends attached to, the several classes of shares respectively.

Number and amount of shares and debentures issues within the 2 years preceding the date of this statement as fully or partly paid up otherwise than for cash or agreed to be so issued at the date of this statement.	**1.** shares of $ fully paid.
	2. shares upon which $ per share credited as paid.
	3. debenture $
Consideration for the issue of those shares or debentures.	**4.** Consideration -
Number, description and amount of any shares or debentures which any person has or is entitled to be given an option to subscribe for, or to acquire from a person to whom they have been allotted or agreed to be allotted with a view to his offering them for sale.	**1.** share of $ and debentures of $
Period during which option is exercisable.	**2.** Until
Price to be paid for shares or debentures subscribed for or acquired under option.	**3.**
Consideration for option or right to option.	**4.** Consideration
Persons to whom option or right to option was given or, if given to existing shareholders or debenture holders as such, the relevant shares or debentures.	**5.** Names and addresses.

Names and addresses of vendors of property (1) purchased or acquired by the company within the 2 years preceding the date of this statement or (2) agreed or proposed to be purchased or acquired by the company, except where the contract for its purchase or acquisition was entered into in the ordinary course of business and there is no connexion between the contract and the company ceasing to be a private company or where the amount of the purchase money is not material.

Amount (in cash, shares or debentures) paid or payable to each separate vendor.

Amount paid or payable in cash, shares or debentures for any such property, specifying the amount paid or payable for goodwill.

Total purchase price
$
Cash.........................$
Shares.......................$
Debentures................$
  _____
Goodwill................$
  _____

Short particulars of any transaction relating to any such property which was completed within the 2 preceding years and in which any vendor to the company or any person who is, or was at the time thereof, a promoter, director or proposed director of the company had any interest direct or indirect.

Dates of, parties to, and general nature of every material contract (other than contracts entered into in the ordinary course of business or entered into more than 2 years before the delivery of this statement).

Time and place at which the contracts or copies thereof may be inspected or (1) in the case of a contract not reduced into writing, a memorandum giving full particulars thereof, and (2) in the case of a contract wholly or partly in a foreign language, a copy of a translation thereof in English or embodying a translation in English of the parts in a foreign language, as the case may be, being a translation certified in the prescribed manner to be a correct translation.

Names and addresses of the auditors of the company.

Full particulars of the nature and extent of the interest of every director in any property purchased or acquired by the company within the 2 years preceding the date of this statement or proposed to be purchased or acquired by the company, or where the interest of such a director consists in being a partner in a firm, the nature and extent of the interest of the firm, with a statement of all sums paid or agreed to be paid to him or to the firm in cash or shares, or otherwise, by any person either to induce him to become or to qualify him as, a director, or otherwise for services rendered or to be rendered to the company by him or by the firm.

Rates of the dividends (if any) paid by the company in respect of each class of shares in the company in each of the 5 financial years immediately preceding the date of this statement or since the incorporation of the company whichever period is the shorter.

Particulars of the cases in which no dividends have been paid in respect of any class of shares in any of these years.

(Signatures of the persons above-named as directors or proposed directors or of their agents authorized in writing.)

....

....

....

Date:

PART II - Reports To Be Set Out

1. If unissued shares or debentures of the company are to be applied in the purchase of a business, a report made by accountants (who shall be named in the statement) upon-

> *(a)* the profits or losses of the business in respect of each of the 5 financial years immediately preceding the delivery of the statement to the Registrar; and

> *(b)* the assets and liabilities of the business at the last date to which the accounts of the business were made up.

2.(1) If unissued shares or debentures of the company are to be applied directly or indirectly in any manner resulting in the acquisition of shares in a body corporate which by reason of the acquisition or anything to be done in consequence thereof or in connexion therewith will become a subsidiary of the company, a report made by accountants (who shall be named in the statement) with respect to the profits and losses and assets and liabilities of the other body corporate in accordance with sub-paragraph (2) or (3), as the case requires, indicating how the profits or losses of the other body corporate dealt with by the report would, in respect of the shares to be acquired, have concerned members of the company, and what allowance would have fallen to be made, in relation to assets and liabilities so dealt with, for holders of other shares, if the company had at all material times held the shares to be acquired.

(2) If the other body corporate has no subsidiaries, the report referred to in sub-paragraph (1) shall-

> *(a)* so far as regards profits and losses, deal with the profits or losses of the body corporate in respect of each of the 5 financial years immediately preceding the delivery of the statement to the Registrar; and

> *(b)* so far as regards assets and liabilities, deal with the assets and liabilities of the body corporate at the last date to which the accounts of the body corporate were made up.

(3) If the other body corporate has subsidiaries, the report referred to in sub-paragraph (1) shall-

> *(a)* so far as regards profits and losses, deal separately with the other body corporate's profits or losses as provided by sub-paragraph (2), and in addition deal either-

>> **(i)** as a whole with the combined profits or losses of its subsidiaries, so far as they concern members of the other body corporate; or

>> **(ii)** individually with the profits or losses of each subsidiary, so far as they concern members of the other body corporate;

> or, instead of dealing separately with the other body corporate's profits or

losses, deal as a whole with the profits or losses of the other body corporate and, so far as they concern members of the other body corporate, with the combined profits or losses of its subsidiaries; and

  (b) so far as regards assets and liabilities, deal separately with the other body corporate's assets and liabilities as provided by sub-paragraph (2) and, in addition, deal either-

    (i) as a whole with the combined assets and liabilities of its subsidiaries, with or without the other body corporate's assets and liabilities; or

    (ii) individually with the assets and liabilities of each subsidiary;

and shall indicate as respects the assets and liabilities of the subsidiaries the allowance to be made for persons other than members of the company.

PART III - Provisions Applying To Parts I And II Of This Schedule

3. In this Schedule the expression "vendor" includes a vendor as defined in Part III of the Third Schedule and the expression "financial year" has the meaning assigned to it in that Part of that Schedule.

4. If in the case of a business which has been carried on, or of a body corporate which has been carrying on business, for less than 5 years, the accounts of the business or body corporate have only been made up in respect of 4 years, 3 years, 2 years or 1 year, Part II of this Schedule shall have effect as if references to 4 years, 3 years, 2 years or 1 year, as the case may be, were substituted for references to 5 years.

5. Any report required by Part II of this Schedule shall either indicate by way of note any adjustment as respects the figures of any profits or losses or assets and liabilities dealt with by report which appear to the persons making the report necessary or shall make those adjustments and indicate that adjustments have been made.

6. Any report by accountants required by Part II shall be made by accountants authorized under this Ordinance for appointment as auditors of a company and shall not be made by any accountant who is an officer or servant, or a partner of or in the employment of an officer or servant, of the company, or of the company's subsidiary or holding company or of a subsidiary of the company's holding company; and for the purposes of this paragraph the expression "officer" shall include a proposed director but not an auditor.

7. For the purposes of Part I, the description of a person, that is to say, his profession, trade or other occupation shall be stated with particularity and precision; and the description "Company Director" shall be inadequate unless supplementary information is provided stating the nature of the relevant company's business.

8. For the purposes of Part I, "address" in the case of a natural person means the place of his usual residence.

THIRD SCHEDULE

[ss. 38 & 342]

Matters To Be Specified In Prospectus And Reports To Be Set Out Therein

PART I - Matters To Be Specified

1. The general nature of the business of the company, and if the company carries on 2 or more activities which are material having regard to profits or losses, assets employed or any other factor, information as to the relative importance of each such activity.

2. The authorized share capital and the description and nominal value of the shares into which it is divided, the amount of share capital issued or agreed to be issued, and the amount paid up on the shares which have been issued.

3. Sufficient particulars and information to enable a reasonable person to form as a result thereof a valid and justifiable opinion of the shares or debentures and the financial condition and profitability of the company at the time of the issue of the prospectus.

4. The number of founders or management or deferred shares, if any, and the nature and extent of the interest of the holders in the property and profits of the company.

5. The number of shares, if any, fixed by the articles as the qualification of a director, and any provision in the articles as to the remuneration of the directors.

6. The names, descriptions and addresses of the directors or proposed directors.

7. Where shares are offered to the public for subscription, particulars as to-

    (a)   the minimum amount which, in the opinion of the directors, must be raised by the issue of those shares in order to provide the sums, or if any part thereof is to be defrayed in any other manner, the balance of the sums, required to be provided in respect of each of the following matters-

        (i)   the purchase price of any property purchased or to be purchased which is to be defrayed in whole or in part out of the proceeds of the issue;

        (ii)   any preliminary expenses payable by the company, and any commission so payable to any person in consideration of his agreeing to subscribe for, or of his procuring or agreeing to procure subscriptions for, any shares in the company;

        (iii)   the repayment of any moneys borrowed by the company in respect of any of the foregoing matters;

        (iv)   working capital;

but, so long as the general purpose of the issue is clearly stated and the issue is fully underwritten, this sub-paragraph need not be complied with, and

(b)   the amounts to be provided in respect of the matters aforesaid otherwise than out of the proceeds of the issue and the sources out of which those amounts are to be provided.

8.   The date and time of the opening of the subscription lists.

9.   The amount payable on application and allotment on each share, and, in the case of a second or subsequent offer of shares, the amount offered for subscription on each previous allotment made within the 2 preceding years, the amount actually allotted, and the amount, if any, paid on the shares so allotted.

10.   The number, description and amount of any shares in or debentures of the company which any person has, or is entitled to be given, an option to subscribe for, together with the following particulars of the option, that is to say-

(a)   the period during which it is exercisable;

(b)   the price to be paid for shares or debentures subscribed for under it;

(c)   the consideration (if any) given or to be given for it or for the right to it;

(d)   the names and addresses of the persons to whom it or the right to it was given or, if given to existing shareholders or debenture holders as such, the relevant shares or debentures.

11.   The number and amount of shares and debentures which within the 2 preceding years have been issued, or agreed to be issued, as fully or partly paid up otherwise than in cash, and in the latter case the extant to which they are so paid up, and in either case the consideration for which those shares or debentures have been issued or are proposed or intended to be issued.

12.(1)   As respects any property to which this paragraph applies-

(a)   the names and addresses of the vendors;

(b)   the amount payable in cash, shares or debentures to the vendor and, where there is more than 1 separate vendor, or the company is a sub-purchaser, the amount so payable to each vendor;

(c)   short particulars of any transaction relating to the property completed within the 2 preceding years in which any vendor of the property to the company or any person who is, or was at the time of the transaction, a promoter or a director or proposed director of the company had any interest direct or indirect.

(2) The property to which this paragraph applies is property purchased or acquired by the company or proposed so to be purchased or acquired, which is to be paid for wholly or partly out of the proceeds of the issue offered for subscription by the prospectus or the purchase or acquisition of which has not been completed at the date of the issue of the prospectus, other than property-

> *(a)* the contract for the purchase or acquisition whereof was entered into in the ordinary course of the company's business, the contract not being made in contemplation of the issue nor the issue in consequence of the contract; or

> *(b)* as respects which the amount of the purchase money is not material.

13. The amount, if any, paid or payable as purchase money in cash, shares or debentures for any property to which paragraph 12 applies, specifying the amount, if any, payable for goodwill.

14. The amount, if any, paid within the 2 preceding years, or payable, as commission (but not including commission to sub-underwriters) for subscribing or agreeing to subscribe, or procuring or agreeing to procure subscriptions, for any shares in or debentures of the company, or the rate of any such commission.

15. The amount or estimated amount of preliminary expenses and the persons by whom any of those expenses have been paid or are payable, and the amount or estimated amount of the expenses of the issue and the persons by whom any of those expenses have been paid or are payable.

16. Any amount or benefit paid or given within the 2 preceding years or intended to be paid or given to any promoter, and the consideration for the payment or the giving of the benefit.

17. The dates of, parties to and general nature of every material contract, not being a contract entered into in the ordinary course of the business carried on or intended to be carried on by the company or a contract entered into more than 2 years before the date of issue of the prospectus; and a statement that a copy of every such material contract has been delivered to the Registrar for registration.

18. The names and addresses of the auditors, if any, of the company, and, if the prospectus invites the public to subscribe for debentures which are stated in the prospectus to be guaranteed, the names and addresses of the auditors, if any, of the guarantor corporation.

19. Full particulars of the nature and extent of the interest, if any, of every director in the promotion of, or in the property proposed to be acquired by, the company, or, where the interest of such a director consists in being a partner in a firm, the nature and extent of the interest of the firm, with a statement of all sums paid or agreed to be paid to him or to the firm in cash or shares or otherwise by any person either to induce him to become, or to qualify him as, a director, or otherwise for services rendered by him or by the firm in connexion with the promotion or formation of the company.

20. If the prospectus invites the public to subscribe for shares in the company and the share capital of the company is divided into different classes of shares, the right of voting at meetings of the company conferred by, and the rights in respect of capital and dividends attached to, the several classes of shares respectively.

21. In the case of a company which has been carrying on business, or of a business which has been carried on for less than 3 years, the length of time during which the business of the company or the business to be acquired, as the case may be, has been carried on.

22. The contents or a sufficient summary of the contents of the articles of the company with regard to any borrowing powers exercisable by the directors and the manner of variation of such powers.

23. Particulars of any bank overdrafts or other similar indebtedness of the company and its subsidiaries, if any, as at the latest practicable date or, if there are no bank overdrafts or other similar indebtedness, a statement to that effect.

24. Particulars of any hire purchase commitments, guarantees or other material contingent liabilities of the company and its subsidiaries, if any, or, if there are none such, a statement to that effect.

25. Particulars of the authorized debentures of the company and its subsidiaries, if any, the amount issued and outstanding or agreed to be issued, or if no debentures are outstanding a statement to that effect.

26. If the prospectus invites the public to subscribe for debentures of the company-

      (a)   the rights conferred upon the holders thereof, including rights in respect of interest and redemption, and particulars of the security, if any, therefor;

      (b)   the designation of such debentures which shall incorporate -

            (i)   in the case of debentures not secured by a charge on assets of the company -

                (A)   the word "unsecured" if the designation is in English;

                (B)   the expression in Chinese "...." if the designation is in Chinese; or

                (C)   both such word and expression respectively if the designation is both in English and Chinese; and

            (ii)   in the case of debentures secured to a substantial extent by a specific mortgage or charge -

                (A)   the word "mortgage" if the designation is in English;

>> *(B)*   the expression in Chinese "…" if the designation is in Chinese; or

>> *(C)*   both word and expression respectively if the designation is both in English and Chinese;

> *(c)*   particulars of any guarantee subsisting in respect of the debentures, including the name and address of the guarantor, and the designation or any description of the debentures shall only incorporate the word "guaranteed" or the expression in Chinese "…." if they are guaranteed to a substantial extent by a legally enforceable guarantee.

27.   A statement as to the gross trading income or sales turnover (as may be appropriate) of the company during the 3 preceding years including an explanation of the method used for the computation of such income or turnover, and a reasonable break-down between the more important trading activities; but a bank, discount house or other company whose business is in the opinion of the directors of a character that such a statement is either not practicable or not of value may instead include an explanation of the absence of such a statement.

28.   If the prospectus offers shares in the company for sale to the public-

> *(a)*   the names, addresses and descriptions of the vendor or vendors of the shares, or, if there are more than 10 vendors, the like particulars of the 10 principal vendors and a statement of the number of other vendors;

> *(b)*   particulars of any beneficial interest possessed by any director of the company in any shares so offered for sale.

29.   The name, date and country of incorporation, whether public or private (if applicable), the general nature of the business, the issued capital and the proportion thereof held or intended to be held, of every company the whole of the capital of which or a substantial proportion thereof is held or intended to be held, or whose profits or assets make or will make a material contribution to the figures in the auditors' report or to the next accounts of the company.

30.   A statement of the persons holding or beneficially interested in any substantial part of the share capital of the company and the amounts of the holdings in question.

PART II - Reports To Be Set Out

31.(1) A report by the auditors of the company and of any guarantor corporation referred to in the prospectus with respect to-

      (a)   profits and losses and assets and liabilities of the company and of any guarantor corporation referred to in the prospectus in accordance with sub-paragraph (2) or (3), as the case required; and

      (b)   the rates of the dividends, if any, paid by the company in respect of each class of shares in the company in respect of each of the 3 financial years immediately preceding the issue of the prospectus, giving particulars of each such class of shares on which such dividends have been paid and particulars of the cases in which no dividends have been paid in respect of any class of shares in respect of any of those years;

and, if no accounts have been made up in respect of any part of the period of 3 years ending on a date 3 months before the issue of the prospectus, containing a statement of that fact.

(2)   If the company or the guarantor corporations have no subsidiaries, the report shall-

      (a)   so far as regards profits and losses, deal with the profits or losses of the company and of the guarantor corporations referred to in the prospectus in respect of each of the 3 financial years immediately preceding the issue of the prospectus; and

      (b)   so far as regards assets and liabilities, deal with the assets and liabilities of the company and of the guarantor corporations referred to in the prospectus at the last date to which the accounts of the company and of the guarantor corporations were made up.

(3)   If the company or the guarantor corporations have subsidiaries, the report shall-

      (a)   so far as regards profits and losses, deal separately with the company's and the guarantor corporations' (other than subsidiaries) profits or losses as provided by sub-paragraph (2) and, in addition, deal either-

            (i)   as a whole with the combined profits or losses of their subsidiaries;

            (ii)   individually with the profits or losses of each subsidiary;

      or, instead of dealing separately with the company's profits or losses, deal as a whole with the profits or losses of the company and of the guarantor corporations and with the combined profits or losses of their subsidiaries; and

(b)   so far as regards assets and liabilities, deal separately with the company's and the guarantor corporations' (other than subsidiaries) assets and liabilities as provided by sub-paragraph (2) and, in addition, deal either-

    (i)   as a whole with the combined assets and liabilities of its or their subsidiaries, with or without the company's assets and liabilities; or

    (ii)   individually with the assets and liabilities of each subsidiary;

and shall indicate as respects the profits or losses and assets and liabilities of the subsidiaries the allowance to be made for persons other than members of the company.

32.   If the proceeds, or any part of the proceeds, of the issue of the shares or debentures are or is to be applied directly or indirectly in the purchase of any business, a report made by accountants (who shall be named in the prospectus) upon-

(a)   the profits or losses of the business in respect of each of the 3 financial years immediately preceding the issue of the prospectus; and

(b)   the assets and liabilities of the business at the last date to which the accounts of the business were made up.

33.(1) If-

(a)   the proceeds, or any part of the proceeds, of the issue of the shares or debentures are or is to be applied directly or indirectly in any manner resulting in the acquisition by the company of shares in any other body corporate; and

(b)   by reason of that acquisition or anything to be done in consequence thereof or in connexion therewith that body corporate will become a subsidiary of the company,

a report made by accountants (who shall be named in the prospectus) upon-

    (i)   the profits or losses of the other body corporate in respect of each of the 3 financial years immediately preceding the issue of the prospectus; and

    (ii)   the assets and liabilities of the other body corporate at the last date to which the accounts of the body corporate were made up.

(2)   The said report shall-

(a)   indicate how the profits or losses of the other body corporate dealt with by the report would, in respect of the shares to be acquired, have concerned members of the company and what allowance would have fallen to be made, in relation to assets and liabilities so dealt with, for holders of other shares, if the company had at all material times held the shares to be acquired; and

(b)   where the other body corporate has subsidiaries, deal with the profits or losses and the assets and liabilities of the body corporate and its subsidiaries in the manner provided by paragraph 31(3) in relation to the company and its subsidiaries.

34.(1) This paragraph shall apply in the case of every company whose accounts at the last date to which the accounts have been made up disclose that either a value exceeding 10 per cent of the value of the assets of the company or a value of not less than $3,000,000 is placed on the company's interests in land or buildings.

(2)   A valuation report with respect to all the company's interests in land or buildings which shall include the following particulars of each property-

(a)   the address;

(b)   a brief description;

(c)   the use at the date of the report;

(d)   the nature of the tenure;

(e)   a summary of the terms of any sub-leases or tenancies, including repair obligations, granted by the company;

(f)   the approximate age of buildings;

(g)   the present capital value;

(h)   the estimated current net rental, being the estimated average net annual income from the property accruing to the company over a long period of years (not being less than 3 years) before taking into account tax and any interest or mortgage expenses but after taking into account management and maintenance expenses.

(3)   A report for the purposes of sub-paragraph (2) shall state-

(a)   whether the valuation-

(i)   is the current value in the open market, stating whether-

(A)   on an investment basis, or

      (B)   on a development basis, or

      (C)   on a future capital realization basis;

    (ii)   is the current value as an asset of a going concern;

    (iii)   is the value after development has been completed; or

    (iv)   has any other basis (which should be stated);

  (b)   where the valuation is based on value after development has been completed-

    (i)   the date when the development is expected to be completed;

    (ii)   the estimated cost of carrying out the development or (where part of the development has already been carried out) the estimated cost of completing the development; and

    (iii)   the estimated value of the property in the open market in its present condition.

(4)   If the company has obtained more than one valuation report regarding any of the company's interests in land or buildings within 6 months before the issue of the prospectus then all other such reports shall be included.

PART III - Provisions Applying To Parts I And II Of Schedule

35.   Paragraphs 15 (so far as it relates to preliminary expenses) and 19 shall not apply in the case of a prospectus issued more than 2 years after the date at which the company began to carry on business.

36.   Every person shall, for the purposes of this Schedule, be deemed to be a vendor who has entered into any contract, absolute or conditional, for the sale or purchase, or for any option of purchase, of any property to be acquired by the company, in any case where-

  (a)   the purchase money is not fully paid at the date of the issue of the prospectus;

  (b)   the purchase money is to be paid or satisfied wholly or in part out of the proceeds of the issue offered for subscription by the prospectus;

  (c)   the contract depends for its validity or fulfilment on the result of that issue.

37.   Where any property to be acquired by the company is to be taken on lease, this Schedule shall have effect as if the expression "vendor" included the lessor, and the expression "purchase money" included the consideration for the lease, and the expression "sub-purchaser" included a sub-lessee.

38. References in paragraph 10 to subscribing for shares or debentures shall include acquiring them from a person to whom they have been allotted or agreed to be allotted with a view to his offering them for sale.

39. For the purposes of paragraph 12 where the vendors or any of them are a firm, the members of the firm shall not be treated as separate vendors.

40. If in the case of a company which has been carrying on business, or of a business which has been carried on for less than 3 years, the accounts of the company or business have only been made up in respect of 2 years or 1 year, Part II shall have effect as if references to 2 years or 1 year, as the case may be, were substituted for references to 3 years.

41. The expression "financial year" in Part II means the year in respect of which the accounts of the company or of the business, as the case may be, are made up, and where by reason of any alteration of the date on which the financial year of the company or business terminates the accounts of the company or business have been made up for a period greater or less than a year, that greater or less period shall for the purposes of that Part be deemed to be a financial year.

42. Any report required by Part II shall either indicate by way of note any adjustments as respects the figures of any profits or losses or assets and liabilities dealt with by the report which appear to the persons making the report necessary or shall make those adjustments and indicate that adjustments have been made.

43. Any report by accountants required by Part II shall be made by accountants qualified under the Professional Accountants Ordinance (Cap. 50) for appointment as auditors of a company and shall not be made by any accountant who is an officer or servant, or a partner of or in the employment of an officer or servant, of the company or of the company's subsidiary or holding company or of a subsidiary of the company's holding company; and for the purposes of this paragraph the expression "officer" shall include a proposed director but not an auditor.

44. For the purposes of paragraph 6, the description of a person, that is to say, his profession, trade or other occupation shall be stated with particularity and precision; and the description "Company Director" shall be inadequate unless supplementary information is provided stating the nature of the relevant company's business.

45. For the purposes of this Schedule, "address" in the case of a natural person means the place of his usual residence.

46. Any valuation report required by Part II

    (a)   shall not state or imply that any land or building has been professionally valued unless the valuation is made by a professionally qualified valuation surveyor who is subject to the discipline of a professional body;

    (b)   shall not be made by a person who is an officer or servant or proposed director

of the company or the company's subsidiary or holding company or of a subsidiary of the company's holding company; and

(c)   shall not be made by a company which-

    (i)   is the company's subsidiary or holding company or a subsidiary of the company's holding company; or

    (ii)   has either a paid up capital of less than $1,000,000 or the assets of which do not exceed liabilities by $1,000,000 or more as shown in the company's last balance sheet.

47.   For the purposes of Part II, "guarantor corporation" in relation to a company, means a corporation that has guaranteed or has agreed to guarantee the repayment of any money received or to be received by the company in response to an invitation to the public to subscribe for or purchase debentures of the company.

FOURTH SCHEDULE

[s. 43]

Form Of Statement In Lieu Of Prospectus To Be Delivered To Registrar By A Company Which Does Not Issue A Prospectus Or Which Does Not Go To Allotment On A Prospectus Issued, And Reports To Be Set Out Therein

PART I - Form Of Statement And Particulars To Be Contained Therein

THE COMPANY ORDINANCE

Statement in lieu of Prospectus delivered for registration by

[Insert the name of the company]

Pursuant to section 43 of the Companies Ordinance

Delivery for registration duly authorized by (Insert the name of every director who has authorized and signed this Statement).	
The nominal share capital of the company.	$
Divided into	Shares of $ each
	Shares of $ each
	Shares of $ each
Amount (if any) of above capital which consists of redeemable shares.	Shares of $ each
The earliest date on which the company has power to redeem these shares.	
Names, descriptions and addresses of directors or proposed directors.	
If the share capital of the company is divided into different classes of shares, the right of voting at meetings of the company conferred by, and the rights in respect of capital and dividends attached to, the several classes of shares respectively.	
Numbers and amount of shares and debentures agreed to be issued as fully or partly paid up	**1.** shares of $ fully paid.

otherwise than in cash.

The consideration for the intended issue of those shares and debentures.

Number, description and amount of any shares or debentures which any person has or is entitled to be given an option to subscribe for, or to acquire from a person to whom they have been allotted or agreed to be allotted with a view to his offering them for sale.

Period during which option is exercisable.

Price to be paid for shares or debentures subscribed for or acquired under option.

Consideration for option or right to option.

Persons to whom option or right to option was given or, if given to existing shareholders or debenture holders as such, the relevant shares or debentures.

Names and addresses of vendors of property purchased or acquired, or proposed to be purchased or acquired by the company except where the contract for its purchase or acquisition was entered into in the ordinary course of the business intended to be carried on by the company or the amount of the purchase money is not material.

Amount (in cash, shares or debentures) payable to each separate vendor.

Amount (if any) paid or payable (in cash or shares or debentures) for any such property, specifying amount (if any) paid or payable for goodwill.

Short particulars of any transaction relating to any such property which was completed within

2.   shares upon which $ per share credited as paid.

3. debentures $

4. Consideration

1.   shares of $ and debentures of $

2. Until

3.

4. Consideration

5. Names and addresses-

Total purchase price
$
Cash............ $
Shares..........$
Debentures $_____
Goodwill......$_____

the 2 preceding years and in which any vendor to the company or any person who is, or was at the time thereof, a promoter, director or proposed director of the company had any interest direct or indirect.

Amount (if any) paid or payable as commission for subscribing or agreeing to subscribe or procuring or agreeing to procure subscriptions for any shares or debentures in the company; or	Amount paid. Amount payable.
Rate of the commission....................................	Rate per cent.

The number of shares, if any, which persons have agreed for a commission to subscribe absolutely.

Estimated amount of preliminary expenses.	$

By whom those expenses have been paid or are payable.

Amount paid or intended to be paid to any promoter.	Name of promoter Amount $
Consideration for the payment..........................	Consideration-
Any other benefit given or intended to be given to any promoter.	Name of promoter- Nature and value of benefit-
Consideration for giving of benefit.	Consideration-

Dates of, parties to and general nature of every material contract (other than contracts entered into in the ordinary course of the business intended to be carried on by the company or entered into more than 2 years before the delivery of this statement).

Time and place at which the contracts or copies thereof may be inspected or (1) in the case of a contract not reduced into writing, a memorandum giving full particulars thereof, and (2) in the case of a contract wholly or partly in a foreign language, a copy of a translation thereof in English or embodying a translation in English of the parts in a foreign language, as the case may be, being a translation certified in the prescribed manner to be a correct translation.

Names and addresses of the auditors of the company (if any).

Full particulars of the nature and extent of the interest of every director in the promotion of or in the property proposed to be acquired by the company, or where the interest of such a director consists in being a partner in a firm, the nature and extent of the interest of the firm, with a statement of all sums paid or agreed to be paid to him or to the firm in cash or shares, or otherwise, by any person either to induce him to become, or to qualify him as, a director, or otherwise for services rendered by him or by the firm in connexion with the promotion or formation of the company.

_____

(Signatures of the persons above-named as directors or proposed directors, or of their agents authorized in writing.)

....

....

....

Date:

PART II - Reports To Be Set Out

1.　　　Where it is proposed to acquire a business, a report made by accountants (who shall be named in the statement) upon-

　　　　　　(a)　　　the profits or losses of the business in respect of each of the 5 financial years immediately preceding the delivery of the statement to the Registrar; and

　　　　　　(b)　　　the assets and liabilities of the business at the last date to which the accounts of the business were made up.

2.(1)　　　Where it is proposed to acquire shares in a body corporate which by reason of the acquisition or anything to be done in consequence thereof or in connexion therewith will become a subsidiary of the company, a report made by accountants (who shall be named in the statement) with respect to the profits and losses and assets and liabilities of the other body corporate in accordance with sub-paragraph (2) or (3), as the case requires, indicating how the profits or losses of the other body corporate dealt with by the report would, in respect of the shares to be acquired, have concerned members of the company, and what allowance would have fallen to be made, in relation to assets and liabilities so dealt with, for holders of other shares, if the company had at all material times held the shares to be acquired.

(2)　　　If the other body corporate has no subsidiaries, the report referred to in sub-paragraph (1) shall-

　　　　　　(a)　　　so far as regards profits and losses, deal with the profits or losses of the body corporate in respect of each of the 5 financial years immediately preceding the delivery of the statement to the Registrar; and

　　　　　　(b)　　　so far as regards assets and liabilities, deal with the assets and liabilities of the body corporate at the last date to which the accounts of the body corporate were made up.

(3)　　　If the other body corporate has subsidiaries, the report referred to in sub-paragraph (1) shall-

　　　　　　(a)　　　so far as regards profits and losses, deal separately with the other body corporate's profits or losses as provided by sub-paragraph (2), and in addition deal either-

　　　　　　　　　(i)　　　as a whole with the combined profits or losses of its subsidiaries, so far as they concern members of the other body corporate; or

　　　　　　　　　(ii)　　　individually with the profits or losses of each subsidiary, so far as they concern members of the other body corporate;

　　　　　　　　　or, instead of dealing separately with the other body corporate's profits or losses, deal as a whole with the profits or losses of the other body corporate and, so far as they concern members of the other body corporate, with the combined profits or losses of its subsidiaries; and

(b) so far as regards assets and liabilities, deal separately with the other body corporate's assets and liabilities as provided by the last foregoing sub-paragraph and, in addition, deal either-

(i) as a whole with the combined assets and liabilities of its subsidiaries, with or without the other body corporate's assets and liabilities; or

(ii) individually with the assets and liabilities of each subsidiary;

and shall indicate as respects the assets and liabilities of the subsidiaries the allowance to be made for persons other than members of the company.

PART III - Provisions Applying To Parts I And II Of This Schedule

3. In this Schedule the expression "vendor" includes a vendor as defined in Part III of the Third Schedule, and the expression "financial year" has the meaning assigned to it in that Part of that Schedule.

4. If in the case of a business which has been carried on, or of a body corporate which has been carrying on business, for less than 5 years, the accounts of the business or body corporate have only been made up in respect of 4 years, 3 years, 2 years or 1 year, Part II shall have effect as if references to 4 years, 3 years, 2 years or 1 year, as the case may be, were substituted for references to 5 years.

5. Any report required by Part II shall either indicate by way of note any adjustments as respects the figures of any profits or losses or assets and liabilities dealt with by the report which appear to the persons making the report necessary or shall make those adjustments and indicate that adjustments have been made.

6. Any report by accountants required by Part II shall be made by accountants authorized under this Ordinance for appointment as auditors of a company and shall not be made by any accountant who is an officer or servant, or a partner of or in the employment of an officer or servant, of the company or of the company's subsidiary or holding company or of a subsidiary of the company's holding company; and for the purposes of this paragraph the expression "officer" shall include a proposed director but not an auditor.

7. For the purposes of Part I, the description of a person, that is to say, his profession, trade or other occupation shall be stated with particularity and precision; and the description "Company Director" shall be inadequate unless supplementary information is provided stating the nature of the relevant company's business.

8. For the purposes of Part I, "address" in the case of a natural person means the place of his usual residence.

FIFTH SCHEDULE

Repealed

SIXTH SCHEDULE

*Repealed*SEVENTH SCHEDULE

[s. 5]

POWERS

1. To carry on any other business which may seem to the company capable of being conveniently carried on in connexion with its business or calculated directly or indirectly to enhance the value of or render profitable any of the company's property or rights.

2. To acquire and undertake the whole or any part of the business, property, and liabilities of any person or company carrying on any business which the company is authorized to carry on, or possessed of property suitable for the purposes of the company.

3. To apply for, purchase, or otherwise acquire any patents, patent rights, copyrights, trade marks, formulas, licences, concessions, and the like, conferring any exclusive or non-exclusive or limited right to use, or any secret or other information as to, any invention which may seem capable of being used for any of the purposes of the company, or the acquisition of which may seem calculated directly or indirectly to benefit the company; and to use, exercise, develop, or grant licences in respect of, or otherwise turn to account, the property, rights, or information so acquired.

4. To amalgamate or enter into partnership or into any arrangement for sharing of profits, union of interest, co-operation, joint adventure, reciprocal concession, or otherwise, with any person or company carrying on or engaged in or about to carry on or engage in any business or transaction which the company is authorized to carry on or engage in, or any business or transaction capable of being conducted so as directly or indirectly to benefit the company.

5. To take, or otherwise acquire, and hold, shares, debentures, or other securities of any other company.

6. To enter into any arrangements with any Government or authority, supreme, municipal, local, or otherwise, that may seem conducive to the company's objects, or any of them; and to obtain from any such Government or authority any rights, privileges, and concessions which the company may think it desirable to obtain; and to carry out, exercise, and comply with any such arrangements, rights, privileges, and concessions.

7. To establish and support or aid in the establishment and support of associations, institutions, funds, trusts, and conveniences calculated to benefit employees or directors or past employees or directors of the company or of its predecessors in business, or the dependants or connexions of any such persons; and to grant pensions and allowances; and to make payments towards insurance; and to subscribe or guarantee money for charitable or benevolent objects, or for any exhibition, or for any public, general, or useful object.

8. To promote any other company or companies for the purpose of acquiring or taking over all or any of the property, rights, and liabilities of the company, or for any other purpose which may seem directly or indirectly calculated to benefit the company.

9. To purchase, take on lease or in exchange, hire, and otherwise acquire any real and personal property and any rights or privileges which the company may think necessary or convenient for the purposes of its business, and in particular any land, buildings, easements, machinery, plant, and stock in trade.

10. To construct, improve, maintain, develop, work, manage, carry out, or control any buildings, works, factories, mills, roads, ways, tramways, railways, branches or sidings, bridges, reservoirs, watercourses, wharves, warehouses, electric works, shops, stores, and other works and conveniences which may seem calculated directly or indirectly to advance the company's interests; and to contribute to, subsidize, or otherwise assist or take part in the construction, improvement, maintenance, development, working, management, carrying out, or control thereof.

11. To invest and deal with the money of the company not immediately required in such manner as may from time to time be thought fit.

12. To lend and advance money or give credit to any person or company; to guarantee, and give guarantees or indemnities for the payment of money or the performance of contracts or obligations by any person or company; to secure or undertake in any way the repayment of moneys lent or advanced to or the liabilities incurred by any person or company; and otherwise to assist any person or company.

13. To borrow or raise or secure the payment of money in such manner as the company may think fit and to secure the same or the repayment or performance of any debt, liability, contract, guarantee or other engagement incurred or to be entered into by the company in any way and in particular by the issue of debentures perpetual or otherwise, charged upon all or any of the company's property (both present and future), including its uncalled capital; and to purchase, redeem, or pay off any such securities.

14. To remunerate any person or company for services rendered, or to be rendered, in placing or assisting to place or guaranteeing the placing of any of the shares in the company's capital or any debentures, or other securities of the company, or in or about the organization, formation, or promotion of the company or the conduct of its business.

15. To draw, make, accept, endorse, discount, execute, and issue-

> (a) promissory notes, bills of exchange, bills of lading, and other negotiable or transferable instruments;

> (b) prescribed instruments within the meaning of section 137B of the Banking Ordinance (Cap.155).

16. To sell or dispose of the undertaking of the company or any part thereof for such consideration as the company may think fit, and in particular for shares, debentures, or securities of any other company having objects altogether or in part similar to those of the company.

17. To adopt such means of making known and advertising the business and products of the company as may seem expedient.

18. To apply for, secure, acquire by grant, legislative enactment, assignment, transfer, purchase, or otherwise, and to exercise, carry out, and enjoy any charter, licence, power, authority, franchise, concession, right, or privilege, which any Government or authority or any corporation or other public body may be empowered to grant; and to pay for, aid in, and contribute towards carrying the same into effect; and to appropriate any of the company's shares, debentures, or other securities and assets to defray the necessary costs, charges, and expenses thereof.

19. To apply for, promote, and obtain any statute, order, regulation, or other authorization or enactment which may seem calculated directly or indirectly to benefit the company; and to oppose any bills, proceedings, or applications which may seem calculated directly or indirectly to prejudice the company's interests.

20. To procure the company to be registered or recognized in any country or place outside Hong Kong.

21. To sell, improve, manage, develop, exchange, lease, dispose of, turn to account, or otherwise deal with all or any part of the property and rights of the company.

22. To issue and allot fully or partly paid shares in the capital of the company in payment or part payment of any real or personal property purchased or otherwise acquired by the company or any services rendered to the company.

23. To distribute any of the property of the company among the members in kind or otherwise but so that no distribution amounting to a reduction of capital shall be made without the sanction required by law.

24. To take or hold mortgages, liens, and charges to secure payment of the purchase price, or any unpaid balance of the purchase price, of any part of the company's property of whatsoever kind sold by the company, or any money due to the company from purchasers and others.

25. To carry out all or any of the objects of the company and do all or any of the above things in any part of the world and either as principal, agent, contractor, or trustee, or otherwise, and by or through trustees or agents or otherwise, and either alone or in conjunction with others.

26. To do all such other things as are incidental or conducive to the attainment of the objects and the exercise of the powers of the company.

EIGHTH SCHEDULE

[ss. 304, 318 & 360]

Table Of Fees To Be Paid To The Registrar Of Companies

I - By A Company Having A Share Capital

(a)   for registration of company $1,450

And, in addition, for every 51,000 or part of $1,000 of the nominal share

capital .... $ 6 *(b)*

for registration of every increase in nominal share capital made after

the first registration of any company, for every $1,000 or part of $1,000

of such increase.. $ 6

Provided that where a company has paid an additional fee under paragraph

(c)(ii) in respect of shares allotted at a premium, no fee shall be payable

under this paragraph in respect of any increase in the nominal share capital

of that company where such increase is made for the purpose of capitalizing

the whole or any part of that premium and is applied to that purpose.

And, in addition, in the case of a company having on the 1 June 1955

a nominal share capital in excess of $3,000,000, on the first such increase

after the said date, for every $1,000 or part of $1,000 of such excess

nominal share capital as remains unissued immediately before such

increase.. $ 4

Provided that no additional fee shall be payable under this sub-paragraph by

a company which has paid the additional fee under paragraph (ba).

(ba)   in the case of a company having on the 1st day of June, 1955 a

nominal share capital in excess of $3,000,000, for every $1,000 or part

of $1,000 of such excess nominal share capital as remains unissued as at

the date of payment of this fee.. $ 4

The fee under this paragraph shall be paid on or before the 1st day of

January, 1977:

Provided that no fee shall be payable under this paragraph by a company

which has increased its nominal share capital and paid the additional

fee under paragraph(b).

(c)   for registration of a return of allotments .... $ 17

And, in addition-

(i)   in the case of a company having on 1 June 1955 a nominal share

capital in excess of $3,000,000, for every $1,000 or part of $1,000

of such excess nominal share capital allotted after the said date.......$ 4

Provided that no additional fee shall be payable under this sub-paragraph by a company which has paid the additional fee under paragraph (b) or (ba);

(ii) in the case of company which allots shares at a premium, whether for cash or otherwise, for every $1,000 or part of $1,000 of the aggregate amount or value of the premiums paid or payable on such shares .... $ 6

(ca) for registration of a prospectus under section 38D or 342C $1,000

(d) for registration of any existing company, except such companies as are by this Ordinance exempted from payment of fees in respect of registration under this Ordinance, the same fee as is charged for the registration of a new company.

(e) annual registration fee (to be paid on delivery of annual return under section 107)-
for a private company having a share capital-

(i) if delivered within 42 days after the anniversary of incorporation......$ 75

(ii) if delivered more than 42 days after but within 3 months after the anniversary of incorporation..$ 715

(iii) if delivered more than 3 months after but within 6 months after the anniversary of incorporation..$1,450

(iv) if delivered more than 6 months after the anniversary of incorporation..$2,200
for any other company-

(v) if delivered within 42 days after the annual general meeting.......... $ 75

(vi) if delivered more than 42 days after but within 3 months after the annual general meeting..$ 715

(vii) if delivered more than 3 months after but within 6 months after the annual general meeting..$1,450

(viii) if delivered more than 6 months after the annual general meeting $2,200

(f) for registering a notice of any change in particulars of directors pursuant to section 158 (4)... $ 17

II - By A Company Not Having A Shape Capital

For registration of a company whose number of members as stated in the articles does not exceed 25.. $ 145

For registration of a company whose number of members as stated in the articles exceeds 25, but does not exceed 100...................................... $ 285

For registration of a company whose number of members as stated in the articles exceeds 100 but is not stated to be unlimited, a fee of $285 with an additional $17 for every additional 50 members or less after the first 100

For registration of a company in which the number of members is stated in the articles to be unlimited... $ 860

For registration of any increase on the number of members made after the registration of the company in respect of every 50 members, or less than 50 members, of that increase... $ 17

Provided that no company shall be liable to pay on the whole a greater fee than $860 in respect of its number of members, taking into account the fee paid on the first registration of the company.

For registration of any existing company, except such companies as are by this Ordinance exempted from payment of fees in respect of registration under this Ordinance, the same fee as is charged for registering a new company.

Annual registration fee (to be paid on delivery of annual return under section 108)... $ 75

For registering a notice of any change in particulars of directors pursuant to section 158(4…………………………... $ 17

III - By A Company To Which Part XI Of This Ordinance Applies

(a)   For the issue of a certificate of registration under section 333(3)...................$ 715

(b)   For registering an annual return delivered to the Registrar under section 336(1)…………………………………………….......... $ 100

(c)   For registering any other document required to be delivered to the Registrar under Part XI of this Ordinance.. $ 17

IV - By A Company Requiring A Licence, Consent Or Approval Under This Ordinance

(a)   for a consent under section 20(2)...…… $ 715

(b)   for a licence under section 21...……. $1,450

(c)   *(Repealed)*

(d)   for a licence under section 93(2)..……. $ 285

V - Miscellaneous Fees

(a)-(b) *(Repealed)*

(c)   for inspecting-

   (i)   by virtue of section 305(1), a copy of all documents relating
           to one company kept by the Registrar and registered in respect of
           one calendar year, for each inspection ....$ 17

   (ii)   by virtue of section 305(1), where a copy is not available, the
           register or any file or any other document, kept by the Registrar,
           for each inspection .... $ 17

   (iii) the register of charges kept under section 83, for each
           inspection.................…………......................................…….. $ 17

(d)   for issuing under section 305(1)-

   (i)   a certificate of incorporation..…..................... $ 145

   (ii)   a copy or extract of any other document or part of any other document-

       (A)   by photostatic means, per sheet or page...............................$ 4

       (B)   where the copy or extract is made other than by
               photostatic means per folio of 100 words or part
               thereof...$ 4
           For each additional copy or extract after the first or top copy, per folio
           of 100 words or part thereof.. $ 4

(e)   for certifying a copy or extract of any document...…………….................... $ 110

(f)   for registering-

   (i)   under Part III of the Ordinance any charge required to be
           registered thereunder whether created by a company or existing on
           property acquired by a company ....…...$ 285

   (ii)   particulars of a series of debentures under Part III of the
           Ordinance ....…..$ 285

(iii)	the appointment of a receiver or manager, or a mortgagee's entering into possession, under section 87..	$ 33

(g) for endorsing the words "satisfaction entered" or the expression in Chinese "...." upon an instrument of charge under section 85 ………….…..................... $ 33

(h) for furnishing a copy of a memorandum of satisfaction under section 85...…... $ 33

(i) for the completion of or giving effect to any dealing, transaction or matter relating to a defunct company, by any act done or caused to be done by the Registrar under section 291B ....…….............. $1,650

(j) for an authorization under section 111(1)........………….…….......................... $ 715

(k) for making a single search (using person or company as the key) of the index of directors, kept by the Registrar ....$ 10

(l) for issuing a print out of the index of directors, kept by the Registrar, showing all directorships in companies incorporated in Hong Kong or registered under Part XI of the Ordinance held by a single person………………………….. $ 20

(m) for making a single search of the register of disqualification orders, kept by the Registrar ……………………….….. $ 10

NINTH SCHEDULE

[s.168]

Provisions Relating To Acquisition Of Minority Shares After Successful Take-Over Offer

PART I - Right of company to buy out minority shareholders

1. If, in a case in which the offer does not relate to shares of different classes, the transferee company has, during the period of 4 months beginning on the date of the offer, acquired not less than nine-tenths in value of the shares for which the offer is made (by virtue of acceptances of the offer or, if the shares are listed on the Unified Exchange, by virtue of acceptances of the offer or otherwise), the transferee company may give notice to the holder of any shares to which the offer relates which the transferee company has not acquired that it desires to acquire those shares.

2. If, in a case in which the offer relates to shares of different classes, the transferee company has, during the period of 4 months beginning on the date of the offer, acquired not less than nine-tenths in value of the shares of any class for which the offer is made (by virtue of acceptances of the offer or, if the shares are listed on the Unified Exchange, by virtue of acceptances of the offer or otherwise), the transferee company may give notice to the holder of any shares of that class which the transferee company has not acquired that it desires to acquire those shares.

3. Any notice under this Part shall be given in the specified form and in the specified form and in the prescribed manner and not later than 5 months after the date of the offer; and where such a notice is given to the holder of any shares the transferee company shall, subject to paragraph 4, be entitled and bound to acquire those shares on the terms of the offer.

4. Where a notice is given under this Part to the holder of any shares the court may, on an application made by him within 2 months from the date on which the notice was given, order that the transferee company shall not be entitled and bound to acquire the shares or specify terms of acquisition different from those of the offer.

5. Where an offer is such as to give the holder of shares a choice of terms, any notice under this Part shall give particulars of the choice and state-

(a) that the holder of the shares may within 2 months from the date of the notice exercise that choice by letter sent to the company at an address specified in the notice; and

(b) which terms are to be taken as applying in default of his exercising the choice as aforesaid,

and the terms of the offer mentioned in paragraph 3 shall be determined accordingly.

6. Where an offer is such that the holder of shares in the transferor company is to receive shares or debentures of the transferee company but with an option to receive instead some other consideration to be provided by a third party-

(a)   the terms of the offer mentioned in paragraph 3 shall not include that option unless the transferee company in its notice under this Part indicates that the option is to apply; and

(b)   if the transferee company does not so indicate it may, if it thinks fit, offer in that notice a corresponding option to receive some other consideration to be provided by that company,

and, if the transferee company offers such a corresponding option and the holder of the shares within 2 months from the date of the notice exercises that corresponding option by a letter sent to the company at an address specified in the notice, the terms of the offer mentioned in paragraph 3 shall be determined accordingly.

For the purposes of this paragraph, consideration shall be deemed to be provided by a third party where it is made available to the transferee company on terms that it shall be used by the transferee company as consideration pursuant to the offer.

7.   Where a notice has been given under this Part and the court has not, on an application made by the person to whom the notice was given, ordered to the contrary, the transferee company shall, on the expiration of 2 months from the date on which the notice has been given or, if an application to the court is then pending, after that application has been disposed of-

(a)   transmit a copy of the notice to the transferor company together with an instrument of transfer executed on behalf of the shareholder on whom the notice was served by any person appointed by the transferee company; and

(b)   pay or transfer to the transferor company the amount or other consideration representing the price payable by the transferee company for the shares which by virtue of this Part that company is entitled to acquire,

and the transferor company shall thereupon register the transferee company as the holder of those shares; but no instrument of transfer shall be required for any share for which a share warrant is for the time being outstanding.

8.   Any sums received by the transferor company under paragraph 7 shall be paid into a separate bank account, and any such sums and any other consideration so received shall be held by that company on trust for the several persons entitled to the shares in respect of which the said sums or other consideration were respectively received; but any such sum or other consideration shall not be paid out or delivered to any person claiming to be entitled thereto unless he produces the share certificate of such shares or other evidence of his title thereto, or a satisfactory indemnity in lieu of such certificate or other evidence.

PART 2 - Right of minority shareholders to be bought out by company

9. If the offer does not relate to shares of different classes and not later than the expiration of the period within which the offer can be accepted the transferee company is the holder of not less than nine-tenths in value of all the shares in the transferor company or, if the offer relates to a class of shares, not less than nine-tenths in value of all the shares of that class, the holder of any shares to which the offer relates who has not accepted the offer before the expiration of that period may by letter addressed to the transferee company require it to acquire those shares.

10. If the offer relates to shares of different classes and not later than the expiration of the period within which the offer can be accepted the transferee company is the holder of not less than nine-tenths in value of the shares of any class for which the offer is made, the holder of any shares of that class who has not accepted the offer before the expiration of that period may by letter addressed to the transferee company require it to acquire those shares.

11. Within 1 month of the expiration of the period within which the offer can be accepted the transferee company shall give notice in the specified form and in the specified form and in the prescribed manner to a person having rights under this Part calling on him to decide whether or not to exercise them, but he shall not be entitled to exercise them later than 2 months after the date on which the notice is given.

12. Where the holder of any shares exercises his rights under this Part the transferee company shall be entitled and bound to acquire the shares on the terms of the offer or on such other terms as may be agreed or as the court, on the application of the holder of the shares or the transferee company, thinks fit to order.

13. Where an offer is such as to give the holder of shares a choice of terms and he requires the transferee company to acquire the shares under this Part without the company having given him a notice under paragraph 11, the requirement shall not have effect unless it indicates an exercise of that choice.

14. Where an offer is such as to give the holder of shares a choice of terms and the company gives him a notice under paragraph 11, the notice shall give particulars of the choice and state-

> *(a)* that he may exercise the choice in making a requirement under this Part; and

> *(b)* which terms are to be taken as applying if he makes such a requirement without exercising the choice,

and the terms of the offer mentioned in paragraph 12 shall be determined accordingly.

15. Where an offer is such that the holder of shares in the transferor company is to receive shares or debentures of the transferee company but with an option to receive instead some other consideration to be provided by a third party-

> *(a)* the terms of the offer mentioned in paragraph 12 shall not include that option

unless the transferee company in a notice under paragraph 11 indicates that the option is to apply; and

(b) if the transferee company does not so indicate it may, if it thinks fit, offer in such a notice a corresponding option to receive some other consideration to be provided by that company,

and, if the transferee company offers such a corresponding option and the holder of the shares exercises that corresponding option in his requirement under this Part, the terms of the offer mentioned in paragraph 12 shall be determined accordingly.

For the purposes of this paragraph, consideration shall be deemed to be provided by a third party where it is made available to the transferee company on terms that it shall be used by the transferee company as consideration pursuant to the offer.

TENTH SCHEDULE

Accounts

Preliminary

1. Paragraphs 2 to 12 apply to the balance sheet and 13 to 17 to the profit and loss account, and are subject to the exceptions and modifications provided for by Part II in the case of a holding or subsidiary company and by Part III in the case of companies of the classes there mentioned; and this Schedule has effect in addition to the provisions of sections 161 to 161C of this Ordinance.

PART I - General Provisions As To Balance Sheet And Profit And Loss Account

Balance Sheet

2. The authorized share capital, issued share capital, liabilities and assets shall be summarized, with such particulars as are necessary to disclose the general nature of the assets and liabilities, and there shall be specified-

> *(a)* any part of the issued capital that consists of redeemable shares, the earliest and latest dates on which the company has power to redeem those shares, whether those shares must be redeemed in any event or are liable to be redeemed at the option of the company and whether any (and, if so, what) premium is payable on redemption;

> *(b)* so far as the information is not given in the profit and loss account, any share capital on which interest has been paid out of capital during the financial year, and the rate at which interest has been so paid;

> *(c)* the amount of the share premium account;

> *(d)* particulars of any redeemed debentures which the company has power to reissue.

3. There shall be stated under separate headings, so far as they are not written off,-

> *(a)* the preliminary expenses;

> *(b)* any expenses incurred in connexion with any issue of share capital or debentures;

> *(c)* any sums paid by way of cohesion in respect of any shares or debentures;

> *(d)* any sums allowed by way of discount in respect of any debentures; and

> *(e)* the amount of the discount allowed on any issue of shares at a discount.

4.(1) The reserves, provisions, liabilities and assets shall be classified under headings appropriate to the company's business:

Provided that-

    (a)   where the amount of any class is not material, it may be included under the same heading as some other class; and

    (b)   where any assets of one class are not separable from assets of another class, those assets may be included under the same heading.

(2) Fixed assets, current assets and assets that are neither fixed nor current shall be separately identified.

(3) The method or methods used to arrive at the amount of the fixed assets under each heading shall be stated.

5.(1) The method of arriving at the amount of any fixed asset shall, subject to sub-paragraph (2), be to take the difference between-

    (a)   its cost or, if it stands in the company's books at a valuation, the amount of the valuation; and

    (b)   the aggregate amount provided or written off since the date of acquisition or valuation, as the case may be, for depreciation or diminution in value;

and for the purposes of this paragraph the net amount at which any assets stand in the company's books at 1st October 1975 (after deduction of the amounts previously provided or written off for depreciation or diminution in value) shall, if the figures relating to the period before 1st October 1975 cannot be obtained without unreasonable expense or delay, be treated as if it were the amount of a valuation of those assets made at 1st October 1975 and, where any of those assets are sold, the said net amount less the amount of the sales shall be treated as if it were the amount of a valuation so made of the remaining assets.

(2) Sub-paragraph (1) shall not apply-

    (a)   to assets for which the figures relating to the period beginning with 1st October 1975 cannot be obtained without unreasonable expense or delay; or

    (b)   to assets the replacement of which is provided for wholly or partly-

        (i)   by making provision for renewals and charging the cost of replacement against the provision so made; or

        (ii)   by charging the cost of replacement direct to revenue; or

(c)   to any listed investments or to any unlisted investments of which the value as estimated by the directors is shown either as the amount of the investments or by way of note; or

(d)   to goodwill, patents or trade marks.

(3) For the assets under each heading whose amount is arrived at in accordance with sub-paragraph (1), there shall be shown-

(a)   the aggregate of the amounts referred to in paragraph (a) of that sub-paragraph; and

(b)   the aggregate of the amounts referred to in paragraph (b) thereof.

(4) As respects the assets under each heading whose amount is not arrived at in accordance with sub-paragraph (1) because their replacement is provided for as mentioned in sub-paragraph (2)(b), there shall be stated-

(a)   the means by which their replacement is provided for; and

(b)   the aggregate amount of the provision (if any) made for renewals and not used.

6. The aggregate amounts respectively of reserves and provisions (other than provisions for depreciation, renewals or diminution in value of assets) shall be stated under separate headings:

Provided that-

(a)   this paragraph shall not require a separate statement of either of the said amounts which is not material; and

(b)   the Financial Secretary may direct that it shall not require a separate statement of the amount of provisions where he is satisfied that that is not required in the public interest and would prejudice the company, but subject to the condition that any heading stating an amount arrived at after taking into account a provision (other than as aforesaid) shall be so framed or marked as to indicate that fact.

7.(1) There shall also be shown (unless it is shown in the profit and loss account or a statement or report annexed thereto, or the amount involved is not material)-

(a)   where the amount of the reserves or of the provisions (other than provisions for depreciation, renewals or diminution in value of assets) shows an increase as compared with the amount at the end of the immediately preceding financial year, the source from which the amount of the increase has been derived; and *(b)*   where-

           (i)   the amount of the reserves shows a decrease as compared with the amount at the end of the immediately preceding financial year; or

           (ii)   the amount at the end of the immediately preceding financial year of the provisions (other than provisions for depreciation, renewals or diminution in value of assets) exceeded the aggregate of the sums since applied and amounts still retained for the purposes thereof; the application of the amounts derived from the difference.

(2) Where the heading showing the reserves or any of the provisions aforesaid is divided into sub-headings, this paragraph shall apply to each of the separate amounts shown in the sub-headings instead of applying to the aggregate amount thereof.

8. If an amount is set aside for the purpose of its being used to prevent undue fluctuations in charges for taxation, it shall be stated.

9.(1) There shall be shown under separate headings-

      (a)   the aggregate amounts respectively of the company's listed investments and unlisted investments;

      (b)   if the amount of the goodwill and of any patents and trade marks or part of that amount is shown as a separate item in or is otherwise ascertainable from the books of the company, or from any contract for the sale or purchase of any property to be acquired by the company, or from any documents in the possession of the company relating to the stamp duty payable in respect of any such contract or the conveyance of any such property, the said amount so shown or ascertained so far as not written off or, as the case may be, the said amount so far as it is so shown or ascertainable and as so shown or ascertained, as the case may be;

      (c)   the aggregate amount of any outstanding loans made under the authority of section 47C(4)(b) and (c);

      (d)   the aggregate amount of bank loans and overdrafts, and the aggregate amount of loans, other than bank loans or overdrafts, made to the company which-

           (i)   are repayable otherwise than by instalments and fall due for repayment after the expiration of the period of 5 years beginning with the day next following the expiration of the financial year; or

           (ii)   are repayable by instalments any of which fall due for payment after

the expiration of that period;

     (e)   the aggregate amount which is recommended for distribution by way of dividend.

(2)   Nothing in head (b) of sub-paragraph (1) shall be taken as requiring the amount of the goodwill, patents and trade marks to be stated otherwise than as a single item.

(3)   The heading showing the amount of the listed investments shall be subdivided, where necessary, to distinguish the investments as respects which there has, and those as respects which there has not, been granted a listing on the Unified Exchange.

(4)   In relation to each loan falling within head (d) of sub-paragraph (1) (other than a bank loan or overdraft), there shall be stated by way of note (if not otherwise stated) the terms on which it is repayable and the rate at which interest is payable thereon:

Provided that if the number of loans is such that, in the opinion of the directors, compliance with the foregoing requirement would result in a statement of excessive length, it shall be sufficient to give a general indication of the terms on which the loans are repayable and the rates at which interest is payable thereon.

10.   Where any liability of the company is secured otherwise than by operation of law on any assets of the company, the fact that that liability is so secured shall be stated, but it shall not be necessary to specify the assets on which the liability is secured.

11.   Where any of the company's debentures are held by a nominee of or trustee for the company, the nominal amount of the debentures and the amount at which they are stated in the books of the company shall be stated.

12.(1)   The matters referred to in the following sub-paragraphs shall be stated by way of note, or in a statement or report annexed, if not otherwise shown.

(2)   The number, description and amount of any shares in the company which any person has an option to subscribe for, together with the following particulars of the option, that is to say-

    (a)   the period during which it is exercisable;

    (b)   the price to be paid or shares subscribed for under it.

(3)   The amount of any arrears of fixed cumulative dividends on the company's shares and the period for which the dividends or, if there is more than one class, each class of them are in arrear.

(4)   Particulars of any charge on the assets of the company to secure the liabilities of any other person, including, where practicable, the amount secured.

(5)   The general nature of any other contingent liabilities not provided for and, where practicable, the aggregate amount or estimated amount of those liabilities, if it is material.

(6) Where practicable the aggregate amount or estimated amount, if it is material, of contracts for capital expenditure, so far as not provided for and, where practicable, the aggregate amount or estimated amount, if it is material, of capital expenditure authorized by the directors which has not been contracted for.

(7) In the case of fixed assets under any heading whose amount is required to be arrived at in accordance with paragraph 5(1) (other than unlisted investments) and is so arrived at by reference to a valuation, the years (so far as they are known to the directors) in which the assets were severally valued and the several values, and, in the case of assets that have been valued during the financial year)-

> *(a)* the names of the persons who valued them or particulars of their qualifications for doing so, and

> *(b)* the bases of valuation used by such persons.

(8) If there are included amongst fixed assets under any heading (other than investments) assets that have been acquired during the financial year, the aggregate amount of the assets acquired as determined for the purpose of making up the balance sheet, and if during that year any fixed assets included under a heading in the balance sheet made up with respect to the immediately preceding financial year (other than investments) have been disposed of or destroyed, the aggregate amount thereof as determined for the purpose of making up that balance sheet.

(9) Of the amount of fixed assets consisting of land, how much is ascribable to-

> *(a)* land in Hong Kong in each of the following categories-

>> **(i)** land held on long lease;

>> **(ii)** land held on medium-term lease;

>> **(iii)** land held on short lease;

> *(b)* land outside Hong Kong in each of the following categories-

>> **(i)** land held freehold;

>> **(ii)** land held on long lease;

>> **(iii)** land held on medium-term lease;

>> **(iv)** land held on short lease.

(10) If in the opinion of the directors any of the current assets have not a value, on realization in the ordinary course of the company's business, at least equal to the amount at which they are stated, the fact that the directors are of that opinion.

(11) The aggregate market value of the company's listed investments where it differs from the amount of the investments as stated, and the stock exchange value of any investments of which the market value is shown (whether separately or not) and is taken as being higher than their stock exchange value.

(12) If a sum set aside for the purpose of its being used to prevent undue fluctuations in charges for taxation has been used during the financial year for another purpose, the amount thereof and the fact that it has been so used.

(13) If the amount carried forward for stock in trade or work in progress is material for the appreciation by its members of the company's state of affairs or of its profit or loss for the financial year, the manner in which that amount has been computed.

(14) The basis on which other currencies have been converted into the currency in which the balance sheet is expressed, where the amount of the assets or liabilities affected is material.

(15) The basis on which the amount, if any, set aside for Hong Kong profits tax is computed.

(16) Except in the case of the first balance sheet laid before the company after 1st October 1975, the corresponding amounts at the end of the immediately preceding financial year for all items shown in the balance sheet other than any item the amount for which is shown-

> *(a)* in pursuance of sub-paragraph (8), or

> *(b)* as an amount the source or application of which is required by paragraph 7 to be shown.

Profit and Loss Account

13.(1) There shall be shown

> *(a)* the amount charged to revenue by way of provision for depreciation, renewals or diminution in value of fixed assets;

> *(b)* the amount of the interest on loans of the following kinds made to the company (whether on the security of debentures or not), namely, bank loans, overdrafts and loans which, not being bank loans or overdrafts,-

>> **(i)** are repayable otherwise than by instalments and fall due for repayment before the expiration of the period of 5 years beginning with the day next following the expiration of the financial year; or

>> **(ii)** are repayable by instalments the last of which falls due for payment before the expiration of that period;

> and the amount of the interest on loans of other kinds so made (whether on the security of debentures or not);

(c)   the amount of the charge to revenue for taxes imposed by the Inland Revenue Ordinance (Cap. 112) and, if that amount would have been greater but for relief from double taxation, the amount which it would have been but for such relief, and the amount of the charge for taxation imposed outside Hong Kong of profits, income and (so far as charged to revenue) capital gains;

(d)   the amounts respectively provided for redemption of share capital and for redemption of loans;

(e)   the amount, if material, set aside or proposed to be set aside to, or withdrawn from, reserves;

(f)   subject to sub-paragraph (2), the amount, if material, set aside to provisions other than provisions for depreciation, renewals or diminution in value of assets or, as the case may be, the amount, if material, withdrawn from such provisions and not applied for the purposes thereof;

(g)   the amounts respectively of income from listed investments and income from unlisted investments;

(h)   if a substantial part of the company's revenue for the financial year consists in rents from land and buildings, the amount thereof (after deduction of ground-rents, rates and other out-goings);

(i)   the amount, if material, charged to revenue in respect of sums payable in respect of the hire of plant and machinery;

(j)   the aggregate amount of the dividends paid and proposed.

(2) The Financial Secretary may direct that a company shall not be obliged to show an amount set aside to provisions in accordance with sub-paragraph (1)(f), if he is satisfied that that is not required in the public interest and would prejudice the company, but subject to the condition that any heading stating an amount arrived at after taking into account the amount set aside as aforesaid shall be so framed or marked as to indicate that fact.

(3) If, in the case of any assets in whose case an amount is charged to revenue by way of provision for depreciation or diminution in value, an amount is also charged by way of provision for renewal thereof, the last-mentioned amount shall be shown separately.

(4) If the amount charged to revenue by way of provision for depreciation or diminution in value of any fixed assets (other than investments) has been determined otherwise than by reference to the amount of those assets as determined for the purpose of making up the balance sheet, that fact shall be stated.

14. The amount of any charge arising in consequence of the occurrence of an event in a preceding financial year and of any credit so arising shall, if not included in a heading relating to other matters, be stated under a separate heading.

15.   The amount of the remuneration of the auditors shall be shown under a separate heading, and for the purposes of this paragraph, any sums paid by the company in respect of the auditors' expenses shall be deemed to be included in the expression "remuneration".

16.(1)   The matters referred to in sub-paragraphs (2) to (4) shall be stated by way of note, if not otherwise shown.

(2)   The turnover for the financial year, except in so far as it is attributable to the business of banking to business of such other class as may be prescribed for the purposes of this sub-paragraph.

(3)   If some or all of the turnover is omitted by reason of its being attributable as aforesaid, the fact that it is so omitted.

(4)   The method by which turnover stated is arrived at.

17.(1)   The matters referred to in sub-paragraphs (2) to (6) shall be stated by way of note, if not otherwise shown.

(2)   If depreciation or replacement of fixed assets is provided for by some method other than a depreciation charge or provision for renewals, or is not provided for, the method by which it is provided for or the fact that it is not provided for, as the case may be.

(3)   The basis on which the charge for Hong Kong profits tax is computed.

(4)   Any special circumstances which affect liability in respect of taxation of profits, income or capital gains for the financial year or liability in respect of taxation of profits, income or capital gains for succeeding financial years.

(5)   Except in the case of the first profit and loss account laid before the company after 1st October 1975 the corresponding amounts for the immediately preceding financial year for all items shown in the profit and loss account.

(6)   Any material respects in which any items shown in the profit and loss account are affected-

> *(a)*   by transactions of a sort not usually undertaken by the company or otherwise by circumstances of an exceptional or non-recurrent nature; or

> *(b)*   by any change in the basis of accounting.

PART II - Special Provisions Where The Company Is A Holding Or Subsidiary Company

Modifications of and Additions to Requirements as to Company's own Accounts

18.(1) This paragraph shall apply where the company is a holding company, whether or not it is itself a subsidiary of another body corporate.

(2) The aggregate amount of assets consisting of shares in, or amounts owing (whether on account of a loan or otherwise) from, the company's subsidiaries, distinguishing shares from indebtedness, shall be set out in the balance sheet separately from all the other assets of the company, and the aggregate amount of indebtedness (whether on account of a loan or otherwise) to the company's subsidiaries shall be so set out separately from all its other liabilities and-

> *(a)* the references in Part I to the company's investments (except those in paragraphs 12(8) and 13(4)) shall not include investments in its subsidiaries required by this paragraph to be separately set out; and

> *(b)* paragraphs 5, 13(1)(a) and 17(2) shall not apply in relation to fixed assets consisting of interests in the company's subsidiaries.

(3) There shall be shown by way of note on the balance sheet or in a statement or report annexed thereto the number, description and amount of the shares in and debentures of the company held by its subsidiaries or their nominees, but excluding any of those shares or debentures in the case of which the subsidiary is concerned as personal representative or in the case of which it is concerned as trustee and neither the company nor any subsidiary thereof is beneficially interested under the trust, otherwise than by way of security only for the purposes of a transaction entered into by it in the ordinary course of a business which includes the lending of money.

(4) Where group accounts are not submitted, there shall be annexed to the balance sheet a statement showing-

> *(a)* the reasons why subsidiaries are not dealt with in group accounts;

> *(b)* the net aggregate amount, so far as it concerns members of the holding company and is not dealt with in the company's accounts, of the subsidiaries' profits after deducting the subsidiaries' losses (or vice versa)-

>> **(i)** for the respective financial years of the subsidiaries ending with or during the financial year of the company; and

>> **(ii)** for their previous financial years since they respectively became the holding company's subsidiary;

> *(c)* the net aggregate amount of the subsidiaries' profits after deducting the subsidiaries' losses (or vice versa)-

(i)   for the respective financial years of the subsidiaries ending with or during the financial year of the company; and

(ii)   for their other financial years since they respectively became the holding company's subsidiary;

so far as those profits are dealt with, or provision is made for those losses, in the company's accounts;

(d)   any qualifications contained in the report of the auditors of the subsidiaries on their accounts for their respective financial years ending as aforesaid, and any note or saving contained in those accounts to call attention to a matter which, apart from the note or saving, would properly have been referred to in such a qualification, in so far as the matter which is the subject of the qualification or note is not covered by the company's own accounts and is material from the point of view of its members;

or, in so far as the information required by this sub-paragraph is not obtainable, a statement that it is not obtainable:

Provided that the Financial Secretary may, on the application or with the consent of the company's directors, direct that in relation to any subsidiary this sub-paragraph shall not apply or shall apply only to such extent as may be provided by the direction.

(5)   Sub-paragraph (4)(b) and (c) shall apply only to profits and losses of a subsidiary which may properly be treated in the holding company's accounts as revenue profits or losses, and the profits or losses attributable to any shares in a subsidiary for the time being held by the holding company or any other of its subsidiaries shall not (for that or any other purpose) be treated as aforesaid so far as they are profits or losses for the period before the date on or as from which the shares were acquired by the company or any of its subsidiaries, except that they may in a proper case be so treated where-

(a)   the company is itself the subsidiary of another body corporate; and

(b)   the shares were acquired from that body corporate or a subsidiary of it;

and for the purpose of determining whether any profits or losses are to be treated as profits or losses for the said period the profit or loss for any financial year of the subsidiary may, if it is not practicable to apportion it with reasonable accuracy by reference to the facts, be treated as accruing from day to day during that year and be apportioned accordingly.

(6)   Where group accounts are not submitted, there shall be annexed to the balance sheet a statement showing, in relation to the subsidiaries (if any) whose financial years did not end with that of the company-

(a)   the reasons why the company's directors consider that the subsidiaries'

financial years should not end with that of the company; and

> *(b)*   the dates on which the subsidiaries' financial years ending last before that of the company respectively ended or the earliest and latest of those dates.

19.(1)   The balance sheet of a company which is a subsidiary of another body corporate, whether or not it is itself a holding company, shall show the aggregate amount of its indebtedness to all bodies corporate of which it is a subsidiary or a fellow subsidiary and the aggregate amount of indebtedness of all such bodies corporate to it, distinguishing in each case between indebtedness in respect of debentures and otherwise, and the aggregate amount of assets consisting of shares in fellow subsidiaries.

(2)   For the purposes of this paragraph a company shall be deemed to be a fellow subsidiary of another body corporate if both are subsidiaries of the same body corporate but neither is the other's subsidiary.

Consolidated Accounts of Holding Company and Subsidiaries

20.   Subject to the following paragraphs of this Part, the consolidated balance sheet and profit and loss account shall combine the information contained in the separate balance sheets and profit and loss accounts of the holding company and of the subsidiaries dealt with by the consolidated accounts, but with such adjustments (if any) as the directors of the holding company think necessary.

21.   Subject as aforesaid and to Part III, the consolidated accounts shall, in giving the said information, comply so far as practicable, with the requirements of this Ordinance as if they were the accounts of an actual company.

22.   Sections 161 and 161B shall not, by virtue of paragraphs 20 and 21, apply for the purpose of the consolidated accounts.

23.   Paragraph 7 shall not apply for the purpose of any consolidated accounts laid before a company with the first balance sheet so laid after 1st October 1975.

24.   In relation to any subsidiaries of the holding company not dealt with by the consolidated accounts-

> *(a)*   paragraph 18(2) and (3) shall apply for the purpose of those accounts as if those accounts were the accounts of an actual company of which they were subsidiaries; and

> *(b)*   there shall be annexed the like statement as is required by paragraph 18(4) where there are no group accounts, but as if references therein to the holding company's accounts were references to the consolidated accounts.

25.   In relation to any subsidiaries (whether or not dealt with by the consolidated accounts), whose financial years did not end with that of the company, there shall be annexed the like statement as is required by paragraph 18(6) where there are no group accounts.

PART III - Exceptions For Special Classes Of Company

26.(1) A banking company shall not be subject to the requirements of Part I other than-

- *(a)* as respects its balance sheet, those of paragraphs 2 and 3, paragraph 4 (so far as it relates to assets), paragraph 9 (except sub-paragraphs (1)(d) and (4)), paragraphs 10 and 11 and paragraph 12 (except sub-paragraphs (7), (8), (9), (11) and (12)); and

- *(b)* as respect its profit and loss account, those of sub-paragraph (1)(h) and (j) of paragraph 13, paragraphs 14 and 15 and sub-paragraphs (1) and (5) of paragraph 17;

but, where in its balance sheet reserves or provisions (other than provisions for depreciation, renewals or diminution in value of assets) are not stated separately, any heading stating an amount arrived at after taking into account a reserve or such a provision shall be so framed or marked as to indicate that fact, and its profit and loss account shall indicate by appropriate words the manner in which the amount stated for the company's profit or loss has been arrived at.

(2) The accounts of a banking company shall not be deemed, by reason only of the fact that they do not comply with any requirements of Part I from which the company is exempt by virtue of this paragraph, not to give the true and fair view required by this Ordinance.

(3) In this paragraph the expression "banking company" means any company which carries on banking business and holds a valid banking licence granted under the Banking Ordinance (Cap.155) authorizing it to do so in Hong Kong.

27. (1) An insurance company shall not be subject to the following requirements of Part I, that is to say-

- *(a)* as respects its balance sheet, those of paragraphs 4 to 7, sub-paragraphs (1)(a) and (3) of paragraph 9 and sub-paragraphs (4), (5) and (7) to (11) of paragraph 12;

- *(b)* as respects its profit and loss account, those of paragraph 13 (except sub-paragraph (1)(b), (c), (d) and (j)) and paragraph 17(2);

but, where in its balance sheet reserves or provisions (other than provisions for depreciation, renewals or diminution in value of assets) are not stated separately, any heading stating an amount arrived at after taking into account a reserve or such a provision shall be so framed or marked as to indicate that fact, and its profit and loss account shall indicate by appropriate words the manner in which the amount stated for the company's profit or loss has been arrived at:

Provided that the Financial Secretary may direct that any such insurance company whose business includes to a substantial extent business other than insurance business shall comply with all the requirements of Part I or such of them as may be specified in the direction and shall comply therewith as respects either the whole of its business or such part thereof as may be so specified.

(2) Where an insurance company is entitled to the benefit of this paragraph, then any wholly owned subsidiary thereof shall also be so entitled if its business consists only of business which is complementary to insurance business of the classes carried on by the insurance company.

(3) The accounts of a company shall not be deemed, by reason only of the fact that they do not comply with any requirement of Part I from which the company is exempt by virtue of this paragraph, not to give the true and fair view required by this Ordinance.

(4) For the purposes of this paragraph a company shall be deemed to be the wholly owned subsidiary of an insurance company if it has no members except the insurance company and the insurance company's wholly owned subsidiaries and its or their nominees.

28. *Repealed*

29. Where a company entitled to the benefit of any provision contained in this Part is a holding company, the reference in Part II to consolidated accounts complying with the requirements of this Ordinance shall, in relation to consolidated accounts of that company, be construed as referring to those requirements in so far only as they apply to the separate accounts of that company.

PART IV - Interpretation Of Schedule

30.(1) For the purposes of this Schedule, unless the context otherwise requires

   (a)   the expression "provision" shall, subject to sub-paragraph (2), mean any amount written off or retained by way of providing for depreciation, renewals or diminution in value of assets or retained by way of providing for any known liability of which the amount cannot be determined with substantial accuracy;

   (b)   the expression "reserve" shall not, subject as aforesaid, include any amount written off or retained by way of providing for depreciation, renewals or diminution in value of assets or retained by way of providing for any known liability or any sum set aside for the purpose of its being used to prevent undue fluctuations in charges for taxation;

and in this paragraph the expression "liability" shall include all liabilities in respect of expenditure contracted for and all disputed or contingent liabilities.

(2)   Where-

   (a)   any amount written off or retained by way of providing for depreciation,

469

renewals or diminution in value of assets, not being an amount written off in relation to fixed assets before 1st October 1975; or

(b) any amount retained by way of providing for any known liability,

is in excess of that which in the opinion of the directors is reasonably necessary for the purpose, the excess shall be treated for the purposes of this Schedule as a reserve and not as a provision.

31. For the purposes aforesaid,-

(a) the expression "listed investment" means an investment as respects which there has been granted a listing on the Unified Exchange, or on any stock exchange of repute outside Hong Kong, and the expression "unlisted investment" shall be construed accordingly;

(b) the expression "lease" includes an agreement for a lease;

(c) in relation to land in Hong Kong-

 (i) the expression "long lease" means a lease in the case of which either-

  (A) the portion of the term for which it was granted remaining unexpired at the end of the financial year is not less than 50 years, or

  (B) if the lease is a renewable Crown lease, the portion of the said term remaining unexpired at the said date when added to the term for which the lessee is entitled to renew the lease amounts to a period of not less than 50 years from the said date;

 (ii) the expression "medium-term lease" means a lease in the case of which either:-

  (A) the portion of the term for which it was granted remaining unexpired at the end of the financial year is less than 50 years but not less than 10 years, or

  (B) if the lease is a renewable Crown lease, the portion of the said term remaining unexpired at the said date when added to the term for which the lessee is entitled to renew the lease amounts to a period of less than 50 years but not less than 10 years from the said date;

 (iii) the expression "short lease" means a lease which is not a long or a medium-term lease;

(*d*)   in relation to land outside Hong Kong-

    (i)   the expression "long lease" means a lease in the case of which the portion of the term for which it was granted remaining unexpired at the end of the financial year is not less than 50 years,

    (ii)   the expression "medium-term lease" means a lease in the case of which the portion of the term for which it was granted remaining unexpired at the end of the financial year is less than 50 years but not less than 10 years,

    (iii)   the expression "short lease" means a lease which is not a long or a medium-term lease;

(*e*)   a loan shall be deemed to fall due for repayment, and an instalment of a loan shall be deemed to fall due for payment, on the earliest date on which the lender could require repayment or, as the case may be, payment if he exercised all options and rights available to him.

ELEVENTH SCHEDULE

Accounts Of Certain Private Companies Under Section 141D

1. This Schedule has effect in addition to the provisions of sections 161 to 161C of this Ordinance.

2. The authorized share capital, issued share capital, liabilities and assets shall be summarized, with such particulars as are necessary to disclose the general nature of the assets and liabilities, and there shall be specified-

> *(a)* any part of the issued capital that consists of redeemable shares, the earliest and latest dates on which the company has power to redeem those shares, whether those shares must be redeemed in any event or are liable to be redeemed at the option of the company and whether any (and, if so, what) premium is payable on redemption;

> *(b)* so far as the information is not given in the profit and loss account, any share capital on which interest has been paid out of capital during the financial year, and the rate at which interest has been so paid;

> *(c)* the amount of the share premium account;

> *(d)* particulars of any redeemed debentures which the company has power to reissue.

3. There shall be stated under separate headings, so far as they are not written off,-

> *(a)* the preliminary expenses;

> *(b)* any expenses incurred in connexion with any issue of share capital or debentures;

> *(c)* any sums paid by way of commission in respect of any shares or debentures;

> *(d)* any sums allowed by way of discount in respect of any debentures; and

> *(e)* the amount of the discount allowed on any issue of shares at a discount.

4.(1) Fixed assets, current assets and assets that are neither fixed nor current shall be separately identified.

(2) The method or methods used to arrive at the amount of the fixed assets shall be stated.

5. There shall be shown under a separate heading the aggregate amount of any outstanding loans made under the authority of provisos (b) and (c) to section 48(1).

6. Where any liability of the company is secured otherwise than by operation of law on any assets of the company, the fact that that liability is so secured shall be stated, but it shall not be necessary to specify the assets on which the liability is secured.

TWELFTH SCHEDULE

[s. 351]

Punishment Of Offences Under This Ordinance

Section creating offence	General nature of offence	Mode of prosecution	Punishment	Daily default fine (if applicable)
8(8)	Company failing to deliver to the Registrar notice or other document following alteration to its objects	Summary	$5,000	$200
10(3)	Company without a share capital failing to give notice of an increase of number of members beyond the registered number	Summary	$5,000	$200
21(9)	Failure by a body to alter its name on the revocation of a licence to use the words "Chamber of Commerce" etc. in its name	Summary	$5,000	$500
22(6)	Company failing to change name on the direction of the Registrar	Summary	$50,000 and 6 months	$500
22A(4)	Company failing to change name on the direction of the Registrar on the grounds that the name is misleading	Summary	$10,000	$500
26(2)	Company failing to send to one of its members a copy of the memorandum or articles when required by the member	Summary	$5,000	-
27(2)	When a company's memorandum is altered, issuing a copy of the	Summary	$5,000	-

memorandum without
alteration

30(2)	Failing to give notice, register prospectus or otherwise failing to comply with section 30(1) or (1A) on ceasing to be a private company	Summary	$25,000	-
30(2A)	Authorizing a statement in lieu of prospectus under section 30(1) containing an untrue statement	On indictment	$100,000 and 2 years	-
		Summary	$25,000 and 6 months	-
38(1B)	Issuing a company prospectus that does not comply with section 38(1) and (1A)	Summary	$25,000	-
38(3)	Issuing a company prospectus that does not comply with section 38	Summary	$50,000	-
38B(3)	Advertising an abstract from or an abridged version of a company prospectus	Summary	$50,000	-
38C(2)	Issuing a company prospectus with an expert's statement in it, he not having given his consent	Summary	$50,000	-
38D(8)	Issuing a company prospectus without delivering a copy to the Registrar or without the requisite endorsements	Summary	$50,000	$200
40A(1)	Authorizing the issue of a prospectus containing an untrue statement	On indictment	$500,000 and 3 years	-
		Summary	$100,000 and 12 months	-
43(4)	Allotting shares before the 3rd day after delivering a statement in lieu of	Summary	$50,000	-

prospectus to the Registrar

43(5)	Authorizing a statement in lieu of prospectus under section 43(1) containing an untrue statement	On indictment Summary	$250,000 and 2 years $100,000 and 12 months	- -
44A(4)	Allotting shares before the 3rd day after the issue of a prospectus	Summary	$50,000	-
44B(3)	Company failing to keep money in separate bank account when received under a prospectus stating that stock exchange listing is being applied for	Summary	$25,000	-
45(3)	Company failing to deliver return of allotments, etc., to the Registrar	Summary	$25,000	$500
46(5)	Company failing to deliver to the Registrar the specified from disclosing the amount or rate of share commission	Summary	$10,000	-
47A(3)	Company giving financial assistance for the acquisition of its own shares	Summary	$100,000 and 12 months	-
47F(4)	Company failing to register statutory declaration under section 47E	Summary	$25,000	$1,000
47F(5)	Director making statutory declaration under section 47E without having reasonable grounds for the opinion expressed in it	Summary	$25,000 and 6 months	-
47G(10)	Company failing to give the Registrar notice, or copy of	Summary	$5,000	$200

court order, of application
under section 47G

49G(6)	Default by company's officer in registering return disclosing purchase by company of own shares	On indictment Summary	$50,000 $10,000	$500 $200
49G(7)	Default by company to keep copy contract, etc., at registered office; refusal of inspection to person demanding it	Summary	$10,000	$200
49K(6)	Director making statutory declaration under section 49K without having reasonable grounds for the opinion expressed in it	On indictment Summary	$100,000 and 2 years $25,000 and 6 months	- -
49M(6)	Refusal of inspection of statutory declaration and auditors' report under section 49K	Summary	$10,000	$500
49N(4)	Company failing to give the Registrar notice, or copy of court order, of application under section 49N	Summary	$5,000	$200
50(3)	Company failing to disclose in a prospectus particulars of discount allowed on the Issue of shares	Summary	$5,000	$200
54(2)	Company failing to give notice of reorganization of share capital	Summary	$5,000	$200
55(3)	Company failing to give notice of increase of share capital	Summary	$5,000	$200
57A(3)	Company failing to disclose on share certificates the class of share or the	Summary	$5,000	$200

	prohibition or restrictions of voting rights for the share			
57B(6)	Director knowingly and wilfully allotting shares without the company's prior approval in general meeting	Summary	$25,000 and 6 months	-
58(1B)	Company reducing share capital in breach of section 58	On indictment	$1,000,000 and 5 years	-
		Summary	$100,000 and 12 months	-
63	Officer of a company concealing the name of a creditor entitled to object to a reduction of capital, or wilfully misrepresenting the nature or amount of the debt or claim	On indictment	$100,000 and 2 years	-
		Summary	$25,000 and 6 months	-
64(5)	Company failing to forward a copy of an order of the court to the Registrar under section 64 within 21 days	Summary	$5,000	$200
69(2)	Company failing to forward notice of refusal to register a transfer to the parties or otherwise failing to comply with section 69	Summary	$5,000	$200
70(2)	Company failing to issue certificates on allotment	Summary	$5,000	$200
71A(9)	Company failing to publish notice of issue of replacement certificate	Summary	$5,000	$200
74A(4)	Company failing to keep register of debentures or to give notice of the place where it is kept	Summary	$25,000	$500
75(4)	Company refusing to allow	Summary	$5,000	$200

	inspection or copy of register of debenture holders			
81(3)	Company failing to register particulars of charge	Summary	$25,000	$1,000
82(2)	Company failing to register particulars of an existing charge over property acquired	Summary	$25,000	$1,000
87(3)	Person appointing, etc., a receiver or manager, etc., failing to give notice to the Registrar	Summary	$5,000	$200
88(4)	Company failing to keep a copy of a charge at the registered office or failing to notify the Registrar where charges are kept	Summary	$25,000	$500
89(4)	Company failing to keep a register of charges or failing to notify the Registrar where the register of charges is kept	Summary	$25,000	$500
89(5)	Officer knowingly and wilfully permitting the omission of an entry in the register of charges	Summary	$25,000 and 6 months	-
90(2)(a)	Officer refusing to allow inspection of the register of charges or instruments of charge	Summary	$5,000	$200
91(4)	Company incorporated outside Hong Kong failing to register a Hong Kong property charge	Summary	$25,000	$1,000

92(3)	Company failing to notify the Registrar of registered office	Summary	$5,000	$200
93(3)	Company failing to affix its name outside its place of business, etc.	Summary	$5,000	$200
93(4)	Company failing to use its company name, seal, etc., correctly	Summary	$5,000	-
93(5)	Officer or other person authorizing the use of improper seal, etc.	Summary	$5,000	-
95(4)	Company failing to keep a register of members or failing to notify place where register is kept	Summary	$10,000	$500
96(3)	Company failing to maintain index to register of members	Summary	$5,000	$200
98(3)	Company refusing inspection of register of members	Summary	$5,000	$200
99(4)	Company failing to supply certificate as to closure of the register of members	Summary	$5,000	-
103(7)	Company keeping register of members outside Hong Kong without licence	Summary	$5,000	$200
104(7)	Company failing to keep a copy of the branch register with the principal register or that copy up to date	Summary	$5,000	$200
109(4)	Company failing to comply the requirements for completing and filing annual returns	Summary	$25,000	$500

111(5) (relating to sub- sections (1) and (2))	Company failing to hold Annual General Meeting	Summary	$25,000	-
111(5) (relating to sub- section (4)	Company failing to notify the Registrar of resolution by company to treat a meeting as an Annual General Meeting	Summary	$5,000	$200
114C(3)	Officer failing to give notice of the right to proxies with notice of meeting	Summary	$5,000	-
114C(5)	Officer authorizing an invitation to appoint proxies at company expense to only some of the members	Summary	$5,000	-
115A(7)	Officer failing to circulate members' resolutions, etc.	Summary	$25,000	-
117(5)	Company failing to lodge copies of special resolutions, etc., with the Registrar	Summary	$5,000	$200
117(6)	Company failing to lodge copies of special resolutions, etc., with the Registrar	Summary	$5,000 per copy	-
119(4)	Company failing to enter minutes of certain meetings	Summary	$5,000	$200
119A(3)	Company failing to keep minutes, etc., at its registered office or failing to notify the Registrar where they are kept	Summary	$25,000	$500
120(3)	Company failing to allow	Summary	$5,000	$200

	minutes, etc., to be inspected			
121(4)	Director failing to take reasonable steps to ensure that proper books of account are kept	Summary	$200,000 and 12 months	-
122(3)	Director failing to take reasonable steps to ensure that accounts are tabled at the Annual General Meeting	Summary	$200,000 and 12 months	-
123(6)	Director failing to take reasonable steps to ensure that accounts tabled at the Annual General Meeting comply with section 123	Summary	$200,000 and 12 months	-
124(3)	Director failing to take reasonable steps to ensure that group accounts tabled at the Annual General Meeting comply with section 124	Summary	$200,000 and 12 months	-
128(6)	Company failing to annex particulars to a return taking advantage of section 128(4)	Summary	$50,000	$200
129(6)	Company failing to annex particulars to a return taking advantage of section 129(4)	Summary	$50,000	$200
129B(3)	Company failing to have balance sheet signed before issue, etc.	Summary	$10,000	-
129C(3)	Company failing to annex required documents to balance sheet before issue, etc.	Summary	$100,000	-

129F	Director failing to take reasonable steps to secure compliance with sections 129D and 129E	Summary	$100,000 and 6 months	-
129G(3) (relating to sub-section (1) or (2A))	Company failing to circulate balance sheet, etc., to members or to supply a copy of a statement	Summary	$5,000	-
129G(3) (relating to sub-section (2))	Company failing to supply a copy of last balance sheet on request of a member, etc.	Summary	$25,000	$200
131(7)	Company failing to give notice of resolution to remove an auditor	Summary	$5,000	$200
133(2)	Subsidiary or holding company failing to give auditors information	Summary	$5,000	-
134(1)	Officer recklessly or knowingly making false statements, etc., to auditors	On indictment	$100,000 and 2 years	-
		Summary	$25,000 and 6 months	-
140(5)	Body corporate acting as auditor	Summary	$25,000	-
140A(7)	Company failing to give notice of resignation, etc., of auditor	On indictment	$100,000 and 2 years	-
		Summary	$25,000 and 6 months	-
140B(3)	Director failing to convene a meeting on the requisition of the auditor	On indictment	$100,000 and 2 years	-
		Summary	$25,000 and 6 months	-
141D(4)	Director failing to take reasonable steps to ensure	Summary	$25,000 and 6 months	-

directors' report is attached
to balance sheet

152A(4)	Company, etc., failing to produce books, etc., to Financial Secretary when required under section 152A	Summary	$25,000 and 6 months	-
152B(4)	Person interfering with execution of a search warrant issued under section 152B	Summary	$25,000 and 6 months	-
152C(2)	Person disclosing information gathered under section 152A contrary to section 52C	On indictment Summary	$100,000 and 2 years $25,000 and 6 months	- -
152D(1)	Person destroying, etc., documents required under section 152A	On indictment Summary	$1,000,000 and 3 years $100,000 and 12 months	- -
152E	Person falsifying documents required under section 152A	On indictment Summary	$1,000,000 and 3 years $100,000 and 12 months	- -
153(3)	Company failing to have at least 2 directors	Summary	$5,000	$200
155(5)	Unqualified person acting as a director	Summary	$5,000	$200
155A(5)	Director failing to take reasonable steps to prevent the carrying into effect of proposals specified in section 155A without the approval of the company in general meeting	Summary	$25,000 and 6 months	-
155B(3)	Director failing to give notice of material interest in a matter, the subject of a	Summary	$50,000	-

resolution to be discussed at a general meeting or meeting of a class of members, which affects the matter differently from the interest of the company

155B(4)	Company failing to give notice of a director's material interest in a matter, the subject of a resolution to be discussed at a general meeting or meeting of a class of members, which affects the matter differently from the interest of the company	Summary	$50,000	-
156(1)	Undischarged bankrupt acting as a director, etc.	On indictment	$500,000 and 2 years	-
		Summary	$100,000 and 12 months	-
157J(3)	Company entering into a loan, etc., contrary to section 157H	On indictment	$100,000 and 2 years	-
		Summary	$25,000 and 6 months	-
158(8)	Company refusing to permit inspection of register of directors and secretaries or failing to keep or maintain the register	Summary	$5,000	$200
158A(3)	Company failing to keep register of directors and secretaries at registered office or failing to notify the Registrar of place where register is kept	Summary	$25,000	$500
158B(2)	Director, etc., defaulting in giving notice to the company of such matters	Summary	$50,000	$500

required under section 158

159(3)	Director, etc., defaulting in giving notice that liability of a director, etc., is, by provision in the memorandum, unlimited before the position is filled	Summary	$10,000	-
161A(2)	Director failing to take all reasonable steps to ensure amounts required to be included in the company's accounts, etc., show the previous year's equivalent amount	Summary	$25,000 and 6 months	-
161BA(7)	Director failing to take all reasonable steps to ensure the company, if an authorized financial institution, maintains a register of agreements	Summary	$25,000 and 6 months	-
161BA(11)	Company failing to permit inspection or to send a copy as required of the register of agreements for an authorized financial institution	Summary	$5,000	$200
161C(3)	Director failing to disclose matters required under section 161 or 161 B	Summary	$25,000	-
162(3)	Director failing to disclose material interest in a contract	Summary	$25,000	-
162A(2)	Company failing to disclose, etc., management contract relating to the management of the whole or a substantial part of company business	Summary	$5,000	$200

163B(2)	Director, etc., failing to disclose payment for loss of office, etc., in connection with transfer of shares in company	Summary	$25,000	-
166(4)	Company failing to deliver order sanctioning compromise to the Registrar	Summary	$500 per copy	-
166A(4)	Company failing to give statement of effect of compromise, etc., with notice of meeting or where notice is by advertisement, failing to give notice of place of meeting or place where such details may be obtained	Summary	$25,000	-
166A(5)	Director, etc., failing to give details of matters relating to himself relevant to section 166A	Summary	$25,000	-
167(3)	Company failing to give notice of an order under section 167 to the Registrar	Summary	$5,000	$200
168A(4)	Company failing to give the Registrar an office copy of an order altering, etc., the company's memorandum or articles on petition of a minority group	Summary	$5,000	$200
168M	Person contravening a disqualification order	On indictment	$100,000 and 2 years	-
		Summary	$25,000 and 6 months	-
190(5)	Person failing to comply with requirements to give	Summary	$25,000	$200

	information, etc to Official Receiver under section 190			
227(3)	Liquidator failing to deliver dissolution order to the Registrar	Summary	$25,000	$200
228A(2)	Director declaring that company cannot continue in business by reason of its liabilities without having reasonable grounds to do so	Summary	$25,000 and 6 months	-
228A(3A) (relating to subsection (3)(b))	Director failing to appoint a provisional liquidator or deliver evidence of appointment	Summary	$25,000	-
228A(3A) (relating to subsection (3)(c))	Director failing to cause meetings of the company or creditors to be summoned	Summary	$25,000	-
228A(4B)	Provisional liquidator failing to deliver to the Registrar the notice of appointment required under section 228A(4A)	Summary	-	$200
229(2)	Company failing to advertise in the Gazette notice of resolution to wind up voluntarily	Summary	$5,000	$200
233(3)	Director declaring that company being wound up voluntarily can meet its debts within the time set out in the declaration without having reasonable grounds to do so	Summary	$25,000 and 6 months	-
237A(3)	Liquidator failing to call a meeting on forming the	Summary	$5,000	-

opinion that a company in voluntary liquidation will not be able to meet its debts within the time stated in the declaration made under section 233

238(2)	Liquidator failing to call a general meeting at the end of any year	Summary	$5,000	-
239(3)	Liquidator failing to send the Registrar a copy of accounts, etc., on completion of the winding up	Summary	$5,000	$200
239(5)	Person failing to deliver an office copy of an order under section 239 to the Registrar for registration	Summary	$5,000	$200
239(6)	Liquidator failing to call a final general meeting under section 239	Summary	$5,000	-
241(6)	Company, etc., failing to comply with the requirements to call creditors' meeting, etc., after a meeting which proposes to wind up the company voluntarily	Summary	$25,000	-
247(2)	Liquidator failing to call annual meeting of creditors	Summary	$5,000	-
248(3)	Liquidator failing to send copy account or return of holding of final meeting to the Registrar	Summary	$5,000	$200
248(5)	Person failing to deliver an office copy of an order under section 248 to the	Summary	$5,000	$200

Registrar for registration

248(6)	Liquidator failing to call a general meeting of the company or of creditors as required by section 248	Summary	$5,000	-
253(2)	Liquidator failing to publish notice of his appointment in the Gazette	Summary	$5,000	$200
271(1) (relating to paragraph (o))	Officer, etc., failing to comply with section 271 (offences by officers of companies in liquidation)	On indictment Summary	5 years 2 years	- -
271(1) (relating to any other paragraph)	Officer, etc., failing to comply with section 271 (offences by officers of companies in liquidation)	On indictment Summary	$100,000 and 2 years $25,000 and 6 months	- -
272	Officer, etc., falsifying, etc., books, etc.	On indictment Summary	$100,000 and 2 years $25,000 and 6 months	- -
273	Officer acting with intent to defraud creditors by giving, etc., or concealing, etc., property of company in liquidation	On indictment Summary	$100,000 and 2 years $25,000 and 6 months	- -
274(1)	Officer failing to keep books for the 2 years prior to winding up of company	On indictment Summary	$100,000 and 2 years $25,000 and 6 months	- -
275(3)	Person being a party to carrying on the business of a company with intent to defraud creditors	On indictment Summary	Fine (unlimited) and 5 years $100,000 and 12 months	- -
278	Undischarged bankrupt or body corporate acting as	Summary	$100,000	-

liquidator

278A	Person corruptly inducing appointment of liquidator	Summary	$100,000	-
280(2)	Company, etc., failing to notify on invoice, etc., that it is in liquidation	Summary	$5,000	-
283(4)	Person contravening general rules made for the destruction, etc., of books, etc., of liquidated company	Summary	$5,000	-
284(3)	Liquidator failing to send prescribed particulars with respect to the proceedings in and position of the liquidation during the liquidation to the Registrar,	Summary	$5,000	$500
290(2)	Person failing to deliver an office copy of an order under section 290 to the Registrar for registration	Summary	$5,000	$200
297(2)	Body corporate acting as a receiver	Summary	$25,000	-
297A	Undischarged bankrupt acting as a receiver	On indictment	$100,000 and 2 years	-
		Summary	$25,000 and 6 months	-
299(2)	Company, etc., authorizing, etc., the issue of invoices, etc., without reference to its being in receivership, etc.	Summary	$5,000	-
300A(7)	Receiver failing to give notices, etc., as required under section 300A	Summary	$5,000	$200
300B(5)	Persons defaulting in	Summary	$5,000	$200

	complying with requirements of section 300B (special provisions as to statement submitted to receiver)			
301(2)	Receiver, etc., failing to deliver accounts to the Registrar	Summary	$5,000	$200
337B(7)	Oversea company carrying on business after being given notice under section 337B	Summary	$50,000 and 6 months	$500
340	Oversea company failing to comply with Part XI	Summary	$25,000	$500
342D	Person responsible for issue, etc., of prospectus, etc., contravening sections 342 to 342C	Summary	$100,000	-
342F(1)	Authorizing the issue, circulation or distribution in Hong Kong of a prospectus relating to shares in or debentures of an oversea company containing an untrue statement	On indictment Summary	$500,000 and 3 years $100,000 and 12 months	- -
348C(4)	Company failing to take adequate precautions against falsification, etc., of registers, etc.	Summary	$5,000	$200
349	Person making a false statement	Summary	$50,000 and 6 months	-
349A(1)	Person dishonestly destroying, etc., registers	On indictment 7 years		-
349A(2)	Person wilfully or maliciously destroying, etc., registers	On indictment Summary	$100,000 and 2 years $25,000 and 6 months	- -

350	Person improperly using "Limited", etc.	Summary	$5,000	$200
350A	Company failing to state paid-up capital at the time of stating authorized capital	Summary	$5,000	-
360J	Person obstructing Official Receiver	Summary	$100,000 and 6 months	-

THIRTEENTH SCHEDULE

[ss. 49BA, 58 & 168B]

Provisions Relating To Acquisition Of Minority Shares After Successful Buy Out By Share Repurchase

PART 1- Right Of Repurchasing Company To Buy Out Minority Shareholders

1. In a case where a shareholder, or a number of shareholders (in this Schedule referred to as the "relevant shareholder"), gives notice to all other shareholders in the repurchasing company not later than the date that notice of the meeting called for the purpose of authorizing the proposed offer is given that the relevant shareholder shall not tender any of the shares held by it for purchase by the repurchasing company, if, during the period of 4 months beginning on the date of the offer, the repurchasing company buys nine-tenths of the shares (other than the shares held by the relevant shareholder) for which the repurchasing company has made the offer, the repurchasing company may, subject to paragraphs 2 and 3 being complied with, give notice to the holder of any shares to which the offer relates, and which the repurchasing company has not acquired, that it desires to purchase those shares.

2. The relevant shareholder shall not tender any of its shares under the offer.

3. The repurchasing company shall not give notice to the relevant shareholder of its desire to purchase any of the relevant shareholder's shares.

4. Where the repurchasing company gives notice under paragraph 1, it shall do so in the specified form not later than 5 months after the offer; and shall be entitled and bound to purchase those shares on the terms of the offer.

5. The repurchasing company shall pay to any holder to whom it has given notice under paragraph 1, the amount of the offer for the shares on receipt of-

      (a)   the share certificate;

      (b)   satisfactory evidence of his title; or

      (c)   a declaration as to the loss or destruction of the share certificate together with a suitable indemnity.

6. Where the repurchasing company has given notice under paragraph 1 to the holder of any shares, the court may, on an application made by the holder of the shares within 2 months from the date on which the notice was given, order that the repurchasing company shall not be entitled and bound to purchase those shares or specify terms of purchase different from the terms of the offer.

7. Where an offer is such as to give the holder of shares a choice of terms, the repurchasing company shall in any notice which it gives under paragraph I state the particulars of the choice and-

(a)   that the holder of the shares may within 2 months from the date of the notice exercise that choice by letter sent to the repurchasing company at the address specified in the notice; and

(b)   which terms are to be taken as applying in default of his exercising the choice as set out in the offer.

8.   Where the repurchasing company has given notice under paragraph 1 and the court has not ordered to the contrary, the repurchasing company shall on the expiration of 2 months from the date of the notice, or if an application to the court is pending after that application has been disposed of, cancel any outstanding shares the subject of the notice, and pay the moneys due for their purchase into a separate bank account in trust for the persons entitled to the shares for which the moneys were received.

9.   A person who claims to be entitled to any funds in the account referred to in paragraph 8 may apply to the repurchasing company for payment on production of-

(a)   the share certificate;

(b)   satisfactory evidence of his title; or

(c)   a declaration as to the loss or destruction of the share certificate together with a suitable indemnity.

PART 2 - Right Of Minority Shareholders To Be Bought Out By Repurchasing Company

10.   If not later than the expiration of the period within which the offer can be accepted, the total of-

(a)   the share holding of the relevant shareholder; and

(b)   the shares purchased by the repurchasing company,

is not less than nine-tenths in value of the shares, or shares in a class, as the case may be, of the repurchasing company as at the date on which the offer was made, the holder of any shares to which the offer relates (other than the relevant shareholder) may by letter addressed to the repurchasing company require it to purchase those shares.

11.   Where a shareholder exercises his rights under paragraph 10, the repurchasing company is entitled and bound to purchase the shares on the terms of the offer, or as may be agreed, or as the court may, on the application of the holder or the repurchasing company, order.

12.   Within 1 month of the expiration of the period within which the offer can be accepted the repurchasing company shall give notice in the specified form and in a manner specified by the Registrar to a person having rights under this Part calling on him to decide whether or not to exercise them, but he shall not be entitled to exercise them later than 2 months after the date on which the notice is given.

13.   Where an offer is such as to give the holder of shares a choice of terms, the repurchasing company shall in any notice given under paragraph 12 state the particulars of the choice and-

> *(a)*   that the holder of the shares may exercise that choice in making a requirement under this Part; and

> *(b)*   which terms are to be taken as applying if he makes such a requirement without exercising the choice,

and the terms of the offer mentioned in paragraph 11 shall be determined accordingly.

FOURTEENTH SCHEDULE

[ss. 98 & 360]

Table Of Fees To Be Paid To A Company

1. By a non-member for inspecting the register of members.......................... $1

2. By a member or non-member for making a copy of the register of members by photostatic means-

    (a)   per sheet or page of size equal to or smaller than
            210 mm x 330 mm.. 80 cents

    (b)   per sheet or page of size greater than
            210 mm x 330 mm.. $3

3. By a member or non-member for making a copy of the register by any other means-
    per record of each member..50 cents

FIFTEENTH SCHEDULE

[s. 168K]

Matters For Determining Unfitness Of Directors

PART I

Matters Applicable In All Cases

1. Any misfeasance or breach of any fiduciary or other duty by the director in relation to the company.

2. Any misapplication or retention by the director of, or any conduct by the director giving rise to an obligation to account for, any money or other property of the company.

3. The extent of the director's responsibility for any failure by the company to comply with any of the following provisions-

  (a)   section 81;

  (b)   section 95;

  (c)   section 96;

  (d)   section 107;

  (e)   section 108;

  (f)   section 109;

  (g)   section 119A;

  (h)   section 121;

  (i)   section 158; and

  (j)   section 158A.

4.   The extent of the director's responsibility for any failure by the directors of the company to comply with sections 122 and 129B.

PART II

Matters Applicable Where Company Has Become Insolvent

1. The extent of the director's responsibility for the causes of the company becoming insolvent.

2. The extent of the director's responsibility for any failure by the company to supply any goods or services which have been paid for (in whole or in part).

3. The extent of the director's responsibility for the company entering into any transaction or giving any preference, being a transaction or preference liable to be set aside under section 182 or 266.

4. The extent of the director's responsibility for any failure by the directors of the company to comply with section 241.

5. Any failure by the director to comply with any obligation imposed on him by or under any of the following provisions-

> *(a)*   section 190;

> *(b)*   section 211;

> *(c)*   section 228A;

> *(d)*   section 241;

(da)   section 274; and

> *(e)*   section 300A.

FOREIGN CORPORATIONS ORDINANCE

CHAPTER 437

FOREIGN CORPORATIONS

An Ordinance to provide for the corporate status in Hong Kong of bodies established or formerly established under the laws of certain territories outside Hong Kong.

Short title

1.   This Ordinance may be cited as the Foreign Corporations Ordinance.

Recognition of corporate status of certain foreign corporations

2.(1)   If at any time-

    (a)   a question arises as to whether a body, which purports to have or which appears to have lost corporate status under the laws of a territory outside Hong Kong which is not at that time a recognized State, should or should not be regarded as having legal personality as a body corporate under the law of Hong Kong; and

    (b)   it appears that the laws of that territory are at that time applied by a settled court system in that territory,

that question and any other material question relating to the body shall be determined (and account shall be taken of those laws) as if that territory were a recognized State.

(2)   For the purposes of subsection (1)-

    (a)   "a recognized State" is a territory which is recognized by Her Majesty's Government in the United Kingdom as a State;

    (b)   the laws of a territory which is so recognized shall be taken to include the laws of any part of the territory which are acknowledged by the federal or other central government of the territory as a whole; and

    (c)   a material question is a question (whether as to capacity, constitution or otherwise) which, in the case of a body

corporate, falls to be determined by reference to the laws of the territory under which the body is established.

(3)   Any registration or other thing done at a time before the coming into operation of this section shall be regarded as valid if it would have been valid at that time, had subsections (1) and (2) been in operation.

PARTNERSHIP ORDINANCE

(as amended)

CHAPTER 38

ARRANGEMENT OF SECTIONS

Dissolution of Partnership and Its Consequences

To codify the law relating to partnership.

Short title

1. This Ordinance may be cited as the Partnership Ordinance.

Interpretation

2. In this Ordinance, unless the context otherwise requires-

"business" includes every trade, occupation, or profession;

"court" includes every court and judge having jurisdiction in the case.

NATURE OF PARTNERSHIP

Definition of partnership

3.(1) Partnership is the relation which subsists between persons carrying on a business in common with a view of profit.

(2) But the relation between members of any company or association which is-

> *(a)* registered as a company under any Ordinance relating to the registration of joint-stock companies; or
>
> *(b)* formed or incorporated by or in pursuance of any other Ordinance, or any Act of Parliament, or letters patent, or Royal Charter,

is not a partnership within the meaning of this Ordinance.

Rules for determining existence of partnership

4. In determining whether a partnership does or does not exist, regard shall be had to the following rules-

> *(a)* joint tenancy, tenancy in common, joint property, common property, or part ownership does not of itself create a partnership as to anything so held or owned, whether the tenants or owners do or do not share any profits made by the use thereof;
>
> *(b)* the sharing of gross returns does not of itself create a

partnership, whether the persons sharing such returns have or have not a joint or common right or interest in any property from which or from the use of which the returns are derived;

(c) the receipt by a person of a share of the profits of a business is *prima facie* evidence that he is a partner in the business, but the receipt of such a share, or of a payment contingent on or varying with the profits of a business, does not of itself make him a partner in the business; and in particular-

(i) the receipt by a person of a debt or other liquidated amount, by instalments or otherwise, out of the accruing profits of a business does not of itself make him a partner in the business or liable as such;

(ii) a contract for the remuneration of a servant or agent of a person engaged in a business by a share of the profits of the business does not of itself make the servant or agent a partner in the business or liable as such;

(iii) a person being the widow or child of a deceased partner, and receiving by way of annuity a portion of the profits made in the business in which the deceased person was a partner, is not, by reason only of such receipt, a partner in the business or liable as such;

(iv) the advance of money by way of loan to a person engaged or about to engage in any business on a contract with that person that the lender shall receive a rate of interest varying with the profits, or shall receive a share of the profits arising from carrying on the business, does not of itself make the lender a partner with the person or persons carrying on the business or liable as such:

Provided that the contract is in writing and signed by or on behalf of all the parties thereto; and

(v) a person receiving, by way of annuity or otherwise, a portion of the profits of a business in consideration of the sale by him of the goodwill of the business is not, by reason only of such receipt, a partner in the business or

liable as such.

Postponement of rights of person lending or selling in

consideration of share of profits in case of insolvency

5. In the event of any person to whom money has been advanced by way of loan upon such a contract as is mentioned in section 4, or of any buyer of a goodwill in consideration of a share of the profits of the business, being adjudged a bankrupt, entering into an arrangement to pay his creditors less than twenty shillings in the pound, or dying in insolvent circumstances, the lender of the loan shall not be entitled to recover anything in respect of his loan, and the seller of the goodwill shall not be entitled to recover anything in respect of the share of profits contracted for, until the claims of other creditors of the borrower or buyer for valuable consideration in money or money's worth have been satisfied.

Meaning of firm and firm-name

6. Persons who have entered into partnership with one another are, for the purposes of this Ordinance, called collectively a firm, and the name under which their business is carried on is called the firm-name.

RELATIONS OF PARTNERS TO PERSONS DEALING WITH THEM

Power of partner to bind firm

7. Every partner is an agent of the firm and his other partners for the purpose of the business of the partnership; and the acts of every partner who does any act for carrying on in the usual way business of the kind carried on by the firm of which he is a member bind the firm and his partners, unless the partner so acting has in fact no authority to act for the firm in the particular matter, and the person with whom he is dealing either knows that he has no authority or does not know or believe him to be a partner.

Partners bound by acts on behalf of firm

8. An act or instrument relating to the business of the firm and done or executed in the firm-name, or in any other manner showing an intention to bind the firm, by any person thereto authorized, whether a partner or not, is binding on the firm and all the partners:

Provided that this section shall not affect any general rule of law relating to the execution of deeds or negotiable instruments.

Partner using credit of firm for private purposes

9. Where one partner pledges the credit of the firm for a purpose apparently not connected with the firm's ordinary course of business, the firm is not bound, unless he is in fact specially authorized by the other partners; but this section does not affect any personal liability incurred by an individual partner.

Effect of notice that firm will not be bound by acts of partner

10.   If it has been agreed between the partners that any restriction shall be placed on the power of any one or more of them to bind the firm, no act done in contravention of the agreement is binding on the firm with respect to persons having notice of the agreement.

Liability of partners

11.   Every partner in a firm is liable jointly with the other partners for all debts and obligations of the firm incurred while he is a partner; and after his death his estate is also severally liable in a due course of administration for such debts and obligations, so far as they remain unsatisfied but subject to the prior payment of his separate debts.

Liability of firm for wrongs

12.   Where, by any wrongful act or omission of any partner acting in the ordinary course of the business of the firm or with the authority of his co-partners, loss or injury is caused to any person not being a partner in the firm, or any penalty is incurred, the firm is liable therefor to the same extent as the partner so acting or omitting to act.

Misapplication of money or property received for or in custody of firm

13.   In the following cases, namely-

    (a)   where one partner, acting within the scope of his apparent authority, receives the money or property of a third person and misapplies it; and

    (b)   where a firm in the course of its business receives the money or property of a third person, and the money or property so received is misapplied by one or more of the partners while it is in the custody of the firm,

the firm is liable to make good the loss.

Liability for wrongs joint and several

14.   Every partner is liable jointly with his co-partners and also severally for everything for which the firm while he is a partner therein becomes liable under section 12 or 13.

Improper employment of trust property for partnership purposes

15.   If a partner, being a trustee, improperly employs trust property in the business or on the account of the partnership, no other partner is liable for the trust property to the persons beneficially interested therein:

Provided as follows-

> *(a)*   this section shall not affect any liability incurred by any partner by reason of his having notice of a breach of trust; and

> *(b)*   nothing in this section shall prevent trust money from being followed and recovered from the firm, if still in its possession or under its control.

Persons liable by "holding out"

16.   Every one who, by words spoken or written or by conduct, represents himself, or who knowingly suffers himself to be represented, as a partner in a particular firm is liable as a partner to any one who has, on the faith of any such representation, given credit to the firm, whether the representation has or has not been made or communicated to the person so giving credit by or with the knowledge of the apparent partner making the representation or suffering it to be made:

Provided that where, after a partner's death, the partnership business is continued in the old firm-name, the continued use of that name or of the deceased partner's name as part thereof shall not of itself make his executors or administrators, estate or effects, liable for any partnership debts contracted after his death.

Admissions and representations of partner

17.   An admission or representation made by any partner concerning the partnership affairs, and in the ordinary course of its business, is evidence against the firm.

Notice to acting partner to be notice to firm

18.   Notice to any partner who habitually acts in the partnership business of any matter relating to partnership affairs operates as notice to the firm, except in the case of a fraud on the firm committed by or with the consent of that partner.

Liabilities of incoming and outgoing partners

19.(1)   A person who is admitted as a partner into an existing firm does not thereby become liable to the creditors of the firm for anything done before he became a partner.

(2)   A partner who retires from a firm does not thereby cease to be liable for partnership debts or obligations incurred before his retirement.

(3)   A retiring partner may be discharged from any existing liabilities by an agreement to that effect between himself and the members of the firm as newly constituted and the creditors, and this agreement may be either express or inferred as a fact from the course of dealing between the creditors and the firm as newly constituted.

Revocation of continuing guarantee by change in firm

20. A continuing guarantee given either to a firm or to a third person in respect of the transactions of a firm is, in the absence of agreement to the contrary, revoked as to future transactions by any change in the constitution of the firm to which, or of the firm in respect of the transactions of which, the guarantee was given.

RELATIONS OF PARTNERS TO ONE ANOTHER

Variation by consent of terms of partnership

21. The mutual rights and duties of partners, whether ascertained by agreement or defined by this Ordinance, may be varied by the consent of all the partners, and such consent may be either express or inferred from a course of dealing.

Partnership property

22.(1) All property and rights and interests in property originally brought into the partnership stock or acquired, whether by purchase or otherwise, on account of the firm, or for the purposes and in the course of the partnership business, are called in this Ordinance partnership property, and must be held and applied by the partners exclusively for the purposes of the partnership and in accordance with the partnership agreement:

Provided that the legal estate or interest in any land which belongs to the partnership shall devolve according to the nature and tenure thereof and the general rules of law applicable thereto, but in trust, so far as necessary, for the persons beneficially interested in the land under this section.

(2) Where co-owners of an estate or interest in any land, not being itself partnership property, are partners as to profits made by the use of that land, and purchase other land out of the profits to be used in like manner, the land so purchased belongs to them, in the absence of any agreement to the contrary, not as partners, but as co-owners for the same respective estates and interests as are held by them in the land first mentioned at the date of the purchase.

Property bought with partnership money

23. Unless the contrary intention appears, property bought with money belonging to the firm is deemed to have been bought on account of the firm.

Conversion into personal estate of land held as partnership property

24. Where land or any interest therein has become partnership property, it shall, unless the contrary intention appears, be treated, as between the partners (including the representatives of a deceased partner), and also as between the heirs of a deceased partner and his executors or administrators, as personal and not real estate.

Procedure against partnership property for

partner's separate judgment debt

25.(1) A writ of execution shall not issue against any partnership property except on a judgment against the firm.

(2) The court or a judge may, on the application by summons of any judgment creditor of a partner, make an order charging that partner's interest in the partnership property and profits with payment of the amount of the judgment debt and interest thereon, and may, by the same or a subsequent order, appoint a receiver of that partner's share of profits (whether already declared or accruing), and of any other money which may be coming to him in respect of the partnership, and direct all accounts and inquiries, and give all other orders and directions, which might have been directed or given if the charge had been made in favour of the judgment creditor by the partner, or which the circumstances of the case may require.

(3) The other partner or partners shall be at liberty at any time to redeem the interest charged, or, in case of a sale being directed, to purchase the same.

(4) This section shall apply in the case of a cost-book company as if the company were a partnership within the meaning of this Ordinance.

Rules as to interests and duties of partners, subject to special agreement

26. The interests of partners in the partnership property, and their rights and duties in relation to the partnership, shall be determined, subject to any agreement, express or implied, between the partners, by the following rules-

> *(a)* all the partners are entitled to share equally in the capital and profits of the business, and must contribute equally towards the losses, whether of capital or otherwise, sustained by the firm;
>
> *(b)* the firm must indemnify every partner in respect of payments made and personal liabilities incurred by him-
>
> > **(i)** in the ordinary and proper conduct of the business of the firm; or

(ii) in or about anything necessarily done for the preservation of the business or property of the firm;

(c) a partner making, for the purposes of the partnership, any actual payment or advance beyond the amount of capital which he has agreed to subscribe, is entitled to interest at the rate of eight per cent per annum from the date of the payment or advance;

(d) a partner is not entitled, before the ascertainment of profits, to interest on the capital subscribed by him;

(e) every partner may take part in the management of the partnership business;

(f) no partner shall be entitled to remuneration for acting in the partnership business;

(g) no person may be introduced as a partner without the consent of all existing partners;

(h) any difference arising as to ordinary matters connected with the partnership business may be decided by a majority of the partners, but no change may be made in the nature of the partnership business without the consent of all existing partners; and

(i) the partnership books are to be kept at the place of business of the partnership (or the principal place, if there are more places than one), and every partner may, when he thinks fit, have access to and inspect and copy any of them.

Expulsion of partner

27. No majority of the partners can expel any partner, unless a power to do so has been conferred by express agreement between the partners.

Retirement from partnership at will

28.(1) Where no fixed term has been agreed upon for the duration of the partnership, any partner may determine the partnership at any time on giving notice of his intention to do so to all the other partners.

(2) Where the partnership has originally been constituted by deed, a notice in writing, signed by the partner giving it, shall be sufficient for this purpose.

Where partnership for term is continued over, continuance on old terms presumed

29.(1) Where a partnership entered into for a fixed term is continued after the term has expired, and without any express new agreement, the rights and duties of the partners remain the same as they were at the expiration of the term, so far as consistent with the incidents of a partnership at will.

(2) A continuance of the business by the partners or such of them as habitually acted therein during the term, without any settlement or liquidation of the partnership affairs, is presumed to be a continuance of the partnership.

Duty of partners to render accounts, etc.

30. Partners are bound to render true accounts and full information of all things affecting the partnership to any partner or his legal representatives.

Accountability of partners for private profits

31.(1) Every partner must account to the firm for any benefit derived by him, without the consent of the other partners, from any transaction concerning the partnership or from any use by him of the partnership property, name, or business connexion.

(2) This section applies also to transactions undertaken after a partnership has been dissolved by the death of a partner, and before the affairs thereof have been completely wound up, either by any surviving partner or by the representatives of the deceased partner.

Duty of partner not to compete with firm

32. If a partner, without the consent of the other partners, carries on any business of the same nature as and competing with that of the firm, he must account for and pay over to the firm all profits made by him in that business.

Rights of assignee of share in partnership

33.(1) An assignment by any partner of his share in the partnership, either absolute or by way of mortgage or redeemable charge, does not, as against the other partners, entitle the assignee, during the continuance of the partnership, to interfere in the management or administration of the partnership business or affairs, or to require any accounts of the partnership transactions, or to inspect the partnership books, but entitles the assignee only to receive the share of the profits to which the assigning partner would otherwise be entitled, and the assignee must accept the account of profits agreed to by the partners.

(2) In the case of a dissolution of the partnership, whether as respects all the partners or as respects the assigning partner, the assignee is entitled to receive the share of the partnership assets to which the assigning partner is entitled as between himself and the other partners, and, for the purpose of ascertaining that share, to an account as from the date of the dissolution.

DISSOLUTION OF PARTNERSHIP AND ITS CONSEQUENCES

Dissolution by expiration or notice

34.(1) Subject to any agreement between the partners, a partnership is dissolved-

> *(a)* if entered into for a fixed term, by the expiration of that term; or
>
> *(b)* if entered into for a single adventure or undertaking, by the termination of that adventure or undertaking; or
>
> *(c)* if entered into for an undefined time, by any partner giving notice to the other or others of his intention to dissolve the partnership.

(2) In the last-mentioned case the partnership is dissolved as from the date mentioned in the notice as the date of dissolution, or, if no date is so mentioned, as from the date of the communication of the notice.

Dissolution by bankruptcy, death, or charge

35.(1) Subject to any agreement between the partners, every partnership is dissolved as regards all the partners by the death or bankruptcy of any partner.

(2) A partnership may, at the option of the other partners, be dissolved if any partner suffers his share of the partnership property to be charged under this Ordinance for his separate debt.

Dissolution by illegality of partnership

36. A partnership is in every case dissolved by the happening of any event which makes it unlawful for the business of the firm to be carried on or for the members of the firm to carry it on in partnership.

Dissolution by the court

37. On application by a partner, the court may decree a dissolution of the partnership in any of the following cases-

> *(a)* when a partner is found lunatic by inquisition, or is shown, to the satisfaction of the court, to be of permanently unsound

mind, in either of which cases the application may be made as well on behalf of that partner by his committee, or next friend, or person having title to intervene as by any other partner;

(b)   when a partner, other than the partner suing, becomes in any other way permanently incapable of performing his part of the partnership contract;

(c)   when a partner, other than the partner suing, has been guilty of such conduct as, in the opinion of the court, regard being had to the nature of the business, is calculated to affect prejudicially the carrying on of the business;

(d)   when a partner, other than the partner suing, wilfully or persistently commits a breach of the partnership agreement or otherwise so conducts himself in matters relating to the partnership business that it is not reasonably practicable for the other partner or partners to carry on the business in partnership with him;

(e)   when the business of the partnership can only be carried on at a loss; and

(f)   whenever in any case circumstances have arisen which, in the opinion of the court, render it just and equitable that the partnership be dissolved.

Rights of persons dealing with firm against

apparent members of firm

38.(1) Where a person deals with a firm after a change in its constitution, he is entitled to treat all apparent members of the old firm as still being members of the firm until he has notice of the change.

(2)   An advertisement in the Gazette as to a firm whose principal place of business is in the Colony shall be notice as to persons who had not dealings with the firm before the date of the dissolution or change so advertised.

(3)   The estate of a partner who dies, or who becomes bankrupt, or of a partner who, not having been known to the person dealing with the firm to be a partner, retires from the firm, is not liable for partnership debts contracted after the date of the death, bankruptcy, or retirement respectively.

Right of partner to notify dissolution

39. On the dissolution of a partnership or retirement of a partner, any partner may publicly notify the same, and may require the other partner or partners to concur for that purpose in all necessary or proper acts, if any, which cannot be done without his or their concurrence.

Continuing authority of partners for purposes of winding-up

40. After the dissolution of a partnership, the authority of each partner to bind the firm, and the other rights and obligations of the partners, continue, notwithstanding the dissolution, so far as may be necessary to wind up the affairs of the partnership, and to complete transactions begun but unfinished at the time of the dissolution, but not otherwise:

Provided that the firm is in no case bound by the acts of a partner who has become bankrupt; but this proviso does not affect the liability of any person who has, after the bankruptcy, represented himself or knowingly suffered himself to be represented as a partner of the bankrupt.

Rights of partners as to application of partnership property

41. On the dissolution of a partnership, every partner is entitled, as against the other partners in the firm and all persons claiming through them in respect of their interests as partners, to have the property of the partnership applied in payment of the debts and liabilities of the firm, and to have the surplus assets after such payment applied in payment of what may be due to the partners respectively, after deducting what may be due from them as partners to the firm; and for that purpose any partner or his representatives may, on the termination of the partnership, apply to the court to wind up the business and affairs of the firm.

Apportionment of premium where partnership prematurely dissolved

42. Where one partner has paid a premium to another on entering into a partnership for a fixed term, and the partnership is dissolved before the expiration of that term otherwise than by the death of a partner, the court may order the repayment of the premium, or of such part thereof as it thinks just, having regard to the terms of the partnership contract and to the length of time during which the partnership has continued; unless-

> *(a)* the dissolution is, in the judgment of the court, wholly or chiefly due to the misconduct of the partner who paid the premium; or

> *(b)* the partnership has been dissolved by an agreement containing no provision for a return of any part of the premium.

Rights where partnership dissolved for fraud or misrepresentation

43.   Where a partnership contract is rescinded on the ground of the fraud or misrepresentation of one of the parties thereto, the party entitled to rescind is, without prejudice to any other right, entitled-

> *(a)*   to a lien on, or right of retention of, the surplus of the partnership assets, after satisfying the partnership liabilities, for any sum of money paid by him for the purchase of a share in the partnership and for any capital contributed by him, and is

> *(b)*   to stand in the place of the creditors of the firm for any payments made by him in respect of the partnership liabilities, and

> *(c)*   to be indemnified by the person guilty of the fraud or making the representation against all the debts and liabilities of the firm.

Rights of outgoing partner in certain cases to share

profits made after dissolution

44.   Where any member of a firm has died or otherwise ceased to be a partner, and the surviving or continuing partners carry on the business of the firm with its capital or assets without any final settlement of accounts as between the firm and the outgoing partner or his estate, then, in the absence of any agreement to the contrary, the outgoing partner or his estate is entitled, at the option of himself or his representatives, to such share of the profits made since the dissolution as the court may find to be attributable to the use of his share of the partnership assets, or to interest at the rate of eight per cent per annum on the amount of his share of the partnership assets:

Provided that where, by the partnership contract, an option is given to surviving or continuing partners to purchase the interest of a deceased or outgoing partner, and that option is duly exercised, the estate of the deceased partner or the outgoing partner or his estate, as the case may be, is not entitled to any further or other share of profits; but if any partner assuming to act in exercise of the option does not in all material respects comply with the terms thereof, he is liable to account under the preceding provisions of this section.

Retiring or deceased partner's share to be a debt

45.   Subject to any agreement between the partners, the amount due from surviving or continuing partners to an outgoing partner or the representatives of a deceased partner in respect of the outgoing or deceased partner's share is a debt accruing at the date of the dissolution or death.

Rules for distribution of assets on final settlement of accounts

46.   In settling accounts between the partners after a dissolution of partnership,the following rules shall, subject to any agreement, be observed-

> *(a)*   losses, including losses and deficiencies of capital, shall be paid first out of profits, next out of capital, and lastly, if necessary, by the partners individually in the proportion in which they were entitled to share profits; and

> *(b)*   the assets of the firm, including the sums, if any, contributed by the partners to make up losses or deficiencies of capital, shall be applied in the following manner and order-

>> **(i)**   in paying the debts and liabilities of the firm to persons who are not partners therein;

>> **(ii)**   in paying to each partner rateably what is due from the firm to him for advances as distinguished from capital;

>> **(iii)**   in paying to each partner rateably what is due from the firm to him in respect of capital; and

>> **(iv)**   the ultimate residue, if any, shall be divided among the partners in the proportion in which profits are divisible.

Saving for rules of equity and of common law

47.   The rules of equity and of common law applicable to partnership shall continue in force, except so far as they are inconsistent with the expressprovisions of this Ordinance.

LIMITED PARTNERSHIPS ORDINANCE

Arrangement of Sections

CHAPTER 37

LIMITED PARTNERSHIPS

To establish limited partnerships.

Short title

1.   This Ordinance may be cited as the Limited Partnerships Ordinance.

Interpretation

2.(1)   In this Ordinance, unless the context otherwise requires-

"firm", "firm name", and "business" have the same meanings as in the Partnership Ordinance (Cap. 38);

"general partner" means any partner who is not a limited partner as defined by this Ordinance.

"Registrar of Companies" means the officer appointed for the registration of companies under the Companies Ordinance (Cap. 32).

Application

(2) This Ordinance shall apply to such partnerships carrying on business in the Colony as in the opinion of the Registrar of Companies can properly be described as non-Chinese partnerships.

Definition and constitution of limited partnership

3.(1)   Limited partnerships may be formed in the manner and subject to the conditions by this Ordinance provided.

(2) A limited partnership shall not consist in any case of more than 20 persons, and must consist of one or more persons called general partners, who shall be liable for all debts and obligations of the firm, and one or more persons to be called limited partners, who shall at the time of entering into such partnership contribute thereto a sum or sums as capital or property valued at a stated amount,

and who shall not be liable for the debts or obligations of the firm beyond the amount so contributed.

(3) A limited partner shall not during the continuance of the partnership, either directly or indirectly, draw out or receive back any part of this contribution, and if he does so draw out or receive back any such part, shall be liable for the debts and obligations of the firm up to the amount so drawn out or received back.

(4)   A body corporate may be a limited partner.

Registration of limited partnership required

4. Every limited partnership must be registered as such in accordance with the provisions of this Ordinance, or in default thereof it shall be deemed to be a general partnership and every limited partner shall be deemed to be a general partner.

Modifications of general law in case of limited partnerships

5.(1)   A limited partner shall not take part in the management of the partnership business, and shall not have power to bind the firm:

Provided that a limited partner may by himself or his agent at any time inspect the books of the firm and examine into the state and prospects of the partnership business, and may advise with the partners thereon.

(2) If a limited partner takes part in the management of the partnership business, he shall be liable for all debts and obligations of the firm incurred while he so takes part in the management as though he were a general partner.

(3) A limited partnership shall not be dissolved by the death or bankruptcy of a limited partner, and the lunacy of a limited partner shall not be a ground for dissolution of the partnership by the court unless the lunatic's share cannot be otherwise ascertained and realized.

(4) In the event of the dissolution of a limited partnership its affairs shall be wound up by the general partners unless the court otherwise orders.

(5) Application to the court to wind up a limited partnership shall be by petition under the Companies Ordinance (Cap. 32), and the provisions of that Ordinance relating to the winding-up of companies by the court and of the rules made thereunder (including provisions as to fees) shall, subject to such modification (if any) as the Governor in Council may by rules provide, apply to the winding-up by the court of limited partnerships, with the substitution of general partners for directors.

(6) Subject to any agreement expressed or implied between the partners-

> *(a)*   any difference arising as to ordinary matters connected with the partnership business may be decided by a majority of the general partners;

> *(b)*   a limited partner may, with the consent of the general partners, assign his share in the partnership, and upon such an

> assignment the assignee shall become a limited partner with all

the rights of the assignor;

(c)   the other partners shall not be entitled to dissolve the partnership by reason of any limited partner suffering his share to be charged for his separate debt;

(d)   a person may be introduced as a partner without the consent of the existing limited partners;

(e)   a limited partner shall not be entitled to dissolve the partnership by notice.

Law as to private partnership to apply

6.   Subject to the provisions of this Ordinance, the Partnership Ordinance (Cap. 38), and rules of equity and of common law applicable to partnerships, except so far as they are inconsistent with the express provisions of the last- mentioned Ordinance, shall apply to limited partnerships.

Manner and particulars of registration

7.   The registration of a limited partnership shall be effected by sending by registered post or delivering to the Registrar of Companies a statement signed by the partners containing the following particulars-

(a)   the firm name;

(b)   the general nature of the business;

(c)   the principal place of business;

(d)   the full name of each of the partners;

(e)   the term, if any, for which the partnership is entered into, and the date of its commencement;

(f)   a statement that the partnership is limited, and the description of every limited partner as such;

(g)   the sum contributed by each limited partner, and whether paid in cash or how otherwise.

Registration of changes in partnerships

8.(1)   If during the continuance of a limited partnership any change is made or occurs in-

(a)   the firm name;

(b) the general nature of the business;

(c) the principal place of business;

(d) the partners or the name of any partner;

(e) the term or character of the partnership;

(f) the sum contributed by any limited partner;

(g) the liability of any partner by reason of his becoming a limited instead of a general partner or a general instead of a limited partner,

a statement, signed by the firm, specifying the nature of the change shall within 7 days be sent by post or delivered to the Registrar of Companies.

(2) If default is made in compliance with the requirements of this section, each of the general partners shall be liable on summary conviction to a fine of $50 for each day during which the default continues.

Advertisement of certain changes

9. Notice of any arrangement or transaction under which any person will cease to be a general partner in any firm and will become a limited partner in that firm, or under which the share of a limited partner in a firm will be assigned to any person, shall be forthwith advertised in the Gazette, and until notice of the arrangement or transaction is so advertised the arrangement or transaction shall, for the purposes of this Ordinance, be deemed to be of no effect.

10. *(Repealed)*

Making false returns to be misdemeanor

11. Any person who makes, signs, sends or delivers for the purpose of registration under this Ordinance any false statement known by him to be false or any incomplete statement known by him to be incomplete shall be guilty of an offence triable upon indictment.

Registrar to file statement and issue certificate of registration

12. On receiving any statement made in pursuance of this Ordinance and upon receipt of the prescribed fee payable in respect thereof, the Registrar of Companies shall cause such statement to be filed, and he shall send by registered post to the firm from whom such statement has been received a certificate of the registration thereof.

Register and index to be kept

13. The Registrar of Companies shall keep at his office, in proper books to be provided for the purpose, a register and an index of all the limited partnerships as aforesaid, and of all the statements registered in relation to such partnerships.

Inspection of statements registered

14.(1) Any person may, on payment of the fee specified in the Schedule-

(a) inspect the statements registered under this Ordinance; and

(b) require to be issued-

    (i) a certificate of the registration of any limited partnership;

    (ii) a copy of or extract from any registered statement;

    (iii) a copy of or extract from any registered statement duly certified by the Registrar of Companies or one of the deputy registrars.

(2) A certificate of registration, or a copy of or extract from any statement registered under this Ordinance, if duly certified to be a true copy under the hand of the Registrar of Companies or one of the deputy registrars (whom it shall not be necessary to prove to be the Registrar or deputy registrar) shall, in all legal proceedings, civil or criminal, and in all cases whatsoever, be received in evidence.

Rules

15. The Governor in Council may make rules providing for-

(a) *(Repealed)*

(b) the duties or additional duties to be performed by the Registrar of Companies;

(c) the performance by deputy registrars and other officers of acts by this Ordinance required to be done by the Registrar of Companies;

(d) forms; and

(e) generally the conduct and regulation of registration under this

Ordinance and any matters incidental thereto.

Fees

16.(1) There shall be paid to the Registrar of Companies in respect of the several matters set forth in the Schedule the several fees therein specified.

(2)   The Governor in Council may by order amend the Schedule.

SCHEDULE

Table of Fees Payable to The Registrar of Companies

Item	Matter in respect of which a fee is payable	Fees
		$

1.   For registering a limited partnership 285.00
        And, in addition, for every $1,000 or part of $1,000 of the
        sum contributed by each limited partner...................................8.00

2.   For registering a statement of any change within the meaning
        of section 8 occurring during the continuance of a limited
        partnership 22.00
        And, in addition-

        (a)   in the case of a statement of increase of the sum
                contributed by any limited partner: for every $1,000
                or part of $1,000 of such increase 8.00

        (b)   in the case of a statement specifying that a general
                partner or any other person has become a limited
                partner: for every $1,000 or part of $1,000 of
                the sum contributed by such limited partner.........................8.00

3.   For inspecting under section 14(1) any statement filed by the
        Registrar of Companies, for each inspection.............................11.00

4.   For issuing under section 14(1) a certificate of the registration
        of any limited partnership 38.00

5.   For issuing under section 14(1) a copy of or extract from
        any registered statement or part thereof by photostatic means,
        per sheet or page 4.00

6.   For issuing under section 14(1) a copy of or extract from
        any registered statement or part thereof where the copy or
        extract is made other than by photostatic means, per folio of
        100 words or part thereof of the first or top copy 4.00

        For each additional copy or extract after the first or top copy,
        per folio of 100 words or part thereof 2.00

7.   For certifying a copy of or extract from any registered statement...........75.00

HONG KONG

BUSINESS REGISTRATION ORDINANCE

(as amended)

CHAPTER 310

ARRANGEMENT OF SECTIONS

To amend the law relating to the registration of businesses in Hong Kong.

Short title

1.   This Ordinance may be cited as the Business Registration Ordinance.

Interpretation

2.(1)   In this Ordinance, unless the context otherwise requires-

"business" means any form of trade, commerce, craftsmanship, profession, calling or other activity carried on for the purpose of gain and also means a club;

"certification" means certification by the Commissioner under section 19;

"club" means any corporation or association of persons formed for the purpose of affording its members facilities for social intercourse or recreation and which-

> *(a)*   provides services for its members (whether or not for the purposes of gain); and

> *(b)*   has club premises of which its members have a right of exclusive use;

"Commissioner" means the Commissioner of Inland Revenue appointed under the Inland Revenue Ordinance (Cap. 112);

"duplicate" in relation to a branch registration certificate means a duplicate thereof issued under regulations made under section 14;

"levy" means the amount prescribed in item 3 of Schedule 2;

"place of business" includes in relation to -

> *(a)*   a company incorporated in Hong Kong under the Companies Ordinance (Cap. 32), its registered office; and

> *(b)*   a company to which Part XI of the Companies Ordinance (Cap. 32) applies, the address of any person whose name has been delivered to the Registrar of Companies for registration under that Part;

"prescribed branch registration fee" means the fee prescribed in item 2 of Schedule 2;

"prescribed business registration fee" means the fee prescribed in item l of schedule l;

"prescribed certification fee" means the fee for certification prescribed by regulations made under section 14;

"Protection of Wages on Insolvency Fund" means the fund deemed to be established and continued in existence under section 6 of the Protection of Wages on Insolvency Ordinance (Cap. 380);

"register" means the register of businesses kept by the Commissioner;

"valid branch registration certificate" means a certificate which is issued by the Commissioner under section 6, or any duplicate branch registration certificate, and which has not expired;

" valid business registration certificate" means a certificate which is issued by the Commissioner under section 6 or had been issued under the Business

Regulation Ordinance 1952 (14 of 1952), or any duplicate business registration certificate, and which has not expired.

(1A)   For the purposes of this Ordinance a company which is-

       (a)   incorporated in Hong Kong under the Companies Ordinance (Cap. 32) or to which Part XI of the Companies Ordinance (Cap. 32) applies; and

       (b)   not otherwise liable to be registered under this Ordinance,

shall be deemed to be a person carrying on business and shall be liable to be registered under this ordinance.

(2)   The duties imposed on and the powers granted to the Commissioner under this Ordinance may be carried out and exercised by any officer of the Inland Revenue Department authorized by the Commissioner either generally or particularly and subject to his instructions.

Persons answerable for doing all acts, etc. required to be done

3.(1)   The expression in this Ordinance "person carrying on business" means-

       (a)   in the case of a single person or corporate body, such person or corporate body;

       (b)   in the case of a business carried on by a partnership, all partners; and

     (c)   in the case of a business carried on by any other body of persons, the principal officers of such body:

Provided that no person who, for the purposes of section 8 of the Inland Revenue Ordinance (Cap. 112), is deemed to have an office or employment of profit shall by reason solely thereof be deemed to be carrying on business for the purposes of this Ordinance.

(2)   *(a)*   Any act or thing required by or under this Ordinance to be done by any person carrying on business shall, if such person is an incapacitated person or is absent, be deemed to be required to be done by the trustee of such incapacitated person or by the agent of such absent person, as the case may be.

           (b)   For the purposes of this subsection a person shall be deemed to be absent where, the Commissioner having posted a registered letter to such person's place of business, he fails to attend during ordinary office hours the place specified therein within 7 days of the posting of such letter.

(3)   Where the person carrying on business who is required under this Ordinance to do any act or thing is a company, the secretary, manager, or any director of such company shall be answerable for the doing of such act or thing.

(4)   Where the Commissioner serves notice on any person to the effect that he will be deemed to be a person carrying on business, he shall be so deemed unless within 1 month from the date of service of such notice he proves to the satisfaction of the Commissioner that he is not carrying on business.

(4A)   A notice under subsection (4) shall include a statement of the reasons for the service of the notice and where such person fails to satisfy the Commissioner as provided in that subsection he may appeal in the manner provided by section 17.

(5)   For the purposes of this section-

"agent" in relation to an absent person includes-

        (a)   the agent, attorney, factor, receiver, or manager in Hong Kong of such person; and

        (b)   any person in Hong Kong through whom such person is in receipt of any profits or income arising in or derived from the business;

"incapacitated person" means any minor, lunatic, idiot, or person of unsound mind;

"trustee" includes any trustee, guardian, curator, manager or other person having the direction, control, or management of any property on behalf of any person, but does not include an executor.

Official secrecy

4.(1) Except in the performance of his duties under the Inland Revenue Ordinance (Cap. 112) or under this Ordinance, every officer of the Inland Revenue Department shall preserve and aid in preserving secrecy with regard to all matters relating to the affairs of any person that may come to his knowledge in the performance of his duties under this Ordinance, and shall not communicate any such matter to any person other than the person to whom such matter relates or his executor or the authorized representative of such person or such executor, nor suffer or permit any person to have access to any records in the possession, custody or control of the Commissioner.

(2) Every officer of the Inland Revenue Department shall, before acting under this Ordinance, take and subscribe before a justice of the peace an oath or affirmation of secrecy in the prescribed form.

(3) Except as may be necessary for the purpose of carrying into effect the provisions of the Inland Revenue Ordinance (Cap. 112) or of this Ordinance, no officer of the Inland Revenue Department shall be required to divulge or communicate to any court any matter or thing coming to his notice in the performance of his duties under this Ordinance, or to produce in any court any document pertaining to such matter or thing other than a document required to be kept by the Commissioner under this Ordinance.

(4) Information given to the Commissioner under section 3(4) or 8(4) shall not be receivable in evidence against the person giving such information in any criminal proceeding save in a prosecution for an offence under section 15(1)(i).

(5) Notwithstanding the provisions of this section information received by officers of the Inland Revenue Department for the purposes of this Ordinance may, together with copies of returns, accounts or other documents used for such purposes be communicated to the Commissioner of Rating and Valuation, to the Collector of Stamp Revenue or to the Estate Duty Commissioner.

(6) Notwithstanding anything contained in this section, the Commissioner may permit the Director of Audit or any officer of that department duly authorized by the Director of Audit in that behalf to have such access to any records or documents as may be necessary for the performance of his official duties. The Director of Audit or any officer so authorized shall be deemed to be an officer of the Inland Revenue Department for the purpose of subsection (2).

Application for registration

5.(1) Every person carrying on any business not registered under the provisions of the Business Regulation Ordinance 1952, or commencing to carry on any business, or carrying on any business to which this Ordinance is made to apply shall make application to the Commissioner in the manner prescribed for the registration of that business.

(2) An application under subsection (1) shall be made within 1 month of the coming into operation of this Ordinance or of the commencement of such business or of the date on which this Ordinance is made to apply to a business, as the case may be, whichever is the later:

Provided that the Commissioner may extend such period if he sees fit.

(3) Every person carrying on business at a branch of a business to which subsection (1) applies shall, except where that branch has been registered under section 6(1A) before its amendment by the Business Registration (Amendment) Ordinance 1992, make application to the Commissioner in the manner prescribed for the registration of that branch.

(4) An application under subsection (3) shall be made within 1 month of the commencement of business at the branch, or the coming into operation of the Business Registration (Amendment) Ordinance 1992, as the case may be, whichever is the later.

(5) The Commissioner may extend the period referred to in subsection (4) if he thinks fit.

Registration of business and issue of business registration certificate

6.(1) Upon application being made under section 5(1) the Commissioner shall register each business in the manner prescribed.

(1A) Upon application being made under section 5(3) the Commissioner shall register each branch in the manner prescribed.

(2) Businesses registered under the Business Regulation Ordinance 1952 shall for the purposes of this Ordinance be deemed to have been registered under this section.

(3) Upon payment of the prescribed business registration fee and levy under section 7 or under an order of a magistrate under section 15 or upon the granting of an exemption under section 9 the Commissioner shall issue a business registration certificate in respect of each business.

(3A) Upon payment of the prescribed branch registration fee and the levy under section 7 or under an order of a magistrate made under section 15 the Commissioner shall issue a branch registration certificate in respect of the branch.

(4) The Commissioner shall not be required to register any business or branch of a business or to issue a business registration certificate or a branch registration certificate where application is made for registration-

> *(a)* of a business or a branch which is unlawful;

> *(b)* by a name which suggests that the business is incorporated with limited liability when it is not; or

> *(c)* by a name which suggests a connection with the Government or any public body when no such connection exists or has existed.

(4A) Where the Commissioner has decided not to register a business for the reason specified in subsection (4)(b) or (c), he shall notify the applicant in writing of his decision and the reason for it, and the applicant shall within 1 month of such notification make a new application to the Commissioner for registration under a different name.

(5) A business registration certificate and a branch registration certificate shall be valid until the expiry date endorsed thereon, and no such certificate shall be valid unless it bears an endorsement to the effect that-

> *(a)* the prescribed business registration fee or the prescribed branch registration fee, as the case may be, and the levy have been paid; or

> *(b)* in the case of a business registration certificate, no fee is ayable.

(6) The issue of a business registration certificate or a branch registration certificate in respect of any business shall not be deemed to imply that the requirements of any law in relation to such business or to the persons carrying on the same or employed therein have been complied with.

Payment of fees

7.(1) The Commissioner may by notice call upon any person-

> *(a)* carrying on business-

>> **(i)** in respect of which he is not in possession of a valid business registration certificate; or

>> **(ii)** which he intends to continue carrying on after the expiry of a valid business registration certificate in respect of such business,

to pay by a date specified in the notice the fee prescribed in item 1 of Schedule 1 and the levy; or

(b) carrying on business at a branch-

(i) in respect of which he is not in possession of a valid branch registration certificate; or

(ii) at which he intends to continue carrying on such business after the expiry of a valid branch registration certificate in respect of such branch,

to pay by a date specified in the notice the fee prescribed in item 2 of Schedule 2 and the levy,

except that in the case of a notice under paragraph (a)(ii) or (b)(ii) the date so specified shall be a date not earlier than the day following the date of expiry of the valid business registration certificate or branch registration certificate.

(2) Where on the expiry of-

(a) a business registration certificate issued in respect of a business; or

(b) a branch registration certificate issued in respect of a business carried on at a branch,

no notice under subsection (1)(a)(ii) or (b)(ii) has been received, every person carrying on such business shall so notify the Commissioner in writing within 1 month of such expiry.

(3) The Commissioner may by notice call upon any person who has carried on business, or carried on business at a branch, at any time during the 6 years immediately preceding the issue of the notice without being in possession of a valid business registration certificate or branch registration certificate (as the case may be) in respect of the business or branch, to pay by a date specified in the notice any fee or levy which would have been payable by him had the provisions of this Ordinance been complied with.

(4) Every person to whom a notice under subsection (1) or (3) is addressed shall comply with that notice on or before the date specified in the notice.

Information to be furnished

8.(1) Where there occurs any change in the particulars of a business as set out in the form of application for registration (whether such form was submitted under this Ordinance or under the Business Regulation Ordinance 1952), any person carrying on such business shall within 1 month of such change notify the Commissioner in writing thereof.

(2) Where a business ceases to be carried on, any person who was carrying on such business shall, within 1 month of the cessation, notify the Commissioner in writing thereof.

(2A) Where a person gives notice to the Commissioner in any return or other document submitted in accordance with the Inland Revenue Ordinance (Cap. 112) of any matter required to be notified under subsection (1) or (2), such notice shall be treated as notification by that person for the purposes of those subsections.

(3) *(Repealed)*

(4) To obtain full information for the purposes of this Ordinance, the Commissioner may give notice in writing to any person, appearing to him to be a person able to furnish information, requiring him-

    (a)   to supply such particulars as the Commissioner may deem necessary; or

    (b)   to attend at a time and place to be named by the Commissioner for the purpose of being examined respecting such information.

(5) In this section references to a business include references to a branchof that business.

Exemption from payments of fees for small businesses

9.(1) Upon application being made to the Commissioner in the manner prescribed, he shall exempt from the payment of the prescribed business registration fee and levy any person carrying on a business which is shown to his satisfaction -

    (a)   in the case of any business except a new business or any business whose profits are derived primarily from the sale of services to have total sales not exceeding an average of the sum specified in item 2 of Schedule 1; or

    (b)   in the case of any business whose profits are derived primarily from the sale of services except a new business, to have total sales or receipts not exceeding an average of the sum specified in item 3 of Schedule 1; or

    (c)   in the case of a new business is unlikely to have total sales or receipts, as the case may be, exceeding the averages referred to in paragraph (a) or (b) respectively.

The average in each case shall be based on the sales or receipts for the period of 6 months immediately preceding the making of the application or on such other information as the Commissioner may see fit to accept.

(2) An application under this section shall be made not later than-

> *(a)* 1 month before the date of expiry of a current business registration certificate; or

> *(b)* in the case of a new business 1 month after application for the registration of such business under section 5:

> Provided that the Commissioner may extend such period if he sees fit.

(3) Where an exemption is granted under subsection (1) the Commissioner shall issue a business registration certificate endorsed to that effect, and such exemption shall apply to the period of 12 months immediately following the date of commencement endorsed thereon or to such further period or periods not exceeding 3 years as the Commissioner may direct.

(4) The liability to pay the prescribed business registration fee and levy shall not be affected by the making of any application under subsection (1) unless the Commissioner shall otherwise direct, and where an exemption is granted after the prescribed business registration fee and levy have been paid such fee and levy shall be refunded.

(5) Where an exemption is not granted under subsection (1) the Commissioner shall so notify the person making the application therefor by notice in writing served either personally or by registered post and such person may appeal in the manner provided by section 17.

(5A) A notice under subsection (5) shall include a statement of the reasons why an exemption is not granted.

(6) This section shall not apply to any company which is incorporated in Hong Kong under the Companies Ordinance (Cap. 32) or to which Part XI of the Companies Ordinance (Cap. 32) applies.

Businesses carried on by same persons

10.(1) Where 2 or more businesses are carried on by the same person or persons the following provisions shall have effect-

> *(a)* *(Repealed)*

> *(b)* *(Repealed)*

> *(c)* no such business shall be entitled to exemption from payment

of fees under section 9.

(2) For the purposes of this section 2 or more businesses shall be deemed to be carried on by the same persons only where all such persons carrying on each of such businesses are identical and no other person carries on any of them.

Penalty for non-payment of fees

11.(1) Where any prescribed business registration fee or prescribed branch registration fee, as the case may be, and levy have not been paid within the time specified for payment under section 7 the Commissioner may by notice in writing to any person liable therefor order that the sum specified in item 1 of Schedule 2 be added to the fee and levy and recovered therewith.

(2) (*Repealed*)

(3) The Commissioner may in his absolute discretion-

(a) extend the time specified for the payment of any fee or levy; and

(b) remit any sum that he has ordered to be added to any fee or levy under subsection (l).

Display of certificates

12.(1) A valid business registration certificate shall be displayed at the place of business to which such certificate relates.

(2) A valid branch registration certificate shall be displayed at the branch to which such certificate relates.

Inspection

13.(1) The Commissioner may authorize in writing any public officer to be an inspector.

(2) Any business registration inspector and any inspector appointed under subsection (1) shall, for the purpose of ascertaining whether the provisions of this Ordinance are being complied with, have power at all reasonable times to enter any premises at which he had reason to believe any business is being carried on and there to make such examination and inquiry as may be necessary for such purpose.

Regulations

14.(1) The Governor in Council may by regulation provide for-

(a) the manner in which application for registration of a business and its branches shall be made;

(b)   the manner in which application for exemption from the payment of fees and levy shall be made;

(c)   the information to be furnished to the Commissioner;

(d)   the form of and the particulars to be entered in the register;

(e)   the forms of business registration certificates and branch registration certificates;

(f)   the issue of duplicate business registration certificates and duplicate branch registration certificates and the fees therefor;

(g)   the exemption of any person or category of persons or business either wholly or in part from the provisions of this Ordinance;

(h)   fees for certification and issue of documents;

(i)   generally for the carrying into effect of the provisions of this Ordinance in relation to any matter, whether similar or not to those in this subsection mentioned.

(2)   Any regulation made under this Ordinance may provide that a contravention thereof shall be an offence and may provide penalties for such offences not exceeding a fine of $1,000 and imprisonment for 6 months.

Offences

15.(1) Any person who-

(a)   acts under this Ordinance without taking an oath of secrecy as required by section 4(2);

(b)   acts contrary to the provisions of section 4(1) or to an oath taken under subsection (2) thereof;

(c)   fails to make any application required under section 5 or 6;

(d)   fails to pay any fee or levy required under section 7, and any sum added thereto under section 11;

(e)   fails to notify the Commissioner of the non-receipt of a notice by the Commissioner under section 7(2);

(f)   fails to furnish any information required under section 8 or to comply with any notice or requirement of the Commissioner under such section;

(g)   fails to display a valid business registration certificate or a valid branch registration certificate as required under section 12;

(h)   commits forgery of any document provision for which is made in this Ordinance;

(i)   makes any statement or furnishes any information to the Commissioner under the provisions of this Ordinance whether such statement or informatio is verbal or in writing, which is false in any material particular or by reason of the omission of any material particular and which he either knows or has reason to believe to be false;

(j)   or resists or obstructs an inspector in the performance of his duties under this Ordinance,

shall be guilty of an offence, and shall be liable to a fine of $5,000 and to imprisonment for 1 year.

(1A) Where a person is convicted of an offence under subsection (1)(c) or (f) the magistrate may, in addition to any penalty that may be imposed, order that the person shall within a time specified in the order do the act which he has failed to do, and a person who does not comply with such an order commits an offence and is liable to a fine of $5,000 and to imprisonment for I year.

(2)   *(a)*   Where any person is convicted of any of the acts or omissions set out in subsection (1)(c), (d), (e), (h) or (i) the magistrate shall, in addition to any penalty that may be imposed, make an order that such person shall pay to the Commissioner the fees and levy and any sums added thereto by the Commissioner, which would have been payable by him over the period of the preceding 6 years had the provisions of this Ordinance been complied with and had he committed no offence thereunder.

          (b)   In making an order for payment under paragraph (a) the magistrate-

               (i)   shall require that the amount payable in respect of the 2 years immediately preceding the date of conviction be paid forthwith to the Commissioner; and

               (ii)   may allow time for the payment of the remainder of the amount specified in the order in accordance with the provisions of section 41 of the Magistrates Ordinance (Cap. 227); and

(iii) may impose a period of imprisonment for non-payment of the amount specified in the order calculated in accordance with the provisions of section 68 of the Magistrates Ordinance (Cap. 227).

(c) For the purposes of this subsection, the Commissioner shall be deemed to have-

(i) called upon the person making application to pay the prescribed business registration fee or prescribed branch registration fee, as the case may be, and levy in accordance with section 7(1); and

(ii) imposed the sum to be added to the prescribed business registration fee or prescribed branch registration fee, as the case may be, and levy for the non-payment thereof in accordance with section 11.

(3)   No prosecution under this section shall be commenced save within 6 years from the date of the commission of the offence.

(4)   In this section, "forgery" has the meaning assigned to that term by Part IX of the Crimes Ordinance (Cap. 200).

Exemptions

16.   The provisions of this Ordinance shall not apply to-

(a) any charitable, ecclesiastical, or educational institution of a public character where-

(i) any profits derived from any trade or business of such \ institution are applied solely for its charitable, ecclesiastical or educational purposes and not expended substantially outside Hong Kong; and

(ii) either such trade or business is exercised in the course of the actual carrying out of the expressed object of such institution, or the work in connexion with such trade or

business is mainly carried out by persons for whose

benefit such institution is established;

(b) *(Repealed)*

(c) the business of-

(i) agriculture including market gardening;

(ii) breeding or rearing livestock including dairy farming, poultry including the production of eggs, bees including the production of honey, or fish including crustaceans and oysters;

(iii) fishing:

Provided that this paragraph shall not apply to any company which is incorporated in Hong Kong under the Companies Ordinance (Cap. 32) or to which Part XI of the Companies Ordinance (Cap. 32) applies;

(d) such other businesses as the Governor in Council may from time to time exempt by regulation made under section 14.

Appeals

17. Any person wishing to appeal under section 3(4A) or 9(5) may-

(a) in the case of an appeal under section 3(4A), within 28 days of the Commissioner informing him that the Commissioner is not satisfied that that person is not carrying on business; and

(b) in the case of an appeal under section 9(5), within 28 days of the Commissioner informing him that the Commissioner will not grant an exemption under section 9(1),

appeal to the Administrative Appeals Board.

Amendment of Schedules

18.(1) The Legislative Council may by resolution amend Schedule 1.

(2) The Financial Secretary may by order published in the Gazette amend Schedule 2.

Certification and issue of documents

19.(1) The Commissioner shall, upon request by any person and on payment of the prescribed fee, certify and issue to that person as soon as practicable-

(a)   a copy of a valid business registration certificate or a valid branch registration certificate;

(b)   an extract of any information on the register.

(1A)   An extract of information for the purpose of subsection (1)(b) may be supplied in any or any combination of the following-

(a)   where the information is contained in a form submitted to the Commissioner under this Ordinance or the Business Regulation Ordinance 1952, by supplying a copy of the form;

(b)   where the information is contained in a microfilm image of a form referred to in paragraph (a), by supplying a copy of the microfilm image in printed form; or

(c)   where the information is recorded on a computer, by supplying such information in printed form,

as the Commissioner sees fit, and where an extract of information is supplied under paragraph (c) the Commissioner's certificate for the purpose of subsection (1) shall state that the information supplied corresponds to information submitted to him under this Ordinance and shall state the section of the Ordinance pursuant to which the information was so submitted.

(2)   A copy of any certificate or extract of any information certified by the Commissioner to be a true copy or extract thereof shall be, in all legal proceedings civil or criminal, prima facie evidence as to the facts stated therein. Any such copy or extract purporting to be certified by the Commissioner shall be deemed, until the contrary is proved, to be certified by him.

(3)   In this section, "computer" means any device for storing, processing or retrieving information.

Service of notices

20.   Any notice to be served under this Ordinance may be served by delivering copy-

(a)   personally; or

(b)   by post addressed to the last known address of the business or residence of the person to be served.

Payment of levy

21.   The Commissioner shall, subject to any refund of levy to be made under this Ordinance, pay all moneys received from the levy to the Protection of Wages on Insolvency Fund.

SCHEDULE 1

	Item	Sum	Section

1. Fee payable on registration of business, or issue of further business registration certificate, where application for registration is made or certificate expires-

		Sum	Section
(a)	before 1 April 1974	$25	7
(b)	on or after 1 April 1974 and before 1 April 1975	$50	7
(c)	on or after 1 April 1975 and before 1 April 1979	$150	7
(d)	on or after 1 April 1979 and before 1 April 1983	$175	7
(e)	on or after 1 April 1983 and before 1 April 1985	$350	7
(f)	on or after 1 April 1985 and before 1 April 1987	$500	7
(g)	on or after 1 April 1987 and before 1 April 1989	$550	7
(h)	on or after 1 April 1989 and before 1 April 1990	$630	7
(i)	on or after 1 April 1990 and before 1 March 1993	$900	7
(j)	on or after 1 March 1993 and before 1 April 1994	$1,000 7	
(k)	on or after 1 April 1994	$2,000 7	

2. Average of total sales to exempt a business other than a new business, or a business whose profits derive primarily from the sale of services — $15,000 9(1)(a) per month

3. Average of total sales or receipts to exempt a business whose profits derive primarily from the sale of services — £4,000 9(1)(b) per month

SCHEDULE 2

[ss.2, 7, 11 & 18]

Item	Sum	Section

1. Penalty to be added for non-payment-

   (a)   of a prescribed branch registration fee and levy $71   11(1)

   (b)   of a prescribed business registration fee and levy $300   11(1)

2. Fee payable on registration of branch, or issue of further branch registration certificate, where application for registration is made or certificate expires on or after the coming into operation of the Business Registration (Amendment) Ordinance 1984 (56 of 1984) $73   7

3. Levy payable on registration of business or branch, issue of further business registration certificate or issue of further branch registration certificate $250   7

INTERPRETATION AND GENERAL CLAUSES ORDINANCE

CONTENTS

Part VIII - Public Officers and Public Contracts

Part IX - Crown, Governor and Governor In Council

Part X - Time and Distance

Part XI - Imperial Enactments

Part XII - (Repealed)

Part XIII - Miscellaneous

CHAPTER 1

INTERPRETATION AND GENERAL CLAUSES

To consolidate and amend the law relating to the construction, application and interpretation of laws, to make general provisions with regard thereto, to define terms and expressions used in laws and public documents, to make general provision with regard to public officers, public contracts and civil and criminal proceedings and for purposes and for matters incidental thereto or connected therewith.

PART I - Short Title And Application

Short title

1. This Ordinance may be cited as the Interpretation and General ClausesOrdinance.

Application

2.(1) Save where the contrary intention appears either from this Ordinance or from the context of any other Ordinance or instrument, the provisions of this Ordinance shall apply to this Ordinance and to any other Ordinance in force, whether such other Ordinance came or comes into operation before or after the commencement of this Ordinance, and to any instrument made or issued under or by virtue of any such Ordinance.

(1A) The inclusion of the substance of a provision of this Ordinance in another Ordinance does not imply the exclusion of the application of any other provision of this Ordinance to the other Ordinance.

(2) This Ordinance shall be binding on the Crown.

PART II - Interpretation of Words and Expressions

Interpretation of words and expressions

3. "act", when used with reference to an offence or civil wrong, includes a series of acts, an illegal omission and a series of illegal omissions;

"Administrative Appeals Board" means the Administrative Appeals Board established under the Administrative Appeals Board Ordinance (Cap. 442);

"adult" means a person who has attained the age of 18 years;

"aircraft" means any machine that can derive support in the atmosphere from the reactions of the air;

"alien" means a person who is neither a Commonwealth citizen nor a British protected person nor a citizen of the Republic of Ireland;

"amend" includes repeal, add to or vary and the doing of all or any of such things simultaneously or by the same Ordinance or instrument;

"arrestable offence" means an offence for which the sentence is fixed by law or for which a person may under or by virtue of any law be sentenced to imprisonment for a term exceeding 12 months, and an attempt to commit any such offence;

"Attorney General" means the Attorney General of Hong Kong;

"British citizen" means a person who has the status of a British citizen under the British Nationality Act 1981 (1981 c. 61 U.K.);

"British Dependent Territories citizen" means a person who has the status of a British Dependent Territories citizen under the British Nationality Act 1981 (1981 c.61 U.K.);

"British Overseas citizen" means a person who has the status of a British Overseas citizen under the British Nationality Act 1981 (1981 c.61 U.K.);

"British protected person" means a person who has the status of a British protected person under the British Nationality Act 1981 (1981 c.61 U.K.);

"British subject" means a person who has the status of a British subject under the British Nationality Act 1981 (1981 c. 61 U.K.);

"Chief Justice" means the Chief Justice of Hong Kong;

"Chief Secretary" means the Chief Secretary of Hong Kong;

"Clerk to the Executive Council" includes any person appointed by the Governor to be Deputy Clerk to the Executive Council;

"Clerk to the Legislative Council" means the Secretary General of the Legislative Council Secretariat appointed under section 15(1) of The Legislative Council Commission Ordinance (Cap. 443) and includes the

Deputy Secretary General and any Assistant Secretary General of the Legislative Council Secretariat;

"Colony" and "Hong Kong" mean the area of land and the area of Deep Bay and Mirs Bay lying within the boundaries specified in Schedule 2 and the territorial waters appertaining thereto;

"commencement", when used in relation to an Ordinance, or any part or provision thereof, means the date on which the Ordinance, part or provision came or comes into operation;

"committed for trial", when used in relation to any person, means-

(a)   committed to prison with a view to his being tried before the
         High Court; or

(b)   admitted to bail upon recognizances to appear and stand his trial
         before the High Court;

"common law" means the common law of England;

"Commonwealth citizen" means a person who has the status of a

Commonwealth citizen under the British Nationality Act 1981 (1981 c. 61 U.K.);

"consul" and "consular officer" mean any person, including the head of a consular post, recognized by the competent authority of the receiving state as entrusted in that capacity with the exercise of consular functions;

"contravene" in relation to any requirement or condition prescribed in any Ordinance or in any grant, permit, licence, lease or authority granted under or by virtue of any Ordinance includes a failure to comply with that requirement or condition;

"counsel" means a person admitted to practise as counsel before the High Court;

"court" means any court of the Colony of competent jurisdiction;
"Crown Agents" means the persons or body for the time being acting as Crown Agents for

Oversea Governments and Administrations;

"Crown lease" means any lease granted by the Crown, any instrument whereby the term of a Crown lease may have been extended or the provisions thereof varied and any agreement for a Crown lease;

"District Board" means a District Board established under the District Boards Ordinance (Cap.366);

"District Court" means the District Court of Hong Kong;

"District Judge" means a judge of the District Court;

"document" means any publication and any matter written, expressed or described upon any substance by means of letters, characters, figures or marks, or by more than one of these means;

"Executive Council" means the Executive Council of Hong Kong;

"export" means to take out or cause to be taken out of the Colony by air, land or water;

"Financial Secretary" means the Financial Secretary of Hong Kong and theSecretary for the Treasury;

"financial year" means the period from 1 April in any year to 31 March in the immediately succeeding year, both days inclusive;

"full age" means the age of 18 years;

"Gazette" means-

- *(a)* the Hong Kong Government Gazette and any supplement thereto;

- *(b)* the Hong Kong (British Military Administration) Gazette published on or between 12 October 1945 and 1 May 1946; and

- *(c)* any Special Gazette or Gazette Extraordinary;

"general revenue" means the general revenue of Hong Kong;

"Government" means the Government of Hong Kong;

"Government Printer" means the Government Printer of Hong Kong and any other printer authorized by or on behalf of the Governor to print any Ordinance or any other document of the Government;

"Governor" means-

(a)   the Governor of Hong Kong;

(b)   the Acting Governor;

(c)   to the extent to which a deputy to the Governor is authorized to perform on behalf of the Governor any functions of the Governor, the Deputy to the Governor; and

(d)   where the Governor of Hong Kong is not intended, the Governor General, Governor, administrator or other officer for the time being administering the government of any British possession;

"Governor in Council", "Governor in Executive Council" and "Governor with the advice of the Executive Council" mean the Governor acting after consultation with the Executive Council in accordance with Royal Instructions but not necessarily in such Council assembled;

"Harbour" means the waters of the Colony within the boundaries specified in Schedule 3;

"health officer" means-

(a)   the Director, Deputy Director and Assistant Director of Health;

(b)   any person appointed as a health officer by the Governor; and

(c)   any person for the time being performing the duties of a health officer under any Ordinance;

"immovable property" means-

(a)   land, whether covered by water or not;

(b)   any estate, right, interest or easement in or over any land; and

(c)   things attached to land or permanently fastened to anything attached to land;

"imperial enactment" means-

(a)   any Act of Parliament;

(b)   any Order in Council;

(c)   any Letters Patent or Royal Instructions; and

(d)   any rule, regulation, proclamation, order, notice, rule of court, by-law or other instrument made under or by virtue of any Act, Order in Council, Letters Patent or Royal Instructions;

"import" means to bring or cause to be brought into the Colony by air, land or water;

"infant" and "minor" mean a person who has not attained the age of 18 years;

"instrument" includes any publication in the Gazette having legal effect;

"judge" means the Chief Justice, a Justice of Appeal, a judge of the High Court of Justice, a recorder of the High Court of Justice and a deputy judge of the High Court of Justice;

"justice" and "justice of the peace" mean a person appointed to be a justice of the peace for the Colony either by the Governor or by or under any Ordinance;

"Kowloon" means the area specified in Schedule 4;

"Lands Tribunal" means the Lands Tribunal established under section 3 of the Lands Tribunal Ordinance (Cap. 17);

"law" means any law for the time being in force in, having legislative effect in, extending to, or applicable in, the Colony;

"Legislative Council" means the Legislative Council of Hong Kong;

"magistrate" means-

(a)   any person appointed to be a permanent or special magistrate under the Magistrates Ordinance (Cap. 227); and

(b)   2 justices of the peace sitting together, to whom section 7(2) of the Magistrates Ordinance (Cap. 227) applies;

"master", when used with reference to a vessel, means the person (except a pilot) having for the time being command or charge of the vessel;

"medical practitioner", "registered medical practitioner" and any words importing that a person is recognized by any Ordinance to be a medical practitioner in Hong Kong or a member of the medical profession in Hong Kong, mean a person duly registered as, or deemed to be registered as, a medical practitioner under the Medical Registration Ordinance (Cap. 161);

"month" means calendar month;

"movable property" means property of every description except immovable property;

"New Kowloon" means the area specified in Schedule 5;

"New Territories" means the territories leased to Great Britain by the Emperor of China under the Convention dated 9 June 1898;

"oath" and "affidavit" include, in the case of persons allowed or required by law to affirm instead of swearing, affirmation; and "swear" in the like case includes affirm;

"occupy" includes use, inhabit, be in possession of or enjoy the land or premises to which the word relates, otherwise than as a mere servant or for the mere purpose of the care, custody or charge thereof;

"offence" includes any crime and any contravention or other breach of, or failure to comply with, any provision of any Ordinance, for which a penalty is provided;

"official languages" means the English language and the Chinese Language, and a reference to an "official language" shall be construed as a reference to the English language or the Chinese language as the case may be;

"Order in Council" means an order made by Her Majesty in Her Privy Council;

"Ordinance" and "enactment" mean-

> *(a)* any Ordinance enacted by the Governor by and with the advice and consent of the Legislative Council;
>
> *(b)* any proclamation made by the British Military Administration on or between 1 September 1945 and I May 1946; and
>
> *(c)* any subsidiary legislation made under any such Ordinance or proclamation;

"Parliament" and "Imperial Parliament" mean the Parliament of England, the Parliament of Great Britain and the Parliament of the United Kingdom;

"per cent", when used in relation to a rate of interest payable in any circumstances, means the rate of interest specified payable in respect of a year, unless it is expressly provided that it is payable in respect of any other period;

"person" includes any public body and any body of persons, corporate or unincorporate, and this definition shall apply notwithstanding that the word "person" occurs in a provision creating or relating to an offence or for the recovery of any fine or compensation;

"pier" includes every quay, wharf or jetty of whatever description connected to and having direct access to the shore and used or intended to be used for the purposes of a pier, quay, wharf or jetty;

"police officer" and terms or expression referring to ranks in the Royal Hong Kong Police Force shall bear the meanings respectively assigned to them by the Police Force Ordinance (Cap.232);

"power" includes any privilege, authority and discretion;

"prescribed" and "provided", when used in or with reference to any Ordinance, mean prescribed or provided by that Ordinance or by subsidiary legislation made under that Ordinance;

"prison" means any place or building or portion of a building set apart for the purpose of a prison under any Ordinance relating to prisons;

"Privy Council" means the Lords and others for the time being of Her Majesty's Most Honourable Privy Council;

"property" includes-

> *(a)* money, goods, choses in action and land; and

> *(b)* obligations, easements and every description of estate, interest and profit, present or future, vested or contingent, arising out of or incident to property as defined in paragraph (a) of this

> definition;

"public" includes any class of the public;

"publication" means-

(a)   all written and printed matter;

(b)   any record, tape, wire, perforated roll, cinematograph film or other contrivance by means of which any words or ideas may be mechanically, electronically or electrically produced, reproduced, represented or conveyed;

(c)   anything whether of a similar nature to the foregoing or not, containing any visible representation, or by its form, shape, or in any manner, capable of producing, reproducing, representing or conveying words or ideas; and

(d)   every copy and reproduction of any publication as defined in paragraphs (a), (b) and (c) of this definition;

"public body" includes-

(a)   the Executive Council;

(b)   the Legislative Council;

(c)   the Urban Council;

(ca)   any District Board;

(cb)   the Regional Council;

(d)   any other urban, rural or municipal council;

(e)   any department of the Government; and

(f)   any undertaking by or of the Government;

"public holiday" and "general holiday" mean any day which is a general holiday by virtue of any provision of the Holidays Ordinance (Cap. 149);

"public office" means any office or employment the holding or discharging of which by a person would constitute that person a public officer;

"public officer" and "public servant" mean any person holding an office of emolument under the Crown in right of the Government of Hong Kong, whether such office be permanent or temporary;

"public place" means-

    (a)   any public street or pier, or any public garden; and

    (b)   any theatre, place of public entertainment of any kind, or other place of general resort, admission to which is obtained by payment or to which the public have or are permitted to have access;

"public seal" means the public seal of Hong Kong;

"Regional Council" means the Regional Council established by the Regional Council Ordinance (Cap.385);

"registered", when used with reference to a document, means registered under the provisions of any law applicable to the registration of such a document;

"Registrar of the Supreme Court" means the Registrar of the Supreme Court and any Deputy or Assistant Registrar of the Supreme Court;

"repeal" includes rescind, revoke, cancel or replace;

"rules of court", when used in relation to any court, means rules made by the authority having for the time being power to make rules and orders regulating the practice and procedure of such court;

"Secretary of State" means one of Her Majesty's Principal Secretaries of State for the time being;

"sell" includes exchange and barter;

"ship" includes every description of vessel used in navigation not exclusively propelled by oars;

"sign" includes, in the case of a person unable to write, the affixing or making of a seal, mark, thumbprint or chop;

"solicitor" means a person admitted to practise as a solicitor before the High Court;

"statutory declaration", if made-

    (a)   in Hong Kong, means a declaration under the *Repealed* Statutory Declarations Ordinance or the Oaths and Declarations Ordinance (Cap.11);

(b)   in any part of the Commonwealth except the Colony, means a declaration made before a justice of the peace, notary public, or other person having authority therein under any legal provision for the time being in force in such part to take or receive a declaration;

(c)   in any other place, means a declaration before a British consul or person having authority under any Act for the time being in force to take or receive a declaration;

"street" and "road" mean-

(a)   any highway, street, road, bridge, thoroughfare, parade, square, court, alley, lane, bridle-way, footway, passage, tunnel; and

(b)   any open place, whether situate on land leased from the Crown or not, used or frequented by the public or to which the public have or are permitted to have access;

"subsidiary legislation" and "regulations" mean any proclamation, rule, regulation, order, resolution, notice, rule of court, bylaw or other instrument made under or by virtue of any Ordinance and having legislative effect;

"summary conviction" means a summary conviction by a magistrate in accordance with the provisions of the Magistrates Ordinance (Cap. 227);

"Supreme Court" means the Supreme Court of Hong Kong;

"surname" includes a clan or family name;

"territorial waters" means such part of the sea adjacent to the coast of the Colony as is deemed by international law to constitute the territorial waters of Hong Kong;

"treaty" means a treaty, convention or agreement made with a foreign state, and any protocol or declaration attached thereto or independent thereof but referring thereto;

"triable summarily" means triable by a magistrate, in accordance with the of the Magistrates Ordinance (Cap. 227);

"trust territory" means a territory administered by the Government of any part of Her Majesty's dominions under the trusteeship system of the United Nations;
"United Kingdom" means-

(a)   the United Kingdom of Great Britain and Northern Ireland; or

(b)   when used with reference to citizenship or nationality, Great Britain, Northern Ireland, the Channel Islands and the Isle of Man;

"Urban Council" means the Urban Council established by the Urban Council Ordinance (Cap. 101);

"vessel" means any ship or boat and any description of vessel used in navigation;

"Victoria" means the area within the boundaries specified in Schedule 1;

"waters of the Colony", "waters of Hong Kong and "Colonial waters" mean -

(a)   all waters, whether navigable or not, included in the Colony; and

(b)   territorial waters;

"words" includes figures and symbols;

"writing" and "printing" include writing, printing, lithography, photography, typewriting and any other mode of representing words in a visible form;

"year" means a year according to the Gregorian calendar;

"years of age" and words of a like meaning, when used with reference to the age of any person, mean years of age according to the English reckoning of ages.

Definition of "Commonwealth"

4.   "Commonwealth" means collectively-

(a)   the United Kingdom;

(b)   the Channel Islands;

(c)   the Isle of Man;

(d)   the countries mentioned in Schedule 3 to the British Nationality Act 1981 (1981 c. 61 U.K.);

(e)   the British Dependent Territories mentioned in Schedule 6 to the British Nationality Act 1981 (1981 c. 61 U.K.).

Grammatical variations and cognate expressions

5. Where any word or expression is defined in any Ordinance, such definition shall extend to the grammatical variations and cognate expressions of such word or expression.

References to Government property

6. Where reference is made in any Ordinance to property and the expressions used in relation thereto imply that such property is owned by, or belongs to, the Government, or convey a similar meaning, such reference shall be deemed to refer to such of the property of the Crown of the description mentioned as has been appropriated to the use of the Government.

Provisions for gender and number

7.(1) Words and expressions importing the masculine gender include the feminine and neuter genders.

(2) Words and expressions in the singular include the plural and words and expressions in the plural include the singular.

Service by post

8. Where any Ordinance authorizes or requires any documents to be served or any notice to be given by post or by registered post, whether the expression "serve" or "give" or "send" or any other expression is used, the service or notice shall be deemed to be effected by properly addressing, pre-paying the postage thereon and dispatching it by post or by registered post, as the case may be, to the last known postal address of the person to be served or given notice, and, unless the contrary is proved, such service or notice shall be deemed to have been effected at the time at which the document or notice would be delivered in the ordinary course of post.

Chinese words and expressions

9. Chinese words and expressions in the English text of an Ordinance shall be construed according to Chinese language and custom.

References to pounds sterling

10. The amount of Hong Kong dollars equivalent to an amount of pounds sterling referred to in any law shall be calculated at the merchant selling rate of The Hong Kong Association of Banks at the close of business on the relevant day.

PART IIA - General Provisions as To Laws in Both Official Languages

Application of Part IIA

10A. This Part shall apply to an Ordinance-

      (a)   enacted in both official languages; or

      (b)   in respect of which an authentic text is published under section 4B of the Official Languages Ordinance (Cap. 5).

Construction of Ordinances in both official languages

10B.(1) The English language text and the Chinese language text of an Ordinance shall be equally authentic, and the Ordinance shall be construed accordingly.

(2) The provisions of an Ordinance are presumed to have the same meaning in each authentic text.

(3) Where a comparison of the authentic texts of an Ordinance discloses a difference of meaning which the rules of statutory interpretation ordinarily applicable do not resolve, the meaning which best reconciles the texts, having regard to the object and purposes of the Ordinance, shall be adopted.

Expressions of English law

10C.(1) Where an expression of the common law is used in the English language text of an Ordinance and an analogous expression is used in the Chinese language text thereof, the Ordinance shall be construed in accordance with the common law meaning of that expression.

(2) In this section "common law" means the common law and rules of equity in force in Hong Kong.

Name of statutory body corporate

10D. Where an Ordinance establishes a body corporate and in the English language text and Chinese language text of that Ordinance the name of the body corporate is in the form only of the language of that text, the name of the body corporate shall consist of the form of its name in each of the texts of the Ordinance.

Words etc. in the official languages may be declared as equivalents

10E.(1) The Governor in Council may, by notice in the Gazette, declare that any word, expression, office, title (including the short title of any Ordinance), citation or thing therein specified in one official language shall, in relation to the interpretation of an Ordinance, be the equivalent of any word, expression, office, title, citation or thing therein specified in the other official language.

(2) No declaration shall be made under this section unless a draft of the notice has been laid before and approved by resolution of the Legislative Council, and section 34 of this Ordinance shall not apply in relation to any such declaration.

PART III - General Provisions as To Ordinances

Ordinance to be public Ordinance

11. Every Ordinance shall be a public Ordinance and shall be judicially noticed as such.

12. (*Repealed*)

Citation of Ordinance

13.(1) Where any Ordinance is referred to, it shall be sufficient for all purposes to cite such Ordinance by-

> (*a*)   the title, short title or citation thereof,

> (*b*)   its number among the Ordinances of the year in which it was enacted; or

> (*c*)   any chapter number lawfully given to it under the authority of any Ordinance providing for the issue of a revised or other edition of the laws of Hong Kong.

(2)   Any reference made to any Ordinance, in accordance with the provisions of subsection (1), may be made according to the title, short title, citation, number or chapter number used in copies of Ordinances printed by the Government Printer.

14. (*Repealed*)

Reference to Ordinance as amended

15.(1) Where in any Ordinance a reference is made to another Ordinance, such reference shall be deemed to include a reference to such last mentioned Ordinance as the same may from time to time be amended.

(2) Where any Ordinance repeals and re-enacts, with or without modification, any provision of a former Ordinance, references in any other Ordinance to the provision so *Repealed* shall be construed as references to the provision so re-enacted.

Citation of part of Ordinance

16. In any Ordinance a description or citation of a portion of an Ordinanceshall be construed as including the word, section or other part mentioned or referred to as forming the beginning and as forming the end of the portion comprised in the description or citation.

Construction of reference to Ordinance, section, etc.

17.(1) Any reference in any Ordinance to "any Ordinance" or to "any enactment" shall be construed as a reference to any Ordinance for the time being in force.

(2) Where in an Ordinance there is a reference to a section or other division by number, letter or combination of number and letter, and not in conjunction with the title or short title of any other Ordinance, the reference shall be construed as a reference to the section or other division of that number, letter or combination in the Ordinance in which the reference occurs.

(3) Where in a section of an Ordinance there is a reference to a subsection or other division by number, letter or combination of number and letter, and not in conjunction with the number of a section of that or any other Ordinance, the reference shall be construed as a reference to the subsection or other division of that number, letter or combination in the section in which the reference occurs.

(4)-(5) (*Repealed*)

Marginal notes and section headings

18.(1) Where any section, subsection or paragraph of any Ordinance is taken verbatim from, or is substantially similar to, a section, subsection or paragraph of any imperial enactment, there may be added as a note to the section, subsection or paragraph of the Ordinance a reference, in abbreviated form, to such section, subsection or paragraph of the imperial enactment.

(2) A reference added under subsection (1) shall not have any legislative effect and shall not in any way vary, limit or extend the interpretation of any Ordinance.

(3) A marginal note or section heading to any provision of any Ordinance shall not have any legislative effect and shall not in any way vary, limit or extend the interpretation of any Ordinance.

General principles of interpretation

19. An Ordinance shall be deemed to be remedial and shall receive such fair, large and liberal construction and interpretation as will best ensure the attainment of the object of the Ordinance according to its true intent, meaning and spirit.

PART IV - Commencement, Disallowance, Amendment And Repeal

Commencement, etc., of Ordinance

20.(1) An Ordinance shall be published in the Gazette.

(2) An Ordinance comes into operation-

(a) at the beginning of the day on which it is published; or

(b) if provision is made for it to commence on another day, at the beginning of that other day.

(3) If an Ordinance is to commence on, or be repealed from, a day to be notified in the Gazette, the notice may fix different days for different provisions to commence or from which different provisions are to be repealed and different notices may fix different days for different provisions.

Disallowance

21.(1) Where any Ordinance is disallowed by Her Majesty, such disallowance shall be notified by the Governor by notice in the Gazette; and from and after the date of publication of such notice the Ordinance shall cease to have effect.

(2) Where notice of disallowance of any Ordinance is notified in accordance with the provisions of subsection (1), the provisions of section 23 shall apply in respect of such disallowance as if the words "disallowance" and "disallowed" were substituted therein for the words "repeal" and "repealed" respectively.

(3) Any Ordinance repealed or amended by any Ordinance disallowed shall revive and continue in force in its original form with effect from the date of publication of the notice referred to in subsection (1).

22. (*Repealed*)

Effect of repeal generally

23. Where an Ordinance repeals in whole or in part any other Ordinance, the repeal shall not-

(a) revive anything not in force or existing at the time at which the repeal takes effect;

(b) affect the previous operation of any Ordinance so repealed or anything duly done or suffered under any Ordinance so repealed;

(c)   affect any right, privilege, obligation or liability acquired, accrued or incurred under any Ordinance so repealed;

(d)   affect any penalty, forfeiture or punishment incurred in respect of any offence committed against any Ordinance so repealed; or

(e)   affect any investigation, legal proceeding or remedy in respect of any such right, privilege, obligation, liability, penalty, forfeiture or punishment as aforesaid; and any such investigation, legal proceeding or remedy may be instituted, continued or enforced, and any such penalty, forfeiture or punishment may be imposed, as if the repealing Ordinance had not been passed.

Repealed Ordinance not revived

24.   Where any Ordinance repealing in whole or in part any former Ordinance is itself repealed, such last repeal shall not revive the Ordinance or provision previously repealed, unless provision is made to that effect.

Repeal and substitution

25.   Where any Ordinance repeals in whole or in part any other Ordinance and substitutes other provisions therefor, the repealed Ordinance shall remain in force until the substituted provisions come into operation.

26.   (*Repealed*)

Effect of expiry of Ordinance

27.   Upon the expiry or lapse of any Ordinance, the provisions of section 23 shall apply as if such Ordinance had been repealed.

PART V - Subsidiary Legislation

General provision with regard to power to make subsidiary legislation

28.(1) Where an Ordinance confers power on a person to make subsidiary legislation, the following provisions shall have effect with reference to the subsidiary legislation-

(a)   when any subsidiary legislation purports to be made in exercise of a particular power or powers, it shall be deemed also to be made in exercise of all other powers that enable its making;

(b)   no subsidiary legislation shall be inconsistent with the provisions of any Ordinance;

(c)   subsidiary legislation may at any time be amended by the same person and in the same manner by and in which it was made;

(ca)   where the person referred to in paragraph (c) has been replaced wholly or in part by another person, the power conferred by paragraph (c) may be exercised by the other person for all matters in his jurisdiction as if he were the original person;

(d)   where any Ordinance confers power on any person to make subsidiary legislation for any general purpose, and also for any incidental special purpose, the enumeration of the special purposes shall not be deemed to derogate from the generality of the powers conferred with reference to the general purpose;

(e)   subsidiary legislation may provide that a contravention or breach of the subsidiary legislation is an offence punishable on summary conviction by such fine not exceeding $5,000 or by such term of imprisonment not exceeding 6 months as may be specified in the subsidiary legislation or by both such fine and imprisonment;

(f)   subsidiary legislation may amend any forms contained in the Ordinance under which such subsidiary legislation is made and may prescribe new forms.

(g)   (*Repealed*)

(2)   Subsidiary legislation shall be published in the Gazette.

(3) Subsidiary legislation comes into operation-

    (a)   at the beginning of the day on which it is published; or

    (b)   if provision is made for it to commence on another day, at the beginning of that other day.

(4)   A person who makes subsidiary legislation may provide for the subsidiary legislation to commence on a day to be fixed by notice to be given by him or by some other person designated in the subsidiary legislation.

(5)   If subsidiary legislation is to commence on, or be repealed from, a day to be notified in the Gazette, the notice may fix different days for different provisions to commence or from which different provisions are to be repealed and different notices may fix different days for different provisions.

Fees and charges

29.(1A)   Where an Ordinance confers a power on a person to make subsidiary legislation, the subsidiary legislation may impose a fee or charge for any thing in it or the ordinance.

(1)   Where provision is made by any subsidiary legislation in respect of fees or other charges, such subsidiary legislation may provide for all or any of the following matters-

    (a)   specific fees or charges;

    (b)   maximum or minimum fees or charges;

    (c)   maximum and minimum fees or charges;

    (d)   the payment of fees or charges either generally or under specified conditions or in specified circumstances;

    (e)   the exemption of any person or class of persons from the payment of fees or charges; and

    (f)   the reduction, waiver or refund, in whole or in part, of any such fees or charges, either upon the happening of a certain event or in the discretion of a specified person.

(2)   Where any reduction, waiver or refund, in whole or in part, of any fee or charge is provided for by any subsidiary legislation, such reduction, waiver or refund may be expressed to apply or be applicable either generally or specially-

(a)   in respect of certain matters or transactions or classes of matters or transactions;

(b)   in respect of certain documents or classes of documents;

(c)   in respect of the occurrence or the termination of any event;

(d)   in respect of certain persons or classes of persons; or

(e)   in respect of any combination of such matters, transactions, documents, events or persons,

and may be expressed to apply or be applicable subject to such conditions as may be specified in the subsidiary legislation or in the discretion of any person specified therein.

Variation of certain fees and charges

29A.(1)   Where the amount of any fee or charge is for the time being specified in, or otherwise fixed or determined by, subsidiary legislation made by the Governor in Council, subject to subsection (2), the Financial Secretary may by similar subsidiary legislation increase or decrease, or otherwise vary, the amount of the fee or charge.

(2)   (a)   The Governor in Council may by a direction in writing direct the Financial Secretary to exercise, as regards fees or charges specified in the direction, a power conferred on him by subsection (1) either-

        (i)   only with the prior approval of the Governor in Council; or

        (ii)   so as not to exceed limits specified in the direction; or

        (iii)   only in some other manner so specified.

    (b)   For so long as a direction under this subsection is in force the Financial Secretary shall comply with it.

(3)   The powers conferred by subsection (1) are in addition to, and are not in substitution for, any power exercisable by the Governor in Council in relation to fees or charges.

(4)   Where-

    (a)   a power under subsection (1) is exercisable; and

    (b)   the subsidiary legislation by which the relevant fee or charge was specified, fixed or otherwise determined ("the primary instrument") is-

(i)   subsidiary legislation to which section 35 applies or to which section 34 does not apply; or

(ii)   subsidiary legislation of which a draft was required to be laid on the table of the Legislative Council,

then such 1 or more of the following provisions as are appropriate in the particular circumstances shall operate-

(i)   section 35 shall apply to subsidiary legislation made or issued in exercise of the power which amends the primary instrument;

(ii)   section 34 shall not apply to such subsidiary legislation;

(iii)   the enactment requiring or otherwise relevant to so laying the primary instrument shall also apply to subsidiary legislation which is so made or issued and amends that instrument.

30.   (*Repealed*)

Construction of subsidiary legislation

31.(1)   Where any Ordinance confers power to make any subsidiary legislation, expressions used in the subsidiary legislation shall have the same meaning as in the Ordinance conferring the power, and any reference in such subsidiary legislation to "the Ordinance" shall be construed as a reference to the Ordinance conferring the power to make such subsidiary legislation.

(2)   Where in subsidiary legislation there is a reference to a section or other provision by number, letter or combination of number and letter, and not in conjunction with the title or short title of other subsidiary legislation or an Ordinance, the reference shall be construed as a reference to the section or other provision of that number, letter or combination in the subsidiary legislation in which the reference occurs.

(3)   Where in subsidiary legislation there is a reference to a subsection or other subdivision of a provision by number, letter or combination of number and letter, and not in conjunction with the number of any other section or provision of that subsidiary legislation or any other subsidiary legislation, the reference shall be construed as a reference to the subsection or other subdivision of a provision of that number, letter or combination in the section or other provision in which the reference occurs.

Exercise of statutory powers between enactment and commencement of Ordinance

32.(1) Where an Ordinance is to come into operation on a day other than the day of its publication in the Gazette, a power to do anything under the Ordinance may be exercised at any time after its publication in the Gazette.

(2) An exercise of a power under subsection (1) is not effective until the provision in the Ordinance to which it relates comes into operation unless the exercise of the power is necessary to bring the Ordinance into operation.

33. *(Repealed)*

Placing of subsidiary legislation before Legislative Council

34.(1) All subsidiary legislation shall be laid on the table of the Legislative Council at the next sitting thereof after the publication in the Gazette of that subsidiary legislation.

(2) Where subsidiary legislation has been laid on the table of the Legislative Council under subsection (1), the Legislative Council may, by resolution passed at a sitting of the Legislative Council held not later than 28 days after the sitting at which it was so laid, provide that such subsidiary legislation shall be amended in any manner whatsoever consistent with the power to make such subsidiary legislation, and if any such resolution is so passed the subsidiary legislation shall, without prejudice to anything done thereunder, be deemed to be amended as from the date of publication in the Gazette of such resolution.

(3) If the period referred to in subsection (2) would but for this subsection expire-

> *(a)* after the last sitting before the end of a session or dissolution of the Legislative Council; but

> *(b)* on or before the day of the second sitting of the Legislative Council in the next session,

that period shall be deemed to extend to and expire on the day after that second sitting.

(4) Before the expiry of the period referred to in subsection (2) or that period as extended by virtue of subsection (3), the Legislative Council may by resolution in relation to any subsidiary legislation specified therein extend that period or that period as so extended to the next sitting.

(5) Any resolution passed by the Legislative Council in accordance with this section shall be published in the Gazette not later than 14 days after the passing thereof or within such further period as the Governor may allow in any particular case.

(6) In this section-

"sitting", when used to calculate time, means the day on which the sitting commences and only includes a sitting at which subsidiary legislation is included on the order paper;

"subsidiary legislation" does not include a resolution of the Legislative Council.

Approval of Legislative Council to subsidiary legislation

35.   Where any Ordinance provides that subsidiary legislation shall be subject to the approval of the Legislative Council or of any other authority, or contains words to the like effect, then-

> *(a)*   the subsidiary legislation shall be submitted for the approval of the Legislative Council or other authority; and

> *(b)*   the Legislative Council may by resolution or the other authority may by order amend the whole or any part of the subsidiary legislation.

Effect of repeal on subsidiary legislation

36.(1) Where any Ordinance

> *(a)*   repeals any former Ordinance and substitutes other provisions therefor; or

> *(b)*   repeals any former Ordinance and re-enacts such former Ordinance with or without modification,

any subsidiary legislation made under the former Ordinance and in force at the commencement of the repealing Ordinance shall, so far as it is not inconsistentwith the repealing Ordinance, continue in force and have the like effect for allpurposes as if made under the repealing Ordinance.

(2)   Where any subsidiary legislation is continued in force by virtue ofsubsection (1), such subsidiary legislation may be from time to time amended asif it had been made under the repealing Ordinance.

Forms

37.(1) Where any form is prescribed by or under any Ordinance, deviations therefrom, not affecting the substance of such form, shall not invalidate it.

(2)   Where a form is prescribed in any Ordinance in both official languages and the text in one official language is combined in a particular manner with, or is set out separately from, the text in the other official language, the form may be printed and used-

> *(a)*   with the texts combined in any manner; or

> *(b)*   in either official language.

PART VI - Powers

Presumption of lawful exercise of power

38.   Where any Ordinance confers power upon any person to-

   (a)   make any subsidiary legislation;

   (b)   make any instrument; or

   (c)   exercise any power,

and the Ordinance conferring the power prescribes conditions, subject to the observance, performance or existence of which any such power may be exercised, such conditions shall be presumed to have been duly fulfilled if in the subsidiary legislation, the instrument or the document evidencing the exercise of the power there is a statement that the subsidiary legislation or instrument is made, or the power exercised, in exercise of, or in pursuance of, the power conferred by such Ordinance, or a statement to the like effect.

Exercise of powers

39.(1) Where any Ordinance confers any power or imposes any duty, then the power may be exercised and the duty shall be performed from time to time as occasion requires.

(2)   Where any Ordinance confers any power or imposes any duty on the holder of any public office as such, then the power may be exercised and the duty shall be performed by the holder for the time being of that public office.

Construction of enabling words

40.(1) Where any Ordinance confers upon any person power to do or enforce the doing of any act or thing, all such powers shall be deemed to be also conferred as are reasonably necessary to enable the person to do or enforce the doing of the act or thing.

(2)   Without prejudice to the generality of subsection (1), where any Ordinance confers power-

   (a)   to provide for, prohibit, control or regulate any matter, such power shall include power to provide for the same by the licensing thereof and power to prohibit acts whereby the prohibition, control or regulation of such matter might be evaded;

   (b)   to grant a licence, Crown lease, permit, authority, approval or exemption, such power shall include power to impose

reasonable conditions subject to which such licence, Crown lease, permit, authority, approval or exemption may be granted;

(c)   to approve any person or thing, such power shall include power to withdraw approval thereof,

(d)   to give directions, such power shall include power to couch the same in the form of prohibitions.

(3)-(4) *(Repealed)*

Power to issue licences, etc. discretionary

41.(1) Where any Ordinance confers power upon any person to issue, grant, give or renew any licence, Crown lease, authority, approval, exemption or permit, the person so empowered shall have a discretion either to issue, grant, give or renew or to refuse to issue, grant, give or renew such licence, Crown lease, authority, approval, exemption or permit.

(2)   Nothing in this section shall affect any right which may be conferred by any Ordinance upon any person to appeal against a refusal to issue, grant, give or renew any licence, Crown lease, authority, approval, exemption or permit.

Power to appoint includes power to suspend, dismiss, re-appoint, etc.

42.   Where any Ordinance confers a power or imposes a duty upon any person to make any appointment or to constitute or establish any board, tribunal, commission, committee or similar body, then the person having such power or duty shall also have the power-

(a)   to remove, suspend, dismiss or revoke the appointment of, and to re-appoint or reinstate, any person appointed in exercise of such power or duty;

(b)   to revoke the appointment, constitution or establishment of, or to dissolve, any board, tribunal, commission, committee or similar body appointed, constituted or established, in exercise of such power or duty, and to re-appoint, re-constitute or re-establish the same; and

(c)   to specify the period for which any person appointed in exercise of such power or duty shall hold such appointment:

Provided that where the power or duty of such person so to act is only exercisable upon the recommendation, or is subject to the approval or consent, of some other person, then such power shall only be exercisable upon such recommendation or subject to such approval or consent.

Delegation by specified public officers

43.(1) Where any Ordinance confers powers or imposes duties upon a specified public officer, such public officer may delegate any other public officer or the person for the time being holding any office designated by him to exercise such powers or perform such duties on his behalf, and thereupon, or from the date specified by such specified public officer, the person delegated shall have and may exercise such powers and perform such duties.

(2) Nothing in subsection (1) shall authorize a specified public officer to delegate any person to make subsidiary legislation or to hear any appeal.

(3) Where any Ordinance confers any power or imposes any duty upon a specified public officer and such power is exercised or such duty is performed by any other public officer, the specified public officer shall, unless the contrary is proved, be deemed to have delegated the latter public officer under subsection (1) to exercise the power or perform the duty.

(4) In this section "specified public officer" means the person for the time being holding any public office which has been specified, either generally or for the purposes of any particular Ordinance, under this section by the Governor by notice in the Gazette.

Effect of delegation of powers and duties

44.(1) Where any Ordinance confers power upon any person to delegate the exercise on his behalf of any of the powers or the performance of any of the duties conferred or imposed upon him under any Ordinance-

(a) such delegation shall not preclude the person so delegating from exercising or performing at any time any of the powers or duties so delegated;

(b) such delegation may be conditional, qualified or limited in such manner as the person so delegating may think fit;

(c) where the delegation may be made only with the approval of some person, such delegation may be conditional, qualified or limited in such manner as the person whose approval is required may think fit;

(d) the delegation may be to a named person or to the person for the time being holding any office designated by the person so delegating; and

(e) any delegation may be amended by the person so delegating.

(2) The delegation of any power shall be deemed to include the delegation of any duty incidental thereto or connected therewith and the delegation of any duty shall be deemed to include the delegation of any power incidental thereto or connected therewith.

Exercise of powers in special cases

45. Where any Ordinance confers any power or imposes any duty upon the holder of any public office and either-

(a)   that office has been abolished; or

(b)   no person has been appointed to discharge the functions of that office,

those powers and duties may be exercised or performed-

(i)   in the case of making subsidiary legislation, by the Governor; and

(ii)   in any other case, by the holder of such other public office as the Governor may by order direct.

Power to make public instruments and perform acts

46. Where any Ordinance confers power upon any person to make, grant, issue or approve any proclamation, order, notice, declaration, instrument, notification, licence, permit, exemption, register or list, such power shall include power-

(a)   to amend or suspend such proclamation, order, notice, declaration, instrument, notification, licence, permit, exemption, register or list;

(b)   to substitute another proclamation, order, notice, declaration, instrument, notification, licence, permit, exemption, register or list for one already made, granted, issued or approved;

(c)   to withdraw approval of any proclamation, order, notice, declaration, instrument, notification, licence, permit, exemption, register or list so approved; and

(d)   to declare the date of the coming into operation, and the period of operation, of any such proclamation, order, notice, declaration, instrument, notification, licence, permit, exemption, register or list.

Power to relate back appointment

47. Any appointment made under the provisions of any Ordinance may be declared to have effect as from the date upon which the person appointed in fact began to exercise the powers and perform the duties of his appointment, not being a date earlier than the commencement of the Ordinance under which the appointment is made.

PART VII - Boards and Committees

Power of Governor to appoint advisory bodies

47A.(1) The Governor may from time to time by order published in the Gazette establish by law such advisory and other committees and bodies as he considers appropriate in the public interest and may appoint the members thereof.

(2) An order under subsection (1) may contain such provisions relating to the committee or body established by the order as the Governor thinks fit, including the terms of reference of the body, the terms of office of members appointed to that body, the removal or resignation of members, the re-appointment of members, quorums for meetings and similar procedural matters.

Power to appoint chairman

48. Where any Ordinance confers power upon any person to appoint any persons to be members of any board, tribunal, commission, committee or similar body, the person so appointing may appoint a chairman, a deputy chairman, a vice-chairman and a secretary of such board, tribunal, commission, committee or similar body.

Power to appoint public officer to board, etc.

49. Where any Ordinance confers power upon any person to appoint any persons to be members of any board, tribunal, commission, committee or similar body, the person so empowered may appoint any public officer, by his official designation, to be a member of such board, tribunal, commission, committee or similar body, and, on such appointment and until such appointment shall be revoked or otherwise determined, the person for the time being holding the public office in question shall be a member of such board, tribunal, commission, committee or similar body.

Appointment of alternates

50. Where any board, tribunal, commission, committee or similar body is established by or under any Ordinance, any person who is empowered by such Ordinance to appoint any or all of the members thereof may-

    (a)   appoint 1 or more duly qualified persons to be alternate members of the same, and any one such alternate member may attend any meeting of the same when a substantive member is temporarily unable to attend for any reason; and

    (b)   appoint a duly qualified person to be a temporary member of the same in the place of any substantive member who is precluded by illness, absence from the Colony or any other cause from exercising his functions as such,

and when attending any meeting of such board, tribunal, commission, committee or similar body, such alternate or temporary member shall be deemed for all purposes to be a member of the same.

Powers of board, etc. not affected by vacancy

51. Where any board, tribunal, commission, committee or similar body is established by or under any Ordinance, the powers of such board, tribunal, commission, committee or similar body shall not be affected by-

(a) any vacancy in the membership thereof;

(b) any defect in the appointment or qualification of a person purporting to be a member thereof; or

(c) any minor irregularity in the convening of any meeting thereof.

Power of majority and exercise of powers

52.(1) Where any Ordinance confers a power or imposes a duty upon a body or number of persons consisting of or being not less than 3, such power may be exercised or duty performed in the name of that body or number of persons by a majority of those persons.

(2) Whenever such body or number of persons is assembled, the chairman or other member presiding shall have a casting as well as a deliberative vote, in all matters in which a decision is taken by vote by whatever name such vote may be called.

(3) The exercise of any power vested in such body or number of persons may be signified either by the chairman or other person presiding at the meeting or other deliberation at which such power was exercised or at which, as the case may be, authority to exercise it was conferred, or by any person from time to time authorized by such body or persons to signify the exercise of such power.

Seal

53. Where any Ordinance constitutes any board, tribunal, commission, committee or similar body to be a body corporate having perpetual succession and a common seal, and any document requires to be sealed with such common seal, then such common seal shall be affixed by the chairman of such board, tribunal, commission, committee or similar body, or by any member thereof appointed by the chairman for that purpose, and shall be authenticated by the signature of the chairman or such member.

PART VIII - Public Officers and Public Contracts

References to public officer

54.   In any Ordinance, instrument, warrant or process of any kind, any reference to a public officer, or to a person holding a public office by a term designating his office, shall include a reference to any person for the time being lawfully discharging the functions of that office, or any part of such functions, and any person appointed to act in or perform the duties of such office, or any part of such duties, for the time being.

Power to transfer functions of public officers

54A.(1)   The Legislative Council may by resolution provide for the transfer to any public officer of any functions exercisable by virtue of any Ordinance by another public officer.

(2)   A resolution under this section may contain such incidental, consequential and supplemental provisions as may be necessary or expedient for the purpose of giving full effect to the resolution.

(3)   A certificate issued by the Chief Secretary that any property vested in a public officer immediately before a resolution under this section takes effect has been transferred by virtue of the resolution to another public officer shall be conclusive evidence of the transfer.

(4)   In this section-

"functions" includes powers and duties;

"public officer" includes any corporation created for the purpose of incorporating a person for the time being holding a public office.

Change of title of office

55.   The Chief Secretary may, by notice (which may be given retrospective effect) in the Gazette, declare a change in title of any public officer or public body, or of any person referred to in any Ordinance, and the notice may contain provisions substituting the new title in any Ordinance relating to the public officer, public body or person and in any instrument, contract or legal proceedings made or commenced before the date on which the notice takes effect.

Appointment of officers by name or office

56.   Where any Ordinance confers power upon any person to appoint or name a person to have and exercise any powers or perform any duties, the person so empowered may either appoint a person by name or direct the person for the time being holding any office designated by him to have and exercise such powers or perform such duties; and thereupon, or from the date specified by the person so empowered, the person appointed by name or the person holding the office aforesaid shall have and may exercise such powers or perform such duties accordingly until such appointment be revoked or otherwise determined.

Filling vacancy

57.(1) When any Ordinance confers a power or imposes a duty upon a public officer and such public officer is unable to exercise the powers or perform the duties of his office, owing to absence or inability to act from illness or any other cause, the Governor may, by notice in the Gazette, direct that such power shall be had and may be exercised and such duty shall be performed by a public officer named by, or by a public officer holding the office designated by, the Governor, subject to such conditions, exceptions and qualifications as the Governor may direct.

(2) Any direction by the Governor under subsection (1) may be given-

(a) in anticipation of any absence or inability occurring; or

(b) subsequently thereto and may relate back to the commencement of such absence or inability.

(3) Where any Ordinance confers powers or imposes duties upon a public officer and a new post is subsequently created in the same or another Government department, the Governor may, by notice in the Gazette, direct that the said powers and duties or any of them shall be exercised by any holder of the new post so created, either to the exclusion of or in addition to the first named public officer or otherwise.

Power to appoint while holder on retirement leave

58.(1) Where the holder of any public office is on leave of absence pending the relinquishment by him of such office, another person may be appointed to the same public office.

(2) Where 2 or more persons are holding the same public office by reason of an appointment made in accordance with subsection (1), then, for the purposes of any Ordinance and in respect of any power conferred or duty imposed upon the holder of such office, the person last appointed to the office shall be deemed to be the holder thereof.

Contracts by public officer

59. In any contract or other document, signed, executed or made by the Governor or by any public officer on behalf of the Governor or the Government or of any Government department, it shall not be necessary to name the Governor or such public officer, but it shall be sufficient to name the office held by the Governor or such public officer, and the Governor or public officer shall be deemed to be a party thereto as if the Governor or such public officer were a corporation sole with perpetual succession for this purpose.

Effect of past contracts by public officer

60.   Any contract or other document signed, executed or made before the commencement of this Ordinance by the Governor or by any public officer on behalf of the Governor or the Government or of any Government department shall be enforceable as if the office of Governor or such public officer had, at the time of such execution or making, been a corporation sole with perpetual succession for this purpose.

Omission of title after signature of public officer immaterial

61.   The omission to add the title of the public office held by the Governor or any public officer signing or executing any contract or other document after the signature of such officer shall not exclude such contract or other document from the operation of sections 59 and 60.

PART IX - Crown, Governor and Governor in Council

Signification of orders of Governor and Governor in Council

62.(1) Where any Ordinance confers a power or imposes a duty upon the Governor or the Governor in Council to make any subsidiary legislation or appointment, give any directions, issue any order, authorize any thing or matter to be done, grant any exemption, remit any fee or penalty, or exercise any other power or perform any other duty, the exercise of such power or the performance of such duty may be signified-

> *(a)*   in the case of the Governor, under the hand of any public officer specified in Schedule 6;

> *(b)*   in the case of the Governor in Council, under the hand of the Clerk to the Executive Council.

(2)   Notwithstanding the provisions of subsection (1), proclamations shall be made or issued only under the hand of the Governor himself.

(3)   The Governor may, by order published in the Gazette, amend Schedule 6.

Delegation by Governor

63.(1) Where any Ordinance confers powers or imposes duties upon the Governor, he may delegate any person by name or the person holding any office designated by him to exercise such powers or perform such duties on his behalf and thereupon, or from the date specified by the Governor, the person so delegated shall have and may exercise such powers and perform such duties.

(2)   Without prejudice to the provisions of any Letters Patent or Royal Instructions relating to the appointment of a deputy to the Governor, nothing in subsection (1) shall authorize the Governor to delegate any person to make subsidiary legislation, issue proclamations or to determine any appeal.

(3)   Where any Ordinance confers powers or imposes duties upon the Governor and such power is exercised or such duty is performed by any public officer, the Governor shall, unless the contrary is proved, be deemed to have delegated such public officer under subsection (1) to exercise the power or perform the duty.

Appeals and objections to Governor in Council

64.(1) Where any Ordinance confers upon any person a right of appeal or objection to the Governor in Council, such appeal or objection shall be governed by rules made in accordance with subsection (2).

(2)   The Governor in Council may make rules governing the procedure to be followed in appeals or objections to the Governor in Council.

(3) The conferring by any Ordinance of a right of appeal or objection to the Governor in Council shall not prevent any person from applying to the Supreme Court for an order of mandamus, certiorari, prohibition, injunction or any other order, instead of appealing or making an objection to the Governor in Council, where an application for such an order would lie, but no proceedings by way of mandamus, certiorari, prohibition, injunction or other order shall be taken against the Governor in Council in respect of any such appeal or objection to the Governor in Council or any proceedings connected therewith.

(4) The Governor in Council, when considering any appeal or objection to him (whether by way of petition or otherwise, and whether such appeal or objection is made by virtue of any Ordinance or otherwise) shall act in an administrative or executive capacity and not in a judicial or quasi-judicial capacity and shall be entitled to consider and take into account any evidence, material, information or advice in his absolute discretion.

(5) The Governor in Council, when considering any appeal or objection to him (whether by way of petition or otherwise and whether such appeal or objection is made by virtue of any Ordinance or otherwise) against any decision of any person, public officer or public body, may confirm, vary or reverse such decision or substitute therefor such other decision or make such other order as the Governor in Council may think fit.

References to the Sovereign

65. Any reference to the Sovereign or to the Crown shall be construed as a reference to the Sovereign for the time being.

Saving of rights of Crown

66. No Ordinance shall in any manner whatsoever affect the right of or be binding on the Crown unless it is therein expressly provided or unless it appears by necessary implication that the Crown is bound thereby.

PART X - Time and Distance

Hong Kong Time

67.(1) Whenever any expression of time occurs in any Ordinance the time referred to is Hong Kong Time.

(2) For the purposes of subsection (1), "Hong Kong Time" means the time used for general purposes throughout Hong Kong namely, 8 hours, or such other period as may be determined by the Legislative Council by resolution under this subsection or under section 16 of the Oil (Conservation and Control) Ordinance (Cap. 264), in advance of Greenwich Mean Time.

(3) A resolution of the Legislative Council under subsection (2) may determine Hong Kong Time for the whole or part of a year.

(4) Nothing in this section shall affect the use of Greenwich Mean Time for the purposes of astronomy, meteorology, navigation or aviation, or affect the construction of any document mentioning or referring to a point of time in connection with any of these purposes.

68. *(Repealed)*

References to "a.m." and "p.m."

69. The expression "a.m." indicates the period between midnight and the following noon, and the expression "p.m." indicates the time between noon and the following midnight. Where 2 such expressions occur conjunctively in relation to any specified hour or in conjunction with the word "sunset" or "sunrise", they shall be construed as relating to a consecutive period of time.

Provision where no time prescribed

70. Where no time is prescribed or allowed within which any thing shall be done, such thing shall be done without unreasonable delay, and as often as due occasion arises.

Computation of time

71.(1) In computing time for the purposes of any Ordinance-

   (a)   a period of days from the happening of any event or the doing of any act or thing shall be deemed to be exclusive of the day on which the event happens or the act or thing is done;

> *(b)* if the last day of the period is a public holiday or a gale warning day the period shall include the next following day, not being a public holiday or a gale warning day;
>
> *(c)* where any act or proceeding is directed or allowed to be done or taken on a certain day, then if that day is a public holiday or a gale warning day, the act or proceeding shall be considered as done or taken in due time if it is done or taken on the next following day, not being a public holiday or a gale warning day;
>
> *(d)* where an act or proceeding is directed or allowed to be done or taken within any time not exceeding 6 days, no public holiday or a gale warning day shall be reckoned in the computation of that time.

(2) In this section "gale warning day" means any day throughout or for part of which a gale warning is in force, and "gale warning" has the meaning assigned to it by section 2 of the Judicial Proceedings (Adjournment During Gale Warnings) Ordinance (Cap. 62).

Power to extend time

72. Where in any Ordinance a time is prescribed for doing any act or taking any proceeding and power is given to a court, public body, public officer or other authority to extend such time, then the power may be exercised by the court, public body, public officer or other authority although the application for the same is not made until after the expiration of the time prescribed.

Distance

73. In the measurement of any distance for the purposes of any Ordinance, that distance shall be measured in a straight line on a horizontal plane.

Warrants, etc. valid on public holiday

74. Any summons, notice, warrant or other process may be issued, served or executed and any arrest, search or seizure may be carried out or made on any day, whether a public holiday or not, and at any hour of the day or night.

PART XI - Imperial Enactments

Modifications

75.   An imperial enactment shall be judicially noticed as such and shall be read with such modifications as to names, localities, courts, officers, persons, moneys, penalties or otherwise as may be necessary to make the same applicable to the circumstances of the Colony.

Citation of imperial enactments

76.   An imperial enactment may be cited by a short title or citation, if any, or by reference to the regnal or calendar year in which it was passed or by the number assigned to any statutory instrument or statutory rule and order.

Construction of reference to imperial enactment

77.   A reference in any law to an imperial enactment or to any provision, part or division thereof shall be construed as a reference to the same as the same may be from time to time amended on or before 1 January 1994 and as a reference to any imperial enactment or to any provision, part or division of an imperial enactment, substituted for it on or before 1 January 1994.

References to subsidiary legislation under imperial Acts

78.   A reference in any law to any imperial Act shall include a reference to any Order in Council, rule, regulation, proclamation, order, notice, rule of court, by-law or other instrument made under or by virtue thereof and having legislative effect.

79.   *(Repealed)*

Copies of imperial enactments

80.   A copy of an imperial enactment shall, if it-

> *(a)*   is published in the Gazette or purports to be printed by the Government Printer; or

> *(b)*   is contained in any printed collection purporting to be published or printed by authority,

be deemed, until the contrary is proved, to be an authentic copy of the imperial enactment as at the date of such publication or printing.

PART XII

(Repealed)

PART XIII - Miscellaneous

Copies of Ordinances, etc. in Gazette

98.(1) A copy of an Ordinance shall, if published in the Gazette, be deemed to be an authentic copy of that Ordinance as at the date of such publication.

(2) A copy of any other instrument shall, if published in the Gazette or purporting to be printed by the Government Printer, on its production be admitted as prima facie evidence thereof in all courts and for all purposes whatsoever without any further proof.

Rectification of errors

98A.(1) The Attorney General may, by order published in the Gazette, rectify any clerical or printing error appearing in any Ordinance printed or published pursuant to this Ordinance.

(2) Every order made under this section shall be laid on the table of the Legislative Council without unreasonable delay, and, if a resolution is passed at the first sitting of the Legislative Council held not less than 27 days after the sitting at which the order is so laid that the order be annulled, it shall thenceforth be void, but without prejudice to the validity of anything previously done thereunder, or to the making of a new order.

(3) In this section, "sitting", when used to calculate time, means the day on which the sitting commences and only includes a sitting at which subsidiary legislation is included on the order paper.

Reprint of Ordinances

99. The Government Printer may, with the authority of the Governor, print copies of any Ordinance with all additions, omissions, substitutions and amendments effected by any amending Ordinances, and such copies shall be deemed to be authentic copies of the Ordinance so amended as at the date of such printing.

100. *(Repealed)*

Power to increase fines

100A.(1) The Legislative Council may, by resolution, amend an Ordinance so as to increase-

    (a)   the amount of a fine specified in the Ordinance; and

    (b)   the amount of a fine specified in the Ordinance as an amount that may be prescribed in subsidiary legislation made under the Ordinance.

(1A)   The increase under subsection (1) may be expressed as an amount of money or as a level in Schedule 8 to the Criminal Procedure Ordinance (Cap.221).

(2)   A resolution under this section may contain such incidental, consequential and supplemental provisions as may be necessary or expedient for the purpose of giving full effect to the resolution.

Amendment of Schedules

101.   The Governor may from time to time, by notice in the Gazette, amend all or any of the Schedules.

SCHEDULE 1

Boundaries of The City of Victoria

On the north-The Harbour;

On the west-A line running due north and south drawn through the north-west angle of Inland Lot No. 1299 and extending southwards a distance of 850 feet from the aforesaid angle; On the south-A line running due east from the southern extremity of the western boundary until it meets a contour in the vicinity of the Hill above Belchers 700 feet above principal datum, that is to say, a level 17.833 feet below the bench-mark known as "Rifleman's Bolt", the highest point of a copper bolt set horizontally in the east wall of the Royal Navy Office and Mess Block Naval Dockyard, and thence following the said contour until it meets the eastern boundary; On the east-A line following the west side of the Government Pier, Bay View and thence along the west side of Hing Fat Street, then along the north side of Causeway Road to Moreton Terrace. Thence along the west side of Moreton Terrace to the south-east corner of Inland Lot No. 1580 and produced in a straight line for 80 feet, and thence along the north side of Cotton Path and produced until it meets the west side of Wong Nei Chong Road on the east side of Wong Nei Chong Valley and thence to the south-east angle of Inland Lot No. 1364, produced until it meets the southern boundary.

SCHEDULE 2

Boundaries of The Colony

On the south-The parallel of latitude 22°09' north between the points where it is intersected by the meridian of longitude 114°30' east of Greenwich and the line of the western boundary; On the north-A line drawn from the point where the meridian of longitude 113°52' east of Greenwich intersects the parallel of latitude touching the extreme south-west point of the shore of Deep Bay to the said south-west point of the shore of Deep Bay; thence along the high water mark upon the shore of Deep Bay to the estuary of the Sham Chun River; thence by a line drawn as described in the agreement delineating the northern frontier of the New Territories signed by James Haldane Steward LOCKHART and WONG Tsun-shin at Hong Kong on 19 March 1899, and following the high water mark in Mirs Bay to the point where the meridian of longitude 114°30' east of Greenwich intersects the mainland high water mark; On the east-The meridian of longitude 114°30' east of Greenwich between the points where it intersects the mainland high water mark and the parallel of latitude 22°09' north; On the west-The meridian of longitude 113°52' east of Greenwich between the point where it intersects the parallel of latitude touching the extreme south-west point of the shore of Deep Bay and the north coast of Lantau Island. The boundary then follows the western coast line of Lantau Island including the waters appertaining thereto to the extreme south-west point thereof and thence runs in a south-easterly direction to the extreme south-west point of Tai A Chau Island in the Soko Island Group and continues in the same straight line to the point at which it intersects the parallel of latitude 22°09' north.

SCHEDULE 3

Boundaries of The Harbour

On the east-A straight line drawn from the westernmost extremity of Siu Chau Wan Point to the westernmost extremity of Ah Kung Ngam Point (sometimes known as Kung Am); On the west-A straight line drawn from the westernmost point of Island of Hong Kong to the westernmost point of Green Island, thence a straight line drawn from the westernmost point of Green Island to the south-easternmost point of Tsing Yi, thence along the eastern and northern coast lines of Tsing Yi to the westernmost extremity of Tsing Yi and thence a straight line drawn true north therefrom to the mainland.

SCHEDULE 4

Area of Kowloon

"Kowloon" means that portion of the peninsula of Kaulung which was ceded to Great Britain by the Emperor of China on 24 October 1860.

SCHEDULE 5

Area Of New Kowloon

"New Kowloon" means that portion of the New Territories which is delineated in red and shown upon a plan marked "New Kowloon" dated 8 December 1937, signed by the Director of Public Works, countersigned by the Governor and deposited in the Land Registry.

SCHEDULE 6

Public Officers

Chief Secretary
Financial Secretary
Attorney General
Secretary for the Civil Service
Secretary for Constitutional Affairs
Secretary for Economic Services
Secretary for Education and Manpower
Secretary for Health and Welfare
Secretary for Home Affairs
Secretary for Financial Services
Secretary for Planning, Environment and Lands
Secretary for Recreation and Culture
Secretary for Security
Secretary for Trade and Industry
Secretary for Transport
Secretary for the Treasury
Director of Administration
Secretary for Works
Director of Home Affairs
Deputy Secretary
Deputy Director of Administration
Principal Assistant Secretary
Assistant Director of Administration

Hong Kong as a Tax Haven for International Business

by

Adam Starchild

Tax havens are very much in the news, and stories about small- and medium-sized companies mushrooming overnight and multi-national giants amassing fabulous fortunes via tax haven operations are growing. They may sound like Alice in Wonderland fairy tales to most people, but to the sophisticated entrepreneur, use of foreign tax havens for such advantages is an everyday business opportunity.

The use of a foreign corporation domiciled in any one of the famous company tax havens such as Hong Kong, Panama, the Bahamas, or Bermuda (among others, can enhance the profitability of any international business.

Many European and American companies are expanding and diversifying overseas as a means of growth and as a hedge against economic ups and downs in their country of origin. By incorporating a tax haven operation to accumulate tax-free income, accomplishment of multi-national objectives is accelerated. An international trading or freight operation can be established in a tax haven to be used as a conduit for international sales activity and financing. Such operations can accumulate trade discounts, commissions, advertising allowances, etc., completely tax-free while the parent or associated company can assume tax deductions by absorbing administrative and selling costs.

Before getting into the ways in which tax haven operations are used by various types of businesses, it is of eminent importance that the distinct difference is understood between two seemingly similar terms: "tax avoidance" and "tax evasion." Tax evasion has dubious and illegal overtones: for example, a company might falsify its financial statements so as to conceal its full liability to the tax authorities — that would be tax evasion — an infraction of the law and a very serious one.

Tax avoidance, on the other hand, is a legitimate method of minimizing or negating the tax factor. In simple terms, it is utilizing "loopholes" in tax laws and exploiting them within legal perimeters. This is the cornerstone of the tax haven concept.

Certain offshore companies can defer any tax until the profits are repatriated to the investor's home country. These are generally companies actively engaged in the conduct of a local business. In most import-export or other international trade activities, such a definition is especially easy to meet. A retailer, or group of retailers, could set up their own wholesale buying opertion in a convenient tax haven, such as Hong Kong, and put all of their Asian business through it. The profits of the Hong Kong firm would accumulate tax-free, and could be invested in other foreign operations.

593

In addition, a great many countries offer tax holidays of 5 to 20 years for new export manufacturers or assembly operations, often including smaller companies down to as few as ten employees. A company or group of companies could easily invest some of their foreign profits in such a venture, continuing to build for tax-free profits. Such concessions often include an exemption from customs duties on raw materials and equipment.

Most developed countries do tax the current income of certain types of corporations controlled by their residents, such as leasing companies, and other financial enterprises dealing the parent company. But this concept of a controlled foreign corporation applies usually to passive or tax-haven type corporations, not to active businesses. But even for a passive business, a joint venture with foreign partners on a 50-50 basis will allow the income to accumulate tax-free since the company is not controlled by national of either country. If you are leasing equipment, consider a joint venture with your foreign partner whereby you set up a jointly owned company to receive some of the income. You will both profit by it, and have a tax-free pool of funds to invest together in other ventures. Such profits will not be taxed in the country of either partner until they are repatriated, since they are not controlled by either country's citizen.

Countries which have no income tax include Bermuda, the Bahamas, the Cayman Islands, Nevis, and the Turks & Caicos Islands. A number of countries do not tax foreign source income, including Panama and Hong Kong.

Many businessmen looking for tax haven opportunities would envy the daily opportunities open to international traders, and yet most international traders rarely use these opportunities — or even understand them. 100% tax-free dollars will grow a whole lot faster than 50% after-tax dollars.

Setting Up Your Tax Haven-Based Trading Operation

A firm I can personally give my highest recommendation to is ICS Trust (Asia) Limited, based in Hong Kong.

The handover of the former British Crown Colony of Hong Kong to China is complete, and it is now called the Hong Kong Special Administrative Region, generally abbreviated to Hong Kong S.A.R., even on official documents.

As more than one local businessman has put it, "now that the politicians and journalists are gone (from covering the handover), we can get down to *business*." This attitude is typical of Hong Kong, still a true capitalist center. In fact, many of the wealthy who left to obtain second citizenships in Canada, Australia, and elsewhere, have now returned home to continue building their fortunes.

The major advantage of Hong Kong is simply that it is a real business center, not just a tax haven. One of the consequences of that is the ability to add value to services that are provided in only skeleton form in other tax havens. The reinvoicing business is a prime example. Most tax haven jurisdictions host a number of trading companies that do nothing more than reinvoicing. But one Hong Kong firm has now developed this traditional service into a "real" business mode, with an ability to arrange local trade financing. This is a healthy step away from traditional tax havenry into a true offshore **business** center.

ICS Trust Company Limited is part of the ICS International group of companies headquartered in Hong Kong. This highly successful entrepreneurial group was started by Elizabeth L. Thomson. Elizabeth describes herself as "a lawyer by profession" (2 law degrees, a member of 4 Law Societies internationally), "an entrepreneur by choice"! She has helped innumerable people start new enterprises in many parts of the globe and is well known in Hong Kong for her work with women entrepreneurs.

With a staff of 40 at ICS, every aspect of your business is covered — from deciding to incorporate, to obtaining financing from the bank, to managing your paper work including Letters of Credit, to investing your hard earned profits! ICS is truly a "one stop shop" for entrepreneurs.

Their clients range from multinational companies for whom they run Direct Import Programs worth millions of dollars to individuals who seek tax sheltering and estate planning on an international scale. As an entrepreneurial group, they attract many entrepreneurs as clients — business people who have grown their business to a level of maturity and profits that requires expansion into Asia for many diverse reasons.

Instead of just a paper thin traditional tax haven reinvoicing company, with ICS you can develop a real business in Hong Kong. With their extensive banking contacts, ICS professionals will "shop" for the best letter of credit facilities that Hong Kong's competitive banking scene can offer, likely better facilities than you can find at home. Depending upon the client, ICS can often arrange letter of credit banking facilities for clients with either a low or zero margin deposit, usually required by the opening bank. By freeing up your collateral and capital, they provide you with more purchasing power to increase sales and gain higher profits.

Most of these reinvoicing transactions are usually effected such that they are tax free in Hong Kong. There is no withholding tax on dividends so it is often possible to engage in international trade through a HK company and obtain dividends from that company tax free.

ICS will also work with international banks and factors in Hong Kong and overseas to arrange financing, secured primarily on the strength of purchase orders from your clients. Working with banks, factories, shipping companies and freight forwarders, ICS will structure a transaction to increase the likelihood of obtaining flexible, low cost facilities.

The goods do not need to go through HK for us to use a HK vehicle to pass title. Most of their clients ship from a third country direct to their own country.

Although the traditional Hong Kong focus is on firms who trade in goods, it is also possible to use these structures in cases where services are to be provided from overseas. For example, a firm could contract out a study to a company in Hong Kong. This Hong Kong company could then sub-contract out the work to a third party firm and the profit kept in Hong Kong, tax free.

If you import goods from Asia for sale to large chains, ICS can help you expand your credit facilities and increase your domestic sales by establishing and running a Direct Import Program for you. Combined with their international trade finance capabilities, the Direct Import Program is a powerful tool for generating more profits.

The primary goal of the Direct Import Program is to maximize your profits by making your customers perceive that they are buying "direct." This is achieved by:

- setting up a subsidiary company in Hong Kong
- getting your buyers to open their L/C or orders to this subsidiary
- liaising with suppliers to ensure goods are to specification.

The Direct Import Program works because of two powerful reasons:

- The trend in the retail industry is for buyers to "buy direct" from the Orient. Having a subsidiary in Hong Kong which receives orders or L/Cs greatly enhances this perception.

- Large retail chains often can obtain freight and insurance at significant savings because of their economies of scale. Selling FOB Asia can often result in a lower selling price for the importer but with the same profit.

ICS will set up and manage the subsidiary company for you, and prepare financing proposals for presentation to local banks. When everything is complete, goods are shipped directly from the Asian factory to the customer. The fact that you are now seen as an Asian supplier (and not the middleman) is often an important factor that clinches the deal. The added prestige of a Hong Kong office makes the customer think he or she is buying "direct" and therefore receiving the lowest price.

To get started, you should contact ICS with as much detail as possible about your business and its trading activities.

For further information, contact:

Mr. Kishore K. Sakhrani, Director
ICS Trust (Asia) Limited
8th Floor, Henley Building
Five Queen's Road, Central
Hong Kong
Telephone: +852 2854 4544
Fax: +852 2543 5555

You will be well-advised and well-serviced in the hands of this fine company.

Sources of Help for Offshore Investing

Britannia Corporate Management Limited

Another business specializing in the formation of offshore corporations and trusts is Britannia Corporate Management Limited, located in the Cayman Islands. Its president, Gary F. Oakley, is a Canadian with over 18 years of Cayman Islands residency. Britannia is licensed to manage investment holding and trading companies, real estate holding companies, patent holding companies, and insurance holding companies. It is licensed to incorporate and manage corporations registered in the Cayman Islands. As such, the firm can service as the registered office of a corporation, provide its secretary, officers and directors, or undertake any day-to-day functions that may be required. More information can be obtained by writing the following:

Britannia Corporate Management Limited
Attn: New Clients Information
P. O. Box 1968
Whitewall Estates, Grand Cayman
Cayman Islands

Britannia can be reached by fax at +1 345 949 0716, marking your fax "Attention New Clients Information.

Skye Fiduciary Services Limited

Skye Fiduciary Services Limited are among the foremost experts in offshore planning. Under the direction of its chairman Charles Cain, formerly managing director of the second merchant bank to open in the Isle of Man, Skye Fiduciary is the most experienced offshore corporate and trust management business in the jurisdiction. Although Skye offers a full range of company and trust management services, their expertise in designing novel company structures to meet the needs of foreign clients is unique.

For further information, write the following:

Skye Fiduciary Services Limited
Attn: New Clients Department
2 Water Street
Ramsey, Isle of Man 1M8 1JP
United Kingdom

Their telephone number is +44 1624 816117. Fax service is available at +44 1624 816645; marking your fax "Attention: New Clients Information".

JML Swiss Investment Counsellors

One of the leaders in Swiss financial management is JML Swiss Investment Counsellors, a firm which offers a unique style of financial management. Clients can customize and control their own portfolios and still receive comprehensive management advice from some of the world's best experts on financial matters.

Recognizing that investors have differing goals, time frames, and tolerance for risk, JML's managers work with their individual clients to help them target their unique objectives. This naturally requires continued surveillance and analysis of worldwide economic trends, political events, financial markets, currencies, and other factors which could make some investments particularly attractive and others most unfavorable. Few individuals have the time or expertise to undertake this kind of evaluation themselves.

Further information about JML can be obtained by writing the following:

JML Jurg M. Lattmann AG
Swiss Investment Counsellors
Germaniastrasse 55, Dept. 212
CH-8033 Zurich, Switzerland

Their telephone number is (41) 1 368-8233 and their fax number is (41) 1 368-8299, marking your fax "Attention Department 212".

Weber Hartmann Vrijhof & Partners

While there are many excellent Swiss investment financial managers, another one of particular note is the management firm of Weber Hartmann Vrijhof & Partners. Offering management services for the portfolios of both individuals and companies, the firm excels at providing personal attention to its clients. Weber Hartmann Vrijhof & Partners was established in 1992 by Hans Weber, Robert Vrijhof, and Adrian Hartmann. The three men have substantial experience in finance and investment. Weber managed Foreign

Commerce Bank (FOCOBANK) in Switzerland for nearly 30 years as its president and CEO, Vrijhof was a former vice-president and head of FOCOBANK'S portfolio management group, and Hartmann was head of FOCOBANK'S North American subsidiary in Vancouver. Weber Hartmann Vrijhof & Partners offers specialized investment services designed to meet the individual needs of their clients.

The minimum opening portfolio to be managed by this firm is $250,000 or equivalent. The management team here normally recommends that a portion of the portfolio be invested in hard currencies other than the U.S. dollar including the Swiss franc, French franc, German mark, and Dutch guilder. Respected for their conservative approach to portfolio management, the partners assist clients with opening a custodial account at one of the major private Swiss banks, so that all client securities are held by the bank, not the investment manager.

A large percentage of their clients are based in the United States. One of their main goals has always been to get a certain portion of their clients' wealth out of the U.S. dollar and into European hard currencies such as Swiss francs, Deutschmarks, and Dutch guilders, and then build a portfolio with a mix of bonds and shares.

For more information, you can write to the following:

Weber Hartmann Vrijhof & Partners Ltd.
Attn: New Clients Department
Zurichshstrasse 110B
CH-8134 Adilswil, Switzerland

Their telephone number is (41-1) 709-11-15 and their fax number (41-1) 709-11-13, marking your fax "Attention New Clients Department".

Dunn & Hargitt International Group

Recently, many international investors have become dissatisfied with the small annual return on Euro-dollar deposits.

This is why private and institutional investors throughout the world are looking at other areas where returns can be in the area of 20-25% a year, to help offset the high annual rates of inflation on luxury goods.

The Dunn & Hargitt International Group, founded in 1961, has specialized in doing research for developing Portfolio Management Programs that have the potential of providing investors with a high return on their capital by investing in a diversified portfolio trading in the commodity, currency, precious metals, and financial futures markets in the United States and throughout the world.

The Dunn & Hargitt group offers investors the possibilitiy of participating in several of the different pools that are managed by them by investing through the investment programs that are offered by their affiliate, Winchester Life in Gibraltar, but which are actually managed by The Dunn & Hargitt International Group.

At the time of publication they are offering three possible investment alternatives, including The Winchester Life Umbrella Account (which allows 100% of a client's money to be invested in a diversified futures portfolio), The Winchester Life 100% Guaranteed Investment Account (in which Lloyds Bank acts as custodian trustee and US Government Zero Coupon Treasury Bonds are set aside to guarantee the client's capital), and The Winchester Life 150% Guaranteed Investment Account (which is a similar program, but guaranteeing that the client will receive at least 150% of the value deposited with a maturity date at least ten years in the future).

The average net return for the 150% Guaranteed Investment Account over the last six years would have been 22% a year. The average net return on the 100% Guaranteed Investment Account over the last six years would have been 27% a year. The average annual net return for The Winchester Life Umbrella Account over the last twelve years would have been 35% a year.

The minimum accounts accepted are $20,000 for The Winchester Life Umbrella Account, $20,000 for The Winchester Life 100% Guaranteed Account, and $50,000 for The Winchester Life 150% Guaranteed Account.

Although commodities are a speculative form of investment, investors everywhere are diversifying part of their portfolios to take part in the considerable potential profit opportunities that are available in the commodity, currency, precious metals and financial futures markets. The programs devised by the Dunn & Hargitt International Group will make profits if significant trends develop in either direction; i.e. up or down. This does not mean that short term results are always profitable, however the Dunn & Hargitt proven trading systems can provide above average returns over the longer term. Their objective is to make a profit for their clients of between 20% and 40% per annum and their computer trading systems are geared to this level of performance.

For more information, contact:

The Dunn & Hargitt International Group
c/o Dunn & Hargitt Research S.A.
Department S-697
P.O. Box 3186
Road Town, Tortola
British Virgin Islands

The structure of the Dunn & Hargitt Group has been established so that no taxes are withheld from the client's investment on the international commodity, currency, precious metals and financial futures markets. Because of this they can only manage money for investors who are neither citizens nor residents of the United States.

The Dunn & Hargitt International Group offers complete confidentiality to all of its clients, and will not reveal any information on a client or on its accounts to any third parties.

About the Author

This special afterword was prepared by Adam Starchild who over the past 25 years has been the author of over two dozen books, and hundreds of magazine articles, primarily on business and finance. His articles have appeared in a wide range of publications around the world — including *Business Credit, Euromoney, Finance, The Financial Planner, International Living, Offshore Financial Review, Reason, Tax Planning International, The Bull & Bear, Trust & Estates*, and many more.

Now semi-retired, he was the president of an international consulting group specializing in banking, finance and the development of new businesses, and director of a trust company.

Although this formidable testimony to expertise in his field, plus his current preoccupation with other books-in-progress, would not seem to leave time for a well-rounded existence, Starchild has won two Presidential Sports Awards and written several cookbooks, and is currently involved in a number of personal charitable projects.

His personal website is at http://www.adamstarchild.com